# 12,000 Students and Their English Teachers

## *Tested Units in Teaching Literature, Language, Composition*



1968

*Commission on English*
*College Entrance Examination Board*

## *Acknowledgments and Credits*

### *Novels*

Two Plans for Teaching *The Bridge of San Luis Rey*

Thomas Hardy, "Hap" and "The Subalterns." Reprinted with permission of The Macmillan Company from *Collected Poems* by Thomas Hardy. Copyright 1925 by The Macmillan Company.

### *Short Stories*

D. H. Lawrence: "The Rocking-Horse Winner"

D. H. Lawrence, creed in "Benjamin Franklin," from *Studies in Classic American Literature* by D. H. Lawrence. Copyright 1923, 1950 by Frieda Lawrence. All rights reserved. Reprinted by permission of The Viking Press, Inc.

### *Poetry*

Whitman/Cummings, A Comparison of Two Poems

E. E. Cummings, "if everything happens that can't be done." Copyright, 1944, by E. E. Cummings. Reprinted from his volume *Poems 1923–1954* by permission of Harcourt, Brace & World, Inc.

"Fern Hill"

Dylan Thomas, "Fern Hill," from *The Collected Poems* of Dylan Thomas. Copyright 1953 by Dylan Thomas. Reprinted by permission of New Directions Publishing Corporation.

Robert Frost, "Nothing Gold Can Stay." Reprinted with permission of Holt, Rinehart and Winston, Inc.

"The Love Song of J. Alfred Prufrock"

T. S. Eliot, "The Love Song of J. Alfred Prufrock," from *Collected Poems 1909–1962* by T. S. Eliot, copyright, 1936, by Harcourt, Brace & World, Inc.; copyright, ©, 1963, 1964 by T. S. Eliot. Reprinted by permission of the publisher.

"Musée des Beaux Arts"

W. H. Auden, "Musée des Beaux Arts." Copyright 1940 by W. H. Auden. Reprinted from *The Collected Poetry of W. H. Auden* by permission of Random House, Inc.

Four Poems on Death

A. E. Housman, "To an Athlete Dying Young," from "A Shropshire Lad"—Authorised Edition—from *The Collected Poems of A. E. Housman.* Copyright 1939, 1940, © 1959 by Holt, Rinehart and Winston, Inc. Copyright © 1967 by Robert E. Symons. Reprinted by permission of Holt, Rinehart and Winston, Inc.

Thomas Hardy, "After the Last Breath." Reprinted with permission of The Macmillan Company from *Collected Poems* by Thomas Hardy. First published in 1925 by The Macmillan Company.

Dylan Thomas, "After the Funeral," from *The Collected Poems* of Dylan Thomas. Copyright 1939 by New Directions. Reprinted by permission of New Directions Publishing Corporation.

"Sonnet on Hope"

Richmond Lattimore, "Sonnet on Hope." Reprinted with permission of The University of Michigan Press from *The Stride of Time* by Richmond Lattimore.

### *Drama*

*The Book of Job* and *J.B.*

Mark Van Doren, "The God of Galaxies," from *Collected and New Poems 1924–1963* by Mark Van Doren. Copyright © 1963 by Mark Van Doren. Reprinted by permission of Hill and Wang, Inc.

Maxine Green, "A Return to Heroic Man," from *Saturday Review,* August 22, 1959.

*The Glass Menagerie*

E. E. Cummings, "somewhere i have never travelled." Copyright, 1931, 1959, by E. E. Cummings. Reprinted from his volume *Poems 1923–1954* by permission of Harcourt, Brace & World, Inc.

### *Language*

Applications of Grammatical Analysis to Stylistic Analysis and to Writing

John Steinbeck, paragraph from *The Red Pony.* Copyright 1937, © 1965 by John Steinbeck. Reprinted by permission of The Viking Press, Inc.

Diction

George Orwell, "Shooting an Elephant," from *Shooting an Elephant and Other Essays* by George Orwell, copyright, 1945, 1946, 1949, 1950, by Sonia Brownell Orwell. Reprinted by permission of Harcourt, Brace & World, Inc.

Redundancy and Dullness: One Way to Attack Two Related Problems

Joseph Conrad, passage from "The Lagoon." Reprinted with permission of J. M. Dent & Sons Ltd.

The Language of an Essay

Arthur T. Hadley, "Complex Query: What Makes a Good Spy?" Reprinted with permission of the author.

### *Composition*

Attitude and Purpose in Writing

Canterbury Cathedral. Color photograph by Tom Hollyman reproduced with permission of Photo Researchers, Inc.

Canterbury Cathedral. Black and white photograph from *English Cathedrals,* published by Thames and Hudson, Ltd., London, and The Viking Press, Inc., New York. Reprinted with permission of Thames and Hudson, Ltd.

Raoul Dufy, "The Fourteenth of July at Le Havre." Permission SPADEM 1967 by French Reproduction Rights, Inc.

Mark Twain, passages from *The Adventures of Huckleberry Finn* and *Life on the Mississippi.* Reprinted by permission of Harper & Row, Publishers.

Ruth McKenney, "A Loud Sneer for Our Feathered Friends." From *My Sister Eileen,* copyright, 1938, 1966, by Ruth McKenney. Reprinted by permission of Harcourt, Brace & World, Inc.

A Composition Unit Based on Cartoons

Mort Gerberg, "Oh, Gerald, I'm so marvelously discontent!" *Saturday Review,* May 21, 1966. Reproduced with permission of the artist.

Cedric Rogers, "His blood ran cold," etc. Reproduced by permission of *Punch.*

Dale McFeatters, "Let's just say we're adrift," etc. From Strictly Business by Dale McFeatters as published in *The Boston Herald,* August 10, 1966.

An Essay and a Poem on the Same Subject

E. B. White, "About Myself," from *The Second Tree from the Corner* by E. B. White. Copyright 1945 by E. B. White. Originally appeared in *The New Yorker,* and reprinted by permission of Harper & Row, Publishers.

W. H. Auden, "The Unknown Citizen." Copyright 1940 by W. H. Auden. Reprinted from *The Collected Poetry of W. H. Auden* by permission of Random House, Inc.

A Composition Unit in Persuasion

Stephen Leacock, "Americans Are Queer." Reprinted by permission of *The Canadian Forum,* in which it appeared in the April 1931 issue.


---


Copies of this book may be ordered from College Entrance Examination Board, Publications Order Office, Box 592, Princeton, New Jersey 08540. The price is $5.50 per copy.

Other correspondence should be addressed to the Commission on English, 475 Commonwealth Avenue, Boston, Massachusetts 02215.





Library of Congress Catalog Card Number: 67–30437.

Printed in the United States of America

Edward S. Noyes

*who in countless ways worked for the success of the Commission and of all who teach English*

# *Preface*

The teachers who participated in the 1962 summer institutes cosponsored by the Commission on English and 20 cooperating universities produced a great many exercises designed for classroom use. Although the Commission had promised to publish a selection of them, the work was twice postponed. Then in 1965 a committee of English teachers and staff members spent weeks in reading all the materials coming out of the workshops that were a part of the 1962 program.

A report of this 1965 study was made to the Advisory Committee of the Commission: Joan W. Wofford, Cardoza High School, Washington, D.C.; Henry W. Sams, Pennsylvania State University; and George Winchester Stone Jr., New York University. They also read many of the 1962 materials and jointly with the Commission's staff submitted to the College Entrance Examination Board a proposal for a program to be undertaken by the Commission. On authorization of the Board's trustees and president, the executive director of the Commission invited a group of teachers to serve on a Committee on Curriculum Resources. It was agreed that in its work this Committee would use the 1962 institute materials as a point of departure, rather than as a table of contents.

As further guidance to the Committee, Mr. Sams wrote, "We spoke hopefully about the intonation of the book, and about designing it in such a way that teachers using it would assume a participative frame of mind. It seemed that this was not beyond the hope of achievement. The machinery might be to surround each exercise with comments by the selecting teachers so that the reader would automatically join the editors as an additional critic of the basic material." Certainly every person involved in this undertaking has been most desirous to avoid materials that prescribe classroom procedures rather than encourage such a frame of mind.

Many teachers in secondary schools—public, parochial, and private—generously helped in testing and revision. Some teachers who pilot-tested the materials wrote detailed comments on the appropriateness or inappropriateness of each unit for the grade and level designated and, further, frequently suggested ways to improve the materials. Others took part in reading the thousands of students' papers submitted from English classes that used the various units. The students' papers and the teachers' letters from the participating schools provided rich and varied summer reading for a team of school and college consultants invited by the Commission to take all the time needed to make a representative selection of high, average, and below-average student papers for each of the units that had been pilot-tested.

In its own work and in the tasks shared with several hundred teaching colleagues and thousands of students, the Committee on Curriculum Resources has done a commendable service. I shall ever continue grateful to its members and to the Commission's staff for their splendid work in completing a large assignment.

*Floyd Rinker*
Executive Director
Commission on English

## Publications of the Commission on English

*End-of-Year Examinations in English for College-Bound Students, Grades 9–12,* 1963
*Freedom and Discipline in English,* 1965
*Handbook on Summer Institutes in English,* 1965
*Kinescripts*—14 Booklets, 1965, 1967
*Speaking about Teaching,* 1967
*12,000 Students and Their English Teachers,* 1968

The Commission is greatly indebted to the College Board's Director of Publications and his staff for design, editing, and production of all the publications listed and of three brochures no longer in print.

*Freedom and Discipline in English,* the Commission's report, was one of 50 books selected for exhibition in 1966 by The American Institute of Graphic Arts. A British edition was published in 1967, by the University of London Press Ltd.

# *Committee on Curriculum Resources*

Winifred L. Post, *Chairman*
Dana Hall School, Wellesley, Massachusetts

Margueritte Caldwell
Rincon High School, Tucson, Arizona

A. J. Downs
Gilman School, Baltimore, Maryland

Virginia A. Elliott
University of Pittsburgh

James M. Gaither
Crispus Attucks High School, Indianapolis, Indiana

Leslie L. Guster
Commission on English

Michael F. M. Harada
Eagle Rock High School, Los Angeles, California

Robert F. Hogan
National Council of Teachers of English

Ned E. Hoopes
Hunter College High School, New York, New York

Carl Niemeyer
Union College

Edward S. Noyes
College Entrance Examination Board

Floyd Rinker
Commission on English

Webb Salmon
Columbus High School, Columbus, Indiana

# *Contents*

## *Secondary Schools Participating in Pilot Testing, 1966 and 1967*

Abington Senior High School, Abington, Pennsylvania
Academy of Our Lady of Nazareth,
  Wakefield, Massachusetts
Alhambra High School, Phoenix, Arizona
Allegheny High School, Pittsburgh, Pennsylvania
Andrew Warde High School, Fairfield, Connecticut
Arlington High School, Indianapolis, Indiana
Arsenal Technical High School, Indianapolis, Indiana
Arts High School, Newark, New Jersey
Baldwin School, Bryn Mawr, Pennsylvania
Baylor School, Chattanooga, Tennessee
Bellaire High School, Bellaire, Texas
Bethesda Chevy-Chase High School, Bethesda, Maryland
Board of Catholic Education, Cleveland, Ohio
Broad Ripple High School, Indianapolis, Indiana
Burlingame High School, Burlingame, California
Carle Place High School, Carle Place, New York
Central High School, Phoenix, Arizona
Central High School, Tulsa, Oklahoma
Chapel Hill Senior High School,
  Chapel Hill, North Carolina
Charles W. Eliot Junior High School, Cleveland, Ohio
Choate School, Wallingford, Connecticut
Claremont Center High School, Hickory, North Carolina
Clayton High School, Clayton, Missouri
Columbus Senior High School, Columbus, Indiana
Concord-Carlisle High School, Concord, Massachusetts
Crispus Attucks High School, Indianapolis, Indiana
Culver Military Academy, Culver, Indiana
Dana Hall School, Wellesley, Massachusetts
Dana Junior High School, San Diego, California
East High School, Salt Lake City, Utah
East Junior High School, Waynesboro, Pennsylvania
Emerich Manual High School, Indianapolis, Indiana
Ernest W. Seaholm High School, Birmingham, Michigan
Evanston Township High School, Evanston, Illinois
Florida State University High School,
  Tallahassee, Florida
George Washington High School, Denver, Colorado
Germantown Friends School, Philadelphia, Pennsylvania
Gilman School, Baltimore, Maryland
Glades Junior High School, Miami, Florida
Gloucester High School, Gloucester, Massachusetts
Greenville High School, Greenville, Mississippi
Grosse Pointe High School, Grosse Pointe, Michigan
Highland High School, Salt Lake City, Utah
Holliston High School, Holliston, Massachusetts
Holy Name of Jesus Mercy Academy,
  New Orleans, Louisiana
Hunter College High School, New York, New York
Huron High School, New Boston, Michigan
James A. Garfield High School, Garrettsville, Ohio
James Ford Rhodes High School, Cleveland, Ohio
John Burroughs School, St. Louis, Missouri
John F. Kennedy High School, Denver, Colorado
John Marshall High School, Cleveland, Ohio
Kamehameha Schools, Honolulu, Hawaii
Kenwood Senior High School, Baltimore, Maryland
Lake Park High School, Medinah, Illinois
Lansdowne Senior High School, Baltimore, Maryland
Lee High School, Houston, Texas
Los Angeles High School, Los Angeles, California
Louise S. McGehee School, New Orleans, Louisiana
Madison High School, San Diego, California
Marshall High School, Milwaukee, Wisconsin
Marshfield High School, Coos Bay, Oregon
Mary Institute, St. Louis, Missouri
Mather Junior High School, Darien, Connecticut
Mercer Island High School, Mercer Island, Washington
Miami Senior High School, Miami, Florida
Middlesex Junior High School, Darien, Connecticut
Milne School, State University of New York,
  Albany, New York
Mission Bay High School, San Diego, California
Morse High School, San Diego, California
Mount Lebanon High School, Pittsburgh, Pennsylvania
Nathan Hale High School, Tulsa, Oklahoma
New Trier East High School, Winnetka, Illinois
Niskayuna High School, Schenectady, New York
Norfolk Academy, Norfolk, Virginia
Oshkosh High School, Oshkosh, Wisconsin
Parkville Senior High School, Baltimore, Maryland
Pascack Valley High School, Hillsdale, New Jersey
Peabody High School, Pittsburgh, Pennsylvania
Peckham Junior High School, Milwaukee, Wisconsin
Penn Hills High School, Pittsburgh, Pennsylvania

Perry Junior-Senior High School,
Pittsburgh, Pennsylvania
Phillips Academy, Andover, Massachusetts
Pierce Junior High School, Grosse Pointe, Michigan
Point Loma High School, San Diego, California
Pueblo High School, Tucson, Arizona
Punahou School, Honolulu, Hawaii
Reagan High School, Houston, Texas
Rincon High School, Tucson, Arizona
Robert Louis Stevenson School, Pebble Beach, California
Roger Ludlowe High School, Fairfield, Connecticut
Roslyn Heights High School, Roslyn Heights, New York
Royal Oak High School, Royal Oak, Michigan
Sacred Heart High School,
Newton Center, Massachusetts
St. John's School, Houston, Texas
St. Mary's High School, Lawrence, Massachusetts
Sandia High School, Albuquerque, New Mexico
San Marino High School, San Marino, California
Scarsdale High School, Scarsdale, New York
Schreiner Institute, Kerrville, Texas
Shortridge High School, Indianapolis, Indiana
South Junior High School, Ogden, Utah
Southwest Miami High School, Miami, Florida
Staples High School, Westport, Connecticut
Stemmers Run Junior High School, Baltimore, Maryland
Stranahan High School, Fort Lauderdale, Florida
Taft High School, Woodland Hills, California
Taylor Allderdice High School, Pittsburgh, Pennsylvania
Thacher School, Ojai, California
Thomas Carr Howe High School, Indianapolis, Indiana
Thomas Jefferson High School, Denver, Colorado
Thomas A. Jefferson High School, Tulsa, Oklahoma
Tilton School, Tilton, New Hampshire
Towson High School, Towson, Maryland
Tucson High School, Tucson, Arizona
University High School, Los Angeles, California
Waltrip High School, Houston, Texas
Waynesboro Area Junior and Senior High Schools,
Waynesboro, Pennsylvania
Webster High School, Tulsa, Oklahoma
West Junior High School, Waynesboro, Pennsylvania
Westbury High School, Houston, Texas
Westminster Boys High School, Westminster Schools,
Atlanta, Georgia
Westridge School, Pasadena, California
Will Rogers High School, Tulsa, Oklahoma
William H. Hall High School,
West Hartford, Connecticut
Woodlawn Junior High School,
Baltimore, Maryland
Wright Junior High School, Milwaukee, Wisconsin
Yates High School, Houston, Texas

# *Introduction*

This book, like other publications of the Commission on English, attempts to say what English is and to suggest what it should be. This time the Commission, through the efforts of a Committee on Curriculum Resources, deals with the daily practicalities of the classroom but tries to irradiate the humdrum with flashes of the idealism that tells us "fences are made for those who cannot fly." When John Stuart Mill wrote, "We must aim at too much, to be assured of doing enough," he eased into aphorism the interlocked practicality and idealism that animate good English teaching and that this book has tried to embody. Some teachers may prefer Mill rephrased to read, "We must aim too high lest we hit too low." This, too, expresses the intended spirit of this book.

One teacher who helped in the pretesting urged the Commission not to make life so easy for English teachers that all they have to do is send to a central office for a "how-to-do-it" kit every time they start a new piece of work. Then he added, "It seems to me the bond between a teacher and his students is strengthened by the fact that the students know that their teacher has 'cared enough' to prepare his own study guides and questions for their use." The committee members couldn't agree more. To regard any of the material in this volume as a "how-to-do-it" kit is to misconstrue its real purpose. It is here for the use of teachers, but it is only a sampling, a takeoff point for the creation of similar and better materials that are hand-tailored to the needs of a particular teacher, a particular class, and a particular undertaking.

English teaching, no English teacher needs to be told, must always be an intensely private enterprise. No teacher can prescribe with exactitude for another. No "teaching unit" can be guaranteed to work even in two successive classes. Every experienced teacher has lived through the carefully laid lesson plan that worked like a charm with the third period class but failed dismally with the fifth. Teachers, classes, and students are profoundly individual. The packaged plan can never be imposed wholesale on that threefold individuality. Always a teacher must use such material with judicious selectivity and venturesome independence, for unless the strategy of the classroom remains supple, rigor mortis sets in. *12,000 Students and Their English Teachers* fails in its purpose and seriously limits its usefulness if it does not reinforce the idea of creativity in teaching.

Since the persons who prepared these materials are themselves English teachers, the voice of the book is that of one English teacher speaking to another—speaking out of shared experience, a sharing that in no way trespasses on the intensely private enterprise that English teaching is and must be. The book aims to reach all English teachers, not just those who work with grades 9–12. Teachers of younger students should find it illuminating to see the kind of work for which, the Committee hopes, they are preparing their students. College teachers will catch here glimpses of the process that some of their students have experienced. The book should have much to say to the inexperienced teacher and to the graduate student preparing for a career in English teaching. It speaks also to the school principal who wonders what is going on in the English classroom and to the interested layman who questions the jeremiads on the state of English that appear regularly in the magazines and the newspapers.

The Committee began and ended its deliberations with the seemingly insoluble problem of imposing order on what is essentially a sampling, a miscellany. The simplest solution for the insoluble would have been a division of the materials under the headings of "literature," "language," and "composition." For two reasons the Committee rejected this way out of difficulties. First, the division enforced a separation among the three parts of English that exists neither in any well-ordered classroom nor in these materials; and, second, it created the false impression that three quarters of the work deals with literature alone. The Committee explored the possibility of organizing the material by grades, but little was narrowly suited to the needs of a single grade. What would work well in one school with grade 9 might work equally well with grade 10 in another or with grade 11 in still another. The final plan of organization is a compromise, but it is one that represents accurately what goes on in many English classrooms. A teacher doesn't usually say, "I'm doing a unit on literature." He is more likely to say, "I'm doing a unit on the short story"—or on drama or on the novel or on poetry—meaning that he is not only teaching the short story but is also actively engaged with language and composition. The first four sections, then, are in line with practice in English classes, where commonly the program starts with literature, with the work in language and composition deriving from whatever literary work is being studied. Committee members were aware, though, that there are times when the starting point, and the concentration, should be on language or on composition. Hence the fifth section on language and the sixth on composition. In almost every unit, however, all three elements are there.

An English teacher looking over the table of contents may well ask, "But what about the essay?" The essay is not forgotten, but just as some of the most significant work in language and composition occurs in what look like sections on literature, so some of the most significant work in literature occurs in the sections marked language and composition. This is true of the essay. The book provides detailed study suggestions for the exploration of six essays, but four of these are in the composition section and two in the language section.

With misgivings the Committee has included suggested grade levels for each unit, but no teacher should feel bound to abide by these labels. Teachers will need to experiment to discover exactly where each unit best suits their particular program and their particular students. A teacher may find that a unit designed for grade 9 works excitingly well with his eleventh grade class. And teachers should exercise caution in deciding offhand that a unit is too hard for their students. With adaptations, omissions, and additions it may not be. The users of the book should remember that none of the material is intended to be taken over verbatim into any classroom. In a few places, nevertheless, the Committee has urged that a particular unit not be used below the given grade level. The material on *The Book of Job* and *J.B.*, for instance, was exciting for able twelfth graders, but the writing assignments and some of the discussion questions were well beyond the grasp of bright and eager eleventh grade students. Where the gap is too great between the student's reach and his grasp, it is folly to subject him to predictable failure.

Although the discussion questions in each unit appear in what their makers believe is a logical order, no teacher should feel obliged to follow that order, nor should he think that he must proceed laboriously through every question. As long as the spontaneity of class discussion stays alive, teachers must expect surprises that collide with their most careful planning. They must stand ready to move with the unexpected question that opens up a point the study plan overlooked. And especially with a quick class nothing proves more deadly than to push ploddingly through a series of prefabricated questions that the lively intuition of the class has already anticipated. Every teacher develops a sixth sense that tells him when his class is bored, and every teacher develops his own technique for avoiding the needless, always bearing in mind, though, that what is needless in one class may be needful in another.

In looking over the discussion questions for a given unit, teachers may sometimes find that a central point is not covered. The temptation will be to bring it in where logically it seems to belong. Before doing so, however, the teacher should take a look at the writing assignments. Often the discussion questions deliberately omit a vital point in order to let the student discover it through his writing and deal with it in his own way. In fact, a guiding principle throughout the book has been to leave to the student, wherever possible, the fun of making his own discoveries and reaching his own conclusions. The time it takes him is time well spent.

This book is coming into a world already teeming with texts on the teaching of English. Its uniqueness lies in its active involvement of the 250 English teachers and the 12,000 students who gave it substance, shape, and life. To them the Committee is as indebted as it is grateful.

*Winifred Lowry Post*
Chairman for the Committee on Curriculum Resources
Commission on English

# *Notes on the Grading of Student Papers*

Readers familiar with the Commission's *End-of-Year Examinations in English for College-Bound Students, Grades 9–12* will note that in *12,000 Students and Their English Teachers* the readers have abandoned the five-point scale used in rating most of the student answers in the 1965 book and have substituted ratings of *high, average,* and *low.* In this book, too, the readers have felt no obligation to supply a sample at each of the three levels for every assignment.

Within each of the three categories—*high, average,* and *low*—there was often enough range to warrant the use in the comments of such terms as a "high" *low* paper or a "low" *high* paper or a "high" *average* paper. It was also possible for two papers to be *high, average,* or *low* for different reasons. At times, then, the readers have included two papers receiving the same score but accompanied by very different explanatory comments.

This book also differs from *End-of-Year Examinations* in that often students from different grades have attempted the same assignment. The readers naturally expected less from a ninth grader than from a tenth or eleventh grader writing on the same topic.

Also, since here the students are not writing answers to examination questions, and since many of the assignments allow for widely different approaches, the readers have accepted a student's interpretation of the assignment wherever possible and have tried to rate the paper on its use of evidence to support that interpretation. For failure to reckon with the assignment, however, the readers felt lenience was not in order, especially in papers from students in the upper grades.

Because lines of demarcation between *high, average,* and *low* are often difficult to locate, teachers may well disagree with some of the ratings given to student papers. The line between a "high" *low* and a "low" *average,* for instance, is always hard to set, but the comments state the readers' reasons for their ratings, though certainly they make no claim that the ratings themselves are infallible. In fact, if they provoke healthy dispute among teachers, they will have served one of their purposes.

The Committee members generally came to an agreement about ratings. Occasionally, debate did not end in a consensus; for a few samples, therefore, the "dissenting verdict" is included in the comment, with judgment as to which is the better left to the reader of this volume.

# Novels

# *Introduction to the Units on the Novel*

The choice of novels for this part of the book raises the question: Why these four? The answer lies in a combination of practical and professional considerations. The actualities of the school budget dictated the choice of books readily available in inexpensive editions. Limitations of time said an emphatic "no" to the five- or six-hundred page novel; and even if time had not been a factor, we wanted novels short enough to be read quickly, short enough to be examined whole, and talked about whole without the partitioning that sometimes leads to dismemberment. Three other purposes guided our choosing. First, we were looking for a novel commonly taught in both grades 9 and 12, one for which we could set up two separate study plans sharply differentiating what is appropriate for the ninth grade from what is appropriate for the twelfth. Hemingway's *The Old Man and the Sea* was custom-tailored to our needs. Second, we wanted a novel frequently used in high schools and especially susceptible to the over-teaching that takes a work apart, page by page, without ever restoring the strewn parts to a new wholeness. Wilder's *The Bridge of San Luis Rey* looked like what we were after. Finally, we set about tracking down a pair of novels rich in possibilities for comparative study. We first toyed with the idea of mating *A Separate Peace* with *Lord of the Flies,* but second thought suggested the wisdom of finding a novel that speaks out of an age other than our own. At last we decided to pair *Stalky & Co.* with *A Separate Peace;* and although we had qualms about how cordial a reception *Stalky* would get from sophisticated eleventh and twelfth graders, we discovered that with *A Separate Peace* as digestant, *Stalky* went down better than we had dared to hope.

This section of the book now offers five teaching plans: one for *Stalky* and *A Separate Peace;* two for *The Bridge of San Luis Rey;* and two for *The Old Man and the Sea.* Although no one of these five units is specifically marked for the tenth grade, teachers may well find that an able tenth grade class can tackle either *The Bridge of San Luis Rey* or *Stalky* and *A Separate Peace,* whereas the ninth grade unit on *The Old Man and the Sea* should work well with many tenth grade classes.

Here, as in all the sections on literature, both language and composition are a vital part of every unit, and the students' writing is among the most significantly revealing outcomes of the work covered.

# The Old Man and the Sea, *Grade 9*

this unit does recognize that some ninth graders are extraordinarily perceptive. A few questions are here for that kind of student, but the major target is the average ninth grader, with his inescapable limitations and exciting potentialities.

## Preparation

(The preparation will take approximately two class periods.)

Complete your first reading of *The Old Man and the Sea.* As you read, you may want to make notes or mark important passages, but focus mainly on events and characters. After you have read the book and before you begin your class discussion, you will write a paper in class for which you may use your book in any way you wish.

## Writing Assignment One

(The paper will take a full class period.)

### Directions

Write a full, detailed answer to this question: Were you satisfied that the ending of Hemingway's book makes a believable, meaningful, and moving fulfillment of the old man's experience?

For this paper, consider the ending to include all that takes place from the time the first shark comes to the time of the old man's final dreaming of the young lions. Use your book as much as you wish.

### Note to the Teacher

A thorough discussion of these papers, perhaps with a reading aloud of the best ones, might well come when the class has finished its discussion of the questions below and, if possible, before the student writes his final paper outside class.

## Questions for Discussion

1. Suppose someone who had never read the book asked you just what happens in *The Old Man and the Sea.* How would you answer that question in the fewest possible words, still doing justice to the story and leaving out nothing vital to its plot? "Happenings" may be external, as when Santiago fights the sharks, or internal, as when he thinks of Joe DiMaggio. Which kind of "happening" do you think was more important to Hemingway, and why do you think so?

2. How many characters are there in the book? Here you will want to consider how far you wish to stretch the term *character.* This is not a question with a single right answer, but it is an important question to consider as you try to understand the book.

3. Is the entire novel a single unit or does it divide into parts? If it divides into parts, how many parts are there? This, too, is a question that probably has no single right answer, but you may be able to reach a compromise on it.

4. Suppose that someone who has not read the book asks you what kind of person Santiago is. What would you say, and why would you say it? How does Hemingway make you feel about the old man, and how does he do it? How do you think Hemingway himself feels about the old man, and why do you think so?

5. Why does the boy Manolin do so much for the old man, and what does the old man do for the boy? How would you describe their relationship?

6. How would you describe the fish to someone who had never read the book? What changes take place in Santiago's attitude toward the fish from the time he hooks it to the time he brings its skeleton back to Havana?

7. Why does Hemingway have the small bird come to rest on the old man's boat (pages 54–55)?

8. Why does baseball mean so much to the old man, and why does he have such a special interest in DiMaggio?

9. Why does Hemingway interrupt the story to have Santiago recall the arm-wrestling incident with the Negro?

10. After the old man has harpooned the fish, Hemingway writes (page 94), "Then the fish came alive, with his death in him." What is gained or lost by this wording, instead of, "Then the fish rose to the surface of the sea, with the harpoon in him"?

11. Why does the old man go on fighting the sharks even when he knows he has no chance of saving his fish?

12. When the fish has been reduced to a skeleton, the old man thinks to himself (page 120), "It is

# The Old Man and the Sea
## *Grade 9*

*Edition Used:* Hemingway, Ernest. *The Old Man and the Sea.* New York: Charles Scribner's Sons, 1952. The page numbers cited in this unit are those of the Scribner Library paperback edition (SL 104). If possible, use this or the hardbound edition, not the school edition with questions and study aids.

*Approximate Time:* 1½ weeks, or about 7 class periods

### To the Teacher

*The Old Man and the Sea* is a book that can be taught well in grade 9 and also taught well—but differently—in grade 12. The purpose of this unit and the twelfth grade one that follows it is to suggest the kind of teaching, questioning, and writing appropriate for grade 9 and then to demonstrate that wise ninth grade teaching will still leave many exercises that belong more properly in the twelfth grade. For instance, these ninth grade materials steer clear of all talk about symbols. The risks of turning ninth graders loose on a scavenger hunt for symbols are unforgettably illustrated in the sample answer following this unit in which the small bird that lights on Santiago's boat appears first as Veronica, minus her handkerchief, and later as the wife of Pontius Pilate. The exceptional ninth grader probably can play the symbol game without coming to grief, but why make him? Too often the glib ninth grader gives the illusion of understanding when he is merely manipulating words—often our words rather than his. This is why some of the discussion questions in this unit may strike the teacher of sophisticated ninth graders as transparently simple and insultingly obvious. Sample answers to some of the assignments, however, indicate that even simple-seeming questions can provide plenty of exercise for an able student's abilities. For example, some ninth graders resented being asked to tell what "happens" in the book. They saw this only as a check-up on whether or not they had done the reading. Actually, it takes skill to condense the plot of a book without distortion, oversimplification, or vital omissions. The answers on the pretesting showed a wide range of accuracy and skill. At the same time, easy when you are beaten. I never knew how easy it was. And what beat you, . . ."

" 'Nothing,' he said aloud. 'I went out too far.' "

Is the old man right in saying that nothing beat him, that he went out too far? Explain your answer. Does Hemingway mean the reader to feel that the old man ought not to have gone out so far, that he ought to have stayed closer to the shore, along with the other fishermen? Give reasons for your answer.

13. Why does Hemingway bring in the tourists at the end of the book?

14. Now that you have discussed the above questions, go back for a further consideration of the question on Hemingway's ending to which you wrote an answer before you had had any class discussion.

## Writing Assignment Two

(The assignment is to be done outside class.)

### Directions

Choose *one* of the following three assignments.

1. Write a carefully planned paper in which you explore the meaning and the appropriateness of Hemingway's title. In doing this, you will need to examine carefully each word of the title and you will also need to consider other possible titles that Hemingway might have used.

2. Below are two questions, each asked by a ninth grade student in a class discussion of *The Old Man and the Sea.* Choose *one* of these two questions and answer it as fully, as explicitly, as thoughtfully, and as honestly as you can. In doing this you will need to refer continually to the book itself to justify your point of view.

a. "After all is said and done, wasn't Santiago just a stupid, senile old man who had no business doing what he did?"

b. "How do we know Hemingway ever intended to do any more than just tell a simple story about a simple fisherman and make a few bucks?"

3. A character in John Steinbeck's *East of Eden* says, "No story has power, nor will it last, unless we feel in ourselves that it is true, and true of us. . . . If a story is not about the hearer he will not listen." It might at first seem strange that you might find anything "true" about yourself in *The Old Man and the Sea,* but some of your contemporaries have "listened" to this story as if it were about themselves.

Write a carefully prepared paper in which you consider what the book had to say to you, where you came in, what you heard about yourself as you "listened."

Choose this topic *only* if you honestly feel that the book had something to say to you.

## Writing Assignment One
## Sample 1. Grade: High

Hemingway's choice of endings for *The Old Man and the Sea* was most skillfully chosen, for in it the author provides the reader with evidence that although Santiago appears to be defeated he is actually triumphant. Hemingway's ending makes the obvious point that Hemingway himself is much more concerned with the quality of Santiago's resistance to nature than with the nature of the old man's material gains. Through this culmination and Hemingway's literary perception, the reader, in spite of Santiago's apparent defeat and the loss of his prize, is left with the feeling that, nonetheless, the old fisherman has won a great victory. Santiago's victory is one which cannot be measured in pounds of marlin flesh, and would actually be weakened if the marlin had been brought in without damage. If the old man had brought the entire marlin to the village, Hemingway's emphasis of victory would be perverted to one of a base, materialistic nature. The reader feels that, while Santiago is in much the same economic condition at the resolution as he was at the beginning of the book, the old fisherman has still undergone a definite change for the better in that he himself is assured of his manhood and of his skill as a fisherman. The real prize for Santiago is the knowledge that he struggled with, and overcame, a force of nature much greater than himself.

## Writing Assignment One
## Comment on Sample 1. Grade: High

This would be an able piece of work from any high school student. For a ninth grader it is outstanding both in form and in substance. This student looks at Hemingway's ending with a mature awareness of the limitations that realism sets to the old man's triumph. He writes with neither sentimentality nor cynicism, but with a full realization that triumph and defeat are essentially inward, that what happens outwardly to a person matters far less than what the person does inwardly with those happenings—a realization that he expresses with skill when he writes: "Santiago's victory is one which cannot be measured in pounds of marlin." The paper shows quite remarkable powers of generalization, and these help compensate for the absence of references to specific events (the dream and so forth) at the end of the novel.

## Writing Assignment One
## Sample 2. Grade: Average

I am satisfied with the ending of the story because I think it is exactly the way it would happen. Since I have experience fishing for big fish in the Gulf Stream, I know it can be a trying experience. You would have to be a superman not to be exhausted after even a day of hard work. Hemingway's ending for his novel is good because it is up to the reader to use his imagination to know what would happen after the story ends. It is possible that the old man may die from the ordeal, but since the author doesn't tell you this you can think for yourself. After reading the novel I like to think the old man will live to catch more marlin!

## Writing Assignment One
## Comment on Sample 2. Grade: Average

This paper has the clarity of a mind uncluttered by complexities, of a vision undistracted by multiplicities. The writing is as clear and as simple as the thinking. Nothing here is wrong; nothing is distorted. At an unsophisticated ninth grade level, the student has grasped Hemingway's ending. But in comparison with the richness, the depth, and the penetration of the first paper, the limitations, the shallowness, and the omissions of this paper proclaim its averageness. To describe what the old man has lived through as "a trying experience" is ludicrously inadequate, though near the end the student does admit the possibility of the old man's dying "from the ordeal." Nevertheless the recognition that Hemingway's ending leaves the reader to use his imagination is valid and perceptive. So is the awareness implied in the final sentence. But what is most glaringly missing from this paper is any recognition that the most significant struggle in the story is the one that has taken place inside the old man—the recognition that makes the first paper so unmistakably superior as a piece of ninth grade thinking and writing.

## Writing Assignment One
## Sample 3. Grade: Low

Not really, because the story dropped off without really telling you what happened. Also the story didn't come through with a realistic type ending. If the old man was going to die, then I think he (Mr. Hemmingway) should have said so or if he wanted him to be a hero, I think he should have said so there, too. The story is a strong story with adventure and suspense, but the ending drops of to almost nothing. I would that it might be a type of anti-climax.

## Writing Assignment One
## Comment on Sample 3. Grade: Low

In comparison with either the *average* or the *high* paper, this is a spindling response to the assignment. This student evidently thinks a good ending to a novel will leave nothing to the imagination. He therefore sees Hemingway as having muffed his job in leaving the reader to guess whether or not the old man dies. He is disgruntled that Hemingway never tells the reader whether or not to consider the old man a hero. The denial of realism to Hemingway's ending is further evidence of limited understanding. The suggestion that the ending "might be a type of anti-climax" might have been both important and valid if the student had followed it with careful qualification, but he leaves it undeveloped and unsupported. Meanwhile he has apparently missed the whole inner drama of the story, and to miss that is to miss most of what matters.

## Writing Assignment Two, Question 1
## Sample 1. Grade: High

I find the title *The Old Man and the Sea* appropriate in most respects to the book. It is both a summary and explanation of the book, but it functions primarily as a summary; the title can be explained by corresponding references to the book. The title can be taken piece by piece and the meaning of each piece in the context of the book analyzed.

Why is the first part of the title the "Old Man"? Firstly, the "Old Man" is the most important part of the title because he is the most important part of the book, that is, the most important character. It seems odd that Santiago should be called the "old" man after all his efforts not to turn old and earn the retired status. However, Santiago is physically old, and he does not deny that, but, more important, his spirit is young. Santiago is old but not senile. He has withstood the test of time and triumphed; he is more of a hallowed figure than an obsolete figure. Finally, why is he entitled "The Old Man" at all instead of "Santiago" "An Old Man" or "The Old Fisherman". I think he is "The Old Man" because in the book he is spoken of as an entity; he is so old that he is almost timeless. He is a human entity, however, with all the normal hopes and dissapointments, but he is truly a *man*. He might have been portrayed as an entity because Hemingway in him gave an example of the ideal man and his ability to conquer physical old age.

Why is the second part of the title ". .and the Sea"? It is the most important outward relationship in the book, but what sort of a relationship is it? The man depends on the sea for his livelihood; although Santiago thinks of the sea as "giving or withholding great favors", but the relationship is not passive since the old man has to go out on the sea and fight to obtain the fruits of the sea's great favors. He is more of a man than the other fishermen; he goes further out. This is his attitude towards life; in fact, the sea can by symbolic of life. The "and" relationship is the most suitable because neither the old man or the sea are inferior to one another. The old man is not a product of sea, or of life, but a product of himself, and the sea, or life, is not merely the means of livelihood for the old man, but a continual struggle.

Lastly, since the book is about manhood, why not call it *"Courage"* or *Manhood?* This would be more direct, and would make it easier to understand the book, but the book is not merely about manhood, but about how age affects an old man who no longer has a man's phisique, but who has a man's character in his struggle with life.

## Writing Assignment Two, Question 1
## Comment on Sample 1. Grade: High

The thoroughness, the depth of understanding, and the technical competence of this paper rank it as superior ninth grade work. The techniques here are not flawless, but no English teacher is going to lose sleep over a ninth grader's spelling "disappointments" "dissapointments" or his use of a plural verb in a neither-nor construction requiring the singular—not when such slips are weighed against the overwhelming evidence throughout the paper of ability to handle diction and sentence structure with grace as well as competence. The plan for this paper is unobtrusively orderly, providing for an examination of every word in the title, including the initial *the* which this student is acute enough to spot as significant. His use, moreover, of the word "entity" for the old man suggests his awareness that this is not just *an* old man. The comments on *old* and *man* are similarly perceptive. The section on *the sea* sees there the symbolic suggestion of life itself and at the same time senses that the essential contest is not between the old man and the fish but between the old man and the element of Nature that bred the fish and that is, perhaps, the source of all life. The student is also aware that the old man's struggle is not so much for a livelihood as for self-realization, self-respect, human dignity. This is a paper that not only builds a firm case for the rightness of Hemingway's title but also examines other possibilities and demonstrates their inadequacy or their inappropriateness.

## Writing Assignment Two, Question 1 Sample 2. Grade: Average

*The Old Man and the Sea* is an excellent title for this novelette by Ernest Hemingway. It is probably one of the best that could be used. The reason I think the title is a good one is because the old man and the sea are the two basic elements in the story.

The old man is the main character and should of course be included in the title. The sea should be included because it represents the object that the old man's whole life is centered around. Even at the beginning of the book the old man speaks fondly in a fraternal way of the sea as if it were a real person. The sea controls the man's life almost completely. If the sea will not yield a fish then the old fisherman must go hungry. Since the sea is the man's way of life then it must be in the title.

Another title such as "The Old Man and the Fish" would not be as effective. The old man's conflict is not really with the fish but in a sense with the sea. In a way the fish and the sharks represent the sea and are characters acting in its place. Another title that would not meet the necessary requirements is "The Old Man". This title shows no conflict which the whole story is based on. The book is not just a story of a poor old man; it is a story of a conflict between man and the opposing, yet sometimes allied, sea.

As one can see *The Old Man and the Sea* is a very appropriate and meaningful title. It leads the reader into what the book is really about. It introduces an important conflict: Man and the necessary but vengeful sea.

## Writing Assignment Two, Question 1 Comment on Sample 2. Grade: Average

This paper makes the essential points in reasonably clear, competent, correct English. What it lacks is the subtle perception, the detailed analysis, and the unusual writing skill of the first paper. This paper looks at the title as a whole and demonstrates its appropriateness, whereas the first paper examined each word in the title before appraising the total impact. The perfunctoriness and the repetitiveness in the first and last paragraphs also put this paper in a different category from the first one. One of the strengths of this paper, however, is its recognition that the old man talks of the sea as though it were a person, but this student sees the old man's way of talking about the sea as "fraternal." A more perceptive student would have remembered the passage explaining why the old man always thought of the sea as *la mar,* not *el mar;* that is, as a capricious but fascinating woman rather than as a brother.

## Writing Assignment Two, Question 1 Sample 3. Grade: Low

This book's title is a perfect example of Hemingway's craft as a writer. In six words he conveys a picture of the story, the total of the point of the narrative. With each word he paints a picture, and the whole glows with color. In this title Hemingway shows that he is to the pen what Rembrandt is to the brush.

To my mind the words "old man" suggest both the wizened old man and the hot humid stillness of the air in the doldrums. It also suggests the brazen platter of the ocean covered with the bronze kettle of the sky at noon. "And" suggests a battle, in this case a silent contest of wills, strengths, courage, and character. The first "the" signifies instead of a specific man, man as a species. The second "the" signifies not the sea, but land as well. The basics of this conflict could take place anywhere.

These are the reasons for which I feel that no other title could fill or assume the place of this masterpiece.

## Writing Assignment Two, Question 1 Comment on Sample 3. Grade: Low

This is not the work of a dull student. No dull student is capable of such a packed sentence as: " 'And' suggests a battle, in this case a silent contest of wills, strengths, courage, and character." This writer also notes, as no dull student would, that the word *the* in the title "signifies . . . man as a species." The trouble, though, is that the student has let an undisciplined imagination take over and has gone on a metaphorical binge. Much of the paper is a kind of verbal froth. For most of us the title does not "glow with color." The Rembrandt analogy is shopworn, though shopworn language is certainly no high crime in a ninth grader. The "hot humid stillness of the . . . doldrums," however, is a sample of truth sacrificed on the altar of vividness. The "brazen platter of the ocean covered with the bronze kettle of the sky at noon," is daringly imaginative, but it is the kind of imagination that plays fast and loose with the facts of the novel and should, therefore, have no place in this kind of paper. The teaching problem with such a student is to discipline the imagination without stifling it. The readers put this paper in the *low* category not only because of its undisciplined handling of language and imagery but because of the thinness of detail from the book and because it pays no attention to other possible titles although this was an expected part of the assignment.

## Writing Assignment Two, Question 2
## Sample 1. Grade: High

*The Old Man and the Sea* is the story of a man's struggle against the forces of nature and against his own weaknesses. In the beginning, Hemingway's novel shows us the necessity for patience and quiet, resolute hope. During the eighty-four days without a fish, the old man's confidence never wavered. His courage was strengthened by the undying loyalty of the boy Manolin.

Santiago's struggle with the marlin was a difficult one. Steadily his weakness and exhaustion increased until his suffering became acute. He had no one to share his misery with. To ward off the dreadful loneliness and perhaps to give himself confidence, Santiago talked aloud to the sea, to the fish, to his hand, and to himself. Out of his great respect for the fish's strength and cunning, he regarded the marlin as a friend and brother. When his left hand cramped, Santiago could feel nothing but contempt for this unworthy member of his body. Anything so unrealiable was useless and deserved to be cut off. The old man fought to keep a clear head, so he would be able to perceive every movement of the fish and use all that he had to kill him. His persistance finally triumphed. When the sharks came, the old man's resourcefulness was portrayed at its fullest. As one weapon after another failed, his ingenuity provided him with a new weapon. Although he could not save his fish, his effort was truly noble.

Throughout Hemingway's story, society invariably enters into the picture. In the beginning, other fishermen taunted the old man and his unsuccessful efforts. Perhaps they were jealous of his quiet, worry-free way of life. Any pity for the old man went unexpressed. In the closing lines of the novel, when a group of tourists comment on the "pretty shark," we see society's superficiality. Only to the old man himself could the fish and the struggle that went with the fish have any value. . . . and that was all the really mattered.

## Writing Assignment Two, Question 2
## Comment on Sample 1. Grade: High

Although the student never states which of the two options he is dealing with, this is a superior answer because of its comprehensiveness, the clarity of its style and its thinking, and because of its awareness of what matters most in the book. The opening sentence packs the essence of the book into a few words. The closing sentence goes similarly to the heart of the matter. The final paragraph with its commentary on the superficiality of society as reflected in the chit-chat of the tourists may be an echo from class discussion, but the student uses it intelligently to make his final point that for the old man it was the struggle that was really significant and nothing else really mattered. An older student might have moved on to the realization that more is involved here than one old man's struggle, that the book speaks eloquently of all human beings who have struggled with forces greater than themselves. But for a ninth grader, the awarenesses in this paper are keen. It is significant, too, that this student has the good sense not to try to push on to a symbolic level of interpretation for which few ninth graders are ready and to which few should be exposed.

## Writing Assignment Two, Question 2
## Sample 2. Grade: Average

*The Old Man and the Sea* concerns itself with the characteristics of a true man. Santiago shows many of the characteristics which Hemingway believes is the role a man should play in life. Santiago is not passive and strives to overcome the fish in their struggle. Although the sharks ate the Marlin, Santiago still had the skeleton as a symbol for the struggle and victory the old man had. Many people cannot understand the struggle the old man had for they have not experienced it themselves. People are usually unaware of many things until they have personally experienced it.

The struggle between Santiago and the fish is not meant to give Santiago money to obtain food. Santiago has been challanged by another thing and he accepts it and gives every thing in his body and mind in his attempt to overcome the huge fish. This, I believe, is Hemingway's idea of a true man. One who is willing and glad to accept a challange and one who is capable of pushing himself to the utmost. Santiago is able to do this, and no matter how he is feeling he is not willing to quit.

## Writing Assignment Two, Question 2
## Comment on Sample 2. Grade: Average

This paper, like the first, finds the book's significance not in the tangible outcomes of the old man's struggle but in the nobility of the struggle itself. This awareness is one of the paper's strengths. Another is the common sense that keeps it from "going out too far" in pursuit of elusive symbols. This student never misinterprets, but his analysis is less detailed, less searching, less discerning than that of the first paper; and control of writing skills is considerably less firm. He, too, fails to indicate which of the two options he is discussing. For these reasons, the readers saw this as a solid, respectable, but undistinguished response to the assignment.

*Note:* This is one of the assignments for which the readers felt that printing a *low* sample was unnecessary. The readers found no *low* paper not characterized by faulty technique and lack of comprehension, with little else worth discussion.

## Introductory Comment on Question 3
## of Writing Assignment Two

One teacher disliked the assignment; another found it the most "worthy" of the three offerings for grade 9; and still another pointed out the problem of sincerity here and saw the assignment as encouraging unctuous hypocrisy. And this is probably a real danger, though the caution in the directions was meant to forestall it. Many teachers felt that the assignment needed to be spelled out in more detail. The revised version tries to do just that. The assignment is a reminder that possibly we have gone too far in expecting our students, especially our younger students, to come at literature with the analytical objectivity of the scholar. The personal, the emotional response is vitally important, too.

## Writing Assignment Two, Question 3
## Sample 1. Grade: High

Although it apparently deals only with an experience undergone by one elderly Cuban fisherman, it is my opinion that *The Old Man and the Sea* has a much deeper message than merely an adventurous account of a struggle between a man and a fish. For me the struggle between Santiago and the huge fish which he has caught is symbolic of the interminable conflict between Man and Nature, and I believe that Hemingway did an excellent job of portraying this constant strife. Though it may, indeed, be a little more difficult for the general reader to identify with Santiago, since most readers have never actually had to enter a desperate conflict with Nature as did Santiago, I think that with a small amount of imaginative projection the average reader could sympathize with the old man's position.

Through reading Hemingway's symbolic account of Man's struggle for survival, I found myself much more aware of the fact that Nature is truly an awesome force, and that Man is comparitively puny when he is measured against Nature. I do not believe, however, that the author is suggesting a course of submission by Man to Nature, but on the contrary it is my opinion that Hemingway admires a man who is willing to meet Nature in all of her greatness, to face her absolutely alone, and to wrest from her a great prize. It is, therefore, because of the old man's determination that Hemingway thinks of him so highly.

In several side incidences Hemingway provides the reader, by the means of Santiago's remarks and observations, with other skillfully noted insights into the nature of Man's relationship with his surroundings. Hemingway depicts the awesomeness of such things as the sea, which is only a small portion of Nature, through Santiago's perceptive remarks upon the vastness of the sea, the eternal journey of the sun and moon, and especially through the old man's attitude toward the giant marlin.

Despite the obvious value of the above-mentioned aspect of Hemingway's statement upon Life and upon Man's relationship with Nature, I found a more personal application of the novel in the brief passage concerning the two tourists. The description of the tourists' ignorance of the great struggle which had taken place so close to them provides a warning for the perceptive reader, lest he himself become a mere spectator in the wonderful, yet terrifying, battle of Life. To me it is appalling that a human being could become so insensitive and absolutely uninterested in the stimulating environment of our world as these two sub-humans did, and yet I realize that this oblivious attitude toward Life is a stealthy process which takes over the human consciousness only after a long war of attrition. To me this is the most provocative facet of Hemingway's excellent work, *The Old Man and the Sea.*

## Writing Assignment Two, Question 3 Comment on Sample 1. Grade: High

This is an exceptionally fine piece of writing. For this student Santiago's struggle is "symbolic of the interminable conflict between Man and Nature"—a recognition remote indeed from the inanities of the adolescent symbol chaser who has not yet learned to apply the brakes of common sense to his super-charged imagination. The writer of this paper also reveals the maturity of his judgment in his realization that though man looks puny confronting Nature as the old man does, Hemingway's purpose is not to suggest "submission by Man to Nature," but rather to assert human dignity in the face of insuperable odds. The final paragraph on the tourists is probably the clearest evidence of this student's insight. Like most students, he expresses his contempt for the tourists' sideline unconcern and superficiality; but, unlike most students, he senses that neither he nor any one of us is immune to what he calls "a stealthy process which takes over the human consciousness only after a long war of attrition."

## Writing Assignment Two, Question 3 Sample 2. Grade: Average

*The Old Man and the Sea* does have something of importance to say to me. I never before realized what the life of a fisherman can be like. I never realized that it was such a tough, demanding life, often with little reward. I never thought of a fisherman as a real person until I read the *Old Man and the Sea.*

Santiago was one of the most interesting characters I have ever read about in a book. He was just an old fisherman, but nevertheless, a great man. His character, his ideas, his feelings, are admirable. Here was a man who had lived a tough life and had had little reward for it. He lived in a poor shack by the sea, fished for a living, and had few friends. And yet he was a tremendous person. Santiago had not had much of an education. And yet he stood out among people. He was a man among men.

If you think of Santiago in terms of his occupation, in terms of physical things, he is just a poor, low-class, common man. Perhaps he is a failure. But mentally, Santiago is a very intelligent person. He has feelings, intelligent ideas, morals, and makes great use of his mind. I was able to understand that a poor fisherman can be an amazing person after reading this book.

After reading *Old Man and the Sea* I have respect for a fisherman's way of life. Before reading this book, I was just like the tourists at the end of the story, who had no insight into Santiago's way of life or the great fight which had taken place between him and the Marlin. Now I have some insight into the kind of life a fisherman leads and I am able to appreciate such a life more. Now I am able to understand that some poor, common men like fishermen can be intelligent, admirable, and wonderful people. The real message that *The Old Man and the Sea* has for me is that one should never judge a person by the kind of job he has. One should always judge him by his character.

## Writing Assignment Two, Question 3 Comment on Sample 2. Grade: Average

This paper moves at a simpler level than the first. The writing is clear and competent but without the distinction that is part of the first paper's superiority. This student sees clear-sightedly but without the depth or range of the first student. For him the book's essential message is that a man may be "a man among men" even though he has neither wealth nor education nor social position. For a ninth grader this is a valid and important but not very subtle realization. So is the writer's new-found awareness of what it must be like to be a fisherman. Perhaps his subtlest understanding comes at the end when he says he realized that he was "just like the two tourists at the end of the story." In comparison with the first paper, however, this one uses little supporting evidence from the book. The second paragraph mentions the admirableness of the old man's character, ideas, and feelings, but never makes any one of those abstract nouns explicit through examples. A merely *average* rating for a paper as valid, as honest, and as clear-cut as this one in its response to an assignment that invited subjectivity is perhaps ungenerous but unavoidable after the brilliance of the first paper.

## Writing Assignment Two, Question 3
## Sample 3. Grade: Low

In *The Old Man and the Sea* Ernest Hemingway definitely has something to say, but discovering just what Hemingway has to say is the problem. After many hours of contemplative thought, I have settled upon two ideas.

This is the first hypothesis. The old man is Jesus Christ. He takes his boat which is really the apostles out into the sea. The sea is the world. The fisherman has not made haul for a long time, and he must make a catch soon or there can be no salvation. Finally the fisherman hooks the fish. The fish is the salvation the fisherman is looking for, and the fisherman knows he will have to struggle in order to keep the fish. The struggle with the fish lasting for several days is Christ suffering the Passion. During the Passion, on the Way of the Cross, the fisherman meets the bird. The bird is Veronica the woman who wipes the blood from Christ's face. The bird gives comfort to the fisherman. The Albacore with the two Flying Fish in its stomach is the sponge soaked in wine on a reed, this nourishes Christ. The agony on the cross is when the fisherman finally hauls in the fish and wins salvation. The sharks play no specialized part in this theory, but they are significant. The sharks are the ones who over the years have torn, or tried to tear the Church, which is the salvation apart ideologically. Even these great accomplishments of Christ go unnoticed by the common people, the tourists.

This is the second hypothesis. The fisherman is Pontius Pilate. He has hooked into Christ, the great fish. Pontius does not quite know what to do about the fish, and he just rides along with the fish. Pontius has many thoughts about the fish. First he compares the fish as an equal, then he hates the fish, finally he realizes it is part of his job to kill the fish. The bird is Pontius Pilates wife. She warns him that the fish is good, and that Pontius should leave it alone. Pontius says it is too late he has allready hooked the fish. Pontius Pilate finally hauls in the fish.

The first shark, the Mako, is the High Priest who takes the first blow at Christ. The Galanos, the sharks who come in pairs are the regular priests. They mock and abuse the fish. Finally the packs of sharks the common people attack the fish. They thrash, spit upon, and jeer Christ. They finish the job the Mako started. The head and skeleton of the fish represent the now defunct body of Christ. This body is given to Pedrico, who is Joseph of Arimathea. The rest of the world, the tourists see what is left of these remains, but they do not understand.

## Writing Assignment Two, Question 3
## Comment on Sample 3. Grade: Low

This paper is proof that symbolism is far beyond the grasp of the average ninth grader. The first two papers exemplify the thoughtful, valid understandings appropriate for the ninth grade. This student combines a severe case of symbol addiction with a similarly severe case of pomposity. After informing the reader that he has indulged in "many hours of contemplative thought," he is off on a verbal spree that leaves common sense and humor behind. He has a symbolic heyday with the bird that lighted on the old man's boat. By some extrasensory perception, he spots the bird's sex as female and turns it into Veronica—minus her handkerchief. The identification of the flying albacore harboring a couple of flying fish in its innards with the "sponge soaked in wine on a reed" is a further astonishing step in the development of the "hypothesis" that the "old man is Jesus Christ." Yet the most persuasive evidence for this theory—the reference to the sound a man might make when the nails go through his hands—goes unnoted.

The second "hypothesis" is even more extraordinary. The fisherman becomes Pontius Pilate and the fish is Christ. The bird suffers a sea change from Veronica to Pontius Pilate's wife, and the sharks take over as priests. Even Pedrico, who gets the marlin's skeleton, takes on the identity of Joseph of Arimathea.

This kind of symbol-hunting is not confined to ninth graders, but with younger students it is particularly pernicious. And certainly this paper is a reminder that any teaching of symbolism must proceed with caution. If students know the dangers, we may hope that they will not park their common sense outside the door when they enter a work of literature.

## Writing Assignment Two, Question 3
## Sample 4. Grade: Low

To me the old man of the sea is showing us his way of living an exciting life. He is saying faith and hope can take a person a long way to living an exciting, happy and enjoyable life. He is saying people can live maybe a more exciting life with little money. The old man is content with his present possesions and is not stingy with them. The old man says we should all be conscious and fascinated by the beauty of the world God created. He is telling us to talk our problems over with God and try to abide in him. To me he is saying that everyone should be as devoted to his work and have as much faith and hope as he does. He has given me hope and shown me the good people get out of life. When reading this book I put myself in the position of the old man and think how courageous and hopeful he is. This man represents the hard-working, faithful, hopefull and courageous people of the world. He has acquired many of these talents due to his understanding and love of God's Kingdom.

## Writing Assignment Two, Question 3
## Comment on Sample 4. Grade: Low

This paper is a sample of the sanctimonious platitudes the assignment invited from the naïve and the unwary. The writing skills are decent but undistinguished. There are no gross misinterpretations, but rather there is a pious beatification that falsifies most of what matters in the book. In fact there is too little of the book here to give the student much chance to misinterpret, though he used what chances he allowed himself. The reference to the old man as "content with his present possesions" and "not stingy with them" overlooks the bleak facts of a poverty too acute to permit many possessions. The notion, too, that the old man was "living an exciting, happy and enjoyable life" is a simple-minded reading that amounts to distortion. The idea that the old man "is telling us to talk our problems over with God" is another pious fabrication. Still another one is the suggestion that Santiago is reminding us that "we should all be conscious and fascinated by the beauty of the world God created." Apparently this student has missed the central concern with Nature rather than with God and the stress on conflict rather than harmony between man and his environment.

Though only one *low* paper was presented for question 2, two are given for question 3 because they illustrate two quite different kinds of forced and false interpretation.

# The Old Man and the Sea, *Grade 12*

## Questions for Discussion

### Part I. Form, Point of View, Structure

1. Hemingway might have written *The Old Man and the Sea* as a much longer novel, taking Santiago from his early childhood to his final dream of the lions. What would have been lost if he had done this? What gained?

2. Hemingway might also have written *The Old Man and the Sea* as a short story, concentrating on the struggle with the fish, with the sea, and with the sharks—and probably telescoping or omitting the scenes before and after that struggle. What would have been lost and gained?

3. From whose point of view does Hemingway tell the story? Why did Hemingway choose to tell it this way? Did he make the right choice for this particular book? Why or why not?

4. In much of this book the old man is talking to himself. Is this heavy reliance on the introspective monologue a weakness or a strength? Explain your answer. Do you imagine it was a weakness or a strength in the filming of the book? Why or why not?

5. Why, where, and how effectively does Hemingway make use of the flashback technique?

6. In answer to the question, "How many parts are there in *The Old Man and the Sea?*" a ninth grade student wrote: "If the novel were to be divided into sections, there would be three of these. The first part is essentially an introduction to the old man's situation, his relation with Manolin, and actually his dauntless attitude toward his ill fortune. The second part may be considered as the struggle between Santiago and the gallant marlin in which the old man eventually conquers the fish. The third section involves the destruction of the fisherman's prize by the sharks and the old man's return to his village. Although the old man has no material gains from his long struggle he has still proven that he retains his ability as a great fisherman."

Is this ninth grade student's three-part division a logical, accurate description of the structure of Hemingway's book? If your answer is no, what alternative division would you suggest and why do you think it more accurately describes *The Old Man and the Sea?*

7. As Hemingway has built his book, does it end with a climax, an anti-climax, both, or neither? Explain your answer.

### Part II. Style, Sentence Structure, Diction, the Condensed Line

1. Hemingway is famous for his ability to pack meaning into a few simple words. Examine and comment on the following examples. Then try to find others.

a. "He was beautiful, the old man remembered, and he had stayed." (The old man says this of the male marlin who stayed by the boat until he saw that the female had been killed.)

b. "It jumped again and again in the acrobatics of its fear." (This is said of the dolphin who had taken the old man's line.)

c. "Then the fish came alive, with his death in him." (This describes the marlin after the old man has harpooned him.)

d. " 'You're tired, old man,' he said. 'You're tired inside.' "

e. "He had to sit down five times before he reached his shack."

2. Hemingway writes, "The old man had taught the boy to fish and the boy loved him." On page 106, he has the old man say, "The boy keeps me alive." And on page 122, he says, "The boy saw that the old man was breathing and then he saw the old man's hands and he started to cry." Using these three quotations as your evidence, describe the relationship Hemingway establishes between the old man and the boy. Then comment on the means by which he does this. You will have to examine the words, the implications, and the sentence structure. Consider, for instance, the effect of the way Hemingway strings his main clauses together with *ands* on pages 9–10 and pages 121–122—exactly what you may have been taught not to do. In what ways would the effect be different if Hemingway had subordinated one of his clauses and had written, "Because the old man had taught him to fish the boy loved him"? Why doesn't he write on page 122, "When the boy saw that the old man was breathing and when he got a look at the old man's hands, he started to cry"?

3. In describing the scars on Santiago's hands on

# The Old Man and the Sea
## *Grade 12*

*Edition Used:* Hemingway, Ernest. *The Old Man and the Sea.* New York: Charles Scribner's Sons, 1952. The page numbers cited in this unit are those of the Scribner Library paperback edition (SL 104). If possible, use this or the hardbound edition, not the school edition with questions and study aids.

*Approximate Time:* 1½ weeks, 7 or 8 class periods

### To the Teacher

Teachers using these twelfth grade materials should also be familiar with the ninth grade unit on *The Old Man and the Sea,* which precedes this one. Some twelfth grade teachers may even wish to use parts of the ninth grade material before moving on to what is here. In the ninth grade unit the focus is on events and characters. The center of attention here is form, structure, point of view, diction, literary devices, levels of meaning, interpretation, and evaluation. Most teachers will want to select from these study materials only what best suits the needs, interests, and abilities of their students; and certainly no teacher should feel obligated to use all that is here.

## Opening Assignment

(The assignment requires one or two preparation periods.)

Read *The Old Man and the Sea,* preferably at a single sitting.

## Writing Assignment One

(This assignment is to be done outside class after the reading but before any class discussion.)

### Directions

Write a paper in which you comment fully and specifically on the significance for the entire book of Santiago's words, "A man can be destroyed but not defeated." To do this you will need to start with an exploration of possible meanings of the two words *destroyed* and *defeated.*

page 10, Hemingway writes, "They were as old as erosions in a fishless desert." Is the simile appropriate and effective? Why or why not? Is the language as simple as Hemingway's language is supposed to be?

4. Look at the fourth sentence in the paragraph on page 28 beginning "Sometimes someone. . ." Is this the kind of sentence for which Hemingway is noted? Is it appropriate and effective in this context? Explain your answer.

5. Examine the following passage from page 35: "But the bird was almost out of sight now and nothing showed on the surface of the water but some patches of yellow, sun-bleached Sargasso weed and the purple, formalized, iridescent, gelatinous bladder of a Portuguese man-of-war floating close beside the boat. It turned on its side and then righted itself. It floated cheerfully as a bubble with its long deadly purple filaments trailing a yard behind it in the water."

Do you find here the simple wording and short sentences said to be characteristic of Hemingway's style? How do you explain your findings?

6. How does Hemingway communicate to the reader the fact that Santiago thinks and speaks in Spanish?

7. Now look carefully at the wording and the sentence structure of Hemingway's final paragraph. Then describe and explain your findings: "Up the road, in his shack, the old man was sleeping again. He was still sleeping on his face and the boy was sitting by him watching him. The old man was dreaming about the lions."

8. Comment on any other features of Hemingway's diction and idiom that seem important.

9. Now that you have examined this sampling of passages from *The Old Man and the Sea,* what tentative conclusions are you ready to draw about Hemingway's diction and sentence structure? Find other passages that reinforce, modify, or change your present conclusions.

## Part III. Meanings and Interpretations

1. a. Hemingway says of the old man on page 13, "He was too simple to wonder when he had attained humility." How do you interpret this statement?

b. Humility has been defined as "the understatement of a powerful personality." What does this mean and to what extent does it apply to the kind of humility the old man has attained?

2. Discuss the role that *luck* plays in this book and consider the different shades of meaning Hemingway gives to it. (You will find references to luck on pages 9, 13, 32, 75, 116–117, and 125.)

3. Comment on each of the following passages, trying to relate it significantly to the book as a whole:

a. "There was no cast net and the boy remembered when they had sold it. But they went through this fiction every day. There was no pot of yellow rice and fish and the boy knew this too" (page 17).

b. "Why did they make birds so delicate and fine as those sea swallows when the ocean can be so cruel?" (page 29). Whom does the old man mean by "they"?

c. " 'Take a good rest, small bird,' he said. 'Then go in and take your chance like any man or bird or fish' " (page 55).

d. " 'I told the boy I was a strange old man,' he said. 'Now is when I must prove it.'

"The thousand times that he had proved it meant nothing. Now he was proving it again. Each time was a new time and he never thought about the past when he was doing it" (page 66).

e. "But it is good that we do not have to try to kill the sun or the moon or the stars. It is enough to live on the sea and kill our true brothers" (page 75).

f. " 'And pain does not matter to a man' " (page 84).

g. "The *dentuso* is cruel and able and strong and intelligent. But I was more intelligent than he was. Perhaps not, he thought. Perhaps I was only better armed" (page 103).

h. "Fishing kills me exactly as it keeps me alive" (page 106).

## Part IV. Symbolism

Critics have pointed out that it is possible to read *The Old Man and the Sea* at several different levels, starting with the purely literal, which yields a powerful story of physical adventure and courage. What are some of the other levels that will yield a valid and a fruitful reading of the book? For each suggestion you make, consider the extent to which Hemingway's text encourages the kind of reading you are advocating. As you move into symbolic levels, take your common sense along with you; and remember that a good literal reading is better than a symbolic one that does violence to Hemingway's intent. The following questions will serve as guides in your exploration of possible uses of symbolism in *The Old Man and the Sea.* Use them as the starting point for your own further investigations, proceeding always with cautious common sense.

1. Where is the one passage in the book that unmistakably alludes to Christ on the Cross? What does such symbolism add to the novel? Do you find any other passages that may be reinforcing the Christ imagery? Can you be sure that they are doing so? The old man is sometimes taken as a symbol of Christ on the Cross. How do you reconcile this notion with the old man's own comment on page 64, "I am not religious," which he follows up with a perfunctory rattling off of a batch of "Our Fathers" and "Hail Marys"?

2. How much convincing evidence do you find for regarding the old man as a symbol of man in general?

3. How much convincing evidence do you find for regarding the fish as more than just a marlin? If the fish is a symbol, what does he symbolize?

4. Are we justified in interpreting baseball and Joe DiMaggio as more than their literal selves? If so, what do they represent?

5. Does Hemingway encourage us to think of the sea in more than literal terms? If so, what is the sea standing for?

6. How do you interpret the young lions? Are they literal or symbolic or both, and why do you think so? If they are symbolic, what do they symbolize?

7. The great fish come in September, not in May. Santiago catches his big fish in September. Are we to take September only literally? If it is more than literal, what is it standing for?

8. Does Hemingway's text invite us to interpret the sharks as more than literal? If they are more than literal, what do they represent? What is their role in the general human drama?

## Writing Assignment Two

(The assignment is to be prepared outside class. Before the student writes his final paper, it is desirable, if possible, to go over the papers written before the class discussion, clearing up possible misconceptions, perhaps reading aloud some of the best papers.)

*Note to the teacher.* This final assignment and its alternative are replacing an earlier assignment that didn't work when pretested. This is why there are no sample answers; but assignment number 1 below did work well in the one school that tried it.

1. Now that you have examined the form, style, literary devices, levels of meaning, and theme of Hemingway's *The Old Man and the Sea,* the toughest and perhaps the most important question of all remains: *As a literary work, how good is it?*

*Directions:* Write a composition in which you give this question the most detailed, thoughtful, honest answer of which you are capable. Although you cannot force your reader to agree with your judgment, try to win his respect for the thoroughness, the fair-mindedness, and the insight that have gone into the making of that judgment.

2. (Here is an alternative to the above final writing assignment.) In the Preface to his novel *The Nigger of the "Narcissus,"* Conrad says that his task as a writer is "by the power of the written word, to make you hear, to make you feel—it is, before all, to make you *see.* That—and no more, and it is everything."

*Directions:* Write a paper carefully prepared outside class in which you show fully and specifically the extent to which Hemingway in *The Old Man and the Sea* fulfills the writer's task of making you hear, feel, and—above all—*see.* You will want to give special attention to all the possible meanings in that word *see.*

## Writing Assignment One
## Sample 1. Grade: High

*Destroyed but Invincible*

In *The Old Man and the Sea,* Ernest Hemingway presents the fisherman Santiago as the true man—independent in his action, eager to follow his calling, and willing to take chances in life. The old man's most noble attribute, however, appears to be his unquenchable spirit: no matter how his body is beaten, his physical nature destroyed, his spirit remains undefeated, undefeatable, through all trials.

Santiago's body is old and beaten, his very physical existence one of suffering and trial. His clothing and shelter are scanty, his good only what neighbors will give him. In his battle with the great fish, the old man's hands are cut, his back scarred. He returns from his ordeal on the sea—several days' battle against the fish, the sharks, and the weather, with meager provisions and no water—with only the skeleton of his conquest to show. His body is torn, beaten, utterly destroyed.

But no amount of pain or physical abuse can quench Santiago's spirit and pride, which remain invincible through all his trials. Even in his squalid existence, the old man is proud, asserting that he will have fish to eat at home, even though he knows he hasn't any. Santiago chooses of his own accord to go "too far out," to ignore the hardship involved in his duel with the great fish; his catching the fish is a justification of his pride and reliance upon self. The carcass of the fish is devoured by sharks, much as Santiago's body is torn; but the skeleton, along with the old man's inner spirit, remain unconquered.

Santiago's ability to endure the harsh influence of environment is largely a result of his resignation to the belief that "Pain does not matter to a man." If DiMaggio can endure his bone spur, if the great fish can bear to pull the weight of his boat, then he, a simple old man, can at least endure the discomforts of his existence. To Santiago, his hands, unwilling to open, responsive to pain, have minds of their own, and are traitors to his own will. Even when his ordeal on the sea is over, the old man, by himself, must carry home the mast of his ship, a symbol of his burden and suffering.

But with seeming indifference to the harshness of his surroundings, to the pain he endures, Santiago dreams of days gone by—of hand-wrestling and golden lions on the beach. Though his body is destroyed, the old man's eyes remain alive, his spirit forceful, his mind beyond the realm of physical suffering. In Santiago, the true man, the physical and spiritual are truly separated, independent. The body is weak, temporary, easily destroyed; the spirit is enduring, driving, ultimately invincible.

## Writing Assignment One
## Comment on Sample 1. Grade: High

The competent writing, the clear and incisive thinking, and the carefully controlled organization all mark this as the work of a thoroughly capable twelfth grade student. The title, "Destroyed but Invincible," is an uncompromising announcement of the position the paper plans to defend. And that defense is straightforward and uncluttered by pursuit of half-sensed or nonexistent subtleties. This writer sees at once that the distinction is between the eggshell vulnerability of man's body and the enduring impregnability of his spirit. The student's repetition of this distinction is probably a conscious recognition of its centrality. An even abler student might have examined more closely the actual words in the quotation from Santiago, particularly the words "A" and "man." Why not simply "man" in general? And does "man" mean any man? A more searching paper might also have reckoned with the section in which Hemingway writes, "He knew he was beaten now finally and without remedy" (page 119), but shortly afterwards: "And what beat you, . . . 'Nothing,' he said aloud. 'I went out too far.' " And finally, a thorough exploration would look long and hard at Hemingway's ending. What are we to make of the final dreaming of the young lions? What is the significance of the old man's plans to go out with the boy as soon as the weather clears? Nevertheless, within its limitations and in spite of its omissions, this paper is a perceptive and responsible answer to the assignment.

## Writing Assignment One
## Sample 2. Grade: Average

"A man can be destroyed but not defeated." He can be torn down without being overcome or beaten. Thus was Santiago, who faced life with courage, endurance, and hope. Although the failure of losing his fish is a very bitter one, he accepts it. He accepts it in much the same way as he accepts his pain, the sea, and the creatures of the sea. In the epitome of his failure, there is always strength, dignity, and optimism. "Think about something cheerful, old man," he said. "Every minute now you are closer to home. You sail lighter for the loss of forty pounds."

The old man's acceptance of the things that are, and cannot be changed, touches the core of why he is not defeated. "I wish I had a stone for the knife," the old man said after he had checked the lashing on the oar butt. "I should have brought a stone." You should have brought many things, he thought. But you did not bring them, old man. Now is no time to think of what you do not have. Think of what you can do with what there is."

Underlying Santiago's pain and disappointment, there is hope. "It is silly not to hope, he thought. Besides I believe it is a sin."

Finally, the old man comes ashore. He is completely exhausted. Practically all that remains of his great efforts is a skeleton, eighteen feet from nose to tail. "He was stiff and sore now and his wounds and all of the strained parts of his body hurt with the cold of the night." This appears to be the very essence of defeat. Yet is it? The old man says, "It is easy when you are beaten. I never knew how easy it was. And what beat you, he thought. Nothing, I went out too far."

"A man can be destroyed but not defeated," and why is this? Because "Man is not made for defeat."

## Writing Assignment One
## Comment on Sample 2. Grade: Average

This paper is like the first in its clear-sightedness, its responsible interpretation of the text, its technical competence, and its tidy organization. Its comparative slightness is the chief reason for marking it *average* instead of *high.* It does very little with the paradoxical terms "destroyed" and "defeated." It leaves the rest of the quotation entirely unexplored. The patness of the final paragraph verges on superficiality. It juxtaposes the two quotations, "A man can be destroyed but not defeated," and, "Man is not made for defeat," without ever noting the shift from "Man" to "A man." And certainly a more energetic mind would have explored that final assertion that "Man is not made for defeat." Nevertheless, when this student chooses to use specific evidence—as in paragraphs two and three—he uses it appropriately and persuasively. This paper is the work of a potentially able student who needs to be prodded into more thorough searching, more detailed analysis, and a wholesome contempt for the too facile disposal of complexity.

## Writing Assignment One
## Sample 3. Grade: Low

*The Old Man And The Sea*

The Old Man And The Sea is an example of a satire. It creates in one's mind the image of values. The boy stayed with the Old Man because of his sense of values; he would not let his friend be defeated. The wants and needs of the Old Man were few. His ambition was unmeasureable. He believed in the saying "Try, try again."

The Old Man could never really be destroyed because his faith in the future would last eternally.

The parents of the boy didn't respect the Old Man because they probably felt he was a tired, silly old man, losing his touch in fishing. The boy's respect was entirely the opposite to that of his parents, because his respect gave the Old Man satisfaction and enthusiasm, so that in his heart he could never fail his pride or the boy's image of him, by giving up.

The fight with the shark showed the boy he could still fight the sea creatures.

The boy, his personal satisfaction and enthusiasm are the basic reasons I believe The Old Man could never have been defeated or destroyed.

## Writing Assignment One
## Comment on Sample 3. Grade: Low

This is a meager offering, but meagerness is not its only fault. The first paragraph starts with two apparently unrelated sentences. The notion that *The Old Man and the Sea* "is an example of a satire" is wrong in a novel way, but the paper supplies no shred of supporting evidence, though it looks like the statement of the student's thesis. There seems to be no connecting linkage whatsoever between the first paragraph and the second; and the leap from the old man to the boy's parents in paragraph three leaves the reader more than ever at loose ends. Then as the student finally develops his thin and disconnected train of thought, he reveals his total failure to grasp the import of Santiago's words. He tries to reckon with "defeated" but does not see it in opposition to "destroyed." He is apparently too much of an idealist to admit the frailty of human flesh. Rather, he sees the old man as both invincible and indestructible; and in doing so he loses most of the thrust of Hemingway's statement of theme.

*Two Plans for Teaching*
The Bridge of San Luis Rey
*Grades 11 and 12*

a novel. They are also here for comparison with the second teaching plan for *The Bridge of San Luis Rey,* a reaction against what the committee sees as a tendency in English teaching to bleed the text dry. And it is possible that, like most reactions, the second plan goes too far in the opposite direction. In its faith in the resourcefulness of teachers and in the ability of good students to make their own discoveries, it may be giving the student too much to do and offering the teacher too little.

*Purpose of Plan I.* The purpose of Plan I is twofold. First, the unit is an attempt to teach students that there is more to a novel than plot. The discussion questions concern structure, word choice, tone, and imagery as well as characterization, theme, and ideas in the novel. Second, the unit tries to develop writing assignments from the reading. The suggested assignments are intended to be specific enough to prevent the typical comment, "I can't think of a thing to say"—and broad enough to encourage the student to think about and to organize coherently what he finds to say.

## Questions for Discussion (Plan I)

### Part One: Perhaps an Accident

1. What is Brother Juniper's reaction to the breaking of the bridge?

2. What does he expect to prove? Has he any doubts?

3. Is it common in human nature to question God's intentions? Is this a new question? Have you read it in literature before? Does God need justification?

4. What clues to Brother Juniper's character do you find in this section?

5. How does the author tell about the breaking of the bridge? Is he emotional about the horror of it? Does he take an "oh-those-poor-people" attitude?

6. Read the first sentence. What details are given? Where else might you expect to find such an account?

7. Why do you suppose he begins this way?

8. What is the tone of this section?

9. Can you make a generalization about the length of Wilder's sentences? Are they long and rambling? Short and clipped? Average length? How does this affect the tone?

10. Do you notice any of the words and phrases Wilder uses as being unusual or particularly vivid or appropriate?

a. "*precipitated* five travellers"— What image does this create? What if he'd just said *dropped?*

b. "*approximately* collected and *approximately* separated" (the bodies)— What effect does that word give?

c. "Diseases . . . *flitting* in and out"— Effect of this word?

d. "a *twanging* noise" when the bridge broke—What sense does this appeal to?

e. "fling five *gesticulating* ants"— What sense does this appeal to? What do you see?

11. Considering the expressions just discussed, do you find Wilder's treatment of the accident subjective or objective?

### Part Two: The Marquesa de Montemayor

1. Does this section deal exclusively with the Marquesa? Who else is introduced? How does Wilder handle these introductions in so few pages?

2. What is the central passion in the Marquesa's life? What kind of love is this? How does it affect the Marquesa? Does it make her kind? Thoughtless? Strong? Weak?

3. What is so special about the Marquesa's letters?

a. Note especially the passage on Velasquez and Titian. Contrast this passage with one that we might write about the gold chain. What would we probably say?

b. If the teacher could show some prints of these artists' works, the class could discuss the difference in the "*the gray and silvery air*" and "*a more golden light*" (page 18).

4. Does the character of the Marquesa change any during this part? How? What causes the change?

5. How does her death on the bridge affect you?

6. What is the character of Pepita?

7. What is the character of the Abbess? How does she resemble "the swallow in the fable who once every thousand years transferred a grain of wheat, in the hope of rearing a mountain to reach the moon" (page 28)?

8. In what ways would Pepita's death affect the Abbess?

# *Two Plans for Teaching* The Bridge of San Luis Rey *Grades 11 and 12*

*Edition Used:* Wilder, Thornton. *The Bridge of San Luis Rey.* New York: Washington Square Press paperback edition (W 236).
*Approximate Time:* 2 to 2½ weeks (for either plan)

## *The Bridge of San Luis Rey,* Plan I Grades 11 and 12

### To the Teacher

The first of these two plans is offered with respect for its unremitting thoroughness and with the realization that many teachers will welcome this kind of page-by-page questioning designed to lead the student through the text and on to the conclusions implicit in the questions. And at least for average or below-average eleventh and twelfth graders such step-by-step guidance may be needful and can be fruitful if not pushed to the point Wilder himself perhaps had in mind when he noted the irony whereby the Marquesa's letters "have become the text-book of schoolboys and the ant-hill of the grammarians." With able students, however, thoughtful teachers have begun to have misgivings about the dangers of over-teaching the novel, of applying indiscriminately to a book like Wilder's the techniques of line-by-line analysis clearly appropriate to the study, say, of a sonnet of Gerard Manley Hopkins. And some of us can even sense with wry amusement the ultimate irony of forcing our students to dissect Wilder's own protest against such literary dissection in his comment on the Conde's response to his mother-in-law's letters:

". . . he thought that when he had enjoyed the style he had extracted all their richness and intention, missing (as most readers do) the whole purport of literature, which is the notation of the heart. Style is but the faintly contemptible vessel in which the bitter liquid is recommended to the world."

The materials in the first unit have not been tried out in schools. They are here as a sample of what teachers are accustomed to in a detailed study plan for

9. How long does Wilder take to fill in the biographical information on the Marquesa?

10. Note the line, "... hysterical scenes ... recriminations, screams and slamming of doors" (page 11, and again on page 12). What do the rhythm and sound of the line suggest?

11. Note the lines, "... the whole purport of literature ... is the notation of the heart. Style is but the faintly contemptible vessel in which the bitter liquid is recommended to the world" (page 15). Who seems to be speaking here? What does he mean?

12. What is *simile?* Note Wilder's use of simile in these two examples.

a. "The knowledge that she would never be loved in return acted upon her ideas as a tide acts upon cliffs" (page 15). What imagery and meaning are here?

b. "... at last, like a general calling together in a rain and by night the dispersed division of his army she assembled memory and attention ... " (page 23). What is the imagery?

13. What is *metaphor?* Note the passage describing the llama. Is this metaphorical? What is the imagery?

14. In this characterization of the Abbess, what does Wilder mean in the lines, " 'How queerly they dress!' we cry. 'How queerly they dress!' "

## Part Three: Esteban

1. What is the relationship between Manuel and Esteban? Is there anything special or unusual about it?

2. Why is the experience involving the Archbishop and their secret language so horrible to them?

3. What causes a break in the closeness of the twins? Of what significance is it that the Perichole makes Manuel promise to keep the letter a secret from Esteban?

4. What comment on love is made at this point? Who makes it?

5. How does Esteban react to this break? Does Manuel understand?

6. Why does Esteban tell the Abbess he is Manuel after Manuel dies? When does he give his own name? Why?

7. Note Esteban's speech to Captain Alvarado. This is the longest speech he has made, to our knowledge, to an outsider. What is the speech about? Why does he say these things? Read the speech aloud. What expressions, ideas, words give it a child-like quality? Does this quality add to or detract from the effect of the speech?

8. When Esteban tells the Captain he wants to buy the Abbess a present because she once had a serious loss, he says, "Women can't bear that kind of thing like we can." Do you find any irony in that comment? Explain.

9. For what reasons do you think Esteban talked to the Captain when he would talk to no one else?

10. Is the section on Manuel's illness vivid to you? What details particularly impress you?

11. Note the final paragraph in *Part Three.* What is its tone? What attitude toward the accident is shown? Compare this with the final paragraph in *Part Two.* Are they similar?

## Part Four: Uncle Pio

1. "As he approached twenty, Uncle Pio came to see quite clearly that his life had three aims" (page 75). What are these aims? How is he able to realize all of them?

2. What is the relationship between Uncle Pio and the Perichole? How do they both feel toward her work?

3. Why does the Perichole play such an important role in this section?

4. Read the first sentence in the paragraph that begins the description of the Archbishop (page 86). What image of the Archbishop do you get? What effect has the word *something* in the description? Do we often describe a person as *something?*

5. Read the passage about the Archbishop that begins, "The Archbishop knew that most of the priests of Peru were scoundrels" (page 87).

a. Do you find humor in the passage? What seems humorous about the Archbishop?

b. But is the passage just humorous or is there a serious undercurrent perhaps? What? What kind of humor can we call this?

6. What two groups does Uncle Pio divide people into? What is the difference between those who have loved and those who have not?

a. What do you think of this idea?

b. Which group is Camila in? After she has smallpox she feels no one could care for her. Why? Can this be related to the idea that she's never loved anyone? How? Upon what does she place value?

7. Read the passage concerning Uncle Pio's feeling about friendship. Can you contrast his feelings about it with those of another character? Do these two have reasons to feel differently about it? Explain.

8. What reasons can you give to explain why Uncle Pio wanted to take Don Jaime with him?

## Part Five: Perhaps an Intention

1. What character do we meet again? Where did we last hear of him? Why does he appear just at the beginning and the end?

2. What are some of the attitudes toward the Marquesa that Brother Juniper learns? Would you expect this same divergence of opinion about Uncle Pio? Esteban? Why?

3. How do you feel about Brother Juniper's death at the stake? Explain.

4. When Brother Juniper died, ". . . he called twice upon St. Francis and leaning upon a flame he smiled and died" (page 110). What is the effect of the phrase, "leaning upon a flame"?

5. *Part Five* is divided into two parts—why this division?

## Discussion of the Novel as a Whole

1. What is the central passion in the Marquesa's life? In Esteban's? In Uncle Pio's?

2. Do these characters have anything in common?

3. Can we classify their loves as three different types? Explain.

4. Does each die at a turning point in his life? What is the turning point for each?

5. Do Pepita and Don Jaime fit a similar pattern? Do they each have strong love for someone?

6. Have Pepita and Don Jaime reached a turning point in their lives?

7. How might Brother Juniper interpret the fact that each of them had reached a turning point of some type? What would the opposing view of the deaths be?

a. What is meant by *fate?*

b. Does *fate* imply that God has planned something to happen?

8. Is the question of whether or not God plans everything directly answered? Why do you think Wilder does not give an answer? Read again the last paragraph in *Part One.*

9. Who makes the decision that causes a turning point in the Marquesa's life? In Esteban's? In Uncle Pio's? In Pepita's? In Don Jaime's? Can you see any reason for this difference in decision making?

10. We have discussed those who die; how do the deaths affect those left behind—the Abbess, Camila, Doña Clara? Are they changed by the deaths?

11. What do most of the characters seem to have in common? What theme runs through the novel? What different types of love and attitudes toward love are brought out?

12. Even the bridge is connected to the theme—what does it symbolize? Read the last sentence in the novel. What does it mean?

13. What is the physical structure of the novel?

14. Could any or all of the parts stand alone?

15. How does Wilder tie all the parts together?

16. Why do you think Wilder chose this form rather than a more standard form divided into chapters with one chapter leading into the next?

17. In discussing *Part One* what did we say about Wilder's style? Does this apply to the rest of the novel? Examples?

18. Do you notice anything about the conversation of the characters? Look at the conversation between Manuel and the Perichole when she first sends for him. Notice such expressions as (page 49):

"It is because I am an actress, no?"

"Yes, señora."

"Name of the Name, Manuel, anyone would think you were as stupid as an ox."

What impression is Wilder trying to convey to the reader by use of these constructions? Can you find other examples to illustrate this?

19. Discuss the Abbess as a unifying character in the novel.

20. For which character do you have the most sympathy? Give specific reasons.

21. Wilder expresses the idea that in a relationship of love between two people one always loves

more than the other. An extension of this idea is that the one receiving more love is sometimes a cruel or an inferior person. Does this idea apply to any characters in the novel? If so, discuss it, using the characters and relationships to which it applies.

22. Discuss in detail how Wilder brings out the theme of the novel. What characters does he use? How does he use them? What symbols does he use? And so forth.

23. Why is the setting in place and time important to this novel? For an idea of this importance consider what would happen to the novel if it were set in twentieth-century Europe or America.

24. Who do you think is the strongest character (*not* physically strongest) in the novel? Give specific reasons.

25. Who do you think is the weakest character? Give specific reasons.

## Suggested Vocabulary List (Plan I)

| | |
|---|---|
| 1. osier | 26. efficacy |
| 2. usurers | 27. sacristan |
| 3. harangued | 28. interminable |
| 4. divesting | 29. jocose |
| 5. recriminations | 30. stupefaction |
| 6. obsequious | 31. philologist |
| 7. grandiose | 32. tacit |
| 8. hydraulics | 33. calumnies |
| 9. insinuated | 34. pander |
| 10. baroque | 35. reticence |
| 11. posterity | 36. coterie |
| 12. bravura | 37. lachrymose |
| 13. introspective | 38. austere |
| 14. succumbing | 39. veneration |
| 15. indiscretions | 40. polyphony |
| 16. flamboyance | 41. virtue |
| 17. provincial | 42. omniscience |
| 18. felicitous | 43. penury |
| 19. supplanting | 44. efface |
| 20. inertia | 45. puerile |
| 21. dissimulating | 46. dropsical |
| 22. perfunctory | 47. poignant |
| 23. maudlin | 48. cursory |
| 24. importunities | 49. usurpation |
| 25. propitiation | 50. languorous |

## Suggested Writing Assignments (Plan I)

*Part One.* Discuss the relationship of the last paragraph in *Part One* to the rest of *Part One.* Include an interpretation of the meaning of the paragraph and consider it in terms of Brother Juniper's ambition.

*Part Two.* The Marquesa is an intelligent woman. Agree or disagree with this statement, supporting your opinion with specific examples.

*Part Three.* Compare and contrast the characters of Esteban and Captain Alvarado. Don't forget the background of each and the relationship between them.

*Part Four.* Discuss in detail the relationship between Uncle Pio and the Perichole.

## *The Bridge of San Luis Rey,* Plan II Grade 11

### To the Teacher

This plan for teaching Wilder's *Bridge of San Luis Rey* to an eleventh grade college preparatory class is, in part, a protest against the assumption that every novel must be anatomized line by line, page by page, thereby robbing the student of his right to ask his own questions, to make his own discoveries, and ultimately to see the work as a living organism deriving its life and its wholeness from the artful fusion of its parts. The main purpose of this plan, therefore, is to force the student first to see the book whole, then to examine its parts in relation to that whole, and finally to see it whole again. And if the examination of the parts has been fruitful, the second whole that the student discovers should be more significant than the first. This is certainly not the only way to teach a novel. There are many ways, each good with a particular class, a particular teacher, and a particular book. With an able class, a willing teacher, and this book, we believe that this plan is worth trying.

## First Assignment (Plan II)

(Allow about five or six preparation periods.)

A. Read *The Bridge of San Luis Rey* rapidly, preferably at one sitting. The main purpose of this first reading is to get a view of the book's wholeness.

B. Next reread either the whole book or selected parts of it, this time reading slowly, looking for details that confirm, modify, or change the impressions you got from your first rapid reading. As you do this second reading, keep the following questions in mind:

1. Why has Wilder divided the book into five apparently separated parts?

2. Wilder calls the first part "Perhaps an Accident" and the last part "Perhaps an Intention." Why didn't he call the first part "Perhaps an Intention" and the last part "Perhaps an Accident"?

3. Why has Wilder chosen Doña María, Esteban, and Uncle Pio as the title characters for the three middle sections? Why didn't he name one of these sections for the Abbess, who, according to the verdict of history, was one of "the two great women of Peru"? Why didn't he name one of the parts for Pepita instead of Esteban?

4. Does Wilder succeed in fusing the five sections of the book so that they form a significant whole? If so, by what means does he achieve this wholeness? If he does not succeed, what prevents the fusion of the parts?

*Writing Assignment One.* (The assignment is to be done outside class after the reading and rereading of the book.)

*Directions.* Write a paper in which you point out and comment on the significant likenesses in the five people who fell with the bridge.

## Second Assignment (Plan II)

*Writing Assignment Two.* (The assignment is a paper to be written in class under test conditions but with free use of the text of *The Bridge.* Allow a full class period for this paper and do not give out the topic in advance.)

*Directions.* Write a paper in which you point out and comment on the significant likenesses in the three women who lived on after the fall of the bridge: Camila, Doña Clara, and the Abbess.

## Class Work During the First Five or Six Days (Plan II)

*Preparation for Writing Assignment One.* Students should receive the first writing assignment as soon as they get their copies of the book. Many teachers will find that they can profitably spend a good part of the first class period forestalling problems of organization posed by the assignment. Without guidance even eleventh graders are likely to organize their material by characters, treating each of the five in a separate section, often with a perfunctory final section that tries to bring the five together. With help from the teacher, however, students can see advantages in organizing not by characters but by likenesses, with the result that each section of the paper will be handling all five characters under the heading of a well-defined similarity. The possibility of dealing with five characters within a single paragraph does not necessarily occur even to good eleventh grade students. The teacher will also do well to remind students that a likeness that holds for some but not all of the five characters is not valid for this assignment. Without this kind of warning, the shadowy little figure of Don Jaime is likely to get left out of the reckoning. And finally, students will probably ask how long the paper should be. A good answer is, "As long as you have anything important to say," though students will prefer such an answer as, "At least three pages, one side only."

*Class activities before the completion of the reading and the writing.* While the students are reading the book and preparing the first writing assignment, class discussion should stay mainly with the philosophic problem of "accident" or "intention" posed by the opening incident and made explicit by the two section titles "Perhaps an Accident" and "Perhaps an Intention." The question comes alive for students when they themselves come up with examples out of their own experience that reopen the eternal question. They can see, too, that the closer to home the incident the more likely it is to provoke the unanswered "why." Their experience tells them that when you read in the paper of a jet crash in India you give it a perfunctory "oh-dear-how-awful" response and go on with the morning coffee; but if it's a glaring headline announcement of a crash at O'Hare or Kennedy, that is something else again. Another sometimes fruitful approach is to ask what an M.I.T. graduate with an advanced degree in engineering would say in answer to the question, "Why did the Bridge of San Luis Rey fall?" It is worth taking a bit of time to consider the matter of how a bridge is built in terms of presumed strain and stress. And in a good class someone is likely to ask whether human beings are built the same way. And really able students will probably point out that an engineer's answer in terms of strain and stress is not really getting at the deeper problem of "accident" or "intention." Students clamoring for an answer to this philosophic unanswerable will be interested to know that when an eleventh grade class wrote to Wilder and asked if he was giving an answer in *The Bridge of San Luis Rey,* his reply was that each reader must find his own answer to that question. Students interested in doing just that will find it illuminating to discover exactly what happens to Wilder's characters at their times of feeling that they are living in a world without plan and without meaning; and many of his characters experience exactly this feeling of being adrift in an uncaring world.

A study of two of Thomas Hardy's poems, "Hap" and "The Subalterns," will take students even further into differing views on the question of whether ours is a world governed by "Crass Casualty" or by "laws in force on high." A good use of class time would be to divide the students into two groups, each with its elected chairman. Then let one group prepare questions and discussion material on Hardy's "Hap" while the other group is working on "The Subalterns." The teacher should stand ready to serve as consultant if either group wants his help. It would be well to allow at least one class period for the preparation of the questions and discussion material and one or two more class periods for each group's presentation of its findings and its questions. The two poems follow. Teachers will also find the two poems in Laurence Perrine's *Sound and Sense; An Introduction to Poetry,* Harcourt, Brace & World, Second Edition (1963), pages 28–29, with notes and questions (but less complete ones than good eleventh graders will produce under the stimulus of group work).

### *Hap*
Thomas Hardy

If but some vengeful god would call to me
From up the sky, and laugh: "Thou suffering thing,
Know that thy sorrow is my ecstasy,
That thy love's loss is my hate's profiting!"

Then would I bear it, clench myself, and die,
Steeled by the sense of ire unmerited;
Half-eased in that a Powerfuller than I
Had willed and meted me the tears I shed.

But not so. How arrives it joy lies slain,
And why unblooms the best hope ever sown?
—Crass Casualty obstructs the sun and rain,
And dicing Time for gladness casts a moan....
These purblind Doomsters had as readily strown
Blisses about my pilgrimage as pain.

### *The Subalterns*
Thomas Hardy

I

"Poor wanderer," said the leaden sky,
"I fain would lighten thee,
But there are laws in force on high
Which say it must not be."

II

—"I would not freeze thee, shorn one," cried
The North, "knew I but how
To warm my breath, to slack my stride;
But I am ruled as thou."

III

—"To-morrow I attack thee, wight,"
Said Sickness, "Yet I swear
I bear thy little ark no spite
But am bid enter there."

IV

— "Come hither, Son," I heard Death say;
"I did not will a grave
Should end thy pilgrimage to-day,
But I, too, am a slave!"

V

We smiled upon each other then,
And life to me had less
Of that fell look it wore ere when
They owned their passiveness.

Some teachers may prefer to give less time to the problem of "accident" or "intention" and to spend the saved time on the appended list of words from *The Bridge of San Luis Rey,* a list that makes no claims to completeness but that does give the student plenty to work with and that does suggest, incidentally, that the vocabulary as well as the thinking in this book are more suitable for eleventh graders than for eighth or ninth graders, to whom it is sometimes taught.

## Class Activities after Completion of Above Discussion and Two Papers (Plan II)

Only *after* the completion of the two writing assignments is the class fully ready to tackle the question of how Wilder fuses the five parts of his book and then to consider the question of the book's theme or themes, with special exploration of such key passages as the one describing Uncle Pio's doctrine of the "elect," page 89, and the one on page 48 in which Wilder writes: "There may be two equally good, equally gifted, equally beautiful, but there may never be two that love one another equally well." And, just before, ". . . even in the most perfect love one person always loves less profoundly than the other."

The remainder of the class discussion should deal mainly with what the two papers have omitted as well as with what they have included. Then if the papers and the resulting discussion have served their purpose, the next step will be to consider the significant likenesses that include all eight of the main characters, the five who fell with the bridge and the three who survived them. Students should then be ready to move on to the further consideration of the extent to which these likenesses also include the two detached yet involved characters, Brother Juniper and Captain Alvarado. Throughout this discussion students will find it helpful to keep coming back to Uncle Pio's doctrine of the "elect" — a passage that only the exceptional student seems to spot as crucially important. A chapel speaker in an independent school once said, "I have only two things to say. First, every human being in one way or another is lonely; and second, in every human being there is something of greatness." Testing these two statements on each character in *The Bridge of San Luis Rey* is another possible way of moving toward the book's wholeness as long as students understand that they do not have to accept either statement as valid. For this kind of discussion aimed at the book's wholeness, allow two or three class periods.

Most teachers will then want to allow at least one class period and one preparation period for a consideration of Wilder's style, perhaps beginning with a review of such terms as simile, metaphor, diction, understatement, irony, and the condensed line, and then asking students to bring to class examples of each of the following:

1. Unusually effective *word choices.* (For this, students are likely to spot such passages as, "The bodies of the victims were *approximately* collected and *approximately* separated," pages 3–4; or, "There was *something* in Lima that was wrapped up in yards of violet satin," page 86.)

2. The *condensed line,* often coupled with *understatement* and *irony.* (A possible example would be on page 102, where Wilder writes, "Uncle Pio said that when they had crossed the bridge they would sit down and rest, *but it turned out not to be necessary.*")

3. Unusually effective *figures of speech.* (Students may well spot such passages as, "The knowledge that she would never be loved in return acted upon her ideas as a tide acts upon cliffs," page 15; or, "She had let fall upon the boys for a moment the detonation of her amazing eyes," page 46.)

4. Unusually skillful *characterizing phrases.* (Almost certainly at least one student will cite this passage on the Abbess, "Her plain red face had great kindliness, and more idealism than kindliness, and more generalship than idealism," page 28.)

5. Uses of *non-English idiom* to remind readers that Spanish is the language of Peru. (Students will be quick to note such a passage as, " 'It is because I am an actress, no?' " on page 49.)

Beyond the examination of these specific examples many teachers will want to encourage students to take a further look at Wilder's sentence structure, perhaps comparing it with that of other modern writers such as Hemingway, or possibly more profitably, with that of an older writer like Conrad or Hardy.

And finally, many teachers will want to move on from a specific consideration of examples of irony to some of the all-embracing ironies that students will partially uncover in their writing assignments—the irony, for instance, of five deaths as the apparently needful prelude to the redemption of three lives, or the cosmic irony that brought each of the five victims to the bridge just as he believed he was about to enter upon a new phase of his living.

Most teachers will probably not be able to manage more than two writing assignments in the 2 to 2½ weeks of work on *The Bridge,* but the following optional assignment should bring interesting results for those who have the time for it.

*Writing Assignment Three* (optional). For this paper allow one full class period with free use of the text of *The Bridge.*

*Directions:* Choose one of the two assignments below, and write a well-planned paper of approximately 350–500 words.

1. Explore fully and specifically the significance and the appropriateness of Wilder's title *The Bridge of San Luis Rey.* You may wish to compare Wilder's title with other possible ones such as:

"The Great Perhaps"

"Accident or Intention?"

"Fall and Redemption"

2. Answer fully and specifically this question: Was Wilder wise in deciding to write *The Bridge of San Luis Rey* as a novel rather than as a play?

To do this, you will need to consider carefully the differences in the two forms, the novel and the play, with special attention to the freedoms each form permits its user and the limitations it imposes upon him.

## Word List from *The Bridge of San Luis Rey* (Plan II)

| | | |
|---|---|---|
| 1. hallucination | page 3 | "they had the *hallucination* of seeing themselves falling into a gulf" |
| 2. latent | page 5 | "mysteriously *latent* in those lives so suddenly cut off" |
| 3. recriminations | page 11 | "hysterical scenes with her mother, *recriminations,* screams and slamming of doors" |
| 4. complementary | page 13 | "her left cheek angry with a leprous affection, her right with a *complementary* adjustment of rouge" |
| 5. grandiose | page 13 | "to maintain her in the *grandiose* style she fancied for herself" |
| 6. obsequious | page 19 | "It was intended as an *obsequious* flattery of the Condesa" |
| 7. felicitous | page 20 | "she had contrived a few *felicitous* phrases" |
| 8. supplanting | page 21 | "possibilities of injury to the Viceroy, nay with the possibility of *supplanting* him" |
| 9. inertia | page 21 | "the *inertia* of gout" |
| 10. scurrilous | page 21 | "not having heard the *scurrilous* songs" |
| 11. dissimulating | page 22 | "presently she stole larger amounts and tried *dissimulating* their effects from Pepita" |
| 12. assiduously | page 22 | "she . . . cultivated the city *assiduously* for material" |
| 13. perfunctory | page 23 | "Camila had intended to be *perfunctory* and if possible impudent" |
| 14. magnanimity | page 24 | "out of a sort of fantastic *magnanimity,* was playing the farce of not having noticed it" |
| 15. maudlin | page 24 | "It induced a new mood in her; one that must very likely be called *maudlin*" |

| | | |
|---|---|---|
| 16. loquacious | page 24 | "She became *loquacious*" |
| 17. subsidies | page 28 | "so dreadful were the struggles to obtain her *subsidies* from her superiors in the church" |
| 18. cessation | page 28 | "counted the *cessation* of her visits among the compensations for dying" |
| 19. importunities | page 31 | "Doña Clara had foreseen the exhausting *importunities* that this news would waken in her mother and had sought to *mitigate* them by the casualness of her announcement" |
| 20. mitigate | (same) | |
| 21. propitiation | page 32 | "There was an etiquette of *propitiation*" |
| 22. jocose | page 34 | "an affectionate and *jocose* note from her son-in-law" |
| 23. virtuosity | page 34 | "remarks . . . perhaps said for the sheer *virtuosity* of giving pain neatly" |
| 24. pleasantries | page 44 | "they suffered the eternal *pleasantries* with *stolid* patience" |
| 25. stolid | (same) | |
| 26. lachrymose | page 73 | "interpolating . . . some *lachrymose* effects into the austerest music" |
| 27. insatiably | page 76 | "He was *insatiably* curious" |
| 28. versatile | page 77 | "Uncle Pio in Peru was even more *versatile* than Uncle Pio in Europe." |
| 29. nonchalantly | page 80 | "Uncle Pio whistling *nonchalantly*" |
| 30. intermittent | page 82 | "A certain *intermittent* contempt for acting made her *negligent*." |
| 31. negligent | (same) | |
| 32. penury | page 82 | "the little middle-aged woman worn with the cares of *penury*" |
| 33. implacable | page 83 | "a drama of wronged ladies and *implacable* hates" |
| 34. puerile | page 84 | "a pride so vast and *puerile* that he seldom heard anything that was said to him" |
| 35. poignant | page 86 | "the distress of remorse was less *poignant* than the distress of fasting" |
| 36. cursory | page 89 | "her treatment of such passages became more and more *cursory*" |
| 37. parasite | page 90 | "another *parasite* found its way into her mind" |
| 38. ludicrous | page 96 | "Camila had become *ludicrous* in homeliness" |
| 39. discrepancy | page 107 | "The *discrepancy* between faith and the facts is greater than is generally assumed." |
| 40. disinterestedness | page 108 | " 'Why keep this thing alive, this rumor of *disinterestedness?*' " |

## Writing Assignment One
## Sample 1. Grade: High

Among the several characters of Thornton Wilder's novel *The Bridge of San Luis Rey,* five have an unfortunate common bond: death. It occurs as they are passing over the famous century-old bridge in Peru; thus, their deaths are not only personal but national tragedies. Yet these five people had certain similarities when alive, too. It becomes apparent that all had been suffering from unhappiness, and that this was caused by their need for certain other people. Ironically, all were killed just as a point of resolution had been made in their lives.

Traveling over the bridge together on their way back to Lima from the Shrine of Santa Maria de Cluxambuqua were the Marquesa de Montemayor, and her young companion Pepita. The latter was an orphan raised and trained by the Abbess Madre Maria del Pilar to be her successor and Wilder gives several evidences of her unhappiness. Pepita, at fourteen, "had never been taught to expect happiness" (p. 29) and from the servants of the Marquesa's house "suffered a persecution of small discomforts and practical jokes." It is also painful and embarassing at times for her to serve the Marquesa. This becomes more apparent when they journey to the shrine, for in the unfamiliarity "Pepita longed for the dear presence, the only real thing in her life." (p. 35)

The Marquesa's unhappiness was of a different nature. The "constant pain at her heart" (p. 15) was caused by a daughter in Spain who would not return her "nervous attention and . . . fatiguing love." (p. 12) Yet after a disastrous visit to Spain, for the Marquesa, "letter-writing had to take the place of all the affection that could not be lived." (p. 14)

A particularly unfortunate death was that of Don Jaime, the epileptic bastard son of Camila Pericole the actress. His suffering derived from his epilepsy and the shame which it caused him: "he bore his pain with the silent bewilderment of an animal, and like an animal he was mortally ashamed when any evidence of it occured in public." (p. 91) Traveling with him was Pericole's mentor, Uncle Pio. His unhappiness came from his protegee's rejection of his love. To her, living with the Viceroy and edging her way into society was infinitely preferable to her career on the stage and to Uncle Pio. He must always humble himself in order to express the love he feels for her: "He bent his head and mumbled: 'Of course I love you, Camila.' " (p. 95)

The fifth victim of the accident was also connected with La Pericole. His unhappiness was caused by his twin brother's love for the actress. As Esteban and Manuel were twins they had never before been separated by love. To Esteban, the fact that his brother had deserted him meant that "the whole meaning had gone out of their life." (p. 48)

Evidently, each character's unhappiness came from his need for another person. For Pepita, this person was her mentor, the Abbess. When young, the hurts and wounds from the Marquesa would cause the girl to tiptoe "about the palace, silent, bewildered, clinging only to her sense of duty and her loyalty to her 'mother in the Lord,' " (p. 30) "the dear presence, the only real thing in her life." (p. 35)

It is the need for her daughter's love that causes the Marquesa's unhappiness. "She wanted her daughter for herself; she wanted to hear her say: 'You are the best of all possible mothers.' " (p. 16) Consequently, she wrote her famous letters to Dona Clara, although "her daughter barely glanced at the letters." (p. 14)

The need of Don Jaime is less evident. It was, perhaps, for a relief from the embarrassement of his condition, and perhaps for someone who would love him and care for him, giving him attention and consideration as a normal individual rather than as a freak.

His companion, Uncle Pio, was evidently in need of Jaime's mother, Pericole. For, as is shown in numerous episodes, "he longed to be by her as a boy of eighteen would long." (p. 98) Even at the age of fifty he could say, "to have known you is enough for my whole life." (p. 95)

Esteban's bewilderment and unhappiness at his brother's apparent desertion is augmented immeasurably when Manuel dies of an infected leg wound. Left alone for the first time in twenty-three years Esteban is lost. Indeed "it had always been Manuel who had made the decisions." (p. 69)

It is subtly ironic of Wilder that each of these five people are killed in the accident just after they have come to a point of decision, or resolution, in their lives which could possibly have made a significant difference in the future.

For Pepita this turning point is in the form of a letter full of complaints and despair: "all inkstains and incoherence." (p. 35) to her mentor the Abbess, hoping for some support or relief in the burdensome task of accompanying the Marquesa. Yet Pepita will not have the letter sent, and finally tears, conceding only that "It wasn't a good letter . . . it wasn't . . . it wasn't . . .

brave." (p. 38)

For the Marquesa, reading this letter is a revelation of her own emptiness and selfishness. She realized that "she had never brought courage to either life or love." (p. 38) In her shame she cried "tomorrow I begin a new life . . . let me live now . . . let me begin again." Two days later both were killed on their return trip to Lima.

The resolution for Don Jaime's troubles can be combined with that of Uncle Pio because the latter is allowed to take the boy from La Pericole to be educated—to be Uncle Pio's protege as his mother had been. Thus, if he could not have Camila's love, he would have her son, "to love him and take care of him." (p. 101)

For Esteban, the harm was not so easily repaired. In the grief and confusion that persisted in him long after Manuel's death he refused to communicate with anyone, even the Abbess. Eventually she arranged for him to meet Captain Alvarado—for whom the brothers had once worked. Thus it was arranged that Esteban should accompany the Captain on a voyage to England. At the last moment, however, Esteban struggles with his conscience—"it had always been Manuel who had made the decisions and even Manuel had never been forced to make as great a one as this." (p. 67)—but does not succeed in killing himself. That day they go across the Bridge on the way to Lima. However, the Captain climbs down to the stream to supervise the baggage and only Esteban is killed.

Thus, rather as Brother Juniper, in his attempt to find reasons for the five deaths, the reader can find connections between the five victims of that accident—their unhappiness, their need for a loved one, and the irony of their final happiness. As the Abbess thought, "There is a land of the living and a land of the dead and the bridge is love, the only survival, the only meaning."

## Writing Assignment One
## Comment on Sample 1. Grade: High

The choice of a single *high* paper for this assignment was difficult because of the wealth of good ones. There were others more brilliantly written than this one, others more tightly organized and more thrifty with words, but none so thorough or so sound in their judgments as this one. In spite of an occasional misspelling, this is competent eleventh grade writing, and among its strengths is the skillful weaving of wisely chosen quotations into the sentence structure of the paper itself. The grasp of the book revealed in this paper and the painstaking perception with which it explores each of the five characters are exceptional. This paper slights no one of the victims, not even little Don Jaime whose shadowy presence went unnoticed in many of the answers to this assignment. Nor is this an exploration that contents itself with generalities. The pages are packed with specific evidence, frequently reinforced by apt quotation. But the paper is more than a laborious collection of relevant material. This student is fully aware of the fundamental irony of lives cut off seemingly at the very moment of emergence into a new dimension of reality. The handling here of Pepita is unusually sensitive, restrained, and respectful of Wilder's text.

This is the kind of able student who would profit from trying to rewrite this paper in no more than two thirds of the number of words used here, yet without losing anything of worth. Forced economy of language would probably sharpen the style and increase the impact of the already clear, perceptive, mature thinking.

## Writing Assignment One
## Sample 2. Grade: Average

When Brother Juniper collected data to show likenesses between these people he did not do very well. As a matter of fact he burned for it. In his attempt to show the common element of sinfulness he was almost too thorough. He came to the undying conclusion that all people are both good and bad.

The most obvious of the three points I intend to cover is the fact that although there were probably a great number of people in this area during this period the five characters seem to have an indirect yet apparently close relationship. The main connection seems to stem through the Abbess who raised Pepita and Esteban, and therefore knew the Marquesa. While Pio and Camila's son in turn are associated indirectly with Esteban by way of the ardent adventurer Captain Alvarado and even more indirectly through the Perichole's encounter with Dona Maria.

The second and third points are combined to bring out the fives relative innocence in life while their greatest sin was only the adverse or unusual conditions under which they lived and each one's own plaguing problems. While none of these people was pure and saintly they offered no resistance to the natural respect for what is right. Brother Juniper's analysis showed no hardened criminals just misguided people with gross of human problems. The Marquesa was a lonely destitute person at a loss for the one thing she loved, her daughter. Pepita on top of being an orphan was also pulled into the Marquesa's lonely world. Uncle Pio, the dejected vagabond who led a very unstable life devoted to the stage, came for a short time to influence Camila's son who had suffered in the Perichole's isolated and suffering group. Last the most lonely of the group, Esteban, who after losing his brother became just the shell of a man and fell to doing anything to forget. All this shows nothing more than the pattern of humanity.

## Writing Assignment One
## Comment on Sample 2. Grade: Average

This is a flimsy production in comparison with the searching thoroughness and detailed development of the first paper, and the opening comment on Brother Juniper misses the real purpose of Brother Juniper in preparing his book. It also misses the reason for the burning of both the book and Brother Juniper. The second paragraph is right in pointing out that the lives of the five victims were interlocked before the bridge fell, but an abler student would have developed this point in more detail. The third paragraph tapers off into vagueness in its effort to characterize the moral quality of the five characters but does a better job of recognizing the loneliness that blighted the lives of these people. This student has apparently missed the crisis of realization through which each of the five characters had passed before reaching the bridge, nor does he sense the irony of cutting off the lives of five people each of whom has at last emerged from the "malady" of love, "pale and wrung but ready for the business of living." This is, on the whole, a decently written paper with no serious inaccuracies of judgment but stingy in its inclusions and generous in its omissions.

## Writing Assignment One
## Sample 3. Grade: Low

There are many likenesses between the victims of the bridge fall. Whether or not they are significant depends on whether you cosider the collapse to be accidental or the result of a controlling force. Pehaps the likenesses could be explained by the idea that most people are somewhat malajusted to their environment, and are therefore somewhat unhappy.

All of the five were unhappy. They all (probably) loved someone and got more pain than pleasure from it. Dona Maria loved her daughter but clashed with her in temperament and was only used by her. Pepita loved and was afraid of Madre Maria. Manuel loved the Perichole, and this hurt his relationship with his brother as well. Uncle Pio also loved the Perichole, but was perhaps disapointed in her. Don Jaime perhaps loved his undemonstrative mother. It is possible that this shows a certain basic incompatability of the female personality.

There was something ungraceful about all of the characters. Perhaps they're childhood had something to do with this. They tended to be obedient to one thing, although they didn't understand it or life.

In contrast, some of the characters that didn't fall with the bridge, i.e. Madre Maria, the Perichole, & Esteban, also were unhappy. Quite likely this shows something about the novelist's outlook on life: a thing that was a trifle gloomy and picked an accident as a fitting subject to write about in the first place.

## Writing Assignment One
## Comment on Sample 3. Grade: Low

Like the *average* paper, this one is decently written but fails to reckon with important points, and this writer, unlike the other, occasionally slips into illogic and irrelevance. The reasoning that tries to link the three sentences of the opening paragraph is an example of the muddled thinking that puts this paper into a lower bracket than the second one. The second paragraph is the strongest part of the paper. Here the thinking is sound and the writer deals specifically with each of the five characters. The third paragraph slithers off into unsupported or unsupportable generalities. Certainly "ungraceful" is not the word that describes the physical appearance of the five victims. Don Jaime was as beautiful as Doña María was ugly. And what is this writer talking about when he says, "They tended to be obedient to one thing, although they didn't understand it or life"? Just what is this "one thing"? The "In contrast" that ushers in the last paragraph is misleading because it introduces a likeness as well as a contrast. The final speculations on Wilder's gloomy view of life are neither accurate nor relevant.

## Writing Assignment Two
## Sample 1. Grade: High

Several significant likenesses were evident in the three women who survived the fall of the bridge.

Had they been classified by Uncle Pio, all three would

have fallen in category of those who "had not loved." None of them had passed through that "cruel malady" to emerge "ready for the business of living;" none of them had "undergone this initiation."

All three seemed too pre-occupied with the trivia, work, and concerns of their daily lives to cultivate a pure love relationship with those who loved them best; the Mother Abbess with her convent, le Perichole with her acting, and Dona Clara with running her household.

Each had been placed on a pedestel with love and reverence,—the Mother Abbess by Pepita, Camila by Uncle Pio, and Dona Clara by her mother,—and yet these three surviving women had been too involved with their own selfish pursuits to recognize the love offered them and the chance to love in return, each had loved "less profoundly." According to Uncle Pio's standards, perhaps they weren't really "ready for the business of living. And yet, after the bridge fell, each woman underwent a transition, seemingly having found the bridge between the land of the living and the land of the dead. The Mother Abbess "accepted the fact that it was of no importance whether her work went on or not; it was enough to work." Camila came out of her isolation and truly gave of herself, from her heart, for perhaps the first time. And Dona Clara feeling true contrition for her behavior to her mother, learned of the deep forgiving, tolerating powers of love. Perhaps each had now found, "the only survival, the only meaning."

## Writing Assignment Two
## Comment on Sample 1. Grade: High

This paper is outstanding in the completeness of its coverage, in the competence of its writing, in the firmness of its organization, and in the keenness of its insights. Many papers handled this assignment well, but what distinguishes this paper from other good ones is its recognition of the crucial importance of Uncle Pio's division of the world into those who have loved and those who have not. This paper derives its unity and its significance from its awareness that before the fall of the bridge no one of these three women had earned the right to enter Uncle Pio's kingdom of the "elect." No one of them had yet experienced the "cruel malady" of love or emerged from it "pale and wrung but ready for the business of living." And unlike many other papers, this one stresses the convergence of the three women at the convent and the initiation of all three into the kingdom of Uncle Pio's "elect." Particularly for an impromptu class paper this one is remarkably competent in writing techniques and masterful in its control of a tightly interlocked comparative organization.

## Writing Assignment Two
## Sample 2. Grade: Average

The story of the Bridge of *San Luis Rey* is the story of "parent-child" relationships, which evolve out of selfish, possessive, and sometimes distainful ties, into bonds sewn of the strong, generous, and disinterested ropes of love, following the fall of the Bridge.

Summarily, these relationships were between the Abbess and her "daughter," Pepita and her "son," Eteban; Dona Clara and her mother, the Marquesa; and between La Perichole and her "father," Uncle Pio and her son, Jaime. The three survivors of the Fall, Dona Clara, the Abbess, and Camila had many likenesses. Each lost someone very dear; each was left alone, devoid of any meaningful kindred love, regretting the malevolence, virulence, and neglect with which they had accorded their lost loves; and in all there developed—for them, perhaps too late—a newly cast, passionate, love for the vitims of the Bridge.

Dona Clara had always spurned her mother, being hypercritical of everything the Marquesa said and did, motivated, perhaps by the shame and disgust she felt of so obsequious, ugly, self-pitying, socially graceless, weak-willed a mother. The Condesa tossed away her mother—not, I must admit,—completely without some just cause—as one might some old and dirty coat, merely putting up with her mother's letters from a distance that would require the least association possible.

La Perichole also failed to realize the true value of her "father" and her son—she had come to take for granted and, later, to despise Pio and the fact that it was he and only he who had developed her into what she now was. Afflicted with small pox, her beauty destroyed, she withdrew into a shell of self-pity, taking her son in after her. Thus she neglected what duties she might have had to Pio as her "father" and to Jaime as his mother; and it was this failure to return their love that so marked her course of pennance and constructed that posthumous bond between her and her loved ones.

In the case of the Abbess, we have a woman who, like the others, is guilty of neglect and misguided love. Parading the cause of the woman and her place in the world, she became more concerned about finding and developing someone who would carry the banner after she was dead, and too little concerned with the emotional and loving care of her "daughter." In the Abbess' own words: "My affection should have had more of that color. My whole life should had more of that quality. I have been too busy." But it was only after the Fall, when she was alone—alone with her cause, that she was able to fully appreciate this fact.

## Writing Assignment Two
## Comment on Sample 2. Grade: Average

In organization and in style this paper is probably the equal of the first paper, and it comes close to equalling the first in the perceptiveness with which it analyzes the three women. Unlike the first paper, though, this one is marred by a number of mechanical errors. A more significant difference in the two papers, however, is that this one omits the most important element in the aftermath of the bridge's fall—the initiation of all three women into the "cruel malady" of love that wrings the soul dry but leaves its owner "ready for the business of living." This student sees the remorse each woman experiences. He is particularly discerning in his recognition of the subtler nature of the Abbess's remorse. But he fails to see that for each woman remorse is the stepping stone to redemption, to full membership in Uncle Pio's kingdom of the "elect." When Camila and Doña Clara come to the Convent, the Abbess is no longer "too busy" to open her heart to them. Doña Clara is no longer too haughty to care about the Abbess's work and perhaps to contribute to it. Camila is no longer too self-centered to lose herself in service to others. Failure to reckon with this vital part of the assignment is the main reason for rating this paper *average* rather than *high*.

## Writing Assignment Two
## Sample 3. Grade: Low

In *The Bridge of San Luis Rey* by Thornton Wilder, a significant likeness that can be seen is the love that sealed the fate of each character. Each individual pocessed a different type of love, which in turn shaped their future's and demeanor's.

Perichole was one of the most talented actresses in the New World. She was discovered by Uncle Pio and taught her all he knew about acting. In time, she became the most exciting and admired ladies in all Peru. Camilia did not love Uncle Pio as a husband, but had a respect for him, that was mutual. As the book says, "The respected each other deeply, but without passion." Their relationship was more father, daughter with Uncle Pio constantly trying to protect and provide for Camilia. As Perichole's career wore on she discovered there were other material gains in life besides acting such as good food, clothes and other men. She became disinterested in acting and resented all Uncle Pio stood for. Soon Camilia stopped acting and got married. Uncle Pio was unaware of the change, but then became very worried. He tried to persuade Camilia to try acting again, but she refused. She came down with small pox and this marred Camilia's beauty. Perichole still loved Uncle Pio deeply but her vanity had made Camilia very self-conscious and selfish. Her one last "act of gratitude," was giving Don Jaime for one year to Uncle Pio.

Love is usually defined as an affectionate relationship between two people. The Madre Maria de Pilar was one of those persons who have allowed their lives to be gnawed away with a love for an idea. She hurled herself against the idea that woman were inferior to men. The Madre had visions of a woman dominated world, with the female sex dependent on herself, not on men. But always the next morning the Madre would have to face the fact that most women were dependent upon a man for their existence. So the Madre came to *hate* all men because the world was dominated by them. The only time in her life that the Madre rejected this idea was when Esteban and Manuel were left to her. These two were harmless and did not try to dominate or shoulder all the responsabities of life. She came to love Manuel and Esteban because they were dependent upon her for their existence, and glorified her idea.

Not much is written upon Dona Clara and most what follows are logical assumptions. Dona Clara was the Marquesa de Montemayor's daughter. Little Clara was cold and very intellectual. At eight she was calmly correcting her mother's speech and soon regarded her with much distaste. Soon she left for Spain and the nobility of the kings court. Dona Clara rejected her mother completely and was very selfish to the Marquesa. Her mother wrote beautiful letters inquiring of her health, but Dona Clara never wrote at all or a very harsh letter. Once on a visit to Europe the Marquesa was not even greeted by Dona Clara. It was not Dona Clara's love that shaped her character or future but a lack of it.

As one can see these individuals futures and demeanors were shaped through a type of love, or lack of it, each pocessed. these by all means are not the only types of love that exist. As long as man inhabits this planet, love will play a major role in composing man's destiny.

## Writing Assignment Two
## Comment on Sample 3. Grade: Low

This paper is a reminder that illiteracy and incompetence don't necessarily come in small packages. The one valid idea that emerges from the tangled incoherence and garbled plot summary is that love is an important part of the book. The lapses in style and mechanics are too evident to require comment. The organization—what there is of it—treats each woman separately and tells, with precarious unconcern for the facts, something of what happened to her, relying heavily on unchewed chunks of quotation ungarnished with quotation marks. The dealings with the Abbess are specially dubious. The final paragraph, starting with the piously hopeful phrase "As one can see," tapers off into the vacuous as it closes the door on a paper that has missed most of what matters in the assignment.

## Writing Assignment Three, Question 1
## Sample 1. Grade: High

*Reasons Behind the Title*

The title *The Bridge of San Luis Rey* is an important device which Thornton Wilder uses to develop the story in his novel. The bridge acts as a link, raises questions, represents reality and faith, and is a symbol.

The bridge as a link connects the lives of five people: Dona Maria, Pepita, Uncle Pio, Jaime, and Esteban. They all have the incident at the bridge in common; they all were there. Maybe Wilder wanted to write about these five people and needed something to gain unity. By using the bridge, Wilder creates a pivot around which the action is centered.

The fall of the bridge raises some provocative questions. Does a Supreme Being oversee the very breaths we take or regard one person as a mere speck among millions? Along with this question one might ask if we live and die by plan or accident. In forming these questions, Wilder gives the novel an air of mystery which prods the reader to seek the answers.

The bridge represents reality as well as faith. The scientific data, which Brother Juniper gathers, puts all the material about the people and the bridge in physical terms. Brother Juniper's faith tells him that the fall of the bridge was an act of God. He tries to combine the facts with his faith, hoping to prove to the questioning people that life is controlled by the hand of God. He tried too hard, because some things must be believed by faith alone.

The bridge is a significant symbol. It symbolizes the bridge of love between life and death. The people who died had loved and their love endured after their deaths, ultimately to be returned. The bridge had fallen just as the love had failed, and was rebuilt, as love after death was found.

The fall of the bridge symbolizes the force of circumstances or of the meaningless workings of nature, but the passions of the victims act as the primary human cause leading them to the bridge.[1] Using his characters and the bridge in such a manner, Wilder brings about unity and fusion to build what he calls his "magic unity."[2]

---

1. R. D. Burbank, *Thornton Wilder* pp. 44–56.
2. *Ibid.*

## Writing Assignment Three, Question 1
## Comment on Sample 1. Grade: High

The superiorities of this paper are its beautifully clear organization, its full handling of the inseparable significances of the literal and the figurative bridge, and its capable handling of language. In this paper the treatment of Brother Juniper falls into none of the traps that led some students to assume that Brother Juniper's book and Wilder's are one and the same. This student is aware that Brother Juniper "tried too hard," that he consequently missed the "spring within the spring." The other conclusions this paper reaches are similarly discriminating. Here is a student mature enough to resist the temptation to find a final answer in the Abbess's words about the bridge of love or a final answer to the question of chance or intention in our universe. Paragraph five is an example of this student's insight coupled with the ability to state that insight compellingly.

This paper makes no attempt to reckon with the other suggested titles, but the directions merely suggest such a comparison. A second *high* paper follows this one mainly because it does the one thing that this paper did not choose to do.

## Writing Assignment Three, Question 1
## Sample 2. Grade: High

*The Bridge of San Luis Rey:*
The Significance of the Title

As are all other first impressions, the title an author chooses for his book is very important. In choosing *The Bridge of San Luis Rey,* Wilder chose a title that is not only interesting but, more importantly, very appropriate.

This is commendable in the face of several sub-plots that offer attractive possibilities for a title. For instance, Wilder could have called his book *"The Great Perhaps"* or *"Accident or Intention"* in reference to Brother Juniper's story. However, the little priest's story is not the main plot, and his ideas are not the main theme. Wilder devotes only one and a half chapters (the first and one-half of the last) to Brother Juniper's story. His idea of divine plan is also found only in the first chapter and the first half of the last chapter. As the book ends with a completely different idea, it seems safe to conclude that Brother Juniper's concern over a divine intention in the accident is not the major concern of the book.

Another possible title, *"Fall and Redemption"* represents another pitfall in choosing titles. At first glance this title seems very appropriate because it deals with the most important action and the most important idea of the book: the fall of the bridge and the survivors' discovery of love for the victims. This action is only a part of the action in the book however, and this idea is only half of the main idea. To be complete, the title should refer not only to the action of the falling bridge but also to the actions of the five victims as they attempted to win love in return for theirs; it should refer not only to the idea that the survivors discovered love for the victims as a result of the accident, but also to the love that preceded theirs.

The title, *The Bridge of San Luis Rey,* does this in the double usage of the word "bridge." In the physical sense "Bridge" refers to the crude suspension bridge between Lima and Cuzco. Thus, it refers to the most important action of the book, the collapse of the bridge. In a spiritual sense, however, "Bridge" refers to the connection of love between the victims and the survivors: ". . . all those impulses of love return to the love that made them."[1] Thus "Bridge" here brings to mind not only the new found love of the survivors but also the futile love of the victims. Similarly "Bridge" also refers to the attempts of the victims to get love and the attempts of the survivors to find an outlet for their love.[2]

Thus, by interpreting "Bridge" to mean not only a physical object but also a spiritual connection, Wilder developed a title to the complete plot and main theme of his book, *The Bridge of San Luis Rey.*

---

1. Thornton Wilder, The Bridge of San Luis Rey, p. 117.
2. Ibid., p. 116.

## Writing Assignment Three, Question 1
## Comment on Sample 2. Grade: High

This is another clearly capable response to the assignment, and this student, unlike the first one, deals with the suggested alternatives to Wilder's title and does so with intelligent awareness of their limitations and defects. Like the first paper, this one is well written though not brilliant, competent in its organization, accurate in its judgments, sound in its interpretation of the book, and perceptive in its insights. The actual analysis of Wilder's title is less detailed than that of the first paper —a natural consequence of the careful attention given to the rejection of the other titles—a back-handed method, incidentally, of recognizing the rightness of the actual title.

## Writing Assignment Three, Question 1
## Sample 3. Grade: Average

*The Bridge of San Luis Rey*

Why did Wilder choose to title his book "The Bridge of San Luis Rey?" This title is not very original if it is merely about the bridge between Lima and Cuzco. Perhaps the author felt this was the only title worthy of the story. The bridge was the center of the story. Without the bridge there could be no book. By using the name of the bridge, the title is not misleading, except that someone who knows nothing about the story might be led to believe it was a huge, magnificent bridge. Maybe this was an intention by the author, because to the people of Peru the bridge stood for all things immortal.

Perhaps Wilder had a second meaning in his title. He often spoke of the two different "bridges." There was the real bridge between Lima and Cuzco and also we discover that there is a "bridge" between the "land of the living and the land of the dead that does not fall." This is the bridge of love, the only surviver, after death.

Let us compare this title to some others Wilder might have chosen for his book. He might have used the titles of his first and last chapter combined into "Accident or Intention." This is a good idea but much better applied as two chapters of the book. The way Wilder introduces the story by giving the facts like an accident and then he goes on to prove throughout the story that it might have been intentional created suspense and interest. If it had been the title you would have been looking for evidence of intention before the latter chapters. Also the title, "Accident or Intention," gives no clue as to what the story is about. Another title Wilder might have used is "Fall and Redemption." With this title Wilder could have broadened on the fact that maybe these people would be forgiven after death, and also that there really was intention in having these five go together to a better place. Still another title Wilder might have used is "The Great Perhaps." This makes the incident of more importance than the bridge. Actually it was not really so important that these people died except that they were on the Bridge of San Luis Rey when they did die. This is what was so important that after more than a century of use suddenly the bridge should fall. This is why I think the title must be keyed in with the bridge.

## Writing Assignment Three, Question 1
## Comment on Sample 3. Grade: Average

This paper is an example of clear, competent eleventh grade writing, but it misses some of what the first two papers see and in its ending it lacks their unassailable accuracy. In recognizing that the title includes both the literal and the figurative bridge, this writer shares the acumen of the first two, but what he does with his recognition is meager. The paper rightly speaks of the bridge as the center of the story but goes into no detail about the interweaving of the lives of the five who perished on that bridge, nor does it reckon with the effect of the fall of the bridge on the three women who came to terms with themselves as a result of that fall. The handling of the figurative bridge is similarly slight. But this student does explore the alternative titles and gives intelligent reasons for rejecting *Accident or Intention.* In examining *Fall and Redemption,* however, the writer makes the dubious suggestion that maybe the five who died with the bridge would be forgiven after death. This is an oversimplification verging on distortion in its unawareness of the redemptive crisis each of the five has gone through before the fall of the bridge. And why is either Don Jaime or Pepita in need of "forgiveness" in the hereafter? The final section dealing with *The Great Perhaps* skates on even thinner ice in its assertion that "it was not really so important that these people died except that they were on the Bridge of San Luis Rey when they did die."

## Writing Assignment Three, Question 1
## Sample 4. Grade: Low

*Significance and Appropriateness of the Title*

The title, *The Bridge of San Luis Rey,* doesn't seem to express the events or suggest the tragedy that occurred on the Bridge. The title only states the location of the Bridge in Peru. The above title gives the impression to one as the story might be about the history of the Bridge which it is not. Instead the plot is about the lives of the five persons who were killed by accident or intention.

Other titles: *The Great Perhaps, Accident or Intention,* or *Fall and Redemption* do not seem to correspond with the Bridge as compared to the title Wilder used.

When a person reads the title—*The Great Perhaps,* he might ask himself, "The great perhaps of what?" On the contrary, some people might want to read a novel titled this, due to curiosity. The title, *The Great Perhaps,* does not seem appropriate relating to the events that took place in this novel, *The Bridge of San Luis Rey.* Also, another question a person might ask himself is, "What was 'great' about whether perhaps it was an intention or an accident?"

The title—*Accident or Intention* would not be a good title either because it does not state, *Accident or Intention* of what. Also this title does not suggest the Bridge, which is important because it ties or connects the novel with the five victims who were on the Bridge.

The title, *Fall and Redemption* does not express itself fully either and would not be good. The reasons why it wouldn't be, correspond much the same as the reasons stated under the other two titles. This title, though, might be suitable because the word, 'Fall,' is related to the Bridge, and 'Redemption,' to the victims.

A better title might be, *The Bridge of Tragedy.* This title, thus, expresses the point that death occurred on the Bridge. Notwithstanding, this title does not relate whether the fall of the *Bridge of San Luis Rey* was an 'accident or an intention.' Nor does the title, *The Bridge of Tragedy* give the location of the Bridge, but this may not be important to some readers. On the whole, I would chose the title to be *The Bridge of Tragedy.*

## Writing Assignment Three, Question 1
## Comment on Sample 4. Grade: Low

Confused thinking, unsound judgment, vagueness, and technical weaknesses drop this paper into a lower category than the papers that precede it. This paper differs from the *average* one in its unawareness that Wilder is using the term *Bridge* figuratively as well as literally. In fact the literal-mindedness that objects to Wilder's title on the grounds that it merely tells the location of the bridge in Peru plagues this writer throughout his grapplings with the alternative titles. The reasons for rejecting *The Great Perhaps* are obscured by illogic and by lack of connectives to take the reader from sentence to sentence. The next section, though not strongly persuasive in presenting reasons for rejecting *Accident or Intention,* does wind up with the most sensible sentence in the entire paper, the one pointing out that the bridge "is important because it ties or connects the novel with the five victims who were on the Bridge." In rejecting *Fall and Redemption* for "much the same . . . reasons stated under the other two titles," the writer merely extends the previous weaknesses in reasoning. In his expression of preference for his own title, *The Bridge of Tragedy,* he overlooks the network of ironies by which Wilder suggests that the bridge was not so much the perpetrator of a tragedy as the means of redemption for the three women who had not learned to "live" until after the bridge fell. The accumulated weaknesses in this paper stem largely from the student's failure to reckon with anything but literals.

## Writing Assignment Three, Question 2
## Sample 1. Grade: High

*Rather A Novel*

"Lessons of wisdom have never such power over us when they are wrought into the heart through the groundwork of a novel which engages passion."—Lawerence Sterne

With The Bridge of San Luis Rey, Thornton Wilder demonstrates his preference of novel rather than play form in relating the complexities of life; but, what is Wilder's reasoning behind selecting the novel rather than the play form?

The novel, one of the most powerful engines of civilization ever invented, can capture and expound upon the low, medium, and high crests of the incidental as well as the paramount spots—overall, the novel presents a limitless scope. One example of such scope is that of Wilder's freely discussing the deteriorating emotional ties between the Marquesa and Dona Clara. Could a play, during the same scene, accomplish this feat with such a finished luster?

A play of a very high caliber could only include a generalization of this sequence. For example, those moments on the "death" bridge and the few days and hours, which proceeded the actual fall of the "death" bridge, would have to be written in the play with a coated, superficial glammar in order to please the audience. But those same scenes ARE shown in Wilder's novel as a quick and unexpected accident without a crude introduction—a true and uncovered picture of life's reality. These moments in play form would tend to drag with a heavy, imposed drama, which does lessen the signifance and drive of the original intention of the sequence.

The responsibility of the play director, like that of the novel writer, is to interpret and develop with insight each character in that particular scene—but, how can we expect both the writer of the novel and the director of the play to conclude all interpretations, similiarly? The play director must follow a tight, logical pattern from the significant to the more significant in order to entail the created atmosphere, but a Novel writer may wander as life wanders, pause as life pauses, and stop to reach back and discuss the background for each different scene. Wilder's novel, *The Bridge of San Luis Rey,* does this: the novel explains and develops the distinct characters of the Marquesa, Esteban and Uncle Pio along with the minor roles; in contrast, a play does not, in favor of the audience, successfully use such a detailed character sketch within the performance time of a few hours. The famous playwright, Budd Schulberg, states the following: "A play must strive for success, and it is most successful when it concentrates upon one character in a short period of time . . . much like that of a short story."

*The Bridge of San Luis Rey* "enters" the heart and mind of each personage to "hear" their private prayers of many a sleepless night, to "see" their hopes and desires, and to understand their moral crises. But, a play could present only an outside appearance of the various emotions, completely excluding the effective reality of religion upon the minds of men; one example would be the exclusion of the real deepness of thought behind the Marquesa's visit to the shrine. Henry L. Mencken opines: "The primary aim of the novel . . . is the representation of human beings . . . ; no other art form clings to that aim so faithfully."

These various thoughts, for and against the novel or

play, entered the mind of Thornton Wilder, and Wilder chose the novel form rather than the play structure.

The novel will always superexcell the play in correlating the emotional, human passions of various characters, such as those in *The Bridge of San Luis Rey*.

## Writing Assignment Three, Question 2
## Comment on Sample 1. Grade: High

Solid worth and sharp insight offset the occasional pretentiousness of this paper. The quotations from Sterne, Schulberg, and Mencken are not here merely to impress the reader. The student has made them an integral and contributing part of his analysis of Wilder's book. He at once makes the vital point that the novel can capture "the low, medium, and high crests of the incidental as well as the paramount," whereas the play's business is with the paramount only. In his eagerness to build a strong case for the preferableness of the novel form, he probably underestimates the potentialities of dramatic form, especially in paragraph three, but the general drift of his argument is both persuasive and valid. The student's command of language is part of the persuasiveness in such a sentence as "but a Novel writer may wander as life wanders, pause as life pauses," or "*The Bridge of San Luis Rey* 'enters' the heart and mind of each personage to 'hear' their private prayers of many a sleepless night, to 'see' their hopes and desires, and to understand their moral crises." The ending of the paper thins out weakly in comparison with the muscularity of sentences like those just quoted, but otherwise this is an unusually discerning, incisive penetration of the assignment.

## Writing Assignment Three, Question 2
## Sample 2. Grade: Average

*"Fallen Bridge—Destructed Novel"*

"The Bridge of San Luis Rey" is not an unqualified success as a novel. Its most noticeable weakness is the episodic structure which, though thematically unified, obviates progression in a single narrative line. Characters are developed in one episode only to be dropped almost entirely in the next one and replaced by a new cast. Another weakness—its most important technical one—is the sometimes obtrusive presence of the omniscient author, who judges and interprets as he narrates the histories and inner lives of the main characters. This subjective, arbitrary narration weakens the dramatic structure of the book, although it is compensated for to a degree by the fact that the dramatic scenes embody or suggest much of what the author says about the characters. Wilder was aware of the defects of the omniscient author narration and came to favor the stage over the novel as an art form partly because he was convinced that dramatic narration eliminates the subjective presentation that he felt was inherent to the novel.

Wilder's style of writing is a possible setback for the conversion of the drama into a novel. The author often employs the devices of amalgamating characters from myth, folklore, religion, and from history. For this reason, it might be difficult to use the employed allusions such as the Spanish Inquisition without leaving part of the audience behind. The reader, on the other hand, can make use of specific footnotes at the bottom of the page, and also of the introduction and afterward in the book.

The characters themselves set up a strong barrier against novel transition. All are portrayed with considerable realism and clarity as individuals. From the standpoint of response to the promptings of the flesh, and susceptibility to forces of environment and heredity, they are conceived with enough naturalism to allay any charges that the author ignores life. He insists, however, that the inner life—the passions, the intellect, the hopes and aspirations—is a mystery whose workings defy rationalization. Stage characters could not be probed from within to give the audience a true picture of them. Aside from actions, unnecessary words must be inducted into the play to try to convey a clearer picture. In the book, Juniper is convinced that the fall of the bridge is an intention of God. The audience would not grasp the idea of a fallen bridge and the crisis it entails quickly. The omniscient author steps in to recount these intimate facts although he admits that it is "possible that even I have missed the very spring within the spring." The readers move, then, from the extrinsic motivations revealed by Juniper's investigation to the intrinsic motivations in the minds and hearts of the victims.

Scenery is also a technical disadvantage. Between the first chapter and the last, three flashback chapters recount the lives of the three chief victims. It would be difficult to switch from the plains of Spain to the mountains of Peru. Also, many different settings are involved in the life of each person. An example is Uncle Pio and Camilla. The switch would go from Spain, to cafe's of Spain, to the theater, to the home of Camilla as he begs her for Jamie. Then scenery must him to the fateful bridge where he dies. This could possibly be done with a small platform with a major dwelling and temporary scenery on it. The remainder of the stage would serve as another country. This method, however, would be quite confusing to an unknowing audience. Lighting would be put to use by flashbacks and future incidents. The letters of the Marquessa could be set over a type of P.A., often called a symograph. This machine produces a deeper voice much like a tape recorder would do, only it uses the voice as an insturment to convey what the marquessa felt.

In summation, I am convinced that the production of a play would involve too many technical entanglements, and also involve too much material wise. A great burden would be placed upon the knowledge and memory of the audience, and with this comes a loss in the translation of the theme.

## Writing Assignment Three, Question 2
## Comment on Sample 2. Grade: Average

The pretentiousness of the first paper was controlled. The pretentiousness here is not always controlled, though the glib assurance and apparent knowledgeableness can be hypnotic in their effects on the unwary. The writer has an extensive vocabulary and much of the time uses it with intelligence, but the occasional inexactness or actual misuse of a word pulls the reader up short. The title "Fallen Bridge—Destructed Novel" is a glaring example. Even more disturbing, though, is the writer's occasional indulgence in sound without sense. "The readers move, then, from the extrinsic motivations revealed by Juniper's investigation to the intrinsic motivations in the minds and hearts of the victims." This sounds impressive, but precisely what does it mean? Brother Juniper's concern was with facts, and we know very little of what he discovered except that Wilder tells us at the outset that he missed the "spring within the spring." And what little we do know, we discover at the end of the book, and it has little bearing on motivations "extrinsic" or "intrinsic." By that time, moreover, Wilder has already taken us in and out of the "minds and hearts of the victims" himself, so that we do not move from Brother Juniper's findings to Wilder's revelations. There is a fine rhythmic sweep in the sentence, "It would be difficult to switch from the plains of Spain to the mountains of Peru," but in turning *The Bridge* into a play, no dramatist would dream of bothering himself about the "plains of Spain." They simply don't figure significantly in the story.

The suggestions this student makes for overcoming some of the difficulties of translating this novel into play form are both practical and ingenious, though occasionally the difficulties are trumped up to enable the writer to propose a remedy.

The most serious weakness, however, in a paper that at times verges on excellence is the failure to establish a thesis and to develop it consistently. The first paragraph deals with the failures of *The Bridge* as a novel, pointing out the intrusiveness of Wilder's subjectivity and stating that Wilder's awareness of this weakness was what turned him to the writing of plays. The reader naturally expects after such an opening that the paper will go on to make a case for the preferableness of dramatic form for this novel, but the second paragraph seems to do an about-face with its switch to the difficulties of dramatizing such a novel as this. The third paragraph—where clarity probably most suffers from obscuring pretentiousness—makes the valid point that Wilder's focus on the inner life of his people might well be lost in the play form. The final paragraph tackles practical problems of staging with a background of knowledge most students don't share.

For the sake of logic and consistency, the wisest course would probably have been to drop the opening paragraph entirely. It sets up expectations that the rest of the paper makes no attempt to satisfy.

## Writing Assignment Three, Question 2
## Sample 3. Grade: Low

*A Novel: A Play*

There is a definite distinction between a novel and a play. As in *The Bridge of San Luis Rey,* a novel deals with various vital characters which are also vitally important in every play. But overlooking this one linking factor, the likenesses between a novel and a play are few. A play is based on a definite plot which is directly followed throughout the story, whereas, a novel can be based a singular idea which is developed in any means the author sees fit.

In *The Bridge of San Luis Rey,* Wilder attempts to project a basic idea by presenting various illustrations and allowing the reader to join ideas. This method of establishing a general theme allows the reader to stem individual branches in a story which create extensions from the one idea. Had this novel been written as a play, the importance of Wilder's idea could not have been stressed. The vitalness of using the five examples in the book could not be captured by the reader unless the reader was given the opportunity to observe these five people as they became involved with their personal struggles. By observing, I refer to a indulgance into the very depths of each character wherein the reader is allowed to clearly understand their individual motives. This observation could not be made by hearing a mere dialoge, but only by obtaining a full account of the innermost beings through an implicit description as done by Wilder.

## Writing Assignment Three, Question 2
## Comment on Sample 3. Grade: Low

This paper is also pretentious—disastrously so. Its mechanics are fairly respectable. The weaknesses are mainly in diction and idiom. The word "singular" near the end of the first paragraph is probably the writer's notion of an elegant variant of "single." "*In* any means" is a sample of shaky idiom. And just how a reader is "to *stem*" the various branches from a story (paragraph two) is a bit of a mystery. The reader is later confronted with a puzzling reference to "a indulgance into the very depths of each character." Some but not all of the content of the paper is valid and sensible. It starts with the obvious recognition that both plays and novels require characters. The further suggestion that plays have a definite plot whereas novels latch onto an idea is not entirely wrong, but it needs the careful qualification that this student fails to give it. Where the content of this paper seriously falls down, though, is in its notion that a play cannot convey an idea, that it cannot present the personal struggles of its people, and that it cannot reveal depths within depths of motivation to its audience.

Among the most valuable results of this assignment was its bringing into the open so many surprising misconceptions about what a play can and cannot do. In its misconceptions, this paper had plenty of company, and some of the misconceptions were cruder than anything here. Meanwhile, though, this paper fails to make some of the crucial distinctions between the novel and the play—the very distinctions that most persuasively argue Wilder's wisdom in choosing the novel form for *The Bridge of San Luis Rey*.

*A Comparative Study of*
Stalky & Co. *and* A Separate Peace
*Grades 11 and 12*

short stories about the same characters, presented in chronological order, making a single point, not necessarily a novel?

## Writing Assignment One

(The assignment is to be done after the reading of both books but before students begin class discussion of likenesses and differences in the two works. This paper should be prepared outside class.)

### Directions

Write a carefully prepared paper in which you compare the attitudes toward war in *Stalky & Co.* and *A Separate Peace.* To do this you will need to refer to and to interpret relevant evidence from both books.

## Questions for Discussion

*Note to the teacher.* Especially with able classes, teachers may like to let the students take over the direction of the class discussion, assigning each of the questions to one or two students who will then lead the discussion for that particular question.

1. Both novels are books about school. How large a part does the classroom play in each book?

2. Knowles's Devon, though American, is actually a considerably older school than Kipling's. How much attention is paid to tradition and the past in either book?

3. Authority is almost a necessary part of school life. In which book does authority play a larger role? What are the sources of authority in each book? (For Finny's view of authority see page 11.)

4. What is the role of sports and games in each book? Are you surprised that Stalky & Co. do not like cricket? Explain your answer.

5. "The battle of Waterloo was won in the playing fields of Eton," said the Duke of Wellington. What did he mean? Would Kipling have agreed? Would Knowles? Give reasons for your answers.

6. Which author tells us more about the background of his characters (in other words, where they come from, details about their families)? Is such information important in these works? Would we understand Gene better if we knew more about what he did before he came to Devon? Would we understand Beetle better if we knew more about his earlier experience? Why or why not?

7. Just what are the attitudes toward war in *Stalky* and *A Separate Peace?* (Since students have already written on this topic, the teacher may want to have some of the best papers read aloud and may wish to clear up possible misconceptions that have cropped up in the papers.)

8. Finny believes (or claims he believes) that war does not exist (pages 106–107); it is a trick "they" play on us. "They," he explains further, are "The fat old men who don't want us crowding them out of their jobs." What character later in the novel is an illustration of Finny's remark? Who are the equivalent people in *Stalky?*

9. One of the few times Kipling makes an explicit comment in the book is on page 41, where he says the boys "were learning, at the expense of a fellow-countryman, the lesson of their race, which is to put away all emotion and entrap the alien at the proper time." Who is the "alien"? How does this concept of "the alien" show up in Kipling's stories? Do we find it anywhere in Knowles?

10. "All companies of boys have an argot, a lingo, a code by which they exclude others and help to identify themselves." To what extent do the boys in both books use their language to exclude others and to identify themselves? What likenesses and what differences do you find in the language spoken by the boys in both books?

11. Finny makes two self-revealing remarks in the novel (pages 40 and 108). Why would none of the Kipling boys have said such things?

12. Gene says on page 178, "But I could not hear, and that was because I did not exist." What does he mean by "exist"? Does he "exist" at the end of the novel? Why do you think he does or does not? Would Stalky or Beetle ever have made such a remark? Explain.

13. Is self-understanding a problem for Stalky, Beetle, and Turk, as it is for Gene?

14. Kipling makes much of the practical joke or "rag." Cite a few of these. Have they any equivalent in the Knowles story?

15. There are obviously symbolic elements in the Knowles fiction: the tree, the two rivers, the seasons.

# *A Comparative Study of* Stalky & Co. *and* A Separate Peace *Grades 11 and 12*

*Editions Used:* Kipling, Rudyard, *Stalky & Co.* New York: Collier paperback edition, 1962. Knowles, John, *A Separate Peace.* New York: Bantam paperback edition, 1966.

*Approximate Time:* 3 to 3½ weeks

## To the Teacher

Probably most teachers will prefer to assign *A Separate Peace* first, since it is more nearly contemporary and, despite subtlety and complexity, presents fewer incidental problems. And many teachers will want to discuss *A Separate Peace* by itself before moving on to the comparative discussion of the two books, focusing on important aspects of *A Separate Peace* that the study materials here do not cover. Scenes particularly rich in discussion material are Finny's first fall, the first trial scene, the second trial, and Finny's second fall. Such discussion can profitably take place at the same time that students are reading *Stalky.*

*Stalky* may not have the immediate appeal for students that *A Separate Peace* does. In fact many teachers discovered that interest in *Stalky* came only as the class began to consider it in comparison with *A Separate Peace.* Teachers will probably do well to prepare students for the difficulties with the language of Stalky and his friends. Students also need to know that *Stalky* is not really a novel; rather, it consists of nine short stories about the same characters. Since in this collection Kipling omitted the five or six other Stalky stories that he had written, we may infer that he regarded these particular ones, in the order in which he arranges them, as forming a coherent unit, which justifies our regarding the book as a near novel. One of the contingent benefits of using the Knowles and the Kipling together is the possibility of pointing out the differences between a collection of short stories and a novel. If the teacher is interested in this kind of structural problem, he may want to ask himself and his students this question: Why is a group of

How do you interpret them? What others do you find? Does Kipling use symbols in the same way? For example, in "In Ambush," which is about fox-hunting, or about the fox-hunting ethic, why should the school sergeant be named "Foxy"? What point is there in the Aladdin pantomime in the second and the last stories? Note the reference to a real lamp on pages 208 and 209. Are these significant? (*Note to the teacher.* For a complete discussion of Knowles's use of symbolism, see James Ellis, "*A Separate Peace:* The Fall from Innocence," *The English Journal,* LIII, No. 5 (May 1964), 313–318. Since symbol-hunting can be easily overdone, the teacher will want to be on guard in the discussion of symbols in these two books. He will also want to make sure that students realize that an important difference between Kipling and Knowles is that Kipling does not use symbols the way a modern writer does.)

## Writing Assignment Two

(The assignment is to be prepared outside class.)

*Note to the teacher.* Number 2 below is offered as a replacement for the original second writing assignment (number 1), which did not work out well. Number 2 has not been pretested, but teachers may wish to try it with good eleventh and twelfth grade classes. The sample answers for this writing assignment are in response to number 1, and the first of them is followed by a note explaining our reasons for dropping the original assignment.

1. "All companies of boys have an argot, a lingo, a code by which they exclude others and help to identify themselves."

a. Show the extent to which the boys in both books use their language to exclude others and to identify themselves.

b. Discuss the likenesses and differences in the language spoken by the boys in both books.

2. There is devilishness in Finny's innocence and there is innocence in Stalky's devilishness.

Write a carefully organized paper in which you state and then defend your agreement, your partial agreement, or your disagreement with the above statement. In developing your paper, give special attention to the terms "innocence" and "devilishness." In defending your views, make full use of relevant evidence from both books.

## Background Material for the Teacher

*A Separate Peace* and *Stalky & Co.* belong to an old and respected genre, the school novel. Though 60 years apart in time and set against very different backgrounds, they both show characteristics of this form. School novels are generally about a group of boys rather than about an individual, though one of these boys generally stands out from the others, as does Stalky in the Kipling, as does Finny in the Knowles. The group is always tightly knit and exclusive. Note, for example, the hostility of Study Number Five to the rest of the school; then note too how Knowles both narrows and enlarges *his* group—the outsiders are everybody but Finny and Gene, but in a curious sort of way the reader comes to think of both Leper and Brinker as being members of the group too. Brinker is not allowed to become an outsider (like Quackenbush) even though he arranges for the crucial trial scene at the end. (How, incidentally, does Knowles keep him from becoming an outsider?)

Since teachers are obviously essential to a school, they appear in the school novel usually as authoritarian or faintly ridiculous though undeniably learned, like King in the Kipling stories. One of the themes of fiction of this kind is the attempt of the boys to circumvent or outwit the teacher. The teacher, however, may also be a friend or confidant, like the chaplain in *Stalky* or Dr. Stanpole in the Knowles; but readers may observe that in the American book teachers play far less of a role, for either good or bad, than in the English one. (N.B., does this throw any light on the backgrounds out of which these two books came? Is the modern, American master or teacher less authoritative—or less learned!—than his English counterpart of the 1880s?)

Since this is young people's fiction, sports and even violence always play a part in it, and the exact role of sport in both books under discussion might be noted. One of the "inside" characters is generally bookish (Beetle in Kipling, Gene himself in the Knowles) and sometimes also faintly ridiculous, though still likeable. This clown role is largely filled by Leper in the Knowles. There is too the convention of the remote outsider, that is, someone from the world beyond the school, who is valuable because he can serve an ironic purpose. Kipling, for instance, builds the whole story of "The Flag of Their Country" around two outsiders: the well-meaning general and the obtuse MP; the insensitivity of the latter is used to bring out the fineness of the boys' feelings. Note a somewhat comparable use of Mr. Hadley in *A Separate Peace.* (Contrast this kind of "remote outsider" with the retired colonel of "In Ambush," who is used so the boys may score off the masters or authority.)

There are other conventions of this type of fiction, which the students may find for themselves. They may even discover that part of an author's success consists in accepting the conventions, then stretching or violating them to achieve something more effective. Reference might here be made to the use of conventions in other forms of writing, for instance, drama, poetry, the short story itself.

### *Stalky & Co.* (1899)

*Stalky & Co.* is available in a paperback edition (Collier books, 1962, $.95), edited by Steven Marcus. The nine stories included do not comprise all Kipling wrote about Stalky and his friends. The book is about life at the United Services College in Devonshire, a school founded in 1874 by a group of officers to provide a good, inexpensive education for their sons. Kipling was a student there from January 1878 to September 1882. He had just turned 12 when he arrived; he left three months before his seventeenth birthday. The Stalky stories are autobiographical and anyone wishing to trace their real-life background should read C. E. Carrington, *The Life of Rudyard Kipling* (1955), chapter 3, pages 16–33, where identification of the major characters is given. Beetle of course is Kipling himself.

The stories are quite typical Kipling and are subject to the objections always made about his work. Because, for instance, he uses the direct method of reporting, seldom making comments of his own, the stories are often difficult to follow, for the author allows us to infer from the information he gives what he wants us to think. (He probably does not do this so subtly as does, for example, Joyce in *Dubliners,* but he may be profitably compared in this respect with de Maupassant or Chekhov — not always perhaps to his advantage.) The stories also make use of a professional vocabulary; Kipling had a high regard for the reporter and prided himself on getting right the jargon of the particular trade or group whom he might be writing about. The slang of the boys in *Stalky & Co.* may sound somewhat out of date now, as old slang always does, but it was probably accurate for the school of the 1880s. For these reasons some teachers may wish to assign only a selection of the nine stories, although all of them should be read if one is to get a full notion of Kipling's intentions.

The first story, "In Ambush," centers upon the sport of fox-hunting and the idea (curious to American readers not acquainted with the etiquette of the hunt) that the fox must be spared for the hunters, not shot down like vermin, as the wicked keeper does in the story. Although the second story, "Slaves of The Lamp—Part I," gets its title and some of its background from the Christmas pantomime of Aladdin, unfamiliar to American students even if they know about Aladdin, it must be read, since the concluding story with the same title makes Kipling's major point in the book—how the ingenuity displayed by the brighter boys in the school is precisely what makes them brilliant and effective officers when they enter the Army. The story also shows well Beetle's peculiar attitude toward the classics master, King. King and the unfortunate Rabbits-Eggs are the victims of a practical joke, and he appears as a master whom the boys dislike; readers should note, however, that the boys also respect him; indeed Beetle learns much about language from him (compare pages 62, 84, 194).

Some teachers may wish to omit "The Moral Reformers," in which two older boys are repaid in kind for the brutality with which they have treated a younger boy. Kipling, who would have been horrified by the explicit use of sex in modern fiction, describes physical brutality with a relish and a devotion to detail that some readers still find distasteful. Not to be omitted are "A Little Prep." or "The Flag of Their Country." The former documents the boys' high opinion of the headmaster, in real life Cormell Price, to whom the book is dedicated. Price appears in most of the stories, but his heroism in saving a boy's life is his finest moment. Students who read this book may notice that usually when the head appears in a story he is a punisher, often one who punishes unjustly. A discussible question, on which Steven Marcus throws some light in his introduction, is why he commands so completely the boys' admiration and affection. "The Head's a downy bird," says Stalky (page 117), and no one contradicts him.

Kipling's chief aim, as has been suggested, is to show how the life of the "public school" (in the English sense) prepares boys for the world of conflict and empire-building. But the enemies they will have to face are not necessarily the natives, whom Kipling (compare the last story) seems rather to regard as children to be rightly led and guided; the less obvious enemies than the Khye-Kheens and the Malots are (page 221) "The other side. The gentlemen who go to the front in first-class carriages." Like many English writers of fiction, Kipling sees life as a conflict between the right sort and the wrong sort (compare with E. M. Forster, for example, who otherwise is remote from Kipling). It is profitable to look at these stories (and other Kipling stories for that matter) to try to find who the right sort are and why. Sometimes, here, as in life itself, the right and wrong sort get mixed up (most conspicuously with the masters); but those who have read *Lord Jim* and remember Marlow's emphasis on the fact that Jim was "one of us" (in other words, the right sort) may notice the same phrase in "A Little Prep." (page 151), when Crandall recovers Duncan's dead body.

*Note*: The Browning references on pages 58–59 are to "Waring" (the title character who, by the way, has some of the glamour and charm of Stalky), "Soliloquy of the Spanish Cloister," and "Caliban upon Setebos." The name Gigadibs is from "Bishop Blougram's Apology." For how Kipling himself acquired it, see Carrington, page 25.

## *A Separate Peace* (1959)

John Knowles's book was first published in England in 1959 and in America later that year. References in what follows, however, will be to the Bantam paperback (1966, $.75). The setting is a New England school called Devon (reminiscent of Kipling?), presumably Phillips Exeter Academy, Knowles's own school. *The Book Review Digest* for 1960 includes excerpts from both English and American reviews. Teachers who have access to a file of *Cosmopolitan* for 1956 will find in the May issue of that year (pages 74–79) a story by Knowles entitled "Phineas," which is the novel in embryo. An interesting student exercise would be to compare the novel with this short story, which unfortunately for our purposes has never been reprinted. It parallels the events of the novel up to page 59 and leaves Gene standing on Finny's threshold, still undecided what to tell him. Knowles has said that the title of the novel was not taken from *A Farewell to Arms* (*Wilson Library Bulletin,* 39, No. 4, Dec. 1964, 347). It was not. The phrase "a separate peace" comes from the prelude to chapter six of Hemingway's *In Our Time,* when the desperately wounded Nick says to the desperately wounded Rinaldi: "You and me we've made a separate peace . . . We're not patriots."

The novel has attracted a good deal of attention, and good discussions of it may be found in John K. Crabbe, "On the Playing Fields of Devon," *The English Journal,* LII, No. 2 (Feb. 1963), 109–111; James Ellis, "*A Separate Peace:* The Fall from Innocence," *The English Journal,* LIII, No. 5 (May 1964), 313–318; Paul Witherington, "*A Separate Peace:* A Study in Structural Ambiguity," *The English Journal,* 54, No. 9 (Dec. 1965), 795–800; Jay L. Halio, "John Knowles's Short Novels," *Studies in Short Fiction* 1 (1963–64), pages 107–112; and John Knowles, "The Young Writer's Real Friends," *The Writer,* 75, No. 7 (July 1962), 12–14, 37. Of these the most useful is probably the Ellis, which puts particular though not undue emphasis upon the symbolism. It is interesting to note what Knowles has written in his article in *The Writer* (*loc. cit.*): "I now began to write another novel called *A Separate Peace,* and if anything as I wrote tempted me to insert artificial complexities, I ignored it. If anything appeared which looked suspiciously like a symbol, I left it on its own."

One way of approaching *A Separate Peace* as a single novel (not in connection with *Stalky*) would be to regard it as a story about a young man and his double and make comparisons with Poe's "William Wilson" or Dostoevsky's *The Double.* Students might be encouraged to find passages where Finny and Gene seem two parts of the same person, or parts of one another. Note for instance Finny's "courageous" confession (page 40); Gene's donning Finny's clothes after the fall (page 54); Finny's "need" of Gene (page 100); his attempt to realize his athletic ambitions through Gene (page 109); and Gene's significant remark on page 171. More simply, however, the novel is the story of two boys in prep school: one a superb athlete, innocent of primal evil; the other a good student, but conscious of evil. The jealousy that the student feels of his friend Finny he attributes to Finny himself, who is quite innocent of it. Unable to bear Finny's unconscious superiority, Gene destroys him; and the act of destruction is more frightening because as Knowles shapes the incident of the jostled tree limb (page 52), Gene does not act with either malice or deliberation; some unknown part of him takes over and acts for him. The writing of this passage should be studied carefully in the light of what Knowles says later of Gene's guilt feelings about what he has done. Note also that Knowles uses this incident, by implication, when Gene says (page 193) "that wars were made instead by something ignorant in the human heart." (In this respect Knowles is making a point similar to William Golding's in *Lord of the Flies.*)

The three strongest scenes of the novel are Finny's fall from the tree (page 52), Gene's visit to Leper (chapter 10), and the trial scene (pages 156–169). It is not altogether clear how these three scenes cohere and supply the novel's structure. At the end of the book (page 196) Gene is made to say of his war service, "I never killed anybody and I never developed an intense level of hatred for the enemy. Because my war ended before I ever put on a uniform; I was on active duty all my time at school; I killed my enemy there." Knowles indicates that the novel is about a boy's growing up to a self-understanding. A discussible question is just what he means by the quoted sentence. Gene has certainly killed Phineas, or has set in motion the train of events that led to his death. In what sense is Finny his enemy? If Finny is innocence, is Knowles saying that a mature man must kill the innocence in himself before he becomes an adult? (*A Separate Peace* is a framework story. Gene after the war returns to Devon—pages 1–6—and remembers what happened; hence the whole novel is told with the reader aware of an adult looking back upon a crucial experience of his boyhood.) Or is what Gene kills simply something in his own self: his jealousy and mistrust? If the point of the novel is that Gene grows up by learning to appreciate Finny's innocence, though at the price of Finny's life, why is Leper given so much emphasis? In part he is certainly meant as a contrast to Finny (page 194): "All others at some point found something in themselves pitted violently against something in the world around them. With those of my year this point often came when they grasped the fact of the war. When they began to feel that there was this overwhelmingly hostile thing in the world with them, then the simplicity and unity of their characters broke and they were not the same again." That is, he "breaks" because he cannot face the fact of the army; Finny breaks because his "best pal" (page 40) smashes him. But there should be something in Leper more organic to the novel than this. These questions are meant to suggest that we cannot make a definitive and final reading of the Knowles as we can of *Stalky & Co.* Does our inability imply a flaw in Knowles's mastery of his form and subject?

## Writing Assignment One
## Sample 1. Grade: High

*Boys At War*

John Knowles's *A Separate Peace* and Rudyard Kipling's *Stalky & Co.* were written sixty-seven years apart. That the chasm that divides their comment on the maturation process seems much greater re-emphasizes the giddy rapidity of change in the modern world and the necessity of historical perspective.

The boyhood that Kipling bisects into *fag*dom and young manhood is otherwise unvarying and flows smoothly into adulthood. In Knowles's novel, however, a boy suddenly matures in his senior year, in a moment of crisis. In each book the assessment of maturity rests on the boys' preparedness for war, and, while warfare is almost the *zeitgeist* of Kipling's day, World War II is a separate war, requiring a separate peace. War has remained the same reality. The difference is that by Knowles' time it has been proscribed by liberal humanism in whose light Stalky's antics appear inhumane. The very sportingness with which Stalky and company confront their enemies reminds one of gladiatorial combat or bull fighting. The game that Stalky pursues as school warfare is in sharp contrast with the warfare that Gene and Phineas make of the school game.

In both books the word war has an ambiguous meaning. It is first used literally as the armed conflict of nations in which citizens must participate, then as the personal conflict of individual personalities, whose ambivalence compells them to clash. There is a difference in the two authors' applications of *war* to personal conflict. While Kipling has Stalky refer to it explicitly as war, Knowles' characters never do. The reason for the difference is summed up competently elsewhere in Riesman's *The Lonely Crowd,* where he characterizes people of Stalky's day as *inner-directed,* containing their goals and justifications within themselves, eager to compete with their fellows in the success race of their day. This sort of conflict has about it the life-or-death quality of real war. The *other-directed* type of modern times measures his success by his ability to relate well to other people, by their approval of him. He is, relatively, lacking in goals and incapable of self-justification, but he is keenly attuned to other people and is a most social creature. He is averse to viewing inter-personal relations as war.

At the United Services College the purpose behind education is to produce officers. Education itself is of secondary importance, academic pursuits are ridiculed, and non-military "Old Boys" are never accorded honor. The poet, Beetle, is given prominence only because Kipling felt he himself had harmonized art and destruction, but one may question the feeling's validity. From the book's concluding story one learns that the important occupations are not those promoted by the pedantic masters, but the games the boys play with the masters, that sharpen their wits and enthusiasm for crushing the enemy. Mere routine ball games could never suffice. The stakes are not high enough, and the games are, after all, mere devices of the masters. The games Stalky and company play are games of personality conflict. The crucial distinction between their games and Phineas' games is that there is no personality crisis involved. Because each recurrent confrontation has rules and rewards which are independent of the confrontation itself, and which will be carried over into all later serious endeavors, the games do not become an end unto themselves and there is no chance of crisis. Adhering to the gentleman's code (as when they submit to the Head's canings uncomplainingly, knowing them to be fair, though there are no school rules covering them) and striving to be courageous and resourceful are ends which surpass the gratification of triumphing over King or Talke. In short, Stalky and company possess ideals.

At Devon School the situation is reversed. The glory of success is vested in study and athletics. Honor to Gene and Phineas is to be had in being first in the class or setting the school swimming record (even if it is not vaunted). Phineas not only participates in games Stalky would have scorned, he even invents one, blitzball, which is the symbol for personal conflict at Devon. Blitzball and the sport of leaping from the tree are performed in preparation for the war. Yet they differ from games at United Services College in that, unlike cricket or soccer, they are spontaneous and, unlike Stalky's games nearly irrelevant to the real war. They are ends unto themselves, with rules composed haphazardly as they proceed.

While Stalky's games are plainly part of his growing up, the games at Devon are rather symbolic of the psychological process of maturing. The view that Gene and Phineas are two sides of the same character might better be put that Gene is an ego-symbol and Phineas an id-symbol. Thus in the end Phineas is not so much killed as subordinated to practical necessities, such as coming to grips with the war of personalities. It is plain that Phineas continues to live through Gene, and the Gene-Phineas character thereafter survives as Gene is able to deal with the ambivalences of interpersonal relations. But the maturation comes all in a moment, in a crisis, as a consequence of one of the war games. It is a traumatic occurrence after which Gene can only hope to maintain his separate peace with himself and all men. Contrast Gene's state on achieving adulthood with that of Stalky for whom growing up has been gradual and relatively painless.

The missing element in the psychological symbolism, the super-ego, may explain the different processes and results. For Stalky the adult world is not the enemy, as Phineas would have it. Brinker Hadley's father may have his counterparts in the masters who comprise Stalky's collective *they,* but for the Head there is no counterpart in *A Separate Peace.* Stalky and company love, fear, and emulate the Head, who represents to them an ideal of virtue. They have assimilated and reverenced his values well, so that for them "knowing what to do" is a matter of innate decency, easily outraged by the panderings of the Member of Parliament, who, incidentally, bears affinities to Mr. Hadley. On the Devon campus there is a dearth of authority, no one to emulate. There the decline of the father-image is complete, and the boys are on their own to discover their own values. In the absence of higher authority, their games assume primary importance, and, since the games are of personality conflict, their highest values will be concerned with the personality. (Again, Phineas' death is meant only to preserve the sanctity of the Gene-Phineas personality.)

Stalky has no need of a separate peace or any peace at all. His values are ideal and unconcerned with mere personality. He will kill and be killed in pursuit of his ideal, using the lessons he learned fighting King as a means to that end. Courage, integrity, and self-sacrifice are his virtues. Stalky, however, is also a tyrannical leader, cold and unfeeling. If one is driven to conclude that Gene is somewhat emasculated, he must also be seen as more human for lacking the strength of character that Stalky possesses.

Stalky in *Stalky & Co.* and Gene in *A Separate Peace* each emerge from school to face two different kinds of war. Stalky is a fine soldier, but, if not a failure, mediocre as a human being. Gene serves in the army, but never kills anyone, and can face the world having made his separate peace with it and himself. Perhaps each is too much a product of his time to be condemned or praised. Perhaps the desirable process for maturing lies somewhere between them, or perhaps beyond them. For the present and immediate future, the heirs to the legacy of Gene and Stalky do well to see them juxtaposed.

## Writing Assignment One
## Comment on Sample 1. Grade: High

With the sure insight of an exceptionally discerning mind, this student sees the multiple meanings lurking in the key term *war* and then writes into his paper the richness and the complexity of what he sees. The less gifted student will treat war in this assignment in the usual sense of a national or world war with literal battlefields and literal winnings and losings. The more imaginative student will extend the term war to include "the mimic warfare of the playing field." A superior student will see that at least for *A Separate Peace* the most significant war is the inner conflict of the human personality. This paper is clearly the work of a superior student, one who perceives all these shades of meaning in the term *war* and who then deals with them in a superbly organized sequence of thought. The length of the paper, its sustained excellence, its tightly knit comparative organization, its penetration, and its largeness of outlook—these are all the marks of the exceptional twelfth grade student.

## Writing Assignment One
## Sample 2. Grade: Average

*Attitudes Toward War*

In John Knowles' *A Separate Peace* and in Rudyard Kipling's *Stalky & Co.,* one discovers that the attitudes of the two different groups of boys toward war differ greatly. However, there are various events that obviously affect these attitudes.

A major factor in relation to both books is the actual closeness of the wars in which England and the United States are involved. In *A Separate Peace,* there is actually a World War going on, and yet one gets the feeling that the war is completely removed. This atmosphere causes much indifference toward the Great War. The American Devon is not a military school, and the parents of the boys are also not connected with the military. This definitely reduces the full awareness of the war.

In the English Devon, as presented in *Stalky & Co.,* it is quite different as far as future purpose is concerned. There the boys are actually being prepared to fight on the battlefield, and one must remember that England is not even participating in a "hot" war at the time of this book's setting. The great interest in the "outside" war is also evidenced by the presence of "crammers" who are trying to get into Sandhurst, the equivalent of the United States' West Point Academy.

In Knowles' book, the participation of the boys in such games as blitzball is merely for fun, although they often revealed very important things about certain characters. For example, through blitzball one learns that Leper cannot face reality.

However, in Kipling's book, one realizes that the boys are not just playing games. They are learning valuable strategy that can possibly be used later in the military futures of these boys. One finds it hard to forget the statement that "he thinks marbles is just a game."

Another matter of importance lies in the determination of who the enemy actually is. In *A Separate Peace,* it is difficult to really pinpoint the enemy, for the references to an enemy are quite broad. Narrowing it down as much as possible, the entire adult world, especially the "theys" or the Bunkers'-father type may be considered the enemy.

On the other hand, the term enemy is not so broad in *Stalky & Co.* Anyone who is too hypocritic, arrogant, superior, or authoritative is the enemy. Of course King ranks highest in these categories.

All in all, Knowles' *A Separate Peace* and Kipling's *Stalky & Co.* are quite different insofar as their attitudes toward war.

## Writing Assignment One
## Comment on Sample 2. Grade: Average

It would be hard for almost any paper to be anything but an anticlimax to the first one, and the perfunctory banality of this paper's final paragraph automatically puts it into a different category from the first paper in spite of the clear, competent writing, the tidily effective organization, and the perceptive awareness that the term *war* can include the games at both schools as well as the conflict of generations in both. It is worth noting, though, that this paper nowhere recognizes the concept of a war going on inside the individual, the element with which the first paper deals with such extraordinary insight. This paper, however, shows acumen in noting the irony of the concern for war in a country not actually engaged in a "hot" war and the comparative apathy toward war in another country actively involved in a struggle that was to reach to the ends of the earth. This writer is also discriminating in his differentiation of the role played by games in the two schools. The paper then moves on to an intelligent consideration of just who the "enemy" is in both books and rightly points out that it is hard to "pinpoint" the "enemy" in *A Separate Peace* because the concept of the "enemy" in the modern book is both broader and less discernible than in *Stalky.* The writer of this paper is the kind of student who sometimes wants to know why his paper didn't get an A. The best answer is just to let him read a paper like the first one, if possible!

## Writing Assignment One
## Sample 3. Grade: Low

*A Young Man's War (Attitudes Toward War)*

In both stories, *A Separate Peace,* and *Stalky And Co.,* War is presented on two different veiwpoints. In *A Separate Peace,* which takes place in the United States the boys aren't a part of the war. They're only affected when the draft grows near and so the envolvement they have in the war is begun only then. The war is concidered a joke by most while in *Stalky And Co.* since the Military idea is predominate in the school the war is a little more than a joke. But it is very little because the boys involved are younger and not affected like the boys portrayed in *A Separate Peace.*

## Writing Assignment One
## Comment on Sample 3. Grade: Low

In comparison with the average paper, this one provides pretty lean pickings, and beside the first paper it is nothing but skin and bone. The slips in style and mechanics alone put this paper in a different bracket from the first two. Beyond this, the single-paragraph organization suggests the paucity of material and the immaturity of the thinking. And slight though the material is some of it raises serious questions of validity. In *A Separate Peace* the war is not "concidered a joke by most." Such an unqualified statement is both naïve and superficial. The comment that the boys in *A Separate Peace* "aren't a part of the war" is similarly sweeping and similarly undiscerning. The assumption that in *Stalky* there is an actual war going on—in the usual sense of war—is further evidence of this student's naïveté and inaccuracy.

## Writing Assignment Two, Question 1
## Sample 1. Grade: High

*Outline*

Thesis: The language of the schoolboys is used as an identity force and as an exclusive force in both *Stalky & Co.* and *A Separate Peace.*

I. The schoolboy language is used to a large extent in *Stalky & Co.*

A. The use of terms having to do with the school and the boys themselves serves as an identifying and excluding force.

B. The use of French and Latin serves as an identifying and excluding force.

C. The use of sarcasm serves as an identifying and excluding force.

D. The use of nicknames serves as an identifying and excluding force.

E. The use of questioning to get a desired answer serves as an identifying and excluding force.

F. The use of a type of speech that avoids emphasizing patriotism or emotion serves as an identifying and excluding force.

II. The Schoolboy language is used to a less obvious extent in *A Separate Peace.*

A. The language concerning the school and boys is not so recognizable as an identifying and excluding force.

B. The use of some French serves as an identifying and excluding force.

C. The use of sarcasm serves as an identifying and excluding force.

D. The use of talk about the Super Suicide Society of the Summer Session serves as an identifying and excluding force.

E. The use of the revelation of emotion served as an identifying and excluding force.

F. The use of a kind of careless talk served as an identifying and excluding force.

The language of the schoolboys has both an identifying and an excluding power in Kipling's *Stalky & Co.* and in Knowles' *A Separate Peace.* This language is used to a large extent in Stalky & Co. where the use of terms having to do with the school and the boys themselves serves as a factor of identification and exclusion. The terms identify their users as English schoolboys and exclude all others. The reader is especially excluded if he is American, since he has had no contact with the terms of the English schoolboys. The use of French and Latin in conversation is another force that has both identification and exclusion powers. It identifies the speaker as a student of languages and shows that he is a member of a group that accepts this form of speech, and it excludes people who are not able to use the language in the way that the boys do or who cannot understand them. Sarcasm serves as both an identifying and excluding force, too. The boys in *Stalky & Co.* identify themselves by their sharp wit and cutting sarcasm, inflicted on each other and on other associates, and at the same time, others are excluded, since the boys are so clever that sometimes their victims do not even know what is happening. The boys' use of nicknames also has both identifying and excluding powers. It defines the boys as a group separate from the masters or outsiders, while some are excluded by a lack of knowledge of their nicknames. The use of a certain kind of question to get a desired answer serves as an identifying and excluding force, too. Repeatedly Stalky says, "Tell me. Isn't your Uncle Stalky a great man?", and the use of intense questioning is evident in the bullying scene with Campbell and Sefton. The boys' unwritten rule that patriotism and emotion are not to be talked about identifies them as a group which accepts these feelings as too sacred to discuss, and it excludes the flag-wavers and speech-givers like the visiting lecturer.

The language of the boys in *A Separate Peace* also serves as both an identifying and excluding, although it is a less obvious one than in *Stalky & Co.* The language having to do with the school life is not so evident as a force of identification and exclusion, especially since the American reader is familiar with these terms and feels that they are common to everyone. The use of some French serves as an identifying and excluding force in much the same way as in *Stalky & Co.,* but Gene and Finny seem to be less proficient than Beetle, for instance. Sarcasm has identifying and excluding powers in *A Separate Peace,* too, and it is used alternately with and against other boys, identifying them all as a group, but sometimes excluding the innocent victim. The whisperings and plans concerning the "Super Suicide Society of the Summer Session" and its "charter members" provide an identifying and excluding force, with "the charter members," Finny and Gene, being the identified group and all others being excluded. The manner in which the boys express deep emotion also has both identifying and excluding powers. When Finny tells Gene that he is his best friend, Gene says, "It was a courageous thing to say. Exposing a sincere emotion like that at the Devon School was the next thing to suicide." The revelation of emotion identifies Gene and Finny as best friends who have this understanding, and it excludes all the others who might have laughed at Finny's statement. Finny's and Gene's careless manner of speech, expressing total disregard for regulations or traditions, has identifying and excluding powers, too. Speaking of Finny, Gene says, "Then in the everyday, mediocre tone he used when he was proposing something really outrageous, he added, 'Let's go to the beach.' " The beach was completely out of bounds, and this kind of disregard identified Finny and Gene as individualists and it excludes all the bound-makers and rule-followers. So the use of a type of schoolboy language provides a source of identification and exclusion in both *Stalky & Co.* and *A Separate Peace.*

## Writing Assignment Two, Question 1 Comment on Sample 1. Grade: High

This is an orderly, conscientious, detailed, and repetitious response to part *a* of the assignment, but it does little with part *b* except by indirection. The tidy finality of the outline foreshadows both the strengths and the limitations of the paper. Transitions in the paper itself are dutiful, perfunctory. The sequence of topics is obvious and unimaginative. Like others, this student finds little to say, for instance, about the use of Latin or French except that it excludes those who don't know the language and includes those who do. And, actually, what else is there to say? The limitations of the assignment are reflected in the limitations of this paper which, in its thoroughness, in its careful breakdown of the different uses of language, was the best the readers discovered. The adequacy, clarity, and competence—without brilliance—of the style was another reason for the tentative rating of ***high.***

## Reasons for Dropping the Original Writing Assignment Two

The sample just given was the best the readers could find. It is undeniably dull, though the student who wrote it was clearly a thoughtful person. Something must have been wrong with the assignment, which, at first sight, looks promising. From a reading of the papers a number of suggestions for the failure of the assignment to evoke good results appear.

1. No paper dealt satisfactorily with both part *a* and part *b*—in answering *a,* students evidently believed that they were also answering *b.*

2. The question seems to imply that boys' groups have "an argot" which they use exclusively, whereas both books indicate that boys adapt their language to their audience and the occasion.

3. Many students confused "code" (a lingo) with "code" (a moral ideal)—with unhappy results.

4. It is difficult to take from the books evidence of "the extent" to which the languages are used for exclusion or identification, other than the simple statement that use of Latin words excludes the non-Latinist. Such statements lead to painful repetition.

## Writing Assignment Two, Question 1 Sample 2. Grade: Average

Thesis: It is found that most boys have an argot, a lingo, and a code by which they communicate with one another. Why?

A. An argot, a lingo, and a code are a means of communication between boys.

B. These boys use this "special language" to exclude others.

C. These boys use this "special language" to identify themselves.

D. This "special language" is a means of self-recognition.

Boys have an argot, a lingo, and a code they use to communicate with each other. An argot is defined as a slang or speech used to exclude others. A lingo and a code are slangs used to "individualize" or isolate the speaker or speakers from others.

Boys often times use this "special language" to exclude others. In *A Separate Peace,* Gene and Phineas have a language or a slang they use to permit themselves privacy from others in their conversations. As Gene and Finny were returning from the river, Gene broke into what Finny called his "West Point Stride." This term was used by Phineas to describe a certain way Gene walked or trotted when he was in a hurry. Very few people would be able to understand what was meant, unless they were friends of the boys. Anyone else such as a teacher or underclassmen wouldn't understand the classification. Later in the summer, Finny created a club called the "Super Suicide Society of the Summer Session." As the word club implies the organization was for members only. The name would exclude non-participants and such people as the faculty who would witness this club as an infraction of the rules. In other cases there is no attempt by the boys of a book to purposely exclude others. In *Stalky & Co.,* Stalky, McTurk, and Beetle didn't "invent" a language to mistify their superiors, instead they would outwit them by talking in circles and for the most part completely confusing the listener. But this is a code by which they lived. It was used as a prevention of punishment and always established them superior to most anyone they came in contact with.

The boys used this "special language" to identify themselves. Finny was recognized by his conversation with Gene. He made such statements as "You always win at sports" and "Say your prayers just in case there is a God." By what he said, Finny was identifiable. He was seen to have a highly optimistic outlook on life which can be revealed through his belief in that "you always win at sports." It is also revealed that he had a limited view of what sports actually were. Finny established himself as a person who can invent for his own needs. Finny created a game called "blitzball" which was exactly suited to his abilities and which was suited to his saying that "you always win at sports," as there was no loser in his game. This was the code that enabled the reader to recognize Phineas. Finny was identifiable through what he said and his true identity was reflected in his speech, that portrayed his thoughts. In *Stalky & Co.* the boys could be identified as they were able to verbally defeat any opponent or opposition that arose before them. They lived and existed by this code, and as can be seen in the last chapter of the book, was the means by which they were able to establish themselves as superior in war matters, which often call for the outwitting of the enemy.

It can be seen then that boys in general have a way of using their language as a code of their life. This code is the beginning of what they will be like as men. This lingo, argot, or code may be either slang expressions or a manner of speech used to "outwit" others and is essential to a boy's life as a means of identification and separation which result in self-recognition.

## Writing Assignment Two, Question I
## Comment on Sample 2. Grade: Average

Like the first paper, this one focuses on part *a* and slights part *b*. Though it describes some of the uses of language in both books fairly well, it is less competent than the first paper in several ways. First, this student takes the word "code" in the sense of ethics or a standard of personal behavior and as a consequence slips off into irrelevance—or near-irrelevance. The section on how Phineas defines his personality by the words he uses is valid in itself, but its relevance to the key idea of an "in" group and an "out" group is peripheral or nonexistent. Second, the paper is repetitive; the whole final paragraph is excess baggage. And third, this writer is less sure, less methodically competent in his organization than the first, as well as less thorough and less discerning in his coverage.

## Writing Assignment Two, Question I
## Sample 3. Grade: Average/Low

Thesis: The language of the boys in *Stalky & Co.* has many similarities, as well as many differences, to the language used by the boys in *A Separate Peace.*

I. There are many similarities between the language used by the boys in *Stalky & Co.* and the boys in *A Separate Peace.*

A. The boys in both books occasionally spoke in a language other than English.

B. Correctness of grammar on both sides seemed to be equal.

C. The boys in both books had fairly extensive vocabularies and had a good command of words.

D. Poetry played a part in the language of both books, but it seemed to be more often used in *Stalky & Co.*

II. There are many differences in the language used by the boys in these two books.

A. The boys in *Stalky & Co.* used quotes and evidences of their knowledge in their conversation while the boys in *A Separate Peace* rarely did.

B. The boys in *Stalky & Co.* seemed to use more slang expressions than those in *A Separate Peace.*

C. The boys in *Stalky & Co.* had more common school terms than boys in *A Separate Peace.*

D. The English brogue was more evident in *Stalky & Co.* than in *A Separate Peace.*

E. The boys in *A Separate Peace* sweared whenever they felt like it, while the boys in *Stalky & Co.* never did.

F. The boys in *Stalky & Co.* used the power of suggestion instead of lying while Finny in *A Separate Peace* was not afraid of making up a story to fit his needs.

III. There are several possible reasons as to the likenesses and differences of the language used.

A. The location of the schools is one of the reasons

for differences.

B. The emphasis of the school is also responsible for the differences.

C. The schools are probably responsible for the boy's vocabularies.

D. The discipline of the school has some effect on the language also.

The language of the boys in *Stalky & Co.* has many similarities, as well as many differences, to the language that the boys in *A Separate Peace* use. One of the similarities is the fact that the boys from both books occasionally speak in a language other than English. Although this seems to be more true in *Stalky & Co.,* it occasionally comes out in *A Separate Peace,* also. In *Stalky & Co.* French and Latin are both often put to use. Usually the second language is combined with the first to come up with something like, "Je vais gloater. Je vais gloater tout le blessed afternoon." One of Stalky's favorite phrases is the Latin phrase, "loco parentis." For the most part grammar and pronunciation used by the boys in both books is good. The one exception to this seems to be that the boys in *Stalky & Co.* almost always leave the "g" off of "ing" forms of verbs, and McTurk often uses the word "ain't." The boys in both books have fairly extensive vocabularies and have a good command of words. An example from Stalky is, "Don't mind us, Orrin; sit down. You don't know how we respect and admire you. There's something about your pure, high young forehead, full of the drams of innocent boyhood that's no end fetchin'." Poetry plays a part in the language of both books, but it seems to be used more often in *Stalky & Co.* Beetle is the poet in *Stalky & Co.* and often employs his poetry in his conversation. The only poetry used in *A Separate Peace* is that composed by Brinker.

There are also many differences in the language used by the boys in both books. The boys in *Stalky & Co.* often use quotes and evidences of their knowledge in their conversation while the boyls in *A Separate Peace* rarely do. For example, McTurk says, "And, besides, he's a Philistine, a baskethanger. He wears a tartan tie. Ruskin says that any man who wears a tartan tie will, without doubt, be damned everlastingly." The boys in *Stalky & Co.* seem to make use of many more slang expressions than the boys in *A Separate Peace* do. Many of their popular expressions are common school terms, such as "fag," "brolly," and "blub." Their conversation and use of these terms makes their English brogue seem more apparent. The boys in *A Separate* Pease swear whenever they feel the urge, but the boys in *Stalky & Co.* never curse. The boys in *A Separate Peace* are not afraid of constructing a story to fit their needs. However, the boys in *Stalky & Co.* never resort to a lie. Instead, these boys rely upon the power of suggestion as their means of evading the actual truth. For instance, when Abanazar accuses Stalky of drinking and bribing Rabbits-Eggs to rock King's room, Stalky firmly denies bribing Rabbits-Eggs. He manages to overlook the other part of the accusation, however, and thus avoided some suspicion. On the other hand, when Finny is trapped by Mr. Patch-Withers at the tea, he invents a story to suit his predicament.

There are several possibilities as to reasons for these likenesses and differences in the language. One of the main reasons would probably have to be the difference of location of the two schools. Since one is located in England, and the other is located in New Hampshire, it can only be expected that there would be a difference in the school terms and in the ways the boys express themselves. The school itself also has some bearing on the question. Since the emphasis at Kipling's school seems to be more academic than that of Devon is, it does not seem strange to hear quotes coming from the mouths of Stalky and his friends. The schools are probably also responsible for the fact that the boys in both books speak more than one language and have good grammar and vocabularies. Kipling's school seems to be a much more strict school than Devon, so this probably explains why Stalky and his friends don't curse or lie. The school seems to be the determining factor in the language of the boys.

## Writing Assignment Two, Question 1
## Comment on Sample 3.
## Grade: Average/Low

Unlike the first two papers, this one deals with part *b* without even a bow in the direction of part *a.* In a plodding way, this writer assembles a phalanx of facts about the language the boys in each school employ, but the paper is less sure of its ground when it moves out from the facts to the reasons for them and their significance. The naïveté of this student is evident in the reference to Brinker's literary productions as "poetry." The writing here is reasonably competent. The paper has a simple, clear plan, as its elaborate outline indicates it will. It also has the lifelessness that such a confining outline comes close to guaranteeing. Beyond this, the justification for a lower rating here than in the other two papers is that failure to reckon with part *a* seems a more serious flaw than failure to reckon with part *b,* though under ordinary circumstances no paper would rate *high* that failed to come to terms with all parts of the assignment. That the assignment was at fault in making too many demands is now the concern of the Commission on English.

# Short Stories

# *Introduction to the Units on the Short Story*

The five stories on which these lessons are based are drawn from a paperback anthology, *The Best Short Stories of the Modern Age,* as noted at the beginning of each unit. The stories are presented in the order in which they might best be taught, beginning with the relatively simplest. Each of the first four stories should be given a full period. The fifth story, James Joyce's "The Dead," will require at least two periods, probably more.

The discussion questions for these five stories are heuristic; that is, they are intended to lead the students toward a particular understanding of each story. They are *not* intended to invite random personal comments and reactions. It is hoped that the questions will keep the students working toward a thoughtful recognition of what the authors are saying, leaving little or no class time for a general airing of the students' personal opinions.

The questions are sequential; each should be answered before the next is raised. Occasionally, however, a question is introduced early that is meant to be challenging and perhaps unanswerable for the moment. (Some of these have been pointed out, but not all.) Such questions should be left unanswered, hovering in the backs of the students' minds; the questions immediately following will lead to the answers.

The questions do not presume to exhaust the meanings and techniques of the stories or to cover them in every detail. It is to be hoped that each class will range beyond them.

The questions on language are meant only to show certain highlights in each author's style. Another important way to start discussions of language is to ask the students where they were confused or impressed or most deeply moved in each story. Examining the language in those passages should be profitable.

The composition assignments for each story are of two kinds: the first assignment builds on a problem of *technique* that the story illustrates, and the second challenges the student to deal with *content* related to that of the story. *Only one of each pair should be assigned.* (For one rationale of this approach, see the transcript of the kinescope "A Student Writing Assignment Based on 'Fire Walking in Ceylon' " by Arthur J. Carr, published by the Commission on English of the College Entrance Examination Board, New York, 1965, 29 pages.)

These assignments are intended as homework, *not* as in-class exercises, and no more than one assignment should be given in any one week (or, preferably, two weeks).

It is essential to remember that this is a guide for the teacher and that all questions have been phrased for conciseness as well as exactness. The phrasing of the questions in the classroom will, of course, vary with the teacher's style and with each class. Even more far-reaching adaptations may be appropriate. For example, more clues should perhaps be built into the discussion questions for some classes, or perhaps the discussion and language questions should be interwoven. Even the sequence of the discussion questions will vary to some extent in each class, since in each the natural flow of the discussion will be unique.

*Edgar Allan Poe:*
*"The Tell-Tale Heart"*
*Grades 11 and 12*

tions? If he is projecting, what does this reveal about his relationship with the old man?

9. Why does the veiled eye disturb the speaker so? What does he say about it? Does this explain why he is so disturbed? Let's put some facts together: (1) he goes to kill the old man at midnight; (2) many nights, at midnight, he is beset by terrors that make him groan aloud; (3) he must look at the eye again before he can murder the old man; (4) he hates the eye because whenever it fell upon him, his blood ran cold; and (5) he is skillful at keeping his secrets concealed. What do these facts suggest? Does he kill the old man or the eye? What kind of eye does a man face alone in the dark of night, especially a man with guilty secrets? What is the speaker really trying to destroy?

10. Whose heart is the speaker hearing? Why does he think it is the old man's? The power of conscience, which he felt in the old man's eye, moves into the speaker's heart when that eye is killed. In this shift, what is Poe implying about the conscience?

11. When the police come, why do they stay so long? Is it really a short time, which seems long to the speaker; or have the police sensed something, and are they staying to break him down? Why don't they notice his gasping for breath, his pacing the floor, and so on—or do they? Or aren't his actions as obvious as he fears? Are their smiles actually mocking, derisive, hypocritical—or do they just seem so to the speaker? What evidence does the story offer for each of these interpretations? Which do you feel is decisive? How does your choice affect the meaning of the story?

12. Why does the speaker break down so fast?

## Questions on Language

1. The speaker is talking directly to you, and Poe uses a number of devices to make the style conversational. What are some of them? Study carefully the points at which the speaker refers directly to the reader (as in the first sentence). What effect does this have? Note the speaker's frequent use of interjections and exclamations. What impression do these create?

2. Why does the speaker use only indirect discourse in telling of his morning conversation with the old man and his talk with the police? What effect does this have on the focus of the story? On your judgment of his sanity or insanity?

3. Perhaps the most striking linguistic device that Poe uses in this story is repetition of words and phrases close together; there are dozens of such repetitions in this very short story. (In the first paragraph, for example: "nervous—very, very dreadfully nervous" and "why *will* you say that I am mad? . . . How, then, am I mad?") How many such repetitions can you find? In each case, what idea or feeling is Poe emphasizing? Taking them all together, what mood do they create, and what do they tell you about the speaker?

## Writing Assignment One

In one or two sentences, describe a person (different from yourself) who is feeling a very strong emotion. Identify precisely what that emotion is. Then write a passage of at least 300 words in which that person is the speaker and in which he sustains that emotion without interruption from beginning to end. (This will be harder than you may think.)

## Writing Assignment Two

Describe in some detail an incident in your own life where you planned very carefully an action that you knew was wrong. Make clear your thoughts and feelings as you planned. Carry your essay to the point where you were about to act on your plans, and stop there. (If you prefer, you may make up a fictional incident, but write it so that it sounds real.)

# *Edgar Allan Poe: "The Tell-Tale Heart" Grades 11 and 12*

*Book Used:* Angus, Douglas, ed. *The Best Short Stories of the Modern Age.* New York: Fawcett (World Library) Premier (m309), 1962.

## Questions for Discussion

1. When you finished reading the story, did you feel glad or sorry that the speaker had been caught? Why? As far as you can tell, is this what Poe intended you to feel? What clues do you find to Poe's intention? (Or aren't there any?)

2. During most of the story, Poe obviously means you to feel tense—and often scared. Did you? Why, or why not?

3. Is the speaker of the story mad? What evidence does he adduce to prove his sanity? Does this evidence *prove* that he is sane? Why, or why not? Note especially his discussion of his sense of time. Why does this seem to him a proof of sanity? How does it compare with the "normal" person's sense of time? Apart from the evidence he offers, what clues do you find to his sanity or insanity? What do they show?

4. Why does Poe have the speaker assume that you already consider him mad? How does this affect your attitude and mood as you read the story?

5. What difference does it make whether the speaker is sane or insane? If he is sane, what does the story imply about human nature? If he is insane, what does it imply?

6. Apart from the question of his sanity, what kind of man is the speaker? How can you tell?

7. What do you know about the old man? Why does Poe tell you so little?

8. What is the relationship between the speaker and the old man? How does the speaker act toward him while the old man is awake? What are his feelings toward the old man, apart from the filmed eye? Note carefully the passages in which the speaker identifies himself with the old man by telling what emotions they share. Does the speaker *know* the old man's emotions, or is he projecting his own emo-

## Writing Assignment One
## Sample 1. Grade: High

*A Good Man Feeling Bad*

It was a cold, windy night, and a drizzling rain was continuing to fall as it had steadily throughout the day. On a muddy road through the level camp, a lone, bareheaded figure made his way slowly back to his shack. As he walked, he talked resentfully and despairingly to himself, sometimes in a low mumble, often in thought only, but occasionally boldly and loudly.

"Sho' is cold! Been cold and mis'able all day. Wish to de Lord I'd stayed back home where I belong on dat ole farm! Dis ole worl' been a hell to me ever since I started to roam. Ever'body always after me now, jus' like dat damn cap'n. Tol' him my hands was cold. What's he say? 'God damn your hands, it ain't quittin' time yet!' Then when de whistles startes blowin' he keeps on workin' me. An' he tol' me he wouldn't never work me in de rain all day!

"An' jus' wait'll I try to collect my pay. Ain't never been no nigger around here able to get his pay when it's due. An' if he did it wouldn't be 'nuff to live any better than some ole weasel off in his hole. How long's it been since I et a good meal? Three, four weeks? Had to pawn my watch an' chain for dat. What I'd give for one bran' new dollar bill in my han'!

"Got de wors' job anywheres, but it's all anyone'll give dis po' nigger. An' its sho' lucky de boss ain't found out I was on de chain gang. Fire me fo' sho'! an jus' 'cause I got in one li'l fight. Put in jail wid my mouth all pushed in. Then, jus' cause I'm black an' ain't got no money for my fine, dey stick me in de county gang.

"Sho' is hard to be a nigger! Look at ole Jake. Won dat money from dat white guy an' 'fraid to take it. Should'a had 'nuff sense not to git in a card game wid no white man. And when pay day come, white man say you ain't worked 'nuff to git payed.

"Rather be dead. Rather be in my grave. If I'd died when I was young, wouldn't had to suffer all dis. De cap'n worked ole Zeke to death, and' dey carried him off to cemetery wid all dose peoples standin' 'roun'. An' after de preacher says amen, dey lays his po' body down. Now he jus' lies dere takin' it easy. Sho' better off dan me. Sometimes I'se felt like suicide. What I got to live for, ennyway? Tired of livin'! Dis po' man's life nothin' but misery. Clothes all dirty and tore to pieces. Shoes wore out, so's my feet touch the groun'. I'se broke and hungry and ragged and dirty. Lonely an' a long ways from home, an' there ain't nobody to pity po' me! Bes' time I ever had was gittin' drunk an' bein' sick in de street all night long. Guess that's what I'll do tonight. Ain't no use livin', so I'll jus' go an' drink 'till I dies. Corn whiskey gonna kill me dead.

"Mebbe tomorrow de ole sun come out."

## Writing Assignment One
## Comment on Sample 1. Grade: High

Successful compliance with the exactions of the assignment is one of this paper's major claims to distinction. This student not only sees the difficulties but forestalls criticism in his opening paragraph by making clear that his character is talking "resentfully and despairingly to himself, sometimes in a low mumble, *often in thought only,* but occasionally boldly and loudly." The use of dialect can be disastrous in unskillful hands, but this student carries it off without notable lapses in accuracy or taste. As a consequence of his fidelity to the speech of the character, the consistent maintenance of the initial tone of long-stored but finally overflowing resentment, and the choice of unexpected and tangential details, this student's monologue seems thoroughly credible, just the sort of thing such a person might say to himself, at such a time.

The introduction is an integral part of the paper, not a mere bow in the direction of the assignment. The cold, the wind, the drizzling rain are an appropriate backdrop for the monologue, even perhaps its prompting agents. The surprise turn at the end suggests this possibility.

A final merit of the paper is its command of the technique of dramatic monologue. This is no mere outpouring of random rage. The student is adept at hinting without fully telling—as in the reference to the jail term. Like a dramatist, he makes every detail count. It is true that in real life no one reveals this much of himself in 300 words, yet the contrivance of the revelation is too skillfully concealed to chip away the reader's acceptance.

Some readers would deny this paper a *high* rating because its persona is such a stereotype, exhibiting traits and language typical of characters in nineteenth-century melodrama, and because they feel that the paper's contrivance is by no means as well concealed as it appears to be to the readers who graded the paper *high.* There may also be a difference in judgment of the following paper.

## Writing Assignment One
## Sample 2. Grade: High

*Anger*

She stormed out of the classroom and confronted me, absolutely boiling with rage. Her face was red with anger and her whole body trembled, as though she was fighting to keep herself under control. She tried to blink back the hot, angry tears as she blurted out the story.

"How could he? How could he? Do you know that, that . . . miserable excuse for a teacher actually accused me of cheating? I am so furious that I can hardly control myself. That man, I could kill him! He humiliated me so, and in front of the whole class, too. I always suspected that he disliked me. He is never nice to me, and no matter how hard I try he always gives me a "C." He seizes every opportunity to make a fool out of me in front of the class. This is positively the last straw! I've had all I can take out of that man. I will never, ever go back to that class again! I just couldn't face anyone in there after such gross humiliation. Boy, he has really done it this time. I wish I had enough courage to tell him off. The worst part of it was that I was *not* cheating. If I had I would have deserved to be completely humiliated and put down in front of the whole class. We were taking a test and I was sitting there minding my own business, doing the test. I got stuck on one question and I looked out the window, and tried to figure out the answer. Mary happened to look up and she made a face at me about the test. I made a face back and then Mr. Johnson practically exploded. He screamed that he had finally caught me in the act of cheating. He said he had suspected me for a long time, and knew he would catch me sooner or later. He went into a long dissertation about what a horrid person I was—no integrity, no honesty—just the type of student he despised. All that time I had been trying to protest that I had not been cheating. He said that lying was almost as bad as cheating. Then he commanded me to get out of his classroom and stop contaminating his other students. I ran out of the room and slammed the door as hard as I could. I wish I would have broken a few windows, it would have serve him right. How could he be so cruel and unfair? There was not one ounce of truth in any of his accusations. I am so humiliated that I could die! Well, I'll fix him. Just you wait. When I get through with him, he won't be able to teach anywhere in the state. The very idea, I have never cheated in my life. Right now, I am going to call my mother and tell her what happened. Then I am going to see the principal and then the School Board. Boy, I can hardly wait to put the squeeze on him. He'll be sorry, I'm going to fix him up good."

## Writing Assignment One
## Comment on Sample 2. Grade: High

This student chooses a situation from school life, and manages a progression from humiliation through outraged innocence to vindictiveness, a natural movement of strong emotion under the circumstances. An audience (of one) is provided; if it seems unlikely that the tirade should not have been interrupted, one should remember that such interruptions were not allowed by the assignment. The paper maintains a consistency of tone with mood; it tends to repetition of ideas, however rephrased; but such repetition could well be characteristic of an angry schoolgirl. As she gets some of the emotion off her chest, she tends to talk more colloquially and naturally—note the final sentences. A sustained dramatic monologue.

Some readers would deny a ***high*** rating to this paper mainly because they feel that the language and style of the monologue are not characteristic of an angry schoolgirl. Such judgments obviously depend primarily on the previous experience of their makers.

## Writing Assignment One
## Sample 3. Grade: Average

*Happiness*

My friend is a lucky girl, she sees what many of us fail to see and she's very happy because of it.

This feeling I have is so intense, it so deep, it's, well actually, it's hard to put into words like most days feeling are you know. Its the kind of feeling that makes me fairly gasp for air, good grief, sometimes I just have to leap up and yelp for joy. It comes and goes, pretty much ruled by my environment. Take last night for example, I was riding along in a convertable, perched on the upper edge of the back seat. One breath of the fragrant evening air sent my arms flinging in the breeze. From deep down inside a funny sensation grew within me, it welled up and burst forth in a stream of garbled shouts. I think about it now and I know I must have made a complete fool of myself. But you know, I don't really care, I was enjoying myself so much. I seemed to be so much more aware than I usually am, you know, sitting around thinking of the past or the future or something dumb like that. I felt I was really appreciating, really feeling deeply. I could hear every minute sound, I could feel the wind blowing hard on my face and wipping through my hair. I'd actually reach out my arms to everything I saw as though God were handing it to me as a gift. I don't know why it's these small things that give me such a complete feeling of joy. They've been around all my life but so much of the time I've never noticed I guess. Actually it doesn't have to be a warm evening, whizzing along in an open car, it can just as well be a rainy, drizzly day in the middle of town and the same thing happens, all I have to do is open my eyes and take a look.

## Writing Assignment One
## Comment on Sample 3. Grade: Average

The writer of this paper tackles a difficult problem—to describe the causes and effects of the emotion of happiness—and makes the solution more difficult by choosing what seem like causes too small to produce such effects. She fails to make a transition between the introductory sentence and the subsequent monologue; her spelling and punctuation are not impeccable; there is some vagueness. Nevertheless, the tone is consistently kept, and there seem to be enough positive qualities in her use of words to rate her paper as low *average.*

## Writing Assignment One
## Sample 4. Grade: Low

This is about a man who's son has been sent to Vietnam. He feels proud but yet he is sad and angry because of the War, and afraid for the fear That his son may come to harm.

My son takes pride in fighting and risking his life for The freedom of his Country and the freedom of others. My heart swells with pride in my son. But I am so afraid for him, Why can't we live in peace, Why must this World be so unkind. I feel anger within my breast for Those Ignorant people who don't even appreciate That our men are dying and suffering for Their benefit. They Lie, cheat, spy, and kill our men for the benefit of Their enemy. My heart pitys Those poor ignorant people. But My body Tenses up with anger. My Son and The son's of millions of others are suffering more than we will ever know, if There was only something In which I could do. All That I am able to do is pray, and write To him. He is only a Boy, a boy of eighteen, Oh My God my dear God, he has'nt even begain to live or to see the world, The beautiful side of the world. All he can see now is hate, greed, death, and dirt. Will all their suffering be in Vain? Will They win? If we lose it will be the begaining of the end. And if we win it will be the begaining of what I hope will be happiness. Yes . . . That's it the begaining of happiness. But My boy will never obtain That happiness which he is fighting for. He will never share in what may be a free and wonderful World nor will I or anyone living Today. He must be out there now in That dirty, damp, wild swamp, every step he takes is a step Closer to death, every breath he takes may be his last. What a foolish old man I am, and how very selfish I must be. But I Love my son, my only boy. How clear That day is to me, The sunny day in which he left. He was not sad, nor was he afraid. The minute had come for us to say good bye. He Turned to me and said: Dad, I will miss you ever so much. But I must go, I want to go. Those people over there need me, But most of all my Country needs me. I will suffer, but I will suffer happily, I may die But I will die with Pride, in knowing That I die for a worthy cause, for something worth dying for. Then he was gone. Yes my son, Those people need you, And yet They defy you. Yes Boy, your Country needs you, yet There are Those of us americans who do you and Millions of other soldiers wrong. Yes, you are suffering for Those who don't care, Who say you are suffering in Vain. But we know different, we know what must be done, and we know why we must do it. Oh God! My dear God have mercy on my Son, have mercy on us all.

## Writing Assignment One
## Comment on Sample 4. Grade: Low

The student tried to express two or three emotions—pride, anger, and fear—rather than one, as directed by the assignment. Unfortunately, only clichés came to mind as means of expression, and the result is confused, bad melodrama rather than dramatic emotion. A single paragraph covering three pages makes the lack of organization more evident than it might otherwise have been. Errors in spelling, punctuation, capitalization, and grammar exist, but are less serious than the inability to avoid stilted language, which makes the emotions presented seem artificial.

## Writing Assignment Two
## Sample 1. Grade: High

*The Sewing Machine*

When I was small, about five years old, I had an argument with my little brother. We had both been drawing pictures, and I knew that mine was by far superior to his; but when we showed them to my mother, she would not admit it. She kept insisting that she could not tell which was the better, because they were both so good. I thought that she was showing favoritism to him (that she loved him more) since she would not admit to the superiority of my picture. So I told him that she had told me that mine was much better than his. Over this we had our quarrel, and since he would not believe what I said, I was determined to have revenge.

Now my mother had a very old sewing machine. To make its needle move up and down one had to work a pump and wheel manually. She kept it set up in an out-of-the-way room. It was here that I lured my brother on a friendly pretense. I told him that I wanted to show him something. In my mind, I knew that I could convince him to put his tender little finger under the needle.

So I led him there with sweet, friendly words, like a Siren lures men to their deaths with her sweet singing, and he fell for the trap which I had carefully planned. Through all my coniving remarks, I finally induced him to ask how the machine worked. My delight at this innocent question was sadistic! "Oh," I said, "put your finger under the needle, and I will show you!" Again and again he refused, suspecting some treachery. But my voice became more honeyed, his curiosity was aroused, and to my joy, my dear little brother, whom I hated vehemently, slipped his chubby, little forefinger under the needle! My hand and foot were poised on the wheel and pump, like a cat poised to strike.

## Writing Assignment Two
## Comment on Sample 1. Grade: High

This is not an impeccable paper: there is some uncertainty of diction; the use of "like" in the third paragraph will disturb many teachers; and there are at least two misspellings. On the other hand, the paper meets the requirements of the assignment fully and plausibly: an action known to be wrong is carefully planned, and the narrative stops at precisely the point demanded—where the action is about to take place. The thoughts and feelings of the planner are made clear. The writing has a simplicity appropriate to the youth of the children in the incident; none of the flaws mentioned above is serious. Better papers on this topic could easily be imagined, but one who judges ability to satisfy the demands of an assignment as a major criterion for grading can hardly keep this paper from the *high* bracket.

## Writing Assignment Two
## Sample 2. Grade: Average

At ten o'clock, when only the girl was at home, we would go and ring the doorbell. As she opened the door, we would chloroform her and keep her until her parents would pay us the money. I could feel her squirming under my grip and I laughed out loud at the though. First there would be the struggle, and then the limp body. Who would ever guess that we would abduct the mayor's daughter?

It wasn't really for the money, we had plenty of money, but just for the thrill of committing a perfect crime. We had even contemplated returning the money and telling the family that we had done it—just to see their facial expressions. They wouldn't prosecute us because we had known the family for a long time. In fact, my father and the mayor were best friends. What irony this perfect little scheme contained.

There was no way to get caught. Everything had already been planned. At nine thirty, we drove by the house. Her parents had gone to a party so she was alone. At ten o'clock, we walked up to the door. With chloroform in hand, we pushed the doorbell. Our blood began to rise as we heard her approrching footsteps.

## Writing Assignment Two
## Comment on Sample 2. Grade: Average

This paper seems to fit the definition of a middle or low *average* rating; it is fairly clean, but it lacks either the imagination or the clear and plausible satisfaction of the assignment's demands that characterize the *high* paper. The idea of an abduction shows some imagination, but the paper fails to make it plausible. Someone else is concerned, but we are never told who. We are told that "Everything had already been planned," but aside from the planner's glee at the thought of the actual chloroforming of the mayor's daughter, there is little evidence of the thoughts and feelings of the planner while the plan was being formed. The whole second paragraph, for instance, has little to do with the assignment. The style is plodding and unimpressive.

## Writing Assignment Two
## Sample 3. Grade: Low

I don't think my older brother, Ray, liked my idea too much, but I knew he'd go along with it. He had a hundred reasons why we shouldn't do it. First, it was a neighborhood grocery store in the neighborhood where we had always lived. Second, it probably had a burglar alarm. Third, what little money that would be in there was not worth the risk. My answers, however, were good and he finally consented to help in my daring robbery.

There was not a great deal of planning necesary. I agreed on his plan of entry, which was to come down from behind the old, brick building and breack the large, plate glass window at the side. Once we were inside, he was to take care of the cash register, while I collected all the candy and other goodies I could carry. From there, we would play it by ear.

As I had fought all my mental battles with conscience, sense of right, and training before proposing the plan to Ray, all that remained was to wait out his internal struggles, and then we were all set.

## Writing Assignment Two
## Comment on Sample 3. Grade: Low

This paper is rated in the *low* group for several reasons. First, there is very little about the actual plan—in fact, we are told that "not a great deal of planning" was necessary. Second, the plan, such as it was, apparently owed at least as much to the writer's brother as to the writer. Further, the thoughts and feelings of the writer are condensed into a single clause in the final sentence, as already disposed of. To Ray's objections we are told that "my answers . . . were good," but we are never told what they were. In other words, the paper fails to meet the requirements of the assignment. There is nothing in its style or technique sufficient to raise it from the *low* group.

*D. H. Lawrence:*
*"The Rocking-Horse Winner"*
*Grades 11 and 12*

7. What is the relationship between Paul and his mother? What are the complexities in his feelings toward her? In her feelings toward him? How do their feelings change in the course of the story? How much can you tell about Paul's relationship with his father? Why does Lawrence tell us so little? Why do the voices in the house become insatiable after the mother receives her 5,000 pounds? What leads Paul to misuse his powers? If he were older, would he have known better? How would he have learned? What did kill Paul? What drove him to the final, intolerable ride?

8. Why might it be significant that Paul goes through a final agony of self-sacrifice, that his dying lasts for three days, and that then he is gone—and the supernatural glory is gone with him? How does Paul resemble Christ? How are they different? Why does this difference matter?

9. At the human level, in what sense is Paul lucky? In what sense is he unlucky? As Paul's mother listens to Uncle Oscar's last statement, would she consider herself lucky or unlucky? Why?

10. Thus far we have been considering the religious aspect from the point of view of the characters in the story, especially Paul and Bassett—that is, from a Christian point of view. But Lawrence's religious beliefs were different. Here is one statement of them (from his essay "Benjamin Franklin"):

"Here's my creed. . . . This is what I believe:

" *'That I am I.'*

" *'That my soul is a dark forest.'*

" *'That my known self will never be more than a little clearing in the forest.'*

" *'That gods, strange gods, come forth from the forest into the clearing of my known self, and then go back.'*

" *'That I must have the courage to let them come and go.'*

" *'That I will never let mankind put anything over me, but that I will try always to recognize and submit to the gods in me and the gods in other men and women.'* "

What new light does this creed cast on the story? How are Paul's gods coming into his known self? How does he betray them? Only by trying to compel them, rather than submitting to them? How does one "recognize and submit to the gods . . . in *other* men and women"? What light does this cast on the characters other than Paul and on their relationships to the gods in Paul and in themselves?

## Questions on Language

1. Lawrence's vocabulary and syntax in this story are exceptionally simple, yet he communicates some subtle impressions and ideas. One of his secrets is iron control over his underlying images, which are often not stated explicitly. Study, for example, the description of Bassett in the death-room ("The gardener . . . dying child," page 104). To what is Lawrence comparing Bassett? Why is that comparison appropriate in this scene?

2. Study all the adjectives that Lawrence uses to describe Paul's eyes. What do they tell us about Paul? How do the descriptions vary? What does that variance tell us about Paul? Study all the descriptions of Paul's mother. What is the underlying image in the descriptions, and how is it related to the image of Paul's eyes?

3. Study the three paragraphs in which Paul's mother reads the lawyer's letter ("She was down . . . and absent," pages 99–100) and the paragraph in which she stands listening outside Paul's door ("She stood . . . what is was," page 103). In each case, how does Lawrence use a string of adjectives to convey a mood? How does he break the string so that it will not become monotonous? What other examples of his use of strings of adjectives catch your attention?

4. Examine some of the passages in which Lawrence's words are extremely precise and some in which they are vague and full of suggestion. How are the words related, in each case, to the effect Lawrence wants to create?

## Writing Assignment One

Write a story of at least 500 words in which you convey a change from one subtle but intense mood to another through very simple language. (*Note to the teacher.* After these stories are collected, ask the students what difficulties they encountered in this as-

## *D. H. Lawrence: "The Rocking-Horse Winner" Grades 11 and 12*

*Book Used:* Angus, Douglas, ed. *The Best Short Stories of the Modern Age.* New York: Fawcett (World Library) Premier (m309), 1962.

### Questions for Discussion

1. When you finished reading the story, did you believe that Paul had actually learned the winners' names by riding his rocking-horse? Lawrence certainly means us to accept this as a fact. How does he establish it as a fact? And why does he have Uncle Oscar at first doubt Paul, even to the point of laughing, and then become convinced that Paul is telling the truth?

2. But do you believe that a boy can learn the winners' names by riding a rocking-horse? We are dealing, then, with a reality that is not realistic in the usual sense. What kind of reality is this? (Leave this question hanging unless the answer comes at once.)

3. How do the children know, at the start, that the house needs money? How does Paul's mother know, near the end, that he is in trouble? Why does she resist this feeling? Why does it win out? How are these inner intelligences similar to—and different from—Paul's knowledge of the winners?

4. Who told Paul that he was lucky? What impression does Paul's luck make on Bassett? Find and list all the references to God, Heaven, church, and so forth in Bassett's speeches or associated with them. What is Lawrence telling us?

5. If Paul, then, is receiving his knowledge from God, what does his frenzied riding of the rocking-horse mean? Study the descriptions carefully. What kind of state does riding throw Paul into?

6. But if Paul, in a mystical trance, is receiving knowledge from God, why is he also a "poor devil" (page 105)? Is the word "devil" just slang, or does it have some meaning in the story? What should a man use his God-given powers for? Does Paul use his powers for that spiritual purpose? What *does* he use them for? Why?

signment and what this shows about the relationship of language to feeling.)

## Writing Assignment Two

In a carefully organized essay, discuss an incident in your life where you felt sure of something (and turned out to be right) even though you didn't know how you knew. Focus your essay on other people's reactions to your intuition and what their reactions made you think and feel. (If you prefer, you may make up a fictional incident, but write it so that it sounds real.)

## Writing Assignment One
## Sample 1. Grade: High

*Decay*

"Dan, come in here and help me with the dishes, please."

"OK, I'm coming." ("If I want to have a chance of getting out tonight," he thought, "I'd better try to get her in a good mood.") He knew that it wasn't often that his mother let him go out on Sunday nights, and that with a D in math and a low C in French his chances were even slimmer. Still, he could always hope.

As he walked into the kitchen he forced a cheerful tone—"All right, where can I start?"

"You know the dish towels are in the drawer."

("Uh-oh, she's in a bad mood.")

They worked on in silence for a while, as Danny dried in rapid succession a casserole, two spoons, and a salad bowl. He opened his mouth as he reached over to take a still steaming-and-sudsing dinner plate, then shut it again as he caught a glimpse of her eyes.

Five minutes later he was drying a carving knife as he sat on the counter, looking down on the back of her blond head.

"Mom."

"Yes."

"I talked to Jerry Graves late this morning while you were still at church, and he said he was having some guys over tonight. Can I take the car over there?"

"Do you really think you ought to after that D in Math? I talked to Mr. Jenkins last Friday and he said you were lucky to get that C in French, too."

"He snatched the pot lid she held out to him. "Well, the only reason he said that is because he doesn't like me. As for math, I know the stuff, I just make careless errors on the tests. So what's the big sweat? I'm passing everything."

"But how do you expect to get into a good school with bad grades?"

"Did it ever occur to you that *you're* worrying a lot more about my getting into college than I am?" He slammed down the lid. "Suppose I don't go to a big-name school. What if I want to join the Army? Don't I have a say?"

"Of course you do, dear, but it's just. . . ."

"Then why can't I go over to Jerry's?"

"Because . . . because I'm your mother and I know what's best for you and as long as you live in this house you have to do what I say and I say you can't! And that's final!"

The boy casually flipped the knife he was drying back into the dishwater, balled up the towel and tossed it aside, and walked out of the room. On his way out she heard him mutter, "Thanks a lot. I'll do you a favor some time."

Her last command came as he was disappearing down the hall. "Dan, go call Jerry right now and tell him you're not coming."

To make sure he obeyed she followed him down the hall and stood at his door. She heard "Hello, Jerry. . . ." and the door slammed in her face. She returned to the kitchen."

A half-hour later she noticed a draft coming from his end of the house. She traced it to his door, shouting in to him, "Dan, is your window open." Her only answer was the final chord of "Satisfaction."

She opened the door to find the room empty. The window was open and the screen removed. On his desk, beneath the unfinished model Messerschmidt, lay a scrap of paper: "Mom, please leave this window open so the glue on my model can dry." As she tremblingly replaced the model on the sheet of paper, there was a small snapping sound, and the fuselage split apart down the middle. The wings, however, remained mockingly attached to the plastic shell—upside down.

## Writing Assignment One
## Comment on Sample 1. Grade: High

The skillful use of the dramatic method, the restraint, the power of saying by what it leaves unsaid, the suggestiveness of the title, and the unforced symbolism at the end are the evident strengths of this unusual paper. The use of a decaying mother-son relationship indicates the writer's closeness to the Lawrence story he has been studying. The conversation and the detail in the dishwashing scene are skillful. Instead of just saying that Danny dried the stack of dishes, this student cites the "casserole, two spoons, and a salad bowl." Danny's starting to speak but then shutting up when he gets a glimpse of his mother's eyes spells out the relationship in all its wrongness, as does the boy's earlier awareness of his mother's mood merely from the tone in which she tells him the towels are in the drawer. The mother's golden hair and morning church attendance, her visit to the school to check on the boy's grades, her following him to make sure he does what he is told, and her tampering with the model the boy has made still further define the relationship without need for comment from the writer.

A problem that may puzzle the reader is whether the paper is dealing with the mother's change of mood or the boy's. Actually it presents both. The boy moves from a mood of coaxing subservience to one of bitter defiance that collides with his mother's cherished hopes and values. The mother presumably shifts from her role of masterful manipulator of her son's life to at least a partial awareness of the bankruptcy of this outworn technique as she "tremblingly replaced the model on the sheet of paper" and "the fuselage split apart down the middle." The final sentence ingeniously summarizes the mother-son relationship through the symbol of the mocking wings and "the plastic shell—upside down."

## Writing Assignment One
## Sample 2. Grade: Average

*Flight of Fear*

The man was still visibly shaken from his recent harrowing experience as he related his story.

"I had the disturbing feeling that my late arrival at the airport was an omen for my trip to come. However, since I am not a superstitious man, I shrugged off my uneasiness as I rushed to catch the plane.

Moments later we were flying smoothly over the kaleidoscoping landscape. Since the flight was to be only two hours long, my previous feeling of dread was soon gone, soothed by the monotonous humming of the motors of the plane. Suddenly my reveries were shattered by the voice over the loudspeaker. 'Ladies and gentlemen, this is your Captain speaking. One of our motors is out! We must turn back. Please fasten your seat belts, as we have a rough ride ahead of us.'

As I began to realize the grave danger we were in, my heart seemed to pound louder and faster than ever before. The plane bounced up and down, then would veer to the left, and back to the right. The idle motor was no help in stabilizing our flight.

Fear quickly seized the minds and hearts of all the passengers, and the growing terror seemed to fill the air as the plane was jostled back and forth. Loud groans escaped even the bravest-appearing passengers. We were all comrades in our terror and suffering.

I had, of course, felt fear before but never a fear like this. My heart seemed to be leaping. I could not control myself. My hands shook, and as I said reassuring things to those around me, I felt they were only empty words.

Thoughts and memories of my family plagued my mind as my senses grew numb from my extreme nervousness. The unbearable thought that I might never see them again affected me greatly.

As we approached the landing field, the muffled sound of sobs and private prayers filled the plane. The plane seemed to jolt more uncontrollably as we flew on. The noise grew and seemed to deaden my eardrums and make me unconscious of anything but my own heartbeats. As we started losing altitude, I closed my eyes and prayed, not opening them until I realized the plane had landed safely. This, as you can undoubtedly see, was one of the luckiest days of my life."

## Writing Assignment One
## Comment on Sample 2. Grade: Average

This paper fulfills the demands of the assignment. The details of the incident justify an intense mood of fear, and the safe landing, after all, brings a natural reaction. There is no indication of the speaker's audience—his monologue is apparently addressed to thin air. What keeps the paper in the *average* category is the stiffness and conventionality of the phrasing—for instance, the fear that "quickly seized the minds and hearts of all"; the thought of never again seeing his family "affected me greatly"—a feeble understatement. The writing is free from technical errors.

## Writing Assignment One
## Sample 3. Grade: Low

I was silently reading a magazine when suddenly the phone rang and startled me out of my little world. Indifferently I answered the phone, not realizing the importance of that moment. It was a nurse from Mercy Hospital, who, regretedly told me that my younger brother had been in an automobile accident. Dazedly I listened to her directions to contact my parents and please come to the hospital if possible. As I hung up the phone, the tears began to flood my cheeks. The nurse had not told me exactly what injuries he had received, but would only tell me it was serious. It seemed as though my heart was draining for the possible loss of this brother would leave me empty. I tried to collect my thoughts and get hold of Dad at the office and Mom at a friends. I could imagine the strain it would be on Dads' heart since he had recently had two bad attacks. News like this would not go over lightly.

After contacting each, I raced across the street, breaking the news to my cousin Shirley and requesting that she drive me to the hospital.

It took us twenty minutes to drive there and every minute caused a passing of all the memories I had of my brother. He was only 16, still in my eyes a baby, too young to have a mishap like this to ruin his life.

We rushed into the entrance of the hospital and asked for news of Jimmy Rankins' condition. The nurse said he had internal bleeding, a slight concusion, two broken ribs and a broken leg. He was still in the emergency operation room now for they were trying to stop the internal bleeding for he already had a heavy loss of blood. It caused a nauseating feeling in the pit of my stomach and I hurried to a chair before my feet gave out. Ten minutes passed and I saw both parents rush into the hospital and then to the waiting room where I limply sat. No words were passed between us—none were needed to express the grief and sympathy for my brother.

Another hour passed and two doctors entered and asked for Mr. and Mrs. Rankin. My parents stood up and blankly stared at the doctors, waiting for the worst. The doctors said Jimmy was "A-ok," the bleeding had been stoped and he was coming out of the anesthetic. It seemed like air began to flow again and breath could be inhaled without causing a quickening of the pulse and a lump in the throat. If we waited about ten minutes we could see him, but only for ten minutes as he would need to get some rest.

Soon we entered my brothers room and stared sympathetically, as thought we each felt his pain and it had been us who had received the injuries.

As Jimmy told the story of the accident, I suddenly wondered what automobile he had been driving. I had lent him my Volvo earlier but he was supposed to had left it off at the garaged to have a new transmission put in.

Upon my questioning, my dread was answered. My Volvo was demolished! My car, my only car, my pride and joy, everything I had saved for the past year had been used for parts on it! Anger welled up in me and I could not help the fury that steamed through my words. Sure, Jimmy was sorry, but what was I going to do. I stood by his bedside with my teeth gritting and my fists clenched. The only thing I could think of was unkind and unsympathetic words for my brother and trying to hold myself back from saying something that would anger my parents. I felt like finding the most valuable possesion my brother had and deystroying it with my own bare hands to get the satisfaction of hurting my rotten, bratty little brother. Just to make him cry, make him sorry for doing this to me. I staled out the hospital room, angry, yet relieved, and still yet—wanting to make an apology.

## Writing Assignment One
## Comment on Sample 3. Grade: Low

This student does more with changes of mood than the assignment requires: from placidity to great anxiety, to sudden relief, and, finally, to anger. The violence of her wrath at the loss of her automobile seems overstated, under the circumstances; that, when her parents rushed into the hospital, "No words were passed between us," also seems improbable. The errors in spelling, punctuation, and grammar are frequent enough to justify a rating of *low,* since they are not balanced by any exceptional content.

## Writing Assignment Two
## Sample 1. Grade: High

Sunday was a very exciting day at our house. Tammy, our cat, had her first litter. The Five Little Peppers (that's what we dubbed them)—three butterscotch, one vanilla, and one licorice. What a combination! They were so tiny and helpless, and their pinkish eyes were still closed. Mom had planned an all-day beach picnic, but *I* wanted to stay home and keep an eye on the kittens. Outvoted twelve to one, I found myself at the beach within the hour. After lunch we watched some guys practicing karati. Karati is a sport which requires a lot of intense concentration, and I guess by watching the boys some of it rubbed off on me. I kept thinking about the Five Little Peppers. Despite my attempt to ward it off, I couldn't rid myself of an uneasy feeling.

"Mom, how soon are we going home?"

"I don't know. What's the matter?"

"Well . . . I . . . I'm worried about the kittens."

"Oh, don't be absurd. What could possibly happen to them?"

"A million things!" Fido could have broken into the house through the back screen, or one might have fallen out of the basket and broken its leg, or . . ."

"All right, all right. We'll go as soon as we bury the campfire."

On the way home, I kept getting more nervous. My stomach was working itself into a tight little knot.

"Dad, hurry!" I cried.

"Hold your horses, sister!"

We rounded the bend and sped along the wooded path to the front door. Dad said, "See, everything's O.K. All that worrying for noth. . ."

The first to hop out of the car, I had been greeted by billows of black smoke gushing out the front door.

"Don't go in there!" my father shouted.

Undaunted, I gulped in fresh air and then darted to the kitchen. Tammy was frantic. I scooped up the basketful of kittens and hurried out again, with Tammy close behind. Mom had used the phone in the summer house to call the fire department and dad, who had hooked up a garden hose, was making his way back in, squirting a stream in the general direction of the kitchen. An Easter basket near the stove had caught fire and the flames had spread to newspapers. With ten children smothering the flames with beach blankets, the blaze was out before the firemen arrived. I'll never forget Dad's story to the reporters: "We were having a family picnic when I sensed something was wrong at home. I could just feel it in my bones . . ."

## Writing Assignment Two
## Comment on Sample 1. Grade: High

The charm of this paper lies in its skillful use of simple ingredients and its satirical ending. The writer handles conversation with a realistic awareness that often people don't get a chance to finish their sentences. The disaster the "I" senses is plausible and the vagueness of the initial apprehension does not violate our credulity as an exact foreknowledge of the impending danger would have done. The paper would be merely good if it had ended with the fire and the rescue of the vanilla, butterscotch, and licorice kittens. What gives it distinction is the mischievous mockery lurking behind the apparently dry, factual account of "Dad's story to the reporters." It should be noted, however, that the paper's "Focus . . . on other people's reactions to your intuition" is minimal.

## Writing Assignment Two
## Sample 2. Grade: Average

One summer I had the opportunity to work for a great painter. My job was very insignificant for I was to run errands, and generally clean up after the absent-minded artist. Never the less, I felt honored that I was allowed to be around the man.

At the time I was employed, the artist was interviewing men to pose for a painting of Jesus Christ. This, to me, was an important job and I found myself intruding upon the artist's selection by offering my opinion of each man.

The painter talked to hundreds of people and each had some or many mannerisms and characteristics that should be on canvas as the Divine Master. After many weeks, the painter was at his wit's end. He just couldn't find the right man. Then one day, during a routine interview, the master of the brush came in and with a quick glance at the prospective models, he pointed his slender finger in the direction of a man waiting by the door. "That's him! That's him! Look at that face. Look no further. I have found him!" I gazed at the man with awe; he was the most beautiful speciman I had ever seen. He was sitting there, very stately and masterfully as if he himself were Jesus.

The resemblance to a Biblical character was very evident in his simple clothes, his rugged face and his long, thick hair. Yes, he was a personage from the Bible, but the more I looked at him, the more unsure I became that the Biblical character this man resembled was Christ. In the reading I have done in the Bible, I remembered a description which fit this man perfectly. However, no matter how hard I tried, I could not place this face with a name.

It was something I couldn't put my finger on, but this wasn't the right man for the painting. I became very sure of my decision and decided I would tell the artist my thoughts. But when I mentioned my feelings to the artist he became furious and I was fired. He told me that he was the artist and he would pick his subjects as he liked them. To him, I was just a kid and could not know a good model if I saw one, so I was let go.

I left, very upset. I was disappointed of course, but more over I was really frightened that something terrible would happen if that man was chosen as the model.

I lost contact with the artist and began visiting the galleries regularly, searching for the face. Just yesterday, while in one art gallery, I spotted it immediately. There was no mistaking that face, but it wasn't the beautiful, flowing, graceful face I had seen that day. It was a face twisted, and snarled with self-hate and stricken by grief. It was only when I glanced at the title of the painting that I recognized the person as he really was. I was right, the man did resemble a Biblical character other than Jesus, and the title was not *Jesus* as was intended to be, but simply *Judas*.

## Writing Assignment Two
## Comment on Sample 2. Grade: Average

This paper fails to achieve complete plausibility partly because of its incidents, partly because of its style. It seems rather improbable that an errand boy should be allowed to voice his opinion of many candidates for the job of modeling, without correction, and then infuriate the artist by objecting to the final choice. It is also improbable that a "master of the brush" should select a model for Jesus, but use him as a model for Judas. And where, in the Bible, did the writer find "a description which fit this man perfectly"—this "most beautiful specimen I had ever seen"? The diction tends a bit toward inflation.

On the other hand, the writer of this paper strove earnestly to fulfill the requirements of the assignment, and there are enough positive values to justify a rating of *average.*

## Writing Assignment Two
## Sample 3. Grade: Low

My boyfriend asked me two weeks in advance for a date on a Friday night because he didn't have a band job that night. So when I was at school I would tell my girlfriends that I knew something would happen and he will break our date. My girlfriends kept reassuring me that he wouldn't, that he wouldn't ask me for a date just to break it. But I had the feeling he would.

Thursday night before that Friday he had a band job, and my girlfriend and I went. He talked to me during the breaks and asked me if I still wanted to go out Friday night. I was glad that he had asked me again, but I still had the same feeling. When he took me home that night and walked me to my porch, and he said that he would pick me up at seven-thirty.

The next day, the feeling was stronger than ever. I just knew that he was going to break our date. My girlfriends and I talked about it for a while, and I told them that he is probably going to stand me up, and they were all saying how ridiculous I was being. So when I got home from school I took the phone off the hook. I guess I just didn't want to face reality. I didn't want him to call me and make up some excuse why he couldn't make it. Then, just in case we were going out, I washed my hair and sat under the dryer. The phone was still off the hook. It was about 6:30 when I started getting ready. Then at 7:00 I took the phone off the hook and it rang about three minutes after. I was hesitant to answer the phone. Then I went over to pick it up. It was my girlfriend. We talked for about fifteen minutes and then the phone rang again. It was a guy that I knew. We talked for a few minutes and then I told him I had to go because I have a date. So by that time it was about 7:30 and he didn't come. I stayed up until 8:30 and then I went to bed.

Monday when I went to school my girlfriends asked me how my date went. I told the, "Oh, great, just fine. I went to bed at 8:30." From what I had said, they all knew what had happened, but they just couldn't understand how I knew.

## Writing Assignment Two
## Comment on Sample 3. Grade: Low

This student technically meets the requirements of the assignment. She has an intuition; she tells (though very little) about other people's reactions to it; and she turned out to be right. Further, there are not many errors in the writing. On the other hand there is little focus either on the others' reactions or the writer's own thoughts and feelings about them. There is a flatness, an immaturity of style, a monotony, that makes this paper seem *low* for a twelfth grade student. Whether the incident was actual or fictitious, the writer failed to make it seem real.

*Anton Chekhov: "Gooseberries"*
*Grades 11 and 12*

7. Who is living the way Ivan advocates? Is Alyohin living that way from a conscious purpose? What is his reaction to Ivan's long sermon? What does this contrast tell you about Alyohin? About Ivan?

8. Is the character Burkin necessary to the story? What is his relationship with Ivan? What sort of life is he living? At the end of the story, what is keeping him awake? Is it only the smell from the pipe?

9. What specifically does the title refer to? What broader meaning might it have?

10. What does Chekhov want you to feel about Ivan? What questions does he want you to ask about yourself?

## Questions on Technique[1]

1. What are the three major sections of the story? Why does Chekhov divide the story that way?

2. Where are Ivan and Burkin when the story opens? How does this affect your first encounter with Alyohin? With Nikolay?

3. Suppose that the rain had not interrupted Ivan at the beginning and that he had told about his brother before he went to Alyohin's. How would this affect the emotional impact of the story?

4. Identify and examine some of the echoes in the story, such as Ivan's two nights in others' homes (Nikolay's and Alyohin's) and the linking at the beginning and end of the story of Ivan's pipe and the rain. What effect does each echo have? How does Chekhov create this effect?

5. Why does Chekhov have Ivan mention, in passing, the loss of his father's estate in childhood? How might this help you to understand Nikolay? To understand Ivan?

## Writing Assignment One

Write a carefully planned story or essay in which the speaker (who may be yourself, or who may be fictional) tells a group of people about an important memory of his past. Do *not* have him explain why the memory is important to him or what he learned from it. Instead, have the environment in which he is talking serve as a contrast to the memory, so that it is clear that his life has become better or worse in some specific way.

## Writing Assignment Two

In one clear paragraph, restate in your own words Ivan's belief about happiness, drawing on all his speeches for your information. Then write a formally organized essay in which you prove convincingly, first, that Ivan is right and, second, that Ivan is wrong. Support both your proofs with examples from the life of one person, perhaps yourself. In a very brief conclusion, indicate whether you personally agree with Ivan or not, and why.

1. Questions on language are inappropriate for a translation.

## *Anton Chekhov: "Gooseberries" Grades 11 and 12*

*Book Used:* Angus, Douglas, ed. *The Best Short Stories of the Modern Age.* New York: Fawcett (World Library) Premier (m309), 1962.

### Questions for Discussion

1. On which character is Chekhov's attention centered? How do you know? Where does Chekhov show specifically that you are to concentrate on Ivan rather than on Nikolay?

2. The story is based on Ivan's reactions to two estates and their owners. What is his relationship with each man?

3. What sort of man is Alyohin? What sort of man is Nikolay? What does each want out of life? How does he go after it? What does he end up with? What contrasts are shown in their physical condition? In their estates? In their attitudes toward work? In their sense of social status? In their manners toward the peasants who work their estates? What other contrasts are shown between them? What is the contrast in the effect each has on the lives of people around him?

4. What lesson does Ivan draw from this contrast? How does he believe men should live, and for what purpose? How should men *not* live, and why?

5. Measuring himself and his own life against these two men, what conclusion does Ivan draw? How is he living? What is his profession, and how hard does he work at it? How does he spend his leisure time? What effect does he have on the lives of people around him? What does he keep exclaiming while he is swimming (and while the peasants are working at the mill)? Why? What does he say as he falls asleep? Why?

6. How does Ivan excuse himself for not living as he believes a man should live? How old *is* he? (The clues in the story will tell you within a few years.) Why does he consider this too old? Reread the description of Ivan's swim. Is this an old man? Why does Chekhov include this incident and emphasize it?

## Writing Assignment One
## Sample 1. Grade: High

*Box Car*

The rhythmic swaying of the moving box car worked with a hypnotic effect upon its occupants. The car was empty save for some straw and scraps of newspaper which had once been used as packing materials. In one corner beside a dimly flickering lantern one could see the dark shapes of four persons reclining or sitting in twisted positions which suggested that they had not been able to find more comfortable accomodations. The shadows of the group danced like some kind of dervish on the walls of the freight car as the lantern was shaken by the motion of the train. The group was dressed in thread-bare garments which, though in that condition, suggested having had better days under the same owners. The shoes of the four betrayed that they had been walking much but lacked that subtle distinction between walking shoes and work shoes. It was August and the intense heat, even of the night, was too much too allow the motion of the train to rock the men asleep; they remained motionless but awake.

The first man, fairly heavily built, wearing a dark well-worn, double-breasted suit lay on his side with his back to the light and gazed at the floor of the car. In the scraps of newspaper in front of him a particular piece caught his eye; he picked up that fragment and read aloud:

Mr. Leon R. Ronov . . . died late yesterday suddenly in his office. Doctors say he suffered a probable heart attack. Mr. Ronov had long been a prominent member of the community and had served in his later years as Chief Consultant to the Government Food Agency. He arrived in this country in 1908, having emigrated from Latvia. After working as an errand boy for his father's fruit stand, Leon earned enough money to invest in the stock market. Rising in a "Horatio Alger" manner, Ronov started his own fruit stand, then a chain and finally saw his company grow into the Great Eastern Coffee Company, one-time largest importer of fresh fruits and vegetables. As recently as August, in an interview Ronov told of how he had reached the top: 'Buy low, sell high and work, work, work.' Some have blamed the recent financial turmoil for his death; Ronov always worked a twelve-hour day, six days a week until stricken yesterday. The corporate holdings of his firm, although they have been declining rapidly in the past weeks, will be maintained by the board of directors . . . Here the scrap was torn off and only the smudged date "Nov 3, 1929" was visible. Just less than three years had passed.

"Whattaya readin that stuff for?" came the voice of a second man. This voice betrayed the speaker's youth and elocutional inadequacy. The first man remained silent for a moment and then spoke sullenly.

"I once knew that man."

"Oh?" The inquisitive tone of a third man's voice suggested that he had been listening to the reading.

"We were in business together. Since both of us had been brought over from the old country together, we started that first fruit stand in the fall of '09. Leon and I saved almost all of our income to invest in stocks. It was an obsession with him. We would often work from before dawn until after dark only to return to his flat and pour over the pages of the 'journal' which we would spread out on the floor under a single bulb. He would often tell me how important our work was, and for a long time I believed him. His thirst for work almost matched mine for liquor—"

"Ha! that's you all right." The third man laughed deeply.

"We had already built our little venture into a major outlay by the time the War broke out. The highest hope of Ronov always had been to have his own stock listed on the big board. Many of his business partners sneered at him, myself included. Like a man chasing a will-o'-the-wisp, Ronov became consumed in his work. With the war came prosperity, and our corporation grew from a street-side concern to a global marketing firm. I had tagged along with Leon for a dozen years now; just by being with him you could sense success. His clothes were the finest (perhaps these remnants attest to our taste), and his lust for expansion seemed insatiable. Our company was listed for the first time in '23; we had finally made the grade. At this time our stocks began their phenomenal surge. Even when Leon was chairman of the board he entered long hours in the office. I was relegated to a vice-presidency, I suspect more for sentimental than practical reasons. He seemed to enjoy having me around; I probably had done nothing useful in my life save supplying him with capital at the company's inception."

"I can believe that," said the third man, speaking as though a break in the narrative was called for.

"In 1926 my position was dissolved and I was released, on pension of course; Leon always cared for me. I did not mind; I had not worked for anything I had received, and then it was no different. I began to wander and lost touch with the Wall Street world. After the crash I heard little of Great Eastern."

"You must admit that riding the rails is better than twelve hours a day working in a lousy office." The fourth man made his presence known for the first time.

"I guess so . . ." said the first hesitantly.

The first rays of dawn were beginning to streak through the cracks in the box car and the images of the dervishes on the walls disappeared as the men fell asleep at last. The swaying of the box car had a hypnotic effect.

## Writing Assignment One
## Comment on Sample 1. Grade: High

Both the story and the environment in which it is told are clearly presented. The narrator does not explain why the memory is important to him. Whereas many students focused on a single past incident, the writer of this paper chose a protracted period of affluence to tell about, but makes the memory quite plausible. The brief comments of his listeners add to the plausibility of the tale. The story is nicely rounded off by the second reference to the dervishes, recalling the introduction. The writing is generally accurate and competent, suggesting ability well above average. This suggestion is borne out by the unusually precise fulfillment of the conditions set by the assignment.

## Writing Assignment One
## Sample 2. Grade: Average

*One of Those Things*

As the evening train sped on toward the suburbs, George advanced toward his two comrades in the smoking car. He was drawn almost magnetically toward the cherry glow that marked Bill's pipe. Bill was nursing the glowing tobacco in the pipe bowl toward total combustion; John was just settling back to enjoy the trip home. Nods all around as George eased himself into the third chair. Its softness enveloped him and he was content to remain silent for a few precious moments. Bill shifted his position so that George was staring down the barrell of the lighted pipe.

A cloud of sweet smoke emerged with each word as Bill broke the silence. "George, you'd just begun to tell me something before we were separated this morning."

"It was nothing really. Just something I saw in New York that keeps coming back to me as if it should mean something. I was going to tell you about it, but after we were separated I thought differently. It's nothing."

"George, it sounded interesting; give it a whorl."

"Go ahead, George." John shifted his position so that he could hear clearly over the muffled clattering of the train. Bill leaned back and took a long pull from the pipe.

"As I left my hotel that first morning in New York, I saw a snowy haired gentleman, possibly of Balkan origin, sitting on a fireplug. His shoes were beside him and he was in the process of removing a sock. I was on the other side of the street; as I passed him he removed a sock and carressed his foot with his hands. He was strangely out of place in the morning rush; yet he might have been any one who had stopped to remove a rock from his shoe.

"When I returned to my hotel about noon, I saw him again. He seemed to be talking to his feet. He was propped against the hydrant and was putting on a sock. He did this with such infinite slowness that he was obviously out of place. He acted as if he had been stationed there.

"When I left the hotel a little while later, I saw him again. This time I was sure that he was talking to the foot propped in his lap. For the first time I noticed his face. He must have been in his fifties; yet he was tired and worn beyond his days. Dark circles and bushy eyebrows framed his tired eyes. The few people on the streets seemed to pass on the other side. He looked at no one and no one seemed to notice him.

"That evening I passed him again. He was staring down at his feet; his shoes were on, but untied. I almost wanted to speak to him. I couldn't tell if he was thinking or—or just existing. I'm not sure what I would have said. I was afraid to disturb him so I waited a few moments. Slowly he got up and moved off through a crowd coming from a subway exit.

"When I caught my taxi the next morning, he was just taking his shoe off." George felt strangely self-conscious in the silence that followed. He wasn't sure if they had understood at all. He looked around and added, "That's it."

Bill shifted in his chair and took a long pull on his pipe. It was he that broke the silence. "This seems to have arroused more than mere pathos." George felt weak and knew that his palms were clammy. "We'd all get out of this insurance racket and do something more rewarding and beneficial if it didn't cost so much to raise a family." It seemed an eternity between phrases. "I think you're bothered because you didn't do anything; what could you do? It sounded as if the man needed full-time —uh—help. You haven't got the time or the resources. Your responsibilities to your family are too big. Forget about it, George; it's just one of those things."

George excused himself weakly and moved toward the rear of the train. It was funny. He'd never been sick commuting before.

## Writing Assignment One
## Comment on Sample 2. Grade: Average

Part of the assignment—telling a group about an important memory of the past without explaining why it was important—this paper fulfills, although it is a series of memories in the very recent past. The only change indicated in the speaker's life is that, for the first time ever, he feels ill on the train, after he has told the story. Thus, a second requirement of the assignment is barely met, if at all. The story does not reveal a number of points one might like to know—why the snowy-haired gentleman ("possibly of Balkan origin") haunted the fireplug, why he concentrated on his socks, shoes, and feet, and why these actions, as George tells them, rouse emotion in George and, to a lesser extent, in his listeners. This student's use of his title in the conversation indicates his effort to achieve unity; his final paragraph is allowed to imply rather than describe its meaning; his writing is generally adequate, though not distinguished.

Several readers rated this paper *low* on its failure to meet the demands of the assignment. The readers further based this *low* rating on the writer's failure to indicate that George's life was better or worse. There is an oddly expressed but trite comment on indifference in the rat race, but it is nothing more than that.

## Writing Assignment One
## Sample 3. Grade: Low

*On the Dark Side*

My friend, John Davis, and I had just come in from a long and hard journey. We were now in our hotel room ready for a much needed night's sleep. It was then we met into an old friend Joel Sims. He seemed nervous and unnatural. Though we were exhausted, we invited him in for a drink. As we sat around drinking and talking, Carl began talking in a slow monotone and we became quiet.

"I was at my father's house the other day. He died two years ago and left the home in the peaceful valley to me. The home was a haven for rest and joy in the simplicity of life. But I was ambitious and I could not even think of even wasting myself away on a farm so I let it go to waste. I got a job with a chemical company. I would make money and achieve fame.

"Now I've worked two years for the company. All this time I've been on the road. I've made money to live comfortably so I went to the old home last week. I watched the trees sway with the breezes and the water flow through the country. I watched the birds fly overhead and heard them sing gaily. I danced in the fields for a whole day. And the next day went back on the road for the chemical company. I passed by the house again this morning and saw it in all of the rustic beauty. I urge you both to forget ambition. Ambition is sometimes good, but is dangerous if it brings you harm. Not only should you live life, but you should also enjoy it."

As he finished, I noticed a tear in his eye. But John and I were exhausted and we needed rest. Joel left the room and John and I went to bed. I thought nothing of Joel's story at the moment, but I couldn't sleep. I kept seeing those dull gray walls and the bare black dresser, symbols of a traveling salesman and took heed of Joel Sims. Maybe he was right. Well, I had to start early in the morning so I finally went to sleep. I had not noticed but John had also been awake. Maybe it was just the hum of the air conditioner that kept him awake.

## Writing Assignment One
## Comment on Sample 3. Grade: Low

This paper seems *low* on all counts. Its technical weakness is suggested by the phrase in the opening paragraph "we met into an old friend Joel Sims." In the same paragraph Joel, without warning, becomes Carl, to the reader's confusion. The picture of Carl's dancing "in the fields for a whole day" might possibly have been made plausible, but is not. In general, the salesman's praise of "rustic beauty," which brings, we are told, "a tear in his eye" sounds artificial. Finally, the assignment forbade an explanation of the meaning of the memory, but this student devotes part of the third paragraph to just such an explanation.

## Writing Assignment Two
## Sample 1. Grade: High

*Gooseberries*

Ivan, in Chekhov's *Gooseberries,* does not think that personal happiness should be allowed to overrule what he considers is man's purpose to be, that of doing good. Ivan has been impressed by the differences between his brother Nikolay and his friend Alyohin. After visiting Nikolay, he can say that "there is an element of sadness . . . mingled with my thoughts of human happiness," because for every happy man who lives at his ease there are many unhappy ones who are unknown because for every happy man who lives at his ease there are many unhappy ones who are unknown because of their silence. It is not right, he says for men to be happy and not to worry about the welfare of others. What he has come to realize is best expressed by his speech to Alyohin:

". . . don't quiet down, don't let yourself be lulled to sleep! As long as you are young, strong, alert, do not cease to do good! There is no happiness and there should be none, and if life has a meaning and a purpose, that meaning and purpose is not our happiness but something greater and more rational. Do good!"

Although Ivan has discovered this, he does not attempt to follow his idea; he is, he says, too old. Therefore his soul is in torture, he bewails a misspent life.

Ivan is correct in a way, but he is also wrong. It seems that he uses *two* definitions of happiness, combining them into one. On one hand, he says that happiness is wrong because it invites complacency, and takes one out of touch with the world's problems. This is true. Chekhov must have seen and reflected upon the life of the Russian nobility in the late nineteenth century, for he describes it accurately. The wealthy and the aristocrats were fat and complacent, and when the Revolution in 1905 and 1917 hit them full in the face, they were rewarded for their neglect by death. Chekhov acts as a prophet of the Revolution in this story, issuing a jeremiad to the nobility.

Ivan believes, however, that happiness must be banished for fruitful work, and here he is wrong. The happiest people in the world are the self-givers. To prove this it is only necessary to ask a Peace Corpsman if he is happy in his work. Our government has had much difficulty in readjusting the returning Corpsmen to our self-seeking manner of living. Many of them want to remain in the Corps, but are prevented by law.

According to psychiatrists, it is the man who drinks *alone* who becomes an alcoholic. It is neurotic not to care for the needs of others.

## Writing Assignment Two
## Comment on Sample 1. Grade: High

Although the Notes on the Grading of Student Papers specifies that a major criterion is the student's ability to follow the requirements of the assignment, this paper is an exception. One requirement was to support proof both that Ivan was right and that he was wrong with examples from the life of one person. No student who wrote on this topic—and there were many—was able to meet this demand. With some reluctance, the readers concluded that this part of the assignment was too difficult.

This *high* paper at least uses illustrative material that is appropriate, even if not what the assignment asked for—the Russian nobility and the returning Peace Corpsman. The writer seems to have understood the story, a feat beyond the power of some eleventh graders; he writes with competence and intelligence, although he is logically inconsistent at one point. For, though he recognizes the complete dichotomy Ivan makes between "happiness" and "doing good" (see his fourth paragraph), he does not realize that it invalidates his own ingenious theory that Ivan "uses *two* definitions of happiness."

## Writing Assignment Two
## Sample 2. Grade: Average

In the story, *Gooseberries,* Ivan Ivanych Chimsha-Himalaisky was saddened at the thought and sight of human happiness. Whenever he saw a happy man, he felt that the only reason the man was happy was because someone else paid for this happiness in silent suffering. He knew that without this mute acceptance of life's burdens, happiness would be an unknown commodity. To remedy this situation, he advocates a constant reminder to happy people that there are those who are not so well endowed with good fortune, and that the happiness will not last; one must eventually succumb as have all others. Finally, he states that there is no true happiness at all, and that this is good; for life's purpose should be somthing higher and more noble.

Now this theory is at once both easily defended and just as easily torn down. First, we shall defend Ivan's theory. Materialistically, money may cause a person to be happy. But the question is then raised as to how this money is raised. If work provided it, then a certain amount of suffering must have been its foundation. The executive, by Marxist theory, benefits from the sweat and toil of his "wage slaves." As for beauty that causes one to be happy, consider a painting. However much pleasure and aesthetic contentment this work may result in, it was created by the painful concentration of the artist. Even a good meal causes suffering. The vegetables were grown by the calloused hands of a farmer, and the meat may have been taken from an animal that was cherished as a pet. This, then, is the argument supporting Ivan Ivanych.

But on the reverse side of the coin is proof, just as conclusive, that Ivan was wrong. Happiness is a valued thing, true, but what goal is nobler than happiness? The "wage slave" of Marxism is almost non-existant in the America of today. It is possible that both the worker and the executive profit from their work. Not many workers died of starvation last year. And not many beggars are seen roaming the friendless streets. The most opressive thing I see in Ivan's speech is his unbearable pessimism.

Happiness can be obtained where no one could possibly suffer. For me, a lake shimmering in the moonlight causes both happiness and content. How have people been hurt by a natural thing of beauty? A good book is satisfying to me. Is not its completion a worthy and rewarding goal for its author? I once knew a man who desired nothing more than a small plot of land to farm in his old age. Has this wish caused anyone suffering?

My own feelings are that Ivan was definitely wrong. His unbearable pessimism reflects badly on Chekov. If this is a sample, I can see why his writing is often regarded as heavy going. To me, happiness for all is a goal worth striving for, somthing as noble as can be created by the mind of man.

## Writing Assignment Two
## Comment on Sample 2. Grade: Average

This paper starts well. The opening paragraph shows an unusually accurate understanding of Ivan's beliefs about happiness. From that point on, however, the logic becomes faulty. The student's illustrations used in defense of Ivan's theory are threefold, instead of being drawn from the life of a single person. His remarks about the painter and the farmer seem far-fetched. His third and fourth paragraphs again fail to present an illustration from an individual's life, and his remarks about the author of a good book contradict his earlier comment about the "painful concentration of the artist." Having set the stage for a really high paper, the student goes farther and farther away from the assignment and from his previous summary of Ivan's beliefs. From the point of view of style, the paper is *average* or better; from that of content, *low,* except for the first paragraph. Rating—a low *average.*

Despite the excellent first paragraph, a statement of Ivan's belief, which is not carried to the point of final precision (happiness is an illusion), some readers rated this paper *low.* The student does not support and rebut from the life of one individual, as required—and argumentation seems politically and historically absurd.

## Writing Assignment Two
## Sample 3. Grade: Low

*Happiness*

Ivan's belief about happiness is three-fold. First of all, he believes that to be happy a person must be good, both in his actions and his thoughts. Secondly, that the only kind of true happiness a person can get is through doing things for others. Thirdly, he believes that a person must go looking for happiness and work to achieve it.

Ivan's kind of happiness can be proven to be right in the following example. A nurse does many things for other people. It is her whole profession. The things that she does, such as comforting a child or easing the pain of an injury, make her happy because she is helping someone else. But to find this happiness she has really had to work to achieve it through schooling and hours of practice. This is the happiness that Ivan believes a person should have.

However, now on the other hand, Ivan's belief can be proven wrong. For instance, take a plumber. He does things for people everyday, such as cleaning out pipes and fixing sewers, but I doubt whether he gets much happiness out of it. He is working but not to achieve happiness.

I firmly agree with Ivan's feelings of happiness. I am happiest when I am helping other people and in this way I am also working toward happiness. Certainly, happiness is present in our lives most of the time but it takes a mature and understanding person to recognize it in the little everyday things.

## Writing Assignment Two
## Comment on Sample 3. Grade: Low

This paper shows lack of understanding both of Chekhov's story and of the writing assignment. The first paragraph makes three statements about Ivan's definition of happiness, each of which is definitely wrong. The assignment calls for an illustration supporting and rebutting Ivan's belief, but drawn from the life of a single individual. The student uses a nurse in one place, a plumber in the second; different types, not individuals. The actual writing in the paper is better than that in many papers rated *low,* but the content is so incorrect that a *low* grade is inevitable.

*William Faulkner:*
*"A Rose for Emily"*
*Grades 11 and 12*

way, trying to recreate a dead past with her father. How has her father been taken from her by threats of force? How does she attempt to restore that loss?

5. Why do the townspeople express pity for "Poor Emily"? What do they mean? How does Faulkner show that their suspicions are wrong?

6. What reasons does Miss Emily have for loving Homer Barron? For hating him? What does the druggist write on the package of arsenic? What does Judge Stevens say is probably causing the smell? What is the narrator's irony here?

7. How does Miss Emily's appearance change over the years? Find all the descriptions and fit them together in chronological order. Now, how much time passes between Homer Barron's death and the time Miss Emily's hair turns iron-gray? When a hair has fallen from the head, does it change color over the years? What is the horror of the last sentence of the story?

8. We've observed that the narrator leaps back and forth in time, rather than following a strict chronological sequence. How does the story gain or lose power through this technique?

9. Are there any indications in the story that Faulkner means this to be more than just a thriller about an insane woman? Who narrates the story? Whom is he referring to when he says "we"? What events does he report as part of the common knowledge of the town? At which events does he seem to have been present himself? Are there any ways in which the townspeople share Miss Emily's reluctance to accept the past as dead? Her unwillingness to change with the times? Where do we see in the townspeople the same tendencies that are pushed to an insane extreme in Miss Emily?

10. From what you know about the South—especially the South of the white aristocracy—with its antebellum legend and its postwar history, what comment does Faulkner seem to be making about the South?

11. Incidentally, what does the title of the story mean? (We don't know, and we've never found anyone who does.)

## Questions on Language

1. How do you feel about Faulkner's use of the word "nigger"? What attitude on the part of the townspeople (through the narrator) does this convey? Why does the narrator link together "niggers and mules and machinery" (page 221)? Study carefully the character of Tobe, the Negro man-servant. Is he presented disrespectfully? (What sort of man is he? How is he different from the white townspeople? Why does he keep Miss Emily's secret all the years, or doesn't Faulkner say?)

2. "Yankee," in the society of this story, is also a term of contempt, almost as strong as "nigger." ("Northerner" and "Negro" are the more polite terms.) Reread the passages concerning Homer Barron with this in mind. Do the townspeople's bewilderment and indignation seem more vehement now?

3. One secret of Faulkner's extraordinary style is that he feels free to use in prose many of the rhetorical devices that are usually reserved for poetry. In the second paragraph, for example:

"But garages and cotton gins had . . . obliterated even the august names . . ."

Obviously, they had obliterated the *houses,* not the names. What device is Faulkner using here? Again:

"Miss Emily's house was left, lifting its stubborn and coquettish decay . . ."

What device is he using here? What other striking examples of poetic devices can you find in the story, and how does each affect the story?

4. How does Faulkner have the narrator keep an objective distance from the events he is recounting? Which incidents does he report wholly without comment? In which incidents does he report the town's comments without revealing his own feelings? In which incidents does he indicate his own feelings, however quietly (as in the first sentence of section II)? What kinds of phrasing does Faulkner use to make these distinctions clear?

## Writing Assignment One

Write a story or an essay about an individual who is both admirable and pitiful, or both frightening and

# *William Faulkner: "A Rose for Emily" Grades 11 and 12*

*Book Used:* Angus, Douglas, ed. *The Best Short Stories of the Modern Age.* New York: Fawcett (World Library) Premier (m309), 1962.

## Questions for Discussion

1. What is the horror of the last sentence of the story? Why does Faulkner stress the fact that the hair is iron-gray and long? (Don't force an answer if the students aren't sure.)

2. Let's start by making sure we follow the chronological sequence of the events that the narrator reports. Here are some of the key events in the order in which he mentions them (these might be on the blackboard when the class starts):

Miss Emily dies. (At what age? Where?)

Miss Emily's father dies. (Year?)

A deputation visits Miss Emily about her tax delinquency.

People complain about the smell in Miss Emily's house.

Miss Emily turns 30.

Miss Emily cuts her hair.

Homer Barron courts Miss Emily.

Miss Emily buys poison.

Homer Barron enters Miss Emily's house, disappears.

Miss Emily's hair turns iron-gray.

Miss Emily closes off the top floor of her house.

In what sequence do these events take place? How much time elapses between them?

3. Let's consider a few of these events in chronological order. First, when Miss Emily's father dies, how does she act? This refusal to acknowledge the dead as dead turns up on two later occasions. Where does Faulkner mention it specifically? What is the third occasion?

4. Why is Miss Emily attracted to Homer Barron? Whom does he closely resemble? In what ways? What impact had her father had on her life? In riding with Homer Barron, then, Miss Emily is, in a

pitiful. Write it in such a way that both impressions are strong and neither dominates the other.

## Writing Assignment Two

In a thoughtful and carefully planned essay, describe a time in your life when you tried to shut out the fact that someone or something close to you had died or ended. How did you try, and why? Conclude your essay by describing the moment when you finally accepted the fact. How did that happen, and how did you feel then? (If you prefer, you may create a fictional situation, but write it so that it sounds real.)

## Writing Assignment One
## Sample 1. Grade: High

"Oh, Granny, what she can do; oh, Granny, she'll murder you," sang the children as they trooped down the trail. Their song was muffled by the dense woods, which smelled of green August earth and sassafras trees. When they reached Vine Valley the children stopped singing and moved carefully through the leaves. Salamanders skittered away and the birds grew suddenly silent.

"You think she'll shoot at us?" whispered the second boy.

"Not if she doesn't see us," said the leader.

Across an unkempt yard was a large gabled house, its white paint peeling off in wide strips. The second story windows were broken, and the back porch, supported by cobweb-filled cement blocks, sagged in the middle. Overhanging oak trees clawed at the house and dropped acorns which clattered on its roof in autumn.

"Think she saw us?"

"I don't know," said the leader. He crouched down and led the way along a dilapidated cross-bar fence enclosing the yard. An ancient car, wheels half-sunken in the spongy earth and entangled in creepers, listed in the yard. Beside the house were four markers of rain-worn sandstone; the names could barely be read: Sarah Lee Wilson, b. Nov. 30, 1899, d. Oct. 4, 1900; Elizabeth Ann Wilson, b. June 22, 1902, d. July 18, 1902; Charlotte May Rice, b. August 31, 1881, d. Feb. 5, 1904; Donald Rice Wilson, b. Feb. 5, 1904, d. March 21, 1908.

The boys crept Indian-file along the fence, snapping twigs and scuffling in spite of themselves. All of the sudden a gunshot shattered the afternoon. The boys stood stock still, then turned and ran helter-skelter through the woods.

The back door opened and the porch creaked as a bent old man carrying a shotgun shambled out of the house.

"Gabe. Gabe? What was that?"

"Only children," said the old man.

The whining query came again. "What did you say? I can't hear you."

Gabe leaned the gun against the wall and crept into the house. It was dark, and smelled of oatmeal, dust, and rotten wood. At the end of a long hall was the living room. One wall was paneled with mahogany and the other three were splotched with layers of peeling wall paper. The furniture in the room was heavily upholstered and covered with yellowed doillies. An oil lamp burned on the mantel, flickering on the suffering countenance of Mary, Queen of Martyrs. In the center of the room a wizened old woman sat in a rocking chair, motheaten blankets covering her legs. Her thin mouth was pursed with righteousness and the skin of her face crinkled like parchment. Her restless hands fingered the edges of the blankets.

She began her litany. "Gabe? Where —"

"What do you want, Ada?"

"Come here where I can see you."

Gabe shuffled around to the front of her chair.

"You know I'm ill," Ada whined. "Since Sarah and Elizabeth died it's taken so much effort just to stay alive." She coughed for emphasis.

"Yes, Ada," he said.

"Don't use that tone of voice with me, Gabriel. You haven't done much to help me all these years. First it was the children and then Charlotte, my very own sister, called here to take care of me after they died. Sins of the flesh, Gabriel." She coughed heavily, wheezing the last words. "But, one must abide and bear what crosses God in His wisdom bestows upon us. . . . Charlotte. . . . May she rest in peace." Ada closed her eyes and rested her head on the back of the chair.

Gabe turned away and trudged down the hall. May she rest in peace. Fifty-one years she's been dead and Ada still won't leave her buried. When he'd married her, Ada had been all a man could desire. Sarah and Elizabeth had come and died, and he'd wanted other children to make up for the hurt he knew Ada felt. But she bore burdens instead of children, and her sister, Charlotte, had come to stay with them. Ada's world, peopled with Sarah and Elizabeth, was closed to him, but she knew what was happening. He loved Charlotte, and she died giving birth to his only son, Donald.

From that time on Ada never walked again. Except once. Her room used to be on the second floor and Donald played in the sunsteps beside her bed each afternoon. One day, while he was working in the garden, Gabe heard a scream from the house. He ran in and saw Ada standing halfway down the stairs. "Donald fell," she said.

Gabe flew to the crushed and broken body in the backyard. Donald was dead. When Gabe brought the frail body into the house, Ada had already gone back to her room. She never mentioned Donald again.

## Writing Assignment One
## Comment on Sample 1. Grade: High

This is an exceptional achievement for an eleventh grader. The irony of the children's song, followed by the gunshot that "shattered the afternoon," becomes fully apparent only when the reader has finished the story. The story grows even better with a second reading. The descriptive details such as the skittering salamanders, the "cobweb-filled cement blocks," the car wheels "half-sunken in the spongy earth and entangled in creepers," and the "rain-worn sandstone" of the four gravestones are indicative of this student's command of language, his ability to manipulate atmosphere and create a single impression of sinister disintegration. The writer manages the children's talk skillfully and is even more skillful with the dialogue between Gabe and Ada. The religious suggestiveness of the picture of Mary, Queen of Martyrs, and the term "litany" for Ada's interchange with Gabe are heavy with the irony that is one of the many strengths of the paper. The reference to Ada's having borne "burdens instead of children" is a masterly touch. So, too, is the quiet skill with which the writer lets us know that Gabe "loved Charlotte, and she died giving birth to his only son, Donald." And the death of Donald sends the reader back to the children's opening song, " 'Oh, Granny, what she can do; oh, Granny, she'll murder you,' " only this time those words have double, perhaps treble meanings.

## Writing Assignment One
## Sample 2. Grade: Average

My grandmother is, to me, a rather outstanding example of a person who is both frightening and pitiful. These characteristics, though quite different, can nevertheless be distinguished simultaneously when describing my grandmother.

The person most frightened by my grandmother was my mother, her adopted daughter. In fact, up until she was almost thirty years of age, my grandmother was a symbol of fright, rather than love and protection, to my mother. Possessing a violent temper, my grandmother's agile palm often left its painful sting on my mother, sending her halfway across the room at times. Such an action done once can easily terrify a child for quite a while, so it is not hard to tell the extent of my mother's fright. Even after my mother was grown, this woman did not cease to be terrifying. She constantly threatened to do drastic things if my mother married, had a second child, moved to a new house, and so on. Although these more than likely turned out to be idle threats, which my mother sensed, they were still the cause of much unhappiness and consternation. The feeling of fright was transferred to my sister and I as well as my mother, because, unfortunately, my grandmother has lived with our family ever since my mother and father were married. She has now passed her nintieth birthday, become senile, and constantly expresses her discontent with her way of living, a disheartening thing for all of us. Although her violence has quieted with age, she still possesses a bitter temper, and is unable to remember any of the pleasant memories or nice things people have done for her.

Even though her personality is as I have described, the members of our family, and especially those outside the family cannot help, at times, to feel pity for my grandmother. Here she is, a very old person with actually no place in the society of today, who must live in the past because she is incapable of finding any joy whatsoever in the present. She has brought herself, through her own actions, to the point where she is unloved by her own family and the very people she lives with. She has very few friends except a small number with thom she corresponds by mail, because of the fact that not many people her age are alive and able to communicate or travel about. We feel this pity, but are virtually unable to do anything about it.

## Writing Assignment One
## Comment on Sample 2. Grade: Average

A noticeable difference between this paper and the first is that this one is entirely expository, whereas the first is dramatic. This paper "tells," whereas the other tries to "show." Here the characterization is entirely by the author's say-so and by the woman's reported actions. Apparently the student was unaware of the possibility of using monologue or dialogue as a way of giving life to a character. Nevertheless, this student deserves credit for his awareness that senility is both frightening and pathetic. It is "frightening" rather than "pitiable"—possibly an indication that this paper never quite strikes a balance between the two impressions.

## Writing Assignment One
## Sample 3. Grade: Low

Many people think of Jacqueline Kennedy as being both admirable and pitiful. After considering her physical aspects, I too am one of those people.

Although I don't know Mrs. Kennedy personally, I have read many articles and have seen many descriptive pictures. In my opinion EVERYONE is pitiful in one way or another and therefore Mrs. Kennedy is NO exception. I admire Mrs. Kennedy very much, but I don't claim her to be perfect. She is a very brave and ambitious person. I know that she never had many beau's before John Kennedy came along and *they* didn't have a beautiful courtship. She is an intelligent person and can speak some foreign languages fluently. But to see their marrage develope successfully and be brought to an end so abruptally is very, very pitiful. She is not a pretty women, due to her size and plain expression, but she took great care in her appearance. A person who is this careful, intelligent, and ambitious, deserves far better than she received.

## Writing Assignment One
## Comment on Sample 3. Grade: Low

This student tries to show Mrs. Kennedy as both admirable and pitiful, as required by the assignment. The paper was also to be written "in such a way that both impressions are strong," but fails in this respect. The writer knows too little about his subject to bring any specific evidence for his statements, except his own feelings. Vagueness begins early; why would "considering her physical aspects" make the writer agree with those who think Mrs. Kennedy both admirable and pitiful? Short as the paper is, it is not free from technical errors, for which there is no compensation either in content or in style.

## Writing Assignment Two
## Sample 1. Grade: High

I was eating breakfast, the big, soggy, French Toast breakfast that a thirteen year old alone can conquer. There were forty laughing, syrup-smeared collegues inside the ranch's mess hall. The day was sunny, and we had a long, dirty, sweaty, joyous ride ahead of us. The bell for mail call rang, and I scrunched and crawled my way out from between the table and the bench to receive the usual packet of scrawled post cards and letters addressed to me, the carefree camper. Folding myself back onto the bench, I turned—ready to be disappointed, expectant eyes on the return addresses. There was one fat, pink envelope, boasting bright red ink, from a good friend. The pink seeming to hold the greatest possibility for the excitement I knew the letter wouldn't hold, I tore it open first. I read, and my French Toast got soggier. I read, and the French Toast became stone cold. I read further and my ooky breakfast, the glee surrounding me, and the red and white checked table clothes melted away, then came back in a gray lump to choke me. My world was an unbelievable swamp of stagnant pink and red. My mind raced to a hospital room visit, now a week-old remembrance. Four giggling girls stood around the bed where a frail blond, their friend, Cindy, lay pinned down by the awesome, frightening mechanism of intravenous feeding. We were planning a party for Cindy's homecoming, a party where all our friends would welcome her back. All the while, Cindy's mother sat in the corner, a magazine hiding her face. Cindy was my best friend, Cindy was thirteen, too, and the pink and red letter said Cindy had died.

The letter tried to convince me that God chose Cindy because He wanted her before He wanted the bad people in the world. I wasn't convinced. I remembered grade school when a bully pushed Cindy into the ditch and chased me, throwing rocks. I was afraid of pelting rocks, but I ran back for Cindy, anyway, because she was my friend. In seventh grade there were boys, and giggles, and wild imaginations.

I ran, the pink and red letter with me, for the comfort of my bunk. I was crying, but I wasn't thinking of death. I was thinking of friendship, and laughter, and vitality, and teen-age crises. My grandfathers had died, my grandmother had died, aunts and uncles had died, but I was a child and they were much older. I had never shared my life with them, I had never sacrificed for them, I had never told them my secrets. I loved each one dearly, but they had never been essential parts of my life.

I rode horses day and night, not thinking of a loss, just saving any feeling I would have until I returned to my real world on a street on Mercer Island. On my way home at the end of the week, I sang ranch songs with the rest of my companions and I laughed and talked, because I wasn't home yet, not quite yet. The bridge, the turn-off, the bumpy road leading to my house, and it wasn't yet time for reality. I could push awareness of the hole in my life away for a few more moments. I was a child and I wasn't ready to lose my best friend. We stopped, I opened the big front door. I hugged my mother, telling her what fun I'd had, saying I just had to go back next summer. Then there were the words: ". . . happened last Thursday," and "internal lung cancer," and "mother and sister now alone." In that instant I knew. I knew I wouldn't talk about boys again with Cindy, or giggle with Cindy, or tell my secrets to Cindy. And I felt at last, that God really must have wanted her first.

## Writing Assignment Two
## Comment on Sample 1. Grade: High

In this paper such occasional flaws as the pompous conventionality of the letter "*boasting* bright red ink" sink to insignificance before the impressive skill which eludes possible sentimentality with the sharp thrust of honest feeling. The job would have been easier if the writer had been writing from the viewpoint of someone his own age, but perhaps the most admirable element in the paper is the sureness with which it takes the reader inside the mind and heart of a 13-year-old girl. The ordering of detail here is highly competent. The use of the French toast before and after the reading of the letter has more impact than any amount of direct description of the speaker's grief. The simpleness of much of the wording and much of the sentence structure is right both for felt grief and for a 13-year-old girl's way of expressing it. The memories of Cindy could easily be mawkish. They aren't. The noting of the exact moment of acceptance of an end purposely left unrecognized until that moment is still further indication of this student's awareness of the demands of the assignment. This writing is strong in its inclusions and right in its omissions.

## Writing Assignment Two
## Sample 2. Grade: Average

When I first heard the news that my family was planning to move from New York to Fort Lauderdale, I refused to accept the possibility that it might be true. I couldn't visualize myself giving up a city which I loved for one which I pictured as a sand dune spotted with swimming pools.

That night I said I was going to a movie, we lived in an apartment near the theatre district, but instead I spent a few hours walking through as much of the town as I could cover. I went down seventh avenue to a Times Square subway station and started out on what I had intended to be a round trip. I cut it short, though, transfered to another train, and came out on eighth avenue. I started moving toward Central Park, the neon lighting my way, and when I got there, I walked through it for a while, hugging the outside edges for safety's sake. I couldn't understand what I was feeling at the time, but now I think I do. I believe I was trying to get involved with the city, to get so wrapped up in it that it would be impossible for anyone to pry me loose.

On the way down, I kept expecting the plane to turn around in mid air and head back, resounding with the laughter of my family as they told me it was all a joke. It didn't, however, and we arrived seven minutes ahead of schedule, an unnecessary piece of efficiency, I thought. As we drove along the beach to our house, however, my hostility began to soften. Finding out that your new neighborhood looks like something out of South Pacific can't help but brighten your outlook. In the following weeks my liking for Fort Lauderdale increased greatly, but I still had a vein of subdued longing for New York. The last ties were broken, however, when we went back to visit some relatives. Looking at the city for the first time as a visitor rather than a resident, I was surprised to find how dirty and full of pale, sickly-looking people it had become in my absence. The flaws which I had never seen before had suddenly become shockingly noticeable. I was suddenly aware that I had lost my status as a New Yorker. As we boarded the plane to return to Florida, I realized that, instead of leaving home, I was going there.

## Writing Assignment Two
## Comment on Sample 2. Grade: Average

The writer of this paper is somewhat off the target in two ways. What he tries to shut out—the dread of leaving New York—is in the future, not something that has already taken place. Further, if one accepts the neat final sentence as describing "the moment when you finally accepted the fact," one has also to accept the previous part of the paper as answering the questions "How did it happen?" and "How did you feel then?"—again a divergence from the suggested time scheme. The paper has also some errors in punctuation and sentence structure; it lacks a transition from the second to the third paragraph. Against these defects, one may put an effort to abide by the rules set forth, even though not wholly successful, a skillful contrast between New York and Fort Lauderdale, and phrasing that is at times distinctly good.

## Writing Assignment Two
## Sample 3. Grade: Low

*—Depths—*

Death. Grief. Death. Melancholy. Death. Dejection. Death. . . . .

Does one accept the inevitable—death? Does one reject the proposal completely?

Death. One year. Loss. Termination. Death.

My grandmother passed away and I felt a profound loss although I was still only a child. In varying degrees, my grandmother's friends and family felt the sorrow and the loss.

Despair. Acknowledgment. Death.

My grandfather took the blow the hardest. Acceptance was difficult and he still suffers periodic fits of deep depression.

Perhaps acknowledging her death was difficult because of the duration of their marriage. Perhaps because he was constantly reminded of their life together; each trying episode, each joyful moment. Being only a child, I could, I can, I will, only guess.

Time. Empty moments. Time. Vacantness.

How does an older person, grief-stricken, not as spry now as in youth, fill the interminable spare moments of the day? My poor, pitiful grandfather; he tries desperately to leave a heritage—a heritage it took him years to acquire—and a heritage for which the youngsters lack the patience to understand and accept. Where do the two worlds meet? Youth and the aged?

. . . . . . . . A rift forms.

Time. Vacantness. Time.

Injustice. Anger. Death. Unforseen. Death.

I find him sometimes, sitting in the dark. Just staring out. Vacantly. Expressionless. What is he thinking?

—He was always the sicker of the two. He had always prepared to die first. Death. Why had *life* left him behind?

Why had *death* left him behind? Life. Death. Why?

He lashes out sometimes in sheer boredom to change his monotonous pace of life.

Boredom. Monotony. Pity.

Pity for those—all those who are forced to experience death of someone close. Sympathy. Sympathy for those unable to acknowledge the fact. Pity for those young, but especially those old, who are unable to occupy the empty, vacant moments. Pity—for death.

Death. Life.

Grief and depression—these are found in abundance in death, and life. Death. Grief. Depression. Death. Sorrow.

Death. So consuming. Death.

## Writing Assignment Two
## Comment on Sample 3. Grade: Low

The writer of this paper refuses to comply with the requirement of writing in the first person. The bereaved individual turns out to be grandfather; even if one accepts this deviation, one looks in vain for a description of "the moment when" he accepted the fact—the essay covers an indefinitely long period. It is not easy to write on this topic without sentimentality and bathos; this writer's use of variations on a refrain tends to heighten the impression of rather artificial sentimentality. The writer needs badly to learn the value of restraint and understatement, and the dangers of repetition.

*James Joyce: "The Dead"*
*Grades 11 and 12*

pocket when he arrives at the party? (How might this help to explain his reaction to Lily's bitter statement, page 121?) How does he plan and replan his speech; and in each case, why? What build-up for the speech is shown at the dinner table? When the speech is given, does Joyce make it seem quite short or quite long? (How?) What is the main purpose of the speech? Why does he say the same thing every year? Where is Gabriel sincere in the speech, and where not? How does Joyce comment ironically on this in his "emphasis" on part of the song that follows? What effect will Gabriel's speech have on the lives of the people at the table?

6. What one sentence did Michael Furey speak to Gretta that has given her whole life a special meaning? How does this one sentence force Gabriel to reevaluate his own life?

7. How does Michael Furey's one sentence weigh against all of Gabriel's long speech? What are the *deepest* differences between the two men?

8. What do we see of Gabriel's relationship to Gretta at the opening of the story? What insight are we given after Gabriel's quarrel with Miss Ivors? (What do they quarrel about? Where is Gabriel going, in reverie, as the story ends?) Why is Gabriel captivated with Gretta when he sees her on the stairs? To what extent is his change of mood spontaneous? To what extent is he responding to a change in her mood? As they walk in the snow after the party, what is he remembering, and why?

9. Gabriel imagines what might happen in their hotel room. Does it happen? When it does happen exactly as he had imagined, how does Gabriel follow through? Why does he fail Gretta—and himself? In contrast, how did Michael Furey *not* fail?

10. In the hotel room, when Gabriel sees himself in the cheval-glass, what does he see? How does he later describe the man inside that appearance? Why does he include "well-meaning" among the words of scorn born of his self-hatred? (Isn't it a virtue to be well-meaning? Why not, in terms of this story?) The word "cheval-glass" is Joyce's way of alluding to an earlier link between Gabriel and a horse, when he acted out the part of one to amuse a crowd. Looking back, what is the resemblance between Gabriel and Johnny? Does it seem funny now?

11. At the end, Joyce says that Gabriel "stretched himself cautiously along under the sheets and lay down beside his wife." He is apparently lying straight and narrow along his edge of the bed. How has Joyce prepared us for this image in an earlier discussion that then seemed quite irrelevant? Why did the monks sleep in their coffins? What, then, is this bed for Gabriel? In what sense? And what is he remembering?

12. In Gabriel's last reverie, what is the meaning of "his journey westward"? What meaning can we draw from the snow, which is falling everywhere? (Examine the many earlier references to snow and our reactions to it. What irony do they now convey?) Why does Joyce refer to the churchyard in which Michael Furey is buried as being characterized by crosses, spears, and thorns? What does Joyce mean by "the snow falling faintly . . . and faintly falling. . ."?

13. In the last part of the story, Joyce includes one sentence in which he contrasts Gabriel and Michael's ways of life and states a moral for the reader. What is that sentence? What is "that other world"? Why is it better, according to Joyce, to live "in the full glory of some passion, than fade . . . with age"? In what sense can death come, for most people, before they die? In that sense, who are "the dead"?

## Questions on Language

1. At the time he wrote this story, Joyce was concentrating on the use of exact, naturalistic gestures that imply some deeper, but unstated, reality in a character. (He called such gestures "epiphanies.") The most obvious example is that of Gretta standing on the staircase in the Misses Morkan's home. What details does he give in the first paragraph? What implications does he draw in the second paragraph? Compare this with the description of Gretta on the staircase in the hotel. What implications are suggested there? Another obvious example is Aunt Julia's singing "Arrayed for the Bridal" (pages 133–134). What details are given? What deeper reality is implied? What are some other important epiphanies in the story?

2. The story is very rich in ironies, most of which become apparent only on a second reading. We've talked about some, such as Gabriel's early, indignant

# *James Joyce: "The Dead"*
# *Grades 11 and 12*

*Book Used:* Angus, Douglas, ed. *The Best Short Stories of the Modern Age.* New York: Fawcett (World Library) Premier (m309), 1962.

## Questions for Discussion

*Note to the teacher.* Keep the students close to the text. With almost every question, ask where—in one place, or in a combination of several places—the answer is found in the story.

1. Who is or are "the dead"? (Establish some possibilities, but do not settle on an answer. Remember that there are at least three levels in the meaning of the title.)

2. At the end of the story, as Gabriel lies in bed, what is his mood? What does he think about himself? About Gretta? About Michael Furey? About his aunts? At the beginning of the story, when he arrives for the party, what does he think about himself? About Gretta? What is he planning to say about his aunts? What does he really think of them?

3. What is the decisive event that changes Gabriel's feeling about himself? What is Gabriel's mood during the half-hour or so before Gretta's revelation? How does this mood increase the shock-effect on Gabriel? What does Gretta do after she has told about Michael Furey? What does Gabriel *do* (his actions, not his thoughts and feelings)?

4. The story shows a marked contrast between Gabriel and Michael Furey. Let's identify some of the more striking aspects of this contrast. What does Gabriel's face look like when he sees it in the hotel mirror? A few paragraphs later, Gretta describes Michael Furey's face. What are the differences? How is Gabriel dressed for the bad weather? Does this suggest any contrast with Michael? What does this tell you about the two men? Study the long passage on the dinner and the reference to Gabriel's weight. How do these descriptions contrast with our image of Michael Furey?

5. More important, study the many passages leading up to Gabriel's speech. What is in his waistcoat

refusal to set out on a journey westward and Lily's comment about men's "palaver." What precisely is the irony in each of these statements? Another obvious example is the paragraph of Gabriel's speech beginning "But yet, . . ." (page 142). What does Gabriel mean when he says this? What is he feeling? What is the irony in his saying these words without real meaning or feeling? Of the dozens of similar ironies in the story, which catch your attention? Why?

3. One of Joyce's most remarkable skills is that of writing long passages in which characters are speaking boringly or stupidly yet which are, to a responsive reader, entertaining and important. What are some important examples? How does Joyce keep them interesting?

4. Another of Joyce's great skills is control of *pace* in his language. Read aloud the dialogue between Gabriel and Miss Ivors. How does Joyce arrange words so that her speeches race and his are restrained and ponderous? What is the pace of Aunt Kate's complaint after Aunt Julia's song? Of Gabriel's speech? Of the conversation between Gabriel and Gretta in the hotel room? Of the closing reverie? How does Joyce control this pace? Where else in the story is pace essential?

## Writing Assignment One

Write a carefully developed short story in a realistic style in which an ironic statement carries the main point—or the moral, if there is one. A central character should make the statement early in the story, not realizing how it is or will become important. Near the end, he should make the statement again or encounter it again in some form, this time with a full and intense awareness of its meaning. But do *not* state this meaning at any point in the story; write the story so the reader can recognize it himself.

## Writing Assignment Two

Write a personal essay (or a story) in which you (or someone very like you) learn about the death of someone you scarcely know and are thereby forced to reevaluate your own way of life. Dig deep.

## Writing Assignment One
## Sample 1. Grade: High

*Jerry*

For Ray, Saturday morning was pure bliss: no alarm clock going off at six followed by shouts of "Get up, get dressed, eat breakfast, brush your teeth;" no silly schedule to follow in school; no track practice with coach's unending criticism; no homework and no nagging to be home early. Ray loved Saturday, and as usual, had the whole day planned.

As he lay in bed he could see the sun was bright outside. It was a good day for the beach. On the way he could stop and get the radiator fixed. Then he could drop by Patsy's and ask her to the show tonight. Sounded good to him—a whole Saturday to himself.

"Ray, Ray, wake up!"

"Darn it, Jerry, can't ya' see I'm not even out of bed yet? You blind or somethin'? What goes?"

"Ray, Mom says you'll take me to the matinee. Will you, Ray? Please! Please!"

"Sorry, small fry, but big brother's got a big day all planned and a big night tonight. Maybe tomorrow you can go see it."

"Aw, Ray, Mom promised you would."

"Tomorrow, okay?" He gave Jerry a shove out the door and dressed.

Ray was right about the weather. It was a great day for the beach, but he was annoyed. As he headed toward the filling station, he thought of his mother planning his Saturday's and it irked him. It was time she recognized that both he and Jerry were growing up. He was sixteen and Jerry was almost seven. In the first place a sixteen year old boy had no obligation to take his kid brother everywhere he went. Besides that, Jerry was old enough to go to the matinee by himself. Mom was definitely over protective.

"Hey, Bud, what can you do about this radiator?"

"Hi, Ray. I don't know. Let me take a look. Where ya' headed?"

"Beachward, to see what I can pick up." They both laughed. Ray laughed because he had a whole Saturday but Bud had to work. Bud, who was eighteen laughed at Ray's "pick somebody up." He knew Ray only said it to be wise.

"Sorry, pal, but there's a leak in the water hose. Pretty busy today. Couldn't get to it until at least five if you feel like leavin' it. Or you can bring it in Monday. It'll run okay if you take it easy."

"Leave it until five—Bud must be crazy," thought Ray. It's Saturday and how can you have any fun without a car? "Okay, Monday afternoon, but thanks anyhow."

The beach was great, just as Ray had anticipated. The water was cool and the sun warm. Too bad there weren't any girls around. Ray decided since he couldn't find anybody to suit his taste he might as well wander over to the basketball court and find the guys. That was strange, too. The basketball court was empty except for some junior high kids playing big deal. He glanced up at the clock on the bank building across the street and saw it was close to noon. Ray showered quickly in the bathhouse, changed his clothes and combed his hair. This was indeed fortunate. He could drop over to Patsy's, ask her out, and she would be so overjoyed she would ask him to stay for lunch. Great!

He took it easy driving to Patsy's. A leaky hose wasn't anything to fool around with. Dad would just have to lend him the Chevy for tonight. Besides, he wouldn't consider taking Patsy out in a heap with a busted radiator.

Patsy answered the door. She looked cute. Ray liked to drop in unexpectedly because then she always appreciated him more. When she saw him she quickly ran her hand down her hair to smooth it down. She had on white shorts and a pink blouse. The outfit showed off her tan great. "She sure is cute," thought Ray.

"Oh, hi, Ray. I was ironing. Sorry I look such a mess, but come on in." She smiled that sweet smile he loved and a pink glow seemed to come to her cheeks.

"Don't be silly. Ya' look great, Patsy. How are ya'?"

"Oh, fine. Busy, but fine. Great day."

"Yeah, great. All the kids are at the beach. Just came from there."

"I wanted to go, too. But my mother's out shopping and so I said I'd watch Melinda till she got back. Since I was home I decided to do the ironing for her, too." She smiled.

Patsy sure was a sweet girl. She was good as gold. "Hey, Pat, like to take in a show tonight?"

She blushed furiously and looked down. Ray knew she was so thrilled he had asked she could hardly speak for joy.

"Gosh, I'm sorry, Ray. But Carl and I are going to dinner. Perhaps some other time."

"Yeah, yeah, maybe some other time."

He left quickly and started driving. The car was acting up again. Ray decided he had better head home. Besides he still hadn't had any lunch. It was one o'clock. Ray decided to take Jerry to the natinee. If he hurried they could just make it. It would make the little kid happy.

The house was quiet when he entered. "Hey, Mom, I'm home. Mom! Jerry!" There was no answer. That was strange. The quiet was nerve racking for Jerry was always making noise, and where was Mom? Something else was wrong. Mom always locked the house up when she went out, but all the doors were open. Ray knew she'd be home soon. He wondered where Jerry had gone to. Ray opened the refrigerator. He was disgusted when he found his mother hadn't even made him a sandwich for lunch.

The phone rang.

"Hello."

"Ray, darling, I'm so glad you're home...

He cut her off. "Where the heck are you? I'm starved. And where's Jerry. I'm taking him to see the matinee. He better get home in a hurry or else he'll miss it."

"Ray, Jerry won't be able to...

He interrupted again. "Wouldn't ya' know it. Come home just to take the kid to the matinee and now he's too busy. Oh, well, I'll take him tomorrow."

"Ray, listen to me. I'm at the hospital." Her voice chocked and a sudden panic gripped Ray. "Jerry was playing with his chemistry set and something exploded, I don't know what..." She was crying then. "But Jerry's eyes. He can't see. He'll never see again. Ray, call your father at the office and both of you come down here at once. Please, Darling."

Ray hung up the phone. He was numb. He couldn't think. He heard his mother over and over again "Jerry can't see . . . can't see . . . can't see..." It echoed over and over in his ears until he could hear nothing else. All he could remember was Jerry waking him up and begging him to go to the natinee. But now there would never be another matinee for Jerry. Ray remembered his little brother in a flash of memories . . . the day he went to kindergarten and drew a picture and gave it to him, the day he said "When I grow up I want to be just like Ray," the day Jerry had given him his life's savings of five dollars to help pay for the car. All these things had been acts of love that Ray had been blind to. Blind. Jerry had lost his sight but for the first time Ray could see. Ray saw not only Jerry, but himself—a self-centered, egotistical, lying boy.

He was cold and numb. For the first time his heart ached and stabs of guilt pierced his mind. "Jerry can't see . . . can't see . . . can't see..." Over and over like a broken record the words sounded and vibrated about the room. Ray placed his hands on his face. His cheeks were burning and his eyes wet with tears.

Slowly he picked up the phone and dialed his father's office. "Dad, this is Ray. I don't know how to tell you, but. . . .

## Writing Assignment One
## Comment on Sample 1. Grade: High

The assignment called for a repetition, at the end of the paper, of the key statement—and this writer apparently forgot that demand. But it is the only sign of failure to meet an exacting series of requirements, and all the others are met so fully and skillfully that the readers, for once, decided to abide by the spirit of the law. The dialogue is excellent, as natural as life; the incidents are probable and made more so by the vividness of their description. The writer plays on meanings of "see" and "blind" throughout the story, but in such a way that the irony at the end becomes greater and more complex. With the addition of one sentence at the end ("you blind or somethin' ") as Ray recalls earlier episodes, the paper would be well-nigh perfect. Even without this, it deserves a rating of *high*.

## Writing Assignment One
## Sample 2. Grade: Average

"No man is an island.—No man is an island," muttered the man as he sat drinking with his friends. They had been ship-wrecked on this island for twenty years and had hoarded a case of vodka for a special occasion. Now, it had come; their rescue. The man who had been muttering spoke to the silent companions, sharing the small shack with him. "You know, if it hadn't been for you, I'd have gone mad. If any one of us had been alone he'd have gone mad by now. No man is an island." His companions silently agreed with him. They had all been hushed, strangely quiet since a small plane had spotted their distress signal and dropped a message that a rescue ship would get to them by the following day. It was almost dawn of that day now. Twenty years he had spent with these men, he knew them as he knew himself. He knew them as he had never known a human being before the shipwreck. It was growing dawn now and the recue party would arrive soon. The grey of the dawn began to lap at the dark of the sand floor. Tomlinson began to sing, then the others. When the rescue party came into the shack five minutes later, they found Tomlinson drinking vodka and singing; sitting on the sand floor alone.

## Writing Assignment One
## Comment on Sample 2. Grade: Average

The student complies with only part of the requirement — the ironic statement is made twice, early in the story, but is not repeated, with full awareness, near the end. One more sentence could have done this. Moreover, the situation is not made plausible: such things as hoarding vodka for twenty years, how the man stayed alive that long, whether he ever did have companions or not—all these make the reader unwilling to suspend disbelief.

On the other hand, the use of the quotation from Donne is ingenious, some of the handling is adroit, and the final revelation is unexpected, but commands respect for cleverness. The paper is really not typically *average* in any respect, yet on balance, *average* seems a more appropriate rating than either *high* or *low.*

Some readers felt this paper should be rated only *low,* arguing that the student does not meet, even tangentially, the requirements of the assignment; and that the character never reencounters an earlier statement, never gains any awareness of its meaning.

## Writing Assignment One
## Sample 3. Grade: Low

*L S D the Crazy Drug*

In a dark alley on one of the back streets of town I overheard A Conversation between two people. They were talking about L. S. D, the powerful new drug that was making people go crazy. One of the boys was trying to tell the other that L. S. D's were all-right to take and it wouldn't do your body any harm, it just lets you go on a trip for eight or ten hours And when your off you don't feel a thing. So the boy finially agreed to go on a trip off of the drug that night In the other boy's house, there were also going to be more than these two boy's over At the house there would be about fifteen or twenty more people. The boy's walked home and I decide to follow them to watch there reaction's off of the drug. I knew that the boy who had gotten talked into taking the drug was not Very smart, because if he had read the news papers or something he would have known that L. S. D would make you go crazy.

When the two boys finially reached the point where they were going to have their tripping party, I watched them go in And Alot of other people too from the Cornor where I sat on the silk green grass. When It started Getting dark, I walked home and fixed me something to eat in a hurry, so I could go back and see the reaction's of the people in the house since about four or five hours had passed. When I finished eating I went as fast I Could to the spot where I was before, When I Arrived I didn't see Any Action so I decided to walk in the house and act as one of them, once inside I could tell that they were tripping because everyone was laughing, All except one of the boys who had been talked into it by his friend, he laid on the floor sweating & pulling his hair out And yelling out loud I wish I were dead. I Couldn't stand the sight of the people, so I ran out And went to the nearest telephone booth & called the police, I told them the whole story And what was going on in the house. The police arrived at the house in About ten minunets And arrested everyone, they were still laughing as they got into the paddy wagon's All except the same boy who had gotten talked into the drug by his friend. I followed them to the police station & watched them go into three cells, they took the boy to a medical hospitial where he was tied down And had test ran on him. I played like his uncle so I could talk to the Doctor and ask him what was wrong with him, the Doctor told me that he had taken the drug the wrong way and it messed up his mind, instead of going on a happy trip he went on a trip of trying to kill himself And he would be like that the rest of his life, because when you take the powerful new Drug L. S. D. your mind will react the same and make you go crazy.

## Writing Assignment One
## Comment on Sample 3. Grade: Low

Only with some stretching does this paper meet the requirements of the assignment. It is a narrative, told in the first person, but there is no dialogue directly stated. The third sentence tells what "One of the boys" said to another, but this statement hardly seems ironic; a doctor (in the last paragraph) partly repeats the statement, as required by the assignment; again, real irony is missing. Spelling, punctuation, capitalization, grammar, and sentence structure are all weak enough to justify a *low* rating even if the content had met the requirements squarely: the errors are flagrant and almost constant.

## Writing Assignment Two
## Sample 1. Grade: High

*"The Dead"*

One day, while I was going through the new issue of Down Beat, I saw an item which said that George Neuman had died in Berlin. The story had a recent picture of him, showing him to be a rather aged-looking man, though he was still in his thirties, and gave some of the circumstances of his death. It said that after he failed to show for his regularly scheduled performance, the other members of the quintet had called his hotel. The manager checked George's room, found him on the bathroom floor, and called a doctor, who pronounced him dead and said that he probably had been for over two days.

The news had a surprisingly strong effect on me, considering how little I really knew about George. I knew that he had been Milt Jynan's pianist for a while because of an old Jynan album that I had. The linear notes had spoken briefly of the influence Bud Powell had had on his playing and of his preference to play in Europe. Although he was given very few solos, I liked his playing very much. He didn't have an excessively flashy technique, but he was very inventive, and somehow, the simplicity of his style served to accentuate the originality of his improvizations and the beauty of his phrasing. I tried to find out more about him, but without much success. All I found were some pretty involved critiques of his music and the often repeated news that he liked performing in Europe. Faced with this lack of information, I used my imagination. Neuman, in my eyes, became something of an idol, a "jazzman on the continent" figure who lived by his piano until two A.M. and then consumed satyrian quantities of wine and women until sunup. He symbolized escape from the responsibility I was beginning to dread as I approached adulthood, renouncement of the nine-to-five rut that I feared falling into.

This article, however, didn't fit in with the image I'd created. Living from day to day was one thing, but lying on a hotel room floor, with no one knowing you were dead, and with only the men who needed you for their rhythm section caring to check, was quite another. I did some serious thinking on the matter, and gradually, nine-to-five began to win out over tomorrow-do-thy-worst. The responsibility of the one was frightening, but the emptiness waiting at the other was even more so.

## Writing Assignment Two
## Comment on Sample 1. Grade: High

What distinguished this paper from most of the other responses to the assignment was its plausibility, its apparent sincerity, and its lack of histrionics. The pianist who dies might well have filled the role of "idol" for an adolescent, a " 'jazzman on the continent' figure who lived by his piano until two A.M. and then consumed satyrian quantities of wine and women until sunup." The student might well have pictured himself as going into an emotional tailspin at the news of his idol's death. Instead, he is quiet about it, almost understating it, and the more convincing by reason of his quietness. His writing is nowhere showy, especially in the opening paragraph, but as he moves in on the assignment, the style becomes tighter, stronger, first as he draws his imaginary picture of his idol and then as he draws the contrasting picture of the sordid death on the bathroom floor of the Berlin hotel.

## Writing Assignment Two
## Sample 2. Grade: Average

*The Dead Man*

Perhaps it seems a little trite to talk about the assassination of President Kennedy any longer. Perhaps. Yet I don't think that any recent event has left such a mark on the public conscience, or on an individual conscience such as my own.

In the days that followed the shooting that November, a lot of us were forced to reevaluate our own lives in terms of the life of the man who had just died.

The brutality of that murder lay in the haste of its performance, in the way it cut jaggedly across the life of a young man, a man who was becoming the symbol of the new American spirit.

The lesson that was really brought home to me, as it must have been to others, was that of the shortness of life. President Kennedy was fortunate. His forty-five odd years of life were packed with more worth, more quality, than most people have in ninety years. Yet I have nearly half his years, and have no worthy achievements. The assassination was a call to duty, a call to equal the young man's tremendous output.

Too, it was a reminder of the futility of life and the fickleness of fate. Since one cannot say when death or immobility may strike, one should live with day to day goals in mind, letting the future take care of itself.

Although the President was a man all of us scarcely knew, his death was deeply wounding. The nation did not die; one of the most obvious of all things caused by the assassination was the quickness of recovery. No, it was more the death of a spirit, a charisma, that was once ours after the revolution, and may not again be ours for *another* two hundred years.

When we lost the President, we lost a part of our souls. And it was all the work of a madman.

## Writing Assignment Two
## Comment on Sample 2. Grade: Average

As far as technique goes, this paper is clearly more free from errors than the paper graded *high;* some who read this volume may wish to reverse the ratings. Part of this writer's difficulty arises from his choice of the death of President Kennedy as his illustration. Although this choice meets part of the requirements—"someone whom you scarcely know"—so much has been written about the assassination that the paper can show little freshness or originality. Further, since the death was a matter of tremendous national importance, it is difficult for the writer to limit himself to the reevaluation of his own way of life; much of the paper deals with the effect on others. Finally, the writer's "lessons" from the assassination—"the shortness of life," making it important to seek "worthy achievements"; "the futility of life" (which would deny the possibility of worthy achievements); and "the fickleness of fate," which should make us "live with day to day goals in mind"—these lessons involve contradictions of which the writer seemed totally unaware. There is some clever phrasing—possibly remembered from what had appeared in print. But the reason for grading this paper *average* is that it is not really "a personal essay."

## Writing Assignment Two
## Sample 3. Grade: Low

Last year the man that I had known for 3 years and had been a good friend of, died of a heart attack. He was around sixty five years old and a very active person. He had had his first heart attack many years before when he was an ice skater. The doctors told him that so active a sport may cause him other attacks. I guess that because of this he moved from Illinois to Texas and took up archery more seriously. Archery is a sport that is not near so active as ice skating yet it is a tiering sport. He became a professional and worked at a summer camp and made arrows and equiptment at home. I spent much of my time at his house discussing differnt things about archery. He did not heed the warnings of the doctors as well as he should have. He shot every day and did a great deal of hunting. One night he was out very late and caught a good case of the flu. This weakened him a great deal, but the first chance he got he was out of bed and shooting again. Leonard eased off on the hunting, but still shot just as much as ever. In another couple months he had another attack. This time he remained in the hospital for a number of weeks where he died.

Due to his death I came to some conclusions about my own life. I realized that he was a very stubborn person and did things that he did like and no one could stop him. He did not drink or smoke and he seemed to be very proud of the fact. He atributed his excelent physical condition to the fact that he got plenty of exercise and didn't smoke or drink. He did not realize that he could posibly get too much exercise for a man of his age. He seemed to feel that merely because he was a nonsmoker and non-drinker nothing could hurt him. Now I wonder if he would be alive today if he had smoked and drank yet not taken so much exercise. Now that he is dead I realize that too much of anything can be fatal. Even though he was in excelent condition for his age he did not realize that he was to old to go and be as active as everyone else. I see now that I should take notice of the reasons for his death. I feel that if I do the same as he did and overdo some phase of my life I may suffer for it. From his death I learned that moderation would benefit me more than over activity in a field. Now I try to use moderation in all things that I do.

## Writing Assignment Two
## Comment on Sample 3. Grade: Low

It may be useful to compare this paper with the other two on this same assignment. Like the paper rated *high,* this one has errors in technique, but they are far more frequent here and involve more serious grammatical mistakes. The paper rated *average* shows evidence of an attempt to meet the requirements of the assignment, even though the attempt is only partly successful. This paper begins with a flat denial of the requirements: Leonard is not "someone you scarcely know," but has been a good friend for three years. On these two counts alone the paper goes into the *low* category. It should be pointed out, however, that the writer tries hard to meet that part of the requirement involving reevaluation of his own life. The paper is marred by long-windedness and dullness, but the student's effort should be recognized.

# Poetry

# *Introduction to the Units on Poetry*

The poetry units in this section appear to be neglecting the tenth grade, but actually the original units on "My Last Duchess" and on the Whitman/Cummings poems were planned for grade 10 as well as for grade 9. In fact, some teachers may find that the materials work better with the tenth grade than with the ninth. And although "Fern Hill" and "Musée des Beaux Arts" are now earmarked for grades 11 and 12, we got reports that both poems worked excitingly well with good tenth grade classes. Here, as elsewhere, teachers will discover, by feeling their way, exactly where each unit can best serve them.

The term "sampling" is particularly appropriate for a poetry section limited to only 11 poems. Easy availability and established familiarity partly dictated our choices. Except for Richmond Lattimore's "Sonnet on Hope," the poems here are old friends of English teachers. We were aware of the lush growth of study materials already on hand for such poems as "My Last Duchess" and "Fern Hill," but with the optimism or the effrontery of inexperience, we rolled up our sleeves and set about the job of trying to inject freshness into the familiar. Nowhere did we get sharper or more helpful criticism than in the teachers' comments on these poetry units as they first went out to the schools for pretesting. Teachers are no longer satisfied—nor should they be—with a haphazard assortment of questions on a poem. They want an orderly sequence moving steadily toward a recognizable climax. They are quick to spot the question that tries to bypass a knotty problem. They are impatient with pursuit of the obvious and elaboration of the trivial. They welcome questions that stretch their students. The revised versions of these materials, therefore, are heavily indebted to all those teachers who took time out of their end-of-year busyness to send us the detailed suggestions that have enabled us to better our work.

# *Whitman / Cummings: A Comparison of Two Poems Grade 9*

## To the Teacher

For most teachers three class periods will be about the right time for this unit on Whitman's "When I Heard the Learn'd Astronomer" and Cummings' "if everything happens that can't be done." It will probably take the first two of these class periods to introduce the unit, to read and discuss the Whitman poem, and to listen to the Cummings poem read aloud. After the discussion of the Whitman poem, the student should prepare his paper on a comparison of the two poems. The papers can then form the basis for a full class period of discussion of Cummings' poem.

There are several reasons for the choice of these two poems for this comparative study. Not only is the central idea in both poems alike, but the idea itself is one which, as one teacher who used the unit has said, "is specially congenial to adolescent iconoclasts." But though the themes of the two poems are alike, both the treatment and the form present striking differences, and good ninth graders delight in discovering these differences. And once they have discovered the differences they can be helped to realize that the form in both poems is a revolt against the poetic conventions of the time, that Whitman's free verse was probably as jolting to his age as Cummings' syntactical and typographical distortions are to ours. Nor is it beyond the powers of an able ninth grader to come up with the understanding that in each poem the unconventional form is in itself a rebellious way of rebelling against the conventional reverence for books and science. But the ninth grader needs also to discover that though each poem is a rebellion against conventional form, neither is casual, haphazard, or formless. The more the student examines the poems the more evidence he will uncover of each poet's meticulous concern for form. It is particularly important for the student to unearth the intricate patterns of rhyme and rhythm in the Cummings poem and to see how these patterns fit the theme and the content.

*Whitman / Cummings:*
*A Comparison of Two Poems*
*Grade 9*

The first aim in this unit is to guide a student's study of the Whitman poem by confronting him with a series of questions concerning Whitman's theme, purpose, form, and diction. After the discussion of the Whitman poem, the student should receive a copy of the Cummings poem for which no discussion questions have been supplied. Hearing the poem read aloud several times should be the student's only preparation before he does the composition assignment calling for a comparison of the two poems. In this paper he has the chance to apply to his examination of Cummings some of the techniques and skills he has picked up in his guided exploration of Whitman.

The amount of preliminary work a teacher may wish to do with poetic form will depend on the extent and the depth of the students' previous experience with poetry. The student does need to know something about rhyme and rhythm. The study materials define "free verse." Beyond that the student can make headway with these two poems without any need for additional technical terminology given by his teacher.

### *When I Heard the Learn'd Astronomer*

Walt Whitman

When I heard the learn'd astronomer,
When the proofs, the figures, were ranged in columns
  before me,
When I was shown the charts and diagrams, to add,
  divide, and measure them,
When I sitting heard the astronomer where he lec-
  tured with much applause in the lecture-room,
How soon unaccountable I became tired and sick,
Till rising and gliding out I wander'd off by myself,
In the mystical moist night-air, and from time to time,
Look'd up in perfect silence at the stars.

## Questions for Discussion of Whitman's Poem

1. Who is the speaker in this poem? Where is he at the time the poem starts? What is going on? What is the occasion? How does the speaker feel about what is going on?

2. How do the others present on this occasion feel about what is going on, and how do you know?

3. What part of speech is "unaccountable" in line 5 and what do you think it modifies? Why do you think so?

4. After dealing with question 3, you are now ready to answer these questions: What action does the speaker finally take? Why does he take it?

5. The poem presents two sharply contrasted ways of coming to terms with the stars. Describe these two opposed views fully enough to show exactly how they are opposed.

6. For which one of these two ways of coming to terms with the stars is the speaker trying to arouse the reader's sympathy and by what means does he go about winning this sympathy? To answer this question you will need to look at the wording he uses to make this viewpoint seem natural, right, sensible, and attractive.

7. By what means does the speaker try to make the reader share his distaste for the other way of viewing the stars? Here, too, you will want to cite particular words and phrases to show how they serve his purpose.

8. Why does the poet begin each of his first four lines with the word *When?*

9. Is the main concern in this poem to indicate two opposing ways of looking at the stars and to express distaste for one and endorsement of the other? Give full, specific reasons for your answer to this question. To do so you will have to reckon with what the poem suggests as well as with what it states. And if you think the poem is concerned with more than a presentation of two opposed ways of looking at the stars, then make clear what else the poem is trying to do.

10. If you examine Whitman's poem and especially if you read it out loud, you will discover that it has no rhyme. You will also find that it has no fixed metrical patterns, no set number of stressed syllables in each line. This kind of poetry is called "free verse" because it has shaken off the restrictions that rhyme and meter impose on the free expression of thought. Is "free verse" an appropriate form for this particular poem? Why or why not?

11. What is the effect of having the poem consist

of one single long sentence? Do you think Whitman would have done better to break it up into several shorter sentences? Why or why not?

12. You have discovered that Whitman's poem presents two opposed attitudes or ways of looking at things. Are these the only two possible attitudes or viewpoints? Must they be mutually exclusive? Or is there a third attitude or viewpoint for an intelligent person to adopt? If so, what is this third attitude or viewpoint and why might it seem reasonable to an intelligent person?

### *if everything happens that can't be done*

e. e. cummings

if everything happens that can't be done
(and anything's righter
than books
could plan)
the stupidest teacher will almost guess
(with a run
skip
around we go yes)
there's nothing as something as one

one hasn't a why or because or although
(and buds know better
than books
don't grow)
one's anything old being everything new
(with a what
which
around we come who)
one's everyanything so

so world is a leaf so tree is a bough
(and birds sing sweeter
than books
tell how)
so here is away and so your is a my
(with a down
up
around again fly)
forever was never till now

now i love you and you love me
(and books are shuter
than books
can be)
and deep in the high that does nothing but fall
(with a shout
each
around we go all)
there's somebody calling who's we

we're anything brighter than even the sun
(we're everything greater
than books
might mean)
we're everyanything more than believe
(with a spin
leap
alive we're alive)
we're wonderful one times one

## Writing Assignment

### Directions

After a careful examination of the poem by E. E. Cummings, write a well planned paper in which you show how this poem is like and unlike Whitman's poem. You will want to discuss each poet's ideas, attitudes, language, and poetic form.

### Note to the Teacher

These papers should serve as the basis for a class discussion of the Cummings poem designed to pick up points that students have missed and to clarify any misconceptions. In this final discussion, teachers may find the sample ninth grade answers printed with this unit helpful.

## Writing Assignment
## Sample 1. Grade: High

*A Comparison of a Poem by Walt Whitman to Another by E. E. Cummings*

In Walt Whitman's poem, "When I Heard the Learn'd Astronomer," Mr. Whitman is presenting his point of view on how people should live their lives. He speaks through a main character, referred to only as "I." "I," while listening to "a learn'd astronomer" analyze the stars and disect them (as one would a frog in biology class), suddenly feels tired and ill. He goes outside into the cool night air, and occasionally looking up at the stars, realizes he knows all he wants to from studying their beauty for himself. He doesn't feel that this beauty warrants explanation from any books, because then it is blanketed by scientific facts.

Walt Whitman used free verse in writing his poem. This is the best thing he could have done, since by rhyming it or making it precisely rhythmic, he would have endorsed what he was persecuting. He would have patterned it "scientifically" instead of simply letting its beauty and meaning shine through.

Mr. Whitman repeats the word "when" in the first four clauses. By this, he uses repetition to make the reader feel as bored as "I" did during the period of time which the clauses are discussing.

Mr. Whitman's poem was shocking to many people living at the time when it was written. The style was defiant of all poetic laws being followed at that time in several ways. Using free verse was, in itself, revolutionary. On top of that, the whole poem was one overgrown sentence! Whitman spelled some words oddly too. He wrote "siting" for sitting, "learn'd" for learned, "wander'd" for wandered, and "look'd" for looked. By doing these things, he used his poetic license to the utmost.

The form E. E. Cummings uses in his poem, "if everything happens that can't be done," is as startling to us now as Whitman's was to his contemporaries. It has rhyme and rhythm, but uses a minimum of punctuation and is void of capitalization.

Cummings is telling us several things in his poem. The main theme is somewhat similar to Whitman's, in that it implies that you shouldn't use books as portals through which you see the world. Instead, you should go out and enjoy it for yourself. It also implies that you shouldn't be bound by fences past which noone has yet ventured, since you can't possibly know what wonderful adventures lie on the other side of them unless you cross them. Furthermore, Cummings seems to consider life a vast carousel which anyone can ride and enjoy if they only want to (as surely everyone does).

In the first part of his poem, Cummings calls his hero who is living life to the fullest "one" (just as Whitman refers to him main character as "I"). But to do the latter, "one" must be in love, so then "one" becomes "we."

Cummings uses repetition even more than Whitman did. In each of his five stanzas, he keeps his various themes going, separated by parentheses. In each stanza he shows his contempt for books in the first set of parentheses. In these sections, he implies that the boundaries which books set up should be burst. From the pattern of the second sets of parentheses, Cummings seems to be comparing life to a great merry-go-round. In all but the last stanza, he uses the word around, referring to the movement of "one" or "we." In the last stanza he says, "alive we're alive." This relates the carousel to living.

As Whitman defies scientific patterns by using free verse, so Cummings defies grammatical laws by leaving out capitalization completely. Just as Whitman spelled sitting "siting," Cummings spelled shutter "shuter."

Cummings scorns the normal way of using the English language. He puts words into phrases which at first seem to make very little (if any) sense. Once you get used to this mode of speech, though, it makes a great deal of the latter. Cummings seems to be trying to break the barrier between people which is set up because our language in its accepted form isn't always sufficient to convey one person's emotions to another.

## Writing Assignment
## Comment on Sample 1. Grade: High

This paper is an able response to an assignment that many teachers felt was beyond the powers of any ninth grader. A hasty glance suggests an unsophisticated organization dealing first with Whitman and then with Cummings but never really fusing the two. Actually, though, this student relates almost every comment on Cummings to a previous comment on Whitman, thus heeding the demand for comparison and contrast more competently than at first appears. It is true, though, that there were other ninth grade papers that did a neater job of presenting the material in a point by point comparative analysis, but no other paper equaled this one in richness of detail or sharpness of perception of the linkages between form and content in both poems. The explanation in paragraph two of why free verse is an appropriate form for Whitman's poem is an example of this ninth grader's acuteness, and so is the awareness of the aroundness of the Cummings "merry-go-round" figure or the recognition that in Cummings' poem to live life fully " 'one' must be in love, so . . . 'one' becomes 'we' " and yet is still "wonderful one times one." The detailed awareness of pattern in the parenthetical portions of the Cummings poem as well as in what precedes and follows them is further evidence of this student's superior command of the relationship between form and content.

## Writing Assignment
## Sample 2. Grade: High

*A Comparative Study of Two Philosophical Poems*

The two poems, "When I Heard A Learn'd Astronomer" and "if everything happens that can't be done," both contain deep philosophical meaning. They impress upon the reader the importance of an individual experience as opposed to a second-hand report. The problems and the questions posed by these two poets are important today in our complex society.

In his poem, Walt Whtman wishes to emphasize the need for individual and private experiences. The weakness in the astronomer's lecture, according to Whitman, is the fact that he attempts to explain the stars in terms of scientific facts and mathematical figures. Whitman believes that it is not necessary to comprehend all of the facts, but rather first, to enjoy and appreciate the awesome beauty of the stars.

Like Whitman, Cummings also criticizes the second-hand knowledge concerning life. However, his interpretation is in a broader sense and expresses more abstract ideas. The joy and meaning of life cannot be recorded in a book but must be experienced. Since a book cannot grow, hear or love, it is only a poor substitute in telling about these. These can only be comprehended by a living being. Books can quote facts but cannot relay the joy that can come only through living.

Walt Whitman uses direct language to express his point. He tells the the reader that the astronomer's lecture makes him sick by employing the use of a direct statement. However, the arrangement and choice of words in this poem are chosen to create an atmosphere of meditation and awe.

Cummings uses abstract words and meanings to convey his philosophy. In order to give his reader his desired picture, he uses many examples. Each example is aimed at the object of not only criticizing books and showing their limitations, but also, the limitations of a secondary source of information. This is exemplified by the phrase "we're everything greater than books might mean." Each word or phrase is a piece of this complex pattern and every piece is essential for the completed picture.

Whitman uses words and groups of words in such a way as to convey the prevailing mood and feelings. The use of the word 'when' in the first four lines implies a feeling of boredom and non-exciting material. However, the shorter, crisper, concluding lines reflect a change in the mood. The sentence variety and the smooth rhythm convey a feeling of meditation and awe.

Cummings uses parenthetical phrases to convey the mood of the poem. They reflect a light, gay, vibrant atmosphere. This atmosphere is representative of life. The rhythm is not as set as in Walt Whitman's poem, yet it does have a definite ebb and flow. This rhythm emphasizes the contrasts of life as a reality and life as described in books.

Cummings uses a definite, set rhyme scheme while Whitman does not. In the poem "if everything happens that can't be done," the first and last lines rhyme as well as the fifth and eighth. Whitman employs a device known as blank verse in creating his mood and establishing his philosophy.

As a modern poet, Cummings defies all rules of punctuation in his poem. These typographical distortions direct the reader's eye to the most important and outstanding portions of the poem. This enables the poet to guide the reader as he forms his interpretation of the poem.

Each of these poems consist of deep philosophical meanings. To comprehend these, the poem must be broken apart so that the meaning can be seen. The freedom of the individual in forming opinions concerning different aspects of life is the principle idea that these two men are defending.

## Writing Assignment
## Comment on Sample 2. Grade: High

Both this paper and the first are surprisingly good but different. Their differences are the reason for including both. This paper is superior to the first in its command of language and sentence structure. Its organization is more obviously and more tidily comparative than that of the other paper. The one possible weakness in the organization is a final paragraph that merely repeats what the first paragraph has said and what the intervening paragraphs have set out to exemplify. The one flaw in the content is the description of Whitman's form as "blank verse." Like the first writer, this one points out skillfully the theme of each poem and notes the likeness. Where this paper falls short of the first is in its lack of any detailed exploration of the relationship between form and content in the Cummings poem. The needed generalizations are here, but too often they stand without the support of examples or are left with the flimsy support of a single example. Nor does this student catch the carousel figure in Cummings and the gay whirling words that express its joyous abandon. These, though, are minor flaws in the clearly superior work of an able ninth grade student wrestling with an admittedly tough assignment.

## Writing Assignment
## Sample 3. Grade: Average

*Comparison of Two Philosophical Poems*

Whitman and Cummings are both trying to put across the same basic idea, that real knowledge is gained not from books, charts or scientists, but from nature. In Whitman's poem "When I Heard the Learn'd Astronomer," he is talking about the charts and formulas which were set before him; and he's mocking the way people try to understand complicated answers to questions when all the time a simple answer was waiting to be found in nature. Cummings, in his poem "If Everything Happens that Can't Be Done," is really stating the same belief. He says that nature holds more secrets than anything else and more knowledge can be gained from nature than from books.

Walt Whitman brings across his theory by relating an incident, and he uses irony as a tool to produce a sarcastic effect. An example of this is his use of the expression "the learn'd astronomer," meaning learn'd only from books. Cummings comes right out and tells the reader what he thinks, but uses a style which has the outward appearance of being non-sensical. He also uses metaphore in line one of stanza III

"so world is a leaf, so tree is a bough"

Personification is used in several places, for instance:

"(and buds know better
than books
don't grow)"

Whitman's poem doesn't appear to have much form, but there are several significant patterns. The poem is a complex sentence beginning with four adverbial clauses. The last four lines of the poem have a pattern of eight words, then ten words, ten words again and then eight words in a line. The first and last lines have four beats and the second, fifth and seventh lines have five beats. There are no rhyme patterns.

Cummings' poem has many patterns. The first three lines of each stanza don't rhyme, but the last line and the first do. Stanzas II and III have rhyme patterns which are alike, the rhyme patterns of the first five lines in stanzas II, III and IV are alike. Each first line has four beats, each second line has two, the third and fourth lines have one beat each, the fifth line has four beats, the sixth and seventh lines each have one beat, the eighth line has two beats and the ninth one has three. Each second line with the exception of the last stanza begins with "and." Every sixth line begins with the word "with" and all seventh lines have only one word. Each third line contains the word "books." Cummings pay no attention to capitalization rules, and he combines many words. Whitman uses conventional style throughout his poem.

## Writing Assignment
## Comment on Sample 3. Grade: Average

Neither of the first two papers goes at the visible aspects of form in the two poems with the diligence of this student, who subjects each poem to a line by line computation of its number of beats and dutifully catalogues the rhyme patterns in the Cummings poem. And this is good, but it is not enough—not even for a ninth grader. The same relentless pursuit of facts appears in the treatment of figurative language. This student can spot a metaphor and quote it, but there he stops with no comment on how the metaphor relates to or illuminates the theme of the poem. The paper ends abruptly with a reference to Cummings' indifference to the rules for punctuation, followed by the statement that "Whitman uses conventional style throughout his poem." Here then is a painstaking assemblage of facts without insights, except for the important recognition that both Whitman and Cummings are saying that "more knowledge can be gained from nature than from books."

## Writing Assignment
## Sample 4. Grade: Low

*Two Views of Poetry*

The two poems apparently say the same thing. The first says it in standard English and the second in in a conglomeration that it uses the same word symbols (with different meanings) and has some relation to English sentence structure. The authur has decided that punctuation and capitalization is beneath his dignity, a anachroism that does not fit modern poetry.

The authur has gone so far in his flight from specifics: and the few general referants to the real world are used in a manner so contrary to English that they are nonsense.

Walt Whitman use a referance in this world, a meeting which he leaves. This is not the universal idea that in trying to make understandable to everyone is made understandable to no one.

Poetry to be enjoyed must be understood: and to be understood it must be in terms that make sense to the reader, not some non-english that takes a semester of study to understand.

## Writing Assignment
## Comment on Sample 4. Grade: Low

Except for its final paragraph, this paper is illiterate and incoherent. It opens with the statement that "The two poems apparently say the same thing," but the reader is left to guess just what that "same thing" is. The student then objects to Cummings' refusal to punctuate and his indulgence in high jinks with the English language. The reader looks in vain for examples. The one explicit comment on Whitman is that he was at a "meeting" and left. The student is disgruntled with both Whitman and Cummings but lacks the skill to articulate his disgruntlement.

*Robert Browning:*
*"My Last Duchess"*
*Grades 9 and 10*

Decca-Parnassus DL9040. Many teachers may wish to begin the study of the poem by having the students follow the text while they listen to the record. A repetition of the record at the end of the class discussion and before the composition work would be highly desirable. If no record is available, the teacher's own reading will serve, but it is imperative that the student hear as well as see this particular poem.

Before moving to the discussion questions, the class will probably need definitions of the following words:

*officious:* meddlesome, line 27
*lessoned:* taught a lesson, line 40
*munificence:* generosity, line 49
*disallowed:* refused, line 51
*avowed:* admitted openly, confessed frankly, line 52

### *My Last Duchess*

Robert Browning

That's my last Duchess painted on the wall,
Looking as if she were alive. I call
That piece a wonder, now: Frà Pandolf's hands
Worked busily a day, and there she stands.
Will't please you sit and look at her? I said
"Frà Pandolf" by design, for never read
Strangers like you that pictured countenance,
The depth and passion of its earnest glance,
But to myself they turned (since none puts by
The curtain I have drawn for you, but I)
And seemed as they would ask me, if they durst,
How such a glance came there; so, not the first
Are you to turn and ask thus. Sir, 'twas not
Her husband's presence only, called that spot
Of joy into the Duchess' cheek: perhaps
Frà Pandolf chanced to say "Her mantle laps
Over my lady's wrist too much," or "Paint
Must never hope to reproduce the faint
Half-flush that dies along her throat": such stuff
Was courtesy, she thought, and cause enough
For calling up that spot of joy. She had
A heart—how shall I say?—too soon made glad,
Too easily impressed; she liked whate'er
She looked on, and her looks went everywhere.
Sir, 'twas all one! My favor at her breast,
The dropping of the daylight in the West,
The bough of cherries some officious fool
Broke in the orchard for her, the white mule
She rode with round the terrace—all and each
Would draw from her alike the approving speech,
Or blush, at least. She thanked men,—good! but thanked
Somehow—I know not how—as if she ranked
My gift of a nine-hundred-years-old name
With anybody's gift. Who'd stoop to blame
This sort of trifling? Even had you skill
In speech—(which I have not)—to make your will
Quite clear to such an one, and say, "Just this
Or that in you disgusts me; here you miss,
Or there exceed the mark"—and if she let
Herself be lessoned so, nor plainly set
Her wits to yours, forsooth, and made excuse
—E'en then would be some stooping; and I choose
Never to stoop. Oh sir, she smiled, no doubt,
Whene'er I passed her; but who passed without
Much the same smile? This grew; I gave commands;
Then all smiles stopped together. There she stands
As if alive. Will't please you rise? We'll meet
The company below, then. I repeat,
The Count your master's known munificence
Is ample warrant that no just pretense
Of mine for dowry will be disallowed;
Though his fair daughter's self, as I avowed
At starting, is my object. Nay, we'll go
Together down, sir. Notice Neptune, though,
Taming a sea-horse, thought a rarity,
Which Claus of Innsbruck cast in bronze for me!

## Questions for Discussion

1. You have been told that the setting for this poem is Renaissance Italy, in the sixteenth century. What details in the poem establish this setting?

2. Who is the speaker in the poem? To whom is he speaking and how do you know?

3. In what part of the palace are the speaker and his visitor when the poem begins? Where have they been and where are they going? What business is being transacted and how do you know?

4. Try reading the title of the poem in three different ways. First read it stressing the word "My."

# *Robert Browning: "My Last Duchess" Grades 9 and 10*

## To the Teacher

In these study materials for Browning's "My Last Duchess," both the inclusions and the omissions are an attempt to recognize the limitations as well as the capacities and the interests of ninth grade students. That is why the focus here is on the situation, the story, and the people rather than on poetic devices and poetic form. In the questions for study the focus is even more narrowly on the Duke's unconscious revelation of his own character, thus leaving the student, in writing assignment two, to figure out the character of the Duchess.

In attempting this poem with ninth graders, the teacher will need to supply some of the background material before the students try to read the poem. Ninth graders need to know that the story takes place in Renaissance Italy, in the sixteenth century. With a good ninth grade class a teacher may want to mention Machiavelli's *Prince* or the subtle practices of the Borgias and the Medici. Ninth grade students also need to know the marriage customs of the time. For many ninth graders the "dowry" is an unknown practice. Possibly, too, the teacher will wish to comment on the relationship existing between the Renaissance nobleman and the artist. And certainly the class will need to know what a dramatic monologue is. The term itself is not important as long as the students understand that in this kind of poem only one person speaks, though the reader can deduce from what gets said who is listening and what is happening. The students need to see that the poet is limited to a single person's speech as a means of defining character, implying dramatic action, and usually indicating the presence of an audience. Ninth graders will grasp the difficulties of this form if they compare its restrictions with the freedoms open to the short-story writer.

There are several good recordings of "My Last Duchess," among them Arnold Moss's reading of the poem in "Famous Poems that Tell Great Stories,"

When you read it this way, what does the title suggest about the Duke's attitude toward the Duchess? Next read the title stressing the word "Last." What different meanings does this reading give to the title? Now read with the stress on "Duchess." What further meanings do you find in the title when you read it this way? Try reading the first line of the poem and see which of the three title words you stress. If you listened to a recording of the poem, which of the three words was stressed?

5. The word "Frà" (in lines, 3, 6, and 16) refers to a monk and means "brother." How does the Duke feel toward Frà Pandolf and how do you know? What do these feelings reveal about the Duke?

6. How do you account for the Duke's being able to state so fluently what Frà Pandolf probably said to the Duchess while he was painting her portrait?

7. What does the Duke reveal about himself when he says he is the only one to draw the curtain covering his wife's picture? (lines 9–10)

8. What further indications of the Duke's character do you discover in the phrase "if they durst," line 11?

9. In lines 13–34 the Duke paints a portrait in words of his "last Duchess" in which he states the reasons for his displeasure with her. In picturing the Duchess, however, he also presents the reader with a portrait of himself. What qualities of his character do you discover through what he says about the Duchess?

10. In lines 34–43 the Duke explains why he never told his wife that she displeased him. What do these reasons tell us about his character?

11. In line 45 the Duke says, "I gave commands." What do you think these commands were? What makes you think so? Should the poem have told you instead of leaving you to guess? Why or why not? In answering these questions use all the clues the poem provides.

12. What do lines 49–54 suggest about the size of the dowry the Duke is expecting from his next Duchess? Is the Duke sincere when he tells the Count's representative that he is primarily interested in the Count's daughter rather than in the amount of the dowry? Give reasons for your answer.

13. Why does the Duke call his visitor's attention to the statue of Neptune taming a sea horse? How do the two final words "for me!" complete the picture the entire poem has been creating of the Duke's character?

## Writing Assignment One

(The assignment should be written during a class period.)

Write an impromptu composition in which you present what you imagine the Count's envoy—that is, his representative or go-between—might report to the Count about his visit with the Duke. Since the envoy is silent throughout the poem and since the poem tells little about the Count, you will have to use your imagination in determining what the two men were like, what their relationship was, and then what questions your imagined Count would be likely to ask of your imagined envoy and what answer your imagined envoy would be likely to give. Your major problem may be to decide just how honest the envoy will dare to be, but take into account all that the envoy has seen and heard, what his resulting impressions of the Duke must be, what he must realize the Duke is after, and how he must feel about the Duke's trustworthiness. Although you will have to make full use of your imagination, try to keep your imaginings in line with what the poem has told you.

## Writing Assignment Two

(This assignment should be prepared outside class.)

In a composition that you prepare at home, tell what kind of person you think the Duchess was and why you think so. Of course the poem shows you the Duchess only as the Duke sees her, but reading between the lines of the poem, try to come up with your own interpretation of what the Duchess was really like.

## Writing Assignment Three

(This assignment is optional for honors or advanced students.)

Try writing a composition in which you have a single speaker reveal himself solely by what he says—perhaps by what he leaves unsaid. Provide this speaker with both an occasion and a hearer—probably an audience of one. Through the speaker's words make clear to the reader the situation, the character of the speaker, and the relationship between the speaker and his audience. Make every word contribute to the reader's understanding of the speaker's character.

## Introductory Comment on Writing Assignment One

Most teachers who used this assignment reported that their students liked it because it gave them a chance to exercise their imagination. Like the writing assignments that go with the short story unit, this assignment is intended to suggest that textual analysis is not the only way to get at a student's understanding of a work of literature.

## Writing Assignment One Sample 1. Grade: High

*To Be or Not to Be*

"Good afternoon, Count," greeted the envoy, bowing low. "I have just returned from the Duke's palace. It was indeed a thing of beauty. The treasures held in his possession were varied and valuable. Your daughter would have all the valuable items to see every day and show off to guests when entertaining. One such treasure was a statue of Neptune taming a sea-horse . . . there is a message in that statue." This last was murmured so low that the Count could scarcely hear it.

"What's that you say?" demanded the Count.

"Oh, nothing, sir, I was just clearing my throat. To continue, the Duke had a magnificent picture of his last Duchess. She looked so lifelike, almost as if she would begin to talk and breathe in the next moment. Fra Pandolph has done a masterpiece."

"All this is very well, very well," said the Count irratably. I know all about the Duke's priceless wonders. What I wish to know is what you, personally, thought of the Duke as a match for my daughter. You have been in my service a long time, and your opinion is valued highly."

The envoy hesitated, as if searching for the right words.

"Well, sir, I would say he is a man of the world, well-versed in antiques and knowing the correct clothes to wear and the art of conversation. He seemed proud of his name and all the things that lay behind it."

"Yes, yes, I know all that. But what I want to know is *your* opinion of the Duke. Do you think he will be a good match for my daughter?"

Again the envoy hesitated. Then, as if he had come to a decision, he heaved in a deep breath, squared his shoulders, and started in:

"Personally, sir, I was very impressed with the Duke. At the beginning when he showed me all the treasures I said to myself, 'What a fine match this would be. The Count's daughter will bask in all these glories. Then suddenly, when the Duke was showing me his last Duchess's painting, a change came over him. The model loving Duke became a beast, not so much by his actions as by the implication behind his words. He indicated that he was ashamed of her. I got the impression he was a callow person. He seemed to want your daughter's dowry first, next your daughter. That, sir, is my opinion."

With that the envoy bowed quickly and left the room.

## Writing Assignment One Comment on Sample 1. Grade: High

This student's reconstruction of a scene we can only guess at by reading between the lines of the poem is lively, dramatic, and imaginative. Both the envoy and the Count emerge in the course of the dialogue: the emissary's subservience tinctured with a dash of audacious sincerity; the Count's impatient irritability with his emissary's suppression of vital facts. The reader senses the relative social positions of the two men without the writer's stating it—or needing to. The reference to the statue of Neptune taming a sea horse is one of several unexpected insights in this tenth grade paper, and certainly one of the deftest touches is the envoy's insistence that he was only clearing his throat. The persistent thrust of the Count's questions is dramatically alive, and so is the envoy's final reluctant decision to speak his mind and then make a discreet getaway. The attempt to emulate the courtly formality of Browning's own language, the energy of the dialogue, the linkage to actual details in the poem, the avoidance of any palpable violation of probability—all mark this as an admirable answer to an assignment demanding imagination, creative power, and an understanding of the poem.

## Writing Assignment One Sample 2. Grade: Average

*My Last Duchess*

In all probability, the Count received an unfavorable account of the Duke from his emissary. Considering the levity of the mission, and the high ranking nobility involved, the reader may reasonably assume that the Count sent an intelligent envoy, possibly a friend or advisor, possibly a minor noble. In any case, anyone but a churl could detect and clearly understand the Duke's slips, intentional or not, and his subtle threats. In his report, the envoy could not help but inform the Count of the Dukes overbearing and imperious attitude, his overpowering egocentricity, and his cruel snobbishness. Also, the emissary would take into account the rigid standards which the Duke measures everything by, finding almost everything lacking. The cold indifference with which he treated everything from royalty to dogs. The cold, couldn't-care-less treachery beneath his pompous face. All these and much more would the Count be told as his ally reported. Then, in addition, and perhaps more important, was the Duke's attitude toward marriage, wives and women. Keeping them in their place, keeping them if they amused him, casting them out if they did not. Treating the marriage more like a certificate of ownership than the ultimate union. Treating wives like women, cold, impartial, disinterested, occasionally bored. Getting more pleasure out of a painting of a "loved one" than from her warmness in flesh. In his pompous splendor wishing to control his spouses thoughts, feelings, and emotions as if she were an automaton. Then, thwarted, remove the evidence of a—failure. For failure he could not stand.

All this, the Count would be told, and he would have another side of his son-in-law to be exposed to him. Exposed now, so that misery could be prevented, rather than later, when it could not.

## Writing Assignment One
## Comment on Sample 2. Grade: Average

In its grasp of the Duke's character, this paper is probably more sophisticated and more penetrating than the first one, as is indicated by such phrases as "The cold, couldn't-care-less treachery beneath his pompous face" or "Treating the marriage more like a certificate of ownership than the ultimate union." Unfortunately, though, this student misses his chance to create the Count and the envoy through dialogue as the first paper did. In the first paper three people come to life, the Count, the envoy, and the Duke. In this paper only the Duke does. What we have here really amounts to a character sketch of the Duke, and the assignment asked for more than that. The writing in this paper also raises questions that the first paper did not. Frequently the diction is superbly precise, and certainly the student, when he wishes, can manipulate a variety of sentence structures. But the use of the word "levity" in place of "gravity" in the second sentence suggests that some of the verbal sophistication here is superficial. The constant use of fragments as sentences is even more serious. No doubt this was deliberate, perhaps a way of representing the thinking out loud of the envoy as he readies himself for his report to the Count; but in a paper that deliberately adopts the essay form, this playing fast and loose with sentence structure for a whole page or more is certainly ill-advised.

## Writing Assignment One
## Sample 3. Grade: Low

*The Report*

Sir, I have spent many a happy moment at His Highnesses estate. Also I have spent an equal amount of nerve-wracking moments. Sir, I am convinced that there is something wrong with the Duke. At any moment he may spring from a calm passive mood into a fit of uncontrolable temper. By the way, that is what happened to the late Duchess. A handsome guard, one of His Highnesses personal guards, I think, made eyes at the Duchess. Now they are both in their graves. Not to mention the state of ruin he left part of his mansion. Now I shall get on to more pleasant things.

He has the most marvelous wardrobe in the land. Cloaks of all colors and shapes, shoes by the dozen are all his. He own thousands of acres of good land. And as many head of cattle and sheep. He is rich beyond my wildest dreams. He collects taxes by the dozen from his people. Although he is not a harsh ruler he is strict.

Sir, my report is finished, but if I may, I would like to advise you to weigh the value of your daughters life.

## Writing Assignment One
## Comment on Sample 3. Grade: Low

A comparison with the *high* paper is illuminating. Both papers use the dramatic method; both are creative and imaginative; but the first paper stays carefully within the boundaries of probability. This one does not. The reference to the handsome guard who "made eyes at the Duchess," the categorical statement that both are now in their graves, and the reference to the ruins in which the Duke left part of his mansion have no validity because nothing in the poem indicates that the envoy could have derived any such information. This student seems not to realize that the Duke reveals himself and his affairs only by indirection. The emphasis on the Duke's fabulous wealth is evidence of this student's unawareness that the Duke is deeply concerned with the amount of the dowry he will annex through his new Duchess. It is only fair, though, to point out that this paper is the work of a ninth grader, whereas the first two came from tenth graders. Teachers, moreover, may disagree on what constitutes an unwarranted use of imagination.

## Writing Assignment Two
## Sample 1. Grade: High

*Characterization of the Duchess*

The Duchess was indeed a rarity in those days in which a person's behavior was based on the class he was born or married into.

The Duchess was a beautiful woman outside as well as from the inside. The Duke knew this and was insanely jealous and selfish because of this. He often spied on her and never let the public view her lovely face. I feel that perhaps she could not perceive her husband's feelings and in this way she was ignorant of more complicated feelings and emotions of others.

If people could get out of life what the Duchess did it would be a better place to live in. She was a simple, uncomplicated creature who enjoyed the little things in life we so often take for granted. She took and saw delight in a golden sunset, a white mule, and a kind offer of help.

She was a congenial person for she often talked with the help around the castle. This shows she was not too proud to talk or wear a warm smile. Her friendly smile was greeted by other smiles.

To sum up her whole behavior would be to say that she loved life and all parts consisting life. Such people are oblivious to the evil around them.

## Writing Assignment Two
## Comment on Sample 1. Grade: High

The writing in this paper is neither brilliant nor flawless, but it stands out among the ninth grade papers on the Duchess because of its modest willingness to stay inside Browning's text, its refusal to use the poem as the taking-off point for a binge of ill-timed imagination, its use of appropriate detail from the poem, and its combined accuracy and restraint in drawing its inferences. The writer gets to the center of the Duchess's character in seeing her as too uncomplicated to understand the "more complicated feelings and emotions of others." The closing of the third paragraph is evidence of the student's ability to pack three important allusions into a single sentence—a rare feat among ninth graders! The last sentence in the paper is a brief but discerning summary of the tragedy that lurks behind the lines of the poem.

## Writing Assignment Two
## Sample 2. Grade: Average

*The Duchess*

I think the Duchess was probably a very beautiful and popular lady. She was popular with all the common people because of her warmth and friendliness towards them. The Duke became jealous and finally killed her because of it.

After reading the poem I see her as a very gay and happy person. I think she loved her husband and didn't realize her flirting bothered him so much. She probably didn't even consider her friendliness with everyone flirting.

She was probably happy at the beginning of her marriage but slowly became unhappy as he became jealous.

## Writing Assignment Two
## Comment on Sample 2. Grade: Average

What chiefly distinguishes this paper from the first is its lack of illustrative detail. It rests its case on unsupported generalizations. It assumes that the Duke had his wife killed, and certainly this is possible, but the student leaves the evidence unexplored. Most of the assumptions about the Duchess are likewise possible but unsubstantiated.

## Writing Assignment Two
## Sample 3. Grade: Low

*The Last Duchess*

The beautiful Duchess loved not one, but all. She was a young maiden. Married against her will.

This fair young maiden had eyes of blue, black hair, lips of rose red. She was the one who stole the men's hearts. The last Duchess was the one they loved. Their gifts made her happy.

Now she is gone, gone to the other world. Oh, how they miss her beauty, and her little smile of joy. Now she is gone.

## Writing Assignment Two
## Comment on Sample 3. Grade: Low

This paper, like the *average* one, gravitates to the unsupported generalization, but here the generalizations themselves are dubious. Nothing in the poem suggests that the Duchess was married "against her will." More questionable is the description of the Duchess as "one who stole men's hearts"—a phrase that turns the lady into a designing hussy. Most serious, though, is the failure even to mention the Duchess's relationship with the Duke. The final paragraph is an extended wail rather than a reasoned analysis.

*Robert Browning:*
*"My Last Duchess"*
*Grade 12*

That piece a wonder, now: Frà Pandolf's hands
Worked busily a day, and there she stands.
Will't please you sit and look at her? I said
"Frà Pandolf" by design, for never read
Strangers like you that pictured countenance,
The depth and passion of its earnest glance,
But to myself they turned (since none puts by
The curtain I have drawn for you, but I)
And seemed as they would ask me, if they durst,
How such a glance came there; so, not the first
Are you to turn and ask thus. Sir, 'twas not
Her husband's presence only, called that spot
Of joy into the Duchess' cheek: perhaps
Frà Pandolf chanced to say "Her mantle laps
Over my lady's wrist too much," or "Paint
Must never hope to reproduce the faint
Half-flush that dies along her throat": such stuff
Was courtesy, she thought, and cause enough
For calling up that spot of joy. She had
A heart—how shall I say?—too soon made glad,
Too easily impressed; she liked whate'er
She looked on, and her looks went everywhere.
Sir, 'twas all one! My favor at her breast,
The dropping of the daylight in the West,
The bough of cherries some officious fool
Broke in the orchard for her, the white mule
She rode with round the terrace—all and each
Would draw from her alike the approving speech,
Or blush, at least. She thanked men,—good! but thanked
Somehow—I know not how—as if she ranked
My gift of a nine-hundred-years-old name
With anybody's gift. Who'd stoop to blame
This sort of trifling? Even had you skill
In speech—(which I have not)—to make your will
Quite clear to such an one, and say, "Just this
Or that in you disgusts me; here you miss,
Or there exceed the mark"—and if she let
Herself be lessoned so, nor plainly set
Her wits to yours, forsooth, and made excuse
—E'en then would be some stooping; and I choose
Never to stoop. Oh sir, she smiled, no doubt,
Whene'er I passed her; but who passed without
Much the same smile? This grew; I gave commands;
Then all smiles stopped together. There she stands
As if alive. Will't please you rise? We'll meet
The company below, then. I repeat,
The Count your master's known munificence
Is ample warrant that no just pretense
Of mine for dowry will be disallowed;
Though his fair daughter's self, as I avowed
At starting, is my object. Nay, we'll go
Together down, sir. Notice Neptune, though,
Taming a sea-horse, thought a rarity,
Which Claus of Innsbruck cast in bronze for me!

## Questions for Discussion

1. Describe the patterns of rhyme and rhythm that Browning uses in this poem and comment on the effectiveness of Browning's use of them. To do this you will need to reckon with these questions: (a) Is the reader likely to notice the rhyme when he first reads the poem? Why or why not? (b) Do the endings of Browning's sentences usually coincide with the ends of his lines of verse? Account for what you discover. (c) Do the requirements of the rhyme and rhythm prevent the poem from sounding like talk? (d) Are most of Browning's lines easy to scan? Is their meter regular most of the time?

2. If this scene were being played on the stage, the envoy, as well as the Duke, would speak and act. Because this is a dramatic monologue he does neither. By what devices and with what success does Browning cope with this difficulty inherent in the dramatic monologue?

3. In what ways is the situation of Browning's poem ironic?

4. Verbal irony occurs when the speaker says one thing but means the opposite. What examples of verbal irony do you find in this poem, and what does each contribute to your understanding of the Duke's character?

5. Compression—the condensed line—is likely to be present in all drama, but in the dramatic monologue it is indispensable. Find examples of Browning's use of such compression and point out how each example contributes to the total impression the poem seeks to create.

6. In line 2 the Duke uses the words "Looking as if she were alive" to describe the painting. Later in lines

## *Robert Browning: "My Last Duchess" Grade 12*

### To the Teacher

One purpose of these materials on Browning's "My Last Duchess" is to explore the possibilities for teaching the same poem at two different grade levels and to suggest the different kinds of approaches appropriate for those different levels. In using the poem with twelfth grade students, some teachers may wish to cover quickly and selectively the material prepared for the ninth grade before moving on to the questions and assignments designed for the twelfth grade. The one caution in using this ninth grade material is not to let it anticipate what writing assignment one in this unit is asking of the twelfth grader.

The ninth grade materials deliberately focus on *what* Browning is doing in the poem. These materials are more concerned with how he does it—with his means, techniques, and devices. The aim here is to compel more searching exploration of the text and to induce subtler insights than are to be expected from ninth graders. The questions are designed to force the student to examine the implications behind the words and to sharpen his awareness of both the potentialities and the limitations inherent in the dramatic monologue. The concern here with voice, tone, mood, and form is appropriate for the twelfth grade but would be too difficult for the ninth.

Many teachers may want to make a comparative study of "My Last Duchess" and "The Love Song of J. Alfred Prufrock," using Browning's poem first as an introduction to the subtler problems posed by Eliot's poem. In using both poems, the Commission on English realizes the rich possibilities of such a comparative study. Neither set of study materials presupposes the student's familiarity with the other.

### *My Last Duchess*

Robert Browning

That's my last Duchess painted on the wall,
Looking as if she were alive. I call

46–47, he says, again of the painting, "There she stands / As if alive." In line 2 why does the Duke say "were" instead of "was"? Why does Browning have the Duke use almost exactly the same words in lines 46–47? What are the overtones of these words and how are they useful in the structure of the poem?

7. The Duke, in explaining the reasons for his never having told the Duchess why he was dissatisfied with her, says in lines 42–43, "and I choose / Never to stoop." How do you reconcile this with his later words to the envoy, "Nay, we'll go / Together down, sir"? Remember that because the Duke is of superior rank, protocol demanded that he go first and that the envoy follow him.

8. Consider the possibility of interpreting the "curtain" of line 10 as a metaphor. If you read it as a metaphor, how does it clarify the structure of the poem?

9. As the poem ends, the Duke calls attention to a piece of bronze statuary (lines 54–56). Why do you think he does so? Browning could have made this piece of bronze statuary almost anything he wanted. Why, then, did he choose to make it a statue of Neptune "Taming a sea-horse"?

10. Why does the Duke value the statue of Neptune? Why does he value the portrait of his former wife? Is he a connoisseur of art? Is he a lover of art? Give reasons for your answers.

## Writing Assignments

The first of these assignments should be prepared outside the classroom and should prove suitable for average as well as honors sections of college preparatory twelfth graders. The second assignment should be written in the classroom during a class period and may well be the kind of assignment suitable for only an honors or Advanced Placement class. In its pretesting, it proved a hopeless stumbling block for the naïve high school senior but valuable and stimulating for the able student.

### Writing Assignment One

Write a carefully planned, fully developed composition in which you point out the differences between the kind of person the Duke thinks he is and the kind of person you as reader believe he really is. In your composition consider how the tone and diction reveal both what the character thinks of himself and what you think he unwittingly reveals about himself.

### Writing Assignment Two

Write one or two paragraphs explaining what change of tone occurs in lines 48–51, "I repeat, . . . will be disallowed," and showing what purpose is served by this change. To do this you will need to take into account the tone of the lines that precede and the lines that follow, but make the tone of lines 48–51 central to your paper.

## Introductory Comment on Writing Assignment One

If this assignment called for only what is defined in its first sentence, then it might well be suitable for younger students. What raises it to the twelfth grade level is the second sentence with its insistence upon a reckoning with tone and diction as conditioners of the dual vision the reader gets of the Duke. Teachers who feel that this assignment is not "challenging" enough for their twelfth grade students will be interested to know that the readers had to dig for a paper they were willing to call a *high.*

## Writing Assignment One Sample 1. Grade: High

THE DUKE

*or*

*"I love myself*
*I think I'm grand*
*I go to the movies*
*I hold my hand."*

The Duke sees himself as being a very important person and accordingly thinks he sports a very dignified air about him, while, in contrast, the reader is more apt to consider His Grace as an arrogant mercenary in light of his attitude toward the Duchess's likeness and his later remarks concerning the dowry from the Count.

The mood of the story shows that the Duke believes himself to be quite a person. The dramatic monlogue makes it seem as though the speaker is doing all of the talking, and the conversation is very much one-sided. This apparent verbosity supports the idea that the Duke considers himself important, for, by use of the monologue, it appears that he likes to dominate conversations.

The Duke's tone again shows that he believes himself to be a king, but the tone also, in the closing ten lines, brings out the Duke's true character, rather self-centered. His Grace's first plain exhibition of the arrogant attitude is his matter-of-fact remark that no one draws the curtain around the Duckess save for himself. His haughty attitude is most evident, however, when he emphasizes that the Duckess ranks his "gift of a nine-hundred-years-old name/ With anybody's gift." (lines 33–34) The tone borders on conceit with the emphasis on the 900-year-old name; the Duke could easily have deleted the "900 years" or reworded the way he said it, but not the Duke. At this point the reader, though he may still agree that the Duchess owed the Duke more than a common smile, cannot help but see the Duke as quite self-centered as exemplified by his lordly tone. The Duke further reveals his self-admiration and pompous attitude and tone by remarking, "I choose/ Never to stoop." (lines 42–43) Finally, in lines 48–51, the Duke destroys all semblance of objectivity and bluntly displays his arrogance when he says, "I repeat,/ The Count your Master's known munificence/ Is ample warrant that no just pretense/ Of mine for dowry will be disallowed." The quotation drips with pure, unadulterated conceit in the haughtily unemotional demand that the Count pay whatever dowry the Duke wishes. The tone, then is casually supercilious, like most Englishmen are stereotyped as.[1] The Duke, without once praising himself openly, establishes such a complacent manner of speaking and so matter-of-factly demands a dowry, that the reader cannot avoid characterizing the Duke as extremely egotistic.

The Duke further displays his arrogance and puts the reader against him with his choice of words and clever speeches. "Munificence" may or may not be an attempt by the Duke to insert a fancy word for the more common "generosity," but by calling someone who offered his wife cherries an "officious fool," he shows that he quite possibly is jealous and again haughtily deems himself far superior to those fools who offer cherries to his wife. In lines 35–39 the Duke subtly praises himself when he declares:

> . . . Even had you skill
> In speech— (which I have not) —to make your will
> Quite clear to such an one, and say, "Just this
> Or that in you disgusts me; here you miss,
> Or there exceed the mark . . . .

First His Grace says that a skillful speaker, which he claims not to be, would have said "Just this . . ." which, of course, he himself has just created; in other words, he says it took skill to say what he has just said. Also, the Duke's speeches involve a bit of sly name-dropping, not so much concerning Fra Pandolf as dealing with Claus of Innsbruck. The Duke casually points out the sculpture as a rarity and drops the name of the artist, probably a famous one. Thus, with the use of degrading adjectives and nouns, subtle accolades, and name-dropping, the Duke not only shows that he is conceited and arrogant, but becomes detestable in the eyes of the readers.

---

1. The tone, like that of the stereo-typed Englishman, is casually supercilious.

The combination of a monologue, a smugly supercilious tone, some derogatory adjectives, subtle praise, and some name-dropping more than proves that the Duke of Ferrara thinks himself to be a god and also makes the readers realize that the Duke is a villainous, mercenary, jealous, arrogant egoist.

## Writing Assignment One
## Comment on Sample 1. Grade: High

This is not a flawless paper, but its substantial merits outweigh its occasional lapses in diction and idiom. The student is also too fond of words. The terms "arrogant" and "egotistical" describe a vital part of the Duke's personality, but their overuse here is part of a general repetitiveness that deprives this paper of the thoroughbred leanness of other *high* samples. For this student the exercise of cutting his paper to two-thirds of its present length without loss of important concepts could be invaluable. It is true, though, that much of the writing is highly competent in its control of language and in its mastery of varied, complex sentence structure. The handling of tone and diction is outstanding, especially the comment on the Duke's back-handed self-praise in saying he has no skill in speech and then going on to state precisely what a person skilled in speech would say. The awareness that the reference to Claus of Innsbruck is a bit of "name-dropping" is further evidence of insight, and the quoted lines with which the paper starts denote this student's amused recognition of the Dukes of Ferrara who grow in the twentieth century.

## Writing Assignment One
## Sample 2. Grade: Average

MY LAST DUCHESS
*by Robert Browning*

In this theme, I shall discuss certain aspects of the character of the Duke. I think the Duke was too critical of the Duchess; also, I thought that he was posessive, domineering, and proud. The Duke saw himself as being always right and fair-minded. He even thought he was being a bit democratic.

I thought he was too critical because he exaggerated small or imagined faults of the Duchess. For example, lines 21–25 show that he was too critical. In his opinion it was undignified for his wife to be happy over small things that pleased her. Or, it was terrible for her to have some varied interests that the Duke didn't have.

Also, I thought the Duke was possessive. He liked to show off his beloved painting even though he was critical of the subject. He did not seem to think of the Duchess as a person in her own right. The Duke also called attention to a bronze statue.

He was also domineering, in my opinion. For example, in line 45 he says, "I gave commands. Then all smiles stopped together." It is not clear whether she stopped smiling long before she died through his having made her unhappy, or whether the smiles were stopped by death.

The Duke was proud. In line 33, he spoke of his "gift of a nine-hundred-year-old name." He did not speak of any "gift" the Duchess gave to him. She was obviously a warm-hearted, kind and gracious lady. But he did not appreciate these qualities.

He thought he was always right. But this was not so, since he missed the good qualities of the Duchess.

Also, he thought he was fair-minded and generous. In lines 49–51, he indicated that he was not greatly interested in a dowry. Actually, he probably thought he was great; because he was never wrong he deserved a big dowry.

The Duke fancied himself as being a bit democratic! He permitted the envoy to walk beside him downstairs. But taking his arrogant behavior into account, he probably looked down on the envoy.

In conclusion, I think the Duke was one mess of a character. He was critical, self-righteous possessive, domineering, and proud. The Duke thought of himself as always being right and fair-minded.

## Writing Assignment One
## Comment on Sample 2. Grade: Average

A hasty reading suggests that this student paid no attention to the assignment's demand for a consideration of tone and diction as indicators of what the Duke thinks of himself and of what the reader is to think of him. It is probable, though, that the student thinks he has at least done his duty by diction in speaking constantly of *what* the Duke says. But there is no attempt here to deal with *how* the character says what he has to say. The strengths that put this paper into the ***average*** category are the correctness and clarity of the writing, the tidiness of the organization, and the accuracy of the assumptions. The student sees the Duke as critical, possessive, domineering, and proud. And certainly the text supplies abundant evidence of these qualities although the student has availed himself of only a small portion of this evidence. He also supports, but not liberally, his accurate contention that the Duke pictures himself as always right, fair-minded, and even a bit democratic. The general plan of organization, the nine tiny paragraphs, and the obvious paragraph transitions all suggest the uncomplicatedness of the mind at work in this paper.

## Writing Assignment One
## Sample 3. Grade: Low

*My Last Duchess*
*by Robert Browning*

In this poem the Duke plays an important role, for he is the person who carries the action throughout the whole of the poem.

The Duke as he sees himself is loyal, humble, and loving, but the picture that he transfers to the reader is one of a completely different nature. The reader pictures the Duke as a selfish, proud, man, who gets everything he wants, and if something should get in his way; he rebels.

As the story progresses I feel that the reader really can't see whether or not he truly loved the Duchess, because in some instances he does, while in others it seems he doesn't.

The Duke portraits himself as a very immature and insecure individual. This is pointed out very clearly by his jealous nature. His wasn't the slight jealousy that comes with true love, but rather a frenzy with him. He felt that if he wasn't the only one that could look upon the Duchess' beauty; he would rid everyone else of the privilege.

The Duke was only concerned with what was for the Duke. He wanted all good thing for himself which he didn't want to share.

The mood in this poem is a fairly pleasant one, while the tone is in some parts melancholy, some parts happy, and still in others it was depressing.

The diction throughout the poem depicts the thoughts with regard to his selfishness, not only for the Duchess but also for wealth and personal satisfaction.

Just by the Duke's actions and revealed thoughts the reader can see his weaknesses, his likes and dislikes. But I, as a reader, feel sorry for the Duke, because of his intense pride and selfishness. Maybe he didn't realize how he was acting. However, I don't feel that the Duke should be completely rejected, because people like him should be pitied rather than put down because these evils probably came about by habit, and everyone has habits whether good or bad.

Therefore the Duke, selfish and thoughtless though he was, played a main role in this poem, and without him the poem wouldn't have had any meaning.

## Writing Assignment One
## Comment on Sample 3. Grade: Low

It is, perhaps, unfair to compare an eleventh grade paper with two twelfth grade ones, especially on an assignment that the readers agreed belongs at the twelfth grade level; but the defects here seem to stem from incompetence rather than from immaturity. In two ways this paper is inferior to the *average* one. First, the generalizations go unsupported, the valid as well as the dubious ones. Second, the paper lacks accurate writing skills. The next to last paragraph makes an abortive effort to whitewash the Duke's character by claiming that his sinister qualities "probably came about by habit, and everyone has habits whether good or bad." An illogical "Therefore" ushers in the self-evident final statement.

## Writing Assignment Two
## Sample 1. Grade: High

In "My Last Duchess", by Robert Browning, the aristocratic Italian duke, the speaker of the dramatic monologue, obviously thinks of all other human beings as instruments to be used for his pleasure. In his egoistical, egotistical world, he is not happy unless he is the center of all attentions. This attitude can be seen in his total ignorance and neglect of the feelings of his late wife. He has no warmth or love for her; he wants her to be cold, haughty, grateful for his gift of a name—not a warm, loving wife.

He considers marriage a social necessity, to be conducted in a business-like and properly unemotional manner. This feeling of transacting a business deal is emphasized in the sentence: "I repeat/ The Count your Master's known munificence/ Is ample warrant that no just pretense/ Of mine for dowry will be disallowed". It is apparent that the Duke sees nothing unacceptable or inconsiderate in his statements—rather, he feels his attitude is quite acceptable. He is not deliberately cruel—it just never occurs to him to consider anybody else. There is a transition in tone when the Duke makes the statement quoted above. The reader feels in the abrupt change that he is shutting the door on any further discussion of his wife, again showing his absolute authority. He assumes a colder, louder tone, as if picking up the conversation after a parenthetical digression about his wife. His words show his unemotional properness and business-like attitude. Instead of saying merely, "I confess this dowry may play a part in my decision", he uses the most magnificent and diplomatic language, to demonstrate his position. He then changes the subject again, as if to prove that brides and dowries are beneath him.

By his language and the transition in tone produced by the language, the Duke ends the conversation about his wife with finality, assumes a new, brisker tone to show, perhaps unconsciously, that the feelings of his future wife and even his future wife herself are not vitally important to him, and proves again his very self-centered, selfish attitude.

## Writing Assignment Two
## Comment on Sample 1. Grade: High

Admittedly this is a tough assignment addressed only to the sophisticated twelfth grader. Even this paper slips into near irrelevance in its first paragraph with the obvious reminder that the Duke is egotistical and heartless in his relations with others. If the student had heeded the request for a single paragraph, he could easily have dispensed with his first paragraph, condensing his third paragraph and fusing it with the second. Nevertheless, this paper does a sensitive job of analyzing the transition in tone and describing it as suggesting that the Duke was "picking up the conversation after a parenthetical digression about his wife." The writer notes here the brisker tone and the "business-like attitude" but notes also the "most magnificent and diplomatic language" that the Duke employs to make his position clear. An abler student would have sensed the apparent inconsistency between the magnificent diplomatic language and the brisk, business-like tone, and would then have set about reconciling them. But this student's mere awareness that all these elements mingle in the Duke's tone is probably evidence of unusual perceptiveness. What even this student misses, though, in the Duke's tone is the unctuousness that cloaks the sinister implications noted in the final paragraph of this paper.

## Writing Assignment Two
## Sample 2. Grade: Average

The poem *My Last Duchess* has a tone which changes and intensifies from the beginning on. The Duke's first words are casual—"That's my las Duchess painted on the wall". He is simply telling his visitor about the picture of his last wife. As he goes on speaking, the Duke becomes more emotionally involved in his description of the Duchess' behavior. He is insulted by the fact that she seemed to treat his "gift of a nine-hundred years old name/With anybody's gift." He speaks of considering himself above stooping to tell his wife of her offensive behavior, but instead gives order that she change. By the line—"This grew; I gave commands;/Then all smiles stopped together"—we can see a tone of anger and offended pride on the Duke's part. The emotional intensity of tone at this point is high. The tone, however, then relaxes with the words concerning the dowry. The words "munificence", "warrent", "pretense", all sound very businesslike; the Duke has reverted to his greed for money, a kind of greed that we have already seen in relation to his wife's attentions. It is obvious, though the Duke denies the fact, that his interest in the Count's daughter stems from the size of her dowry. Whether wrapped in emotion, or casually handling monetary business, we see selfishness as the Duke's outstanding characteristic.

## Writing Assignment Two
## Comment on Sample 2. Grade Average

This student uses three quarters of the paper for a preliminary exploration of the shifts in tone throughout the poem up to the passage in question. When he finally comes to terms with the passage itself, he sees a relaxation of tone as the Duke shifts to money matters—an observation that may well be valid but needs amplification and justification. The writer then cites " 'munificense', 'warrent', 'pretense' " as evidence of the "businesslike" tone. A subtler comment would have noted that this overblown language serves as a delicate wrapping for the ugliness of the money motif. The first paper notes the grandiloquence of the "diplomatic language." This student stops short of any such insight, though he recognizes that the Duke's main interest is in the size of the dowry.

## Writing Assignment Two
## Sample 3. Grade: Low

In the poem, "My Last Duchess", the Duke has killed or done away with last wife. During his romance with his last wife, the Duke laid laws on what his wife could do when around other people. He was very jealous of her. Once she smiled at a man, and the Duke got mad and had her done away. Now there is only her picture in which he remembers her by. In the lines, "I repeat, The Count your Master's known munificence Is ample warrent that no just pretense of mine for dowry will be disallowed;" the Duke is getting set to marry another women and tells the go between what he wants of her and that she must obey him. The tone of this poem changes from the first, when he is telling of how bad is first wife was, to when he is telling the go between how good he is.

## Writing Assignment Two
## Comment on Sample 3. Grade: Low

The readers chose this sample to demonstrate their point that this assignment is a waste of time except for the able and sophisticated twelfth grader. This paper combines feeble content with a juvenile style and a liberal sprinkling of crude errors in mechanics. The student merely supplies a summary of what happens in the poem, with a halfhearted nod in the direction of the assignment.

*Dylan Thomas: "Fern Hill"*
*Grades 11 and 12*

Golden in the heydays of his eyes,
And honoured among wagons I was prince of the apple towns
And once below a time I lordly had the trees and leaves
Trail with daisies and barley
Down the rivers of the windfall light.

And as I was green and carefree, famous among the barns
About the happy yard and singing as the farm was home,
In the sun that is young once only,
Time let me play and be
Golden in the mercy of his means,
And green and golden I was huntsman and herdsman, the calves
Sang to my horn, the foxes on the hills barked clear and cold,
And the sabbath rang slowly
In the pebbles of the holy streams.

All the sun long it was running, it was lovely, the hay-
Fields high as the house, the tunes from the chimneys, it was air
And playing, lovely and watery
And fire green as grass.
And nightly under the simple stars
As I rode to sleep the owls were bearing the farm away,
All the moon long I heard, blessed among stables, the night-jars
Flying with the ricks, and the horses
Flashing into the dark.

And then to awake, and the farm, like a wanderer white
With the dew, come back, the cock on his shoulder: it was all
Shining, it was Adam and maiden,
The sky gathered again
And the sun grew round that very day.
So it must have been after the birth of the simple light
In the first, spinning place, the spellbound horses walking warm
Out of the whinnying green stable
On to the fields of praise.

And honoured among foxes and pheasants by the gay house
Under the new made clouds and happy as the heart was long,
In the sun born over and over,
I ran my heedless ways,
My wishes raced through the house-high hay
And nothing I cared, at my sky blue trades, that time allows
In all his tuneful turning so few and such morning songs
Before the children green and golden
Follow him out of grace,

Nothing I cared, in the lamb white days, that time would take me
Up to the swallow-thronged loft by the shadow of my hand,
In the moon that is always rising,
Nor that riding to sleep
I should hear him fly with the high fields
And wake to the farm forever fled from the childless land.
Oh as I was young and easy in the mercy of his means,
Time held me green and dying
Though I sang in my chains like the sea.

---

3. *dingle:* small wooded valley
8. *daisies and barley:* common decorations in Welsh harvest festival
25. *night-jars:* night birds
26. *ricks:* haystacks

## Questions for Discussion

1. Who is the speaker in this poem? Why does he speak in the past tense throughout the poem and in what kind of tone does he speak?

2. What uses does the poet make of the two colors "green" and "gold" in the course of the poem? (You will find the word "green" in lines 2, 10, 15, 22, 35, 44, and 53. The word "golden" occurs in lines 5, 14, 15, and 44.) In your consideration of Thomas's uses of these two color words, you may find that the poem

# *Dylan Thomas: "Fern Hill"*
# *Grades 11 and 12*

## To the Teacher

A superficial exposure to the torrential flow of Dylan Thomas's poetry is likely to leave a student vastly more aware of the liberties the poet is taking with language than of the discipline he is imposing upon it. Interpretation, then, in the student's eyes, becomes a free-for-all where anything goes. A searching exploration, however, of such a poem as "Fern Hill" should dissipate all notion that Thomas is indulging in a spree of ungoverned emotion. The deeper the exploration the more impressive is the evidence of order, structure, sequence, and pattern. Nothing in "Fern Hill" is random though at first reading the poem may sound like a spontaneous outburst. Nor can interpretation be random, for although flexibility and associative value characterize poetic language, especially in such a poem as this, the poet, by his infinitely painstaking selection of exact diction and carefully patterned structure, sets limits to his meanings. The reader's job is to sense those limits, to accept the text itself as the final court of appeal, and to recognize that a good poem yields its wealth of meaning only to the most patient, responsible, sensitive reading the reader can give it. The questions that follow are designed to help the student in that kind of patient, sensitive, and responsible reading. He should have these questions to work with on his own before any class discussion takes place, and he should hear a good oral reading of the poem by a selected student, by the teacher, or, if possible, by the poet himself (Caedmon record TC1002, Houghton Mifflin, Boston).

### *Fern Hill*

Dylan Thomas

Now as I was young and easy under the apple boughs
About the lilting house and happy as the grass was
        green,
    The night above the dingle starry,
        Time let me hail and climb

"Nothing Gold Can Stay," by Robert Frost, is helpful.

*Nothing Gold Can Stay*
Robert Frost

Nature's first green is gold,
Her hardest hue to hold.
Her early leaf's a flower;
But only so an hour.
Then leaf subsides to leaf.
So Eden sank to grief,
So dawn goes down to day.
Nothing gold can stay.

3. How do you interpret the phrase "lamb white days" in line 46? What shades of meaning would have been lost if the writer had written "snow white" instead of "lamb white"? What new shades of meaning would be introduced?

4. The speaker's conception of time pervades the entire poem. Do time's characteristics change in the course of the poem or only the speaker's concept of them? In arriving at your answer examine lines 4–5; lines 13–14; lines 41–45; lines 46–47; line 50; and lines 53–54. Before reaching any final answer you may want to explore questions 6, 7, 8, and 9 below, since these questions also deal with the role of time in the poem.

5. What familiar sayings about time has the poet used in lines 7, 19, and 50? By what means does he give freshness to their familiarity?

6. In what way is the passing of time associated with night and sleep? In line 24 why does the speaker say that he "rode to sleep" rather than "fell asleep"? In line 49 is he talking about the same kind of "sleep" and the same kind of "riding"? How do "night-jars / Flying with the ricks" and "horses / Flashing into the dark" (lines 25–27) reinforce the idea of the passing of time?

7. In what sense does time lead "the children green and golden . . . out of grace" (lines 44–45)? What does "grace" mean here and is there any synonym that could adequately replace it? (For this you will need to consult your dictionary.) What story-book character is time being likened to, by implication, in the description of his leading "the children . . . out of grace"? In what ways is this comparison appropriate?

8. What are the "chains" in the last line, and what is the effect of the simile "like the sea"?

9. The poem at several points touches upon the theme of awakening, a theme closely connected with the treatment of time. With what does the speaker compare waking after sleep in lines 28–36? By what details does he develop this comparison? Is the comparison valid and appropriate? Would this comparison be as effective if the poet had chosen an urban instead of a rural setting?

10. What kind of "waking" is the speaker talking about in line 51? Why had "the farm forever fled from the childless land"? Why was the farm "childless"? What connection is there between this "waking" and the allusion to "Adam and maiden" in line 30?

11. Poetry is for both the ear and the eye. Without actually rereading the poem, take a look at the appearance of each of the six printed stanzas. What does your eye tell you about the patterning, the shape of these stanzas? Now try reading one of them aloud. What does your ear tell you that your eye could not detect?

12. Further evidence of the pains Thomas has taken with the form of this poem is the rich use of repetition with variation. You have already discovered some examples of this device in your exploration of the poet's uses of "green" and "gold." What other examples do you find? What does each add to the poem?

13. What liberties has the poet taken with diction, syntax, and sentence structure? What effects does he achieve by such devices?

## Writing Assignments

Each of the following assignments calls for a carefully planned paper written outside the classroom with plenty of time for revision, rewriting, and proofreading. Each student should write on only *one* of these assignments.

### Writing Assignment One

"Fern Hill" might be considered as a kind of initiation poem, a discovery of one's own nature in relation to the world about one. Compare and contrast the treatment of this theme in "Fern Hill" with that of a prose work such as "The Garden Party," by Katherine Mansfield; "The Silver Horn," by Thomas Sancton; or "Sophistication," from *Winesburg, Ohio,* by Sherwood Anderson.

### Writing Assignment Two

Compare the poet's treatment of a similar theme in his poem "The Force That Through the Green Fuse Drives the Flower." Comment fully on the poetic devices, language, structure, and allusions in developing your comparison.

## Writing Assignment One
## Sample 1. Grade: High

OUT OF THE GARDEN

The naïveté, simplicity, and joy of childhood that one must leave behind with the passing of time and the gaining of experience and knowledge is portrayed by two twentieth-century British writers, Dylan Thomas and Katherine Mansfield, in the poem "Fern Hill", by Thomas, and the short story "The Garden Party", by Miss Mansfield. "Fern Hill" emphasizes the bondage of time, from which the innocence of green and golden youth and even its beautifully expressed memory is an escape. "The Garden Party" shows that the unclouded joy of the young must pass and should give way to a deeper "sympathy" and understanding of life's complexity, its pain, and its possibilities of beauty.

Both pieces use the image of the garden for youth. In "Fern Hill" the poet as a boy is "young and easy under the apple boughs", "it was all/Shining, it was Adam and maiden". The image is that of the Garden of Eden, "that first spinning place", but the simple, homey apple tree is there too. In "The Garden Party" Laura is the daughter of a wealthy family who own a garden full of green grass, lilies (a symbol of purity), fragrant lavendar, splendid exotic kanakas, and, under a golden-hazed, cloudless sky, green bushes "bowed down as though they had been visited by archangels". The happy young boy at Fern Hill loves the "morning songs", when the sun is born over and over and seems to grow round for the first time each day. The sun makes everything green and golden, but it is the sun that is his chains, for it marks the passage of time. Time mercifully allows him the green and the gold, but it holds him "green and dying", though he sings "in his chains like the sea". The sun, the moon, and Time allow him and the sea an innocent, naive joy. In the same way, that which gives Laura joy leads her out of the joyful but shallow attitude of youth. She loves the garden and the party, the "happiness it is to be with people who are all happy, to press hands, press cheeks, smile into eyes". She enjoys the workmen who come to set up the marquee, finding them friendly, easy, and cheerful. She loves her large, gay family too. When she hears of the death of a workman who lives nearby, she is suddenly catapulted into a situation where attitudes and decisions are complex, and upsetting. In sympathy, she tries to get the party put off, but runs into opposition from her mother, a woman who still has the attitudes of childhood, defining sympathy as not ruining anyone's enjoyment. Experiencing ambivalence, Laura finds herself talked into enjoying the party, but she has had the experience of having a feeling different from the rest of her family. When she takes a basket of food to the widow, she sees in the dead man one who was marvelous and beautiful, *beyond* garden parties and lace frocks, and finds that a deeper contentment can come than the frivolous joy of childishness. Life is so much more than she thought it could be, that she cannot begin to express herself. An echo of youth's inability to express what life is is the line in "Fern Hill", "All the day long it was running, it was lovely . . ."; a vague word like "lovely" often is the best one that will come out in such a case.

A major difference between the two points of view is that the boy is alone in his garden while Laura is surrounded by others. One reason is that the boy is probably younger. Looking back, the poet sees himself as "prince of the apple towns", "blessed among stables", and "famous among the barns". The comparison to Adam shows the glory Thomas felt as a child, alive, loving the night and the day of the farm. Laura, as an adolescent, feels the interaction of other people strongly. She too is lordly, though, directing the workmen, and alone in her idea of sympathy and her discovery of new values. Noticing and loving the spots of sun and the air she is alone. As a new adult and yet as a child still, she finds comfort in the sympathy and understanding of her brother.

## Writing Assignment One
## Comment on Sample 1. Grade: High

This student had the advantage of having chosen Katherine Mansfield's "The Garden Party," a work adapted to this assignment. The choice of title for the paper is an indication of this student's astuteness in spotting significant links between "Fern Hill" and "The Garden Party," and as the paper progresses the reader realizes that the figurative garden is the center of the comparison. The directness of the opening sentence is an immediate indication of the writer's competence in spite of the singular verb for the plural subject—a lapse occurring again in the second sentence and about the only technical weakness in an otherwise correctly written paper. The strengths that put this paper into the *high* bracket are its tightly interwoven comparative organization, its skillful shuttling between illuminating generalization and firmly supporting illustration, its precise diction and controlled sentence structure, and its discerning penetration of both the poem and the story without ever doing violence to the text except possibly in the assertion that Laura "too is lordly" in her direction of the workmen, whereas, in fact, she is too unsure of herself to issue orders and can only acquiesce in the "royal suggestions" of the workmen.

## Writing Assignment One
## Sample 2. Grade: Average

*"Fern Hill" Compared With "The Garden Party"*

Dylan Thomas' "Fern Hill" and Katherine Mansfield's "The Garden Party" are concerned with like subjects. Each is expressive of an outlook on life which only youth can enjoy. Only the young are innocent of harsh realities. Youths can search for happiness and find their objective in simple ways. A deep joy of living is prevalent in the mind of the carefree youth; to the giver of life a sense of gratitude for the irreplaceable gift of vitality is felt. The young person is concerned with the present, for worry of the future is non-existant in his mind. Thus, there is a farm boy who found great pleasure in the participation of simple activities: riding a wagon of apples to market, viewing daisies, running about the hills and farms, and settling into a deep sleep after a tiring, yet always lovely, day. Laura Sheridan of "The Garden Party" finds great enjoyment when she plans an afternoon party with a marquee, beautiful flowers, and delightful food. She is very pleased with a new hat, a spontaneous gift from her mother. Laura, like the youth of "Fern Hill", has an innocent love of a simple life.

"Fern Hill" and "The Garden Party" differ in one respect. The youth of "Fern Hill" is apparently unaware of any life but that of a carefree boy. Responsibility is not present in his limited world, nor has tragedy shown itself in any form. Laura Sheridan, however, is exposed to a grim reality of the world: the death of a man who is a neighbor. She is introduced to the idea, but it is only after her afternoon of gaiety that the meaning of tragedy is fully comprehended by her. When she discovers real grief, she finds that life is not what she had thought it to be, and Laura is no longer a child living in a world of unreality. The reader is not told when the youth of "Fern Hill" discovers a life which differs from that which was familiar to him on the farm. The time of the metamorphosis is not important, however. Dylan Thomas is nostalgic of that time prior to the young boy's awakening; Katherine Mansfield is telling of an awakening. Both deal with the child's worry-free dream world of bliss. In both cases a child has passed out of naïveté and into knowledge, necessarily, with time. Each feels the pain of growing and, especially, its meaning; in each case the author has expressed it extremely well.

## Writing Assignment One
## Comment on Sample 2. Grade: Average

The writing in this paper is quite competent, and the content accurate as far as it goes. The title is clear but prosaic. The writer is seldom inaccurate, but he is simply incapable of the depth and maturity of understanding shown in the previous paper. This paper, also, does not recognize fully the changing attitude toward time, in the speaker of "Fern Hill," and does not attempt to differentiate between his carefree world and Laura's—which is not precisely "a simple life." On the whole, a solid performance without distinction; a good *average.*

## Writing Assignment One
## Sample 3. Grade: Low

*A Comparative Analysis of "Fern Hill"*

"Fern Hill" by Dylan Thomas is a man's self analysis. The man now past the prime of his life objectively views his past life and comes to a conclusion striking by like the theme of "The Garden Party" by Katherine Mansfield.

"The Garden Party" is the story of a young girl, Laura, whose life is somewhat changed by the death of a poverty stricken neighbor.

In "Fern Hill" the poem's subject reflects on his past life and sees that he lived it carefreely and carlessly giving no thought to the time when he would grow old. Several lines in the first stanza verify this assumption. ". . . I was young and *easy* under the apple boughs . . ./ Time let me hail and climb / Golden in the heydays of his eyes,." Now that he is mature he realizes the futility of what he had accomplished in his playing as time past. The lines "All the sun long it was running . . . / As I rode to sleep the owls were bearing the farm away," give evidence to show that he now realized how foolish he had been. Perhaps even as a young person he realized or partly realized what he was actually doing, but did not care. Such may be assumed from lined found after those just sited. He stated that after his sleep he would awake "and the farm . . . comeback, the cock on his shoulder. In his sleep he had seen what was happening but chose not to recognize his weakness when he waked.

In viewing both this poem and "The Garden Party at this point we find a intrusting and a similar situation. Not as in "Fern Hill," in "The Garden Party" the story's main character is still young with all of her life to still look forward to. In one the main character is fairly old in the other it is young, but in each they are seeking themselves. A simielarity may be noted in that in "The Garden Party" Laura wanted to call off the big event in her life, her garden party when she found out about her neighbors death. Here she is given a brief sight of her real self as the man in Fern Hill is when he was asleep; however—she chooses to push it aside in favor of having the garden party just as the man in "Fern Hill refused to recognize what he saw.

As the theme in "Fern Hill" is developed, the man finally comes to realize that he has wasted a good part of his life and thus finds himself in regards to his destiny. This can be easily seen in the last stanza when he says, "Nothing I cared . . . that time would take me/ Nor that riding to sleep/I should hear him fly with the fields/ And wake to the farm forever fled . . ." Indeed he had found himself, but his cognizance of his foolishness had come too late.

Laura in "The Garden Party finds herself too. When she was forced to look upon the dead body of her neighbor she got an insight into life, but unlike in "Fern Hill," the realization determined her future destiny because she still had all of life to look forward to.

## Writing Assignment One
## Comment on Sample 3. Grade: Low

This student shows some comprehension of the similarities and contrasts between the poem and the story. Moreover, he tries to bring in apt quotations to support his statements, a praiseworthy effort. But his picture of the speaker in "Fern Hill" as a man "past the prime of his life" whose "cognizance of his foolishness had come too late" hardly jibes with the speaker's genuine joy in remembering the carefree, golden days of boyhood. Furthermore, we don't know what will happen to Laura Sheridan in later life—but to this student it is clear that "the realization determined her future destiny because she still had all of life to look forward to." These errors, plus doubt that his quotations actually do support the student's statements, plus occasional technical errors, seem to justify a grade of *low*.

## Writing Assignment Two
## Sample 1. Grade: High

*"Green and Dying:" Recognition of Time in Two Poems by Dylan Thomas*

In "Fern Hill" and "The Force That Through the Green Fuse Drives the Flower," Dylan Thomas has developed themes that are similar but not identical. Both poems consider growing older and the passage of time. "Fern Hill" deals with childhood and its ending; it is gay and lively, although it is shadowed by the poet's present recognition of the evanescence of his boyhood. ". . . Green Fuse . . .", which, somewhat differently, is about the recognition of nature's destroying force, dwells upon death and decay; Thomas, who has often managed to sound like a transcendentalist Bob Dylan, has created a more sombre mood.

The first of these two poems reflects happiness, both past happiness and present participation by remembrance of it, tinged by the knowledge that it was not to last. The second is resigned rather than despairing; it admits the poet's inevitable death, his present death through recognition of what is to come (for all of life, in a sense, is one and takes place at once), and his present progress toward that death. In "Fern Hill" he is glad master of the glorious springtime world—or was, for he is a boy no longer. In "Green Fuse" he is one with nature, of nature, bent like the rose and destroyed by the same forces as move the water and nourish the worm. Both poems are faithful to the truth of humanity, the truth of aging, loss, longing, acceptance, and learning. Perhaps they reflect the thoughts of the same man looking back and then forward.

Each of the two poems has unity of mood, and each changes—"Fern Hill" in idea, "Green Fuse" in form—in the last stanza. "Fern Hill" has irregular rhyme and "Green Fuse", some false rhyme:

The force that drives the water through the rocks
. . . . .
How at the mountain spring the same mouth sucks.

More important is the strong rhythm, found in both works, which is so characteristic of Dylan Thomas. Consistent with the differing emphases of the poems, the rhythm of each gives a distinct impression. "Fern Hill" is lilting; "Green Fuse" states calmly. "Fern Hill" has the feeling of quick, forward motion, while the meter of "Green Fuse" is a measured tread. This heightens the contrast between youth and maturity. Thus the last few lines of "fern Hill," in which the recognition is stated, are more sombre than the rest of the poem.

Oh as I was young and easy in the mercy of his means,
Time held me green and dying
Though I sang in my chains like the sea.

The color green and the idea of being an unrecognizing prisoner of time are repeated throughout the first poem. In the second, in which a quiet acceptance is manifest, the mute, inarticulate knowledge of the poet's decay, of his union with all things decaying, as expressed in the lines

And I am dumb to tell the hanging man
How of my clay is made the hangman's line.

is used almost as a refrain:

And I am dumb to tell . . .

Although the language of "Fern Hill" and "Green Fuse" is as different as are gold, sunlight, and ferns from quicksand and fallen blood, both contain metaphors, symbolism, characteristic alliteration, and personifications. Both are constructed with an amazing parallelism. In "Fern Hill", "All the sun long" is followed seven lines later by "All the moon long;" the owls fly away with the farm as does time. "In the sun born over and over" becomes "In the moon that is always rising". Thomas changes the significance of "green" and youth from

Now as I was young and easy under the apple boughs
About the lilting house and happy as the grass was green

to

Time held me green and dying
Though I sang in my chains like the sea.

In "Green Fuse", the poet has used a refrain and the same pattern of lines to give continuity and a certain resignation to the poem. The relation of shroud, sail, and sheet is developed.

The hand. . . .
. . . .that ropes the blowing wind
Hauls my shroud sail.
. . . . . .
And I am dumb to tell the lover's tomb
How at my sheet goes the same crooked worm.

In contrast to the main thought of "Fern Hill", his youth, here, like the "crooked rose", is "bent" by the "wintry fever". Personification is evidenced by two lines, one from each poem:

Love drips and gathers.
Time let me hail and climb.

Thomas has made two skilfully structured poems, each of which is consistent within a different mood. "Fern Hill" is a celebration of youth, green and golden in its words and its meaning, for the boy is no less joyous for the unexpected brevity of his boyhood. "The Force That Through the Green Fuse Drives the Flower" anticipates time's injuries and sees union with all of the world, especially the material world of which the poet will become a physical part in the cycle of life, death, and decay. It is beautiful in its restraint of passion and its acceptance of the inevitable.

## Writing Assignment Two
## Comment on Sample 1. Grade: High

This student handles language with economy, precision, and grace. His sentences are the product of a master-builder. The first paragraph, with its tight comparative organization, its sharp diction, and its easy control of sentence length and sentence rhythm, is an achievement. What follows is no letdown.

Here is a student who has mastered the art of comparing and contrasting not only in every paragraph but even in almost every pair of adjoining sentences, and with no such obvious bits of verbal mucilage as "on the other hand" or "however" planted at the beginning of the sentence. The skillful fusion of the general and the particular is a further indication of linguistic sophistication. Nor does the writer ever thrust a quotation naked at the reader. Always he wraps it in the structure of the sentence in which it occurs, and there it rests so easily that only the quotation marks or the indentations remind the reader that it is not the student's own.

The content is impressive on all counts. The carefully measured judgments and the good taste that protects the writer from irrelevant or unwarranted subjectivity, except for the reference to Bob Dylan, are further indications of an exceptionally strong paper.

## Writing Assignment Two
## Sample 2. Grade: Average

Dylan Thomas has used a similar theme in two of his works, "Fern Hill" and "the force that through the green fuse drives the flower". He has tried to show his close communication with nature. He is almost a part of it, as he is trying to tell us by his use of language, poetic devices, and structure.

The author has used several poetic devices, one of which is metonomy. In "Fern Hill" he is trying to describe where he had so much fun and enjoyment as a child which was, "under the apple boughs". He must have spent hours under the trees playing, and in the trees being lord and master over all he could see, perhaps in a treehouse he had built. The many references of golden are very youthful. He is young and carefree, and enjoys being out in the sun. The sun means happy times to a boy, because he can then be outside playing. Dylan Thomas has also used metonomy in "the force". He speaks of a green fuse. This is a flower stem of the plant, through which the flower must go to bloom. The water is not just being through any rocks, it is being pushed down mountains, along stream beds, and through fields. The meaning is much larger than it appears to be.

The author has tried to carry over his feeling for nature by his use of color. In "the force" the stem of the flower is green, of course. But then life is also labled the same way. It must mean that age is alive and growing, and something beautiful, not to be thought of in a vegetative, passive way. In "Fern Hill" Dylan Thomas was "green and carefree". He has used the color to describe the boy, green and growing, learning, and having fun.

There are four main topics in "the force". Earth, air, fire, and water make this a chemic poem. The force is related to each one of the four elements. Dylan Thomas has used nature to bring out the feeling in "Fern Hill", but not as specifically. He has used the orchard, the sun, the farm, and animals. each one of these is further describing his youthful feeling and exhuberance.

The physical structure of the two poems is basically the same. Each has the shape of an hourglass. Each stanza in "Fern Hill" has nine lines, the first seven of which produce the hourglass effect. The first two lines in each have a total of twenty-eight sylables. The next three have fifteen, and can be considered to be the neck of the glass. Lines six and seven have a total of twenty-eight, which could be the base. The first four stanzas of "the force" each have five lines. The hourglass is even more gradual than in the other. The lines have lenghs of eleven, ten, four, ten, and eleven respectively. The hourglass is the symbol of time, which is constantly running. When a person is young he has much time that he could, in Dylan Thomas' case, devote to the enjoyment of nature. Youth seems to have been made for that purpose. This then implies that middle age is not a time for appreciation but for more materialistic things, but then there is plenty of time as the end of life draws near.

Dylan Thomas has a similar theme, and he has shown it quite well in his structure and usage. These methods have bound the two poems together, producing a deeper, more complete meaning.

## Writing Assignment Two
## Comment on Sample 2. Grade: Average

The mind revealed in this paper moves in a world of the obvious and the uncomplicated, but this is not exactly Dylan Thomas's world. The writing is unexcitingly decent. The organization is neat, obvious, and perfunctory. Transitions call attention to themselves. The initial assertion that the similar theme in the two poems is Thomas's "close communication with nature" is too broad to be vulnerable. The naïveté, the pedestrian accuracy, and the flair for the obvious that permeate all parts of this paper but one are all apparent in this section of paragraph two:

"The many references of golden are very youthful. He is young and carefree, and enjoys being out in the sun. The sun means happy times to a boy, because he can then be outside playing."

The one part of the paper that is out of key with the rest is paragraph five, which explores "The physical structure of the two poems" in terms of their alleged visual resemblance to an hour glass. The glib knowledgeableness of this section comes as a surprise to the reader unless he knows that other students from the same school talked at length and in similar terms about the hour glass. The concluding paragraph subsides into the tame obviousness that dulls the first four paragraphs.

## Writing Assignment Two
## Sample 3. Grade: Low

The poetic devices are somewhat similar since they both arise images. But the manner in which these images are impressed is different. The main device in Fern Hill is the use similies. In the Force that threw the green fuse drives the flower the sensation of images is introduced through irony and the use of personification. The structure of these two poems is based on the same theme of time and are constructed with informative color words both of which stress youth and the innocents. The structure can be very closely linked because many of the same impressionistic words are used in both poems; bearing of course the same thought. The whole spoken and written body of words and method of combining words in these two poems flow from one source and thus reflect a single classified language. The language is truly stricking because it holds deep meaning throughout the context. The language fits the setting since in both it completes the air of time. The language also ties the mixture of nature in full to motivated times. But the success of these poems and fine importance flows through the allusions. Both of these poems function on youth and this love of youth for time. In Fern Hill the poem in composed in the past tense looking on time as a master. The Lord is the dominating person. Giving good to the young share freedom and brings innocents since the young are all good and since are free and unaware of evil. In the Force that threw the green fuse drives the Flower. Is a poem written in the present tense. Show time moving building knowledge in the foundated innocent. This poem is at present and as such bears a duel fight within the man. Life is innocent and as time flows so to does life until verses death. Growth in Life brings information and deals with a revolving function throughout both of these poems.

## Writing Assignment Two
## Comment on Sample 3. Grade: Low

The readers chose this not merely as an example of illiterate writing but as a prime illustration of the weak student's addiction to assertion without proof and to generalization without illustration. The terms "irony," "simile," "personification," and "impressionistic words" jostle one another without a single example of any one of the four. No illustrations attach to such a statement as "The language is truly stricking because it holds deep meaning throughout the context." The latter part of the paper degenerates into incoherence occasionally penetrated by faint glimmerings of insight as in the recognition that "Fern Hill" deals with the past and "The Force" with the present.

*T. S. Eliot:*
*"The Love Song of J. Alfred Prufrock"*
*Grade 12*

Of insidious intent
To lead you to an overwhelming question . . .
Oh, do not ask, "What is it?"
Let us go and make our visit.

In the room the women come and go
Talking of Michelangelo.

The yellow fog that rubs its back upon the window-panes,
The yellow smoke that rubs its muzzle on the windowpanes
Licked its tongue into the corners of the evening,
Lingered upon the pools that stand in drains,
Let fall upon its back the soot that falls from chimneys,
Slipped by the terrace, made a sudden leap,
And seeing that it was a soft October night,
Curled once about the house, and fell asleep.

And indeed there will be time
For the yellow smoke that slides along the street,
Rubbing its back upon the windowpanes;
There will be time, there will be time
To prepare a face to meet the faces that you meet;
There will be time to murder and create,
And time for all the works and days of hands
That lift and drop a question on your plate;
Time for you and time for me,
And time yet for a hundred indecisions,
And for a hundred visions and revisions,
Before the taking of a toast and tea.

In the room the women come and go
Talking of Michelangelo.

And indeed there will be time
To wonder, "Do I dare?" and, "Do I dare?"
Time to turn back and descend the stair,
With a bald spot in the middle of my hair—
(They will say: "How his hair is growing thin!")
My morning coat, my collar mounting firmly to the chin,
My necktie rich and modest, but asserted by a simple pin—
(They will say: "But how his arms and legs are thin!")
Do I dare
Disturb the universe?
In a minute there is time
For decisions and revisions which a minute will reverse.

For I have known them all already, known them all—
Have known the evenings, mornings, afternoons,
I have measured out my life with coffee spoons;
I know the voices dying with a dying fall
Beneath the music from a farther room.
So how should I presume?
And I have known the eyes already, known them all—
The eyes that fix you in a formulated phrase,
And when I am formulated, sprawling on a pin,
When I am pinned and wriggling on the wall,
Then how should I begin
To spit out all the butt-ends of my days and ways?
And how should I presume?

And I have known the arms already, known them all—
Arms that are braceleted and white and bare
(But in the lamplight, downed with light brown hair!)
Is it perfume from a dress
That makes me so digress?
Arms that lie along a table, or wrap about a shawl.
And should I then presume?
And how should I begin?

. . . . .

Shall I say, I have gone at dusk through narrow streets
And watched the smoke that rises from the pipes
Of lonely men in shirt-sleeves, leaning out of windows? . . .

I should have been a pair of ragged claws
Scuttling across the floors of silent seas.

. . . . .

And the afternoon, the evening, sleeps so peacefully!
Smoothed by long fingers,
Asleep . . . tired . . . or it malingers,

# *T. S. Eliot:*
# *"The Love Song of J. Alfred Prufrock"*
# *Grade 12*

## To the Teacher

Although a comparative examination of Eliot's "Prufrock" and Browning's "My Last Duchess" should prove fruitful, especially with advanced students, the study materials for "Prufrock" do not presuppose the students' prior study of "My Last Duchess." Teachers who choose to use both poems will find that many of the same techniques are used in "My Last Duchess" and Eliot's poem. "Prufrock," too, is a type of dramatic monologue, recording the thoughts and revealing the personality of a character in a modern context and through the stream-of-consciousness device. But because "Prufrock" has its own emotional tone, quite different from that of Browning's poem, and because it is so richly detailed, so charged with subtleties, and so multiply allusive, the study of this poem alone can provide even the ablest twelfth grader with plenty of opportunities for achieving new insights and developing new critical skills.

### *The Love Song of J. Alfred Prufrock*

T. S. Eliot

*S'io credesse che mia risposta fosse*
*A persona che mai tornasse al mondo,*
*Questa fiamma staria senza piu scosse.*
*Ma perciocche giammai di questo fondo*
*Non torno vivo alcun, s'i'odo il vero,*
*Senza tema d'infamia ti rispondo.*[1]

Let us go then, you and I,
When the evening is spread out against the sky
Like a patient etherized upon a table;
Let us go, through certain half-deserted streets,
The muttering retreats
Of restless nights in one-night cheap hotels
And sawdust restaurants with oyster shells:
Streets that follow like a tedious argument

---

1. Dante, *Inferno,* Canto XXVII, lines 61–66.

Stretched on the floor, here beside you and me.
Should I, after tea and cakes and ices,
Have the strength to force the moment to its crisis?
But though I have wept and fasted, wept and prayed,
Though I have seen my head (grown slightly bald) brought in upon a platter,
I am no prophet—and here's no great matter;
I have seen the moment of my greatness flicker,
And I have seen the eternal Footman hold my coat, and snicker,
And in short, I was afraid.

And would it have been worth it, after all,
After the cups, the marmalade, the tea,
Among the porcelain, among some talk of you and me,
Would it have been worth while,
To have bitten off the matter with a smile,
To have squeezed the universe into a ball
To roll it toward some overwhelming question,
To say: "I am Lazarus, come from the dead,
Come back to tell you all, I shall tell you all"—
If one, settling a pillow by her head,
Should say: "That is not what I meant at all.
That is not it, at all."

And would it have been worth it, after all,
Would it have been worth while,
After the sunsets and the dooryards and the sprinkled streets,
After the novels, after the teacups, after the skirts that trail along the floor—
And this, and so much more?—
It is impossible to say just what I mean!
But as if a magic lantern threw the nerves in patterns on a screen:
Would it have been worth while
If one, settling a pillow or throwing off a shawl,
And turning toward the window, should say:
"That is not it at all,
That is not what I meant, at all."

. . . . .

No! I am not Prince Hamlet, nor was meant to be;
Am an attendant lord, one that will do
To swell a progress, start a scene or two,
Advise the prince; no doubt, an easy tool,
Deferential, glad to be of use,
Politic, cautious, and meticulous;
Full of high sentence, but a bit obtuse;
At times, indeed, almost ridiculous—
Almost, at times, the Fool.

I grow old . . . I grow old . . .
I shall wear the bottoms of my trousers rolled.

Shall I part my hair behind? Do I dare to eat a peach?
I shall wear white flannel trousers, and walk upon the beach.
I have heard the mermaids singing, each to each.

I do not think that they will sing to me.

I have seen them riding seaward on the waves
Combing the white hair of the waves blown back
When the wind blows the water white and black.

We have lingered in the chambers of the sea
By sea-girls wreathed with seaweed red and brown
Till human voices wake us, and we drown.

## Notes (for the Use of Teacher and Student)

1. The speaker in the Dante passage is a soul damned in hell to be forever encased in a flame that "quivers" when he speaks. He thinks he is speaking to another damned soul; he does not know that Dante, by special grace, is allowed to journey through hell and return to life with the message of what he has learned. The quote translated reads:

"If I believed that my reply might be to a person who would ever return to the world, this flame would quiver no more; but, inasmuch as no living man ever returns from this depth, if what I hear is true, without fear of infamy, I answer you."

2. The repeated phrase "there will be time," lines 23–48, suggests Ecclesiastes 3:1–8. See also Andrew Marvell's poem "To His Coy Mistress" and note 6 below.

3. The phrase "works and days," line 29, is the title of a poem describing agricultural life by the early Greek poet Hesiod. But what "works and days of hands" is Eliot concerned with in this poem?

4. "Voices dying with a dying fall," line 52, recalls

(ironically) the opening lines of Shakespeare's *Twelfth Night.*

5. Lines 81–82 refer to John the Baptist, whose head was presented on a platter to Salome by Herod as an expression of his pleasure in her dancing. For the full story see Matthew 14:1–11.

6. Line 92 is an echo of the last six lines of Marvell's poem "To His Coy Mistress": "Let us roll all our strength and all / Our sweetness up into one ball, . . ."

7. The mention of Lazarus, lines 94–95, may be a reference to the Lazarus in Luke 16:19–31, a beggar who fed on the crumbs from the rich man's table, but who, when he died, "was carried by angels into Abraham's bosom," whereas the wealthy man ended in hell from where he could see Lazarus in Abraham's bosom while he lay in the torments of hell. The rich man begged that Lazarus be sent back into the world to warn the rich man's brothers about the dangers of hell, but Abraham refused the request. Another possibility is a reference to the other Lazarus, the brother of Mary and Martha, who died but was brought back to life by Christ (John 11:1–44).

8. Lines 111–119, the *Hamlet* passage, are sometimes taken to refer to the "attendant lord" Polonius, but they may also include such sycophants as Rosencrantz and Guildenstern and Osric, whose hollowness is of a piece with that of Polonius. The phrase "To swell a progress" means to be a "stately" extra or stand-in in a rather showy "court scene." In Elizabethan English a "progress" was actually a state journey made by royalty or nobility—what we call a "state visit." (See *Macbeth,* I.3.127–129, and *Henry V* Prologue, 3–4.) The phrase "Full of high sentence" means "sententious." (See "The General Prologue" to Chaucer's *Canterbury Tales,* lines 307–308.)

## Questions for Discussion

1. Look carefully at the name J. Alfred Prufrock. What does each part of the name suggest about the speaker? What impression does the complete name convey?

2. What does the diction that he uses reveal about Prufrock and the background from which he comes?

3. What details of Prufrock's physical appearance does the poem supply? Do these details reinforce the impression the reader has already formed from his name and his diction?

4. What is the occasion, what are the circumstances that prompt Prufrock's soliloquy? In answering this question, make full use of the clues the title provides.

5. What ironies do you detect in Eliot's title?

6. Critics commonly assume that the "you and I" of the poem's first line denote two aspects of the personality of the speaker. If you accept this assumption as valid, then what are these two aspects of Prufrock's character? To which one does "you" refer and to which one does "I" refer? Why do you think so? If you do not accept the "you and I" as dual aspects of Prufrock's personality, then how do you interpret them and why?

7. What evidence do you find that the speaker is headed for an afternoon social function? Why, then, does the first stanza talk about "the *evening* spread out against the sky / Like a patient etherized upon a table"? And how do you account for the description in the third stanza of the fog "asleep" because "it was a soft October night"? Read lines 75–78. What parallels do you find there to the description of the evening in lines 1–2 and in lines 21–22? In exploring the question of the time of day in this poem, remember that Eliot is using the stream-of-consciousness technique throughout the monologue.

8. Where is the speaker urging the "you and I" of line 1 to go? How do you know? Does the "visit" in line 12 refer to the visit to the room where "the women come and go / Talking of Michelangelo" or to those "certain half-deserted streets" of lines 4–10? On what evidence in the text are you basing your answer?

9. How does the speaker feel toward the women whom he refers to in lines 13–14, and by what means does he reveal his feelings?

10. In the fourth and sixth stanzas the repeated key phrase "there will be time" is an echo with a difference of Ecclesiastes 3:1–8, which begins: "To every thing there is a season, and a time to every purpose under the heaven." Notice, though, that Ecclesiastes says there *is a* time, whereas Prufrock says "there will be time." What do these differences in tense indicate about the differences between the thinking in

Ecclesiastes and the thinking of Prufrock? Note the items for which Prufrock says "there will be time." What do his choices tell you about him? Do you discover any sequence, any pattern in his assemblage of items for which "there will be time"?

11. Is there any connection between lines 35–36 and the lines immediately preceding them? If so, what is this connection? If not, how do you explain the lack? What effect does Eliot achieve by his repetition of lines 13–14 in lines 35–36?

12. Look again at line 51 ("I have measured out my life with coffee spoons"). What would it do to the impact of the line if Eliot had written instead: "I have measured out my life with table spoons"? Why did he pick "coffee spoons" instead of tea spoons? How do lines 49–54 explain and reinforce lines 13–14 and lines 35–36? As the notes point out, the "voices dying with a dying fall" are an echo of the opening lines of *Twelfth Night*. If you have studied the play, comment on the significance of that echo. What do these "voices" and "a farther room" (lines 52–53) represent for Prufrock?

13. How do lines 55–60 intensify the reader's awareness of characteristics in the speaker already revealed by the preceding stanzas? In developing your answer, give special attention to the words "formulated," "sprawling," "pinned," and "wriggling." Examine carefully the metaphor "spit out all the butt-ends of my days and ways," beginning your examination with the literal "spit out" and the literal "butt-ends," and then moving out to what they are saying and implying about Prufrock's "days and ways."

14. Why, in lines 70–72, does Prufrock recall the "lonely men in shirt-sleeves" in contrast to his recollection of the women's arms in lines 62–66? What do you think the men's arms represent for him?

15. What is the speaker saying about himself in lines 73–74 and why does he say it?

16. What quality of the evening (lines 75–78) appeals to the speaker? Why? How does the image of evening here resemble and differ from the image in lines 2–3? What echoes do you find here of the fog image in lines 15–22?

17. Who is "the eternal Footman" of line 85? Why does he hold the coat and why does he "snicker"?

18. To whom does the phrase "you and me" refer in line 89 and why do you think so?

19. What irony do you sense in the phrase "settling a pillow by her head" (line 96)?

20. Line 104 reads, "It is impossible to say just what I mean!" Is Prufrock commenting here on the inadequacy of language or on his own impotence with words or on both?

21. What relationship do you discover between the nerves thrown "in patterns on a screen" (line 105) and the speaker "pinned and wriggling on the wall" (line 58) or "formulated" in a phrase (line 56)?

22. Describe Prufrock as he characterizes himself in lines 111–119, making use of the note on the Hamlet allusion and of whatever knowledge you have of the play. What is the importance of this characterization for what follows in the rest of the poem? On the basis of your understanding of the whole poem, comment on the validity in this self-portrait.

23. How does Prufrock make his self-evaluation in lines 111–119 more understandable by his allusions to John the Baptist (lines 81–82), to Lazarus (lines 94–95), and to Marvell's poem (line 92)? Do these allusions support and intensify the point he is making about himself?

24. After you have finished reading lines 120–131, do you know what Prufrock is going to do? Can you chart the probable course the rest of his life will take? How do you know? And if you do not know, why does the poem leave you in uncertainty?

25. Now that you have examined the entire poem, describe the speaker's attitude at the beginning of the poem and then describe the speaker's attitude at the end of the poem. Are these attitudes alike? Are they different? Has there been a recognizable emotional progression from one to the other? Give reasons for your answers.

## Writing Assignments

The two composition assignments that follow should be carefully prepared outside class with no time limit set. The student should choose one or the other but not both.

## Writing Assignment One

The epigraph to the poem is from Dante's *Inferno* (Canto XXVII, lines 61–66) and translated means:

"If I believed that my reply might be to a person who would ever return to the world, this flame would quiver no more; but, inasmuch as no living man ever returns from this depth, if what I hear is true, without fear of infamy, I answer you."

Remember that, as your note points out, the speaker thinks he is addressing another damned soul and is unaware that by special grace Dante will return to the world of the living.

*Directions.* Write an essay in which you state convincingly and forcibly:

a. what you think the meaning of the poem is;

b. whether you think Eliot, the poet, is criticizing something, advocating an approach to life, or simply stating a problem;

c. what clue the Dante passage gives to the meaning of the poem and to Eliot's purpose in writing the poem.

## Writing Assignment Two

*Directions.* Write a paper in which you systematically and explicitly consider:

a. what the causes may be for Prufrock's predicament;

b. whether or not he is typical of modern man;

c. how his particular problem may or may not be generalized to represent the complex problems of man in contemporary society.

## Writing Assignment One
## Sample 1. Grade: High

*Prufrock: Lyric Frustration*

T. S. Eliot, the poet, is an artist; and "The Love Song of J. Alfred Prufrock" is a work of art. The poem portrays, through the man's own thoughts, Prufrock and his failures. Eliot's finely patterned lines reveal his speaker's dissatisfaction with himself—especially with the social-sociable side of his nature, his longing for sexual fulfillment and his inability to find it, his vague dislike of the rest of the world and his suspicion that it thwarts him deliberately, and the complete lack of vitality and personal reality in his life. Prufrock reflects both the thoughts of a neurotic man and existential despair, through which he could be made to stand for all of mankind.

Eliot is not a polemicist. He has no easily defined purpose, as does Shaw in showing the shortcomings of the Salvation Army or even Thomas in praising Ann Jones. His poetry creates and exists in feeling. Meaning and purpose unite in his revelation of Prufrock's sensibilities. Yet in presenting Prufrock, the poet does, in a sense, state the problem of man's disconnection from life.

At the beginning of the poem, Eliot has quoted a passage from Dante's *Inferno*. It is, in translation,

If I thought that my response would be addressed to one who might go back alive, this flame would shake no more; but since no one ever goes back alive out of these deeps (if what I hear be true), without fear of infamy I answer you.

When one indulges in exegesis, there is always the danger of finding too much symbolism. And I believe that Eliot, in much of his poetry, is mocking those who hunt for hidden meanings. The first few lines of the poem,

Let us go then, you and I,
When the evening is spread out against the sky
Like a patient etherized upon a table,

are characteristic in their careful destruction of any tendencies toward sentimental romanticism. The evening is not a black cloak or a lovely woman but a rather grotesque and sprawling corpse. The effectiveness of "Prufrock" depends on emotional impact rather than on specific meanings. It is possible, however, to examine how the reference to the Italian poet becomes a part of the total poem. First, easy transition is accomplished from the conversational tone of Dante's lines to that of the poem itself and to the invitation, "Let us go then." The damned one reveals himself only because no listener can ever return to the world; his privacy is guaranteed. And Prufrock opens himself only to one who cannot affect his world and who, indeed, cannot escape his own position as one of the damned, in a sense. We see both men in hell: the speaker of Dante's tale literally damned and Prufrock caught in an aristocratic inferno—a half-life of yellow smoke and frustration. Images of dirt and ugliness reinforce this picture:

The muttering retreats
Of restless nights in one-night cheap hotels
And sawdust restaurants like a tedious argument

. . . the pools that stand in drains,
. . . the soot that falls from chimneys.

Prufrock's hell, too, is inescapable. Thus the passage fits Eliot's mood, which is nearly identical with his purpose, and adds to the poetic effect of "The Love Song of J. Alfred Prufrock".

## Writing Assignment One
## Comment on Sample 1. Grade: High

This paper is mature in its judgments and restrained in its conclusions. The writer is sophisticated enough to realize that a work of art is not a preachment, a protest, or a treatise. The portrayal of a mind, a spirit—even one as vacillating, as abortive as Prufrock's—is enough for the artist. Yet, with exceptional insight, this student sees that implicitly Prufrock voices the depths of "existential despair" and the problem of modern man's "disconnection from life." Further evidence of sophistication is the awareness expressed in paragraph four that what starts as exegesis may end with the extraction of a nonexistent symbol. The treatment of the bond between the Dante passage and the Eliot poem is perhaps this paper's most impressive claim to superiority. The recognition that the "conversational tone of Dante's lines" makes an easy transition to the casual "Let us go then" with which the poem opens is one of those subtle extras that did not crop up in other responses to this assignment. The rest of the commentary on the Dante passage is brief but packed with awareness of the two hells, the two assumptions of guaranteed privacy, and the two damnations—the damnation of the speaker in Dante and the damnation, with a difference, of Prufrock.

## Writing Assignment One
## Sample 2. Grade: Average

*An Analysis of "The Love Song of J. Alfred Prufrock"*

Through his poem, "The Love Song of J. Alfred Prufrock", T. S. Eliot develops a theme concerning the double nature of a man and his relationship to the world about him. This man, J. Alfred Prufrock, is engaged in a struggle within his character, a clash in the extremes of his personality. Prufrock is not satisfied with the life he has led as he is now growing old. This love song is melancholy because Prufrock has not been able to experience love, the love of a woman, the love of living, or any kind of love. As Prufrock admits, he has measured his life with coffee spoons, which indicates that the shy, introspective part of Prufrock has dominated his whole life and his own nature has stifled his relations with others. Prufrock asks himself, "Do I dare disturb the universe?" He is in a rut in life, and even though part of him wants to change, he cannot because he thinks it is too late; Prufrock is afraid of life, afraid to assert himself like Hamlet or Lazarus, so he turns within himself and remains alone. Again, Prufrock alludes to his inability to relate well with others when he says, "Till human voices wake us, and we drown."

When the problems of Prufrock are taken together as a whole, they describe a man's inner turmoil and his lost condition. Prufrock himself confesses that he cannot make a decision on his life. Thus the whole meaning of this poem is the problem of inner conflict and the effects of this condition on a man and his relation to the world and the woman he loves. However, Prufrock feels that he must keep the failures of his life to himself. He knows that he is growing old, yet the many opportunities of life have not been realized by him, and he begins to question the meaning of his life. Nevertheless, Prufrock finally reaches an answer by deciding that his calling was in reality what he is suited for, and in the end, accepts himself as he is.

Throughout this whole poem, T. S. Eliot is presenting a problem through the thoughts of this man, J. Alfred Prufrock. All that Prufrock reveals about himself and his life is confined within his mind. So the problem which Eliot is stating in this poem is psychological in that Prufrock is envolved with a struggle within, and he is afraid to reveal himself to others. Eliot is able to state this problem through Prufrock himself, as he goes through a series of thoughts and discussions within his mind. After several self-revealing thoughts of his place in life, Prufrock finally recognizes and accepts his problem, and all this occurs within his thoughts. Another aspect of the problem is Prufrock's love life. Because his own nature, Prufrock is unable to work up enough courage to even ask the woman he loves to marry him. So this love song is full of problems of indecisions and revisions, but again Prufrock resolves himself to be what he is.

As an introduction the "The Love Song of J. Alfred Prufrock", Eliot uses a quotation from Dante's *Inferno.* This quotation of Dante has a direct bearing on the whole meaning of this poem. In essence, the quotation concerns a question which is asked in hell by a visitor, and the only reason the question is answered is because the visitor will never return to earth and reveal his knowledge of hell. This is relative to the meaning of the poem because Prufrock is the one asking the questions and he answers them because no one else can know his thoughts. Just as the truth of hell will not be revealed, the truth of Prufrock's life will not be revealed because it is locked within his mind. And finally, the quotation also helps show Eliot's purpse in writing this poem. Since the question of hell will not be revealed to the world, Prufrock's own problems, his question's of self-identity, can be discussed under a similar situation in that no one else will become aware of his condition. This is a problem within Prufrock's mind, and he finally justifies himself with *his* world, and is at last resigned to live his life as it may be. Therefore, in the end, J. Alfred Prufrock has found himself.

## Writing Assignment One
## Comment on Sample 2. Grade: Average

This is a clearly acceptable response to a hard assignment, but the thinking here is simpler than in the first paper, and the conclusions certainly less sophisticated. The diction lacks the incisiveness of the first writer's; the paper is too long for what it says. This student can't resist a repetition of his point about Prufrock's blighted love life and of his observation that the revelation of character comes through the words of the speaker himself. The section on the Dante passage lacks the first paper's awareness that Prufrock is as surely in hell as the speaker in Dante's *Inferno.* But what makes this paper clearly inferior to the first is its facile assumption that Prufrock has come to terms with himself after a few verbal reconnoiterings and that he now "resolves himself to be what he is"—a remark that does not acknowledge the vacillation essential to Prufrock's makeup.

## Writing Assignment One
## Sample 3. Grade: Low

What meaning is there in a depressing poem?What constructive purpose is served by a poem descriptive of a stand-offish,sedentary,abnormal and probably unique individual? What actions do we plan after concluding that the poem's meaning is thus and so?The poem was nauseatingly meaningless and ineffective.A description, beautiful or otherwise-in this case otherwise-serves no purpose. In this case,at least,which is not in praise or criticism of anything I recognize as being present in our society the effort is wasted on an unreal world. The fictional and impossible combination of personalities including mixtures of egotism,schizophrenia,neurosis,isolation, and willingness to live like a parasite was a Frankenstein of waste. I felt a hatred toward the interest-parasite J. Alfred Prufrock and the royalty-parasite T.S. Eliot.

It has been said that Eliot built his significance on little insignificances. Baloney!Eliot wrote the insignificances and we have built the significance upon them. Yes, he makes you think.He makes you think up meaning for ambiguous and wordy "poems". I and thou can read meaning,hidden and otherwise,into a blank verse poem of beer ads.Eliot,pop art in print,collects thought fragments and "beautiful words" into an irrelevantly titled love song.Such degeneracy does not deserve the relationship it receives recognition for with art.Our real art is prostituted by such association. English classes should be reading *Popular Mechanics* for credit next.

The fact that Eliot was an innovator of a variety of modern poets using pop art in print can be agreed by most.That more has been read into him than he ever said or intended to say can also be mostly approved as truth. When I have to argue that such drivel is obviously drivel in depth as it is on the surface this will not be easily believed.Any poem that a person can read his own or several meanings into,however,will sell and be well-read. When I declare it for what it is—drivel—it is looked upon, like the Emperor's new clothes,as an unbelievable heresy.

Dante and he probably laugh, or turn over in their graves,as English classes relate their writings.But I am very sure that I will not go to Hell for my next statements. Their validity to me is clear.Eliot feels he has seen the light and,paraphrasing Dante,he wants to relay the vision to the world.Others,under drugs,have seen the same light and felt just as sure they were prophets or seers and have been just as unsuccessful in relaying their vision.Eliot made money while he slept,on his dreams. I can not really blame him.I might be sorely tempted,too, regardless of what prostitution of art it entails.Fame *and* money were his for it.

## Writing Assignment One
## Comment on Sample 3. Grade: Low

Low papers are of two kinds, the dull and the lively. This one is lively. Cantankerous irrelevance usually is. The language here is alive. It smolders with resentment, especially that poignant single-word sentence "Baloney!" Imagination is here, too—unharnessed but here—in the picture of Dante and Eliot chuckling together in the hereafter over the unholy coupling of "Prufrock" and *The Inferno*. The knowledgeable references to pop art and drug addiction suggest a cosmopolitan viewpoint that cannot be confined to the single realm of literature, though the writer erupts literary criticism with an assurance that real critics would never venture to emulate. The opening question, "What meaning is there in a depressing poem?" with its implication that pessimism and meaning are mutually exclusive, is typical of the slippery logic on which this paper careens to its climactic picture of Eliot as a sort of male madam presiding over an establishment for the prostitution of art. The elusiveness of pronoun references throughout the paper is an outward indication of the fuzzy-mindedness that prompts the student's emotings. The reference in paragraph two to "an irrelevantly titled love song" betrays the writer's deafness to the accents of irony. A typical example of the addiction to assertion unpropped by proof occurs in the second and third sentences of paragraph four, "But I am very sure that I will not go to Hell for my next statements. Their validity to me is clear." The compelling illogic of that "to me" needs no underlining.

Although the readers agreed that this is a *low* paper, they also agreed that any mind capable of launching such vigorous prose would be more fun to work with than one that rests its case on warmed-over platitudes and prudential noncommittalism.

## Writing Assignment Two
## Sample 1. Grade: High

*Forgive Me, Mr. Eliot...*

Long before the psalmist first twanged his harp and asked the Divine Wisdom, "What is man . . .?" men have raised this query. This writer now re-echoes, directing his question to the wise heirarcy of the Commission. Since there is no one to answer him, the writer will gleefully pursue a stretching of Eliot's "Prufrock" to embrace Twentieth Century Society (*man?*) with what Martial candidly called a *"rudi ori"*.

Twentieth century man, composing current society, is faced with the same dilemma which confronted Prufrock, that is the dilemma of hollowness, insecurity, and fathomless timidity. Realizing the futility of his existence, man can not complete the effort to shrug his inertia and seek ways of improving the weary pathos of his lot. In like manner, Twentieth Century society, unable to shirk even some of the harsh realities of voidness which it faces, struggles under great tides of inertia.

Utterly unaware of what is going on, Twentieth Century society happily, yet uneasily, moves about in its surroundings, whether in regions of hideous urbanization or in the fields of squalor. Hither and thither it moves, tittering superficial inanities. ("Into the room . . . talking of Michaelangelo.") Assuredly there is time to fritter; has not our society seen its "evenings, mornings, afternoons" and measured its existence "with coffee spoons", never drinking life's offerings to the leas, rather insipidly sniffing or blowing them.

Society realizes its position of aloneness. No longer have we the cocky assuredness of former societies who could "talke the world by the tail" and spin it in whatever direction suited their fancy. Timorous of the eyes of the past and future (though a great regiment of current society seriously doubts that the eyes of those gone before are viewing our present plight), it makes no decisive moves. The uneasy comfort of current society's personal corner is too great an inducement for society to deaden. The voices keep echoing and flailing hollow nothings about the atmosphere. There is decidedly talk, talk, talk, but little else. Talk seems the *leit motif* of Twentieth Century society. Ah! only if society might assume the identity of some minor order of the bestial world, perhaps the crustaceans, then there would be no worry. What use is there of worry, anway?

Twentieth Century Society is certainly no prophet and by all means no St. John the Baptist; it seeks to prepare the way for no one. This society, too, has become timorous and quickly inert at the smirk of the "eternal footman". Would it have been worthwhile or should it be worthwhile for our society to "raise its voice"? Evidently not. Surely no individual *man* should, for the mass of society sorely lacks "ears to hear".

Current society is no Hamlet. It shall never become that which is it is not already, even if in so doing it might shape history or successfully right some of its malvolent ills. Rather, it is a Polonious, running hither and yon, filled with ridiculous talk. No latent forces within this society will be evidenced, no matter how rewarding the end might prove. It grows truly old and approaches the final quarter of a century, determined not to discover a true identity separate from that of other cultures.

How pleasant indeed is Twentieth Century society's sweet dream world in the sea caves of shoddy idealism, far removed from reality or action. Within these caves society with well-waxed cars, ears blunt from talk, talk, talk, talk, may close out the siren voice which would summon it to action. Heaven forbid the day when some human voices manage to awaken Twentieth Century society to that which it has feared all along, its blind, sterile futility and closet full of "might-have-beens". It will probably mourn like a tired, wounded old rhino and clumsily roll over to sleep.

## Writing Assignment Two
## Comment on Sample 1. Grade: High

This is a daring, high-spirited response to an assignment that asks the student to stick his neck out. And this student sticks his neck out in the very process of lambasting a society too timorous to do the same. The wholesaleness of the condemnations and the vitality of the language used to express them are young, despite the surface sophistication of the frequently brilliant style; but youngness as energetic as this is a welcome antidote to the apathy that sleeps its way through many a class. Perhaps that same energy, impatient of proof reading, was responsible for the misspellings.

The title and the first paragraph move less sure-footedly than what follows. The suggestion of prankishness in the title and in the remarks addressed to the Commission are probably the products of excess verbal energy. A quick reading of what follows might suggest that the student is off on a spree of vituperation leveled at an undefined "society" and that he has forgotten his assignment. A more careful reading uncovers his constant awareness of what he is about, his constant but unobtrusive allusions to the poem, as in the mermaid reference in the final paragraph. Here, too, is a writer who avoids the unsubtlety of specific references to each of the three parts of the assignment, and this lack of obviousness in the organization is one of the many superiorities of this paper.

## Writing Assignment Two
## Sample 2. Grade: Average

The probable cause for Prufrock's predicament is his inability to live in the world of society. He fabricates in his mind an unreal world which shields him from the realities of life. During Prufrock's life there might have been an incident which affected his mind and his relationship with other people. Prufrock is definitely very self-conscious which is evident by his appearance as well as his state of mind. A person who is afflicted with a strong feeling of self-consciousness frequently regards himself as an outcast of society. He refuses to comply with the mannerisms of society and as a result is unable to communicate with the people existing in the society.

Prufrock is typical of modern man in the sense that he is forced to live in society, but is unable to cope with its problems.

Today, men living in the modern society are also faced with Prufrock's feelings of self-consciousness and inferiority, but are merely placed in a different setting.

Prufrock's particular problem can be generalized in the sense that during everyone's life, at one time or another, he must cope with his feelings of insecurity and inferiority. Especially today, due to "mass conformity and constant competition, man is forced to live by a series of standards and rules of contemprary society, if he wishes to succeed. Prufrock is an example of a person who is desperately fighting against the formation of a "monolithic society".

## Writing Assignment Two
## Comment on Sample 2. Grade: Average

After the heady prose of the previous paper, this one is something of a down-drop to the obvious and the methodical. Within its limitations it is good. The writing is uncluttered, correct, but unexciting. The organization is so obvious that even the dullest reader cannot miss it. Since the paper deals mainly in evident incontrovertibles, the reader finds little here with which to take issue. One really questionable statement occurs in the first paragraph where the writer claims that Prufrock "refuses to comply with the mannerisms of society and as a result is unable to communicate with the people existing in the society." The poem, however, points rather to the malady of over-compliance on the part of a man who has measured out his life with coffee spoons. Prufrock may be out of touch with society in the broad sense, but—at least in the past—he has been adept at adjusting his face to meet the faces met over cakes and ices. Like the first paper, though at a simpler level, this paper argues that Prufrock is typical of modern man, and the third paragraph prudently qualifies the wholesale generalization. The final statement about Prufrock as "an example of a person who is desperately fighting against the formation of a 'monolithic society' " is another indication that the student has not fully understood the character.

## Writing Assignment Two
## Sample 3. Grade: Low

*"The Love Song of J. Alfred Prufrock"*

J. Alfred Prufrock is a shy introvert who is the product of a high class of society. In Prufrock's social class it is the fashion to go to teas every afternoon and to politely talk about the weather or to gossip about someone who is not at the tea.

Prufrock is tired of this way of life and secretly desires to see how the other half of society lives but is too set in his ways, too old, and too shy to try it; he is afraid of what people might say about him behind his back.

The main cause of Prufrock's emotional standing is his upbringing. Brought up by high class parents, he was never allowed to mingle with the common people but rather had to set himself apart as it was beneath him to associate with the lower classes. By being cut off from life, J. Alfred Prufrock was a human no more but became a vegetable living off of his family name and money.

The world today is increasingly becoming a woman's world and many men are finding themselves in the same position that J. Alfred Prufrock was in. Since women are becoming more dominant in the home and business world, many men are becoming henpecked, mama's boys who are too afraid to stand up for their own rights. They grow up regretting this and long to try the other side of life just to see what it would be like.

There are not a great number of these types of men now but enough to notice the dominance of women. If this trend continues women shall soon hold most of the key positions in this country and men shall become the housewives.

## Writing Assignment Two
## Comment on Sample 3. Grade: Low

This paper moves fairly sensibly along the tracks of its pedestrian thinking in the first three paragraphs but gets derailed in the fourth paragraph and never manages to get back on the track. The style, like the thinking, is uncomplicated. The opening paragraph adds to Eliot its own notions of what goes on at tea parties. The third paragraph deposits the blame for Prufrock's psychological kinks on the doorstep of his parents—probably with greater explicitness than the poem warrants. On the whole, though, the first three paragraphs suggest an accurate though simple understanding of Prufrock's plight. It is in paragraph four that the paper begins to detach itself from Prufrock in its earnest concentration on the growing dominance of women and the alarming increase in "henpecked, mama's boys." In the brief remainder of the paper, Eliot and Prufrock have dropped out of sight, and the shift in ideas is violent enough to warrant a rating of *low.*

*W. H. Auden:*
*"Musée des Beaux Arts"*
*Grades 11 and 12*

preferably outside the classroom, drawing on the ideas arrived at through the small-group discussions of one aspect of the poem. A separate composition is provided for each of the three groups. Ideally this writing should take place after the group discussions and before the final class discussion. Where this is not feasible, then the writing should come last. With an average college preparatory class the time required for presenting the poem and the picture for the small-group discussions and for the final class discussion would probably be three or four class periods, especially if the writing takes place outside class.

*Musée des Beaux Arts*

W. H. Auden

About suffering they were never wrong,
The Old Masters: how well they understood
Its human position; how it takes place
While someone else is eating or opening a window or
just walking dully along;
How, when the aged are reverently, passionately
waiting
For the miraculous birth, there always must be
Children who did not specially want it to happen,
skating
On a pond at the edge of the wood:
They never forgot
That even the dreadful martyrdom must run its course
Anyhow in a corner, some untidy spot
Where the dogs go on with their doggy life and the
torturer's horse
Scratches its innocent behind on a tree.

In Brueghel's *Icarus*, for instance: how everything
turns away
Quite leisurely from the disaster; the plowman may
Have heard the splash, the forsaken cry,
But for him it was not an important failure; the sun
shone
As it had to on the white legs disappearing into the
green
Water; and the expensive delicate ship that must have
seen
Something amazing, a boy falling out of the sky,
Had somewhere to get to and sailed calmly on.

## Group One—Questions for Discussion: Title, Painting, Setting, Speaker, and Occasion

1. "Musée des Beaux Arts" is the Royal Museum of Fine Arts in Brussels. In what ways does the title set the scene for the poem?

2. As the poem begins, where are you to imagine that the speaker is? What is he doing? What prompts him to speak?

3. Using the title and the text of the poem as your guide, explain who "The Old Masters" (line 2) are. Where else in the poem does Auden refer explicitly to "The Old Masters"?

4. According to the speaker, what is it that "The Old Masters" understood about suffering and "Its human position"? How did they demonstrate this understanding?

5. Does the speaker share the views of "The Old Masters" on suffering and on "Its human position" or does he merely state and illustrate these views? Cite evidence from the poem to support your answer.

6. Why is the word *Icarus* italicized?

## Writing Assignment One (for Group One)

"The Fall of Icarus," by Brueghel the Elder, is located in the Royal Museum of Fine Arts at Brussels and was inspired by the Greek myth about Icarus and his father Daedalus, who invented wings attached by wax so that he and his son could escape from the island of Crete by flying. Icarus was warned not to go too near the sun, but he disobeyed; the sun melted the wax; his wings dropped off and he fell into the sea and was drowned. There are several versions of the myth, but all agree that Icarus fell from the sky.

### Directions

Write a carefully prepared paper in which you compare and contrast the myth, Brueghel's painting, and lines 14–21 of Auden's poem. In your paper consider in what way the three treatments are similar and different in content or facts, in purpose, and in tone. Try to explain as specifically as you can in what ways these similarities and differences are important.

# *W. H. Auden: "Musée des Beaux Arts" Grades 11 and 12*

## To the Teacher

The study plan for this poem differs from the usual procedure of having the teacher ask the questions while the entire class tries to arrive at the answers. This plan presents a series of problems for small groups of students to try to solve together before the entire class moves on to its final discussion of the poem as a whole. Although the materials here are designed for grades 11 and 12, the pretesting suggested that an able tenth grade class can make encouraging headway with the poem, the questions, and the writing assignments.

Most teachers will want to begin by reading the poem aloud to the class several times while the class follows with the text. The last part of the poem refers specifically to Brueghel's "The Fall of Icarus," but the first 13 lines allude to other pictures by "The Old Masters." The teacher will do well to ask the students in Group Two to find and bring to class reproductions of other pictures illustrating the points Auden makes in lines 1–13. One, for example, might be Brueghel's "The Skaters"; others could be various depictions of the birth of Christ, the martyrdom of St. Jerome, the Crucifixion, and so forth. Each member of the class should also have time to look carefully at a reproduction of Brueghel's "Icarus." A small print of the picture is in the envelope at the back of this book, but a full-size reproduction in color will be preferable.

The next step will be to divide the class into three groups, each of which will consider a different set of questions and then share its finding with the rest of the class, at which time the teacher and the rest of the class will want to examine, discuss, and perhaps modify the conclusions presented by each group. In assigning students to groups the teacher will want to make sure that at least one or two able students are in each group. This is specially important for Groups Two and Three.

In addition, each student will write a composition,

## Group Two—Questions for Discussion: Happenings and Meanings

1. How do lines 3–4 illustrate the particular aspect of human suffering that the speaker says "The Old Masters" understood so well? How would you characterize the activities mentioned in line 4? How do they contribute to the point the speaker is making about "The Old Masters"?

2. Lines 5–8 are hard to interpret. The following questions are ones with which you will have to grapple in arriving at your own interpretation of these lines. You are to realize that Auden is alluding to various paintings by "The Old Masters."

a. What is meant by "the miraculous birth"?

b. Why are the aged waiting for it "passionately" and "reverently"?

c. What is the "it" that the children did not specially want to happen?

d. Is the speaker bracketing the aged or the children with the people described in line 4? Why do you think so?

e. Is the speaker bracketing the aged or the children with the dogs and the horse of lines 12 and 13? Why do you think so?

3. As you have now discovered, the first stanza of the poem presents examples of suffering and examples of the human response to that suffering that the speaker says "The Old Masters" understood well. What likenesses or differences do you note in the kinds of suffering and the responses to the suffering described in the first stanza? What connection do they have with *"Icarus"* in the second stanza, lines 14–21?

4. In what ways does the painting by Brueghel serve as a "for instance" for the point of the poem?

## Writing Assignment Two (for Group Two)

In a carefully prepared, well-developed paper, do the following:

1. Summarize the meaning of the poem.

2. Show how the specific aspects of the painting named by the speaker might be generalized to stand for common reactions to suffering in the modern world.

3. Explain how, in your opinion, modern attitudes toward suffering resemble or differ from those that "The Old Masters" understood and portrayed.

Be sure to support your generalizations with specific examples.

## Group Three—Questions for Discussion: Language, Structure, Tone

1. Auden said in "Making and Judging Poetry"—included in *Discovering Modern Poetry,* by Elizabeth Drew and George O'Connor (New York, 1961, pages 324–344)—that a poem's "use of language is deliberately and ostentatiously different from talk." In what ways does "Musée des Beaux Arts" demonstrate such a use of language? The questions set below direct your attention to places in the poem where, though he may be using the words of talk, the poet is using those words as a poet would use them, not as a talker would.

a. How does the poet create his word picture by the three adverbs he uses in the last part of line 4?

b. Why does he use the words "reverently" and "passionately" in line 5? Do they modify "the aged" or "waiting" or both? Explain your answer.

c. Why does the poet call the birth "miraculous," and what birth is he talking about? You will want to compare your answers to these questions with the answers of Group Two.

d. What pictures does the poet evoke by the setting he provides for the children in lines 7–8 and the martyrdom in line 10? (Here again you will want to compare your answers with those of Group Two.)

e. Why are the words "leisurely" in line 15 and "expensive delicate" in line 19 appropriate? Show what each of the following words or groups of words contributes to the effectiveness of the poem's description of what happened to Icarus: "splash," line 16; "forsaken cry," line 16; "failure," line 17; "the white legs disappearing into the green / Water," lines 18–19; and "a boy falling out of the sky," line 20.

2. At what points in the poem does the poet deliberately employ the diction and rhythms of talk? Why does he do this?

3. Does the rhyme in the poem call attention to itself? Why or why not? Is the rhyming haphazard?

Cite evidence to support your answer. Is rhyme appropriate in this kind of poem? Why or why not?

4. Read the poem aloud again. How would you describe its meter: regular, irregular; kind of patterns, if any? In what ways do you think its rhythm (including the varying length of lines) contributes to or detracts from the total effect of the poem?

5. Poems often begin with specific instances and move toward a generalization or theme. To what extent does Auden deviate from this structure in this poem? You will need to consider where and how he first states his theme, where he illustrates it, and whether or not there is a tendency toward greater generality or greater specificity as the poem moves on.

6. Tone in literature may be defined as the writer's or speaker's attitude toward his material, his audience, or himself, and the degree to which he is involved with or detached from his subject matter. With this definition in mind, how would you characterize the tone of this poem? On what evidence in the poem are you basing your answer?

7. Is Auden advocating anything in this poem? Is he making a value judgment? Or is he simply stating a problem or defining an attitude? Give reasons for your answers.

## Writing Assignment Three (for Group Three)

Write a carefully prepared paper in which you examine and discuss "Musée des Beaux Arts" in terms of Auden's own statement, "Poetry does not have to be great or even serious to be good." Evaluate the poem and decide whether it is great, serious, or good; or all of these; or none of them. Although this assignment invites your own opinions, be sure to support those opinions by offering specific and convincing reasons for them.

## Writing Assignment One
## Sample 1. Grade: High

*The Fall of Icarus: Myth, Painting, and Poem*

Reading Auden's poem about Brueghel's painting about the mythological fall of Icarus and realizing this history is like coming upon a flower from a seed which has been buffeted by the wind for centuries, and which had finally blossomed—not only once but twice!

The ancient Greek tale about Icarus, the brilliant inventor's son, claims that when the father and son were fleeing from the Cretan labyrinth with wings made from feathers and wax, the boy, ignoring his parent's warning, flew too near the sun. The sun melted the wax, and Icarus fell into the sea and drowned.

Although the sixteenth-century painter and the modern poet utilized this drowning, their emphases were slightly different from each other and quite different from the legend. The legend seem to be scolding boys for foolishly disobeying their wise fathers; Brueghel and Auden had another purpose in mind. Brueghel showed a completely indifferent landscape: a farmer is thoughtfully plowing; a shepherd is absently gazing at the sky; sheep are nibbling the grass; ships are sailing in the cove; farmer, shepherd, sheep, and ships are unaware of each other *and* a boy falling from the sky. Auden picked up the indifference, almost ignored the painter's ironic humor, and added suffering.

Brueghel's picture is rather humorous for several reasons. He painted a prominent literary figure as a pair of kicking legs. No one noticed a boy falling out of the sky, which *was* "something amazing," as Auden said. The fall seems serious and terrible in the poem. Auden called the situation a "disaster;" he heard a "forsaken cry" and saw "green Water." The water in the painting is a quite gay blue; green sound sickening and cold. In the line, "Something amazing, a boy falling out of the sky," the poet shows the only lightness in the poem. He used the painting to illustrate his idea that suffering occurs while "someone else is eating or opening a window or just walking dully along" and that no one notices the unfortunate one.

While reading the legend, I did not think about the splash-down; the poem and the painting, however, depend on it. In the myth, Icarus had a personality since he disobeyed his father; in the other two works, he was a distressed pair of legs. Brueghel's Icarus landed in a sixteenth-century landscape: I doubt that any ancient farmer wore a red shirt under a gathered coat.

All these differences in the general plot make the artists' intent clear. One can discover what the man liked and what he rejected in the previous work.

## Writing Assignment One
## Comment on Sample 1. Grade: High

Compressed style and keen insight are the evident strengths of this unusually competent response to the assignment. An example of this disciplined compression and sharp insight is the reference to Brueghel's and Auden's Icarus as a "distressed pair of legs." The summary of Brueghel's painting and Auden's poem in paragraph three is a sample of the paper's richly packed brevity. The metaphor in the opening paragraph is imaginative, though some might cavil over the appropriateness of a "flower" figure for either Brueghel's painting or Auden's poem. By the very terms of the assignment this and all other papers are, no doubt, indebted to both the small-group discussion and the general class discussion that followed it, but perhaps the freshest touch in this paper is the recognition in paragraph three that Brueghel's picture is tinged with "ironic humor" and the effectively detailed development of that recognition in paragraph four. The comparison of the water's color in the painting and in the poem is another unexpected and discerning touch. Certainly this student has not exhausted the possibilities of the assignment, but what he writes is clear-sighted, valid, and ably expressed.

## Writing Assignment One
## Sample 2. Grade: Average

*"Musée des Beaux Arts"*

Auden's poem, Brueghel's painting, and the myth of Icarus are basically telling the same story. Each is concerned with portraying the suffering of man and the indifference of others toward those suffering. The artist, the story teller, and the writer, in their own way, are expressing their feelings.

Inspired by the Greek myth about Icarus and his father Daedalus, Brueghel set out to express his opinion through art. His painting, *The Fall of Icarus,* contains much more than the mere plight of Icarus. The indifference of the plowman and the sheppard are clearly evident. Their backs are turned away from human suffering. Perhaps they didn't see his fall, but the man leaning over the water throwing pebbles into the sea and those on board the ship can almost reach out and touch him.

Almost following a pattern; first the myth, then a visual interpretation, and lastly the written word, Auden expresses himself in his Poem "Musée des Beaux Arts". From the title of the poem and even from the first sentence we can see that Auden is interpreting a work of art. "Old Masters" who understand the human position and suffering include Auden, Brueghel, and even the ancient Greek myth tellers. Lines 14–21 of Auden's poem are directly concerned with Brueghel's painting. He is merely explicating the great work of art.

No matter how the "Old Masters" show us their understanding of human suffering and the indifference of others their messages will always be clear. Whats so amazing about "a boy falling out of the sky?"

## Writing Assignment One
## Comment on Sample 2. Grade: Average

Admittedly this is the work of an eleventh grade student, but the readers found it more than a year younger in its language and its appraisals than the twelfth grade paper that precedes it. The writing is competent but undistinguished. The organization has the tidy simplicity and the conscious transitions of the carefully taught student. Its shortcomings are in its judgments rather than in its form. This student naïvely assumes in his opening paragraph that the same purpose animates the myth, the painting, and the poem, whereas the first paper sees the ethical lesson as the central aim of the myth, an ironically humorous commentary on human nature as the intent of the picture, and a concerned exploration of the role of suffering in the human scheme of things as the core of the poem. And a sharply discriminating study of the myth, the painting, and the poem would not culminate in the banality of the closing question "Whats so amazing about 'a boy falling out of the sky?' "

Although the paper says much that is acceptable and relevant, the flaws noted in this comment justify a rating of *average*.

## Writing Assignment One
## Sample 3. Grade: Low

"The Fall of Icarus" in the myth, Brueghel's painting and Auden's poem are all very similar because they treat the fall as lightly as possible. The purpose in the three treatments seems to be very much the same also, because the purpose is to show Icarus he must suffer alone no matter how many times he was told and disobeyed, he only received that one chance. This purpose can very easily be applied to our own lives today that we must suffer alone no matter who we tell our problems to and Brueghel's purpose in his portrait may have been depicting this very purpose for the people after Icarus to follow. The myth, as myths often do, depict some moral and point it out and play it up so as to reach the emotions of its readers. In Auden's poem, Auden treats the fall very lightly and sometimes as I think in this poem, (it) the point Auden is trying to make is emphasized more by treating it as light as possible. The tone in the three treatments is similar because it is serious and has an overall tragic (feeling) tone. The tone is serious and somber and in the painting there is a suffering which is depicted in the fall. Particularly, in the painting, this suffering tone makes you interested as a viewer, and stirs some emotion within each individual. The calm and serene atmosphere in the poem and in the painting creates a lonliness which is difficult to explain, but is certainly there. In contrasting Brueghel's painting, Auden's poem and the myth, I find only similarities which are all in themselves very important and shed much light on the meaning, the purpose and the emotional feeling which the painter, the poet and the myth wanted identified.

## Writing Assignment One
## Comment on Sample 3. Grade: Low

This paper earns its right to a *low* score by reason of its feeble writing skills, its illogic, its lack of supporting evidence, and the dubiousness of its inferences. The paper gets off to an inauspicious start with the claim that the myth, the painting, and the poem all "treat the fall as lightly as possible." The reader may find it a trifle hard to reconcile this opening statement with the later pronouncement that "The tone in the three treatments is similar because it is serious and has an overall tragic (feeling) tone." The chief message that has come through to this student is that human beings do their suffering alone. The vagueness about "emotional feeling" in the latter part of the paper is one more symptom of the ineptness with which this student gropes his way through the assignment.

## Writing Assignment Two
## Sample 1. Grade: High

*"Musée des Beaux Arts"*

In his poem, "Musée des Beaux Arts," W. H. Auden discusses the futility of human suffering. The title sets the tone of the poem by bringing to mind the old-world culture of the Royal Museum in Brussels. Auden uses the paintings in the Museum as a vehicle to express his ideas regarding human suffering, ones synonymous to those of the Old Masters.

Auden concludes the poem with a rather arresting nonconvention by adding an octet concerned with a specific example instead of a conclusive generality or a moral. Nevertheless, this backward thematic structure is effective. It leaves the reader, who must, of course, be familiar with Pieter Brueghel's "Icarus," with a visual summation of the more general first stanza. The fact that Icarus, in the painting, is so small compared to the seemingly more dominant figures of the plowman and the ship, implies the insignificance to other people of what is undoubtedly the most significant event in the life of Icarus. "How everything turns away/ Quite leisurely from the disaster; the plowman may/ Have heard the splash, the forsaken cry." To the plowman, however, Icarus' failure is unimportant since it has no direct effect on his life. The ship, that sails calmly on, perhaps symbolizes humanity, which, despite the martyrdoms, the sufferings, or the deaths of individuals, progresses imperiously and calmly on. Brueghel's painting not only shows the attitude of those who witnessed Icarus' fall, but also that of mankind towards any human suffering —an attitude of indifference.

Auden believed that the Old Masters understood, possibly more so than the less artistic and less perceptive masses, the "human position" toward suffering. To create a comprehensive and meaningful expression of humanity, the artist must draw himself away from society in order to view it with proper perspective. The example of "Icarus" shows artistic insight, by means of oils, into the emotions of humanity, as does "Musée des Beaux Arts" by means of poetry.

The Old Masters, like Auden, were perhaps concerned with their own sufferings and assumed that the rest of humanity was also. In any case, they are mocking humanity's traditional irreverence towards the miseries (Icarus' fall) and the greatnesses (Icarus' flight) of individuals.

## Writing Assignment Two
## Comment on Sample 1. Grade: High

The few mechanical flaws in this paper are insignificant beside the impressive evidence throughout the paper of the student's ability to handle language with precision. The phrase "backward thematic structure," for instance, neatly defines the unconventional technique of a poem that culminates in a developed example instead of the expected generalization. The paper then goes on to say of the effect of this reversal that "It leaves the reader . . . with a visual summation of the more general first stanza." Many students would take several lines to say what this student says in his two-word phrase "visual summation." Further proof of the sureness of diction in this paper is the adverb "imperiously" for the progress of "the expensive delicate ship." The wording of this assignment may be partly to blame for the questionable assumption that "The Old Masters," like Auden, "were perhaps concerned with their own sufferings." Certainly neither the poem nor Brueghel's painting provides a shred of evidence to support such a conjecture. A concerned reader might also question the use of the term "irreverence" in the final sentence to describe the common human response to the sufferings of others. Irreverence implies at least a negative kind of awareness, but what Auden is talking about is lack of awareness or indifference that lets us turn away from the pain around us. These are minor flaws, though, in an obviously capable handling of a hard assignment.

## Writing Assignment Two
## Sample 2. Grade: Average

*Human Attitude Toward Suffering in*
*Musée des Beaux Arts*

In *Musée des Beaux Arts,* Auden's theme is concerned with the human indifference to the suffering of others. The "Old Masters", however, understood suffering and its place in life. They understood that life continues on as people overlook those who are "reverently, passionately waiting for the miraculous birth." They never forgot, as most people today forget, "that even the dreadful martyrdom must run its course".

Auden illustrates his theme of human indifference through Brueghel's painting of the fall of Icarus. In this painting, the shepard, the Plowman, and the fisherman all turn away from the drowning Icarus. Perhaps they heard "the splash, the forsaken cry", but they did nothing about it. Also quite unconcerned with Icarus's plight, the "expensive, delicate ship" sails on by without concern. These reactions to the suffering of Icarus are illustrative of the attitude toward suffering in the modern world. There are many situations today in which people do not want to become involved. They are unaware or indifferent to the suffering of others. They may pass a man attacking a woman and walk right by, pretending they didn't see it happen. They won't help and they won't go for help.

The attitude which Brueghel takes in his painting, and which Auden takes in his poem are indicative of great awareness and preception to human attitudes by both men. They illustrate that the human position toward suffering is indifference and non-involvement. This attitude is not a new one concerned only with modern man. *As Musée des Beaux Arts* illustrates, it is an attitude held for centuries. Because man is concerned for himself alone, his attitude of non-involvement will not disappear. He will continue to pass by the attacker and the attacked, he will continue to turn away because he has "somewhere to get to".

## Writing Assignment Two
## Comment on Sample 2. Grade: Average

The opening statement of this paper gets at once to the center of the poem, and the conclusions this student reaches are unassailable, though they lack the penetrating sharpness of the first paper. And technically this paper is clearly the inferior of the first. In the *high* paper no such lapses occur as appear in this paper's third paragraph, where the student writes, "The attitude which Brueghel takes in his painting, and which Auden takes in his poem are indicative of great awareness and preception to human attitudes by both men." This is a student, however, who heeds instructions and who supplies an appropriate example of modern indifference to human suffering, whereas the first student contents himself with a generalization. The paper is near the top of the *average* group.

## Writing Assignment Two
## Sample 3. Grade: Low

This poem's beginning reflects upon how intrepid a meaning the ancient masters had about suffering. They easily correlated it to human behavior patterns, the way it happened and the nonchalance that so often accompanied it.

How when the aged calmly await their inevitable fate theire is always that inexplicable taint of regret. Yet time's sand stops not for any man and what was, has been and thus carries no never ceasing effect.

Those ancient great ones never forgot that even martyrdom makes its stay and calmly saunters away. Yes in some recluse hovel far distant from the normalities of life where even the inadvertently malignant find refuge from life itself.

## Writing Assignment Two
## Comment on Sample 3. Grade: Low

This paper is a prime example of pretentious inadequacy and verbal confusion. The misuse of the word "intrepid" in the opening sentence is the first indication of the pretentious ineptness that reaches its high water mark in the second paragraph with the reference to "time's sand" which "stops not for any man." The second sentence of the first paragraph certainly gets the main idea of the poem and manages to bring it into the world without a linguistic miscarriage. But what follows is a lush growth of elaborate confusions. The one specific reference to the poem mentions the martyrdom that "makes its stay and calmly saunters away." But in the poem it is not the martyrdom that "saunters away," though perhaps this is the student's reading of "must run its course." The heavy reliance on fragments punctuated as sentences is one more weakness in a disturbingly weak paper.

## Introductory Comment on Writing Assignment Three

The basic difficulty with this assignment is that it calls for the manipulation of three slippery terms: great, serious, and good. Each requires a judgment that will be necessarily subjective. In evaluating responses to this assignment, the rudder to which the teacher must cling is the demand for specific reasons to support the subjective judgment. To invite the student's opinion and then to penalize him if his opinion does not chime in with our own would be manifestly unfair. The assignment, then, calls for broad-minded teachers and students willing to stick their necks out. Most of the students, however, were not eager to risk their necks. Most of them hedged or wound up with the prudential assurance that the poem was certainly serious, probably good, but surely not great. Although some of the readers found the results disappointing, they all agreed that we should continue to set this kind of assignment, though perhaps with a word of warning to teachers not to expect too much from their students.

## Writing Assignment Three
## Sample 1. Grade: High

*"Musée des Beaux Arts": A Great Poem?*

"Musée des Beaux Arts" could conceivably be classified as a great poem. Greatness implies a number of things: importance and universality of the poem, the message it carries; timelessness; near perfection of mechanics, in some cases; suitable diction, tone; good style. The usual overall effect of greatness in poetry is that of impressing the reader with the depth, importance (through pertinence to basic questions of life or, specifically human existence), and profundity of the thought contained within the poem. In many cases, the thought or philosophy expounded is actually quite trivial, but masterful presentation, through one means or another, makes it seem otherwise. To state with conviction, however, that a poem possesses greatness or that it lacks it is a matter of considerable difficulty. But if it were necessary to apply one classification or the other, great or not great to "Musée des Beaux Arts", it would be almost necessary to give that work the benefit of obscure doubts and call it great.

The thought it presents involves the human condition of suffering; and it presents that idea in a manner which is attractive and unique. The mood of the poem shows traces of seriousness, humor, frankness and sarcasm delicately combined in a style of light and readable quality. Humor appears with the dogs and their "doggy life", pathos in the "passionate waiting" of the aged; frankness is evident in the opening lines and light sarcasm in the attitude of the witnesses to Icarus' fall. These different qualities bring about a certain artful contrast. And there is also contrast in situations described by the poem: birth awaited by the aged, not wanted by the young; the brilliance of martyrdom in untidy, unsuitable spots; the despair of suffering, rewarded by the indifference of the universe and humanity.

"Musée des Beaux Arts" is a clever poem, a poem presenting a matter of universal importance in a unique, readable manner; it is a good poem, and certainly must be, in the estimation of many, a great poem.

## Writing Assignment Three
## Comment on Sample 1. Grade: High

This student's immediate and intelligent awareness of the central difficulty of the assignment differentiates his paper from most of the others. When the reader realizes that nearly half of this paper is an expanded definition of literary greatness, he may well fear that the student will not do justice to the main job of reaching a value judgment about this particular poem. But the more thoroughly a reader examines the second half of the paper, the more he will be impressed by the wealth of carefully evaluated details, each firmly linked to the initial definition of literary greatness. The second paragraph is a happy fusion of relevant detail and sound generalization. The final paragraph is cautious in its conclusions but ultimately grants the poem's claim to greatness at least in the eyes of some of its readers. Most students were afraid to risk even this much of a commitment. To call the poem "good" and stop there was safer, and many of the papers proceeded on a safety-first basis.

## Writing Assignment Three
## Sample 2. Grade: Average

*Musée des Beaux Arts* is what I consider to be a good, serious poem. Auden is writing on a serious problem which concerns all of mankind and he gives his attitude on the problem. He is quite serious when he says, "Where the dogs go on leading their doggy life and the torturer's horse scratches its innocent behind on a tree". He makes it quite clear that the entire human race is leading the same life as these two animals, not caring what happens to one's fellow man. I consider the poem good because it presents a problem and it shows the attitude of the author to the problem. He discribes, "Brueghel's *Icarus*", as being the example of the problem with the human race. He saw that the problem was everyone's unconcern for their fellow man. The boy drowning in the water was the example of all those who suffer and need help, but do not receive it from others who could help. He shows by saying, "the plowman may have heard the splash, the foresaken cry, But for him it was not an important failure." Auden presented this problem to the human race in his poem and it is up to the reader to understand its solution. This poem is good because it shows those who read it what should be done. The intellegent reader sees that more consideration for his fellow man will blot out the present indiference.

## Writing Assignment Three
## Comment on Sample 2. Grade: Average

The writing in this paper is clear, reasonably correct, but plodding. The understanding of the poem is accurate but without depth or subtlety. The student allows the poem's claim to goodness on the grounds that it conveys the message that "consideration for his fellow man will blot out the present indiference." And certainly this message is not foreign to Auden's poem, but as a summary statement of the poem's claim to approval as a work of art it is inadequate. One can also think of apter examples of Auden's seriousness than his use of the "doggy life" and the horse's "scratching his innocent behind," though, as this student seems to sense in part, the seriousness lies not in the animals themselves but in the human counterparts of their unfeeling absorption with the self.

## Writing Assignment Three
## Sample 3. Grade: Low

*"Poetry does not have to be great or even serious to be good."*
*William H. Auden*

In my opinion Auden's "Musés des Beaux Arts" is not great nor is it good. All too sadly, however, it is very serious.

Auden dilutes a good two-line couplet proverb of Shakespearian greatness which I see in the poem. In Auden himself there must have been better but, for discussion's sake, I have carved all of the fat off of the poem to reveal the one meaty idea of his discourse on Bruegal's *Icarus.*

"The Old Masters . . . . never forgot . . .
the plowman . . . heard the splash."

This brings Auden's accusing words out in clear indictment of apathy as our major trouble. Auden's greatness of mental power is obvious since he thought of the idea. But he wanted to create a hackneyed muddle which would make the comment deep by burying it under torturer's horses, skating children and other barriers of abstract and concrete connotation. This fat was added to make the small idea publishable from a technical viewpoint. Such redundancy compromises efficiency for literary excellence. The adding of sentences about "untidy spots where the dogs go on with their doggy life" ornament his poem to Victorian architectural standards and create the impression of a muddled old man staring at a painting and describing it—only incidentally throwing in a moral.

Because of its serious presentation and lack of real greatness I can see the most doleful Shakespearean actor mournfully and by rote delivering the poem in a hilarious comedy. But I am glad that he tried, anyway.

## Writing Assignment Three
## Comment on Sample 3. Grade: Low

No moralistic platitudes dull the piquancy of this paper. The assignment invited the student to express his opinion and this student has done exactly that. The poet might be surprised at the butchering this student does to the poem in an effort to carve "all of the fat off." Unfortunately, the two lines he comes up with as the "one meaty idea" of his (Auden's) poem look more like chop suey than a slice of defatted beef. And beefing is more the student's province than the poem's anyway, especially when he accuses Auden of wanting "to create a hackneyed muddle" but adduces no evidence of such a muddle. Apparently he has not noted Auden's careful development of his theme by illustrations, though he states the theme of the poem at the beginning of paragraph three, "This brings Auden's accusing words out in clear indictment of apathy as our major trouble." How a student capable of such insight could have gone off on such a binge of rancorous and muddy rhetoric is hard to understand. The lack of supporting evidence, the lack of order or sequence of ideas, the intrusion of such irrelevancies as making "the small idea publishable from a technical viewpoint"—all add up to an incoherent muddle, but a muddle penetrated by occasional insights so sharp as to make any teacher wonder how to save the insights and eliminate the muddle.

*Four Poems on Death, Grade 12*

ship between the speaker in each poem and the person who has died.

*Methought I Saw My Late Espoused Saint*

John Milton

Methought I saw my late espoused saint
Brought to me like Alcestis from the grave,
Whom Jove's great son to her glad husband gave,
Rescued from death by force though pale and faint.
Mine, as whom washed from spot of childbed taint,
Purification in the old law did save,
And such, as yet once more I trust to have
Full sight of her in Heaven without restraint,
Came vested all in white, pure as her mind.
Her face was veiled, yet to my fancied sight,
Love, sweetness, goodness, in her person shined
So clear, as in no face with more delight.
But O, as to embrace me she inclined,
I waked, she fled, and day brought back my night.

Notes (for the Use of Teacher and Student)

1. A few years after Milton became blind he married Katharine Woodcock, who died in 1658 giving birth to a child that also died a few weeks later. Soon after these events Milton wrote this poem in honor of the wife he had never seen.

2. "Alcestis": According to the classic legend, Alcestis, the wife of King Admetus, offered to die in place of her husband but was restored to her husband from Hades by Hercules (lines 2–4).

3. "Washed from spot of childbed taint," (line 5), is a reference to the Old Testament law that regarded a new mother as impure until after "Purification" (Leviticus 12).

## Questions for Discussion

1. What evidence in the poem substantiates the external circumstances that inspired the poem? In what lines and by what means does Milton indicate that he had never *seen* his wife? How does he let the reader know the cause of his wife's death?

2. Why does Milton speak of his dead wife as a "saint"? How does line 9 reinforce and explain this introduction of the wife in the first two lines? (For an explanation of the phrase "vested all in white," see Revelation 19:8.)

3. Is the reference to Alcestis (lines 2–4) an appropriate comparison? Why or why not? Does this classic reference increase or decrease the reader's sense of the sincerity of Milton's emotion? Give reasons for your answer, bearing in mind that when Milton wrote, all educated persons were familiar with the classics.

4. Why is the word "restraint" in line 8 more effective than the words "hindrance," "obstruction," or "interference" would be in this particular context?

5. What is the technical name for the form Milton uses in this poem? Suggest reasons for his having chosen this particular form for this particular poem. How many parts does this kind of poem usually have and where does the division of the parts usually occur? Does Milton's poem follow the usual practice? If so, point out the confirming evidence. If not, then describe just what Milton does with his chosen form and explain what effects are produced.

*To an Athlete Dying Young*

A. E. Housman

The time you won your town the race
We chaired you through the market-place;
Man and boy stood cheering by,
And home we brought you shoulder-high.

Today, the road all runners come,
Shoulder-high we bring you home,
And set you at your threshold down,
Townsman of a stiller town.

Smart lad, to slip betimes away
From fields where glory does not stay
And early though the laurel grows
It withers quicker than the rose.

Eyes the shady night has shut
Cannot see the record cut,
And silence sounds no worse than cheers
After earth has stopped the ears:

Now you will not swell the rout

# *Four Poems on Death*
# *Grade 12*

## To the Teacher

How an individual acts and reacts in the face of death has often been a principal concern of poets. In their responses to death, poets reflect a variety of attitudes: they may see death as a doorway to a continued life, or as an escape from the vanities of man, or as a relief from suffering, or as an occasion for the expression of a profound love. By examining four representative poems on death, students should arrive at an understanding of the universality of the experience and also of the widely divergent human responses to that universal experience. The four poems presented here for study are:

Milton, "Methought I Saw My Late Espoused Saint"

Housman, "To an Athlete Dying Young"

Hardy, "After the Last Breath (J. H. 1813–1904)"

Thomas, "After the Funeral (In Memory of Ann Jones)"

As part of this study, the student will write two compositions, one before and one after the class discussion. He should be given copies of both assignments when he receives his copies of the four poems. Both papers should be written outside class.

*Note to teachers and students.* In dealing both with the composition assignments and with the discussion questions, bear in mind that no one of the four poets expresses directly his general views on life and death. Each poet is responding to the death of a particular person in a particular set of circumstances. The reader can only infer from this specific response to a specific death what the poet's general views on life and death are; but learning to draw such inferences sensitively and responsibly is one of the major tasks of a good reader. In drawing such inferences in writing assignment one, students will want to consider very carefully the tone and voice in which the speaker in each poem speaks, the degree of formality or informality in the language he uses, the emotional involvement or detachment with which he handles his material. Another consideration is the closeness of the relation-

Of lads that wore their honors out,
Runners whom renown outran
And the name died before the man.

So set, before its echoes fade,
The fleet foot on the sill of shade,
And hold to the low lintel up
The still-defended challenge-cup.

And round that early-laureled head
Will flock to gaze the strengthless dead
And find unwithered on its curls
The garland briefer than a girl's.

## Questions for Discussion

1. What happening has prompted the writing of this poem?

2. The first two stanzas are built out of contrasts. What are these contrasts and by what means does the poet emphasize them? How do these contrasts prepare for and lead into the contrast operating throughout the poem?

3. Why is the athlete a "Smart lad, to slip betimes away" (line 9)? What does each of the following represent: the "laurel" (line 11); the "rose" (line 12); and "shady night" (line 13)? In what sense will the athlete's "record" become immortal?

4. In what sense can a name die before the man (line 20)? How do the verbs "slip" (line 9), "withers" (line 12), and "outran" (line 19) prepare the reader for line 20 and increase its impact?

5. In line 26 Housman calls the dead "strengthless." Would "fleshless" serve as well in this context? Why or why not?

6. What is the main theme of this poem? Where is it first introduced? By what means and with what details is it developed? In what ways do the last two stanzas summarize and resolve it? How do the words "unwithered" (line 27) and "briefer" (line 28) reinforce the point being made and bring the main theme into final focus?

7. Describe the form of this poem, including comment on its rhyming, its rhythm, its use of sound effects, the length of its lines, its stanza form. How do these technical aspects of the poem help the poet to achieve his point? In what ways does the poem indicate motion and change through its form?

## *After the Last Breath*
## (J. H. 1813–1904)

Thomas Hardy

There's no more to be done, or feared, or hoped;
None now need watch, speak low, and list, and tire;
No irksome crease outsmoothed, no pillow sloped
        Does she require.

Blankly we gaze. We are free to go or stay;
Our morrow's anxious plans have missed their aim;
Whether we leave to-night or wait till day
        Counts as the same.

The lettered vessels of medicaments
Seem asking wherefore we have set them here;
Each palliative its silly face presents
        As useless gear.

And yet we feel that something savours well;
We note a numb relief withheld before;
Our well-beloved is prisoner in the cell
        Of Time no more.

We see by littles now the deft achievement
Whereby she has escaped the Wrongers all,
In view of which our momentary bereavement
        Outshapes but small.

## Questions for Discussion

1. Hardy wrote this poem in 1904, soon after his mother had died at age 91 from a long and painful illness. By what details does the poet indicate the external circumstances that prompted the poem?

2. What effect is achieved by the use of such words as "medicaments" (line 9) and "palliative" (line 11)?

3. Why is Time likened to a "cell" in lines 15–16?

4. What is the "deft achievement" in line 17? Why does Hardy call it "deft" and what effect does he create by his choice of this word?

5. Who are the "Wrongers all" in line 18, and why does Hardy call them "Wrongers"?

6. What does "by littles" mean in line 17 and "Outshapes" in line 20?

7. Describe the tone of the opening stanza, commenting on particular words and phrases that help to create that tone.

8. Does the second stanza reinforce the tone of the first or modify it? Cite evidence in support of your answer.

9. What tone do you find in stanza three that is not present in stanza one or stanza two? By what words does the poet make this tone apparent? Describe the relationship of the third stanza to the last two, considering the value of the phrase "And yet."

10. What is the dominant tone of the last two stanzas? How would you describe the emotional development that takes place in these two stanzas? How does Hardy signal the change in tone?

11. How does this poem capture the accents of spoken language? Support your answer with examples from the poem.

12. Comment fully on the relation of form to content in this poem, giving special attention to rhyme, rhythm, line length, sentence structure, and punctuation.

## *After the Funeral*
(In Memory of Ann Jones)

Dylan Thomas

After the funeral, mule praises, brays,
Windshake of sailshaped ears, muffle-toed tap
Tap happily of one peg in the thick
Grave's foot, blinds down the lids, the teeth in black,
The spittled eyes, the salt ponds in the sleeves,
Morning smack of the spade that wakes up sleep,
Shakes a desolate boy who slits his throat
In the dark of the coffin and sheds dry leaves,
That breaks one bone to light with a judgment clout,
After the feast of tear-stuffed time and thistles
In a room with a stuffed fox and a stale fern,
I stand, for this memorial's sake, alone
In the sniveling hours with dead, humped Ann
Whose hooded, fountain heart once fell in puddles
Round the parched worlds of Wales and drowned
 each sun
(Though this for her is a monstrous image blindly
Magnified out of praise; her death was a still drop;
She would not have me sinking in the holy
Flood of her heart's fame; she would lie dumb and
 deep
And need no druid of her broken body).
But I, Ann's bard on a raised hearth, call all
The seas to service that her wood-tongued virtue
Babble like a bellbuoy over the hymning heads,
Bow down the walls of the ferned and foxy woods
That her love sing and swing through a brown
 chapel,
Bless her bent spirit with four, crossing birds.
Her flesh was meek as milk, but this skyward statue
With the wild breast and blessed and giant skull
Is carved from her in a room with a wet window
In a fiercely mourning house in a crooked year.
I know her scrubbed and sour humble hands
Lie with religion in their cramp, her threadbare
Whisper in a damp word, her wits drilled hollow,
Her fist of a face died clenched on a round pain;
And sculptured Ann is seventy years of stone.
These cloud-sopped, marble hands, this monumental
Argument of the hewn voice, gesture and psalm,
Storm me forever over her grave until
The stuffed lung of the fox twitch and cry Love
And the strutting fern lay seeds on the black sill.

## Questions for Discussion

*Note.* Ann Jones, a poor but generous and devout woman, died almost unknown in Wales. Thomas wrote this poem about her in 1938. Keeping constantly in mind what goes on during and after a funeral will help you grapple with the first 20 lines of the poem.

1. Who is the speaker in this poem? In answering this question, make use of all the evidence and of your common sense.

2. Into how many parts may the poem be divided? How does the poet let you know where such division occurs? What is the major concern of each part?

3. What do the terms "mule praises, brays, / Windshake of sailshaped ears" (lines 1–2) suggest about the speaker's emotional response to the funeral service?

4. What do "the teeth in black" (line 4) and "The spittled eyes, the salt ponds of the sleeves" (line 5) imply about the emotional response of the other mourners to the funeral ceremonies? What do they imply about the feeling aroused in the speaker by those other mourners' response?

5. What does the phrase "muffle-toed tap / Tap happily of one peg in the thick / Grave's foot" (lines 2–4) indicate that the speaker is hearing at the burial service?

6. What happening is referred to in "Morning smack of the spade that wakes up sleep" (line 6)? What is the underlying irony in these words?

7. What are the feelings of the boy during the funeral and the burial services? Are the phrases "slits his throat" (line 7) and "sheds dry leaves" an appropriate expression of those feelings? If so, why? If not, why not?

8. To what previous word in the poem does the clause "That breaks one bone to light with a judgment clout" (line 9) refer? Is the line talking about a literal bone? How does this line, by implication, reinforce what lines 7–8 have told us about the boy's emotional response to Ann's death?

9. To what do the "feast" in line 10 and the "room" in line 11 refer? What effect does the poet achieve by repeating the word "stuffed" in the phrases "tear-stuffed time" (line 10) and "stuffed fox" (line 11)?

10. Why is the word "sniveling" used to describe the "hours" of line 13? What shades of meaning would be lost if the poet had written "weeping" instead of "sniveling"?

11. What figures of speech, what images does the poet use in lines 14–15 and why does he use them? Why does he call Ann's death "a still drop" in line 17? What does the poet himself realize about the imagery he has been using in lines 14–15? What does he believe Ann's reaction would be to such praise? Why does he use the word "Flood" in line 19 instead of "Warmth" or "Love"? How do you interpret the word "druid" in line 20?

12. Why does the poet call Ann's virtue "wood-tongued" (line 22)? Why does he use the simile "Babble like a bellbuoy" (line 23) to express what he wants Ann's "wood-tongued virtue" to do? Why doesn't he use the expected "Babble like a brook"?

13. What do you think the "four, crossing birds" in line 26 stand for?

14. In line 27 the poet describes Ann's flesh as "meek as milk"? Is "meek" usually a term of approval nowadays? What does it mean here and what feeling on the part of the speaker does it express?

15. What is "this skyward statue" (line 27) and why is it called "skyward"? What is the "room" in line 29 and why does it have "a wet window"? What is the "fiercely mourning house" in line 30 and why does the poet call the year "crooked"?

16. The poet refers to Ann's hands first in line 31 and then again in line 36. What contrasts do you note between the two descriptions and what is the purpose of these contrasts?

17. What does the poet mean when he says in lines 32–33 that Ann's voice, a "threadbare / Whisper," has become "a damp word"? What do you think that "damp word" is?

18. In three different places—line 11, line 24, and lines 39–40—the poet refers to the fox and the fern. Comment fully on the significance of these repeated references, giving particular attention to what happens to the fox and the fern in the two final lines.

19. In what significant ways does the form of this poem differ from the form of each of the three preceding poems? Could Thomas have achieved his purpose as well if he had chosen any one of the forms the other three poets use? Why or why not?

20. For most students this poem is harder to understand than any of the other three death poems. What are the characteristics of this poem that create the difficulties for the reader? If you listened to a recording of Dylan Thomas's reading of this poem, did his reading help you to understand the poem? If you did not hear his reading, do you think it would have been helpful if you had been able to do so? Why or why not?

## Original Writing Assignment One

(This was the original assignment, to be written after the poems had been studied.)

Sometimes a poem appeals to a reader because it states or implies an idea that is congenial to his own. A particular philosophical belief or attitude often provides the basic assumption upon which a particular poem is based. To the extent that you have some notions about life and death, even you might be considered to be, in one sense, a philosopher. What do you think about the poets' ideas on death and life in the four poems? In a well-organized and concrete way, write a paper in which you: (1) state as clearly as possible the poets' attitudes toward life and death, and (2) supply definite examples from the poems to support your statements.

## Reasons for Revising the Original Writing Assignment One

The papers that were written on the original writing assignment—of which three samples follow—show weaknesses in the assignment unsuspected until it was tried out. First, the assignment is too much a repetition of what should be discussed in class. Second, the connection between the introduction and the directions is insufficient. Third, the tone in which the student is addressed is condescending. Finally, the assignment, even for home work, is long and demanding. Even the *high* paper on the original assignment had to skimp the last section (on Dylan Thomas's poem).

The revised assignments, as shown below, endeavor to correct these errors. The first paper—an analytic one—is to be written before class discussion of the poems. The second calls for a personal response to one of the four poems. They have not been pretested.

## Revised Writing Assignment One

(The assignment is to be written before class discussion of the four poems, but after the student has gone as far as he can on his own with the study materials provided in this teaching plan.)

### Directions

In a well-planned essay define the implied attitudes toward life and death of *one* of the four poets by comparing and contrasting his implied attitudes with those of the other three poets. To do this you will need to support your conclusions with illustrations from each of the four poems, but make your chosen poet the center of your paper.

## Writing Assignment Two

(The assignment is to be written after the class discussion has been completed.)

### Directions

Choose the poem in which the implied view of death is most remote from your own previous conceptions. Write a carefully planned paper in which you state and explain your own reaction to the view of death suggested by this poem. Then show how your encounter with the poem has changed, modified, or confirmed your previous conceptions.

## Original Writing Assignment One
## Sample 1. Grade: High

In four poems—"On His Deceased Wife" by John Milton, "After the Last Breath" by Thomas Hardy, "To An Athlete Dying Young" by A. E. Housman, and "After the Funeral—(In Memory of Ann Jones)" by Dylan Thomas—each of which deal with the poet's attitude toward the death of another, various views about life and death are evident. None states general principles about death; and projection always risks inaccuracy. The poet, in every case, has presented a reaction to one death, to the death of a specific personality in a specific set of circumstances. From this beginning it is often possible to speculate and enlarge, gaining some idea of the man's thoughts on life and death in general.

John Milton, author of the sonnet "On His Deceased Wife," is visited in a dream by the wife, dead in childbirth, whom he has never seen. The Puritan poet presents religious ideas tinged with an imaginative mysticism.

Methought I saw my late espoused Saint, establishes a ghostly, dreamlike atmosphere while it refers to the "elect" of Puritanism. The poem indicates a definite belief in an afterlife—specifically in a heaven where he will see his beloved wife. He will no longer be blind; presumably there will be perfection in the mind as well as in the spiritual body.

> . . . As yet once more I trust to have
> Full sight of her in Heaven without restraint.

Milton's life is not happy, as shown in the last line:

> I wak'd, she fled, and day brought back my night.

His misery arises from his blindness and from his separation from his wife and the goodness that she represents, for:

> Love, sweetness, goodness, in her person shin'd,
> So clear . . .

Life, to Milton, is thus an imperfect form of (and almost a preparation for) an afterlife of goodness, love, and beauty.

Housman's "To An Athlete Dying Young" present a view of life and death very much like that of the Greeks.

> And round that early-laureled head
> Will flock to gaze the strengthless dead.

Death is seen as "the road all runners come," a common destiny. The afterlife is an inferior continuation of earthly existence. One can picture behind his words Argive youths wandering sadly in Hades, playing again their accustomed games, but shadows only of their former selves. Housman points out, as well, the evanescence of earthly glory—represented by the laurel—and of love and youth, symbolized by the rose.

> Smart lad, to slip betimes away
> From fields where glory does not stay
> And early though the laurel grows
> It withers quicker than the rose.

Although his reaction to another life's death might be different, in writing of the dead runner Housman appears not to find life ultimately valuable, for to him present fame is better (or at least wiser) than a prolonged life with the glory forgotten.

Hardy's "After the Last Breath" is much like Housman's ballad in its frank lack of any Christian sentiment; one might almost label it pagan. Hardy, however, writes in a tone that is much more restrained and passionless, more pessimistic.

Life is viewed as the conspiracy of evil forces, full of pain and sadistic spirits. Death is a release.

> Our well-beloved is prisoner in the cell
> Of Time no more.
> We see by littles now the deft achievement
> Whereby she has escaped the Wrongers all
> In view of which our momentary bereavement
> Outshapes but small.

Throughout the poem a sense of the purposelessness of life is exhibited.

"After the Funeral—(In Memory of Ann Jones)" is a beautiful poem which memorializes a woman of beautiful spirit, dead at seventy. Her life was one of goodness, kindness, and humility—and this Dylan Thomas, "Ann's bard on a raised hearth," praises.

> I stand for this memorial's sake, alone
> In the snivelling hours with dead, humped Ann
> Whose hooded, fountain heart once fell in puddles
> Round the parched worlds of Wales and drowned each sun.

Her death, generally unnoticed, is the culmination of her life and the reason for his poem, for his proclamation of her living. Her life, ended by her death, is inspiration and example. Thomas does not discuss the death of Ann Jones except as a fact. But he builds from dead Ann

> . . . this skyward statue
> With the wild breast and blessed and giant skull.

And he will mourn loss—the loss of her humble, holy soul—until all the world is transformed into Ann's likeness.

These cloud-sopped, marble hands, this monumental
Argument of the hewn voice, gesture and psalm,
Storm me forever over her grave until
The stuffed lung of the fox twitch and cry Love
And the strutting fern lay seeds on the black sill.

Thus there are similarities and differences in four poets' particular treatment of particular deaths. Milton anticipates paradise; Housman sees the fitness of a well-timed death; Hardy grieves but blesses the beloved's release from painful earth-life; Thomas praises in hope of emulation. Yet all have created poetry in presenting a personally valid situation with truth and beauty.

## Original Writing Assignment One
## Comment on Sample 1. Grade: High

This paper is outstanding in its thoroughness, its grasp of the material, its awareness of the difficulties of the assignment, and its judiciousness in circumventing these difficulties. Other papers used a more sophisticated scheme of organization, but none of them reckoned with some of the vital points that this paper tackles. The organization here is essentially an introduction, a separate section on each of the four poems, and a conclusion; but that final section does an admirable job of packing a wealth of commentary into a very small space.

The precision and economy of the sentence in which the student has expressed his recognition of the essential difficulty are noteworthy, "None (of the four poets) states general principles about death; and projection always risks inaccuracy." Yet this student is also acute enough to realize that it is possible to infer the general from the particular provided you exercise caution in the process.

A hasty glance at the paper might suggest that it leans too heavily on quotations, but a careful reading reveals that the student has made these quotations an integral part of his own thinking. The coverage of each separate poem is not complete, nor could it be, but this is a writer who has developed a sure sense of what to include and what to omit.

## Original Writing Assignment One
## Sample 2. Grade: Average

*Attitudes of Death*

Every individual has his own personal attitude toward death. In the poem "On His Deceased Wife" John Milton is very emotional, due to the fact that his wife died during childbirth. He holds a definate belief in the after-life, and he sees death not as an end, but as a beginning. Any impediment that may have existed on earth will cease to exist in heaven. The author, himself, is blind and has never had full sight of his beloved wife. He believes that in heaven he will see his wife fully, without this physical impediment. For him all his days are nights until his death when he will be united with his wife.

In "To An Athlete Dying Young", A. E. Houseman has an entirely different attitude toward death. He develops a parallel with the race and the athlete to life and death. Houseman believes life is a road race that all runners, or people must enter and participate in. He commends the young athlete for having made something of his life before he reached old age and people forgot him. This athlete had the strength to decide what he wanted from life, and saw his aim accomplished. The weaker athletes running the race of humanity will gaze at the stronger athlete and see what they failed to achieve during their lives.

Thomas Hardy is concerned more with suffering than death in "After The Last Breath". The woman in the poem, Hardy's mother, suffered a long time before her death. The shock those around her bedside experience is contrasted with the relief death brings to her pattern of suffering. Hardy feels that he and the others who sought vainly to keep her alive were wrong in doing so. To him death is an end to suffering and to prolong it is a useless act of cruelty.

Dylan Thomas seems to believe all people are hypocrites. He was only a small boy when Ann Jones, his aunt, died. In "After The Funeral–(In Memory of Ann Jones)" Dylan Thomas tells the impression her funeral and the hypocritical people that attended it had on him. The people did not realize what kind of a person Ann Jones was, and so he alone tries to raise her to the height he feels she deserves. He believes people get their own reward only in heaven, and so her just reward will come only after death.

To me death is a conglomeration of all these ideas. Like Milton, I believe death is not really an ending, but rather a beginning. I also believe each individual must decide what he wants from his life, then set an aim and strive to attain it. Some people would agree with Hardy, that there is no use in prolonging death, but still others would disagree. It does seem cruel to prolong suffering, but no human being may take the life of another. Death is not one of these authors' aspects, but a conglomeration of all of them.

## Original Writing Assignment One
## Comment on Sample 2. Grade: Average

This paper is a dutiful attempt to cover both parts of the assignment. It moves to its ends with a sure command of the obvious and occasional falterings with the more subtle. The style is clear, but unexciting. This student, unlike the first, is not predictably sure in his diction. An example of imprecision is the use of "aspects" in the final sentence, but even more disturbing is the illogic in the sentence of the final paragraph that reads, "Some people would agree with Hardy, that there is no use in prolonging death." Surely the writer must have meant either "prolonging life" or "postponing death." Nor are the judgments in this paper as consistently sound as those in the first paper. The reader may well take issue with the statement in the second sentence that "John Milton is *very emotional,* due to the fact that his wife died during childbirth." The final part of the Housman section in its comment on the "weaker athletes" reads into the poem what Housman probably never intended. The sweeping generalization that Dylan Thomas seems to believe that all people are hypocrites is ingenuous if not inaccurate. Finding in Dylan Thomas the notion that "people get their own reward only in heaven" neatly illustrates the first student's warning that "projection always risks inaccuracy." Despite these defects, however, this student has made a commendable attempt to grapple with the multiple demands of an admittedly difficult assignment.

## Original Writing Assignment One
## Sample 3. Grade: Low

Death is a revitilizing force which shines forth so clear, that it awakens the spirit to the present ecstacy and the past victories of life. The inclination is to turn away from death and not face it realistically or rationally. It may come slowly, as a "still drop" or rapidly while crowds cheer, and carry you shoulder-high. But it must come, the "silence sounds", the undiscriblable nothing that death is, will consume something, and the audience —heretics or sincere lovers pose in suspended andimation over the "broken bones" that will one day be them.

Nature is the only one truly crying, calling "this skyward statue" to clench deaths hand and shovel the storm of lifes grief under its masked duo representation of the earths values. The gestures which the machanical watches shows are things left to them as a tradition and their inner response which the desolate person remains uncommunicable and lay black and still in spirit.

## Original Writing Assignment One
## Comment on Sample 3. Grade: Low

This student makes no direct reference either to the assignment or to the poems. The word "death" occurs several times, but what the student is trying to say about it is never clear. Phrases are quoted (without acknowledgment) from the poems, but to no perceptible purpose. Spelling is weak; weaker still are diction and sentence structure—consider the last sentence of the first paragraph. Unquestionably *low.*

*Richmond Lattimore:*
*"Sonnet on Hope"*
*Advanced Placement, Grade 12*

## To the Teacher

The choice of this poem sprang partly from the realization that the other poetry units pretested in the spring of 1966 included only poems already so familiar to teachers that some of them, such as "My Last Duchess," might be termed "old war horses." None of the poems already tested has the newness for teachers that this one has; none is so immediately close to our own time; and probably none poses such intriguingly difficult problems of interpretation. It was for this last reason that the Commission felt that here was a "challenge" for even the ablest of twelfth grade Advanced Placement students. Another reason for choosing the poem is its exciting fusion of the traditional and the contemporary in a pattern of tightly packed allusion stretching from Odysseus to that peculiarly twentieth-century phenomenon—the baby-sitter.

Writing assignment one is here to give able twelfth graders the chance to wrestle alone with the poem, to gauge its difficulties, and then to record their left-over questions after they have moved as far into the poem as they can without help. The students' own questions should be a vital part of the study of the poem. The extent to which the discussion questions prepared for this unit will be useful will depend on how deeply the students' questions have already probed. The questions offered here deliberately focus on the form of the poem, on its imagery and its allusions, and on the fusion within the poem of the traditional and the contemporary. They leave the student a chance for further discoveries in his final writing assignment.

## Writing Assignment One

Now that you have heard the poem read aloud five or six times, study it further. Then write a paper in which you explore its meanings and its implications as fully and as thoroughly as you can without the help of class discussion. After you have done all you can with the poem, list at the end of your paper any left-over questions or problems that you were not able to answer or solve.

## Questions for Discussion

1. The title tells you that this poem is a sonnet. What kind of sonnet is it? Does it adhere strictly to its chosen form? If not, just how does it vary? Do these variations strengthen or weaken the poem? Give reasons for your answer.

2. What features in the poem give it a more casual tone than is usual in a sonnet? (Here students should notice the almost-but-not-quite-perfect rhymes; the lack of capitalization for the first word in each line that is not the beginning of a sentence; the terms "bedraggled," "barefoot," and "slattern.")

3. Lines 2–3 allude to the Sirens in Homer's *Odyssey.* What does the Hope in this poem have in common with the Sirens in the *Odyssey?*

4. The phrase "counting her sheep" in line 4 may remind some reader of the familiar nursery rhyme:

> Little Bo Peep has lost her sheep,
> And can't tell where to find them;
> Leave them alone, and they'll come home
> And bring their tails behind them.

Do these lines from "Little Bo Peep" relate in any significant way to the rest of the poem? Do you get just as satisfactory a reading of line 4 if you take it to mean merely that Hope is counting sheep in the hope of falling asleep? Are both readings possible? You will need to give carefully considered answers to these questions. (You may want to consider other stanzas of "Little Bo Peep.")

5. What evidence in line 5 suggests that the poet is making a comparison between Hope and Cupid? In what ways are the two similar?

6. What qualities do the Sirens and Cupid have in common? Do these two allusions merely support each other or does each add another dimension to the speaker's concept of hope?

7. The image of "The baby-sitter in the abandoned chair" is a picture drawn from contemporary reality. What evidence is there that the poet thinks of the baby-sitter as a teen-ager? As an older person? Must the reader choose between these two interpretations? Why is the chair "abandoned"? Is there any connection between "The baby-sitter in the abandoned chair" and the situation in the Ithaca of Homer's *Odyssey?*

8. For many readers the most powerful image in

# *Richmond Lattimore: "Sonnet on Hope" Advanced Placement, Grade 12*

*Approximate Time:* 3 class periods and 3 preparation periods

The following time schedule is merely suggestive:

*First class period.* Distribute copies of the poem. Have five or six different students read the poem aloud. Then let the students use the rest of the class period to make a start on the preliminary writing assignment.

*First preparation period.* Students should complete the first paper.

*Second class period.* Use this period for a discussion of the questions students have raised at the end of their papers. Then give out the prepared discussion questions, including the final writing assignment.

*Second preparation period.* Students should study the prepared discussion questions and make a start on the final writing assignment.

*Third class period.* Use the time for as much of the prepared discussion material as is needful and useful. If any time is left, students should work on the final writing assignment.

*Third preparation period.* Students will complete the final writing assignment.

*Sonnet on Hope*

Richmond Lattimore

Bedraggled daughter of Desire and Fear,
she'll glaze your eyes and sing your brain to sleep,
pour siren's wax and honey in your ear.
Hope, self-seduced and simple, counting her sheep.
The painted Hope, blind, whispering, and with wings.
The baby-sitter in the abandoned chair
waiting beside a phone that never rings,
dreaming of cradles and fixed calendars,
and the clock stopped forever, and the glass
sucking its sand back in, the never-was
world come again, new-made and clean of scars.
I fled from Hope and found her everywhere,
barefoot and bold in all her slattern charms,
with a two-headed baby in her arms.

the poem is probably the "two-headed baby" of the final line. What was your first response to that image? After further examination of the poem has your response changed? If so, how and why? The speaker in the poem tells you that he "fled from Hope and found her everywhere . . . with a two-headed baby in her arms"—and that is all he tells you. Now look again at line 1. Does it give you a clue to the meaning of the "two-headed baby" of line 14? If so, how do you now explain that image? Could these lines be seen as two images for the same idea? If so, what does the second image add to what is conveyed by the first?

9. How does the concept of Hope in this poem differ from the usual one? From these differences what can we infer about the purpose of the writer of this sonnet?

## Writing Assignment Two

In a carefully planned paper show the extent to which the speaker's consciousness of Time shapes his understanding of Hope.

## Writing Assignment One
## Sample 1. Grade: High

*An Interpretation of "Sonnet on Hope"*

In his "Sonnet on Hope," Richmond Lattimore presents a very negative view of Hope. Rather than as the maiden who gives man reason and direction in his futile struggling, Hope appears, with the first line, as the "bedraggled daughter of Desire and Fear," who will "glaze your eyes and sing your brain to sleep,/pour siren's wax and honey in your ear." Glazing man's eyes, she impairs his perception of reality, with her wax and honey she entices and deludes him, and singing his brain to sleep she stops his rational thoughts.

Having warned his readers of the ways of Hope, Lattimore presents Hope in two images. The first is of Hope "self-seduced and simple, counting her sheep." Both the image of this line, Hope, self-corrupted and simple, shepherding her deluded, glass-eyed followers, and the way the image is presented, concisely, in not even a sentence with an alliterative repetition of the hissing S sound, present an almost perverse and fiendish Hope. In the succeeding line the reader views the second image of Hope: "painted Hope, blind, whispering and with wings" Painted, Hope again deceives, appearing other than what she really is, and blind with no true goal towards which she might actually lead man. "Whispering and with wings," Hope is quiet, subtle and fleeting.

Juxtaposed with the portrayal of Hope as he envisions her, the next image Lattimore presents is of one taken in by Hope. The baby-sitter, beside "a phone that never rings," is waiting with unfulfillable hope, as she dreams, with equally false hope, of "fixed calendars/and the clock stopped forever, and the glass/sucking its sand back in," of the stoppage and even reversal of time. She dreams of the "never-was world come again new-made and clean of scars," her past life brought back clean of any mistakes or unpleasantness it might have held. Completely deluded by Hope, the baby-sitter sits with her reality-seeking eyes glazed and her reality-contemplating mind asleep, awaiting events beyond reality.

Finally, the poet reveals himself, juxtaposed with the deluded babysitter, as one who, seeing the true nature of Hope, has attempted to flee from her and yet has "found her everywhere/barefoot and bold in all her slattern charms,/with a two-headed baby in her arms." Since Hope has not gathered him among her sheep, with his yet un-glazed eyes the poet sees both Hope, in reality crudely "barefoot and bold" with the seductive charm of a prostitute, and the unnatural (hopes, etc.) to which she gives rise, the two-headed baby in her arms.

The poet, then, views Hope not as the savior of mankind from his misery of futility but rather as the crude seducer of men who blinds men, giving them false expectations.

I am not quite secure in my interpretation of the two-headed child, nor do I totally comprehend the significance of Hope's being the daughter of Desire and Fear, or of her blindness.

## Writing Assignment One
## Comment on Sample 1. Grade: High

The strengths of this paper are its command of diction and sentence structure, its avoidance of the over-reading and misinterpretation so easily possible in this poem, its firm grasp of main points, and its awareness of the pattern of organization the poet has given to these main points. Another paper, from the same school, did an even subtler job of linking the poem's form, structure, and meaning but was less sound than this paper in its total interpretation of the poem. Still other students tracked down the allusions more methodically and more explicitly than this student does. This student, for example, never mentions the *Odyssey* in commenting on the Sirens, but his comment suggests his awareness of the source of the allusion. At the close of his paper he indicates the parts of the poem about which he is doubtful, and in his comment he discreetly interprets only as far as his certainties permit, thus avoiding some of the errors that cropped up in papers where students were too eager to lasso the elusive. This student respects the text and knows the limits of his own knowledge. His style is polished and precise but never pretentious. The last sentence of paragraph two and the last sentence of paragraph three demonstrate the writer's control over sentence form and parallel structure.

## Writing Assignment One
## Sample 2. Grade: High

*Hope Springs Eternal*

From the very first word, "bedraggled," to one of the last words, "barefoot," Lattimore amply supplies images that support his basic idea. He creates the mood that there is something both cheap and easy about resorting to hope. Because hope is the "daughter of Desire and Fear," she was born of Desire and Fear. She was born of the necessity to escape: to escape from fearful realities, to escape *to* desirable illusions. Her actions—"she'll glaze your eyes and sing your brain to sleep, pour siren's wax and honey in your ear."—are measures of blocking the truth out, of separating the "follower" from reality. The words chosen indicate that the person who succumbs to her has made the weak, ignoble choice. Odysseus was similarly tempted by the siren's "singing."

Hope, as personified by Lattimore, is as much taken by her own powers and charms ("self-seduced."). This aspect of her character seems to indicate that those who revel in their reliance upon hope are cruelly self-deceived. Indeed, Hope mocks the regularity and inevitability of many followers by "counting her sheep." "Sheep" also indicates the docile trust of her followers. The seductive qualities of Hope are again emphasized in the next line where she is flaunted as a "painted" woman. "Blind, whispering, and with wings" intensifies the fleeting value of faith put in her.

The next few lines present a spiteful concrete example of one who has succumbed to her charms. The fact that the subject is a baby-sitter offers many important connotations to the reader. First of all, a baby-sitter is a teenage girl, who, no doubt, views herself and her world as extermely imperfect. It may be trivial, but the situation connotes loneliness both by the fact that she is alone in a foreign house and obviously doesn't have a date—the important measure of teenage success. Hope has placed her in a state of expectation—replacing present loneliness with possible future dreams. The dreams are hinged upon a phone call, which would be the first step toward escaping the loneliness. The dreams are simple thoughts of married life, "of cradles" representing children. The babysitter also anticipates "fixed calendars" or a life of regularity like J. Alfred Prufrock's life that was measured out in coffeespoons. Lattimore expertly returns the poem to its previous general level by having the babysitter's thoughts intensify and become more general. Her dreams cease to be the fulfillment of specific desires, and become the universal dreams of all followers of hope. First, she wishes to stop time: "the clock stopped forever, and the glass sucking its sand back in." This idea could also indicate her desire to *keep* her happiness of cradles and calendars after she has attained it. Secondly, she envisions a world of perfection. It is not enough to have *this* world "new-made" without its imperfections—"clean of scars." The world that will return in perfection *is* her dream world—"the never-was world."

In the last three lines, Lattimore returns to his images that exist on two levels. Hope, as she is personified, has both cheap slattern appeal and an aura of mythological power. She seems both a slut and a godess. At any rate, escape is impossible, and the poet changes the voice to first person to intensify the futility. He tried not to succumb, but she was everywhere—charming all those around him with the earthy appeal of a slut, "barefoot and bold," and the enchantment of a godess, "self-seduced and simple." She is holding "a two-headed baby," because all trust in Hope only breeds more Desire and Fear and those who believe in her power to eliminate desire and fear are deceiving themselves.

1. The meaning of the "two-headed baby" was unclear to me.

2. "and with wings" was an image that didn't seem to fit the poem.

## Writing Assignment One
## Comment on Sample 2. Grade: High

The writing here is also competent, though without the sharpness, the seemingly easy brilliance of the first sample. This student, however, examines the poem in greater detail than the first writer. The handling of the Sirens is more explicit and the attack on the "two-headed baby" is more thorough. Another strength of this paper is the constant recognition that Lattimore's concept of Hope is dual, linking the power of a goddess with the sluttishness of a prostitute. Because this writer is venturesomely explicit, he is more vulnerable to error than the first writer, as, for instance, when he interprets "fixed calendars" as meaning "a life of regularity," apparently missing what is happening to Time itself in the phrase, nor does he seem fully aware of the hoped-for reversal of Time in the hourglass figure. These, though, are minor defects in a paper written entirely without the help of class discussion about a sonnet deliberately picked for its multiple difficulties.

## Writing Assignment One
## Sample 3. Grade: Average

The poet has divided this sonnet into three distinct sections. Each section reveals his reactions toward hope as he has experienced it in his life. The first five lines present an elaborate personal definition of hope. Hope, to the poet, is a direct product of desire and fear. Despite the fact that hope is worn with continual use, she still maintains power over humans. The poet appears dissatisfied with the effects of hope. It misguides your emotions and forces you into a dream world, which lacks realness. Hope can have a dual effect on a person. It can bring much happiness into a life and give someone faith in the world. But by believing too strongly in hope, a person might stray too far from reality and will eventually be hurt mentally or physically. Regardless of which case the poet experienced, he feels that to encounter hope in one's life is extremely easy to achieve. This is the reason why many people are involved with hope and use it so automatically.

Up to this point in the sonnet, the poet has explained his personal feelings about the good and the harmful aspects of hope. But his second division in the poem, consisting of lines six through eleven, deals solely with an incident illustrating the ill-effects of hope. The baby-sitter has obviously had hopes in the past of having her own family, but her wish has never come true. All she has left to hope for is that time will stop and she will be able to start her life again. With this example, the poet shows how hope can effect a person's mind and attitude. The usefulness and meaning of hope has become distorted to this person, because she is hoping for something that can never happen. From this incident, the poet emphasizes the fact that hope can be cruel rather than helpful when it becomes too meaningful to a person.

The last section returns to the poet's personal philosophy and again he presents his dual interpretation. In his own personal life, he finds hope inescapable. He expresses, for the time, his dislike for hope. His reference to "her slattern charms" makes me feel that her effects inevitably head to personal destruction. When his dual interpretation appears in the form of "a two-headed baby", he shows again that hope has two effects. He has found the ill-effects more prominent and tries to warn the readers of the poem that hope can effect us in the identical manner.

Questions:

1. What is the meaning of "a two-headed baby in her arms"?
2. What does "fixed calendars" refer to in the sonnet?

## Writing Assignment One
## Comment on Sample 3. Grade: Average

This paper moves in a simpler, more obvious world than the first two. Because it never grapples with the really puzzling parts of the poem, it lacks the sharp insights and the subtle perceptions that put those other two papers in the *high* brackets. Except for an occasional minor slip, the writing skills here are unexcitingly respectable. Nowhere in this comment, though, does the reader sense that the writer is in close touch with the poem. Rather, the sonnet is used as a point of departure for a somewhat colorless paraphrase of its most obvious ideas, eked out by the writer's own notions about Hope. The idea that Hope "can bring much happiness" is certainly the student's rather than Mr. Lattimore's. And the observation that "The poet appears dissatisfied with the effects of hope" is an almost ludicrously mild understatement of the speaker's feelings in the sonnet. This student, like the second, senses the duality of the concept of Hope, but he sees that duality as Hope's power of conferring both happiness and pain. He is aware that the "two-headed baby" is a tough nut to crack, but his only other left-over question concerns the meaning of the phrase "fixed calendars"—a phrase with which an able twelfth grader should be competent to deal. The averageness of this paper lies in its noncommittal generality, its avoidance of gross misinterpretation, its methodical organization, and its failure to achieve either subtlety or thoroughness.

## Writing Assignment One
## Sample 4. Grade: Low

Certainly the picture painted of Hope in this poem is far from a pleasant one. The vision of Hope that I get is a gloomy, dismal one with the theme being that no matter where you go or what you do, the element of Hope is always present. It cannot be avoided. Hope appears in many forms, and when it is at work, it can be rather cruel. How many times have we hoped that something would happen the way we wanted it to, knowing all the while that the chances for it to happen were really very slim, but still hoping nonetheless? The off-chance that it may work out for us, that one glimmer of Hope, keeps the spark alive. Hope is present while we sleep, in our dreams, and it is present in the mind of a baby-sitter who sits by a phone hoping it will ring. The point is that what we hope for and what becomes reality in dreams are two entirely different things, and rare is the case that what we dreamed and hoped for becomes reality. So Hope then, while it can sustain us and keep us going, is really nothing more than an evil agent working against us.

Question: Meaning of "a two-headed baby?"

## Writing Assignment One
## Comment on Sample 4. Grade: Low

In this paper the writing skills are competent. The student nowhere actually misinterprets, but about all he offers is a smooth summary composed more of his own ideas about Hope than Mr. Lattimore's. He never comes to grips with any of the images, except for his recognition that the baby-sitter hopes the phone will ring. In fact, he dismisses the matter of imagery with the assurance that "Hope appears in many forms," leaving untouched the Sirens, the sheep counting, and the "two-headed baby." Nor is there any reckoning here with the duality of Hope in both her parentage and her offspring. For a regular twelfth grader an *average* rating might be right for the paper. But this is an Advanced Placement candidate, one the College Board defines as a sensitive and responsible reader. The student evidences neither sensitive nor responsible reading.

## Writing Assignment Two
## Sample 1. Grade: High +

The concept of Hope is usually thought of in terms of optimism, cheerfulness and expectancy. The main and underlying theme of this poem, however, is not that of Hope's Fruitfulness, nor even of its futility, though this aspect of Hope is emphasized to a certain extent, but rather of Hope's timelessness. And to the poet in this sonnet Hope is not in any way fettered by the conventional time divisions of past, present and future. Normally the concept of Hope itself naturally presupposes a sense of expectation or waiting, in that it is impossible to hope for something that has happened or that is happening, but only for something that will happen. But in this poem the barriers of this conventional restriction and distinction are broken down, and the concept of Hope is intentionally made to wallow in the indefinite and unending swamp of infinity. Its origin and its end are unclear and indeterminable; its existence is undeniable.

This continuous process is here represented as a never-ending cycle of regeneration. Hope procreates herself indefinitely, and her continuous process of recreation is mentioned in this poem, appropriately in the first and last lines. For in line 1 Hope is represented as the daughter of Desire and Fear, the twin elements of Hope that go to make her up, and in line 14 Hope is now seen as the mother of a two-headed baby, the one head representing Desire, and the other Fear. Desire and Fear create hope, which in turn creates Desire and Fear. The cycle is infinite.

The actual construction of the poem itself shows how significantly the poet's consciousness of "Time" has affected the organization of his sonnet on Hope. The sonnet-form in poetry immediately makes the reader think back to the Elizabethan times in England. The poets of that time, and particularly Shakespeare, were the chief exponents of the sonnet in English literature. The form that they used was neat, concise and well-ordered, with a regular metre, and, above all, strictly documented rules about rhyme. The ingenuity with which Lattimore uses these allusions to enhance the effect of his poem is superb.

Having started off with a regular quatrain in iambic pentametres with the customary ABAB rhyming scheme, he inspires in the reader the expectation, or hope, of a regular and well-ordered sonnet, adhering to the Elizabethan format. The reader should have been forewarned by the first word of the whole poem: "bedraggled." Bedraggled is the nature of Hope, and bedraggled is the construction of the sonnet; but its disorder is achieved by the skilful organization and consumate artistry. For the regularity of the poem breaks down after the first four lines, but a pattern remains. The metre remains regular throughout, syncopated at times to give added effect or emphasis; but it is the rhyming scheme that disintegrates, and yet at the same time holds the poem together. For the sense of the poem, together with the time element expressed in it, can be divided into three sections: ll. 1–5, where the allusions and suggested references refer mainly to the past, ll. 6–11, the present, and ll. 12–14, the future: the rhyming scheme (A.B.A.B.C.D.C.E.F.F.E.D. G.G.) is also divided into three sections: ll. 1–4, 5–12, 13–14. In order that the sonnet does not become split into three distinct sections in sense, time, and rhyme, thus creating three isolated units within the constructional whole, the poet has overlapped the central rhyming section so as to incorporate the last line of the first sense and time section and the first line of the last, thus creating one unified whole. And in order that his rhyming scheme may not become stereotyped, predictable, and therefore monotonous, the poet has skilfully syncopated the central rhyming section, thus putting the central lines of the poem slightly off balance. And this whole scheme of apparent disorder, and the deliberate rejection of the conventional form of the Elizabethan sonnet is in keeping with the poet's concept of Hope as being fickle, fleeting and transient in nature.

Although I divided the poem into three sections of time, these divisions, though a very strong case can be made out for them, were purely artibrary and functional for the purpose of illustrating the sonnet's construction. The time element of the poem is, in fact, universal in its scope, in a temporal rather than physical sense, and it flits indiscriminately from past, to present, and to future. And this, in the poet's opinion is just exactly the nature of Hope.

There is only one line in the whole poem (l.13) in which the element of time is not in any way involved. Line 1 refers back to the creation of Hope out of the two elements of Desire and Fear. Line 2 illustrates the ever-present dangers that Hope presents, and her power of unreason over the human mind. Line 3 picks up the classical reference of the Sirens, fabulous monsters of the ancient world, part-woman and part-bird, who were supposed to lure sailors to their destruction by their enchanting singing. In lines 4 and 5 Hope is depicted as deluding herself and as deluding others. I do not think that the suggested allusion to "Little Bo-Peep" has much relevance in the content. The soporific connotations that the metaphor "counting her sheep" implies and its prominent position, rhyming with the "sleep" of line 2, present a much more acceptable interpretation.

Time stands still for the baby-sitter; she is firmly fixed in the present, dreaming vaguely of the past, and hoping fruitlessly for the future. In her, at the centre of the poem, the three elements of time meet, join and intermingle; she incorporates and represents them all. The picture is of a young teen-ager, left alone in a house as a baby-sitter, with nothing to occupy her attention except her dreams, thoughts and hopes. The position of the epithet 'abandoned' is very effective in the content. This is a hypallage, as it is not the chair that is abandoned; but the adjective is really meant to apply to the girl, who has been left alone in the house. She waits, at first optimistically, but then with ever-increasing depression and resignation, for her boy-friend to ring her up. Her hopes are dashed, and the telephone remains mute. The interpretation of the next line (8) is harder: the 'cradles' might conceivably be interpreted as the cradles of the children who are in the girl's charge, but this is very unlikely, and another interpretation, much better in the content of Hope as portrayed in this poem, is that these are the future cradles of her own children. This interpretation continues the idea of hope of her boy-friend's 'phone call, through hope of marriage with him, to hope of having children by him in the future. The 'fixed calendars' probably describe the concept of her hope that time will stand still for her in her hoped-for future happiness, and this idea would be in keeping with the next line and a half, where this concept of the cessation of the passage of time is definitely expressed. This idea progresses in reverse so that in the last image the girl is actually hoping that time will go backwards. The 'glass', of course, is the obconical, sand-filled hour-glass.

The idea expressed in the second half of line 10 and in line 11 is one of the most interesting images in the poem from the point of view of consciousness of "Time"; it is also an extremely difficult one to express, because of its almost impossibly elliptical construction. But the idea is as follows: in her imagination and hope the girl had created an idyllic Utopia that never had, or could, exist. This idealistic image was so strong for her that she actually forces herself to believe that her image of hope existed in the realistic world of her daily life. This explains how she could hope that a world that had never existed except in her hopeful imagination would "return again" from her old self-made utopia to the reality of the present-day world. And not only is she content to transfer something non-existent and abstract into something real and concrete, but her hope is so powerful that she actually wishes her utopia to come "new made and clean of scars." Such is the force of human hope.

The elements of past, present and future, of abstract and concrete, and of vague and dramatically clear imagery intermingle in the last three lines; and the poet's belief in the universality of the scope of "Time" here receives its final statement in the intricate manipulation of Time's different aspects. From this fusion it can be seen that the poet does not intend any distinction to be drawn between the events of yesterday, today and tomorrow; they all occur within the sphere of "Time," which is a single, continuous and indivisable unit, and all events are thus united by their incorporation into this single unity of "Time."

Thus, it can be seen by this analysis of the sonnet that the poet's conception of "Time" is that it is universal and incapable of distinction into the three conventional, sectional divisions of past, present and future. The central figure of the baby-sitter in the poem personifies and expresses this idea. Hope, too, is all-embracing: although the poet realizes that, logically, you can only hope for the future, nevertheless he realizes that Hope is very closely tied up with the past and the present, and, as a result of his consciousness of "Time," the poet believes that Hope, too, can be viewed as a fusion of the three elements of past, present and future.

## Writing Assignment Two
## Comment on Sample 1. Grade: High +

The sustained brilliance, incisiveness, and comprehensiveness of this essay are an example of the exceptional thinking and writing of which some Advanced Placement candidates are capable. The style is compact, firm, balanced, or antithetical as need dictates, precise and sensitive in the use of a diction, as at home with the term "hypallage" as with the phrase "boy friend," and sensing exactly where to use each. The careful ordering of each separate section is as impressive as the master building of the total structure of the paper. The thoroughness and the depth of the analysis are as remarkable as the insights, particularly the exceptional handling of the relation between theme and form in the poem. The reader of this paper will not wonder at the exceptional grade *high+*.

## Writing Assignment Two
## Sample 2. Grade: High

*Time and Hope; or, poetry at Bryn Mawr; or, the Abandoned Chair*

A basic theme of Lattimore's sonnet is that of the relationship of Hope to Time. The poet suggests aspects of this theme through the structure of the sonnet itself and through illustrative personifications of hope. Time, as an absolute force, affords a basis for the study of hope, inasmuch as the latter parallels the former or reacts to it.

The poem's structure is a synthesis of interaction between classical and modern influences. The sonnet form, after all, is generally thought of as a tightly-controlled apostrophication, strict in its conformity to a pattern of rhyme. Its tone tends to idealise its subject. Lattimore deliberately produces a mutation of the sonnet as an analogy to the content of his poem.

He begins with a formal quatrain, and the reader expects the usual Elizabethan structure. The center section starts appropriately, but then seems to degenerate until the introduction of a final couplet. On inspection one senses a subtle decrescendo; as the speaker turns from an allusion to Homeric Sirens and begins the modern illustration of the baby-sitter, the structure loses its accord with classical rules. The borders are not distinct, however; the rhyme scheme tapers off rather than ending abruptly. As regards the parallel between the form and contact, we turn to Lattimore's interpretation of hope.

Lines four and five suggest the self-deluding characteristic of Hope. She is "self-seduced and simple," she paints herself in artificial rejection of beauty's transience, she is blind, and, winged, she can be fleeting and impermanent. (Other readings are equally appropriate, but these point up the relationship to Time especially well, as we shall see.) The last observation is followed by the baby-sitter image, which can be read as a devalued allusion to Penelope of the Odyssey. In contrast to the first Homeric allusion, this illustration is drawn in parody of its model, and becomes almost maudlin in its strained appreciation of the most mundane subjects. The effect is to create in the reader a sense of present futility as opposed to the previous evocation of archaic terror.

Hope, of course, suffers in transition. She is an admitted monster in the first place, the misbegotten offspring of primitive emotions. But in retrospect against past Time she assumes a mythical detachment; as a baby-sitter she is merely immediately fatuous. Time shows up her foolish vanity, for her idealism demands a cessation or reversal of this basic universal constant. Written over the palimpsest of Penelope's two-decade wait, Lattimore's "phone that never rings" sums up the devaluation of Hope.

There is still the Future tense to deal with;;analogous to the return to classical form we see the cyclical inevitability of Hope. For Hope, though devalued, exists in some form throughout Time; it is a "variable constant," a paradox whose justification is its regeneration of the forces that gave it life. Hope confronts the fleeing realist with her monster baby whose two heads remind us of the original Desire and Fear. James Joyce might have called this the "ineluctable modality of the temporal"—for protean Hope, inescapeable, cannot conquer or be conquered by Time—she exists parallel to it, purified by the total experience of her existance: siren, whore, innocent, fool and mother.

## Writing Assignment Two
## Comment on Sample 2. Grade: High

This paper is also superior, though it runs to less than half the length of the first sample and therefore inevitably lacks such amazing thoroughness and richly detailed documentation. In style this sample is probably the equal of the first. If anything, it is even more tightly packed, terse, razor-sharp in its diction, and masterly in its manipulation of sentence structure. Nor is there a hint of superficiality in its brevity. To say so much in so few words is an unusual feat for any high school student. This student achieves unity by focusing on the concept of the "devaluation" of Hope through the offices of Time, a valid and vital part of the poem that many students either overlooked or underplayed. A final strength of this paper is the climactic ending that traces the changing yet unending roles of Hope as "siren, whore, innocent, fool and mother."

## Writing Assignment Two
## Sample 3. Grade: Average

*"Sonnet on Hope"*

In "Sonnet on Hope" the concept of "Time" is as unusual as that of Hope. There is no hint of a Father Time who rushes humanity through life, killing youth and happiness, and driving man to the unwelcome grave. Time sinks into timelessness, and Hope's hopelessness evolves.

If Hope sings the brain to sleep and voids the sense of hearing with wax and honey, humanity loses the ability to reason about Time or to hear of its passing. If Hope has wings, she and her followers can escape the bounds of Time into timelessness. The dulled senses and painted wings of Hope, therefore, evolve from the lack of time-consciousness inherent in a Hope which dumbly sits and waits.

The world of Hope is "never-was", but yet "new-made", that is totally imagined in the fleeting present, dreaming of what never existed in the all-engulfing past. Man can lose his consciousness of time, past and present, and can imagine this "never-was" world because he is embroiled in Hope, which closes his eyes to reality and creates a world of lifeless perfection.

The phone NEVER rings because Hope's world is eternally inactive and insensitive. The author sees an unending life-span, timeless since it cannot be reckoned, which enslaves the man who hopes.

If the calendars are "fixed" and the clocks are "stopped", and if the minute glass has sucked the "sand" back in, invalidating its time-telling ability, it is a world without Time. Time after all is not a self-sufficient entity, but is rather the brain-child of man who invented clocks and calendars, and enslaved himself to them. He need only destroy his inventions to destroy Time. Once Time is stopped, man can hope and dream undisturbed. If no clocks exist to goad man, he need never budge from his "abandoned chair" to work and strive for the better life. He can sit eternally, waiting, just waiting—and hoping.

A lack of Time, therefore, reveals and blends with a Hope which is lifeless and hopeless in "Sonnet on Hope".

## Writing Assignment Two
## Comment on Sample 3. Grade: Average

This paper is *average* only by Advanced Placement standards. By ordinary twelfth grade standards, a student capable of the condensation and paradox in the second sentence of the first paragraph is not average. But in comparison with the searching thoroughness and subtle perceptiveness of the first two papers, the substance of this paper is slight, its thinness verging on superficiality. The fourth paragraph, for instance, sounds impressive after a quick, casual reading; but a closer scrutiny raises uncomfortable questions about its soundness, its accuracy. Is Hope's world, as Lattimore presents it, "eternally inactive and insensitive"? Just what does the student mean by that "unending life-span" which "enslaves the man who hopes"? And at the end of the paper how has the writer managed to miss the underlined femininity of the baby-sitter figure in the "abandoned chair"? Is he confusing Hope with her victims in his phrase, "The dulled senses and painted wings of Hope"? Hope dulls the senses of her dupes, but her own senses are not dulled at all. The closing paragraph is also misleading in its phrase "lack of Time." The poem is talking not so much about "lack of Time" as about the annihilation of Time through the dreams prompted by Hope.

## Writing Assignment Two
## Sample 4. Grade: Low

*Hope*

In Richard Lattimore's Sonnet on Hope, the speaker's consciousness of time shapes his understanding of hope. The speaker is quite conscious of time: time long past, modern time, and the future.

In the first group of lines the speaker shows his awareness of the past in his images of hope. One of his images is of Homer's ancient sirens. Hope, like these seductive women, is enchanting and causes one to lose his reason. Another image shows Ullyses escaping from the Cyclops under one of his sheep. A third ancient image is of Daedalus and Icarus, escaping by their invention of wax wings. Icarus is killed because of his extreme enthusiasm. These images, portraying hope as enchanting, an escape from reality, and enthusiastic, are from ancient literature. This shows the speaker's consciousness of the past.

The next group of lines show the speaker's concept of modern time. His image is of a present-day baby-sitter. She dreams of her future and of eternity, thinking of cradles and stopped calendars. She hopes that the future will be better than the present and is waiting anxiously for it. The reader can picture an hourglass, with the sand being sucked back up into the top half. Time is repeated with hope of improvement the second time. With time stopped one can be eternally hopeful. The second group of images shows the speaker's awareness of present and future time.

The speaker's awareness of time is shown in each of his images of hope. He uses images of the ancient past, of the present, of the future, and of eternity.

## Writing Assignment Two
## Comment on Sample 4. Grade: Low

This is not poor twelfth grade writing. The thinking is neither confused nor grossly inaccurate. A plan of organization is evident. But the ploddingly correct style, the perfunctory organization, and the depthless conclusions reached by superficial scanning of Lattimore's lines mark this paper *low* among Advanced Placement papers. The student is on solid ground in his comment on the Sirens, but he provides no justification—nor could he readily do so—for the flat assertion that "Another image shows Ullyses escaping from the Cyclops under one of his sheep." To convince most readers that such an allusion is there would require the most skillfully persuasive mustering of evidence and rhetoric. The Daedalus and Icarus reference is probably not in the sonnet either, but many students seized upon it when they missed the probable Cupid imagery in "blind" and "winged," and at least a fairly reasonable case can be made for it, though this student's picture of Icarus dying of too much "enthusiasm" is typical of the somewhat naïve treatment throughout the paper. The confrontation with the "baby-sitter" is hardly more than a stringing together of phrases from the poem. The closing of the paper, like the closings for paragraphs two and three, merely restates the obvious.

# Drama

# *Introduction to the Units on the Drama*

The notable omissions in the drama section of this book are another reminder that what we are offering is a sampling, not a complete course. Nothing is here for grade 9. Shakespeare and Greek tragedy are not here. There is no comedy. In our early planning the Committee did play with the possibility of presenting two plans for teaching the same Shakespeare play—one plan for grade 9 and one for grade 12. The problem was to find a Shakespeare play as potentially fruitful for the ninth grade as for the twelfth, a play as validly teachable in its entirety at one level as at the other. In a venturesome or foolhardy moment we decided on *Hamlet* but lived to regret it when we discovered that to make the play accessible to ninth graders we had to omit to the point of distortion—and better no teaching at all than that. The more obvious choice for such a double presentation is *Julius Caesar,* but our courage drooped over the difficulties of infusing new life into such an overtaught play. We bypassed comedy with regret but realized that both *J. B.* and *The Glass Menagerie* have their moments of comedy, particularly the kind that comes tinged with satire or irony and that underlines by contrast the serious intent of the work.

The final choice of *The Book of Job* and *J. B.* was the answer to a search for two works adaptable to comparative study—two works alike yet strikingly different, two with strong appeal for older students. In choosing *The Glass Menagerie,* we were looking for a distinctively modern play different in its view of the world from the Shakespearean and Greek tragedies that are likely to be the staples of the secondary school program in drama. *The Glass Menagerie* comes out of our own time. It speaks to the sensed loneliness of high school students, to their dawning awareness that the human will is often powerless before the onslaught of circumstance, to their new consciousness of the limitations of language and of the baffling failures of human beings to communicate with each other. The responses from both teachers and students suggest that these choices were sound.

In the composition work here, as elsewhere, although we have paid homage to the critical, analytic, expository theme, we have also included assignments that call for other kinds of ingenuity, originality, creativity, and imagination—assignments that let the student express his understanding of a piece of literature by trying to create something like it. In each group of composition assignments the last is of this sort. Admittedly such assignments pose problems of evaluation, and some teachers may prefer not to grade the kind of writing they invite. And certainly in all assignments of this type the final product matters less than the process the student goes through as he writes and the deepened respect he acquires for the professional who does this kind of writing well.

The Book of Job *and* J. B.
*Grade 12*

but yielded disappointing results on the writing assignments.

The plan presented here puts the burden of the initial class discussions primarily on the students, deliberately focusing that initial discussion on significant differences in the two Job stories. The intent is to allow the student to make his own discoveries and to remove from the teacher the temptation to deliver a preliminary lecture on the problem of undeserved suffering. Once the class has grappled with the significant differences in the two works, it should be ready for the further discussion questions and for the writing assignments.

Some teachers may wish to vary the suggested plan, reading and discussing *The Book of Job* first and then moving on to the comparative study with *J.B.* Others may wish to expand the teaching plan to include a study of Sophocles' *Oedipus the King*, and those who have tried it have discovered it works well with a good twelfth grade class.

## First Assignment

The assignment will take about one week. Have the class read *The Book of Job* first and then *J.B.* At the outset, divide the class into five groups, each with its chosen chairman. Each group will focus on those particular differences in the two works for which it is responsible. As part of the week's assignment, each group will prepare a list of the most significant differences it discovers in the two works under the one of the following five headings to which it has been assigned:

1. Differences in plot or action
2. Differences in characters and characterization
3. Differences in setting (including the world setting as well as the local or the stage setting)
4. Differences in themes and the treatment of those themes
5. Differences in style

The class periods should be used for group work and for listening to the recording of *The Book of Job*, which takes from 50 to 60 minutes of class time. (The RCA recording of *J.B.* requires an hour and a half to two hours.)

After finishing the reading and hearing the records, each of the five group chairmen should present his group's listing of significant differences in the two works and should recommend one or two of these for detailed class exploration and discussion. These recommendations should be subject to the approval of the whole class and the teacher, but with an able class most of what matters will be included in the lists presented. If the students have overlooked anything vital, the teacher will need to do some gentle nudging as they prepare the recommendations, but the more he can keep hands off the better.

## Second Assignment

This assignment will take two or three days. Each group will prepare class discussion materials on the one or two significant differences with which it has chosen to deal. These materials may be questions put to the rest of the class; they may be interpretation or comment; they may be a combination of questions and comment. The chairman of each group will probably be the one to present the materials, but all members of the group should act as a sort of panel of "experts." Meanwhile the teacher should collect from each group its original list of significant differences and should have all five lists mimeographed or dittoed as reference material for each member of the class. (For the teacher's use, a list of some of the differences that should show up in the students' work is appended to this teaching plan.)

## Writing Assignment One

While the students are working out their class discussion materials, the teacher may wish to use one class period for writing. Of the two assignments printed below, the student is to choose *one:*

1. Turn Nickles' song ("If God is God . . .") into a piece of formal expository writing.

2. Write a speech for yet another "modern" comforter.

After reading these papers, most teachers will want to use one or two class periods, having the most interesting papers read aloud and discussing questions and problems that the entire set of papers has raised.

# The Book of Job *and* J. B.
## *Grade 12*

*Editions Available:* If possible all students should use the King James translation of *The Book of Job.* The use of a mixture of other translations rules out any significant discussion of literary style. Two paperback editions of Archibald MacLeish's *J.B.* are available, one from Houghton Mifflin and one from Samuel French. Some teachers may prefer the French edition because it embodies the substantial revisions the poet made in collaboration with Elia Kazan, but whichever edition the teacher uses with his class, several copies of the other edition should be made available to permit a comparative examination of the two texts.

*Records:* A vital part of a student's study of *The Book of Job* will be his listening to the excellent recording, Caedmon TC1076, Caedmon Records, 505 Eighth Avenue, New York; or Houghton Mifflin, Boston. Unfortunately, the RCA Victor recording of *J.B.* is no longer available, though some schools using these materials either had the records or managed to borrow them (the number of the recording is LD/LDS 6075); the album includes a booklet with some of Blake's engravings pictured beside equivalent scenes from the production of *J.B.*

*Approximate Time:* 2½ to 3 weeks

Teachers who have tried these materials differed in the amount of time they felt the unit required. One teacher reported that 2½ weeks was more time than he needed, but he was in the unusual position of having 80-minute class periods. Another teacher used four weeks and wished he had had six.

*Poems for Supplementary Study:*

Matthew Arnold, "Dover Beach"

Mark Van Doren, "The God of Galaxies"

(Copies of both poems are included at the end of this unit.)

### To the Teacher

This material is designed for twelfth grade classes. In the pretesting some teachers used it with eleventh grade classes, but according to such teachers' reports either the whole unit was beyond the reach of eleventh graders or else it provoked excellent discussion

## For Further Class Discussion

Each teacher should feel free to use only those topics below that promise to be most fruitful for his particular class.

1. Discuss some of the most striking uses of both literal and figurative *light* and *darkness* in both *Job* and *J.B.*

2. Discuss the uses the two works make of *trees* and *leaves*.

3. Discuss some of the uses in both works of the verb *see* and noun *eye*. Consider whether the *seeing* in both works is literal or figurative or both.

4. Discuss the extent to which *Job* and *J.B.* lose or gain spiritual stature in the scenes of their recantations in response to the voice of the whirlwind.

5. In his poem "Hypocrite Auteur" (1952) MacLeish says that the old metaphors of past history have died with their worlds, and he then calls on modern poets to "Turn round into the actual air: / Invent the age! Invent the metaphor!" Discuss the extent to which MacLeish in *J.B.* follows his own advice to modern poets. Look closely at some of MacLeish's metaphors.

6. Explore this comment on *The Book of Job:* "For sheer power to build metaphor on metaphor, each more powerful than the last, it stands unmatched."

7. Compare the ending of *J.B.* in the French edition with the ending in the Houghton Mifflin edition, keeping in mind that a poet reveals himself in the revisions he makes in his work.

8. Study Arnold's "Dover Beach," noting the parallels between the poem and the last pages of the play, such as the parallel between "The Sea of Faith . . . Retreating" and "The candles in churches are out" and the parallel between "let us be true / To one another!" and "Blow on the coal of the heart."

9. Study Mark Van Doren's "The God of Galaxies" with special attention to its contrast between the world of the Old Testament and the world of the Nuclear Age. Note, though, the differences in Van Doren's ending and MacLeish's.

10. (With a very able class) read and discuss "A Return to Heroic Man," by Maxine Greene, *Saturday Review,* August 22, 1959, pages 10–11, 35–36. This article is particularly useful in shedding further light on *J.B.* It will be doubly useful for a class that includes *Oedipus* in its study of the two Job works.

## Writing Assignment Two

These papers should be prepared outside class; most students will need at least two preparation periods.

### Directions

Choose *one* of the following writing assignments:

1. According to the psychologist Jung, "There is no coming to consciousness without pain." Write a carefully planned composition in which you show the extent to which the story of both the Biblical and the modern Job illustrate Jung's statement. You may wish to start with an exploration of Jung's meaning, with special attention to the term "consciousness."

2. Read the following passage. Then write the paper called for below.

"The Greeks knew that suffering was ineradicable; that innocent men too often died unfairly; that passion could run rampant and destroy. They knew, too, that although these events were part of the nature of things, man ought to take responsibility for his frailties and defeats. . . . They did not root their ideals in a cosmos that was reasonable and just. They recognized injustice, even irrationality, and they challenged them symbolically, by means of tragedy; they created an image of man standing up against the sky."—Maxine Greene, "A Return to Heroic Man," *Saturday Review,* August 22, 1959, page 11.

Write a carefully planned composition in which you examine the extent to which *Job* and *J.B.* embody the knowledge and the recognition that the above passage attributes to the Greeks.

3. Imagine that you are a historian, a theologian, or a writer living in the year 2500 A.D. You have just read *The Book of Job* and *J.B.* (translated, of course, into your future language). Bearing in mind your role as historian, theologian, or writer, and remembering that almost a thousand years have passed since the production of *J.B.,* write a full, detailed comment on the two renderings of the Job story as revelations of the two ages out of which these works came.

## For the Use of the Teacher: A Partial List of Differences in *Job* and *J.B.*

Good students will undoubtedly come up with important differences not included in this list, but these are the differences that the students in most classes are likely to spot.

### Plot

1. All action involving Zuss and Nickles as shelved actors in *J.B.* has no counterpart in *Job.*

2. The Thanksgiving dinner is in *J.B.* and not in *Job.*

3. The handling and the timing of the disasters differ in the two plays.

4. Sarah's contemplated suicide, her physical desertion of Job, and her return are vital to *J.B.,* with no counterparts in *Job.*

5. What happens to Job in the two endings is very different.

### Characters

1. The two portrayals of Job differ sharply.

2. Job's wife plays little part in *Job* but is vitally important in *J.B.*

3. Job's children are merely mentioned in *Job* but individualized in *J.B.*

4. The messengers in *Job* are undefined voices, but in *J.B.* they are characterized, differentiated, and modernized.

5. There are crucial differences in the two portrayals of God.

6. There are likewise crucial differences in the two portrayals of Satan.

7. The two sets of comforters are very different. MacLeish has "updated" his group, tingeing them with a modern cynicism entirely foreign to the intense though mistaken earnestness of the *Job* group.

8. Zuss and Nickles have no counterpart in *Job* when they are playing their own role of actors who "have seen better days." When they play God and Satan, MacLeish defines them as individuals—as the Old Testament story does not. In *J.B.* MacLeish keeps reminding us that they are not God and Satan but merely essaying the roles.

9. In *The Book of Job* there is no counterpart to the women and the children introduced in *J.B.* aft the atomic explosion.

10. There is no character in *J.B.* corresponding Elihu.

### Settings in Time and Place

1. The framework of the folk tale in *The Book* *Job* contrasts sharply with the framework of the circ tent in *J.B.*

2. The ancient rural setting contrasts with th modern urban setting.

3. The small, tidy, personal world of the Old Te tament is a far cry from the vast and apparently u caring world of the Space Age.

### Themes

1. There are marked differences in the two trea ments of undeserved suffering.

2. The implied answers in the two endings are si nificantly different.

3. There are perhaps suggestions in *J.B.* of th Christian doctrine of redemption through atonemen for recognized guilt, though it is worth noting th the idea of a reward in an afterlife gets little atten tion in either work.

4. In *J.B.* there are suggestions of the existentia ist view of life as "absurd"—a concept totally foreig to the Old Testament story.

5. The treatment of God's allowance of evil somewhat different in the two works.

### Style

1. Humor and irony are often present in *J.B.* b practically nonexistent in *Job.*

2. The narrative style of the folk tale framework *Job* has no counterpart in *J.B.*

3. The diction in *J.B.* shifts between the ultr modern and the dignified, poetical, and high charged language of the Old Testament. There is n such jolting juxtaposition of two totally different le els of speech in *Job.*

4. Although both works rely heavily on simile an metaphor, the figures they use are often as differe as the ancient Hebrew world is from our own.

5. The style, diction, tone, and voice of MacLeish messengers are individualized as they are not in *Job.*

*Note.* Overlapping in any such list as this is unavoidable and will undoubtedly occur when the student committees present their five lists. One teacher, in using the unit, found that she got better results by having all five committees deal with a single point when overlapping seemed inescapable, instead of letting each committee present its full list and then having time wasted by needless repetition.

*The God of Galaxies*

Mark Van Doren

The god of galaxies has more to govern
Than the first men imagined, when one mountain
Trumpeted his anger, and one rainbow,
Red in the east, restored them to his love.
One earth it was, with big and lesser torches,
And stars by night for candles. And he spoke
To single persons, sitting in their tents.

Now streams of world, now powdery great whirl-
winds
Of universes far enough away
To seem but fog-wisps in a bank of night
So measureless the mind can sicken, trying—
Now seas of darkness, shoreless, on and on
Encircled by themselves, yet washing farther
Than the last triple sun, revolving, shows.

The god of galaxies—how shall we praise him?
For so we must, or wither. Yet what word
Of words? And where to send it, on which night
Of winter stars, of summer, or by autumn
In the first evening of the Pleiades?
The god of galaxies, of burning gases,
May have forgotten Leo and the Bull.

But God remembers, and is everywhere.
He even is the void, where nothing shines.
He is the absence of his own reflection
In the deep gulf; he is the dusky cinder
Of pure fire in its prime; he is the place
Prepared for hugest planets: black idea,
Brooding between fierce poles he keeps apart.

Those altitudes and oceans, though, with islands
Drifting, blown immense as by a wind,
And yet no wind; and not one blazing coast
Where thought could live, could listen—oh, what
word
Of words? Let us consider it in terror,
And say it without voice. Praise universes
Numberless. Praise all of them. Praise Him.

*Dover Beach*

Matthew Arnold

The sea is calm tonight.
The tide is full, the moon lies fair
Upon the straits—on the French coast the light
Gleams and is gone; the cliffs of England stand,
Glimmering and vast, out in the tranquil bay.
Come to the window, sweet is the night air!
Only, from the long line of spray
Where the sea meets the moon-blanched land,
Listen! you hear the grating roar
Of pebbles which the waves draw back, and fling,
At their return, up the high strand,
Begin, and cease, and then again begin,
With tremulous cadence slow, and bring
The eternal note of sadness in.

Sophocles long ago
Heard it on the Aegean, and it brought
Into his mind the turbid ebb and flow
Of human misery; we
Find also in the sound a thought,
Hearing it by this distant northern sea.

The Sea of Faith
Was once, too, at the full, and round earth's shore
Lay like the folds of a bright girdle furled.
But now I only hear
Its melancholy, long, withdrawing roar,
Retreating, to the breath
Of the night wind, down the vast edges drear
And naked shingles of the world.

Ah, love, let us be true
To one another! for the world, which seems
To lie before us like a land of dreams,
So various, so beautiful, so new,

Hath really neither joy, nor love, nor light,
Nor certitude, nor peace, nor help for pain;
And we are here as on a darkling plain
Swept with confused alarms of struggle and flight,
Where ignorant armies clash by night.

## Writing Assignment One, Question 1 Sample 1. Grade: High

*God Cannot Be Good*

God punishes both the wicked and the good, and because of this he cannot be considered a fair or just God by our standards. If we say that God is good how can we explain the evil that happens to people who seemingly lead a good life, and people who continuely do evil prosper and increase in fortune. Is this a good and just God?

This problem of evil cannot be explained by saying that God is good, for a good God would punish the wicked and reward the good. I could be said that Satan causes the occurance of evil and, it is he who sees to it that the evil men prosper. But God doesn't have to let Satan exist. If one contends that God is good and that Satan is responsible for the evil without God's help, Satan must share some of God's power. God cannot be God and have some of his power taken away by Satan. God to be God must certainly have more power than Satan.

All this leads us back to the same question. How can God be God and be good also? If God's power is limited by Satan, then he is not the omnipotent god we believe in. If God is all the power in the universe, he must be held responsible for the evil done.

In the *Book of Job,* God tells Satan "thou movedst me against him (Job), to destroy him without cause." Would a good God destroy a man if he had all the power to prevent it? A good God would not as in Job's words "destroy the perfect and the wicked." God does this.

## Writing Assignment One, Question 1 Comment on Sample 1. Grade: High

This student resists the temptation to intrude his own comment and is content with merely presenting the intellectual dead ends down which Nickles' song leads us. "Punishes" in the opening sentence is probably not precisely the right word either for a God who merely permits injustice or for one who is powerless to prevent it. In fact the comforters in *J.B.* will have nothing to do with anything so quaint as guilt or condign punishment or guiltlessness and undeserved punishment. The rest of this paper, though, senses that the issue is God's permissiveness of evil, not his deliberate "punishment" of the blameless. By his paragraph transition in the next to the last paragraph this student emphasizes the traplike, vicious, circular logic of Nickles' song. The writing here is not flawless, but flawlessness doesn't usually mate with impromptu writing; and on the whole this is a strong paper, strong in both its inclusions and its omissions; strong in its directness, its clarity, its thoroughness, and its unshrinking recognition of all that the song is saying.

## Writing Assignment One, Question 1 Sample 2. Grade: Average

*The Nature of God*

The view of the nature of God expressed in Nickles's song "If God is God He is not good" is neither recent nor unusual. It maintains that we need only to look around us to see the nature of God. Since God is supposedly omnipotent, he should be able to govern the events in the world around us. The suffering and evil around us leads us to the conclusion that God is either evil or indifferent. These observations have caused many people to think that the God they see in the universe is not good, and that if God is good he is not the omnipotent and omiscient being he is thought to be.

In the second part of the song, Nickles says that he would not choose to live on the earth if he had a choice. The only things that give hope and comfort are the things of nature—the green leaves and the wind. If it were not for the encouragement and promise of better circumstances offered by nature, many people would certainly have committed suicide instead of continuing the fight of existance.

The view of life and of God expressed by Nickles is the view of an experienced man. This man is often bitter because of these experiences, but he may be forced to discover different attitudes which can be more meaningful to the individual.

## Writing Assignment One, Question 1 Comment on Sample 2. Grade: Average

This paper recognizes the central dilemma that Nickles' song poses, but here the student intrudes his own comments instead of merely turning the song into expository prose as the directions demanded. The opening sentence signals the missing of directions that weakens this paper. The opening sentences of the second and the third paragraphs are further evidence of this student's constant intrusion of his own commentary in an assignment that asks him to leave himself on the doorstep when he goes inside to deal with Nickles' song. The writing here is clear, correct, and acceptable; the student understands the song. For these reasons, the readers rated this paper as *average* in spite of its partial failure to follow directions.

## Writing Assignment One, Question 1 Sample 3. Grade: Low

*Nickles' Song in* J.B.
*"If God is God He is not good,*
*If God is good He is not God;"*

This statement is a part of Nickles' song which he sings before he learns that he is to play Satan. He says that a man, sitting upon a dung heap and unable to sleep, has said these words. Apparrantly, Nickles is referring to Job.

If the God that we worship is the one true God, than it is not possible for him to always be good. This does not affect his state of perfection. It means that in the courses of ages, God has ruled man, a creature who is far from good and who must be punished for his evil. God is man's punisher. God's wrath upon mankind makes man more appreciative of God's goodness.

In the same sense, a God who is always good cannot be the God of the Heavens and the Earth. If a God were always good, his people would be unable to appreciate Him. Since the day that Adam and Eve ate of the fruit of the Tree of Knowledge of Good and Evil, God has had to punish mankind for the evil which dwells within. Before the day of such knowledge, it was possible for man to live in peace and love, attended by a God who was good. But now, because man possesses the knowledge of good and evil, he must be ruled by a God who can exhibit both of these attitudes. Man must learn to accept the evil, the odd, along with the good, the even.

Job, while upon his dung heap, is unable to sleep and declares that he would not sleep even if he could. Sleep would be a means of escape for Job from the punishment which God has set up for him. For many years he had basked in God's goodness. Understanding that his God cannot be good all of the time, Job accepts fully God's wrath and does not try to escape. Only after God has finished his punishment will Job be able to sleep. The green leaves in the wood and the wind on the water are Job's hopes of future grace in God's eyes; a time of goodness and of sleep.

## Writing Assignment One, Question 1 Comment on Sample 3. Grade: Low

This is a well written paper. Its sentiments are irreproachable. The only trouble is that they are not Nickles' sentiments as Nickles frames his sentiments in his song. The thinking in this paper is, in fact, close to the viewpoint of the Old Testament comforters, thus missing most of the point of *Job, J.B.,* and Nickles' song. The confused logic of paragraph two, with its insistence that man is a guilty creature who must suffer God's punishment for his wrongdoing, is an indication of how far off base this paper is in its approach to the assignment.

## Writing Assignment One, Question 2 Sample 1. Grade: High

(Zophar . . . The warm at heart, the wilful will corrupting with its foul imagining.) page 126

*A fourth comforter, clean-shaven and with the dress and bearing of a television MC, steps forward, already gesticulating with his hands with obvious agitation.*

Fourth Comforter: Your guilt is the collective guilt of the age; your guilt is the guilt of the atomic bomb and LSD.—

J.B.: But I've never even—

Fourth Comforter: Can't you see? *That doesn't matter!* It is never the *really* guilty who suffer; they never have the consciousness, the awareness. It is always the innocent.

J.B.: What do you mean? Im the scapegoat of the twentieth century?

4th C: No; you are the Christ of the winter of 1956.

Bildad: But how is that different from—

4th C: But it is! This is not Marxist History, or history's guilt; this is J B's guilt, now. This is J. B's consciousness. I am not saying that the universal guilt syndrome is different now; it isn't. The appearances are different —But the fact is the same.

J.B.: But why (falters with puzzlement)
Silence
But why did God choose me?

4th C: Why? Because you are the Modern Man, well fed and shod, and Mainly because you began to Think. You were ready for Guilt and suffering. Your eyes were permanently dilated.

J.B.: What will I do?

4th C: Christ forgave the Romans, and you, J.B. must

forgive the streetwalkers in Minneapolis and the Marijuana ring in East Dakota. Forgive them for the twentieth century And for your awareness.

## Writing Assignment One, Question 2 Comment on Sample 1. Grade: High

This is an able, soundly conceived response to a tough assignment. The jargon of MacLeish's three comforters is so glibly up-to-date that it takes a clever student to "up-date" MacLeish; but this student has done it with his references to LSD and the streetwalkers in Minneapolis. The choice of a television MC as fourth comforter is both obvious and ingenious. It permits a new brand of up-to-the-minute jargon as abrasive to the lacerated feelings of J.B. as anything MacLeish has supplied. The student is also shrewd enough to let Bildad pose the question that may be occurring to the reader: "But how is that different from—"? This provides a chance to differentiate the fourth comforter's brand of moral anodyne from the Marxist variety that MacLeish has offered. The dialogue moves swiftly and sharply, with the final speech forming a smashing climax. For impromptu writing this is surprisingly skillful. It is an example, too, of the possibilities in an assignment that asks the student to express his understanding of a literary work imaginatively rather than analytically.

## Writing Assignment One, Question 2 Sample 2. Grade: Average

*Speech Between J.B. and Another Comforter*

After J.B. asks God to answer him and before the Distant Voice is heard, a fourth comforter interrupts for the first time. The comforter is a funeral director.

Funeral Director: Why dost thou believe that God will answer you?

J.B.: For what have I wronged, for what is all this suffering which I have had put on me by my dear Lord.

Funeral Director: This is not the Lord's way but this is the way of Lady Luck. She was once with you and you were prosperous and you had money, children, and a wonderful wife. But now she has turned her wheels in reverse and your luck has simply changed.

J.B.: Luck! No! God's Way!

Funeral Director: Well, whatever it is you are destined to die. Since your wife has left you and you have no one left to choose your casket, you will have to make the choice. I have a bronze one, or how about a nice simple cedar chest.

J.B.: (mumbling) God! Luck! Bronze . . . cedar chest.

Funeral Director: Since you have picked the cedar chest you will have to be buried high on a hill. I have two beautiful plots in the Oakhill Cemetary. You will rest at ease in that quiet place which overlooks my funeral home.

J.B.: (stronger at first but very weak at the end) If I must die . . . God answer me. I must know why I am to die. Plot. . . . Oakhill Cemetary. . . . Rest at ease. . .

Funeral Director: Yes, you will be very comfortable in the cedar chest high upon the hill. You remember Mrs. Henry, old James Henry's wife who died of overweight or as the Doctor said, "bad heart condition." Well anyway she is buried on the right on you and your plot is the last one on the left side of the hill. That's where a breeze blows nearly all the time.

J.B.: Breeze. . . . Wind. . . . I hear. . . I feel. . . . the wind. Silence.

## Writing Assignment One, Question 2 Comment on Sample 2. Grade: Average

Most *average* papers are too innocuously dull to be controversial. This one is certainly not dull, and it may be controversial. At first the readers did not agree in their judgments of it. It is probably as ingenious, as imaginative, and as wryly amusing as the first paper. Its dialogue is snappy. The choice of a funeral director as fourth comforter at first impresses the reader with the cleverness of its implication that the evasions and the euphemisms of a modern funeral home are a fourth form of modern comfort. The reader's first impulse is to smile at J.B.'s mumbled response to the prospect of a permanent residence in a cedar chest, and the reference to the perpetual breezes on the hilltop of the cemetery neatly foreshadows the coming of God's voice out of the whirlwind. On second thought, though, one questions the appropriateness of a funeral director for the role of fourth comforter. In both *Job* and *J.B.* the comforters' job is to offer forms of solace that the sufferer finds intellectually and emotionally repugnant. At this point in the drama, in the depths of the agony of their lonely pain and doubt, would death have been repugnant to either Job or J.B., or might they not have welcomed it as a termination to their trials? And, furthermore, the choice of the funeral director permits no further probing into the Job tragedy; it in no way extends the modernity of MacLeish's scene. As the readers saw it, this paper is clever but lacks the ballast of serious thought that makes the first paper considerably more than merely clever.

## Writing Assignment One, Question 2
## Sample 3. Grade: Low

*The Fourth Comforter in "JB"*

The play "JB" has only three comforters. These three men do more to hurt JB than they do to help him. There is need of a fourth man to talk to JB. This man would correspond to Elihue in *The Book of Job.*

The fourth comforter in "JB" would have to repudiate what the other three comforters said. Instead of trying to figure out why JB is being punished he would tell JB to just accept his punishment. He would tell JB to accept God's judgement without question. He would explain to JB that God is all powerful and that no mortal man can understand his ways. He would tell JB that, even though he (JB) had no knowledge of his sins, God knows all and is free to punish man as he sees fit.

The fourth comforter would also cut down the other three comforters. He would tell them that they had no right to question God. He would say that they can not understand God and therefore they have no right to question what he does.

## Writing Assignment One, Question 2
## Comment on Sample 3. Grade: Low

The writing skills in this paper are competent; the paper is orderly in its organization; but by using the expository essay form instead of the dramatic form called for, it has missed the point of the assignment. To complicate his problems, the student apparently thought the fourth comforter must be another Elihu translated from his times into ours; and the shadowy figure he creates does nothing but mouth Elihu's sentiments without Elihu's impassioned poetry, and with no discernible modern bias. The timid dullness of this response, its derivativeness, and its total failure to catch the spirit of the MacLeish scene all mark this paper as *low.*

## Writing Assignment Two, Question 1
## Sample 1. Grade: High

*Jung, and Job, and J.B.*

Karl Jung's statement "There is no coming to consciousness without pain" is no revelation in psychology, but it does bear directly on both the Book of Job and Archibald McLeish's modern interpretation of Job, *J.B.* Before the application of Jung's statement is made to the two works, it must be made clear what is meant, in this particular instance, by the words "pain" and "consciousness."

By "pain" Jung does not limit his meaning to physical pain, though physical pain is certainly a very important part of what he means; the term stands for the anguish of any struggle of the body, or the mind, or the spirit. The frustrations of a poet trying to create an image, or of a philosopher trying to conceive infinity are pain as much as a migraine. Pain may also include the normal tensions of living as well as the various hungers (and the quest for their satisfaction) of such things as food and sex.

Consciousness is awareness. It is the ever-improving perspective of human values and a focus of the nature of things. And pain—in the generalized sense above—is the stimulus that provokes consciousness. And if pain may be over-generalized into sensation, then consciousness itself is pain.

The pain and suffering of both Job and J.B. bring about an external awareness, or a more profound understanding, of man and God, and of the relation of one to the other. The awarenesses brought about in the two works are different, and the two types of pain, though the same in their outward appearances, are different in the manner in which the protagonists receive them and in their ultimate effects.

Job's conception of God before he is tested is childishly naive; his only knowledge of God is an inherited formula of laws and customs of whose origin he is uncertain and whose purpose he has never questioned. The pain which Job suffers is simple and obvious—he is not subject to any philosophic or psychological torture, but he is the victim of bodily and circumstantial suffering. This suffering gives rise to another pain, in the form of a conflict between Job's understanding of God's ways and justice and his seemingly incongruous reward.

If Job had not been tested, his theology would have remained as it was, and no amount of re-teaching or explanation could have corrected his idea of the nature of God as well as suffering does, because the human mind grasps much more readily on the concrete level than on the abstract (this is the power of metaphor and simile). However, Job's "consciousness" is only of the increasing significance of his problem and of the fallacy of his previous understanding of God; the loss of his children and the boils from head to foot create a mental tension that is not resolved until Job hears the voice from the whirlwind. But the Book of Job ends in tensionless peace: "So Job died, being old and full of days."

It is in this respect that *J.B.* differs from the Book of Job. J.B.'s philosophical pain (or, more clearly, struggle), embodied in dialogue between J.B. and Sarah in the Thanksgiving dinner scene, begins before his physical pain. It almost seems that J.B.'s philosophical puzzling (if one can consider Sarah as a *poet* of J.B.'s personality) *causes* his physical pain, or that the physical pain is the objective correlative of J.B.'s internal struggle. Thus the *Job* relationship between pain and wonder is reversed in J.B.

Then the resolution of J.B. must necessarily be different from Job. J.B.'s wife returns, but she is the only thing salvaged, including his faith in a human fellowship with God, who is now a distant and inscrutable entity. J.B. is left to "blow on the coals of the heart" and to derive his meaning from love and life itself. The story of Job is a complete life; the story of J.B. is a beginning, from which point forward the reader expects J.B. to reestablish the perspective of his values in humanistic striving and pain infinitely adjusting consciousness.

## Writing Assignment Two, Question 1 Comment on Sample 1. Grade: High

The brilliance and the disciplined control of style in this paper are as impressive as the depth of understanding of the two plays. Possibly the initial definitions of "pain" and "consciousness" are needlessly elaborate and deliberately pretentious, but the directions invited a careful exploration of these two terms, and this student's competence in dealing with them is beyond question. If the paper later skimped on its main job, then such criticism might be in order; but it doesn't. In paragraph four the student moves with masterly skill from his introductory definitions to a tightly interlocked comparison of the distinctions between the awarenesses that Job and J.B. reach by the end of their dramas. He then goes on to what looks like a separate analysis first of Job and then of J.B., in which he traces the inexorable pattern of pain emerging in response to newfound consciousness. The section dealing with Job comes to rest in the beautifully phrased sentence: "But the Book of Job ends in tensionless peace: 'So Job died, being old and full of days.' " The next section turns to *J.B.*, but, in doing so, never forgets that the object of the paper is to relate the two works comparatively to Jung's statement. The ending of the first paragraph dealing with *J.B.* closes with a sentence indicative of this student's awareness of both works as he deals specifically with one: "Thus the *Job* relationship between pain and wonder is reversed in J.B." The final paragraph starts with a similar linkage of the two works: "Then the resolution of J.B. must necessarily be different from Job," after which the paper defines the vitally important difference between a J.B. "left to 'blow on the coals of the heart' " for the comfort he can't find in a remote, inscrutable God, and a Job who ends in "tensionless peace."

## Writing Assignment Two, Question 1 Sample 2. Grade: High

*The Illustrations of Jung's Statement on Consciousness and Pain in* J.B. *and* Job

The psychologist Karl Jung once said, "There is no coming to consciousness without pain." In both *Job* and *J.B.*, the reader finds characters searching for an answer to their questions about the nature of God and of life; these characters in the latter parts of the two works are initiated into this knowledge by God himself, speaking from a whirlwind. In both *J.B.* and *Job* we have an experience which may be investigated for an illustration of Jung's meaning.

If we are to reach a meaningful conclusion, we must interpret Jung's statement and relate its meaning to the actual occurrences in *Job* and *J.B.* In this interpretation the reader is faced with the question, "What does Jung mean by 'consciousness'?" At least in relation to the two works *J.B.* and *Job* "consciousness" refers to an awareness of some important fact—that is, the learning of a fact earnestly sought after. Job wants to know why he is suffering when he knows that he is righteous in the sight of the Lord. When Job learns that the justice of the Lord is too wondrous to be understood, he has "come into consciousness." Jung means by "consciousness" not only a man's learning of an important fact but, even more so, a man's learning of a fact *that will enlighten the man about himself.* Job sees God, but he also sees himself. It is this self-illumination that is important, for by seeing himself in the light of his new knowledge about God, Job is able to change himself. In Jung's statement "consciousness," therefore, means knowledge that enables man to have insight into himself.

What Jung means by "pain" is also essential to the complete understanding of his statement. The "pain" implied by Jung's hypothesis is a mental one in accordance with the mental "coming to consciousness." This "pain" is a mental discomfort, a shrinking away from the truth seen in the "coming to consciousness." When a man sees into himself a disillusionment is the natural outcome; this disenchantment is the direct cause of "pain."

In the ancient *Job* we find illustration of Jung's nineteenth century psychological viewpoint. Job is searching for the reason for his apparently unjust suffering; he is seeking the nature of God. Job has perfect faith in God as the supreme being, but Job's logic and his knowledge of righteousness and justice are not sufficient for him to solve his problem. He does, however, "come to consciousness" when God tells him of His wondrous and infinite ways, incomprehensible to mortal man. This knowledge handed down by the Lord causes Job to see himself as he is; Job learns that as a mere man he must not attempt to justify or understand the Lord.

"Therefore have I uttered things which
I understood not,
Things too wonderful for me, which
I knew not."

Yet even in this realization that the Lord's ways are too wondrous for Job, the ancient Hebrew sees both God and himself more clearly than before; in other words, Job "comes to consciousness."

"I had heard of Thee by the hearing
of the ear;
But now mine eye seeth Thee."

Job feels a definite pain after his initiation into knowledge by the Lord; he best expresses his pain when he says,

"Wherefore I abhor my words, and
repent,
Seeing that I am dust and ashes."

In the modern play *J.B.,* there is an illustration of Jung's statement; this further illustration does not necessarily follow from the fact that *J.B.* is based on the *Job* story. On the contrary, Jung's statement is shown in a different light in *J.B.* by reason of the difference in theme between *J.B.* and *Job*. J.B., like the Biblical Job, is searching for the reason why he is suffering. His "coming to consciousness" occurs as it does in Job with God speaking from a rushing wind. J.B. sees the wondrous infinity of God and the comparative insignificance of man, but he is unable to reconcile his new knowledge with his former faith in God. Unlike Job, who could resume his complete faith and trust in God after his "coming to consciousness," J.B. is disillusioned and, therefore, sees the Lord as a more distant God. J.B. finds pain not only in the fact that he has seen himself a mere mortal whose feeble logic can not possibly equal the infinite nature of God, but also in the fact that as a man he has been left in a hostile environment, the earth, by a God who created him but who is too great to take a personal interest in him. He is left after his "coming to consciousness" with only pain and another question, "How is man to live on earth; how can he survive alone in his hostile environment?" MacLeish uses stage directions to help indicate J.B.'s pain: "J.B. pulls himself painfully to his knees." (Although this pain is physical, its placement in the play during the words of the Distant Voice imply a spiritual pain.) and "His (J.B.'s) face is drawn in agony."

In conclusion, *J.B.* and *Job* illustrate Jung's statement, for in both works the main character "comes to consciousness" and is pained by his experience. J.B., furthermore, must feel a deeper pain than Job. His pain is twofold; it includes the somewhat superficial pain incurred in the realization of man's insignificance, but it also includes the pain concomitant with the horrifying knowledge that man is left to fend for himself in the hostile environment God has made for him.

## Writing Assignment Two, Question 1 Comment on Sample 2. Grade: High

Here is a second paper that all readers rated *high*. It provides further evidence of what an assignment some teachers called too hard could produce when used with the able twelfth grade students for whom the unit was intended. This paper starts less brilliantly, perhaps less pretentiously than the first. Although it does a simpler job of defining the terms "pain" and "consciousness," its analysis of the two plays in terms of the Jung quotation is fuller, more detailed than that of the first paper. Its strategic use of quotations gives it a solidity that perhaps the other paper lacks. Here, too, the organization proceeds from the definitions to an analysis of *Job* and from there to a comparison with *J.B.,* beginning the latter with the recognition that J.B.'s pain derives from a consciousness more complex than the simpler pain of Job's "seeing" God and then "seeing" himself, with the inevitable disenchantment that any such vision of self must entail. This student makes clear that the subtler pain of J.B. springs from the clarity with which he sees God as inscrutable, uncaring, and himself as adrift in a hostile universe. The one significant omission in this paper is the recognition on J.B.'s part that God doesn't love, though man does and "there's the wonder."

## Writing Assignment Two, Question 1 Sample 3. Grade: Average

*The Cause of Job's and J.B.'s Pain*

Jung's statement relating new consciousness and pain actually pertains to the pain of philosophical revelations. The statement simply means that when one realizes that he has been under the influence of incorrect assumptions or reasonings, there is emotional pain. This is because he regrets having lived incorrectly or under false pretenses prior to the revelation.

Both Job and J.B. had thought that it was their purpose to keep God's laws and reap His rewards. But the hideous misfortunes heaped upon Job and J.B. forced them to do away with the idea of having a purpose or meaning in life. They realized their complete lack of understanding God and, because of the events and circumstances, it became meaningless to claim their purpose. So the real issue at Job's and J.B.'s hands was whether any purpose did exist.

With a twinge of uncertainty, Job and J.B. went to God to find out His purpose for His actions. But in their separate talks with God they found no reason for their mistreatment. They thought that if God had no purpose, then they had no purpose. Their uncertainty turned into pain when they realized they had been living for a meaningless purpose. The finality of God's word made it even more painful.

It is as though Job and J.B., sitting on their ash heaps had demanded, "See here, God! What is the meaning of this?"

And God in his whirlwind had replied, "See here, Job and J.B.! This has no meaning!"

## Writing Assignment Two, Question 1 Comment on Sample 3. Grade: Average

This is clear, correct, competent twelfth grade writing. It never misinterprets; its organization is tidy; but in comparison with the first two papers its tidiness is the tidiness of an uncomplex mind; its conclusions are obvious and shallow; its insights are partial. The opening definitions of "pain" and "consciousness" are indicative of the tidy-mindedness that misses subtleties and ignores complexities. Its conclusions are facile. The student deals only in likenesses, seeing nothing of those differences in the final consciousness of Job and J.B. with which the first two papers deal so perceptively. In its inclusions and even more in its omissions, this paper is an innocuous, unexciting, average response to an assignment that cries out for more than tamely negative virtues.

## Writing Assignment Two, Question 1 Sample 4. Grade: Low

*Painful Consciousness in* Job *and* J.B.

There is no coming to consciousness without pain.—Carl Jung.

Sigmund Freud, one of Jung's teachers, believed that the "coming of consciousness" was controlled by the amount of energy invested in the thought and the intensity of the resisting force. This resisting force is always present for a reason and when the supressed thought comes into consciousness by overriding the resisting force there is pain.

In the case of Job in the Bible, faith in his resisting force and doubt is the thought being supressed. The Dartmouth Bible opens the book of Job with a preface entitled, "The Travail of a Perplexed Sufferer," and according to Webster "perplexed" means trouble with doubt. This trouble with doubt comes out in chapter twenty-one when Job says, "Wherefore do the wicked live, become old, yea, are mighty in power?" After Job's apparent "coming to consciousness" it is difficult to distinguish the pain which has already resulted from his material misfortunes and the pain of his doubts. Job says, "Why died I not from the womb?" right after his family has been taken away and before he has begun to doubt God.

In the play *J.B.* by Archibald MacLeish, Jung's point of "coming to consciousness pain" is illustrated much more clearly. J.B. says, "Show me my guilt, O God," in approximately the same place as Job does in the Bible but J.B.'s next line is, "If I had perished from the womb, not having been . . ." His pain seems to be the result of his "coming to consciousness."

The extent to which Jung's statement is illustrated seems much greater in *J.B.* because most of the sorrow for the children is carried by Sarah. J.B. is left to deal with the problems of his faith and it is there for easier to distinguish between the two.

## Writing Assignment Two, Question 1
## Comment on Sample 4. Grade: Low

This paper looks absurdly slight in comparison with the first two. It makes even the *average* paper seem meaty. The writing is clear, respectable, frequently competent twelfth grade work, but the thinking barely grazes the surface of the two plays. The opening paragraph starts impressively with its glib recourse to Freudian terminology, but the treatment of Job in the second paragraph is totally inadequate and distressingly superficial. The paragraph that follows is similarly inadequate and superficial in its dealings with J.B. But up to this point the conclusions, such as they are, have been clear and valid. It is the final paragraph that raises more serious questions about this student's grasp of either *J.B.* or the assignment. It is true that Sarah is the one who voices her sorrow for the children, but J.B. feels it through all his anguished search for a just God. His problems with his faith are not separable from his loss of his children. They stem from that loss. And who are the "two" in the last sentence between whom it is "easier to distinguish"? If it means Job and J.B., the reference is remote. If it means J.B. and Sarah, then the ending misses the central target at which the paper should have aimed.

## Writing Assignment Two, Question 3
## Sample 1. Grade: Average +

*Job and J.B. in the Year 2500*

*J.B.* was an attempt to translate the theme of the book of Job into a modern context, in order to show that it was valid to Christian man in the twentieth century. The effectiveness of *J.B.* hinged on the reader or spectator's belief in a real and active God. A modern-day Job required a modern-day God; for without one there was no point to the play.

The play reflected the changes in the way people thought of God and His relationship to man. The absolute and simple belief of the writer of Job has been replaced by a more sophisticated and less anthropomorphic one which has trouble reconciling itself with the world it lives in. This reconciliation is the purpose of the play. Thus the author does not portray God on the stage but uses symbols instead, so that he does not define what God really is.

Job is the story of a personal God, and of people who can believe in a personal God. The people of the 20th century were beginning to live in an impersonal society. The growth of population and science contributed to a world which attached less and less worth to the individual. It became more and more difficult to define the importance of God in a scientific society; He seemed to be an anachronism, more appropriate with shepherds than computers. *J.B.*, then, is bucking a trend.

The trend today, in the year 2500, has continued. The scientific rather than the supernatural explanation of events now dominates man's thinking. Scientific laws and logic have replaced the outmoded concepts of supernatural forces and divine intervention.

With this decline and eventual replacement of the importance of the supernatural in daily life came a decline in the importance of the question of God's existence.

The theme of the play, therefore, was of little importance to people living in society today. Thus people are not concerned about any statement a play might make on this theme. *J.B.* is not relevant to the people of the present.

In addition *J.B.* was set in the 20th century. This obscures the import of the play behind a cloud of dated detail. Only a student of the era could understand the full impact of the play at the time of its presentation.

*J.B.* is a play that began with the idea of up-dating the story of Job. It is therefore only pertinent to those familiar with the Christian beliefs. Since *J.B.* is an attempt to show the relevance of Job in the 20th century, its effectiveness declined as its readers lived farther and farther away from that time. The year 2500 needs another version, up-dated to the present, for maximum effectiveness. *J.B.* has become as difficult to relate to our own lives as Job was to the people of the time of *J.B.*

This alone is enough to doom the play to obscurity. But the fact is that another version will not be written now because the theme is not important to people of the present. The play was thus not only dated and ineffective, but also on a theme that is dated and irrelevant, and thus uninteresting to people living now in the year 2500.

## Writing Assignment Two, Question 3
## Comment on Sample 1. Grade: Average +

This is a generally well-written paper that would have deserved a *high* rating if its author had followed directions. He is asked to write "a full, detailed comment on the two renderings of the Job story as revelations of the two ages out of which these works came." Instead, he treats the renderings briefly, with very little revelation of their respective ages, and spends the last half of his paper on his own age and the reasons for its neglect of the story. Even here there is some contradiction: after stating that "*J.B.* is not relevant to the people of the present," he says that "The year 2500 needs another version," and then realizes that another version will not be written. He has some difficulty with his tenses, also.

Relatively few schools attempted this topic; this paper is the best that appeared. Perhaps this kind of essay should not be required, but for certain students it may be useful.

## Writing Assignment Two, Question 3 Sample 2. Grade: Average

Job *and J.B.*

The age of *Job* was an age of faith in God. Job, the hero of the book, shows his faith in God and is richly rewarded. The three comforters are the villains of the book because they try to lead Job astray and also because they show their own unbelief.

the play *J.B.* shows an entirely different age. The views of this age are presented by Mr. Zuss and Mr. Nickles. They voiced the doubt and questioning of God that were characteristic of this age. The hero of this story, J.B., was not rewarded for his faith in God as was *Job*. The people of *J.B.*'s age did not trust God to reward them for their faith.

The two ages differ in their closeness to God. The people of *Job*'s time were able to talk with God. They felt his presence in their lives. The people of the time of J.B. were not able to communicate with God. They had somehow grown apart from God.

Perhaps there is some significance in the fact that *Job* was written before Christ and *J.B.* was written after Christ. Before Christ man had hope in a world of peace. He had faith in the prophecy that when Christ came, there would be peace on earth. When Christ came and went and there was still no peace on earth, some men lost faith in God. The peace mentioned in the prophecy was probably a peace of mind found in religion. But this was not enough for some men. At the time of *J.B.*, this resentment was still evident and probably could account for the rift between God and man.

The two different settings show the ways the people lived. In *Job* the people lived in tribes and were sheepherders. In *J.B.* the people lived in a big city where Job was a banker and businessman.

In *Job* the wife and children were not mentioned very much. In *J.B.* they were very important. This reflects on the importance of the family in each of these times. In the time of *Job* families were more institutional or ceremonial. In the time of *J.B.* the family was a very closely knit group. The children were important in *J.B.* because they made a comment on life. They showed the indifference to religion of the people of the age of *J.B.*

## Writing Assignment Two, Question 3 Comment on Sample 2. Grade: Average

This paper meets the demands of the assignment but does so more ploddingly than the first and with little indication of how it feels to be looking back at the twentieth century from the vantage point of five hundred years hence. In fact the paper reads like a 1967 comparison of important differences in the two plays. An imaginative creation of 2500 A.D. is evidently beyond this student's powers, and, moreover, this student is less competent in his analysis of the two plays than the first writer. In his first paragraph, for instance, this writer states that the comforters in Job are "the villains of the book because they try to lead Job astray and also because they show their own unbelief." As an evaluation of the comforters this is unsubtle and misleading. Similarly dubious is the statement in paragraph two that both Mr. Zuss and (Mr.) Nickles "voiced the doubt and questioning of God that were characteristic of this age." The later notion that rancor and doubt of God were engendered by Christ's failure to leave behind him a world at peace and that traces of this rancor account for *J.B.* overlooks the profound faith of the Middle Ages and is probably attributing modern disbelief to the wrong cause. Nevertheless, much of this paper is valid. The organization is simple and clear-cut. Writing techniques are competent. In fact the whole paper suggests a not very imaginative student who indiscreetly picked an assignment calling for a lively and disciplined imagination.

## Writing Assignment Two, Question 3 Sample 3. Grade: Average

*The Relationship of God to Man in the Ages of Job and J.B.*

A theologian's purpose is to study God's relation to man. The relationship of God and men underwent definite changes between the age of Job and the time of J.B.

The affinity between man and God, as shown in the two different ages, is best seen by comparing the attitudes of Job, J.B., their wives, and the comforters toward God.

One important difference between the times of Job and J.B. is the change from fearing God to loving Him. Job's God was a powerful force whose presence was strongly felt; God's nearness to men of Job's time probably caused their fear, for God took immediate action against those who disobeyed Him. Eliphaz asked Job, "Is not your fear of God your confidence. . . ." On the other hand, J.B. ". . . trusts the will of God and loves—" J.B.'s God seemed to be removed from man; His part was played by a human and when God did speak, He was the Distant Voice rather than God. The feeling of a distant God may account for the less fearful attitude of the J.B.'s time. Instead of offering sacrifices to God as Job did, J.B. prayed or thanked God: J.B. said, "The thanks are Part of love and paid like love. . . ."

There were comforters in both Job's and J.B.'s times, and these comforters represent attitudes of their ages toward God. Job's comforters felt he must have sinned against God to receive all his punishment. Eliphaz said to Job, "Think now, who that was innocent ever perished? Or where were the upright cut off? As I have seen, those who plow iniquity and sow trouble reap the same." Bildad said, ". . . if you are pure and upright, surely then he will rouse himself for you and reward you. . ." Zophar went so far as to say, "Know then that God exacts of you less than your guilt deserves." These comforters showed an idea prevalent in Job's day: that man is punished for his evil and, thus, gets what he deserves. The comforters of J.B.'s time showed a different attitude. Bildad did not try to convince J.B. that he deserved his suffering: "At the end there will be justice! On the way . . . it doesn't matter." Zophar felt that J.B. had no more guilt than other men: "All mankind are guilty always." Eliphaz said that all men were ignorant; due to their ignorance men could not be guilty. The great difference in attitudes, as shown by the comforters, is that in Job's time men were convinced of God's justice, while in J.B.'s time they did not claim that God was just nor that one man particularly deserved to suffer.

The dissenting views of the two age are shown by Job and J.B. While job's comforters said that he must deserve his punishment because God is just, Job said, ". . . he destroys both the blameless and the wicked." Job felt that he was righteous, and was being punished for unknown reasons not his own evil. When J.B.'s comforters said that men were all guilty (or ignorant) and that guilt was not God's reason for punishing, J.B. answered that guilt does matter. J.B. would rather have suffered unspeakable suffering knowing he deserved it than to justify nis suffering by innocence or common guilt. J.B. thought he must have deserved his punishment and Job justified himself, rather than God.

In both ages, there were people who turned away from God. The wives of Job and J.B. both said, "Curse God and die." But in both ages there were also men who retained their faith in God, as did Job and J.B.

## Writing Assignment Two, Question 3
## Comment on Sample 3. Grade: Average

This student, like the second, falls short of the first paper in his failure to establish clearly the vantage point of 2500 A.D. and to comment throughout as though from that vantage point. Essentially the paper is reproducing neatly and with copious quotations what the student has picked up through class discussion on the differing concepts of God in the two plays and the differing sets of comforters. The paper is usually accurate in its statements, but the student shows little awareness of the evolution of feeling toward God within the two characters Job and J.B. The paper implies that Job began and ended in fear of a near-at-hand God, whereas J.B. began and ended in love for a distant, impersonal God. This writer seems to have misunderstood the significance of J.B.'s final awareness that God is neither just nor loving and that man's hope lies in the solace of human love. The paper also naïvely assumes that to the end of their stories Job denies his guilt and J.B. affirms his. This is to miss the impact on both characters of the encounter with God in the whirlwind. Job's recantation amounts to an admission of the guilt of presumptuous ignorance, whereas J.B.'s recognition that justice is in man, not in God or in the cosmos, indicates an ultimate awareness that he was not guilty and that his sufferings were not due punishment delivered from on high.

## Writing Assignment Two, Question 3
## Sample 4. Grade: Low

As a historian one has to take into account all the facts of the story before giving any account of what has happened. In the modern translation of Job and J.B. you can see how much alike the two renderings of the same story are, even though the two stories were written centuries apart. There were many resemblances between the stories where one could see that the stories were the same basically.

The two main characters in the stories were very alike and at the same time very different. These two men, one a rich merchant in an ancient arabic land and a well to do business man in New England, are perfect examples of the Upright man. God sees this and says in both cases

"Hath thou considered My servant Job
"There is none like him on the Earth
A Perfect and an upright man, one
That Fearth God and escheweth evil?"

This shows that God has a good deal of respect for Job and J.B. They are upright, they fear God and are very sucessful men. They also have faults in common. One of their common faults is their wifes. They seem to be the exact opposit to their husbands in their attitude toward God. In both stories the wifes told their husband to curse God and die, but both men having such faith in God couldn't do such things. They wanted to find out the reason that they were being punished but the wouldn't curse God and die. As you can see the stories are really very similar in composition. The characters are not exactly the same but they are quite similar.

## Writing Assignment Two, Question 3 Comment on Sample 4. Grade: Low

In its original form this unit had been offered to both eleventh and twelfth grade students, but most teachers agreed that the composition assignments were out of the reach of all but exceptional eleventh graders. The weaknesses here, though, suggest more than mere immaturity. For one thing the student has ignored the directions that ask him to write from the vantage point of the year 2500 A.D. Nothing in the paper even suggests that it is being written at any time other than our own. The substance is thin; the writing is feeble. The one spicy bit in the entire paper is the comment on Job and J.B. that "One of their common faults is their wifes." The emptiness of the ending sentence is a measure of the student's failure to grasp the significance of either work.

The Glass Menagerie
*Grades 10 and 11*

to teach it as though it were a novel. The text of a play is no more the play itself than the score of a symphony is the symphony. The teacher should do everything possible to turn his classroom into a theater. The teacher who is a "ham" at heart may want to try reading all the parts himself. (Caedmon record TC1005 has Williams himself reading most effectively a long excerpt from *The Glass Menagerie.* Even better will be the assigning of parts to members of the class and playing a record of the play itself. Caedmon TRS301M(S) is probably the best record available, though a critical class will not be satisfied with it, especially with the reading of Tom's part.)

2. As much discussion as possible of the questions and study materials that follow. The material in parentheses does not pretend to supply final answers but is merely a guide to directions the discussion may well take.

## Questions and Suggestions for Discussion

Although the material that follows is divided into four parts, these four parts are so closely related that some teachers may prefer to deal with all four aspects simultaneously in a consecutive study of the play.

### The Problem of Communication

With the possible exception of the Tom–Laura pair, no two of the characters in this play can communicate successfully with one another except in brief flashes that, by contrast, make the basic situation of the play even more touching. Below are brief guides on three "pairs" that focus on this problem.

a. *Tom and Amanda.* Read Scene IV (pages 30–44 in the New Directions edition). Find lines in this scene that show that Tom and Amanda are on different "wave lengths." (A few examples: Tom's reaction to Amanda's "Try and you will succeed!"—page 36. He knows it is not true in the way she means it—success at the warehouse. Or Tom's "I will never be a drunkard," page 36. The "Promise" is a joke to Tom. Or Amanda's talk about "Christian adults"; or Tom's talk about "instinct," page 40. The two might as well be talking on separate planets. But is there one of those flashes of genuine communication in this scene? Perhaps, when Tom apologizes, page 35; and surely when they are both at least *aware* of the problem of communication, pages 38–39.)

Look at Tom's speech in Scene II, page 28: "I'm going to opium dens!" and so forth. Does he *mean* what he says? (No. What the speech shows is that he has given up trying to communicate. Incidentally, it is also one of a number of genuinely funny scenes in the play. Williams is a master at mixing humor and pathos; and students will be quick to spot other examples of this blending. Note also that in Tom's hysterical attempt to break away—Scene III—he breaks some of Laura's glass animals, just as his outburst has "broken" part of Laura's dream world. Students will note that Jim does the same thing in Scene VII.)

Look at the last exchange between Tom and Amanda at the end of the play. (It is, of course, the final breakdown of communication between these two.)

b. *Amanda and Laura.* Look over Scene II, pages 13–21. Try to see why it is all but impossible for Laura and Amanda to understand each other. (Amanda has no conception of the neurotic nature of Laura's shyness. Laura is almost incapable of communicating with *anyone.* Amanda's idea of women as gay, flighty, charming—her own no doubt exaggerated picture of herself as queen of the Delta—simply makes Laura more painfully introverted.)

c. *Laura and Jim.* The scene between these two, pages 87–116, requires particularly careful study. Why is it considered the most touching scene in the whole play? (Because it is Laura's only chance to break out of her dream world. The two or three minutes while she dances with Jim, and the kiss, are the climax of her life, the only time she ever really communicates with anyone. And we know that once she learns of Jim's engagement, her life is over. And, incidentally, although it is probably true that Laura and her brother come closer to genuine communication than any other pair of characters, his leaving at the end of the play suggests how little realization he has of the state in which the scene with Jim has left his sister.)

### The Dream Worlds in *The Glass Menagerie*

Since this aspect of the play will be covered in writing assignment one, the students should be left to make their own discoveries insofar as is possible. Each

# The Glass Menagerie
## *Grades 10 and 11*

*Edition Used:* Williams, Tennessee. *The Glass Menagerie.* New York: New Directions, paperback edition, 1966. All page references in this unit are to this edition.
*Approximate Time:* two weeks (10 class sessions)

### To the Teacher

The pretesting suggests that this unit can be used most fruitfully with eleventh grade students or with able tenth graders in the latter part of sophomore year. For such high school students *The Glass Menagerie* is probably the most suitable of Williams' plays for these reasons:

1. It is not at all obscure or obscene.

2. It is not ostentatiously morbid or "sick" as many of his other plays are.

3. It provides a basis for an examination of the use of symbols in the drama, but because in this play Williams has his symbols under tight control, the student gets no invitation to indulge in unrestrained and undisciplined symbol-hunting.

4. It deals with themes that adolescents can understand—indeed are likely to be involved with.

The teacher will probably wish to allow the students two or perhaps three days of outside preparation for the completion of their first reading of the play. For the completion of the two writing assignments at the end of the unit, students will probably need at least three outside preparation periods. Further out-of-class assignments are left to the individual teacher, but some may wish to have students read Williams' short story "Portrait of a Girl in Glass" for comparison with *The Glass Menagerie.* In fact, some schools may wish to substitute a written comparison of the play and the short story for one of the writing assignments suggested at the end of these study materials.

The class periods should be devoted to two main concerns:

1. As much time as can be given to *reading* the play *aloud* together. Plays are intended to be performed. Nothing could be more unfair to a play than

teacher will have to decide how much help a given class needs before it is turned loose to do its own finding of Amanda's "Delta Society," with its beaux, jonquils, romantic duels, picnics, and laughter; Tom's world of adventure and escape from responsibility; Laura's fantasy world of glass animals, who cannot hurt or embarrass her, who are unaware of her infirmity, and whom she can manipulate; Jim's world of the bustlingly efficient executive carving out for himself a chunk of the American dream of "success."

## Symbolism

Students should come to see that symbolism, properly used, is not a hindrance but a help to understanding, a marvelous means of compressing meaning, a sort of dramatic shorthand.

a. Discuss in detail the central symbol of the play, the glass menagerie itself. By the end of the play, how much is Williams able to "say" about Laura by having her pick up a little glass horse and look at it?

b. Is it possible to overwork a symbol? Is Williams guilty of this in the scene where Jim inadvertently breaks the unicorn's horn, thus symbolizing the way his visit has ruptured a part of Laura's dream world? Give reasons for your answer, being sure to reckon with a similar scene earlier in the play.

c. What symbols do you find for Tom's dream world and Amanda's? (The movies, Blue Mountain.) Why are these symbols less fully developed than that of the glass menagerie? (Perhaps because Tom and Amanda are less dependent on them?)

d. Is the "gentleman caller" himself a symbol? (Possibly he symbolizes the "real world" impinging upon Laura's dream world, though students will be aware that Jim, too, is living partly in a nostalgic dream world of his high school successes and partly in a dream world of his future ascent into the executive class.)

e. In the drama, symbols are most often seen in action; therefore, stage directions need careful and imaginative study. Below are questions on Williams' stage directions:

(1) Is the fire escape used symbolically? (Read the second paragraph at the beginning of the play where, in his stage directions, Williams spells out the significance of the fire escape.)

(2) On page 11, and in other places, Williams calls for "clear light" on Laura. Why? (A symbol of purity and perhaps, too, of vulnerability, in contrast to the blackness and "strong," even violent colors of other parts of the set.)

(3) At the beginning of Scene II (page 14), Laura *"touches her lips with a nervous gesture."* Why? (Perhaps through fear of *having* to speak.)

(4) At the start of Scene IV (page 30), Williams provides another striking symbol. What is it? (The big bell and the tiny noisemaker.)

(5) In the last scene (page 114), *"Laura's look changes, her eyes returning slowly from his to the ornament in her palm."* Why? (Probably to mark the beginning of her irrevocable retreat from reality.)

(6) The final scene between Laura and Amanda *"is played as though viewed through soundproof glass."* Why? (Probably to show that they have retreated into the past, that they are now only memories.) Why *"glass"*? And why *"soundproof"*?

## Style

a. Look at Amanda's speech on eating in Scene I (pages 6–7). Why has Williams chosen words like "chew," "stomachs," "mastication," "salivary glands"? Can you find a similar example in another scene? (This is one of Amanda's preoccupations characteristically expressed in pseudoscientific language, a common cloak for half-baked knowledge. More important dramatically, however, is our vision of Tom's appetite diminishing with every word.) Why do Amanda's words affect Tom's appetite as they do?

b. Amanda is a bit of a Mrs. Malaprop. What examples do you find of her malapropisms? ("Turned up their toes to the daisies!" page 10; "up the spout," page 17; ". . . as plain as I see the nose in front of my face!" page 41.)

c. Read Tom's speech on page 27. What is the effect of the words *"celotex interior"* and *"fluorescent tubes"*? (They violently express his sense of his life at the warehouse and its artificiality.)

d. Tom's "soliloquies" have many of the characteristics of poetry, perhaps most importantly in the use of metaphor and in strong rhythmic patterns. What examples do you find? (The blind generation and the Braille alphabet in the opening speech are examples of striking metaphor. If students have had experience with scansion, they will find it a fascinating exercise to rewrite some of Tom's lines as verse. Here, for example, are the last lines of the play, which are, in effect, blank verse:

> For now / adays / the world / is lit / by light / ning!
>
> Blow out / your can / dles, Lau / ra—and so / good-bye. . . .

The hovering accents, the feminine ending, the anapestic substitution—all can be found on almost any page of Shakespeare.)

### Note to the Teacher

These study materials leave untouched aspects of the play that many teachers will want to discuss with their students. For instance, some may wish to discuss the dramatic construction of the play at the outset, having students analyze how each scene culminates in a natural crisis and foreshadows the ultimate outcome. Students familiar with Wilder's *Our Town* may want to compare Wilder's staging with Williams' and Wilder's use of the Stage Manager with Williams' use of Tom as both narrator and actor. Or students familiar with Greek drama may want to compare the use of the chorus there with the use of the narrator in *The Glass Menagerie.* The possibilities are so rich that no single study plan can do more than suggest some of them.

Some teachers may want to use the first class period, before students have begun their reading of the play, for a consideration of salient features of modern drama, of Tennessee Williams as an exponent of this modern drama, and of *The Glass Menagerie* as an example of it. Especially with a class that has previously had limited experience with plays, the teacher's main job will be to make students aware that modern drama reflects attitudes profoundly different, say, from those of Shakespeare, and that these differences reflect the current world view, one aspect of which is our inability to believe that the individual can significantly *influence his environment.*

The teacher can then point out that this is why, by and large, modern playwrights tend to write about "little" people trapped in a world they cannot control—"little" people like Willy Loman, Blanche Dubois, any of Albee's characters, or Beckett's, or most of O'Neill's. Students who have had any experience with Shakespeare or Greek tragedy can see for themselves the difference between the "littleness" of a Willy Loman and the "largeness" of a Macbeth or Hamlet. They can sense the contrast between the proud assumption of responsibility for his own actions in an Oedipus and the implied abnegation of all personal responsibility in a Blanche Dubois. An alert class may want to push on to an exploration of the reasons for a modern view of man that tends to reduce the human situation to an "absurdity." How far the teacher will wish to carry such a discussion will depend on the intellectual level of the class, on the extent of their previous experience with plays, and on the teacher's own sixth sense that tells him when a discussion has run its course.

## Writing Assignments

Two writing assignments appear below. All students should write on the first, which is a revision of the original first assignment. For his second paper each student should choose either question 1 or 2. If possible, both writing assignments should be done outside class, with plenty of chance for revising, rewriting, and proofreading. For both these assignments the student should be allowed to use his copy of *The Glass Menagerie* freely.

### Revised Writing Assignment One

In T. S. Eliot's *Murder in the Cathedral,* the main character, Becket, says, "Human kind cannot bear very much reality."

*Directions.* Write a carefully planned paper, prepared outside class, in which you examine and compare the extent to which the above quotation applies to each of the people in *The Glass Menagerie.* To do this you will need first to arrive at a working definition of "reality" that is appropriate for *The Glass Menagerie.* In developing your paper draw fully and specifically on relevant evidence from the play itself.

## Writing Assignment Two

Choose *one* of the following writing assignments:

1. Write a carefully planned composition, prepared outside class, in which you cope fully and specifically with the problems set below.

The epigraph to the play is the last line of E. E. Cummings' poem, "somewhere i have never travelled." (A copy of the complete poem is included at the end of the unit.) Here is the last stanza of the poem:

(i do not know what it is about you that closes
and opens;only something in me understands
the voice of your eyes is deeper than all roses)
nobody,not even the rain,has such small hands

What may be some of the reasons that Williams chose as his epigraph the line "nobody,not even the rain,has such small hands"? How do these words relate to the play? How might the title and the whole stanza relate to the play? To whom in the play might the "i" and the "you" relate, and why do you think so?

2. You have seen how alive, how individual Williams makes Amanda by the deftness with which he has her reveal herself through her speech—her mannerisms, her malapropisms, her pseudoscientific jargon about mastication and the salivary glands, her medical superstitions about the linkage between hot coffee and cancer of the stomach, her Delta reminiscences, her use of stock phrases mostly repeated without variation, and her shifts of diction as she oscillates between St. Louis and Blue Mountain.

Now try to do a similarly skillful job on a small scale by writing a single speech or a single scene in which a person whom you either know well or imagine vividly, reveals himself by what you have him say and by how you have him say it. Before you start to write decide exactly what traits in the person you want to bring out and try to make every word serve your purpose. You will probably need to provide one or more other people to whom you have your chosen character talking, but keep the spotlight on your main person and his words.

### *somewhere i have never travelled*

e. e. cummings

somewhere i have never travelled,gladly beyond
any experience,your eyes have their silence:
in your most frail gesture are things which enclose
me,
or which i cannot touch because they are too near

your slightest look easily will unclose me
though i have closed myself as fingers,
you open always petal by petal myself as Spring opens
(touching skilfully,mysteriously) her first rose

or if your wish be to close me,i and
my life will shut very beautifully,suddenly,
as when the heart of this flower imagines
the snow carefully everywhere descending;

nothing which we are to perceive in this world equals
the power of your intense fragility:whose texture
compels me with the colour of its countries,
rendering death and forever with each breathing

(i do not know what it is about you that closes
and opens;only something in me understands
the voice of your eyes is deeper than all roses)
nobody,not even the rain,has such small hands

## Introductory Comment on Original Writing Assignment One

The original writing assignment one reads as follows:

By specific reference to the play, arrange the dream worlds of Tom, Laura, and Amanda in a sort of continuum. Which is most insulated from reality? Which least? Which character has the best chance of ultimately reestablishing contact with reality?

Teachers objected to this assignment on the following grounds: 1. the wording is needlessly "formidable"; 2. the directions fail to indicate what kind of "continuum" is meant; 3. the student can only guess about which character has the best chance of reestablishing contact with reality; but 4. if you leave out that part of the assignment, the student is being asked to do little more than to summarize what he has already discussed in class. The revised assignments are an attempt to meet these objections. The samples written in response to the original assignment indicate the students' disagreement about which character is most remote from reality. The usual arrangement is Tom, Amanda, and Laura—in increasing order of remoteness, yet the *high* paper makes a persuasive case for Amanda as the most remote, and one teacher reported that some of his students thought Tom was the most remote because he was still living in a dream world years after the play's ending. Putting aside their personal convictions, the readers tried to rate each paper in terms of how persuasively it presents whatever viewpoint it chooses to present.

## Original Writing Assignment One Sample 1. Grade: High

*Glass Managerie*

There is little doubt as to how I would rate these characters in terms of contact with reality. Tom is the most realistic, followed by Laura, and then Amanda.

Tom is the most realistic. This is evident in his attitudes toward his family, himself, and their relationship with the "outside" world. He has faced the facts: he realizes Laura is crippled, that she is destined to play the victrola for the next 50 years, that his mother is in a lost world, and that he is not moving ahead. He is dissatisfied with his lot—he wishes to do more than stack shoes, smoke and go to the movies. In realizing that his family is in part holding him back, Tom is very much in touch with the real situation.

This being in touch with life, this actual *living* is what distinguishes Tom from Laura. Laura recognized her defects, but resolves to do nothing. She resigns herself to the fact that there will be no gentlemen callers. When questioned by Jim as to what she does, she replies:

"I don't do anything—much. Oh, please dont think I sit around doing nothing! My glass collection takes up a good deal of time. Glass is something you have to take good care of."

In other words, she really *does* do nothing. The fact that she can consider playing with glass a worthy pastime for six years shows she is warped in her sense of judgement. When Jim tries to bring her back to reality, he almost succeeds. But when the truth is known, and he hastily exits, Laura's first reaction is to wind the victrola—proof that she is withdrawing once again, and probably forever.

While Laura at least recognizes the fact that she will receive no gentlemen callers, that she is crippled, and that her mother is living in the past, her mother refuses to accept any of these things. Holding on to the blind faith that *her* children cannot be run-of-the-mill, surely not inferior, but *will* make their way in the world, Amanda shows she is totally lost by saying, ". . . Stay fresh and pretty!—Its almost time for our gentlemen callers to start arriving. How many do you think we're going to entertain this afternoon? . . . . . What? No-one—not one? You must be joking. Not one gentleman caller? It can't be true! There must have a flood, there must have been a tornado.

Aside from this belief that something will happen even if they do nothing, Amanda is also superstitious—constantly referring to ways to stay healthy, or wishing on the moon. She is constantly referring to her past in the Blue Mountains—not realizing that this does not apply to a daughter called Blue Roses because of pleurosis—not her beauty.

In short, Tom is the most realistic as he alone realizes his plight, his surroundings, and attempts to leave them. Laura, too, at times realizes her plight, and, as with Tom, realizes her mother is lost to reality. She, however, is able to withdraw from reality—something Tom cannot do—and what Amanda does almost constantly.

## Original Writing Assignment One Comment on Sample 1. Grade: High

This is a competent, persuasive presentation of the minority opinion that of the three main characters in *The*

*Glass Menagerie* Amanda is the most remote from reality. The logic here is not unassailable. The student makes his case in part by ignoring some of the facts, but almost any paper on this topic will do likewise. The logic of this paper derives from a restricted definition of "being in touch with reality." Closeness or remoteness in relation to reality is gauged in terms of realizations rather than actions, except for the recognition that Tom acts out his realizations. Within the limitations imposed by this definition, the student then examines degrees of awareness of actuality in each character and finds Amanda the most remote of the three. The strengths of this paper are the directness and clarity of its attack on the assignment; the convincing use of judiciously selected evidence; the competent writing skills; the tightness of the total organization; and the firm cementing of paragraph to paragraph. Nor is the paper distorted in its treatment of Laura as any paper might well have been that puts Amanda at a further point from reality than her daughter. This student, however, sees clearly that after Jim leaves, Laura will probably retreat forever to her fragile glass world, but he argues persuasively that she will take with her into that world some realizations that her mother cannot or will not share.

## Original Writing Assignment One
## Sample 2. Grade: Average

*A Family's Dreams*

In the play *The Glass Menagerie,* all of the main characters—Tom, Laura, and Amanda—live in a dream world. The character who seems most insulated from reality is Laura. The one whose dream comes closest to reality is Tom's. Laura's world is one closed in by the walls of her home. Her life consists of her glass menagerie, phonograph records, her scrapbook, and her memories of Jim. The glass menagerie is something she can care for, something to have some pride in. Her phonograph records, which were left by her father, give her the enjoyment which she doesn't receive often at home. Because of her crippled condition, she feels there is a barrier between the outside world and the time she spends at home.

The second of the three main characters is Amanda whose "dream world" is retold in the past. From her seventeen gentleman at Blue Mountain to the Governor's Ball, she expresses her experiences all of wonderful times. She retells them as a dream that most girls would live for. One of her experiences might have been the time when she would pick jonquils and would make gentleman callers get out of their carriages to help her. This is the world she now dreams of. It is a world of love and happiness, which is in her life no longer.

The third and final main character is Tom, whose world lies in present and in the future. The most obvious part of his present dream world is the movies. The movies are his escape from life. They are something he can go and leave all his troubles outside. He gives many reasons for attending the movies so frequently, and his stock explantion is that he likes "adventure". He says he like adventure because it is one thing he sees little of at home or at work. Another one of his escapes is his smoking. He feels that by smoking he can get away from all of the world. For him it is a time to relax his tensions and put himself at ease. His dream of the future is to be a writer. He writes poems in some of his spare time, this is the only hobby he has. It is the only way of expressing himself. Thus the dream worlds of these characters differ and each does something for him.

## Original Writing Assignment One
## Comment on Sample 2. Grade: Average

This is a plodding paper typical of the many that put Laura furthest from reality, Amanda next, and Tom the least remote—probably the arrangement least difficult to justify, though this student does only a mediocre job of justification. The pedestrian paragraph transitions suggest the ordinariness of the organization and contrast with the jet-smooth movement from section to section of the first paper. The writing techniques here are accurate but without distinction in either diction or sentence structure. The descriptions of the three dream worlds are accurate and fairly detailed, but the writer relies mainly on assertion rather than on persuasive evidence in supporting his thesis that Laura is the most insulated from reality and Tom the least. Nor is there any reckoning here with the additional question of which character is most likely to reestablish contact with reality, though possibly this student came from one of the schools that deliberately avoided this part of the assignment and called merely for a description of the three dream worlds of Tom, Amanda, and Laura.

## Original Writing Assignment One Sample 3. Grade: Low

*"The Glass Menagerie"*

The most insulated from reality is Laura. She plays with her glass menagerie, and plays her old records over and over again. As soon as Laura walks into her room, she is in her own little world, shut off from reality. In scene one you start to find a little bit about Laura. Act two scene 1 Jim is introduced into the story and into Laura's life. The name Blue Roses is part of her dream world. Jim called her blue Roses because Laura was sick with pleurosis and when she got back he thought she said Blue Roses. Laura always kept a little scrap Book, it was so neat, and everything had its own little place, just like her dream world.

Amanda dream world was not as insulated as Lauras. By the means of escape she would always talk about her past, Her Gentlemen callers "seventeen" of them so she says. It was up at Blue Mountain she'd always talk about it. She'd want to make a picnic and get away with her family.

Amanda was always busy making some kinds of plans for Laura, either wanting her to date or having to sit and stay neat & pretty for her gentlemen callers. And how excited she got when she heard Tom was bringing home a boy for Laura. She fixed new lamp shades, and went over the furnature a little, she made alot of declious food, and that dress she wore, that dress she had worn on the day She met Laura's father. She was trying to hard to make a good impression. In scene 1 act two is where Amanda fixes the lamps and the furinature. That scene is where she wore that dress.

Toms dream world is filled with adventure thats why he goes to the movies so often, and he also goes by means of escape. Tom's wanting to become a writter in the first few scenes you notice that. He enjoys doing something else besides going to the movies. going out onto the fire escape was another mean of escape for tom. Tom would use the fire escape like the new world, not the world of adventure he see's in the movies. Both Laura and Tom use the fire escape.

It something that they know is always there. Tom snokes alot, sometimes he's nervous and other times he smokes for another escape, throughout the whole play Tom is smoking and using the fire escape, and going to the movies.

In the play the character Tom, I think has the best chance of ultimately reestablishing contact with reality. Tom can face alot of things more than Amanda or Laura can like; facing the fact that by bringing Jim over it wouldn't help or change matters at all, in fact he was aganist it or unconserned about the whole idea from the beginning, because he knew it wouldn't help. He wants to get out on his own you know then that he's trying to feel for something but he's still not sure of what he wants, but he knows he wants to get out into the world. In my opinion I think he will make it.

## Original Writing Assignment One Comment on Sample 3. Grade: Low

The *average* paper is dully innocuous in style, but this one is a jungle growth of misspellings, comma splices, and fragments punctuated as sentences. In putting Laura furthest from reality and Tom closest to it, and also in seeing Tom as most likely to reestablish contact with reality, the student stands on easily defensible territory, but his defense is feeble. So is his organization. In fact, the only organization is by characters, first Laura, then Amanda, and finally Tom, with a concluding section on Tom's chances for reestablishing contact with reality. Within the paragraphs, except for the final one, the reader trips over a tangled assortment of facts. The best part of the paper is its final section. There for the first time the writer has linked his sentences and imposed some sort of orderly progression on his ideas, though the concluding "In my opinion I think" is a final reminder of his stylistic inadequacies.

## Introductory Comment on Writing Assignment Two, Question 1

A number of teachers found this assignment "interesting but hard." Students tended to shy off from it, but, as one teacher pointed out, the occasional student who did tackle it, often produced a surprisingly good paper. The merits of the assignment are that it forces the student to move beyond his class discussion; it has freshness; and it encourages the student to enter the play with sensitivity and imagination. Because a number of teachers wrote the assignment off as too hard, the Committee is presenting two *high* papers, both from tenth grade students. And on this assignment tenth grade papers were about as good as eleventh grade—another unexpected finding.

## Writing Assignment Two, Question 1
## Sample 1. Grade: High

Williams chose this stanza as an expression of the play's idea because it tells how Tom remembers Laura. There is partial understanding here ". . . something in me understands the voice of your eyes is deeper than all roses.)" Laura's delicicy and fragility are noted in the words ". . . small hands".

Still there remains a mystery about the person in question. "(i do not know what it is about you that closes and opens; . . ." Laura, too, is like a rose, a blue rose, in fact. Small, delicate, shy, she unfolds once and then hastily and finally closes again.

The title of the poem, "somewhere i have never traveled" can refer to Tom's travels in an attempt to forget his sister. No matter where he goes or what he does he cannot. "Oh, Laura, Laura, I tried to leave you behind me . . ." he says, trying to forget her. Her memory remains like a piece of glass, in his mind, delicate like the rose but enduring like the rain.

## Writing Assignment Two, Question 1
## Comment on Sample 1. Grade: High

Choosing a *high* tenth grade sample for this assignment was hard because of the surprising number of good responses to a topic that many teachers apparently wrote off as too difficult. What is remarkable in this paper is the richness of its brevity. This student assumes that Cummings' title relates to Tom's travels in the real world "in an attempt to forget his sister," and this is probably a valid inference though it overlooks the other possibility that the "somewhere" Tom has never traveled is the fragile-as-glass world of his sister's mind. Later, however, this student does recognize Tom's merely partial understanding of the elusive delicacy and fragility of his sister's world. And this paper moves beyond many others in its linkage of Cummings' "all roses" with the "blue roses" of *The Glass Menagerie.* The controlled handling of sentence structure and diction throughout the paper is an exceptional achievement for any tenth grader.

## Writing Assignment Two, Question 1
## Sample 2. Grade: High

*"somewhere he has never travelled"*

The epigraph of "The Glass Menagerie" was taken from the poem "somewhere i have never travelled" by e. e. cummings. The poem could actually be a description of Laura by her brother, Tom. The "somewhere" in the title of the poem could refer to Lauras' dream world. Tom has wanted to communicate with Laura but he finds it impossible. Laura also cannot communicate with Tom, but it is possible that she understands him. For in Act One, Scene Five, Amanda says to Tom, ". . . A few days ago I came in and and Laura was crying. She has an idea that you're not happy here." This statement is evidently very true and is substantiated later in the play. In the second, third and forth stanzas, Tom tells about Lauras' gentleness and fragility. However, in the fifth stanza—Tom actually sums up his feelings towards Laura.

The fifth stanza reads, "(i do not know what it is about you that closes and opens; only something in me understands, the voice of your eyes is deeper than all roses) nobody, not even the rain, has such small hands". In the first line, Tom is saying that he cannot understand why Laura is the way she is. He cannot understand her dream world, although he would like to. However, in line two Tom says that something in him (perhaps his sensitivity) understands. The word "understands" must not be misconstrued. For it really connotates empathy rather than understanding. These two lines bring out the love and closeness that Tom feels for Laura. But it is interesting to note that Toms' love for Laura is not blind like Amandas'. For in the play he says, "Laura is very different from other girls . . . she's terribly shy and live's in a world of her own." When Amanda says that Laura is lovely, sweet and pretty, Tom says, "Laura seems all those things to you and me because she's ours and we love her." Tom goes on to say that Laura seems beautiful to him. This is shown by the comparison of "the voice of her eyes" to a rose.

Finally Tom concludes the poem with the epigraph of the play which is, "nobody, not even the rain, has such small hands." The rain connotates the gentility and softness of nature. The small hands signify the time that Laura covered the damaged unicorn in her hands. In sumary, the epigraph means that Laura is more gentle and sensitive than all of nature. In conclusion, the epigraph is appropriate because Tom is aware of Lauras' sensitivity. Yet, he knows that he cannot communicate with her and cannot help her, for Laura lives in a dream world—a world from which she cannot escape and no one else can enter.

## Writing Assignment Two, Question 1
## Comment on Sample 2. Grade: High

This paper does not have the condensed power of the first tenth grade paper, but it has one or two insights that the other lacks and its length is probably a better indication of what the assignment drew out of most tenth graders who tackled it. To present only the first sample and then the even briefer *average* sample would give a distorted impression that sophomores had little to say in response to this topic, whereas many wrote at great length, and eleventh graders wrote at even greater length. This student, with greater subtlety than the first, interprets Cummings' title as a reference to Tom's failure to travel in the mind of his sister Laura. The section on Laura's understanding of Tom verges on irrelevance, but the paper then moves on to the shrewd conjecture that the "something" in Tom that understands is his sensitivity. Equally discerning is the differentiation between understanding and empathy that immediately follows. The comment on the "rain" is another of this paper's high spots. What follows subsides into a perfunctory repetitiveness of which the first writer would never be guilty.

## Writing Assignment Two, Question 1
## Sample 3. Grade: Average

"Nobody, not even the rain, has such small hands." Tennessee Williams chose this last line of E. E. Cummings because it is the theme of the play, describing Laura.

The "closing and opening" refers to roses. Laura is like roses because she opens herself to realistic people and then closes herself again. Jim makes a comment about her pretty hands, small and delicate, as in the poem where it refers to hands.

## Writing Assignment Two, Question 1
## Comment on Sample 3. Grade: Average

This paper is accurate as far as it goes, but it stops far short of the thoroughness of the second paper and the imaginative perceptiveness of the first. Here is brevity, but it is brevity without richness. And there are important omissions. This student gives no heed to the title of the Cummings poem, nor is there any reckoning with the "hands" of the rain. This student recognizes the obvious—the smallness and the delicacy of Laura's hands and her "closing and opening" in the presence of "realistic people."

## Writing Assignment Two, Question 1
## Sample 4. Grade: Low

*"Nobody, not even the rain, has such small hands."*

It seems to me that Williams could not have chosen a more appropriate and well-written statement to be used as the epigraph of his play if he had had a sentence "custom-made for the occasion." E. E. Cummings' line symbolically summarizes the whole theme of *The Glass Menagerie.*

Hands are something which is as common as the number of people—in fact, twice as common; each person has two hands. Rain is infinitely common. I think that what Williams is saying is that each drop of rain, no matter how small, is considered important be each pair of hands (representing a person) has no importance on anyone but those few directly in contact with him.

Tom, Laura, and Amanda represent the tragic commonness of people—lost amongst a crowd of strangers. They live in ". . . overcrowded urban centers of lower middle-class population and are symptomatic of the impulse of this largest and fundamentally enslaved section of American society to avoid fluidity and differentiation and to exist and function as one interfused mass of automatism."

The commonness of them is the tragic flaw in each of them. They each have their problems. Their problems are so common that they seem unreal. Actually, they are only simple problems exaggerated many times. They each have their dreams within which they seek refuge from the cruel reality of life.

Tom lacks ambition but at the same time he wants excitement; he escapes this conflict by going to the "movies" every night and finally leaving his home. Laura is extremely shy and self-conscious of being "crippled"; she hides from people and life by playing her victorola and caring for her glass animals. Amanda wants success for her children; she knows, but won't admit, that this is an impossibility. She denies the truth by imagining Laura's gentlemen callers and Tom's having a successful job and by thinking back over her popular youthful days.

These dreams and desires of Tom, Laura, and Amanda

are not uncommon. Everyone has his own dreams—but they don't hide from the rest of the world in them. They try to overcome the commonness of themselves and become an individual.

## Writing Assignment Two, Question 1 Comment on Sample 4. Grade: Low

This paper is three times the length of the first one; it is well expressed; most of what it says is valid. Unfortunately, though, it uses the Cummings line as a point of departure and likewise as a point of no return. It starts promisingly with the assurance that the Cummings line is " 'custom-made for the occasion' " and that it "symbolically summarizes the whole theme of *The Glass Menagerie.*" And with that the student whisks off on a binge of recollection, presumably of a class discussion, in which the class—perhaps with gentle nudgings from the teacher—arrived at the conclusion that the theme of *The Glass Menagerie* is "the tragic commonness of people." The only linkage with Cummings is the comment that the rain is common and that hands and fingers are common. Possibly the student looked only at the single line from Cummings that appears on the title page of the play and not at the rest of the last stanza quoted in the study materials. At any rate he does nothing with Cummings' title, nothing with the "i" and the "you" in Cummings' lines, nothing with the "something in me understands," and nothing with "the voice of your eyes . . . deeper than all roses." The failure in any way to link Laura with these lines is enough in itself to justify the *low* score. The paper as a whole sounds like the glib regurgitating of a student who has absorbed one important truth about the play—its concern with "the tragic commonness of people"—but who is then apparently powerless to move on under his own steam.

## Writing Assignment Two, Question 2 Sample 1. Grade: High

*Thirty-Four, and You Look Like My Sister*

The material props are not really important, except for one large mirror placed in a strategic point on the stage with a chair facing it. A fasionable loveseat is across the stage, opposite the mirror and a large closet is placed unobtrusively toward the back. The stage is dark, except for one shaft of light focused upon the mirror area. A woman is sitting in front of it first combing her hair and then leaning forward toward the mirror and smoothing out the crow's feet and other inevitable signs of age.

A girl, about thirteen, enters and plops down on the loveseat. She is obviously a bookworm and not noticably attractive. She wears thick glasses and a decidedly unbecoming dress. As she enters, the light spreads to include her.

GIRL: (wearily) Hello, mother.

MOTHER: Oh darling! I'm so glad you're home. I've been simply dying to have someone's opinion on my new shade (she reaches up and lightly touches her mass of curls—a stylish blondish-gray color) Do you like it? As I was sitting under the dryer in the beauty-shop—oh my dear, I thought I'd never get out from under that hot thing—I imagined the complete smash I'm going to make at the Governor's Ball tonight. And my dress! Don't you just adore that lovely maroon color? I can see myself now! Everyone will turn around as I walk in and a hush will sweep over the crowd. I'm certainly going to outshine that Betty Jane Randall. She thinks she just owns everyone. Why last week at the Ladies' Aid meeting she had the gall to say that I. . . .Oh honestly, Sabina, must you wear that horrid dress?

GIRL: Mother, I asked you last week to take me shopping on Monday. That was two weeks ago. (as the girl is talking, the woman gets up and walks to the closet. She takes out the maroon gown along with a matching cape.)

MOTHER: Whaa? . . . Oh yes, shopping. Well next week for sure, honey. Tell me the truth—is this cape a little too-too? I thought maybe it was when I saw it in the store but, well, you know frivolous, spendthrift me. (a squeaky giggle) But I must say, it certainly put me back a pretty penny. That good-for-nothing father of yours better get my alimony payments in soon or will he be sorry. By the way, Sabina, we simply must do something about those glasses—they're too horrible for words. That reminds me, do you know Emmy Johnson's daughter Liz? She's that cute little blond with the lovely blue eyes. Well, anyway, Joan McCloud said that Mary Barton said that Liz used to wear glasses, but Emmy bought her blue-tinted contact lenses. Did you ever hear anthing so quaint and clever in your entire life? We'll just have to do something like that for you. Now, be honest with me, baby, does this dress make me look like I'm thirty-four or not? When I went out with that nice Albert from the office, he's the managers' son, you know, he said I only looked old enough to be your sister! Isn't that too much! He's such a card! (another giggle)

GIRL: (even more wearily than before) Yes, mother, you're a shapely thirty-four and look old enough to be my big sister. (there is a strong note of sarcasm in her voice, unobserved by the woman)

The girl gets up and deliberately stomps out leaving her mother with her young, stylish mirror-image which is as shallow as the woman before it. The darkness closes in again and finally overcomes that one shaft of light, making the stage completely black.

## Writing Assignment Two, Question 2 Comment on Sample 1. Grade: High

This is an exceptionally skillful self-revelation of a mother's coy absorption in her multiple vanities and her multiple illusions—an absorption so complete as to anaesthetize all consciousness of the needs, feelings, and even the words of the unattractive daughter. The initial and the final stage directions deftly set and deftly close the scene. At the end the reader knows the mother well—her feigned girlishness, her extravagance, her concern for her alimony, her flirtations with other men, and her myopic unawareness of the daughter who knows her with the deadly perceptiveness of a neglected 13-year-old. The use of the mirror throughout the sketch is further evidence of the artistry of this characterization.

## Writing Assignment Two, Question 2 Sample 2. Grade: Average

*Poor Old Gal*

Sue's mother is a very pretty woman. With her artistic talent, she enjoys painting in her spare time. Because she is friendly she gets along considerably well with people. It is not surprising that people get tired of hearing one's complaints throughout a conversation. This situation is the case with Sue's mother and their friends. To put it bluntly, the problem of Sue's mother is that she is a hypochondriac. Her family cannot see, through their love for her, that she needs help rather than sympathy. The setting is in the kitchen of Sue's home; Sue has just arrived home from school.

Sue: Hi, ma!

Mother: Hello, dear. How was your day at school?

Sue: Oh, okay. I got a "B" on a Spanish test. If I keep trying, I could get a "B" in the class. How was your day?

Mother: Oh, I went shopping at Century City with Ruth. I have a splitting headache. You know how it is down there, so much noice and shoving and confusion. Just drives me crazy. And with this cold of mine coming on and off again, today didn't help any.

Sue: Yeah, that cold's been bugging you a long time. Why don't you let me fix dinner tonight?

Mother: No honey, I can do it. I'm not an invalid. Besides, we're having a nice dinner tonight—Spencer steak.

Sue: You sure you don't want me to do it mom? I have time.

Mother: No, sweetheart. You go do your homework.

After dinner, Sue, Mother and Father at dinner table.

Father: That dinner was fit for a king.

Mother: Well, thank you, dear. (Putting her hand on her head, leaving the table). That hot kitchen gives me such a headache.

Father: Well I should think it would. (Addresses Sue). Susan, didn't you help your mother?

Sue: I offered, but she didn't need me. She wanted to do it by herself.

Father: Poor old gal—always putting herself out for other people. She sure comes out on the raw end of the deal.

## Writing Assignment Two, Question 2 Comment on Sample 2. Grade: Average

This paper also paints an unpleasant picture of adult self-absorption—this time the self-absorption of hypochondria tinctured with a martyr complex. The irony of the father's final comment puts a neat, clean finish to the dramatic revelation. The introductory section, however, is not quite so neat and clean. This student is not subtle enough to let the scene itself reveal to the reader that the mother is a hypochondriac and that she has her family fooled into baseless pity and crippling sympathy. The reader wonders, moreover, why the introduction drags in the mother's love of painting in her spare time. Is this detail relevant to the impression the scene itself seeks to create? Like a good many introductions, this one tells too much. Unlike the first writer, this one lacks the sure judgment that knows exactly what to leave out.

## Writing Assignment Two, Question 2
## Sample 3. Grade: Low

The scene opens with a mother directing her criticisms at her son. The mother consideres herself quite an athority on Medicene.

Mother: Today the girls gave me a luncheon for my birthday and gave me this beautiful tablecloth (holds up tablecloth). Where do you think you're going? Get back to this table.
Son: I'm going to get some ice water.
Mother: Don't you know that can cause ulcers in the stomach? How many times do I have to tell you that?
Son: You've been telling me that so much that I went to the school doctor to ask him if it were true that drinking ice water could cause ulcers in the stomach?
Mother: What did that so-called doctor tell you?
Son: He told me that that business about ice-water causing ulcers is nothing but an old wives-tale.
Mother: Oh? What does he know!
Son: He's a doctor mother.

## Writing Assignment Two, Question 2
## Comment on Sample 3. Grade: Low

A charitable reader might slip this paper into the *average* slot, but it is clearly less competent than the first two papers, first because of such technical weaknesses as the misspelling of "athority" and "medicene" and second because it is heavily indebted to Tennessee Williams' Amanda, with a mere shift from hot coffee to ice water and from cancer to ulcers. A fussy critic will also wonder why the mother is made to sound off on her birthday lunch and her birthday tablecloth when the stage directions state that the scene opens "with a mother directing her criticisms at her son." The best part of the paper is the son's attempt to confound his mother by citing the school doctor and the mother's asinine imperviousness to the professional verdict.

# Language

# *Introduction to the Units on Language*

No other component of the English curriculum has endured a more varied fate than the study of language. In some schools language study means nothing more than grammar and syntax, grade 12. Dissatisfied with the work and the results, a few schools jettisoned a decade or two ago the formal teaching of any grammar and confined language instruction in their English program to marginal notations on students' papers and to student-teacher conferences on writing. Where syntax continued to be taught, it was and still is drawn from traditional school grammar, structural linguistics, and generative grammar.

Most English teachers are aware that syntax and language study are not synonymous. Many schools have broadened their programs to embrace far more than syntax. Phonology, social and regional dialects, the history of the English language, lexicography, usage, and semantics are increasingly recognized as important elements and incorporated in the courses of study. Moreover, in the absence of any school text that is definitive, teachers are relying on sets of class materials that supplement the basic grammar text or handbook. Teachers frequently combine this work with composition and literature rather than limit language study to separate units.

At such a time, the Committee on Curriculum Resources would err seriously if it took no note of the state of flux that characterizes language study, either by ignoring the new developments or by rushing to premature adoption of a particular program. The materials prepared by members of the Committee give less attention to instruction in syntax than to other aspects of language. In schools where language is taught at all, syntax is already strongly entrenched and probably needs little encouragement. In schools where teachers know one grammar system but want to learn another, a sample lesson plan is hardly the medium of instruction. The effort here is to show how other aspects of language properly demand a time and a place and to suggest how the teacher can fuse language study with the study of literature and composition.

The Committee has tried to produce for various grade levels teaching materials that will reflect both the fluid state of intelligent language programs in the schools and the promising trends noted above. That the materials that follow are a sampler and not a program is both intentional and inevitable.

The work in language assumes that students will have available for consultation various dictionaries, grammars, and reference books. The list given below is by no means complete, but is likely to go beyond the resources of most English classrooms or, indeed, of many school libraries. Works specially useful in the units are starred, and unless most of these can be put in the classroom during the period of work on language units, it is probably wise to omit these units or at least to curtail them.


* *Webster's Second New International Dictionary* (Unabridged).
Springfield, Mass.: G. & C. Merriam Company, 1957.

* *Webster's Third New International Dictionary* (Unabridged).
Springfield, Mass.: G. & C. Merriam Company, 1961.

*The American College Dictionary.*
New York: Random House, 1960.

* *Webster's Seventh New Collegiate Dictionary.*
Springfield, Mass.: G. & C. Merriam Company, 1963.

*Thorndike-Barnhart Comprehensive Dictionary.*
Chicago: Scott, Foresman & Co., 1958.

*The Shorter Oxford English Dictionary.*
New York: Oxford University Press, 1933.

Miscellaneous paperback dictionaries.

Birk & Birk. *Understanding and Using English,* Fourth Edition.
New York: Odyssey Press, 1959.

Bryant, Margaret M., ed. *Current American Usage.*
New York: Funk & Wagnalls Company, 1962.

Corbin, Richard K. and Porter G. Perrin. *Guide to Modern English.*
Chicago: Scott, Foresman & Co., 1955.

Evans, Bergen and Cornelia Evans. *Dictionary of Contemporary American Usage.*
New York: Random House, 1957.

Fowler, H. W. *A Dictionary of Modern English Usage.*
New York: Oxford University Press, 1965.

Mencken, H. L. *The American Language.*
New York: Alfred A. Knopf, 1943.
Pence, R. W. and D. W. Emery. *A Grammar of Present Day English.*
New York: Macmillan Company, 1963.
*Pooley, Robert C. *Teaching English Usage.*
New York: Appleton-Century-Crofts, 1946.

*Dictionary Usage: To Kill a Myth*
*Grade 9*

od, a healthier attitude toward dictionaries and a more accurate understanding of how they work.

Although most students have had dictionary work in the elementary school, the ninth grade teacher cannot safely assume that his students know how to "read" a dictionary, so with many classes the first step before starting this unit may be to review such fundamentals as the more common abbreviations and the keys to pronunciation.

Some teachers may wish to give as homework the first two sections of this unit, "Controversial Words" and "Spelling," with the chance, of course, to check findings in those dictionaries available only in the classroom. Other teachers will prefer to carry on all the work in class, perhaps having students do some of it in pairs or in groups, with eventual reports to the class from each pair or group. The need is to have all the class profitably at work making use of all the dictionaries available but without getting in each other's way and wasting time. Each teacher will want to plan in terms of the size of his class and the materials available in his classroom.

No teacher should feel that he must use every item in each of these units. Once the class gets the point of the exercise, it may be well to move on to the next one before interest flags.

## Controversial Words

For years you may have been telling your teacher that "ain't" is in the dictionary. So it is—along with thousands of other words that many people refuse to use.

1. Look up "ain't." Is it in all the dictionaries? What does each dictionary say about it other than defining it? What labels are attached to show the level of usage of "ain't"? Do all dictionaries have the same attitude toward "ain't"? Point out any differences you find, being sure to identify the dictionary you are using. With which dictionary do you agree? Why? Would it ever be all right to use "ain't" in a composition? If so, when?

2. Look up "soda jerk." If you follow *Webster's New World,* should you ever use it in a composition? If so, when? Under what other circumstances could you use this term if you followed the guidelines of *Webster's New World?*

3. Look up "doodad." What does *The American College Dictionary* say about the word? According to this dictionary, when may you use it? What is meant by the label "colloq."?

4. Look up "crumple." Is there a meaning of this word that *The American College Dictionary* limits in its usage? What is the stand of *Webster's New World* on this particular meaning? Does *Webster's Third* agree?

5. Is "irregardless" in all the dictionaries? Could you ever use this word in conversation? Defend your answer by citing a particular dictionary. Which dictionary gives the strongest support for this word? Why do you think such a word came into being?

## Spelling

The purpose of this section is to answer these questions: Do dictionaries agree on the spelling of words? Is there only one correct way to spell a word?

1. Check the spelling of "caliph." Does it begin with a "c" or a "k"? How many spellings of this word are correct? Which dictionary should you follow? Why? Does one dictionary have more authority than another?

2. Check "cozy" for spelling. Do you find more than one way to spell it? Do all the dictionaries in your classroom agree on the one spelling?

3. Check "judgment." Can this word ever be spelled with an "e" after the "g"? What dictionary could you use to show that it can be spelled two ways? Do the dictionaries that record this second spelling have any explanation for it? Why should the letter "e" be included? Which spelling will you use in your own compositions?

4. May the word "development" be spelled with an "e" after the "p"? Does "develop" have a second spelling with an "e" at the end of the word?

5. What variant spellings are listed for "blond"? If you are studying French how do you explain the second spelling?

6. Check "frankfurter." Which form do you prefer—"frankfurter" or "frankfurt"? Why? Which dictionaries make the distinction? How many spellings are there for "hot dog"? At a restaurant would you order a "hamburg" or a "hamburger"? Which form would you use when ordering from the butcher?

7. Check "carburetor." May you spell this word

# *Dictionary Usage: To Kill a Myth*
# *Grade 9*

*Approximate Time:* 2 class periods, possibly 1 preparation period in addition

*Needed Classroom Materials:* The success of this lesson will depend on each student's having some kind of dictionary and searching out for himself the answers to the questions. If the students are paired off for this exercise, it will be useful if each pair has different dictionaries. By comparing what he finds with what his classmates find, a student should be able to conclude that on some matters dictionaries disagree, and that no dictionary is a law except unto itself. He should also realize that some dictionaries are superior to others and that the cheaper varieties are likely to have serious limitations.

In students' hands, or available in the classroom for all students without dictionaries, there should be at least one copy of each of the following dictionaries (other standard dictionaries may also be included):

*Webster's Second New International Dictionary* (Unabridged).
Springfield, Mass.: G. & C. Merriam Company, 1957.

*Webster's Third New International Dictionary* (Unabridged).
Springfield, Mass.: G. & C. Merriam Company, 1961.

*Webster's Seventh New Collegiate Dictionary.*
Springfield, Mass.: G. & C. Merriam Company, 1963.

*The American College Dictionary.*
New York: Random House, 1960.

*Thorndike-Barnhart Comprehensive Dictionary.*
Chicago: Scott, Foresman & Co., 1958.

*The Shorter Oxford English Dictionary.*
New York: Oxford University Press, 1933. (If possible)

*Webster's New World Dictionary. College Edition.*
Cleveland: World Publishing Company, 1964.

## To the Teacher

One of the most dangerous misconceptions that students pick up early and sometimes carry with them into their adult life is the notion that we consult *the* dictionary, not *a* dictionary, and that *the* dictionary is a dictator, oracle, prophet, or Bible. This unit is designed to help students acquire, by an inductive meth-

with two "t's"? Where should you be living to do this and still be using "correct" spelling?

8. Would you put "catchup," "ketchup," or "catsup" on your "hamburg" or "hamburger"? Is there any difference in the recipe for "catchup," "ketchup," or "catsup"?

9. Is there such a thing as a "preferred spelling"? How did you find out?

*Note to the teacher.* "Somersault," "gipsy," and "sirup" raise similar questions.

## Pronunciation

If you don't know how to pronounce a word, you usually go to the dictionary. How would you pronounce the following:

1. "Creek." Where might you live and never hear /krik/? Might you ever be criticized for pronouncing /krek/ as /krik/? According to which dictionaries? How do *The American College Dictionary* and *Webster's New World* account for the variant spellings on grounds other than usage?

2. "Comparable." How many ways may you pronounce this word? Which dictionaries allow two pronunciations? Why does *Webster's Third* say "*sometimes* ÷ kəm′par-."?

3. "Demonstrative." Can you make an educated guess as to why the pronunciation dē·mŏn′strȧ·tĭv came into being? Does *Webster's Second* agree with *Webster's Third* about the two pronunciations?

4. "Grimace." Should you say grim′əs or grəmās′? According to whom? Which pronunciation is older? How do you know?

5. "Miscellany." Is this word pronounced more than one way? Where would be the best place to use the less known pronunciation?

6. "Nazi." How many ways may you pronounce this word? To what extent do your dictionaries agree about this word?

## Differences among Dictionaries: Contents

(The purpose of this exercise is to find out whether dictionary editors agree on what words should go into a dictionary.)

1. "Kloof." Is "kloof" in your dictionary? If so, is there any special marking in front of it or within the definition? How does *Webster's New World* indicate that a word is foreign? Why isn't "kloof" in all the dictionaries, since it is in some and must therefore be in current usage?

2. "Blitz." Is "blitz" in your dictionary? Who gave us this word? Would it have been in your grandfather's dictionary? Why or why not? How many parts of speech can "blitz" be? Do all dictionaries agree about the use of "blitz"?

3. "Bon mot." Is this word listed in all dictionaries? If not, why not? What difference do you notice in the way *Webster's New World* lists "bon mot" and the way it lists "bon jour" and "bon soir"? How do you explain this difference?

4. "Coup d'état." What special mark or label is given this word if it is in your dictionary? Why does *Webster's New World* mark this word as foreign but not words like "chauffeur" and "visit"?

## Agreement among Dictionaries: Word Meaning

(The purpose of this section is to discover whether or not dictionaries agree about the meaning of words.)

1. Compare the definitions for the word "cryptic" in *Webster's Second* and in *Webster's Third.* Does either agree with definitions in the smaller dictionaries?

2. Look up the definitions of "exotic" in *Webster's Second* and in *Webster's Third* and then in the smaller dictionaries.

3. Do all dictionaries give the same number of definitions? Are the definitions they do give the same, especially in the desk or hand dictionaries?

4. What are the implications behind the discoveries you have made about the meanings of these words?

## Summary

1. What conclusions may you now draw about dictionaries?

2. Why is it not entirely accurate to talk about "*the* dictionary"?

3. What good are dictionaries if you can't count on their all agreeing?

4. What questions about dictionaries do these exercises leave unanswered?

5. Are there different kinds of dictionaries? Explain.

6. How do dictionaries like *Thorndike-Barnhart* and *Webster's New World* differ from the dictionaries many students carry to class with their books?

7. What part do you have in the making of a dictionary?

*Changes in the English Language*
*Grades 9 through 12*

teacher will probably want to work out his own solution for this problem. The plan offered here is merely suggestive. By this plan the teacher will appoint individual students to do most of the dictionary work outside class and to assume the responsibility of reporting their findings for class consideration and discussion. Some use of the dictionaries in the classroom will be needful in response to questions students themselves may raise, especially questions that move beyond the assignments. The nine sections that follow include suggested time schedules and suggested distributions of the homework among the students. With an able class it may be possible to move rapidly, covering this whole unit in three or four days instead of five. No teacher should hesitate to omit parts of the unit that he thinks are not needful for his particular class.

## Section I

## Language Changes through Vocabulary

(The suggested time schedule for this section and for Section II, which follows it, is 1 preparation period and 1 class discussion period. Suggested assignments for Sections I and II are: assign two students to each of the four dictionary assignments—A, B, C, and D—in Section I and two more students to do the dictionary work in Section II, making one of the two students responsible for *Webster's Second* and the other for *Webster's Third.* This dictionary work will be the homework assignment for 10 students, and the rest of the class should do part E of Section I as homework. The class period that follows should be used for reports from each student of his findings and discussion of the significance of these findings.)

The most well-known way in which language changes is through vocabulary. But to what extent is this true? Just how does the meaning of a word change? The following exercises will help to answer these questions.

A. Consider the following: *bebiet, anweald*

1. Do these look like English words?

2. Are they in *Webster's Second New International Dictionary* (Unabridged: hereafter referred to as *Webster's Second*)?

3. Are they in *Webster's Third New International Dictionary* (Unabridged: hereafter referred to as *Webster's Third*)?

4. Look up these two words in *The Shorter Oxford English Dictionary,* if it is available. What do you find?

5. Find the following in *Webster's Second:*
ridiculize
disagreeance
noyous

6. Find the same words in *Webster's Third.*

B. Look up the following words in *Webster's Second* and *Third:*
gate-crasher
globalize
name-dropping
Hoover apron
What did you find? (Not in the *Second.*)

C. Find the following words in *Webster's Second* and *Third:*
hight
creek
disband
schedule
travel

1. Do any of these words have a meaning no longer in current usage?

2. What is the difference between *obsolete* and *archaic?*

D. Compare the meaning of the following words in *Webster's Second* and *Third:*
exotic
alligator
canary
nightgown
iceberg
cohort

E. In magazines such as *Time, Newsweek,* and *Life,* or in the newspaper, find at least five words that are not in the dictionaries (for instance, "peacenik," "Vietnik").

### Final Questions

1. What conclusions can you now draw in answer to the questions raised at the beginning of this section: to what extent is the language changing in vocabulary and just how does the meaning of a word

# *Changes in the English Language Grades 9 through 12*

*Approximate Time:* 5 days (5 class periods and 5 preparation periods)

*Materials Required:*

*Webster's Second New International Dictionary* (Unabridged).
Springfield, Mass.: G. & C. Merriam Company, 1957.

*Webster's Third New International Dictionary* (Unabridged).
Springfield, Mass.: G. & C. Merriam Company, 1961.

*Materials Highly Desirable if Available or Procurable:*

*Student's Dictionary of Anglo-Saxon* (Henry Sweet, ed.).
New York: Oxford University Press, 1896.

Fowler, H. W. *A Dictionary of Modern English Usage.*
New York: Oxford University Press, 1965.

Birk & Birk: *Understanding and Using English,* Fourth Edition.
New York: Odyssey Press, 1959.

Pence, R. W. and D. W. Emery. *A Grammar of Present Day English.*
New York: Macmillan Company, 1963.

Curme, George O. *Syntax.*
Boston: D. C. Heath & Company, 1931.

*The Shorter Oxford English Dictionary.*
New York: Oxford University Press, 1933.

## To the Teacher

Students in modern schools know that the English language has changed since the writing of *Beowulf* and *The Canterbury Tales.* They also know that the language of Shakespeare's plays is in many ways unlike the language of today, though they probably attribute some of the difference to the poetic form of the drama. Most students are also aware that English vocabulary is changing right now. The purpose of this unit is to sharpen the student's awareness that his language is constantly changing, not just in vocabulary but in word order, structure, auxiliaries, spelling, and punctuation. The student's gain from this unit will be greater if he has already done the preceding unit, "To Kill a Myth," or its equivalent.

The major problem that this unit poses is one of classroom strategy. Especially when only one copy of each of the unabridged dictionaries is available in the classroom, the danger is of having the rest of the class idle while two are consulting the dictionaries. Each

change? (These are some of the conclusions the class will probably reach: a. language is constantly changing in word meanings; b. some words drop out of English entirely; c. some new words get added; d. some words drop off certain meanings, or some meanings of words become obsolete and archaic; e. some meanings acquire different statuses.)

2. What influences the meanings of words?

3. Why do some words drop out of the language? Why are new ones added?

## Section II
## Do Words in our Language Change in Pronunciation?

Check the following in *Webster's Second* and *Third:*

arctic
disastrous
theater
lingerie
grievous
mischievous

1. In what year was *Webster's Second* published? In what year was *Webster's Third* published?

2. Do you find any differences in the pronunciation of any of the above words? If so, what are the differences?

3. Do you now have any evidence that language changes through the pronunciation of some of its words?

## Section III
## Is the Language Currently Changing in the Spelling of Words?

(Suggested time schedule and assignments for Sections III and IV: assign the dictionary work in Section III to 10 or 11 students, making sure to use students who did not do dictionary work on the first assignment. Assign as homework for the rest of the class Section IV, part A. The second class period will then be used for reports on dictionary findings, for discussion, and for moving on to the remaining parts of Section IV, skipping parts requiring texts that are not available.)

A. *Sovran.*

1. Find the word *sovran* in *Webster's Second* and in *Webster's Third.*

2. Look up the word *sovereign* in both dictionaries. What notations regarding *sovran* are there?

3. What tentative conclusion can you draw from your findings?

B. *Through.*

1. Does *Webster's Second* list another spelling of this word?

2. Does *Webster's Third?*

3. What evidence do you find from your own observations that this word is not always spelled the same way? Bring in examples to class if you can.

C. *Christmas.*

1. What do both dictionaries say about the spelling *Xmas?*

2. What do the hand dictionaries say about it?

3. What does your English handbook say about this spelling? Or if you have no handbook, find one in your library and see what it says about the spelling *Xmas.*

D. Look up the following words in both unabridged dictionaries:

honor, honour
theatre, theater
programme, program
centre, center
woolen, woollen
moustache, mustache

1. What kind of label accompanies some of these spellings?

2. What generalization do your findings suggest?

3. What explanation do you find about the spellings of certain words in the "Orthography" section of *Webster's Second?*

E. What information can you find about *flier* spelled *flyer?* Look up this word in *The Shorter Oxford English Dictionary,* if possible, and report the date of the latest spelling to the class.

F. Find the following words in both *Webster's Second* and *Third:*

burden
choir
catalogue
willful

1. Do any of these words have another spelling? What is it?

2. Is there any evidence that one spelling is older than the other?

### Final Questions

1. What general conclusions can you draw about spelling on the basis of the evidence accumulated in this section of exercises?

2. Does the fact that some words are being spelled two ways indicate a genuine change in the language?

## Section IV
## Is the Structure of the Language Changing?

A. Examine the following sentences:

I have lost the pen I write my themes with.

He should read the kind of books his parents approve of.

That is nothing to joke about.

He is the old gentleman I gave my warm coat to.

I've forgotten what it was he came looking for.

The child returned slowly having forgotten what he was sent to the store for.

1. Can you rewrite these sentences putting the last word of each elsewhere in the sentence?

2. Which form have you been taught to use in your compositions?

3. What does your language textbook say about putting a preposition at the end of a sentence?

4. Consider the following quotation: "There is no recognized rule of usage which forbids placing a preposition at the end of a sentence; in fact, idiomatic and direct English sometimes require that the preposition come at the end. Students can concentrate on writing clear, emphatic, rhythmical sentences and can let the prepositions fall where they may." Birk and Birk, *Understanding and Using English,* Fourth Edition, page 535.

5. If it is available, see Fowler's *A Dictionary of Modern English Usage,* 1965 edition, for comments on this point.

6. If your home or your library has an old English grammar book, see what it has to say about the order of the preposition and its object.

(*Note to the teacher.* It helps to get the point home to students if you tell them about Winston Churchill's famous retort, "This is something up with which I will not put," in response to someone who objected to his putting a preposition at the end of a sentence.)

B. Examine the following sentences and pick out the verbs:

Please look after your little sister this afternoon.

Children often think up hard questions to ask their fathers.

Every year, the group of young students takes up a collection to buy toys for the orphans at Christmas.

By careful planning, the newlyweds paid off the debt within the year.

1. Are the verbs you picked out composed of more than one word?

2. What part of speech is the second word in the two-word verb?

3. Does *Webster's Second* list both words as a verb?

4. Does *Webster's Third?*

5. Could your finding suggest that the structure of the English sentence is changing?

C. Examine the following sentences and pick out the verbs:

The bullies laughed at my black eye.

We should not make fun of him.

I cannot put up with your conduct any longer.

1. Are the verbs made up of words that are often prepositions in other contexts?

2. Check both unabridged dictionaries to see if they list *laugh at, make fun of, put up with* as verbs.

3. Find out what Pence and Emery have to say about such verb forms in *A Grammar of Present Day English,* 1963, if it is available.

4. Check Curme's *Syntax,* if you have it, to find out if these forms are considered verbs.

D. Here are additional examples of language change (optional if time allows and the students' interest holds).

1. How many entries follow *laugh* in *Webster's Second?* How many in *Webster's Third?*

2. How many new verbs are formed from *laugh* plus a preposition and an adverb?

3. Check the word *lay-by* in *Webster's Second* and then compare it with its entry in *Webster's Third.* May this word now be used as a verb?

4. Which of the two unabridged dictionaries con-

tains more entries for the verb *fly* plus prepositions and adverbs? Do you have an explanation for your findings?

5. What does *fly-over* mean in *Webster's Third?*

6. Do entries other than new verbs indicate that other parts of speech are formed by a fusion of prepositions and/or adverbs? If so, give several examples.

E. In all of Shakespeare's plays you will find places where this order of subject–verb occurs:

Consents he to this?

Saw you not the place?

1. Today how do we form questions that need *yes* or *no* answers?

2. Rewrite the two sentences above as we would normally say them. What additional words do you have to use?

## Section V
## Are Verb Forms Changing?

(Section V will probably need 1 preparation period followed by 1 discussion and question period. The parts requiring use of the two unabridged dictionaries are 5, 6, 7, and 8 under E. Assign one of these to each of four students, leaving the rest of the class to prepare the rest of the material in this section, using such desk dictionaries where needful as *Webster's Seventh New Collegiate Dictionary* and *Webster's New World Dictionary.*)

A. In his stories Hawthorne sometimes uses such sentences as "Couldst thou visit me?" and "Woe to the witch that troubleth thee." Which of these verb forms and auxiliary forms is no longer used in current English?

B. How do verbs such as *dance, wash, print,* and *decide* indicate the past tense?

C. How do *ring, write,* and *eat* form the past tense?

D. Which group in C would be longer if you were able to include all the verbs that belong in each?

E. To which group does *dream* belong?

1. Note this quotation:

"There are more things in heaven and earth, Horatio, Than are dreamt of in your philosophy." (*Hamlet:* I.v. 166–167)

2. What is the past tense of *to dream?*

3. Note these quotations:

"And they said unto him, We have dreamed a dream and there is no interpreter of it." (*Genesis:* 40:8)

"And he slept and dreamed the second time: and, behold, seven ears of corn came up upon one stalk, rank and good." (*Ibid.,* 41:5)

4. The King James version of the *Bible* was published in 1611. *Hamlet* was written about 1602. Why did Shakespeare use *dreamt* and the editors of the *Bible* use *dreamed?*

5. Check *Webster's Second* and *Third* to see what forms of *to dream* are correct today.

6. Is it correct to say, "I dived off the board and hurt myself yesterday," or "I dove off the board and hurt myself yesterday"?

a. Check both unabridged dictionaries.

b. What does your own language or grammar book say?

c. If it is available, find out what Fowler says in *A Dictionary of Modern English Usage.*

7. What are the past tenses and past participles of the following:

x-ray
camouflage
Americanize
tree

Are these fairly recent words? Does their recentness have anything to do with the way they form their past tenses and past participles?

8. Check in both unabridged dictionaries for the past tenses and the past participles of the verbs listed below:

broadcast
burn
bark
spell
fly
swell
hang
dig

9. (Optional: if Pence and Emery or a similar grammar text is available.) Check these verbs in Pence and Emery, *A Grammar of Present Day English,* 1963. What distinction is made regarding certain past tense forms of certain words? Does the dictionary make these distinctions? What may your find-

ings indicate? Note especially Mencken's comment about *to hang.*

10. Is there any logic to Dizzy Dean's saying, "The pitcher throwed to first for the second out," or John Brown's saying in *John Brown's Body,* "But God has digged his saints a grave / Beyond the Western Sky."? Explain.

## Section VI
## Is Usage Changing?

(For Sections VI and VII allow 1 preparation period and 1 class period for questions, discussion, and checking with available sources.)

A. Is it "correct" to say, "It's me"—anywhere or at any time? Give reasons for your answer.

B. Which form is "correct" in the following sentences:

Who–Whom did you take to the dance Friday night?

We were to vote for the three students who–whom had done the most for the school.

Who–Whom can you trust nowadays?

Most of the workers who–whom he supervised admired him.

Who–Whom do you mean?

1. Look in your English handbook or language book.

2. Look in as many of the following books as are available:

Mencken's *The American Language,* page 201.

Fowler's *A Dictionary of Modern English Usage,* page 707.

Corbin and Perrin's *Guide to Modern English,* page 566.

Pence and Emery, *A Grammar of Present Day English,* page 246.

(Any strongly traditional handbook would do.)

C. Is there any chance that the distinction between *who* and *whom* in a certain type of sentence will be lost? In what type of sentence? How careful should people be about distinguishing between *who* and *whom* in informal conversation? In a public speech? In English examinations? Would it ever be better to ignore the distinction in a composition? If so, under what circumstances?

## Section VII
## Are Auxiliaries Showing Evidence of Change?

A. When do you use *shall* and when do you use *will?*

B. Have you had exercises in any of your English classes that insist that you make a distinction between *shall* and *will?*

C. Have you had assignments in a foreign language that required you to distinguish *shall* and *will* in your translations?

D. Does this distinction occur on any school or national test that you have taken or have heard about?

E. Ask your grandparents, your parents, and any college students you know if they remember having to distinguish between *shall* and *will.*

F. What do the unabridged dictionaries say about the meaning of *shall* and *will?*

G. If possible, check Pence and Emery, Mencken, Fowler, and R. C. Pooley's *Teaching English Usage* (1946 edition) to see what they have to say about "correct" usage of *shall* and *will.*

## Section VIII
## Writing Assignment One

(Assign Section VIII to half the class and Section IX to the other half, or let students choose one or the other. Most teachers will want written answers to these two assignments. And most teachers will want to use all of the fifth and final class period for discussion of these two sections. However, with an able class, a teacher may prefer to have all students tackle Section IX since it is far more demanding than VIII. With such a class, oral discussion of VIII should be sufficient.)

Summarize in a carefully planned paper the kinds of changes that the preceding exercises indicate are taking place in the English language.

## Section IX
## Writing Assignment Two

Some persons argue for using *whom* wherever the objective case is indicated and argue for retaining the distinction between *may* and *can* and between *shall* and *will*. Not to do so, they fear, will make language less precise; it will make our statements ambiguous. In a carefully planned paper summarize the extent to which you agree or disagree with this position, and give your reasons for believing as you do.

*Applications of Grammatical Analysis to Stylistic Analysis and to Writing Grades 9 and 10* ters is for each student to go through the experience of analyzing at least some of the sentences and for all students at the end to become conscious of the array of varied structures that Steinbeck achieves with no artificial or self-conscious tinkering with sentence beginnings. At the outset students should realize that this is not a "grammar" exercise for which they will get a grade but rather an exploration of precisely how one professional writer builds his sentences when he is doing much the kind of job that they have already tried to do.

In its second stage the grammatical analysis of the Steinbeck passage focuses on identifying noun modifiers, with a close examination of both the number and the kinds of modifiers Steinbeck uses. These are some of the understandings the student should derive from such a study: (1) that a common characteristic of "spongy" prose is a piling up of such colorless, general, vague adjectives as "pretty" and "nice"; (2) that sometimes a single, sharply specific noun does the job better and more thriftily than a more general noun that leans on adjectives for its definition; and (3) that at other times the use of adjectives is both needful and artistic.

When the student has completed his analysis of Steinbeck's use of noun modifiers, the teacher may wish to take some time to discuss some of the other means by which Steinbeck makes his reader see and know Billy Buck in just 14 sentences. Let students take another look at sentence 6, for instance. How much does it tell us about Billy? Is there a better way of telling us? Or let students comment on the implications of the verb "seen to" in the clause "When he had seen to the weather" (sentence 7). How much does the description in sentence 7 of the way Billy blows his nose tell us about the kind of person he is? What do we learn about him from the way he attends to the two horses (sentence 9)? How much does sentence 13 suggest about Billy's position, his relationship to the Tiflins, and his self-estimate? Students should see—or be helped to see—the extent to which Steinbeck characterizes Billy by what Billy himself does or doesn't do rather than by any direct statement from Steinbeck about the kind of person Billy is.

The student should now be ready to revise and rewrite his first 200-word composition, and it is precisely at this point that the teacher can forestall trouble first by making clear that the object of the revision is not to imitate Steinbeck or anyone else, that the object is not even mainly to achieve a wide variety in sentence length, sentence patterns, sentence structures, and noun modifiers. Rather, the main job is to give the clearest possible picture in the fewest possible words of a middle-aged person engaged in a characteristic activity. Being wisely on guard against monotonous sentences and juiceless adjectives is sound practice for any writer, but this is a different matter from self-consciously counting the number of words in each sentence and after three fairly long sentences, saying, "Ah, yes, now it's time for a short sentence; so here goes." Examining every adjective to make sure it's paying for the room it takes is also sound practice as long as the aim in this paper is to make the person so alive that he steps off the page. The danger always of joining grammatical analysis with the art of writing is that the student will get the notion that writing is mainly a manipulative exercise, instead of seeing manipulation only as a means to an end—the end of saying something that matters and saying it well.

## Writing Assignment One

Write a carefully planned composition of approximately 200 words in which you describe a middle-aged person you know well. The person may be a parent, an aunt or uncle, a neighbor, a family friend, or the like. Have this person engaged in an activity that is typical for him so that the reader not only sees the physical features you describe but also understands through the action something of the personality. As you write, remember that your job is to make your reader see and know the person.

(*Note to the teacher*. Students may well ask, "How old is middle-aged?" One teacher answered that by saying, "Anywhere from 30 to 80." Perhaps a better answer is, "Someone about the age of your parents or your parents' friends." Obviously the term "middle-aged" is both relative and elastic. Several grandmothers were requisitioned for service, and no doubt grandmothers are legitimate in a time when grand-

# *Applications of Grammatical Analysis to Stylistic Analysis and to Writing Grades 9 and 10*

*Approximate Time:* 3 class periods and 3 preparation periods

## To the Teacher

Two common recommendations for student writers are: to vary their sentence structure by beginning with an element other than the subject and to achieve vividness by using adjectives and adverbs. This advice can mislead students. The trouble is that it directs attention to only *one* method for varying sentence structure and only *one* method for achieving vivid modification, whereas the skilled writer demonstrates in his writing an awareness of a number of choices for accomplishing each of these two purposes. The aim of these study materials is to direct the student's attention to these other choices and to show him how to use them in his own writing.

The student's first job is to describe, in about 200 words, a middle-aged person he knows well. Next comes a grammatical analysis of the first paragraph of John Steinbeck's *The Red Pony.* Finally, students reexamine their own 200-word compositions in the light of the richness of options revealed in the grammatical analysis. They then rewrite their papers making full use of whatever insights they have gained from their exploration of the Steinbeck passage.

The grammatical analysis of Steinbeck's sentence structure and sentence variety may be easier and possibly more thorough when students and teachers are familiar with structural linguistics or transformational grammar, as well as the traditional, but the concepts and terms from traditional grammar will serve well enough. Each teacher and each class can use the terms with which they are most familiar and should carry the analysis as far as the students' knowledge and interest permit. If time is short or if the analysis moves slowly, not every student needs to analyze every sentence. Separate groups of students may work singly or together on selected sentences. What mat-

mothers are getting younger every day. It is up to the teacher whether the student writes his paper in a class period or as an outside assignment or as a combination of the two.)

## Sentence Structure in a Paragraph from *The Red Pony*

The following paragraph is the opening passage of Steinbeck's *The Red Pony.* Each sentence has been numbered and after each sentence, in parentheses, is the number of words in that particular sentence.

On a separate sheet of paper, number 1–14, leaving plenty of space between the numbers. After each number say as much as you can in answering these questions about each of Steinbeck's sentences:

a. With what element does the sentence begin (subject, dependent clause, adverbial phrase, and so forth)?

b. What is the structure of the sentence? (Is it simple, complex, compound, compound-complex? Or is it one of these patterns: 1. subject/verb; 2. subject/verb/direct object; 3. subject/verb/indirect object/direct object; 4. subject/linking verb/predicate word?)

The purpose here is to provide you with your own notes for a class discussion on sentence length, structure, and variety in the Steinbeck passage.

1. At daybreak Billy Buck emerged from the bunkhouse and stood for a moment on the porch looking up at the sky. (21)

2. He was a broad, bandy-legged little man with a walrus mustache, with square hands, puffed and muscled on the palms. (20)

3. His eyes were a contemplative, watery gray and the hair which protruded from under his Stetson hat was spiky and weathered. (21)

4. Billy was still stuffing his shirt into his blue jeans as he stood on the porch. (16)

5. He unbuckled his belt and tightened it again. (8)

6. The belt showed, by the worn shiny places opposite each hole, the gradual increase of Billy's middle over a period of years. (22)

7. When he had seen to the weather, Billy cleared each nostril by holding its mate closed with his forefinger, and blowing fiercely. (22)

8. Then he walked down to the barn, rubbing his hands together. (11)

9. He curried and brushed two saddle horses in the stalls, talking quietly to them all the time; and he had hardly finished when the iron triangle started ringing at the ranch house. (32)

10. Billy stuck the brush and currycomb together and laid them on the rail, and went up to breakfast. (18)

11. His action had been so deliberate and yet so wasteless of time that he came to the house while Mrs. Tiflin was still ringing the triangle. (26)

12. She nodded her gray head to him and withdrew into the kitchen. (12)

13. Billy Buck sat down on the steps, because he was a cow-hand, and it wouldn't be fitting that he should go first into the dining-room. (25)

14. He heard Mr. Tiflin in the house, stamping his feet into his boots. (13)

The findings on sentence length are in no way startling. The range between 8 words and 32 is not exceptional, and the general average in the low 20s is probably normal. Students probably will note that the 11-word sentence comes just before the 32-word one and that the 8-word sentence by its position also does a nice job of balancing longer sentences and preventing monotony.

Ninth graders are probably surprised to discover that so many of the sentences begin with the subject and yet without monotonous effect. If they are familiar with sentence patterns, they will not be surprised at the frequency of patterns 2 and 4 (subject/verb/direct object; and subject/linking verb/predicate word). Students working with the traditional terminology may be surprised at the number of compound–complex sentences and at the absence of a compound sentence, especially if they have the notion that Steinbeck, like Hemingway, uses very simple pared-down sentence structure.

If they are surprised that so many sentences start with the subject, they will be interested to know that recent research by Francis Christensen, Professor of English, University of Southern California, shows that professional writers in general are more likely to start their sentences with the subject than students are.

## Steinbeck's Noun Modifiers

This section concerns itself with the kinds of modifiers Steinbeck uses with his nouns. And it is interesting to note that in the course of his 14 sentences Steinbeck provides modifiers (apart from possessives like *Billy's* or *its*) for only 15 of around 60 nouns. For your convenience, here is a list of the nouns that have modifiers (the numbers refer to sentence numbers):

| | | |
|---|---|---|
| 2. man | 3. hat | 9. triangle |
| 2. mustache | 4. jeans | 9. house |
| 2. hands | 6. places | 11. action |
| 3. eyes | 6. increase | 12. head |
| 3. hair | 9. horses | 14. Mr. Tiflin |

Examine first the *adjectives* Steinbeck uses with the above nouns. Often when people think of adjectives, they think of such broad, vague, general words as "pretty," "nice," "bad," or "lovely." How much use does Steinbeck make of such broad, general adjectives? How many of his adjectives look as if they had been made from nouns or verbs, with something of the vigor of nouns and verbs still in them? ("Spiky" and "muscled" are examples.)

Examine next the words that are behaving like adjectives but are actually other parts of speech ("a walrus mustache," for instance).

Then examine all the phrases and clauses Steinbeck uses as noun modifiers.

Note finally the relative frequency of the various kinds of noun modifiers. Is it what you expected? If not, how is it different?

(If interest and time hold out, some teachers may want to make at least a partial exploration of the amount and kinds of modification Steinbeck provides for his verbs.

The class is now ready to draw up a series of conclusions about how Steinbeck puts his sentences together in this passage and with what results. Having one student record these conclusions on the board will be a good way of making sure that all students are fully aware of them.)

## Writing Assignment Two

Now that you have completed your analysis of how one professional writer puts his sentences together in writing a passage in which he is doing much the same thing that you were doing in your 200-word description of a middle-aged person, go back to your own papers, and examine them in somewhat the same way that you have been examining Steinbeck's sentences. Your final job will be to rewrite your paper, making full use of any insights you have derived from your analysis of Steinbeck's passage and your reexamination of your own first draft. The object is not to imitate Steinbeck or any other writer. The main job is to make your middle-aged person as real and as alive as possible and to do so in the fewest words possible and with the most effective possible use of those few words.

### To the Teacher

You may want to have the student begin his revised composition in the classroom where you can be on hand to forestall trouble, but he probably should have the chance to finish the paper outside class where he is not working to a set time limit. Most teachers will prefer to grade the student only on his final product, though probably most teachers will take into account the extent to which he has bettered his first performance and the skill with which he has put to use the insights derived from his study of Steinbeck. One school found it extremely helpful to have students write their final papers on ditto stencils so that eventually every student had a chance to see every other student's work. Ninth graders particularly like to see themselves in print and seem to do a more careful job of editing when they know the rest of the class will have copies of their work.

## A Note on Writing Assignments One and Two

Although these materials were originally intended for grades 10 and 11, a number of teachers tried them with the ninth grade and reported enthusiastically on their results. All the papers printed below are samples of what able ninth graders did with the composition part of the unit.

## Writing Assignment One
## Sample 1. Grade: High

*Grandma's Day*

With her hair falling away from the knot at the back of her neck, she deftly moves about the kitchen humming a favorite tune, that is, favorite about thirty years ago. This is the usual part of the house where you can find Grandma. She doesn't especially like the kitchen the best, as one can tell by the way she scowls at dirty dishes and the yearning way she looks out the window at her garden, but here she must spend alot of her time because of her 'kids' home for vacation. (Her kids range from 36 to 40). She is what one expects most Grandmothers to be, particularly when a small child falls and hurts herself. Grandma gentle carries the little one into the house and carefully cleans and dress the skinned knee or scraped elbow. Then she takes her 'baby' on her lap and holds her until all the tears are gone. These are the things that will be remembered: her slow full smile and tender touch.

## Writing Assignment Two
## Sample 1. Grade: High

*Grandma's Day*

Stately as an elm, Grandma stands in front of the window, looking out at her garden. In her eyes there is a trace of sadness, but the brightness and understanding outshine it by far. Her hands are rough and callused by the long years of housework and gardening, but this can't hide the delicately tapered fingers. Her dress is well worn and some of her activities are shown by the stains of peach juice and cherries. Wiping the final dish, she lays the dish cloth down and takes her gardening gloves. She puts a small cap on her greying curls, leaving some to blow in the gentle spring breeze. Kneeling on one knee, she deftly pours water over her Golden Crysanthemums, the most prized of her flowers. Footsteps on the porch bring her head up with a jerk. She greets the newcomer and starts back into the house to begin again the thrice daily task a preparing a meal for a loving family.

## Writing Assignments One and Two
## Comment on Sample 1. Grade: High

The first of this student's papers is the unrevised version. The second is the revision written after the grammatical analysis of the Steinbeck passage. The relative merits of the two versions are partly a matter of opinion, but the readers feel that some of the freshness, the spontaneity, the apparent artlessness, and the charm of the unrevised version get lost in the too conscious effort of the second to vary sentence length, to use "concrete" adjectives, and to achieve a variety of sentence patterns. The readers decided to print both versions of this paper to point up the possible dangers of making a student so conscious of sentence form that he comes to see composition more as a matter of verbal manipulation than of having something you want to say and then finding the best way of saying it. The other danger in the unit as it originally appeared was of giving students the impression that their job was to imitate Steinbeck—a notion that, according to one teacher, produced "disastrous" results. This is not to say that the revised version of this student's paper is "disastrous." Far from it. Most ninth grade teachers would probably agree that both the unrevised and the revised versions are able ninth grade responses to the assignment. The first paper, however, attempts a simpler job and concentrates on creating a single impression. The second paper in its attempt at greater complexity does more telling and less showing. The slight touch of humor in the first paper—"(Her kids range from 36 to 40)"—is lost in the near-sentimentality of the second. The initial "Stately as an elm" gets the revised paper off to a stiffly conventionalized start to what looks as if it would be just another of those saintly and unforgettable grandmas who bloom lushly in ninth and tenth grade papers. But this Grandma is not just watering her flowers; she is watering her "Golden Crysanthemums." Her hands are not just stained; they are stained with peach and cherry juice. This student has learned the worth of the concrete, and it is just such details as that peach or cherry juice that redeem the paper from ordinariness. The first paper, though, does a more subtle job of letting the reader know that Grandma loved her garden—when it mentions her scowling at the dirty dishes that kept her from her flowers. The "skinned knee or scraped elbow" of the unrevised paper, moreover, shows this student's command of picture-making detail before encounter with the Steinbeck passage. It is true that the first paper has careless writing errors that get cleaned up in revision—along with some of the charm. Possibly this is a student who should be asked a year from now to write a third paper in which he blends the best of these two, perhaps adding some of the skill in writing that has come with one more year of living.

## Writing Assignment Two
## Sample 2. Grade: High

Mrs. Pruitt is the director of the camp I go to, and I think the years up there in the wilderness and the constant exposure to young people have had the same effect on her as the Fountain of Youth. Once a year, on a "Request Night" at camp, she stands on her head in a canoe. It is very exciting for the new girls who haven't seen this and rather tense for those who have.

She chooses a canoe from canoe dock, settles herself in it with ease, and pushes off with her paddle, while the girls gather on the banks and docks. With a somewhat distant, daring smile, she puts her paddle in and begins. One slip and the whole camp gasps. But she is still smiling as she starts again. Putting her head on the middle thwart and her hands on the gunwales, she slowly raises her feet over her head. No one breathes until she is straight from her head to her toes. Then cheers and applause rise from the banks and echo on the far shore. Coming down again, she picks up her paddle, tosses her head and smiles again, as if to say, "It was nothing."

## Writing Assignment Two
## Comment on Sample 2. Grade: High

This student's revision is better than the original (and the original was good). The paper comes from a class that did not attempt some parts of the original unit but instead spent a period discussing exactly how Steinbeck makes his reader see and know Billy Buck by telling how he blew his nose, by describing the notches in his belt and the clothing he wore, and by explaining why Billy felt it unfitting that he should be the first to go into the dining room. And this class before writing their revisions were merely told to make any use they could of insights picked up in the examination of the Steinbeck passage. They were not told to "vary their sentence structure," as the original unit had directed.

This paper does an admirable job of meeting the requirements of the assignment. There are no evident tricks with sentence structure, no dramatic variations of sentence length; but every detail counts; every word pays for the space it occupies, unless someone wants to pounce on "cheers and applause" as wordy, but you cheer with your voice and applaud with your hands. A possible criticism might be that the paper tells very little about the physical appearance of Mrs. Pruitt, but does it need to? The feat performed in the canoe lets us know that we are in the presence of a lady who has never allowed herself to fall victim to the middle-aged spread. The writing in this paper is unusually clean and competent for a ninth grader, and every detail contributes to the creation of a total impression of seemingly nonchalant self-assurance in a situation that could have been ludicrous.

## Writing Assignment Two
## Sample 3. Grade: High

*The Drunk*

I watched from behind as the drunk staggered down the ally, stumbling over tin cans, bottles, and garbage. His hair was greasy, matted, and grew over his ears and down his neck. On his back hung a torn filthy old blue shirt. His pants, which were in the same condition as his shirt, were held up by a thick, old rope. He had on his feet, old wornout, brown leather shoes, and dirty white socks, full of holes, which sagged to his ankles. He was of medium heigth and weight and had huge, filth-caked, hands with wide, split, grimy, chewed-off nails. In one of his hands he held a half-empty fifth of vodka.

He stopped, dropped the bottle, gazed at the darkened sky, tried feebly to balance himself, and then crashed, on his back, into a pile of broken bottles and tin cans. Then it started to rain so I left.

The next morning I went back to the alley to see if he was still there. I found him, in the same place, lying in a foot of garbage and mud, his dialated, blood-shot eyes staring into the bright morning.

## Writing Assignment Two
## Comment on Sample 3. Grade: High

This is not a flawless piece of writing, but the student has grasped the vital parts of the lesson, has tried to apply them, and, at many points, has succeeded. There are minor slips here such as the misspellings "ally" and "dialated," or the lack of parallelism in the series "greasy, matted, and grew over his ears." An unkind critic might point out that the student has learned too well the lesson of using adjectives that make the reader "see" the person he is describing. But this possible overdoing of the adjectives is probably a natural response to the exploration of Steinbeck's adjectives and it occurs only in the first paragraph. The rest of the paper is stripped down and admirably understated. And even in his over-generous use of adjectives in the first paragraph, the student certainly paints his picture of sordidness and filth. His adjective "filth-caked," for instance, to describe the man's hands, is typical of the better-than-usual word choices that frequently showed up in the revised papers. This student has also responded intelligently to the suggestion —in the original unit—that he vary the length and the patterns of his sentences. His final sentence is an example of balanced, rhythmic structure, achieved without apparent artifice.

## Writing Assignment Two
## Sample 4. Grade: Average

*The Good Colonel*

As usual, the middle-aged man slowly rose out of bed in the early morning and immediately put on his robe and slippers. He then proceeded customarily to the bathroom where he showered, shaved, and dressed himself in a gray flannel suit.

He ate his large breakfast with enthusiasm, for in the army he had learned to appreciate a good meal. However, he was not as stocky and rounded as some of his close friends. Towering over most people, he walked erect and held his large, square shoulders high.

As he read the morning paper, he began to reminisce. His twenty-five years in the army were fruitful. After commanding a local installation for some time, he reluctantly retired. He felt that he had made a wrong decision, but he wasn't quite sure.

Momentarily, he glanced at his gold watch out of habit (for he also learned to be punctual). It was spring, and time for his annual physical check-up today. He hastily left.

## Writing Assignment Two
## Comment on Sample 4. Grade: Average

This paper is a clearly acceptable but undistinguished response to the assignment. Perhaps its outstanding strength is its skill in showing the reader, rather than telling him, that the Colonel is a creature of habit. The opening "As usual" strikes the keynote, with later reinforcement from such expressions as "customarily" and "out of habit." The reader also gathers without having to be told that the Colonel is still living over his army days, that army routine governs his doing and his being, and that he is deeply concerned with his physical health. This student is sparing in his use of adjectives and when he does use them, he doesn't choose ones that leap out of the page with aliveness. An abler student would not be content with telling us that the Colonel ate a "good" breakfast, nor would he use such expected adjectives as "large" and "square" for a Colonel's shoulders. In this paper the student is attempting to create a more complex impression, perhaps even to create several impressions no one of which comes through with the sharpness of the single impression another student has created of the "drunk." On the whole, too, this student is less successful than others in varying the length of his sentences. He nowhere demonstrates his ability to handle a long, complex sentence to balance the near monotony of his many two-line sentences. He makes an evident effort, however, to vary his sentence beginnings by making use of participial phrases and dependent clauses. The three-word sentence at the end is an obvious gesture in the direction of variety in sentence length and it does round off neatly the reference to the "annual . . . check-up." Although a title was not part of the requirements for this assignment, it is worth noting that a more ingenious student could surely have found a better adjective than "good" for the title of a paper specifically concerned with discriminating choices of adjectives.

## Writing Assignment Two
## Sample 5. Grade: Low

*The Man From* K.L.A.N.

One cold and windy night I saw a man walking in an alley. He was a bery tall man with thin bones and wearing a black overcoat. As I was sitting on a trash can at the end of the alley he came up to me and asked for some directions as though he were in a hurry. His deep-set eyes looked like cat's eyes as he piered at me. He had a very flat nose that looked like it had been burned alone with another portion of his face. His mouth was small and did not open very wide when he talked. He had hair that was a deep gray in color and it was very long and unkept. It hung down to a curious mark on his neck that extended across it. This mark showed the burns of a rope —or noose.

With out warning he reached up and grabbed me by the arm. His hand felt very peculiar on my arm. All though I could not see his hand it felt as though there was quite a distance between his thumb and his little finger. It felt like he was holding me with two fingers. I looked down at his arm and there, branded on his arm was the mark of a notorious klan that was renown for treachery and heartlessness. Aparently he had been initiated into it. He was a terrible mess.

## Writing Assignment Two
## Comment on Sample 5. Grade: Low

Not all of the many technical errors here can be dismissed charitably as typing slips, nor is the student altogether successful in his attempt to introduce vivid details in a paper whose title prepares the reader for the unconvincing sensationalism that lies waiting for him in the paper. The second sentence of paragraph two, "His hand felt very peculiar on my arm," and the final sentence, "He was a terrible mess," suggest this student's ineptness with language. "A terrible mess" is hardly adequate for a member of "a notorious klan that was renown for treachery and heartlessness," especially when the writer was about to become the victim. And the whole situation stretches to the snapping point the reader's credulity as much as it side-steps the demands of the assignment for a description of a middle-aged person the student knew well. Just what was the student doing on that trash can in the alley, and just how well do you get to know someone who grabs your arm without waiting for the social amenities of an introduction?

*Diction, Grades 10 and 11*

dug
scoured
dredged
furrowed

Making full use of dictionaries, answer these questions: Is *scored* a more appropriate word in this context than any of the other words suggested? Can you find any word not listed that would have been better than *scored?* Examine each of the substitutes to see exactly how it differs from *scored.* Explain why you think the author would have rejected each of the substitute words.

2. "The Burmese sub-inspector and some Indian constables were waiting for me in the quarter where the elephant had been seen. It was a very poor quarter, a *labyrinth* of *squalid* bamboo huts, thatched with palm-leaf, winding all over a steep hillside." — George Orwell

*Directions.* In place of *labyrinth* the author might have used one of the following:

mass of winding streets
complex
maze
tortuous passageway

Which one of these four substitutes is closest in meaning to *labyrinth?* Why might the author not have chosen it? Why do you think he would have rejected each of the other three substitutes? Use your dictionary.

In place of *squalid* the author might have used:

filthy
wretched
unclean
mean
miserable

Is *squalid* a better choice than any one of the substitutes? With the help of dictionaries, be prepared to give reasons for your answers.

3. "Children all day *capered* or squealed by the glazed or *bashing* sea and the steam organ wheezed its waltzes in the threadbare playground in the waste lot, where the dogems dodged, behind the pickle factory." — Dylan Thomas

*Directions.* Explain why each of the following would or would not do as well as or better than *capered* in this passage:

pranced
cavorted
frisked
leaped about

Explain why each of the following would or would not do as well as or better than *bashing* in this passage:

smashing
crashing
knocking
thundering
violently rolling

4. "There were *audacious* young freethinkers, who adored nobody or nothing except perhaps Robespierre and the Koran, and panted for the day when the pale name of priest should shrink and dwindle away before the indignation of an enlightened world." — William Makepeace Thackeray

*Directions.* From the evidence of this passage, how do you think the author feels toward the "young freethinkers"? Why might he have used the word *audacious* to describe them rather than any one of the following substitutes?

daring
bold
reckless
insolent
impudent
rash

5. "I remember sharing the last of my moist buns with a boy and a lion. Tawny and savage, with cruel nails and *capacious* mouth, the little boy tore and devoured. Wild as seedcake, ferocious as a hearthrug, the depressed and *verminous* lion nibbled like a mouse at his half a bun and hiccupped in the sad dusk of his cage." — Dylan Thomas

*Directions.* The author might have used any one of the following words in place of *capacious.* Did he make the best possible choice? Why or why not?

roomy
spacious
commodious
ample
copious
inclusive
magnificent

## *Diction*
## *Grades 10 and 11*

### To the Teacher

This lesson on diction aims to make students more conscious of the options a writer has in choosing his words and to make them realize the dangers of using a thesaurus indiscriminately. Although able tenth grade students have pretested these materials with pleasure and profit near the end of their sophomore year, the unit is probably most useful with eleventh graders whose greater verbal maturity better fits them to cope with subtle distinctions in word meaning. For most teachers the easiest plan for scheduling the time will be to assign each of the four exercises to be done in one preparation period, with a period of class discussion immediately following each assignment. With classes keenly interested in this kind of word study, teachers may want more time both for homework and for class discussion.

### Exercise I

(*Note to the teacher.* In this exercise there are nine passages, each followed by work for the student. Because there is far more work here than any one student could complete in a single preparation period, it will be well to make each student responsible for one or two of the nine passages, thus making sure that all nine passages are covered, each one probably by two or three students, depending on the size of the class.)

1. "The people said that the elephant had come suddenly upon him round the corner of the hut, caught him with its trunk, put its foot on his back and ground him into the earth. This was the rainy season and the ground was soft, and his face had *scored* a trench a foot deep and a couple of yards long." — George Orwell

*Directions.* The author might have used any one of the following words in place of the word *scored* in the above passage:

notched
gashed
pitted

Is *verminous* a better word for the lion than any one of the following? Why or why not?

filthy
offensive
flea-bitten
bedbug-ridden
lice-infected
malodorous
rank

6. "I was sub-divisional police officer of the town, and in an aimless, petty kind of way anti-European feeling was very bitter. No one had the *guts* to raise a riot, but if a European woman went through the *bazaars* alone somebody would probably spit betel juice over her dress." —George Orwell

*Directions.* Why might Orwell have chosen *guts* in this context rather than any one of the following?

pluck
courage
force
perseverance
moral stamina
fortitude

Why is *bazaars* a better choice here than any one of these substitutes?

market places
shopping malls
shops
stores
ateliers

7. "What is new, if anything, about this old sordid story is that college athletics today have won full acceptance as legitimate university activities, and with acceptance, *tacit* approval of practices which even a backward school, much less (Is 'less' the right word here?) a major university, might have frowned upon twenty-five years ago." —Kenneth Eble

*Directions.* Explain why each of the following substitutes would do as well as or less well than or better than *tacit* in the above context:

unspoken
silent
uncommunicative
taciturn
implicit

8. "For university presidents facing the necessity of distilling raw animal spirits into purer forms, football seems a likely *expedient.*" —Kenneth Eble

*Directions.* Is *expedient* a better word than any one of these? Why or why not?

means to an end
makeshift
resource
device

9. "In the second place, college and university faculties are singularly *inept* at doing anything about their problems." —Kenneth Eble

*Directions.* Examine each of the following words and then explain why each is as good a choice as *inept* or a better choice or a worse choice:

unfit
foolish
inefficient
awkward
clumsy
unsuitable

## Exercise II

(*Note to the teacher.* As this exercise was originally set up, students were simply given this passage by George Orwell with no clue to which of the words were substitutes for Orwell's. Some teachers may still prefer to use the exercise that way, especially with an unusually able class; but with many classes this procedure would degenerate into a time-consuming game of guesswork.)

The paragraph that follows is from George Orwell's essay "Shooting an Elephant." There are 17 words or phrases in the passage in italics, each of which is a substitute for what the author actually used. These 17 substitutes are all synonyms found in thesauruses, hand dictionaries, and *Webster's Third* (Unabridged). Read the passage carefully for meaning. Examine its diction, giving special attention to the 17 words or phrases in italics. Then answer the questions and do the work set below the passage.

"But at that moment I glanced round at the crowd that had followed me. It was an *enormous* crowd, two thousand at the least and growing every minute. It blocked the road for a long distance on either side. I looked at the sea of yellow faces above the *gaudy* clothes—faces all happy and excited over this bit of fun, all certain that the elephant was going to be shot. They were watching me as they would watch a *sideshow of legerdemain.* They did not like me, but with the magical rifle in my hands I was momentarily worth watching. And suddenly I realized that I should have to shoot the elephant after all. The people expected it of me and I had got to do it; I could feel their two thousand wills pressing me forward, *strong.* And it was at this moment, as I stood there with the rifle in my hands, that I first grasped the hollowness, the *inefficacy* of the white man's *domination* in the East. Here was I, the white man with his gun, standing in front of the unarmed native crowd—seemingly the leading actor of the piece; but in reality I was only *a senseless doll moved by strings* pushed to and fro by the will of those yellow faces behind. I perceived in this moment that when the white man turns *ruler* it is his own freedom that he destroys. He becomes a sort of hollow, posing *figurehead, the rubber stamped version of a master.* For it is the condition of his rule that he shall spend his life in trying to *influence* the "natives," and so in every crisis he has got to do what the "natives" expect of him. He wears a mask, and his face grows to fit it. I had got to shoot the elephant. I had *pledged* myself to doing it when I sent for the rifle. A *master* has got to act like a *master;* he has got to appear *firm in purpose,* to know his own mind and do definite things. To come all that way, rifle in hand, with two thousand people marching at my heels, and then to trail *weakly* away, having done nothing — no, that was impossible. The crowd would *deride* me. And my whole life, every white man's life in the East, was one long *labor* not to be laughed at."

1. As you read, do any of the words in italics seem out of place?

2. Do any of the words in italics draw your attention away from the meaning and to themselves as you read?

3. Are any of the 17 overused? If so, which ones?

Now read the entire essay, "Shooting an Elephant," by George Orwell (below). Locate the passage that has been tampered with. Then answer the following questions calling for comparison of Orwell with the substitutes for his wording.

1. Do any of the substitutes seem as appropriate as the wording Orwell actually uses? If so, which ones?

2. Which ones of the 17 substitutes do not fit the tone of the essay?

3. Which ones do not fit the level of language the author has chosen for his essay?

4. Which of the 17 synonyms is the poorest? Why?

5. Which of the 17 twists the author's intended meaning?

6. What special objections are there to substituting *doll* for *puppet?*

7. Why is *master* a poor substitute for *sahib?*

8. What other words strike you as ineffective synonyms and why?

9. Would any other noun do as well as *sea* in sentence 4? Give reasons.

10. In sentence 6 is there a synonym that would serve as well as Orwell's word *magical?* Give reasons for your answer.

11. Is there any one word in the original passage that you could replace with an equally good synonym of your own choosing? One that the whole class will accept as equally good? Look in the thesaurus for help. Note that you now have the help of the entire context of the essay to guide you in making a choice.

## Exercise III

(*Note to the teacher.* Either before this exercise or before the preceding one, it will be helpful to explain how a thesaurus works to a class unfamiliar with Roget and its kindred. One teacher made transparencies to show as samples of how a thesaurus is set up.)

Like most tools, a thesaurus works well for those who know how to use it, and the first step in knowing how to use it is to realize that synonyms are not necessarily interchangeable and that even in the closest synonyms there may be different shadings of meaning, different connotations with which a careful writer must reckon when he goes to the thesaurus to find exactly the right word for a given context.

Here are the synonyms one thesaurus and several dictionaries give for six of the words replaced in the paragraph of Orwell with which you have been working. If any of these synonyms had been the substitutes, what would the effect have been on the meaning of the sentence? What would the effect have been on the essay as a whole:

| *Original Word* | *Synonyms* |
|---|---|
| immense | limitless, immeasurable |
| garish | dazzling, glaring, tawdry |
| irresistibly | unresistedly |
| absurd (puppet) | irrational, unreasonable, high-flown, paradoxical |
| impress (the natives) | inspire |
| laugh at | (under *laugh*) chuckle, snicker, giggle |

## Exercise IV

1. Which of the following words that Orwell uses are in the dictionary you normally use and which are not?

   Raj
   mahout
   bazaar
   paddy
   sahib
   dahs

2. Where there are English equivalents in this dictionary, why doesn't Orwell use them?

3. Why does Orwell use some words for which there are no English equivalents in this dictionary? Does he wish to impress the reader with his intellectualism? Are there any other possible answers?

4. What two other foreign terms does Orwell use and why does he use them?

5. In this dictionary what is the meaning of *despotism, colonialism,* and *imperialism?* Are they synonyms? In the second sentence of paragraph three, why does Orwell use *imperialism* rather than *colonialism?* Why does he say *despotic governments* rather than *imperial governments?* What does his use of *imperialism* and *despotic* tell us about his attitude, his feelings toward his own country?

6. How much liberty does an author have in defining his own words or in using them to suit himself? What are the advantages and the dangers in this kind of liberty?

7. Take a paragraph from Orwell's essay or from another piece of literature. Keeping in mind the content of the whole unit, replace at least *five* words with the best synonyms you can find in thesauruses or dictionaries. Have you made the passage better or worse? How does your class react to your substitutions?

8. An author takes particular pains with his wording when he uses a simile. Examine each of the following similes that Orwell uses in "Shooting an Elephant":

a. "The friction of the great beast's foot had stripped the skin from his back *as neatly as one skins a rabbit.*" (paragraph 4)

Is Orwell's wording more effective than *as neatly as one peels a peach?* Why?

b. "If the elephant charged and I missed him, I should have about as much chance *as a toad under a steam-roller.*" (paragraph 9)

Is Orwell's wording better than *as a toad in the path of a scythe?* Why?

c. "The thick blood welled out of him *like red velvet,* but still he did not die." (paragraph 12)

Is Orwell's wording better than *like raspberry* Jello? Why?

## Paragraph from George Orwell's "Shooting an Elephant"*

(Teacher's copy for Exercise II)

[1]But at that moment I glanced round at the crowd that had followed me. [2]It was an *immense* crowd, two thousand at the least and growing every minute. [3]It blocked the road for a long distance on either side. [4]I looked at the sea of yellow faces above the *garish* clothes—faces all happy and excited over this bit of fun, all certain that the elephant was going to be shot. [5]They were watching me as they would watch a *conjurer about to perform a trick.* [6]They did not like me, but with the magical rifle in my hands I was momentarily worth watching. [7]And suddenly I realized that I should have to shoot the elephant after all. [8]The people expected it of me and I had got to do it; I could feel their two thousand wills pressing me forward, *irresistibly.* [9]And it was at this moment, as I stood there with the rifle in my hands, that I first grasped the hollowness, the *futility* of the white man's *do-*

* Seventeen words or phrases italicized.

*minion* in the East. [10]Here was I, the white man with his gun, standing in front of the unarmed native crowd—seemingly the leading actor of the piece; but in reality I was only *an absurd puppet* pushed to and fro by the will of those yellow faces behind. [11]I perceived in this moment that when the white man turns *tyrant* it is his own freedom that he destroys. [12]He becomes a sort of hollow, posing *dummy, the conventionalized figure of a sahib.* [13]For it is the condition of his rule that he shall spend his life in trying to *impress* the "natives," and so in every crisis he has got to do what the "natives" expect of him. [14]He wears a mask, and his face grows to fit it. [15]I had got to shoot the elephant. [16]I had *committed* myself to doing it when I sent for the rifle. [17]A *sahib* has got to act like a *sahib;* he has got to appear *resolute,* to know his own mind and do definite things. [18]To come all that way, rifle in hand, with two thousand people marching at my heels, and then to trail *feebly* away, having done nothing—no, that was impossible. [19]The crowd would *laugh at* me. [20]And my whole life, every white man's life in the East, was one long *struggle* not to be laughed at. (paragraph 7)

## *Shooting an Elephant*

George Orwell

In Moulmein, in Lower Burma, I was hated by large 1
numbers of people—the only time in my life that I have been important enough for this to happen to me. I was sub-divisional police officer of the town, and in an aimless, petty kind of way anti-European feeling was very bitter. No one had the guts to raise a riot, but if a European woman went through the bazaars alone somebody would probably spit betel juice over her dress. As a police officer I was an obvious target and was baited whenever it seemed safe to do so. When a nimble Burman tripped me up on the football field and the referee (another Burman) looked the other way, the crowd yelled with hideous laughter. This happened more than once. In the end the sneering yellow faces of young men that met me everywhere, the insults hooted after me when I was at a safe distance, got badly on my nerves. The young Buddhist priests were the worst of all. There were several thousands of them in the town and none of them seemed to have anything to do except stand on street corners and jeer at Europeans.

All this was perplexing and upsetting. For at that 2
time I had already made up my mind that imperialism was an evil thing and the sooner I chucked up my job and got out of it the better. Theoretically—and secretly, of course—I was all for the Burmese and all against their oppressors, the British. As for the job I was doing, I hated it more bitterly than I can perhaps make clear. In a job like that you see the dirty work of Empire at close quarters. The wretched prisoners huddling in the stinking cages of the lock-ups, the grey, cowed faces of the long-term convicts, the scarred buttocks of the men who had been flogged with bamboos—all these oppressed me with an intolerable sense of guilt. But I could get nothing into perspective. I was young and ill-educated and I had had to think out my problems in the utter silence that is imposed on every Englishman in the East. I did not even know that the British Empire is dying, still less did I know that it is a great deal better than the younger empires that are going to supplant it. All I knew was that I was stuck between my hatred of the empire I served and my rage against the evil-spirited little beasts who tried to make my job impossible. With one part of my mind I thought of the British Raj as an unbreakable tyranny, as something clamped down, in *saecula saeculorum,* upon the will of prostrate peoples; with another part I thought that the greatest joy in the world would be to drive a bayonet into a Buddhist priest's guts. Feelings like these are the normal by-products of imperialism; ask any Anglo-Indian official, if you can catch him off duty.

One day something happened which in a rounda- 3
bout way was enlightening. It was a tiny incident in itself, but it gave me a better glimpse than I had had before of the real nature of imperialism—the real motives for which despotic governments act. Early one morning the sub-inspector at a police station the other end of the town rang me up on the 'phone and said that an elephant was ravaging the bazaar. Would I please come and do something about it? I did not know what I could do, but I wanted to see what was happening and I got on a pony and started out. I took my rifle, an old .44 Winchester and much too small to kill an elephant, but I thought the noise might be

useful *in terrorem.* Various Burmans stopped me on the way and told me about the elephant's doings. It was not, of course, a wild elephant, but a tame one which had gone "must." It had been chained up, as tame elephants always are when their attack of "must" is due, but on the previous night it had broken its chain and escaped. Its mahout, the only person who could manage it when it was in that state, had set out in pursuit, but had taken the wrong direction and was now twelve hours' journey away, and in the morning the elephant had suddenly reappeared in the town. The Burmese population had no weapons and were quite helpless against it. It had already destroyed somebody's bamboo hut, killed a cow and raided some fruit-stalls and devoured the stock; also it had met the municipal rubbish van and, when the driver jumped out and took to his heels, had turned the van over and inflicted violences upon it.

4 The Burmese sub-inspector and some Indian constables were waiting for me in the quarter where the elephant had been seen. It was a very poor quarter, a labyrinth of squalid bamboo huts, thatched with palm-leaf, winding all over a steep hillside. I remember that it was a cloudy, stuffy morning at the beginning of the rains. We began questioning the people as to where the elephant had gone and, as usual, failed to get any definite information. That is invariably the case in the East; a story always sounds clear enough at a distance, but the nearer you get to the scene of events the vaguer it becomes. Some of the people said that the elephant had gone in one direction, some said that he had gone in another, some professed not even to have heard of any elephant. I had almost made up my mind that the whole story was a pack of lies, when we heard yells a little distance away. There was a loud, scandalized cry of "Go away, child! Go away this instant!" and an old woman with a switch in her hand came round the corner of a hut, violently shooing away a crowd of naked children. Some more women followed, clicking their tongues and exclaiming; evidently there was something that the children ought not to have seen. I rounded the hut and saw a man's dead body sprawling in the mud. He was an Indian, a black Dravidian coolie, almost naked, and he could not have been dead many minutes. The people said that the elephant had come suddenly upon him round the corner of the hut, caught him with its trunk, put its foot on his back and ground him into the earth. This was the rainy season and the ground was soft, and his face had scored a trench a foot deep and a couple of yards long. He was lying on his belly with arms crucified and head sharply twisted to one side. His face was coated with mud, the eyes wide open, the teeth bared and grinning with an expression of unendurable agony. (Never tell me, by the way, that the dead look peaceful. Most of the corpses I have seen looked devilish.) The friction of the great beast's foot had stripped the skin from his back as neatly as one skins a rabbit. As soon as I saw the dead man I sent an orderly to a friend's house nearby to borrow an elephant rifle. I had already sent back the pony, not wanting it to go mad with fright and throw me if it smelt the elephant.

5 The orderly came back in a few minutes with a rifle and five cartridges, and meanwhile some Burmans had arrived and told us that the elephant was in the paddy fields below, only a few hundred yards away. As I started forward practically the whole population of the quarter flocked out of the houses and followed me. They had seen the rifle and were all shouting excitedly that I was going to shoot the elephant. They had not shown much interest in the elephant when he was merely ravaging their homes, but it was different now that he was going to be shot. It was a bit of fun to them, as it would be to an English crowd; besides they wanted the meat. It made me vaguely uneasy. I had no intention of shooting the elephant—I had merely sent for the rifle to defend myself if necessary—and it is always unnerving to have a crowd following you. I marched down the hill, looking and feeling a fool, with the rifle over my shoulder and an ever-growing army of people jostling at my heels. At the bottom, when you got away from the huts, there was a metalled road and beyond that a miry waste of paddy fields a thousand yards across, not yet ploughed but soggy from the first rains and dotted with coarse grass. The elephant was standing eight yards from the road, his left side towards us. He took not the slightest notice of the crowd's approach. He was tearing up bunches of grass, beating them against his knees to clean them and stuffing them into his mouth.

6 I had halted on the road. As soon as I saw the ele-

phant I knew with perfect certainty that I ought not to shoot him. It is a serious matter to shoot a working elephant—it is comparable to destroying a huge and costly piece of machinery—and obviously one ought not to do it if it can possibly be avoided. And at that distance, peacefully eating, the elephant looked no more dangerous than a cow. I thought then and I think now that his attack of "must" was already passing off; in which case he would merely wander harmlessly about until the mahout came back and caught him. Moreover, I did not in the least want to shoot him. I decided that I would watch him for a little while to make sure that he did not turn savage again, and then go home.

7 But at that moment I glanced round at the crowd that had followed me. It was an immense crowd, two thousand at the least and growing every minute. It blocked the road for a long distance on either side. I looked at the sea of yellow faces above the garish clothes—faces all happy and excited over this bit of fun, all certain that the elephant was going to be shot. They were watching me as they would watch a conjurer about to perform a trick. They did not like me, but with the magical rifle in my hands I was momentarily worth watching. And suddenly I realized that I should have to shoot the elephant after all. The people expected it of me and I had got to do it; I could feel their two thousand wills pressing me forward, irresistibly. And it was at this moment, as I stood there with the rifle in my hands, that I first grasped the hollowness, the futility of the white man's dominion in the East. Here was I, the white man with his gun, standing in front of the unarmed native crowd—seemingly the leading actor of the piece; but in reality I was only an absurd puppet pushed to and fro by the will of those yellow faces behind. I perceived in this moment that when the white man turns tyrant it is his own freedom that he destroys. He becomes a sort of hollow, posing dummy, the conventionalized figure of a sahib. For it is the condition of his rule that he shall spend his life in trying to impress the "natives," and so in every crisis he has got to do what the "natives" expect of him. He wears a mask, and his face grows to fit it. I had got to shoot the elephant. I had committed myself to doing it when I sent for the rifle. A sahib has got to act like a sahib; he has got to appear resolute, to know his own mind and do definite things. To come all that way, rifle in hand, with two thousand people marching at my heels, and then to trail feebly away, having done nothing—no, that was impossible. The crowd would laugh at me. And my whole life, every white man's life in the East, was one long struggle not to be laughed at.

8 But I did not want to shoot the elephant. I watched him beating his bunch of grass against his knees, with that preoccupied grandmotherly air that elephants have. It seemed to me that it would be murder to shoot him. At that age I was not squeamish about killing animals, but I had never shot an elephant and never wanted to. (Somehow it always seems worse to kill a *large* animal.) Besides, there was the beast's owner to be considered. Alive, the elephant was worth at least a hundred pounds; dead, he would only be worth the value of his tusks, five pounds, possibly. But I had got to act quickly. I turned to some experienced-looking Burmans who had been there when we arrived, and asked them how the elephant had been behaving. They all said the same thing: he took no notice of you if you left him alone, but he might charge if you went too close to him.

9 It was perfectly clear to me what I ought to do. I ought to walk up to within, say, twenty-five yards of the elephant and test his behavior. If he charged, I could shoot; if he took no notice of me, it would be safe to leave him until the mahout came back. But also I knew that I was going to do no such thing. I was a poor shot with a rifle and the ground was soft mud into which one would sink at every step. If the elephant charged and I missed him, I should have about as much chance as a toad under a steam-roller. But even then I was not thinking particularly of my own skin, only of the watchful yellow faces behind. For at that moment, with the crowd watching me, I was not afraid in the ordinary sense, as I would have been if I had been alone. A white man mustn't be frightened in front of "natives"; and so, in general, he isn't frightened. The sole thought in my mind was that if anything went wrong those two thousand Burmans would see me pursued, caught, trampled on and reduced to a grinning corpse like that Indian up the hill. And if that happened it was quite probable that some of them would laugh. That would never do.

There was only one alternative. I shoved the cartridges into the magazine and lay down on the road to get a better aim.

10 The crowd grew very still, and a deep, low, happy sigh, as of people who see the theatre curtain go up at last, breathed from innumerable throats. They were going to have their bit of fun after all. The rifle was a beautiful German thing with cross-hair sights. I did not then know that in shooting an elephant one would shoot to cut an imaginary bar running from ear-hole to ear-hole. I ought, therefore, as the elephant was sideways on, to have aimed straight at his ear-hole; actually I aimed several inches in front of this, thinking the brain would be further forward.

11 When I pulled the trigger I did not hear the bang or feel the kick—one never does when a shot goes home—but I heard the devilish roar of glee that went up from the crowd. In that instant, in too short a time, one would have thought, even for the bullet to get there, a mysterious, terrible change had come over the elephant. He neither stirred nor fell, but every line of his body had altered. He looked suddenly stricken, shrunken, immensely old, as though the frightful impact of the bullet had paralysed him without knocking him down. At last, after what seemed a long time—it might have been five seconds, I dare say—he sagged flabbily to his knees. His mouth slobbered. An enormous senility seemed to have settled upon him. One could have imagined him thousands of years old. I fired again into the same spot. At the second shot he did not collapse but climbed with desperate slowness to his feet and stood weakly upright, with legs sagging and head drooping. I fired a third time. That was the shot that did for him. You could see the agony of it jolt his whole body and knock the last remnant of strength from his legs. But in falling he seemed for a moment to rise, for as his hind legs collapsed beneath him he seemed to tower upward like a hugh rock toppling, his trunk reaching skywards like a tree. He trumpeted, for the first and only time. And then down he came, his belly towards me, with a crash that seemed to shake the ground even where I lay.

12 I got up. The Burmans were already racing past me across the mud. It was obvious that the elephant would never rise again, but he was not dead. He was breathing very rhythmically with long rattling gasps, his great mound of a side painfully rising and falling. His mouth was wide open—I could see far down into caverns of pale pink throat. I waited a long time for him to die, but his breathing did not weaken. Finally I fired my two remaining shots into the spot where I thought his heart must be. The thick blood welled out of him like red velvet, but still he did not die. His body did not even jerk when the shots hit him, the tortured breathing continued without a pause. He was dying, very slowly and in great agony, but in some world remote from me where not even a bullet could damage him further. I felt that I had got to put an end to that dreadful noise. It seemed dreadful to see the great beast lying there, powerless to move and yet powerless to die, and not even to be able to finish him. I sent back for my small rifle and poured shot after shot into his heart and down his throat. They seemed to make no impression. The tortured gasps continued as steadily as the ticking of a clock.

13 In the end I could not stand it any longer and went away. I heard later that it took him half an hour to die. Burmans were bringing dahs and baskets even before I left, and I was told they had stripped his body almost to the bones by the afternoon.

14 Afterwards, of course, there were endless discussions about the shooting of the elephant. The owner was furious, but he was only an Indian and could do nothing. Besides, legally I had done the right thing, for a mad elephant has to be killed, like a mad dog, if its owner fails to control it. Among the Europeans opinion was divided. The older men said I was right, the younger men said it was a damn shame to shoot an elephant for killing a coolie, because an elephant was worth more than any damn Coringhee coolie. And afterwards I was very glad that the coolie had been killed; it put me legally in the right and it gave me a sufficient pretext for shooting the elephant. I often wondered whether any of the others grasped that I had done it solely to avoid looking a fool.

# *Redundancy and Dullness: One Way to Attack Two Related Problems Grades 10 and 11*

## First Class Period

A. In the first class period a teacher should begin by reading Conrad's "The Lagoon" to the class. The story will give the students a taste of Conrad's style.

B. Now hand out Passage I and have a student read it aloud.

1. Ask students whether they think this passage is taken from Conrad.

2. Then ask them to tell why this is or is not good writing. Ask them if it makes them eager to read the rest of the story. (Students should speak of the lack of color, the impoverished brevity, the generalities, the failure to draw the reader into the scene, the lack of visualization, and the monotonous sentence structure.)

C. Next give out Passage II and have it read aloud.

1. Ask students whether this passage was written by Conrad.

2. Read again the two opening paragraphs of "The Lagoon" and ask students whether this paragraph and Passage II match in style, force, and color. (Some will probably say yes; others will doubt that Conrad wrote Passage II.)

3. If the length and detail in Passage II mislead the students, point out one obvious weak spot, such as "The boat of a large size" at the beginning of the second sentence. Then ask them to spot other weaknesses.

4. Ask the students just what II says that I doesn't and ask them whether II carries the reader further along in the story than I.

5. Then ask what kinds of revision might improve Passage II.

### Assignment Requiring One Preparation Period

Ask each student to prepare a written revision of Passage II, giving particular attention to loose structures, redundancy, and dull diction.

## Second Class Period

Have each student hand in his own version of Passage II, and then spend the period having the class work out together what they consider the best possible revision. In guiding this class project, the teacher may find some of the following 22 discussion questions useful. They are here merely to suggest the kinds of questions that will come up as the class makes its joint revision. Appoint a student to take down the final revision of each sentence as the class completes it. Then ditto copies of the class revision for distribution at the next class meeting.

### Discussion Questions on Passage II

(Be sure that students realize that length may be merely the result of the kind of wordiness that obscures meaning instead of clarifying it.)

1. Passage II is much longer than Passage I. Is it therefore better?

2. Does sentence length make writing good? Explain your answer.

3. What lines in Passage II are wordy? What words can be omitted by finding another form for expressing the idea?

4. What long, involved phrases can be replaced by a single, precise noun?

5. What phrases are redundant? (Hints about the "spongy" places.)

6. What word might replace "The men who were propelling the boat" in line 1? (Boatmen, Malayans, polers.)

7. What phrase could replace "by means of long poles in their hands" in lines 3–4?

8. What word could replace "of a large size" in line 4?

9. In lines 4–5, how can you rephrase "with swiftness and smoothness and without any noise" so as to make the passage briefer and better?

10. What word in the phrase "in a confusing harsh manner" in line 13 is colorless and needless? Why won't just the word "harshly" do in place of this phrase? What about "noisily," "vociferously," "stridently"?

11. In lines 14–15 how much can you take out with no sacrifice of meaning and clarity?

12. In line 16 can you change the adjective clause "which was bamboo and crude" to a double adjective? Would you put it before the noun or after? Do you need both adjectives? If not, which one would you keep?

13. Is there a single word that will replace "the flat

# *Redundancy and Dullness: One Way to Attack Two Related Problems Grades 10 and 11*

*Approximate Time:* 3 class periods and 3 preparation periods

## To the Teacher

Although this unit has been designated for grades 10 and 11, it might be suitable for an average or slow twelfth grade class.

Students often complain that we ask them to cut out unnecessary words, to rely heavily on nouns and verbs, and to go easy on adjectives and adverbs. Then when they think they have followed our injunctions, we write in the margin of their papers: "dull," "thin," or "you need to flesh out your ideas." Understandably the baffled student resents our apparent unreasonableness and comes to regard the whole business of writing with hopeless distaste.

The purpose of this unit is to show the student that length is not necessarily a valid measure of how good a piece of writing is, that dullness can result from too few words as well as from too many, that packed brevity is not the same as barren brevity, that adjectives and adverbs can be indispensable to the effect a writer wants to create, that skillful use of adjectives and adverbs is altogether different from using them to pad an undernourished thought, and that always the question to ask about any word the writer uses is, "Does it pay its way?"

In attacking the different yet related problems of redundancy and dullness, this unit asks the student to judge three passages and to defend his judgment. The third passage is quoted from Joseph Conrad's "The Lagoon." But before the students see the actual Conrad passage, they examine first a condensed version and then an inflated one. The condensed version is called Passage I; the inflated version is called Passage II; and the actual Conrad passage is called Passage III. The three passages are included at the end of this unit.

wooden flooring" in line 17 without lessening the image? Is "flooring" appropriate in this context?

14. In the phrase "small river boat," line 18, are the words "small" and "river" helpful or needful? (Look back at line 4.)

15. Does the verb "stretched" in line 25 imply the "just able to" of lines 25–26? Are the words "just able to" forceful? Needful?

16. In lines 27–28 would a single adverb telling how they pulled away from the house be strong enough to do in place of the phrase "went out away from the clearing which disturbed them"? How about a more descriptive verb than "went out"?

17. In lines 30–31 can you think of a single word that will serve in place of "ramshackled place"? (Hut?)

18. In line 31 can the phrase "through the opening" be omitted or does it add to the exactness of the description?

19. In lines 30 and 32 the word "was" appears three times. Is the repetition effective? Is it necessary?

20. In line 37 is "outward conduct" wordy? In line 38 do you need the adjective "friendly" in the phrase "friendly welcome"?

21. The final sentence is more than just "awkward." How would you streamline it?

22. Must an author explain the meaning of a foreign term like "Tuan," line 39? When should an author use foreign terms?

### Second Assignment Requiring One Preparation Period

At the end of the second class period, give students the copy of Passage III, the actual Conrad passage, and ask them to use their preparation time to compare the three versions: the condensed, the inflated, and Conrad's own.

## Third Class Period

This will be a comparison of the class's revision of Passage II with the original (Passage III) and a comparison of the unrevised Passage II with Passage III. Give each student a dittoed copy of the class revision of Passage II. If you have had time to glance through the individual revisions, return to each student his own revision. The main purpose of this final discussion is to focus attention on the qualities of Passage III that make it good writing—better writing, presumably, than any of the other versions the student now has before him. The following questions are merely suggestive, and any teacher using them should guard against leaving students with the notion that good style is merely a matter of varying sentence length, eliminating words, or counting the number of adjective clauses used. Students should leave this unit aware that, after all, the most essential part of writing is having something important to say and the desire to say it well.

A. In Passage III do you find any words that you can take out without loss of effectiveness?

B. How many sentences does Conrad have? How many does the class revision have? How many does the unrevised Passage II have?

C. How many words are there in Conrad's shortest sentence? How many in his longest? Answer these same questions for the class revision.

D. What forms of modification does Conrad use?

1. *Adjectives.* Does Conrad use more adjectives than you use in your revision of Passage II? Does he use too many? How do you decide whether or not to use an adjective?

2. *Adjective clauses.*

a. How many adjective clauses does Conrad have?

b. How many does the unrevised Passage II have?

c. How many does your revision of Passage II have?

d. Can adjective clauses be one source of "wordiness"? What can you substitute for them?

3. *Prepositional phrases.*

a. Does Conrad use fewer or more of these than you do in your revision of Passage II?

b. Does he link two or more prepositional phrases? Does he do this frequently? If so, what is the effect?

4. *Adverbs.* List Conrad's adverbs and then go back to the unrevised Passage II to see what happens to his adverbs there. What adverbs do you use in your class revision of Passage II? How do they compare in effectiveness with Conrad's?

### Writing Assignment

This is the third assignment requiring a preparation period outside class.

*Directions.* Do the writing assignment set below, applying to it all that you have learned through this unit about writing and revision.

Write a composition of about 250 words in which you try to make your reader *see* and *understand* a person (or a group of people) in a particular situation and in a particular place. In his preface to *The Nigger of the "Narcissus"* Conrad defines the writer's job as above all to make his reader *see.* Keep this in mind as you write and as you revise. And as you revise, examine each word you have used to make sure that it is paying its way. Here are possible topics, but you are free to choose your own:

1. a hunter coming into a clearing in search of game
2. a fisherman finding a good spot for fishing
3. a shy man about to go through the receiving line at a wedding party
4. a student walking into the wrong class on the first day of school
5. a patient waiting his turn in the dentist's office
6. a person experiencing his first take-off in a jet plane
7. a person driving out of a cloudburst into the sunshine
8. a family arriving at the summer cottage they had rented sight unseen from a newspaper ad

(*Note to the teacher.* In place of the above assignment, or in addition to it, some teachers may wish to ask students to take an old composition and rewrite it, applying to the rewriting the techniques of revision learned through the work on this unit.)

## Passage I: "The Lagoon" (condensed)

They thought about these things as they were going toward the house. When they reached there, they yelled noisily to Arsat, who didn't appear. The man climbed up the ladder but the boss of the boat said they wanted to stay in the boat all night. He got his things and the boat left. He turned around and saw Arsat, who had just come out. He was a strong big man and wore only a sarong. He looked eagerly at the man but calmly asked if he had any medicine.

## Passage II: "The Lagoon" (inflated)

The men who were propelling the boat thought about all these things as they pushed their conveyance through the water by means of long poles in their hands. The boat of a large size slid with swiftness and smoothness and without any noise. When they finally reached the heavy long stakes which had been driven in the ground in the water in order to keep the house which sat on top of them out of the wet mud, they threw the oars down so hard and fast, they rattled. They made loud murmurs and said, "Allah be praised!" The canoe touched the massive stakes gently as the men in the boat lifted up their faces and shouted in a confusing harsh manner: "Arsat! Arsat!" But no one came out of the house in answer to their shouts. The man of white origin started climbing up a ladder which was bamboo and crude but which was the only way to the flat wooden flooring outside the house. The master of the small river boat said to the European, "We would rather cook in our boat and even sleep in it out of the water than stay in or near this ruined house." "Very well," snapped their boss, "but give me my things then. I'll need the stuff for the night." By now he had climbed up out of the boat so he had to kneel down to try to reach the things he wanted. He stretched out his fingers and was just able to grab the bundle. Then the natives pushed their boat away from the wooden stakes and went out away from the clearing which disturbed them. The white man stood up with his bundle clutched in his hand. He faced the door which was low of the ramshackled place. Just then Arsat appeared through the opening. He was a strong young man. His chest was broad and his arms muscular. He had only a sarong on and he stood there with a bare head. His eyes which were soft and also big stared at the white man. Although there was an eager light in them, he did not let his voice or his outward conduct show anything but composure. He did not give the visitor any friendly welcome but called him Tuan, which is the term meaning "sir" and one which the natives apply to all Europeans, and asked directly, "Have you medicine?"

## Passage III: From "The Lagoon" by Joseph Conrad

So they thought, throwing their weight on the end of 1
their long poles. The big canoe glided on swiftly, noiselessly, and smoothly, towards Arsat's clearing, till, in a great rattling of poles thrown down, and the loud murmurs of "Allah be praised!" it came with a gentle knock against the crooked piles below the house.

The boatmen with uplifted faces shouted discord- 2
antly, "Arsat! O Arsat!" Nobody came. The white man began to climb the rude ladder giving access to the bamboo platform before the house. The juragan of the boat said sulkily, "We will cook in the sampan, and sleep on the water."

"Pass my blankets and the basket," said the white 3
man, curtly.

He knelt on the edge of the platform to receive the 4
bundle. Then the boat shoved off, and the white man, standing up, confronted Arsat, who had come out through the low door of his hut. He was a man young, powerful, with broad chest and muscular arms. He had nothing on but his sarong. His head was bare. His big, soft eyes stared eagerly at the white man, but his voice and demeanor were composed as he asked, without any words of greeting:

"Have you medicine, Tuan?" 5

## Writing Assignment
## Sample 1. Grade: High

His head, rolling gently on a large red neck, seemed to follow the weaving pattern of his feet as the drunk threaded his way along the sidewalk. He was a large man, with a big head of gray black hair that curled sweatily onto his flushed face. His clothes possessed that strange air of discomfort one gets in humid weather; they were neither dirty nor especially ruffled, but they oozed an air of disease. The man's face, ludicrous and sad, painfully sought to comprehend its own situation. His brow was furrowed in the deep concentration required to avoid telephone poles. It was sad, his black shoes, his hair, his clothes, his gait, his immense thought—it was unutterably sad. He was amazingly unaware of his tragedy, though. He simply followed the sidewalk, exulting over each crack he crossed, and wondering vaguely where the hell he was.

## Writing Assignment
## Comment on Sample 1. Grade: High

This student has learned the power of packed brevity and knows how to create it. He is rare among adolescents in being able to write about a "drunk" with neither ridicule nor sentimentality. He has also picked up some of Conrad's stylistic tricks and uses them effectively—the painfully exact adverb in the phrase "hair that curled *sweatily* onto his flushed face"; the adjectives tucked in after the noun in "The man's face, *ludicrous* and *sad*"; the Conrad-like "immense" in "his *immense* thought"; and the occasional insertion of a short sentence to forestall the soporific flow of unbroken long ones, as in the sentence "He was amazingly unaware of his tragedy, though." This student has understood the double aim of the lesson: to avoid wordiness without slipping into the opposite fault of undernourished dullness. A stickler for thrift in language would probably jettison a few of the words here and with no loss to the whole, but in making the reader see and feel the combined absurdity and pathos of the man and his situation, this paper does an exceptionally skillful job.

## Writing Assignment
## Sample 2. Grade: Average

*Insufficient Welfare*

Right on schedule the gleaming, inconspicuous, pink Volks Wagon skimmed around the corner and turned into the designated street. The automobile sympathized with the character of its owners, being an economical asset to any budget and simultaneously catered to their female eccentricity, as it was a radient pink.

The two Medicare-eligible, grandmotherly, spinsters in the front seat gossiped amicably as their car drew to a full stop in front of an epitome of the residence of an upper class, American family, complete with a shrub-lined, stone walk and a crew-cut lawn.

"Ready, Muriel?" the driver asked her sister.

"Ready, Gertrude," her sister replied.

Thus, the two women stepped out of the car and walked up to the main entrance. Both were well-dressed, including diamond and furs, however, both were wearing pink sneakers. Perhaps to be mentioned is the fact that one carried a gunny sack and the other a suspicious-looking, gold-plated flashlight.

## Writing Assignment
## Comment on Sample 2. Grade: Average

An *average* paper is likely to be respectable but dull. This one is among the tastiest bits the readers unearthed in the course of their delvings. Here is a student who can write with imagination, humor, and such an occasional deft touch as the choice of names for the two "Medicare-eligible" ladies—a pair of names out of fashion just about long enough to mark their owners as of Medicare vintage. And the phrase "Medicare-eligible" is in itself a condensed characterization. This same capacity for terse phrasing is evident in this interchange:

" 'Ready, Muriel?' the driver asked her sister.

" 'Ready, Gertrude,' her sister replied."

And no doubt these two Medicare-eligible ladies shared Hamlet's awareness that "the readiness is all," as they pink-sneakered their way past that "crew-cut lawn" on business best known to themselves. The quiet matter-of-factness of the climax is another strength that will make readers wish they could have the fun of working with this student.

For several reasons, though, the paper just misses the *high* category. In fact some people after a quick reading might relegate it to the lower regions because of its preposterous situation. A more valid charge, perhaps, is that although it is clever its cleverness never quite comes off, nor is the cleverness a means of accomplishing anything that is of real importance. In the readers' minds, too, is the realization that the writing techniques are not as consistently strong as in most of the papers ranked *high*. "Sympathized" in paragraph one and "epitome" in paragraph two just miss the sure precision of the unusually competent writer, and the sentence fragment in the final paragraph is an even more serious blemish. Certainly, though, no paper should be classed as *low* that has the vitality and the imagination to conceive of two pink-sneakered ladies in a "radient pink" "Volks Wagon" doing their bit to right a topsy-turvy economy.

## Writing Assignment
## Sample 3. Grade: Low

*Embarassing Situation*

In the following composition an attempt will be made to describe the reaction of a student walking into the wrong class on the first day of school.

I chose the above topic because, at one time I also walked into the wrong classroom. I can remember it distinctly. It was the first day of school back in seventh grade, and like most school openings they began on a Wednesday.

In homeroom, our teacher gave us roster cards to fill out, which were schedules of the time and periods we were to attend our classes.

The halls of Harrington Junior High at the time, seemed so big and there, I was amongust all those students, as I walked down the hall, in an attempt to find my class. When to my surprise there I was in a room, which I was sure was on my schedule. The first thing I noticed, was a boy who lived down the street from me. Bobby was the type of boy who thought everything, was a joke, including me, standing there with a puzzled look on my face. I quickly ran from the room, and stood in the hall deciding what to do. There I was reading my roster card, trying to figure out what I did wrong.

When a teacher approached me in hopes of getting me to class. She then told me that today was Wednesday, and I was looking at the schedule for Monday. The teacher showed me how to get to my next class. So again, I started down the halls laughing at myself, for what I had done.

## Writing Assignment
## Comment on Sample 3. Grade: Low

This paper combines the redundancy of the fat version of the Conrad passage and the dullness of the lean one, adding an occasional touch of illiteracy for good measure. The first paragraph and half of the second could have gone into the wastebasket with no loss. The passive voice of the initial "an attempt will be made" adds to the feebleness of the unneeded opening. And since the paper is to be about the writer's experience of finding himself in the wrong classroom, why tell the reader that he has chosen the topic because he once had such an experience? The dawdling indecisiveness irritates the reader before he ever reaches what meat the paper has to offer. And since paragraph three is more fat than meat, cutting out the excesses would make a good exercise in linguistic thrift for almost any eleventh or twelfth grade class. In the remainder of his paper the student exhibits his fondness for sentence fragments and needless commas.

*The Language of an Essay*
*Grades 11 and 12*

may well be the key to successful use of this material with a given class.

## Class Procedure

I. The teacher should read the essay to the class, directing them to listen, enjoy, and absorb the major points the author makes. Before reading the essay he should tell the class when it was written, that it appeared in *The New York Times Magazine,* and that it is an example of informative prose, indeed the kind of writing assignment they themselves might have attempted. Some teachers may wish to give out copies of the essay at this point so that students can follow the text as they listen to the reading, and thus experience a simultaneous assault on their ears and their eyes. If students do have copies of the essay before them, they may wish to make notations as the reading goes on.

II. The teacher should take a few minutes to discuss the substance of the essay and to answer any questions students may raise. (With a very able class this step can be taken very quickly or not at all.)

III. Before moving to an examination of the language of this essay, students need to be conscious of the specific audience for whom Hadley was writing and the extent to which his awareness of that audience conditioned what he said and how he said it. A first question should be, What kinds of people read *The New York Times Magazine* and why do they read it? What are they looking for? How much do most of them know about Hadley's subject before they read his essay? In what sort of tone would you address such an audience? What kind of "voice" should you use? What kind of wording? How much technical language? Is the subject one that sells itself or is the author going to have to sell it to this particular audience? To what extent will this determine his opening strategy?

IV. The class is now ready for a preliminary discussion of what they have gathered from a first hearing of the essay. Questions such as these should lead them from the substance of the essay to its style. (In judging style, they must always bear in mind Hadley's audience—the readers of *The New York Times Magazine.*)

A. Is the essay well written? Is it lively? Are its words vigorous?

B. How might a topic like A Modern Spy be written dully? What makes writing dull? Is the dullness sometimes in the reader?

C. Is Hadley's rhythm varied, melodic, monotonous, crisp, heavy, swift? What words would you choose to describe your general impressions of the style?

D. Could you tell whether the author varies the length of his sentences? Did the intonational patterns of any one passage catch your attention? Did you notice any choppy sentences? Did any of the sentences make you wait a long time for a breath? If so, why would a writer use such a sentence?

E. Does Mr. Hadley have an effective vocabulary?

1. Is his vocabulary hard to understand? Would it be for his *New York Times* readers?

2. Were there words you didn't know?

3. Did you notice any specially striking phrases?

4. Any unusual word combinations?

5. What tone does Hadley use? Does he use the same tone throughout the essay?

V. If time permits, go back and reread aloud the first five paragraphs of the essay, perhaps discussing some of the following points:

A. Would the opening sentence be sharper, better, if it read: "The secret agent's world is solitary"? Give reasons.

B. In his very brief first paragraph, Hadley uses the word "world" four times. Why does he do this? Why does he repeat this same word in the last sentence of paragraph 5?

C. In his third sentence Hadley writes "with the tension of a high note held too long." Would it improve the passage if he had written "with the tension of an elastic stretched too far"? Why or why not?

D. In paragraph 3, the essay refers to "those fat, contented years." What is the reference and is Hadley right in assuming that his readers will recognize it?

E. In the next to the last sentence of paragraph 3, the author uses the word "peace" twice. Would it have been better to substitute "serenity" in one of the places where he has used "peace"? Why or why not?

# *The Language of an Essay*
# *Grades 11 and 12*

*Essay Used:* "Complex Query: What Makes a Good Spy?" by Arthur T. Hadley. *The New York Times Magazine,* May 29, 1960, pages 12, 43–44.

*Approximate Time:* From 3 to 5 class periods, depending on the stamina of the teacher and the staying powers of the class. Since most of this work requires class discussion rather than outside preparation, teachers may wish to have students reading other essays as their outside assignment or writing an essay of their own.

## To the Teacher

Although the essay is the form we most commonly ask our students to use in their own writing, it is the form we are least likely to teach them in their literature. Thus in our concentration on the other literary forms, we are slighting the one that could be most explicitly helpful to students in the kind of writing we most frequently require of them. And too often, if we do teach the essay, we deal with its ideas and let it go at that. The student needs also to examine the form of essays: their organization, their amplification, their sentence structure, the devices other than the adjective by which they achieve their modification, their use of metaphorical language to clarify or to reinforce an abstraction, and—above all—their subtle adaptations of diction, tone, and voice to their audience and to their purpose. The double aim of this unit, therefore, is to focus attention on essays in general and to provide a close, analytic study of the language and structure of one essay in particular. If the teacher can use this material merely as one part of a larger study of the essay, so much the better.

There are probably more questions here than teachers will want or need to use. What will fascinate an Advanced Placement class may bore a slow section. Each teacher should sense the point at which his particular class is growing restless and should then move at once to the next section. With an able class the teacher may want to skip the less demanding questions, which may be exactly the ones most useful with a slow section. Complete coverage of every question is neither needful nor desirable. Judicious omission

## Analysis

(*Note to the teacher.* The statistical exercises and questions center mostly on just one section of the essay, paragraphs 6–12—only the sentences in these paragraphs are numbered—since any attempt at a close stylistic analysis of the whole essay would be too time consuming and, for most classes, too tedious. Some of the questions, though, do lead the student out of the single section and into other parts of the essay. If the teacher wishes, almost any one of the questions can do this. Teachers may find it wise to have groups of two or three students working on just one or two paragraphs of the marked section instead of having every student answer questions on every one of the seven paragraphs.)

### I. Sentence Length

A. Do the sentences vary in length? Test your answer by counting words in what look to you like the longest and the shortest of Hadley's sentences.

B. Is it by accident or design that almost all the paragraphs have about the same range? (The range is from 2–33 unless you want to have numbered sentence 12 include the definitions following it.)

C. If you have some of your own writing in your notebook, pick out a paragraph of typical length and see what the range is between your shortest and your longest sentence. Do you imagine that a professional writer thinks consciously about the length of his sentences as he writes, or does the variety in length just happen if he is a good writer? Do you think consciously of sentence length and variety in length when you are writing?

D. What effect does Hadley create when he uses a very short sentence?

### II. Rhythm

Sentence length is an obvious source of rhythm in an essay. Here are other sources:

A. *Word order* (normal and inverted word order).

1. What is normal word order in an English sentence? How many sentences here have normal word order?

2. Are some of the remaining sentences less obviously inverted than others? Why? (We hardly think of sentences beginning with "there" as inverted, and Hadley uses many of these.)

3. Why do writers use inverted word order?

4. What happens to style if a writer overuses inverted word order? Try inverting several contiguous sentences and then listen to how they sound.

B. *Structure.*

1. What elements in sentence structure other than inversion can influence the rhythm of the sentence?

2. How many sentences here have structures in front of the subject even though there is normal word order?

3. How many sentences in this excerpt have varied beginnings other than subject and verb? Is this kind of variation good writing strategy? Is it good if it calls attention to itself or should it sound as though it just happened that way?

4. What do compound elements or parallelism do to sentence rhythm? Sentences 21 and 22 are good examples of compound subjects. Read them aloud for rhythm.

5. How much use does Hadley make of participial phrases as a means of varying his sentences?

6. Does Hadley omit words, especially verbs in a compound sentence? Why might a writer choose to do this?

7. What is the source of uncommon rhythm in sentence 7? (Subject separated from verb.) How frequently does Hadley use this device? If a writer carries this too far, what danger does he run? (The danger of weakening syntax.)

8. What changes the rhythm in sentence 30? (The contrasting verb set off with commas.) Would it be more effective to say, "He must outthink rather than outfight the enemy." Explain.

### III. Diction

(*Note to the teacher.* If this topic comes up spontaneously before rhythm, treat it first; certainly the two are linked. Often a writer will choose one word rather than another because of what it does for the rhythm of his sentence, a fact that students should be made to realize as they move from rhythm to diction—or from diction to rhythm. The material in this section is grouped under five headings: nouns, pronouns, modifiers, verbs, and figurative language. Many teachers may wish to use the material under only two or three of these headings. Others may wish to make their own selection of material under all five sections. It will be better to do a small amount well than to risk boredom through trying to cover too much.

To make them realize the link between rhythm and diction, have students take one or two of Hadley's sentences and try substituting synonyms to see what happens to rhythm. For instance change sentence 23 to, "Underneath the panoply of technological competence reside the quintessential basic characteristics." And, incidentally, students should notice that more than rhythm suffers a change in the substitution. Or change sentence 18 to, "Being a tea imbiber, he did not know that piece of equipment.")

A. *Nouns.*

1. Select several of what you think are Hadley's most successful choices of nouns. ("Argot," sentence 2; "isolation," sentence 5; "fanatic," sentence 12; "glibness," sentence 24 are possible examples.)

2. Give a dull synonym for one or two of these unusually good choices. What happens when you read the sentence aloud with your synonym?

3. Do most of the nouns have referents? List examples on the board. (The purpose here is not to show noun *identification* but rather to emphasize noun *evaluation* and effects.)

4. Which nouns have marked connotations? ["Powers," "Soviet Union," "cold war" (taken as a noun?)]

5. What kind of noun is "situation" (sentence 26)? Try using it in a series of unrelated sentences. Does it mean the same thing in each context you give it? What happens if you substitute a more specific word? Is it always possible to use a more specific word without changing the meaning and intent of the sentence?

6. Does Hadley use other relatively unspecific nouns? ("Qualities," sentence 8; "attributes," sentence 10.) What might heavy reliance on this kind of noun do to a writer's style?

7. Compare such a noun as "situation" or "qualities" with nouns like "urn," sentence 17; and "matches," sentence 21. Why not use the "urn"/"matches" type all the time?

8. Which of the two types does Hadley use more often?

9. In the sentence "His balance must be self-sustaining, an internal gyroscope. . . ." (paragraph 16), doesn't "gyroscope" repeat the idea in "self-sustaining"? Why does Hadley add "gyroscope"?

10. Can you find other examples in the whole essay of the author's pinning down an abstraction with a figure of speech?

B. *Pronouns.*

1. Does Hadley use many pronouns?

2. Why might a good writer go easy on pronouns, especially the indefinite pronouns? Try writing a sentence or two using pronouns in place of all nouns? What does this do to the style?

C. *Modifiers.*

(*Note to the teacher.* The type and amount of modification is one of the major stylistic points of this essay and is a main source of the tight, packed style. Before starting this section, ask students for a list of half a dozen words that first come to their minds when they think of *adjectives.* Their list will probably contain such words as *good, big, pretty, nice,* or *interesting.* Keep this list before them as they begin to examine Hadley's adjectives.)

In this excerpt there are roughly twice as many nouns as modifiers, not counting the articles. This means that only half the nouns are modified by adjectives.

1. What does this mean for the job the nouns must do? (Precision must derive from the noun itself, not from other words that change or limit it. It means an exacting choice of each unmodified noun.)

2. Take a look at the adjectives Hadley uses in the paragraph that begins: "Many black agents now are . . ." (sentence 20 ff.). Put the nouns from this paragraph on the board in one column and the modifiers in the other. Then contrast this list of modifiers with the list of adjectives the students produced earlier. In what ways do Hadley's differ from the class's? (The bases of many of the words suggest verbs and nouns. The teacher may wish to introduce the term "nominal" at this point if students don't know it, but the term is not important as long as students see that an adjective can have something of the quality of a verb or a noun.)

3. Does Hadley make use elsewhere in the essay of such adjectives as "black," "radar," "inflatable"? Have you ever been told to be very sparing of adjectives because they weaken your style? Do adjectives like "black," "radar," and "inflatable" weaken style? Explain your answer.

4. Can you find any place where Hadley stacks up several of this kind of modifier in front of one noun? What is the effect?

5. What is the effect of such a compound adjective as in "pip-pip-and-all-that British colonel of spy fiction," sentence 11?

6. Take a look at the phrase "supersecret German torpedo factory" (sentence 17). Note that all these ideas are packed into the one phrase: the factory was supersecret; it was in Germany; it made torpedoes. What would it do to Hadley's style if he had written:

There is a legendary story in intelligence about a British colonel in World War II who, at great hazard, broke into a factory. The factory was supersecret. It was in Germany. It made torpedoes.

7. Examine this sentence: "This necessity for fanaticism makes the role of Westerner-turned-agent particularly difficult," paragraph 33. What part of speech is "this" and what device has Hadley used to make it so? Is it possible to rewrite the sentence just as effectively using other forms for the same idea? Try it.

8. Are adjectives such as "fat," "green," "soft," and "contented" unusual? Fresh? Forceful?

9. Take a look at paragraph 3. "It was a *soft,* mint-julep afternoon in the spring of one of those *fat,* contented years shortly after the Korean war's end."

". . . I broke our rule and said, gesturing at the *soft green* peace of the garden . . ."

Would you modify the answer you gave to question 8? How? Why? What determines whether or not a word is fresh, forceful?

D. *Verbs.*

1. Would you say offhand that *is* and *have* are forceful verbs? Have you ever been told to avoid them in your own writing? Why might an English teacher offer this advice to a student?

2. Hadley uses some form of "to be" many times in the marked passage. He uses some form of "to have" several times. Do they detract from the interest of the essay? Did you notice them when you first heard the essay? How does a good writer decide when to use them and when not to?

3. Do you find any places where Hadley would have written a better sentence if he had replaced a "to be" verb with a more active one? Insert your suggested replacement and listen to the resulting sound of the sentence.

4. Pick out verbs in the marked passage or in the rest of the essay that strike you as particularly good choices. Examine several of these to see why they are good. ("Outthink" and "outfight," sentence 30; "snoop," sentence 15; "relieved," paragraph 28.)

E. *Figurative language.*

1. Would it be possible to write an essay on Hadley's subject without using any figurative language? Why or why not? Have you ever tried it? What are some of the purposes figurative language serves in prose as well as in poetry?

2. Would you say that Hadley makes extensive use of figurative language? Find examples and explain why Hadley uses them. You might start with the "mint-julep afternoon" and the "fat, contented years after the Korean war's end," paragraph 3. Suppose Hadley had written "relaxing" for "mint-julep" and "prosperous, peaceful years" for "fat, contented years." What shades of meaning would he have lost? "The rack on which the Western agent is stretched" (paragraph 35) is another metaphor worth exploring. What shades of meaning would have been lost if Hadley had written, "The predicament in which the Western agent finds himself"?

## IV. Other Devices

A. *Ambiguity* (purposeful?).

In the sentence, "So he sat alone in his separate world, while the peaceful world of the garden went on happily, *not understanding*" (paragraph 5), what do the italicized words modify? If you cannot be sure, does this mean that Hadley is guilty of bad writing? Explain your answer.

B. *Omission.*

1. What word is omitted in sentence 5? Is the sentence better with or without the word? Why?

2. The word "and" in sentence 3 has been left out. Should Hadley have left it in? Why or why not?

## Optional Writing Assignment

Some teachers may wish to conclude this unit by having students write an essay of their own in which they try to apply some of what they have learned through their work with Hadley's essay. Almost any topic requiring informative writing directed to a specific audience—probably the class—should serve. Here are a few suggestions:

1. what it takes to be the head of school government;
2. what makes a good class president;
3. the world of the star athlete;
4. what makes a good parent in the world of 1967;
5. the high price of office-holding.

Students will probably enjoy choosing their own topics, but these are here if any pump-priming is needed.

### *Complex Query: What Makes a Good Spy?*

Arthur T. Hadley

The world of the secret agent is a solitary world. His is the aloneness of the infantryman proceeding up a deserted enemy street. The hostile world stretches out infinitely in all directions around him with the tension of a high note held too long. Within this world he has no friend. He and his fear exist alone. 1

Just so was Francis Gary Powers alone on his U-2 spy-plane mission when he was brought down 1,200 miles within the Soviet borders. 2

I remember sitting in a quiet Georgetown garden with an old friend. It was a soft, mint-julep afternoon in the spring of one of those fat, contented years shortly after the Korean war's end. My friend and I maintain the fiction that I don't know what he does. It's easier. That afternoon he was obviously on the rack. So much so, and this was so unusual, that I broke our rule and said, gesturing at the soft green peace of the garden to indicate the apparent peace of the world. "It must be even rougher, now." 3

"It is," he answered. And then, after an instant: "I blew a nasty one last week. Killed a few people. Must have set the cold war back months." 4

He should not have come out of his world apart and said that to me. But in his own world of secret intelligence there was no one he could talk to. His superiors would have regarded his depression as a dangerous sign of weakness. Intelligence security is so rigid his colleagues couldn't know what he was doing. So he sat alone in his separate world, while the peaceful world of the garden went on happily, not understanding. 5

[1]The official bureaucratic designation for a man who takes on this demanding work is "agent, intelligence, covert." [2]In the argot of his trade he is "opps black"—a "black operator." [3]"White operators," or "agents, intelligence, overt," are those who analyze foreign technical journals, listen to Russian broadcasts, interview refugees. [4]Their work may be secret, but they do not pretend to be something they are not. [5]Theirs is not the extreme isolation and danger. [6]They are not "in black." [7]Agents like Powers, who both pretend to be something they are not and penetrate the Curtain, Bamboo or Iron, are "in deep black."

[8]What mental and psychological qualities make up the ideal black agent? [9]Different nations set different standards. [10]Nevertheless, intelligence agents themselves are in general agreement about the necessary attributes. [11]The man they describe is a far remove from the all-American boy or the pip-pip-and-all-that British colonel of spy fiction. [12]These agents outline their ideal with such observations as:

"Lonely, complicated jobs take lonely, complicated guys."

"The quiet, bookish type, without bravado, sticks longest."

"Team players who don't need the coach or the team."

"The thinking fanatic."

[13]Obviously, the ideal black agent on either side of the cold war must have extreme technical competence. [14]The Soviet Union is a well-guarded, closed society. [15]Those who snoop in or around it cannot be amateurs. [16]The West, while not so secretive, has effective counter-espionage, too. [17]There is a legendary story in intelligence about a British colonel in World War II who, at great hazard, broke into a supersecret German torpedo factory and blew up the coffee urn. [18]Being a tea drinker, he didn't recognize that piece of equipment. [19]Those days, one hopes, are past.

[20]Many black agents now are electronics special-

ists. [21]Parabolic microphones and transistorized radio transmitters the size of a book of matches have changed agents' methods of operation. [22]So has the aqualung, the inflatable airplane, high-speed aerial photography, infra-red and radar detection devices, and the electronic processing of data.

[23]Beneath the armor of technical competence lie 10
the essential basic traits. [24]Intelligence is an absolute must—not quiz-show glibness, but the ability to sit down with a sheet of paper and solve complex, original problems.

[25]Much of the time, the agent has no "book" to go 11
by. [26]The situation he confronts is unique. [27]There is no one to turn to for guidance, no committee to render a considered opinion, no staff to brief him on the big picture. [28]On his decision rests not merely the future of some company, but that awesome entity, the national security.

[29]His intelligence should be imaginative. [30]He must 12
outthink, not outfight, the enemy. [31]Then, there are certain tough basic questions to which the ideal agent has worked out his answers. [32]For example: "Since almost all men talk under torture in time (and women, too, though their psychology enables them to hold out longer), how long should I hold out? [33]And why?" [34]Or: "Since the enemy will stoop as low as necessary to gain his ends, how far should we stoop?"

The ideal agent must have faced up to the possible 13
necessity of suicide. Actually, the dividing line between suicide and other hazards does not appear so great to those inside the black area. There is a macabre joke well-known in intelligence circles about a secret agent going off alone on a particularly dangerous job inside an enemy country. The last words of his chief are: "Hold out, and keep reporting to the last man."

The agent has one overriding security rule: if he 14
knows certain types of information he is to kill himself rather than fall into enemy hands, and he is issued the necessary equipment to do so. Other situations are left to his judgment.

The ideal agent must be a psychologically well- 15
balanced individual—not ordinary, but so well-balanced as to appear normal. He needs the same deep, introspective knowledge of himself that the ideal psychiatrist needs. He should have looked perceptively at himself and the world around him and come up with his own philosophy.

His balance must be self-sustaining, an internal 16
gyroscope. The man who needs praise, fellowship, coaching or even understanding cannot maintain the pace. Nor will the shibboleths of conventional wisdom sustain the agent in his dark hour. Conventional wisdom does not recognize the occasional necessity of murder or suicide.

The introspective intelligence necessary in the ideal 17
agent shows up in the postwar published writings of British black operators about their work. A mystic quality permeates "Hugh Dormar's Diaries." Both W. Stanley Moss' "Ill Met by Moonlight" and Fitzroy Maclean's "Eastern Approaches" are ripe with scholarship.

French resistance leaders had the same intellectual 18
quality. Albert Camus is remembered as a philosopher, not as an agent. The man who called himself Colonel Remy wrote in "How a Resistance Dies"—perhaps the most agonizing tale ever told of ăn agent's work—an excellent antidote for anyone bemused by the glamour of working in black.

Ideal agents are hard to come by. Defectors from 19
the Soviet Union indicate that even Russia has trouble finding them. The West must not only find them, but persuade them to volunteer. Inevitably, many of any country's agents are foreign nationals.

Since good agents are so hard to find, their supe- 20
riors are likely to condone eccentricities in their off-duty behavior—which, to be frank, is often very odd. Two highly successful American black agents spring to mind. One used to borrow suits of armor from a museum and ride through the countryside looking for someone to joust with. (He found people who would, too.) The other would put on a ragged suit of clothes about once every two months and, going to the toughest part of a rather tough town, start a barroom brawl. He didn't always win, but he claimed it kept him in shape and worked off his tensions.

The tensions are constant. The presence of danger 21
not only creates its own anxiety, but heightens the anxiety-producing factors in the agent's other problems.

One is schizophrenia—never letting on in one life 22
what is being done in the other. Several Soviet agents

have defected to the West because their "Western" personalities finally became dominant. One American, whose job is recruiting new agents, greets his friends with the mocking question: "Met any well-balanced schizophrenics lately?"

23 The secrecy of the work produces tensions in another way. An agent knows only his small portion of the job, not where he fits into the whole. He must be able to accept the necessity of performing morally despicable actions in situations of extreme danger over prolonged periods of time without knowing why.

24 The moral horror of certain actions he must take contributes to his psychological malaise. For example: You are a secret agent who has been leading a twenty-man resistance group in a hostile country for two years. You have shared desperate and intimate hardships with your men and have their complete trust. You are now ordered to betray your resistance group into ambush and to make certain none of them survives.

25 The example is not farfetched. In the middle of July, 1944, when it became obvious to the Russians that the war in Europe was won, secret orders went out to Communist agents working with resistance groups in France, Yugoslavia, Poland and Greece to liquidate non-Communist resistance groups. From the French Alps to Mount Olympus, Red agents betrayed their closest comrades to the Germans. In liberated France, it was easier to murder, and explain to the Americans that the murdered were really collaborators.

26 The black operator does not face decisions every day as tough as the example. But even in the easiest, difficult moral choices are there. For some agents, after a time, the decisions become impossible. They break down. Every government in the business maintains special hospital rooms, plus doctors and nurses with security clearances, to handle the emotional problems of agents whom the work has pushed too far.

27 A more subtle form of breakdown that faces the Western agent in particular comes when the decisions all begin to seem easy. The agent has become either brutalized or so fanatical about his cause that his human values have disappeared. As Arthur Koestler has pointed out (and Koestler and George Orwell will be found among the black agents' most quoted authors) the yogi and the commissar, in the end, show the same image to the mirror.

28 Quite a few years ago, I talked to one of America's most famous intelligence agents—famous, that is, within the small circle where such fame is possible. I had sought him out because I had heard that he had accurately forecast what the enemy was going to do before one of America's bitterest military disasters. His warning had been rejected and, after the débâcle, his reports had been destroyed and he had been relieved for having been right.

29 I asked him about the incident. He answered that his superiors were absolutely right to destroy his reports and relieve him. Faith in the national leadership was essential for the war effort and he and his reports jeopardized that faith.

30 I was younger then, and I looked at the man closely for signs of irony or bitterness as he made that statement. I saw none. I concluded that the poor man had been beaten down by the magnitude of his job. I felt, as many reading this may feel, that he needed a good psychiatrist or a tonic to buck him up and help him regain his lost confidence.

31 I now realize the man had that final ingredient of the ideal intelligence agent: a fanatical devotion to duty. He had been absolutely right. His warnings had not been misunderstood or disregarded, but deliberately set aside. The result had been a major American disaster. For the country's future, his retirement had become a necessity. It is not always wise to prove the boss wrong in industry, either.

32 However, when a man has been removed for such reasons, we in America and throughout the West feel he has been treated badly. The ideal agent must feel he has been treated in the only way possible. In Koestler's novel, "Darkness At Noon," the hero, Rubishov, confesses to things he has not done rather than embarrass the regime. He knows his voluntary confession will mean his death.

33 This necessity for fanaticism makes the role of the Westerner-turned-agent particularly difficult. The agent himself, like the criteria by which he is selected, is in large part the product of his environment. We in the West consider many of the actions an agent

must take morally reprehensible. People who do such things, or order them done, or even those who write about the agent's problem with sympathy, are considered ogres or worse. Yet for national survival our agents are ordered to—and do—perform such actions.

But, and the but is crucial, the Western agent can- 34
not just perform the action and forget it. He must, in his "worst" moments, retain his respect for life and human dignity. He is under orders not to become the mirror image of the enemy.

The rack on which the Western agent is stretched 35
is well-described in Shakespeare's "Henry V." King Henry wanders in disguise among his soldiers, conversing with them, just before the battle of Agincourt. The soldiers are debating how they will fight on the morrow. One of them wonders what will happen to his soul if the cause for which he dies "be not good."

"If the King's cause be wrong," replies another 36
soldier, "our obedience to the King wipes the crime of it out of us."

Not so, answers Henry. "Every subject's duty is 37
the King's. But every subject's soul is his own."

Our Western philosophy of freedom and moral re- 38
sponsibility splits the Western-reared agent in two. In societies where the subject's duty and soul both belong to the King, agents don't have the same problems—nor citizens the same freedoms.

The lack of complete fanaticism, the holding to 39
moral values, puts an agent brought up in a free society under a much greater strain than his opposite number elsewhere. As a result, the West will lose rounds in the cold war. The strains and losses are unavoidable.

To combine the West's humanistic heritage of the 40
individual's responsibility and freedom with the need for obedience and service to the state is not easy in 1960. Deciding the proper mix of freedom and responsibility is a problem we all face. The secret agent, the black operator, merely faces the problem in its most acute form. He is our frontiersman in more ways than we realize.

# Composition

# *Introduction to the Units on Composition*

If concern with composition began and ended with the four teaching units that follow, this book would be wide open to the charge of grossly neglecting what should be at the heart of any sound program in English. But every one of the units on literature is profoundly concerned with composition and necessarily linked with language. The same three-in-one fusion occurs in much of the language section. And now here in the composition section every unit is inescapably involved with language, and some but not all of the work derives its impetus from literature.

It is significant that not all of the writing in this section takes literature as its starting point and even more significant that not all of the writing is the critical, analytic, expository, or argumentative breed before which English teachers have been bowing and scraping for the past 10 years or more. Among the most exciting happenings in the field of English is the assault on the exclusive reign of the expository theme. It is no longer the only kind of writing that commands our genuflections. Resourceful teachers are rediscovering other kinds of writing and restoring them to a position of respectability in the English classroom, though this rediscovery of other kinds of writing is by no means a move back to vapid outpourings on "My Most Embarrassing Experience" or "A Day in the Life of a Maltreated Shoestring." We know now that even the freest of free writing needs the restraints of discipline.

The composition materials for this book came out of a full awareness that books are not the only stimulus to writing; that the critical, analytic, expository theme is not the only valid means by which a student may express his understanding of a piece of literature; and that the creative, original, imaginative response that uses literature as its springboard has a validity of its own that merits attention and respect.

Some of the materials here deliberately move away from books to explore the possibilities for composition in photographs, paintings, cartoons, and architecture. In all these units, however, the emphasis is on the relationship between the writer and his audience; on the degree to which the writer's apparent purpose seems to have dictated those choices that are the essence of the writing process; and on the adaptation of tone and voice to purpose, audience, and material. These are not new concepts, but they are a far cry from the conventional text on composition with its absorption in topic sentences, outlines, and paragraphs developed by definition, example, or analogy—all based on the unreliable assumption that a writer knows precisely what he is going to say before he says it. The materials here are concerned rather with writing as an exercise of choice, a strategy, an art, a fusion of the dual processes of seeing and making someone else see what you have seen.

*Attitude and Purpose in Writing*
*Grades 10 and 11*

sary, defend the way he has ordered his descriptions.)

Write two descriptions of a single stationary object located out of doors (a building, statue, tree, lamppost, gate, or fountain, for instance): the first should be a description of the object as it appears in one kind of weather or at one time of day; the second a description as it appears in quite different weather or at a different time of day. Write the first draft of each description while you are observing the object.

Suggestions:

1. Describe only what you see.

2. Indicate the time of day or the weather by statement or by details.

3. Do not write about so large an area as a woods, garden, or beach; keep to a single object.

4. Use detail to individualize your description.

*To the teacher.* On the day the papers are due, have students write in class and attach to their two descriptions the answers to the following questions:

1. Are the differences between your two descriptions in any way a result of a difference in your feeling about the object at the two different times?

2. Are they in any way the result of a difference in purpose?

3. Were your feeling and purpose in each case related?

## Comparison of Two Photographs of Canterbury Cathedral

*Questions for discussion of the color photograph of Canterbury Cathedral.* The aim of the discussion is to explore the possibility that the photographer's choices in making the picture indicate an intent to romanticize the cathedral; and that if such was his intent, it must have governed certain of his choices. The teacher should be sure students understand the place of Canterbury Cathedral in English history and literature. If time permits, students might read either *Becket*, by Anouilh, or *Murder in the Cathedral*, by T. S. Eliot.

1. What choices did the photographer make in planning this picture of Canterbury Cathedral? What were his alternatives? (His most significant choices —color film; a distant point of view that shows the south side and the west end of the building; a slightly blurred focus for the cathedral; obscurity of foreground; sweep of background; evening as the time of day.)

2. Why might the photographer have made each of these choices? (Whatever other answers are given, here are some matters that must be considered:

The distant viewpoint—possibly to show the cathedral's importance in a large area of landscape and to suggest thereby its importance in England's history and religious life. Perhaps also to suggest our historical distance from its days of greatest glory.

The blurred focus for the cathedral—possibly to suggest once sharp lines blurred by time; possibly also to emphasize our physical and symbolic distance from the cathedral.

The blurred foreground—possibly to prevent the foreground's becoming more important than the blurred cathedral. Possibly also to contrast its darkness with the rosy light on the cathedral.

The sweep of pearly sky instead of a clear blue or dark overcast—perhaps to provide color contrast for the cathedral. Perhaps also to romanticize the scene by adding "prettiness." Perhaps also to suggest by the vast sweep of sky the vast sweep of time with the cathedral set against it, a symbol of spiritual power in its age and of spiritual endurance.

Evening as the time of day—the light on the cathedral strikes the main entrance, which, as in most cathedrals, faces west. The time of day, then, is close to sunset. Possibly to give the building a romantic rosy glow from the sunset light. Possibly also to suggest that the cathedral's greatest glory is past, that it is a relic standing in the glow of its ancient splendor.

Color film rather than black-and-white—possibly to strengthen the romantic quality of the picture. Without color, the glow of sunset, the pearly quality of the clouds, and all they suggest would be missing.)

3. What do the choices suggest about the photographer's purpose? His attitude toward the cathedral?

*Questions for discussion of the black-and-white photograph of Canterbury Cathedral.* The aim is to explore the possibility that the photographer in this picture may have wished to show Canterbury Cathedral as dominating the landscape; and that his attitude toward the building may be admiration for its size and strength. It is also to suggest that the two photographs differ because the photographers' atti-

# *Attitude and Purpose in Writing Grades 10 and 11*

*Approximate Time:* 2½ to 3 weeks

## To the Teacher

The student needs to be aware of the choices he makes as he writes. He needs to be aware also that many of these choices will derive from his attitude toward his subject and his purpose in writing. In class discussion the importance of attitude and purpose is easily obscured by necessary work on choices stemming from them—choices of content, sentence structure, or diction. Approaching the problem through a medium other than literature can demonstrate attitude and purpose more clearly as governing factors in an artistic creation. Continuing this emphasis on attitude and purpose in later discussions of literature will then have more meaning for students. This unit, therefore, starts with nonliterary materials, which are supplied in the envelope in the back of the book. It contains the color and black-and-white photographs of Canterbury Cathedral, "The Fourteenth of July at Le Havre" and "The Adoration of the Magi," and photographs of the Strozzi Palace and the *Petit Trianon*.

## Introduction through Visual Materials

### Writing Assignment One

(This assignment is to be given about a week before the opening of the unit and is to be due the day following the completion of this "Introduction through Visual Materials." If students have had no training in writing descriptions, a day or so should be devoted to possible ways of ordering description. Using a chair, desk, or other classroom object as model for a practice description, ask students to discuss possible patterns of organization—from top to bottom, left to right, least important to most important, shape, color, material, and so on—each student trying in his writing the order that he prefers. After writing such a description, students might exchange papers for comment on effectiveness of organization, with, if time permits, class reading of some papers and opportunity for each writer to explain and, if neces-

tudes toward the subject, as nearly as we can determine them, differ, as do their apparent purposes. The responses indicated below are again matters that must be considered by the students, whatever other answers are given.

1. Find the chief similarities and differences in the two photographs. (Similarities—the subject; the approximate point from which the building was photographed; the clouded sky as background; the trees as foreground. Differences in the black-and-white picture—the black-and-white film, which makes the building seem less ethereal and brings out its strong lines more sharply; the time of day, which, from the shadows, would seem to be late morning; its sharpness of focus, the billowing lines of clearly defined trees in the foreground contrasting, like the clouds, with the strong vertical and horizontal lines of the building, giving an impression of the cathedral's strength, in contrast to the impression of fragility and age given by the first picture.)

2. What do you think might be the photographer's purpose in the black-and-white picture? Why do you think so? (The distant view establishes the dominance of the cathedral in the landscape, as does the point of view, which reveals the great length of the building. The clouds in their contrasting softness emphasize the firm, strong lines of the cathedral. The purpose would seem to be to show the cathedral as dominating the landscape.)

3. Is each photographer's attitude toward the cathedral (as far as you can tell) related to the purpose the picture suggests?

## Alternate Comparison of Two Photographs of Canterbury Cathedral

Some readers feel that the questions and suggested answers to the original plan, above, run the risk of ascribing purposes to the photographers that would be difficult to justify. Other answers for the questions are conceivable that would lead to conclusions other than those assumed. At the same time, an exercise in perceiving differences between two photographs of the same building and in seeking to relate these differences to a possible purpose appears to be valuable—hence, a somewhat different assignment is presented.

The teacher should be sure that students underst nd something about the place of Canterbury Cathedral in English history and literature. Some references: St. Augustine, Chaucer, Anouilh's *Becket,* T. S. Eliot's *Murder in the Cathedral,* the *Encyclopedia Britannica.*

The aim of this plan is to perceive the differences in the two pictures of the same building and then to relate those differences that appear significant to a possible purpose of the photographers.

*Questions for discussion.*

1. In two columns (one headed Color, the other Black-and-White) list on the board the differences students can detect. The most obvious, of course, is color. Others may include: treatment of the foreground, of the sky; sharpness and clarity of detail, foreground, clouds, the cathedral itself; time of day when the pictures were taken (the shadows help if the students are told that the main entrance faces west); degree to which other buildings appear or are recognizable; approximate distance from the camera (about the same); presence of scaffolding on the tower of the black-and-white photo; time of year (some evidence of changing color of foliage in the color photo); ways in which the cathedral is made the dominant feature of each photograph.

2. We cannot be sure what the photographers had as main purposes. Here are some possible ones, to be listed also on the board. As they are listed, discuss with the class which picture seems more appropriate for a given purpose, and why; but leave *four* of these purposes not discussed in class.

(a) As an illustration for a guidebook.

(b) As an illustration for a history of Canterbury, town or cathedral.

(c) As an illustration for a treatise on Gothic architecture.

(d) As an illustration for a comparative study of English cathedrals.

(e) As an illustration for a page of an ecclesiastical calendar.

(f) In support of a drive for funds to maintain the cathedral.

(g) As a souvenir of a tourist who first saw the cathedral from this angle—and took the picture.

(h) As the request of a newly appointed Archbishop of Canterbury who wanted a picture of his cathedral in his study.

### Alternate Writing Assignment

Write a paragraph in which you assume that *one of the four purposes not discussed in class* was the actual purpose for taking either the color or black-and-white picture of Canterbury Cathedral, and in which you show how some of the features of this picture that you noted in class are appropriate to the "actual purpose."

### Comparison of "The Fourteenth of July at Le Havre," by Dufy, and "The Adoration of the Magi," by Fra Angelico and Fra Filippo Lippi

The aim of the discussion is to demonstrate that a painter's purpose affects his choices in a painting. Each of the pictures presents a street on a festive occasion. "The Fourteenth of July" shows a French street of the early twentieth century on a national holiday; "The Adoration of the Magi" shows a street supposedly at the time of the birth of Christ, actually at the time of the Italian Renaissance: in the one picture we see patriotic celebration and in the other religious celebration.

1. What are the differences between the painters' treatment of faces?

2. Are these differences related to the painters' differing purposes, as well as you can determine these purposes?

(Dufy seems chiefly concerned with saying, "A street full of flags is a gay sight." The faces are featureless, possibly to avoid weakening this gay observation.

The painters of "The Adoration of the Magi" seem to be saying that the birth of Christ is an event evoking joy, astonishment, adoration; the various expressions in the picture convey such feelings. The great number of people suggests the universality of the rejoicing; the individuality and detail of the expressions may result from the Renaissance emphasis on man.)

*Note to the teacher.* The Committee does not mean to imply that these two pictures are not comparable in other ways.

### Comparison of Two Buildings Designed for Different Purposes (Optional)

The aim is to demonstrate that an architect's purpose governs his choices in designing a building.

1. The Strozzi Palace was built to be both fortress and palace. What characteristics of its design indicate each of its intended uses? (Its use as a palace is indicated by its elegance, size, air of authority. Its use as a fortress is indicated by its massiveness, the thickness of the walls—suggested even in an exterior view—its strong, austere lines, the smallness of the windows in proportion to the rest of the building.)

2. The *Petit Trianon* was designed as a residence for Madame du Barry of the court of Louis XV of France. What characteristics indicate the difference in its purpose from that of the Strozzi Palace? (Instead of the strong lines of the Strozzi Palace, the *Petit Trianon* has elegance of a gentler sort. Its balustrade and its pilasters with Corinthian tops have a feminine look. Tall windows fill most of the facade, giving the building an open, residential appearance, unlike the closed look of the Strozzi. And the Strozzi fills its property, opening directly onto the street; the *Petit Trianon* opens onto a lawn and gardens.)

### Writing Assignment Two

(This assignment should be given about a week before the discussion of two pieces of writing on the same subject by the same author begins; the assignment should be due the day that discussion opens.)

Examine two Monet paintings of the same subject (the cathedral at Rouen, water lilies, a haystack, for instance). Write a paper supporting your judgment as to whether Monet has a different purpose in each of the two paintings.

(*Suggestion to the teacher.* You might read these papers without grading them, noting any serious or frequent problems to be discussed with the class before the next composition assignment.)

## Students' Descriptions of Their Own Classroom

The aim is to demonstrate that the author's purpose and attitude toward his subject, like the photographer's and artist's, determine his choices—such as his selection and treatment of detail, his sentence structure, imagery, diction. It is to demonstrate as well that an author's choices create his speaker: the side of himself he reveals or the personality he creates in a particular work.

## Writing Assignment Three

In 10 to 15 minutes write a brief description of your classroom.

(*To the teacher.* Hold these papers until after the class has discussed the sample descriptions printed below. Then, pass out copies of the descriptions your class wrote. Ask your students to see whether details, diction, and the structure and length of sentences in their papers seem to be related to the author's apparent purpose and attitude.)

## Sample Descriptions

These are excerpts from papers written in a class in about 15 minutes. Copies of the seven excerpts should be distributed to the class so that they can consider the questions that follow them.

A

Room 110 is like any other classroom in the school. It has four walls, a door, and four windows. Its lights are suspended from the ceiling. Its public address speaker is located at the front of the room so that each student can hear plainly what is being said. At the front of the room also is the teacher's desk and cabinet; filling the room from there to the back are thirty-five chairs. At one side, next to the windows, are the radiator and air vent. The radiator manages to crank irritatingly at times, while the air vent normally blows out cold air in cold weather and warm air in warm weather. On the north and east walls of the room are the blackboards.

B

Room 110 is bleak and ugly. Designed only for efficiency and without an eye for aesthetics, it is harsh in its planes, without relief, and cold. Flat blackboards stop against a plain wall; a crazy, uninteresting, and unhappily colored green and red floor clashes with pink walls and a red bulletin board. The desks poke out their angles unpleasantly against the cold look of window panes and glass-paneled book cupboards. The ceiling is hung with lights whose vulgar attempts at design war with the tone of efficiency that otherwise prevails.

C

Heat waves rise from the register in front of the window, and the pane then seems of old blown glass, for the outer world wavers and the lines of the bricks in the wall across the way seem sometimes not to come together. But we are inside, and the red and green tiles (pleasing colors, not harsh) meet square, parallel, and neatly checkered. The yellow-brown of desks and chairs is not discordant with the yellowed pink of the walls, and the books in the cupboards I do not find depressing, even the old faded ones.

D

This room to me has meaning. The hours spent here have taught me many things—the meaning of a poem, of a speech, of an author, even of a word. The paperbacked books tossed on top of our others, carefully folded papers protruding from notebooks, these are symbols of the meaning this room has for me. I can't put it into words exactly, but it is the confidence I have that I didn't have three years ago, the bold stroke of a pen, the understanding of a poem.

E

This room is a rectangular parallelepiped. It has, therefore, six planar surfaces: a ceiling, a floor, and four walls—two pairs of walls, each pair a different length. The front wall is a solid, plastered, pinkly painted surface adorned with objects varying from fire drill signs to symbols of American patriotism to cryptic messages like "Do not open" neatly penciled on drawers of cabinets. In this same planar area hang a pencil sharpener, a calendar, reports of various Student Congress meetings, and a wall telephone. The most dominant element of the front wall is the three-paneled blackboard.

F

Room 110 is not conducive to bright, fresh ideas because it is so drab and dingy. No object in the room has a color one could term bright. The ceiling is white, the absence of all color. The walls are a putrid pink. The blackboards are not a vivid black but a chalk-beaten charcoal. The linoleum is composed of monotonous blocks of tomato-paste red and dirty aqua blue. The filing cabinet is a dark olive green. The one spot of color in the room—the gaily covered paperbacks in the cupboard—are obscured by dust-collecting window glass.

G

The ceiling is twice my height and the walls stand apart to give ideas room to soar—Thoreau-like. A four-windowed wall lets the rolling dipsy doodle outside world into our room. We don't mind the windows because the wind whistles around them sometimes and snips at the panes.

Room 110 is my haven;
I shall not be insecure.
It leadeth me in the paths of contemplation;
It giveth me art.
I set up a desk before me
In the presence of my friends.
Thy pink and thy black,
They comfort me.
My eyes are opened
To the complexities of yonder hill.
Surely goodness and tranquillity
Shall follow me all my English periods,
And I shall dwell in 110 forever.

## Questions for Discussion of the Seven Descriptions

I. *Questions on choice of detail.*

1. Which of the seven papers indicate similar purposes? Do you see a relationship between the indicated purpose of each paper and the author's attitude toward the room?

(B and F suggest the room's unattractiveness; D and G present personal, generalized reactions to experiences enjoyed in the room rather than a reaction to physical elements; A and E are both objective; C stands alone in approving the room's appearance.)

2. You say B and F both show the room as unattractive. Two of the same details they use are the monotony of the floor pattern and the unattractive color combination of the floor. Might some slight difference in purpose between B and F account for the difference in the details presented in each?

(B's terms suggest a dehumanized efficiency; F seems concerned with color problems—"drab and dingy.")

Apply your answer to their differing treatments of the blackboard and the glass panels of the cupboards in the room.

3. B and E both use some geometrical terms to describe the room. What is the difference in their use of them? How do you account for the difference?

(B's aim, seemingly to convey dehumanized efficiency, is accomplished partly through the cold abstraction of geometrical terms; E's aim, seemingly to present the room unemotionally, is aided by the impersonality of such terms.)

II. *Questions on diction and imagery.*

1. Why do you think C says "yellowed pink," F "putrid pink" (note the disapproval added to the tone by the alliterative p's), and B only "plain wall" and "pink walls"? What other words than "putrid" might have been used in F? Why might the author have rejected them?

2. What difference in attitude and purpose might have caused the author of G to use "whistles" and "snips at the panes" to describe the movement of air and the author of A to use "blows out"? How would either effect have changed with a different choice of words?

3. (Optional.) Find other examples of differences in diction that seem to result from differences in attitude and purpose.

(B's "glass-paneled book cupboards" vs. F's "dust-collecting window glass"; the description of the lights in A and B; the description of the blackboards in B, E, and F; the description of the cabinets in A and F.)

4. Why might A have chosen colorless verbs?

(To suggest his opinion that the room is uninteresting.)

5. (Optional.) What difference in purpose might have made the author of G say, "I shall not be insecure" and the author of D, "the confidence I have"? How does the phrase "bold stroke of a pen" serve the apparent purpose of D? What does it suggest about the writer?

III. *Questions on sentence structure.*

1. In what way does the structure of the sentences in A seem related to the purpose and attitude the author indicates? Does the length of the sentences seem also related to these matters?

(Sentences 2, 3, and 4 open with forms of "it"; sentences 3 and 4 repeat "its" as a modifier of the subject, and both follow the subject with a passive verb. Sentences 5 and 6 use the same preposition, "at," as the opening of an introductory phrase, with the subject and verb of the clause inverted. These repetitions emphasize the monotony of the scene and, perhaps, the indifferent attitude of the writer.

As for length, the abruptness of sentences 1, 2, and 3 and their lack of development suggest boredom in the speaker.)

2. Which other descriptions use a series of short sentences, seemingly as a step toward achieving a purpose? What purpose in each case? (F, G.)

IV. *Questions on characteristics of the various speakers.*

1. Do D and G suggest the same kind of person addressing the reader?

[Consider in G the vividness of phrasing: "dipsy doodle outside world," the use of "our" ("our room"), and "we" ("We don't mind"); the reference to friends; the enjoyment of abstract thinking, evident in the reference to ideas that need "room to soar"; the sense of humor, evident in the parody.

Consider in D the admitted earlier insecurity and the enjoyment of accomplishment.]

2. The personality you can identify as addressing you through a piece of writing is called the speaker (or *persona*). It is the side of himself that the author is revealing or a personality that he develops to speak for him.

Characterize the speakers of A, C, and F, noting especially what details, diction, and structure and length of sentences contribute to the personality of each.

## Comparison of Two Pieces of Writing on the Same Subject by the Same Author

The aim is to show that the same author treating the same subject in two different pieces of writing will, if his purpose in each is different and if he is addressing a different audience, create for each a different speaker.

A

Two or three days and nights went by; I reckon I might say they swum by, they slid along so quiet and smooth and lovely. Here is the way we put in the time. It was a monstrous big river down there—sometimes a mile and half wide; we run nights, and laid up and hid daytimes; soon as night was most gone we stopped navigating and tied up—nearly always in the dead water under a towhead; and then cut young cottonwoods and willows, and hid the raft with them. Then we set out the lines. Next we slid into the river and had a swim, so as to freshen up and cool off; then we set down on the sandy bottom where the water was about knee-deep, and watched the daylight come. Not a sound anywheres—perfectly still—just like the whole world was asleep, only sometimes the bullfrogs a-cluttering, maybe. The first thing to see, looking away over the water, was a kind of dull line—that was the woods on t'other side; you couldn't make nothing else out; then a pale place in the sky; then more paleness spreading around; then the river softened up away off, and warn't black any more, but gray; you could see little dark spots drifting along ever so far away—trading-scows, and such things; and long black streaks—rafts; sometimes you could hear a sweep screaking; or jumbled-up voices, it was so still, and sounds come so far; and by and by you could see a streak on the water which you know by the look of the streak that there's a snag there in a swift current which breaks on it and makes that streak look that way; and you see the mist curl up off of the water and the east reddens up, and the river, and you make out a log cabin in the edge of the woods, aways on the bank on t'other side of the river, being a woodyard, likely, and piled by them cheats so you can throw a dog through it anywheres; then the nice breeze springs up, and comes fanning you from over there, so cool and fresh and sweet to smell on account of the woods and the flowers; but sometimes not that way, because they've left dead fish laying around, gars and such, and they do get pretty rank; and next you've got the full day, and everything smiling in the sun, and the song-birds just going it!

—Mark Twain, *Huckleberry Finn*

B

I still keep in mind a certain wonderful sunset which I witnessed when steamboating was new to me. A broad expanse of the river was turned to blood; in the middle distance the red hue brightened into gold, through which a solitary log came floating, black and conspicuous; in one place a long, slanting mark lay sparkling upon the water; in another the surface was broken by boiling, tumbling rings, that were as many-tinted as an opal; where the ruddy flush was faintest, was a smooth spot that was covered with graceful circles and radiating lines, ever so delicately traced; the shore on our left was densely wooded, and the somber shadow that fell from this forest was broken in one place by a long, ruffled trail that shone like silver and high above the forest wall a clean-stemmed dead tree waved a single leafy bough that glowed like a flame in the unobstructed splendor that was flowing from the sun. There were graceful curves, reflected images, woody heights, soft distances; and over the whole scene, far and near, the dissolving lights drifted steadily, enriching it, every passing moment, with new marvels of coloring.

—Mark Twain, *Life on the Mississippi*

Questions for Discussion of an Excerpt
from *Huckleberry Finn*

1. What kind of person do you think the speaker in the excerpt is? If you know the book, how much of his personality do you find Huck reveals here?

(*To the teacher:* Try to keep students to the speaker of *this* passage and away from what they may have read or heard of Huck elsewhere.)

2. What is the relationship between Huck and the author?

(Huck is the speaker created by the author to narrate the story.)

3. What does Huck's level of usage tell you about him? (For instance, "swum," "anywheres," "on t'other side," "them cheats.")

4. What does his sentence structure tell you about him? (For instance, in the sentence "Not a sound anywheres . . . bullfrogs a-cluttering, maybe"; and in the use of "and" from line 30 on.)

(Huck's sentence structure in the quoted passage indicates that he is a simple, unpretentious person.)

How does the construction of the clause "by and by you could see a streak . . . makes that streak look that way" (lines 26–30) resemble the snag the clause describes?

5. What diction besides substandard usage characterizes Huck?

(The rural or Southern "I reckon"; "jumbled-up voices"—boy talk; "a monstrous big river," "little dark spots drifting along," and "the song-birds just going it"—colloquial phrasing.)

6. What details characterize him?

(a. He knows the river: "tied up—nearly always in the dead water under a towhead," lines 7 and 8.

b. He is a person of integrity; he is indignant at "them cheats" who pile the wood so loosely "you can throw a dog through it anywheres," lines 34–35.

c. He enjoys nature: he is sensitive to all the details of the sunrise and to experiences other than sight as well—to cooling off in the water and sitting on the sandy bottom; to the croaking of frogs and the cheerfulness of bird-song; to the fragrance of woods and flowers.)

7. How would you describe Huck's voice in this paragraph? Is it related to the purpose of the paragraph as far as you can discern the purpose?

Questions for Discussion of an Excerpt
from *Life on the Mississippi*

The aim is to show that the author's purpose is very likely not only to describe a sunset but also to please, perhaps even to impress, his *Atlantic Monthly* audience.[1] It is to show the speaker as therefore more pretentious than Huck in diction, imagery, and sentence structure.

1. In this passage, the same author, Mark Twain, is presenting nearly the same subject—this time at sunset.

How much does the first sentence tell you about the speaker?

(It indicates a distance in time from the experi-

---

1. Leonard Kriegel, "Afterword," in Mark Twain's *Life on the Mississippi,* New American Library, 1961, page 377: "Most of Part 1, Chapters IV through XVII, had originally been published as a series of sketches in 1875 in the *Atlantic Monthly* under the title of 'Old Times on the Mississippi.' "

ence. While Huck seems young and very close to both the experience and the audience, the speaker in *Life* seems older, less involved in the experience, and, by his formality, more removed from his audience. Note "I still keep in mind" and "witnessed.")

2. What characteristics of the speaker's language in the rest of the passage reveal him as different from Huck?

(This speaker is more literate and literary, pretentious and sophisticated, as demonstrated in his diction, imagery, and sentence structure.

His diction tends toward the latinate: "unobstructed splendor," "dissolving," "reflected images," "conspicuous," "radiating," as opposed to Huck's "they swum by," "they slid along," and "you see the mist curl up off the water."

To identify the diction, students should be able to understand at least the latinate etymologies in a dictionary. If they can not, a lesson in the roots, prefixes, and suffixes of English words might well precede this discussion and should show latinate diction as likely to be more formal and to characterize the more highly educated speaker.

This speaker's phrasing is more formal in other ways: "witnessed," "a solitary log," "boiling, tumbling rings," "graceful circles and radiating lines," "somber shadow," "the unobstructed splendor that was flowing from the sun," "graceful curves, . . . woody heights, soft distances," "the dissolving lights drifted steadily, enriching it, every passing moment, with new marvels of coloring."

While the speaker in *Life* says "A broad expanse of the river," Huck says "a monstrous big river"; while the speaker in *Life* notes "the forest wall" and says "the shore on our left was densely wooded," Huck says "that was the woods on t'other side"; *Life*'s speaker says "A broad expanse of the river was turned to blood," but Huck, "the east reddens up." *Life*'s speaker says "in the middle distance," but Huck, "aways on the bank on t'other side of the river."

In *Life* the imagery comes often from an experience beyond Huck's: "many-tinted as an opal," "shone like silver"; Huck's imagery is from the simple life: the smell of rank gars, the bullfrog's croaking, throwing a dog through the spaces in a woodpile, "everything smiling in the sun."

Note in the passage from *Life* the number of terms suggestive of art criticism: "middle distance," "many-tinted," "radiating lines," "traced," "graceful curves," "reflected images," "soft distances," "dissolving lights," "coloring"—indicating an educated speaker.

In *Life* the sentences are characterized by more formal constructions than Huck's. Students may reach this understanding best by answering these questions:

a. Which excerpt makes the greater use of adjective clauses?

b. Which excerpt more frequently places sentence elements before the subject?

c. Which excerpt uses more passive verbs?

d. In both passages, Mark Twain uses the same device, the long sentence with its parts marked off by semicolons. How does the structure of sentence parts differ in the two long sentences?

In the long sentence from *Life,* each part is a complete independent clause, relating the ideas of the sentence more closely and giving the whole a formal tightness. The long sentence from *Huckleberry Finn* consists of fragments as well as clauses, the whole loosely stitched together by "and's.")

3. What have you learned from these two passages about the effect of an author's audience on the choices in his writing?

4. Why do you think you were asked to write about two paintings by the same painter and on the same subject just before your discussion of these two paragraphs?

## Writing Assignment Four

Using a piece of your own writing, preferably one written at least a month ago, write an analysis of your "speaker":

1. State the purpose of the writing.

2. Show that choice of details, diction, imagery, sentence structure, and length of sentences are related to your purpose. (If at any point they are not, indicate the changes you would make and your reasons for making them.)

3. Show what kind of speaker these choices created.

4. Show the relationship of the speaker to the purpose.

## Comparative Analysis of Two Essays

The aim is to show by comparative analysis of two complete works on the same subject the role of purpose in determining an author's choices.

### *The Silver Horn*

Thomas Sancton

The scene is a Boy Scout summer camp, thickly grown with pines and cypress. There is a row of green clapboard cabins, with clean floors and neat double-decker bunks; there is an open field and a flag hanging still in the heavy air; and at the field's edge the land drops down a little to the dark water of a bayou. I spent five summers here, from the time I was twelve until I entered college. I did my first real living and my first real thinking in this camp. 1

And I think of it now. Like some reader of a long novel who turns back through the pages to find a forgotten part of the plot, and who comes with a flash of recognition across old scenes and dialogues, and characters who have gone out of the narrative but whose personalities and substance once filled pages and pages, I have gone turning back through the pages of my life. When was it and where was it—I have been asking—that I first began to believe what I now believe about the Southern world I left not many years ago, about Negroes, about democracy, about America, about life and death, about men and all their curious fates? This search has been long and turning. Often it has led me back to the years of my early teens and to the summers I spent in the camp. 2

I was born to the sidewalks and asphalt of the largest city and the widest street in the South. In New Orleans, broad Canal Street was never empty of speeding automobiles and streetcars, even late at night, and of people walking by, their footsteps echoing on the sidewalk. But here on the bayou another world existed. In the morning it was the strange, thin call of a bugle that broke into our sleep. Almost before we were awake we could smell the wet exercise field and the forest. Birds popped from tree to tree, plump and colorful, bluejays, mockingbirds, cardinals, flickers—Audubon had painted in these woods. Rabbits ran into the bushes. Snakes we had no fear of, long thick blue racers and speckled king snakes, slid through the weeds at our approach. 3

Standing in the wet grass, still yawning and sleepy, we took the morning exercises. Night chill was in the air, but behind our backs the sun was rising, and its warmth crept onto our shoulders. After the exercises we raced along a wagon road to the swimming pool, and as we ran up, shouting and excited, two or three startled frogs made tremendous leaps and plumped beneath the glassy surface of the water. After the swim we dried our skinny sunburned bodies and ran to the mess hall.

Most of us in the camp were poor boys, or boys who were almost poor. It was not a welfare camp, but the fees were low, less than a dollar a day for a camper. As a consequence it was filled with boys from modest New Orleans neighborhoods and also from the tough ones. There was always a smattering of the democratic rich: the son of the traction company president came every summer. So did his cousin from Texas, a wild, hard towhead with plenty of money and the soul of a true picaroon. He fascinated and dominated the rest of us. He was the first colorful outlaw I ever knew. But most of the well-to-do families sent their boys to camps in the Maine woods or the North Carolina mountains. Our camp was only forty miles from the city. Department store clerks, streetcar motormen, little grocers could afford the fees.

We had no saddle horses, no golf course, and only a weed-grown tennis court which no one used. For diversion we fell back on nature. In the morning we performed a work detail, cutting a patch of weeds or hauling dirt in wheelbarrows to mend a road. After this we were free to swim, to paddle on the bayou in slender little Louisiana boats called pirogues, to fish for the boisterous black bass and yellow perch and fat blue catfish, and to work for our Boy Scout medals and merit badges, tracking through the grassy cut-over pine lands, cooking dough and bacon on sweet-gum spits, bandaging one another with first-aid splints.

These little medals and bits of colored ribbon 7

meant a great deal to us. We wrote home enthusiastic letters about our progress, describing in detail how we had passed the tests, forwarding the comments of some eighteen-year-old camp officer as though it really mattered. Our parents, most of whom did not have very big events happening in their own lives, were just as eager and simple-hearted about these things, and one or two of the fathers were foolishly ambitious to have their sons win the highest number of merit badges in the area.

Little things that happened during these years seemed of great importance. I remember that in my first year at camp I wore an ill-fitting Boy Scout hat. One of the councillors, a boy five years my senior who seemed to me to belong already to the grown-up world of brilliance and authority, began, in a pleasant way, to tease me about the hat. Every morning for a week he led us to the abandoned logging road and clocked us as we walked and trotted a measured mile. My hat was anchored down by a heavy chin strap; it flopped and sailed about my head as I ran to the finish line. The boy began to laugh at me. He waved his arms and called out, "Come on, you rookie!" The other kids took it up and Rookie became my first nickname. I loved it. I tingled when someone called it out. I painted it on my belt, carved it in my packing case, inked it into my hatband, and began to sign it to my letters home. Years later when we were grown I knew this camp officer again. The gap between our ages had vanished and in real life now he seemed to me a rather colorless young lawyer. He did not remember about the hat. 8

At mealtime we ate ravenously in the mess hall. There were steaming platters of pork and beans and cabbage and stew. As we walked to the long clapboard building with our hair freshly combed and water glistening on our faces, which we washed at the flowing pipe of a big artesian well, we existed in a transport of driving hunger. In the steamy fragrance of the mess hall we set up a clatter of knives and forks and china, and afterward we went to our cabins and flopped on the bunks in a state of drowsy satisfaction. Somehow, fat never formed on our skinny frames. We ran too much. We paddled in the boats. We swam. We cut firewood and played softball after supper. When there was nothing else to do we climbed in the rafters of our cabins, trying to invent complicated monkey swings that no one else could do. Every year some campers broke their arms. 9

## II

A giant Negro named Joe did the camp's heavy work. He cut and trimmed the big trees, dug the deep post holes, mixed the cement, cleaned out the underbrush. His strength was a never-ending fascination for the rest of us. Joe was a light-eyed Negro, with a tan cast of skin and a huge bald dome of a head. One of his grandparents must certainly have been a white man. He lived half a mile down the bayou with his large and hazily defined family, in an old "plantation house." 10

Actually it was not, and never had been, a pretentious place, and I do not know what kind of plantation could have been there. The ground round it was alternately sandy and swampy and there are no plantations where pine trees grow. Pines mean sandy land. In slave days the Negroes had boiled Southern history down to a couplet: 11

Cain't make a living on sandy lan'—
Ruther be a nigger den a po' white man.

Joe's place stood on a cleared bend in the bayou. The weatherboards and shingles were green with age. The house rested on high slender pillars and there were patches of bright red brick where the covering mortar had fallen away. The yard was shaded by two enormous water oaks, hung with gray Spanish moss, and an iron kettle stood beneath the trees where women did the washing. At the bank of the bayou five or six towering cypress trees leaned heavily toward the water, for the slow currents of a century had washed their roots completely bare of soil. To get a new anchorage on the land the trees had sent out a forest of gnarled roots and stubby knees along the shoreline. The house seemed beautiful and somber in these surroundings as we paddled past it on our expeditions down the bayou to the lake. 12

Obviously a white man had built this place long ago, and if he had not been a plantation owner, he had at least been a man of substance. Perhaps this had been the summer home for some wealthy old New Orleans Frenchman in years gone by. Sometimes the camp officers spoke of Joe as "caretaker" on the place. 13

But that was hardly possible. He and his family inhabited every room; chickens roamed freely, and washing hung on lines stretched across the wide porch. It was clear to us that the Negro giant was no caretaker here. He possessed this place, to have and to hold. How he got it and why we never asked him; and his presence there did not seem a very curious thing to us. Already a dark, subjective understanding of Louisiana's history was in our blood and bones.

14 Joe smoked strong cigarettes and chewed tobacco. His teeth were rotted stumps. We delighted in bringing him supplies of smokes from the nearby town on Saturdays to win his quick and genuine appreciation. There were two or three measures of a Cajun French ditty he used to sing, dancing and stomping the ground, waving his hat and swaying his heavy shoulders with real grace. The words and the stomping finished together, with two hard accents. He would do this every time in exchange for a gift. Yet he did it in such a way that we knew always that this was nothing more than a grown-up man doing monkeyshines for children. He enjoyed making us laugh. There was nothing servile about it.

15 He got to be one of the people I liked best of all—not only in the camp but in my whole circumscribed world. I liked Joe very simply because he was a nice man. He recognized me every year when I returned to the camp, and after the second or third year I could tell that he considered me a real friend and was glad to have me back. We talked together often, equally and easily, and when I was sixteen and seventeen and by then a councillor in the camp, Joe would do me the honor of becoming quite serious with me and of placing our whole friendship on a mature plane. I do not remember many of the things we talked about, but I do remember that a conversation with him was a reassurance and a satisfaction; that it was always good to find him walking on the road and to fall in with him.

16 I saw a brief notice in the paper, some years after I had stopped going to the camp, that Joe had died of blood poisoning in the New Orleans Charity Hospital. I thought of those stumps of teeth, and of the many years they had been seeping infection into his system. I thought also of the tall trees I had seen him fell, and that now Joe too had come toppling to the earth. And, though I felt a quiet sorrow, I felt no anguish. Life grew rank and lush along the bayou. His old house was teeming with the spawn of his years. The sun would beat upon the water forever, the trout would break the surface, the rushes would grow thick and green. Joe had done his share of hauling and of digging. Now he could lie down in the warm and sun-drenched earth and sleep.

## III

During those summers in camp a love grew up in me for the rhythms of nature, for tropical rains that came sweeping through the pines and oaks, for the fiery midday sun, for long evenings, and the deep black nights. Great campfires were lit beside the bayou and a rushing column of luminous smoke and sparks ascended to the cypress trees. Fire gleamed in the water where bass were sleeping in the stumps. Campers wandered toward the meeting place, their flashlights swinging in the woods. We sat about the fire, singing, beating deep rumbling tom-toms made of hollowed oak logs, performing an ageless repertoire of skits and mimicry. And after these sessions one leader took the Protestant boys and another the Catholics and, standing in the open fields, in our separate groups, we prayed aloud.

My heart had strayed already from the formal, repetitious praying. A towering pine tree at the field's edge made a silhouette in the starry sky. I knew the constellations, the Giant, the Dipper, the Bear. I looked for the two inseparable stars, Misar and Alcar, horse and rider, and sensed the fact that Arabs named these stars a thousand years before me, and even in my boy's ignorance I felt aware of man's long and varied time upon the earth. I knew this night-filled wilderness had stretched beneath these stars for endless ages before Frenchmen had come in boats to build New Orleans. I thought of the Indians who had fished and hunted here, whose bones and broken pottery we sometimes found in grassy mounds. I felt worshipful of the earth, the pine tree, the night itself.

Sometimes we packed provisions and tents and mosquito bars and paddled down the bayou to the lake, ten miles away. The lake was a great inland finger of the Gulf of Mexico, twenty miles long, ten wide. Twenty miles below us, in prehistoric times, the mouth of the Mississippi river had built up new land, and these watery prairies had pinched off the small inland gulf and made a lake of it, but it connected still through a series of passes with the Mexican Gulf. The lake teemed with croakers, catfish, shrimp, and big blue-clawed crabs. At the northern end, where we camped, a network of tributary bayous emptied into the lake. For the last mile or so of their crooked lengths, where the brackish water of the lake crept into the slow-moving bayous, fish and small life were abundant, bass fed in the rushes, and muskrats built their cities of the plains.

20 There was a relatively high, sandy point near the mouth of the bayou, where we camped. The sun went down red into the lake and left a long, clear twilight. A few stars came out. A salty wind blew in from the Mexican Gulf; it came out of the south every night. The breeze swept over the rushes and made small waves break on the sandy, grassy shore. There was a red beacon light on weather-beaten piles out in the lake and its long reflection shimmered in the water. We sprayed our mosquito netting with citronella and built up a driftwood fire and lay down on canvas bedrolls spread upon the thin, tough grass and sand. The trade wind blew through our tents throughout the night. We listened to the waves. We could smell the vast salt marshes far below us. A yellow moon came out of the gulf. Far down the lake we could see the lights of a railroad bridge. We felt the beauty of this wilderness like a hunger.

21 After two days of fishing and swimming in the lake, our shoulders and faces darker from the sun, we paddled back up the winding bayou.

IV

22 One summer when I was sixteen a party of us, paddling upstream to buy some candy at a crossroads store, came upon three young girls who were bathing in a sandy cove. There were four of us in the long pirogue, all of an age. For a long moment we were speechless. At last we said hello, and they answered in warm gay voices. We drifted the boat into the cove and began to speak to them. Two of the girls were sisters. The three of them had come to visit a relative who kept a fine summer lodge in the woods across the bayou from the camp. One of the sisters was fifteen and the others were seventeen. They were aglow with fresh and slender beauty, and their bathing suits were bright flags of color. Their impact upon us was overwhelming. We grew silly, tongue-tied, said foolish things we did not mean to say, shoved one another about in the boat, and finally overturned it. The loreleis laughed musical little laughs. They seemed unbearably beautiful. We had no idea what to do about it.

23 The girls had been at the lodge for a week. They missed their beaux in New Orleans, they missed the dating and the dancing and the music. It was a gay town in the summertime. The older girls looked upon us as children; but still—they must have reflected—we were not such children at that. The younger sister, a slender child with thick brown hair and heavily crimsoned lips, sat on the bank and regarded us with a happy open face.

24 At last we took courage and asked if we could call on them that night.

25 "Oh, yes!" they cried eagerly. Life at that moment was dazzling.

26 Making this rendezvous was an impulsive thing to do, for it was midweek and we should have to steal away after taps and walk down a path without flashlights through a snake-infested lowland and—because the boats were counted and chained at nightfall—swim across the bayou, holding our clothes above our heads.

27 We crept from our cabins at ten o'clock that night and met in the pine woods. One of us intoned a counting-out rhyme; the loser had to walk first down the path through the snake hole. He cut a long gum sapling and rattled it down the path ahead of us. We walked bunched tightly together, tense with fear, giggling at our own unbelievable audacity, trembling in our eagerness. At the bayou's edge we slipped out of our shorts and shirts and sneakers and, holding them above our heads with one hand, we felt our way round the knees and along the sunken roots of a cypress tree, and pushed off into the bayou and began to swim.

28 The moon had not yet risen. We had only the silhouettes of trees to guide us. We swam closely together, cautioning one another to silence, bursting into convulsive squeals as water lilies brushed against our bodies or when a fish broke the surface near us. We swam upstream from the camp, past two bends,

and waded from the water in the cove where we had met the girls. Now we were laughing with relief and excitement, and popping one another on the backsides. We scraped the glistening water from our bodies, dressed, and combed our wet hair and hurried off down the wagon path into the woods. Long ago the cove had been a landing stage for small schooners which came to load pine firewood for New Orleans.

29 The girls were waiting for us, dressed in bright print cotton dresses and wearing hair ribbons. The soft light gave age and mystery to their youthful shoulders, to their slender bodies; and, like nameless night-blooming vines in the woods about us, they bore a splendid fragrance all their own, a fragrance of youth and cleanliness and fresh cosmetics. They were playing a phonograph on the wide porch of the lodge. This was the summer of Maurice Chevalier's great success in American movies. The little sister sang his song, rolling her eyes, turning out her soft pink lip:

> If ze night-ting gail
> Cood zing lak you . . . .

30 And she sang another:

> . . . you make me feel so grand
> I want to hand the world to you.
> You seem to understand
> Each foolish little dream I'm dreaming, scheme
> I'm scheming . . .

31 I was so in love with her I could hardly catch my breath. I was in love with the other sister, too, and with their friend. All of the boys were in love with all of the girls; the girls—so they said—had crushes on each of us. Our hearts were afire.

32 We walked hand in hand down the wagon trail to the cove and built a bonfire. We stretched out on blankets, laughing, singing. We sang the songs that people always sing by rivers and campfires, "There's a Long, Long Trail A-winding," "The Sweetheart of Sigma Chi," all the rest. We kissed the girls and they held fast to us. Before this night we had been only boys, holding hands with girls in movies, not quite sure why we pursued them and acted silly. Now, lying beneath the open sky, for the first time we understood the poignance and the beauty of the human heritage.

33 Every night for two weeks we came to see them. And when they told us good-by the last kiss was as much a discovery as the first, and we knew that love was a thing that could never grow old. After they had gone we would steal from our cabins to sit on the back porch of the camp hospital, on a hill, where we could see the bayou and the cove and the woods where we had found them; and we sat there talking late into the night, like daemon lovers in the ballads of old. I never passed the cove again, even years later when I would paddle down the bayou fishing, without remembering our meetings with a suddenly racing heart. First love is unforgettable.

## V

I had no lessons to do in those summer months of 3 camp life. There was plenty of time to think. I was living a communal life with other boys. Among us were embryonic bullies, scoundrels, cheats, promoters, Babbitts, Christers, and stuffed shirts; and there were also the boys of good heart, the unselfish, the humorous, the courageous, boys who were the salt of the earth, but who, often in their later lives, would be misled and preyed upon and set against one another by the sharp ones. One and all we lived together, ate together, slept together. Our personalities clashed, fermented, or formed amalgams. Sitting together at night in the lamplit cabins, with darkness and towering woods closing in upon us, we had our first grave talks about religion, about death, about sex. The future stretching before us was wide and fathomless. And all about us, in the grass, in the underbrush, in towering summer skies, we beheld the face of nature and the earth's wide harmonies as they had never been revealed in our city lives. At night we could stretch out upon the field, observe the stars, and grasp for the first time the fact that some were vastly deeper in space than others. In our star-study courses we heard phrases like "light years." It began to seep into the consciousness of many of us that a hundred years or the life of an individual had little meaning in the total universe; and from this point some of us began our first gropings after moral philosophy, gropings for a belief that could give the total universe a meaning in our own lives.

There was a bugler in our camp who was the first 3 consummate expert, in any field, that I had known.

He had no other talent but his music. He was a good-natured, chubby, curly-headed Italian boy, rather lazy, and when he was not back in the woods practicing his cornet he walked round with a dreamy look, as though our own handicrafts could not possibly be of interest to him.

Paolo had a silver trumpet and he preferred it to the bugle. He wanted to be a great musician. He would take his horn and music back into a pine clearing a quarter of a mile from the camp and all day long we could hear him practicing the runs. He blew the trumpet with a clear, sweet tone. We had supreme confidence as we stood at attention on the parade grounds and the flag came down the creaking flagpole pulley in the late afternoon sunlight, and Paolo stood alone, with everyone watching, and bugled. We were proud of him when visitors came. He had that ability of experts to create a sense of possessiveness in others. 36

It was at bedtime that Paolo gathered up into his clear, thin music all the ineffable hungering of our awakening lives. At ten o'clock he climbed a high ladder to a life-guard platform we had nailed into the branches of a tall cypress tree beside the bayou. Paolo lived for this moment and, with the whole camp silent and listening below him in the darkness, he blew taps with a soft and ghostly beauty all his own. Somehow the music spoke for us, uttered the thing we knew but had no words for, set up a wailing in the pine trees of the brevity and splendor of human life. Lying in our bunks in the darkness of the cabin, some of us fell into sleep; but some lay in silence thinking longer, alive to the night, and I was of these. 37

One night some ten years later I entered a smoke-filled tavern in another city where Paolo was playing in a band. By this time he had made a small reputation as a boy with a hot trumpet. I watched his now older face as he tore through the hot routines. He was tired. The silver horn made noise but, though I knew little about it, I could see that he was not a great jazz musician. 38

I did not go to see him any more. I wanted to remember Paolo before he had lost something, before any of us had lost it, a kind of innocence. I wanted to remember him in the land of our first discoveries, when he had climbed into a cypress tree to blow his horn, and there was a kind of Gothic night-drench in our lives. 39

## *A Loud Sneer For Our Feathered Friends*
## (We Go To A Girls' Camp And Don't Think Much Of It. Also About Birds)

Ruth McKenney

From childhood, my sister and I have had a well-grounded dislike for our friends the birds. We came to hate them when she was ten and I was eleven. We had been exiled by what we considered an unfeeling family to one of those loathsome girls' camps where Indian lore is rife and the management puts up neatly lettered signs reminding the clients to be Good Sports. From the moment Eileen and I arrived at dismal old Camp Hi-Wah, we were Bad Sports, and we liked it. 1

We refused to get out of bed when the bugle blew in the morning, we fought against scrubbing our teeth in public to music, we sneered when the flag was ceremoniously lowered at sunset, we avoided doing a good deed a day, we complained loudly about the food, which was terrible, and we bought some chalk once and wrote all over the Recreation Cabin, "We hate Camp Hi-Wah". It made a wonderful scandal, although we were immediately accused of the crime. All the other little campers *loved* dear old Camp Hi-Wah, which shows you what kind of people they were. 2

The first two weeks Eileen and I were at Camp Hi-Wah, we sat in our cabin grinding our teeth at our councillor and writing letters to distant relatives. These letters were, if I say so myself, real masterpieces of double dealing and heartless chicanery. In our childish and, we hoped, appealing scrawl, we explained to Great-Aunt Mary Farrel and Second Cousin Joe Murphy that we were having such fun at dear Camp Hi-Wah making Indian pocketbooks. 3

"We would simply L-O-V-E to make you a pocketbook, dear Aunt Mary", we wrote, "only the leather costs \$1 for a small pocketbook or \$1.67 for a large size pocketbook, which is much nicer because you can carry more things in it, and the rawhide you sew it up with, just exactly the way the Indians did, costs 40 cents more. We burn pictures on the leather but that 4 doesn't cost anything. If we O-N-L-Y had $1 or $1.67 and 40 cents for the rawhide, we could make you the S-W-E-L-L-E-S-T pocketbook."

As soon as we had enough orders for Indian pock- 5
etbooks with pictures burnt on them, we planned to abscond with the funds sent by our trusting relatives and run away to New York City, where, as we used to explain dramatically to our cabinmates, we intended to live a life of sin. After a few days, our exciting plans for our immediate future were bruited all over the camp, and admirers came from as far away as Cabin Minnehaha, which was way down at the end of Hiawatha Alley, just to hear us tell about New York and sin.

Fame had its price, however. One of the sweet little 6
girls who lived in our cabin turned out to be such a Good Citizen ("Camp Hi-Wah Girls Learn to Be Good Citizens") that she told our dreadful secret to our councillor. Our mail was impounded for weeks, and worst of all, we actually had to make several Indian pocketbooks with pictures burnt on them. My pictures were all supposed to be snakes, although they were pretty blurred. Eileen specialized in what she believed to be the likeness of a werewolf, but Cousin Joe who had generously ordered three pocketbooks, wrote a nice letter thanking Eileen for his pretty pocketbooks with the pretty pictures of Abraham Lincoln on them. We were terribly disgusted by the whole thing.

It was in this mood that we turned to birds. The 7
handicraft hour at Camp Hi-Wah, heralded by the ten-thirty A.M. bugle, competed for popularity with the bird walks at the same hour. You could, as Eileen had already somewhat precociously learned how to say, name your own poison. After three weeks of burning pictures on leather, we were ready for anything, even our feathered friends.

So one hot morning in July, the two McKenney 8
sisters, big and bad and fierce for their age, answered the bird-walk bugle call, leaving the Indian-pocketbook teacher to mourn her two most backward pupils. We were dressed, somewhat reluctantly, to be sure, in the required heavy stockings for poison ivy and brambles, and carried, each of us, in our dirty hands a copy of a guide to bird lore called *Bird Life for Children.*

*Bird Life for Children* was a volume that all the 9
Good Citizens in Camp Hi-Wah pretended to find engrossing. Eileen and I thought it was stupefyingly dull. Our favorite literary character at the time was Dumas' Marguerite de Valois, who took her decapitated lover's head home in a big handkerchief for old times' sake. Eileen, in those days, was always going to name her first girl child Marguerite de Valois.

*Bird Life for Children* was full of horrid pictures 10
in full color of robins and pigeons and redbirds. Under each picture was a loathsomely whimsical paragraph describing how the bird in question spent his spare time, what he ate, and why children should love him. Eileen and I hated the book so, we were quite prepared to despise birds when we started off that morning on our first bird walk, but we had no idea of what we were going to suffer, that whole awful summer, because of our feathered friends. In the first place, since we had started off making leather pocketbooks, we were three weeks behind the rest of the Hi-Wah bird-lovers. They had been tramping through blackberry bushes for days and had already got the hang of the more ordinary bird life around camp, whereas the only bird I could identify at the time was the vulture. Cousin Joe took me to a zoo once, and there was a fine vulture there, a big, fat one. They fed him six live rats every day in lieu of human flesh. I kept a sharp eye out for a vulture all summer, but one never turned up at Camp Hi-Wah. Nothing interesting ever happened around that place.

On that first bird walk, Eileen and I trotted anx- 11
iously along behind the little band of serious-minded bird-lovers, trying desperately to see, or at least hear, even one bird, even one robin. But alas, while other bird-walkers saw, or pretended to see—for Eileen and I never believed them for a moment—all kinds of hummingbirds and hawks and owls and whatnot, we never saw or heard a single, solitary feathered friend, not one.

By the time we staggered into camp for lunch, 12
with stubbed toes, scratched faces, and tangled hair, Eileen and I were soured for life on birds. Our bird logs, which we carried strapped to our belts along with the *Guide,* were still chaste and bare, while all the other little bird-lovers had fulsome entries, such as "Saw and heard redbird at 10:37 A.M. Molting."

13 Still, for the next three days we stayed honest and suffered. For three terrible mornings we endured being dolts among bird-walkers, the laughing-stock of Camp Hi-Wah. After six incredibly tiresome hours, our bird logs were still blank. Then we cracked under the strain. The fourth morning we got up feeling grim but determined. We sharpened our pencils before we started off on the now-familiar trail through the second-growth forest.

14 When we got well into the woods and Mary Mahoney, the premier bird-walker of Camp Hi-Wah, had already spotted and logged her first redbird of the morning, Eileen suddenly stopped dead in her tracks. "Hark!" she cried. She had read that somewhere in a book. "Quiet!" I echoed instantly.

15 The bird-walkers drew to a halt respectfully and stood in silence. They stood and stood. It was not good form even to whisper while fellow bird-walkers were logging a victim, but after quite a long time the Leader, whose feet were flat and often hurt her, whispered impatiently, "Haven't you got him logged yet?"

16 "You drove him away", Eileen replied sternly. "It was a yellow-billed cuckoo."

17 "A yellow-billed cuckoo?" cried the Leader incredulously.

18 "Well," Eileen said modestly, "at least *I* think it was." Then, with many a pretty hesitation and thoughtful pause, she recited the leading features of the yellow-billed cuckoo, as recorded in *Bird Life for Children.*

19 The Leader was terribly impressed. Later on that morning I logged a kingfisher, a red-headed woodpecker, and a yellow-bellied sapsucker, which was all I could remember at the moment. Each time, I kept the bird-walkers standing around for an interminable period, gaping into blank space and listening desperately to the rustle of the wind in the trees and the creak of their shoes as they went from one foot to another.

20 In a few days Eileen and I were the apple of our Leader's eye, the modest heroes of the Camp Hi-Wah bird walks. Naturally, there were base children around camp, former leading bird-walkers, who spread foul rumors up and down Hiawatha Alley that Eileen and I were frauds. We soon stopped this ugly talk, however. Eileen was the pitcher, and a very good one, too, of the Red Bird ball team and I was the first base. When Elouise Pritchard, the worst gossip in Cabin Sitting Bull, came up to bat, she got a pitched ball right in the stomach. Of course, it was only a soft ball, but Eileen could throw it pretty hard. To vary this routine, I tagged Mary Mahoney, former head bird-walker, out at first base, and Mary had a bruise on her thigh for weeks. The rumors stopped abruptly.

21 We had begun to get pretty bored with logging rare birds when the game took on a new angle. Mary Mahoney and several other bird-walkers began to see the same birds we did on our morning jaunts into the forest. This made us pretty mad, but there wasn't much we could do about it. Next, Mary Mahoney began to see birds we weren't logging. The third week after we joined the Camp Hi-Wah Bird Study Circle, everybody except the poor, dumb Leader and a few backward but honest bird-lovers was logging the rarest birds seen around Camp Hi-Wah in twenty years. Bird Walks developed into a race to see who could shout "Hark!" first and keep the rest of the little party in fidgety silence for the next five minutes.

22 The poor bird-walk Leader was in agony. Her reputation as a bird-lover was in shreds. Her talented pupils were seeing rare birds right and left, while the best she could log for herself would be a few crummy old redbirds and a robin or so. At last our Leader's morale collapsed. It was the day when nearly everybody in the study circle swore that she saw and heard a bona-fide nightingale.

23 "Where?" cried our Leader desperately, after the fourth nightingale had been triumphantly logged in the short space of five minutes. Heartless fingers pointed to a vague bush. The Leader strained her honest eyes. No notion of our duplicity crossed her innocent, unworldly mind.

24 "I can't see any nightingale," our Leader cried, and burst into tears. Then, full of shame, she sped back to camp, leaving the Camp Hi-Wah bird-lovers to their nightingales and guilty thoughts.

25 Eileen and I ate a hearty lunch that noon because we thought we would need it. Then we strolled down Hiawatha Alley and hunted up Mary Mahoney.

26 "We will put the Iron Cross on you if you tell," Eileen started off, as soon as we found Mary.

27 "What's the Iron Cross?" Mary squeaked, startled out of her usual haughty poise.

28 "Never mind," I growled. "You'll find out if you tell."

29 We walked past Cabin Sitting Bull, past the flagpole, into the tall grass beyond the ball field.

30 "She'll tell," Eileen said finally.

31 "What'll we do?" I replied mournfully. "They'll try us at campfire tonight."

32 They did, too. It was terrible. We denied everything, but the Head of Camp, a mean old lady who wore middy blouses and pleated serge bloomers, sentenced us to no desserts and eight-o'clock bedtime for two weeks. We thought over what to do to Mary Mahoney for four whole days. Nothing seemed sufficiently frightful, but in the end we put the wart curse on her. The wart curse was simple but horrible. We dropped around to Cabin Sitting Bull one evening and in the presence of Mary and her allies we drew ourselves up to our full height and said solemnly in unison, "We put the wart curse on you, Mary Mahoney." Then we stalked away.

33 We didn't believe for a moment in the wart curse, but we hoped Mary would. At first she was openly contemptuous, but to our delight, on the fourth evening she developed a horrible sty in her eye. We told everybody a sty was a kind of wart and that we had Mary in our power. The next day Mary broke down and came around to our cabin and apologized in choked accents. She gave Eileen her best hair ribbon and me a little barrel that had a picture of Niagara Falls inside it, if you looked hard enough. We were satisfied.

## Questions for Discussion

1. Describe the speaking voice of each essay. What does each voice suggest about the attitude of the author toward the subject?

a. What words and phrases in the first four paragraphs of the Sancton essay suggest the author's attitude?

b. In the first two paragraphs of the McKenney essay?

2. How distant from his camp experience is each speaker? How detached from it? How can you tell?

a. What does the structure of the second sentence of Sancton's second paragraph, for instance, or the last sentence in his sixth paragraph, suggest about the maturity of the speaker?

b. What does the structure of the first sentence of the second paragraph of the McKenney essay suggest about the maturity of the speaker?

c. If the speaker in each essay were camp age, what differences would you expect to find in the diction throughout?

(In the Sancton essay, note "dominated" in the fifth paragraph, "diversion" in the sixth, "simple-hearted" in the seventh, "circumscribed" in the fifteenth, and so on.

In the McKenney essay, note "chicanery" in the third paragraph, "bruited" in the fifth, "precociously" in the seventh, and so on.)

d. Rewrite a paragraph (1, 3, 4, 6, or 9) of the Sancton essay to create a different speaker—perhaps a younger speaker who dislikes the camp he is attending or an older speaker who is unwilling to admit his earlier enjoyment of camp.

(This assignment should be due the day following this discussion.)

3. What does the imagery in each essay contribute to the speaking voice?

(Note that in the Sancton essay, the images are chiefly pleasant: no fear of snakes; warmth of the sun; a comic Boy Scout hat; steaming platters of pork and beans and cabbage and stew; the clatter of knives and forks and china; salty wind; Paolo's taps.

Note that in the McKenney essay the images are often strongly unpleasant; vulture; rats; werewolf; snakes; "grinding our teeth"; bird names with the sound of insult; poison ivy and brambles; a decapitated lover's head.)

4. The speaking voice in the Sancton essay may be called nostalgic, and that in the McKenney essay humorous, satirical. What sections in the Sancton essay would probably have been omitted if the author had intended a comic or satirical presentation of his experience at camp?

(The section on spiritual development. The section on Joe. The section on the horn, at least as it is now treated; the horn could no longer symbolize the glory of the life ahead and the failure of fulfillment, as it does now.)

a. Which of the camp activities described in Sancton's essay would lend themselves to ridicule?

(Probably the morning exercises, the work detail, the lack of planned activities, hunting for stars, and the young love episode.)

b. Does Sancton at any point present the comic?

(In paragraph 8.)

Why does he treat this section humorously?

c. What is the difference between Sancton's comedy and McKenney's?

(Sancton's humor in his eighth paragraph lies chiefly in the boy's incongruously ever-enthusiastic reaction to his nickname. Ruth McKenney's humor lies chiefly in diction, irony, situation, and direct, slashing statement.)

d. In the McKenney essay, what do you consider the funniest moment? The funniest sentence?

5. Where, in each story, would you locate the climax? Defend your choice by showing the steps leading to the climax?

a. What is Sancton's subject for each major section? What happens to the movement toward climax if the sections are rearranged?

b. Can you reasonably rearrange any of the paragraphs within sections?

c. Can you rearrange the parts of the McKenney essay without changing the effect? Can you, for instance, interchange the pocketbook-making and bird-walking episodes? Can you put the wart curse before the bird-walking episode?

6. The two essays treat some of the same phases of camp life. How does their treatment of these phases differ—for instance, their treatment of their fellow campers; the relation between the author and an adult connected with the camp; camp food; a bugle call?

7. What attitude does each author seem to have toward his audience?

8. How much do attitude and purpose seem to have affected each speaker's choices?

## Writing Assignment Five

Choose either question 1 or 2 below.

1. If you have been to summer camp, which author's experiences do yours more closely resemble?

Write an essay demonstrating the similarity of your experiences to those of Sancton *or* McKenney. After your essay, add a paragraph stating your attitude toward your subject, your purpose in writing about it, and your tone.

2. If you have not been to summer camp or prefer not to write about your experiences there, what experiences have you had that you now look back on with either nostalgia or distaste? Have any of these experiences contributed to your development as Sancton's experiences at summer camp did to his? Write a paper showing by specific incident and detail the contribution of one such experience.

If you prefer to write about a distasteful experience, decide on a tone of either direct dislike or ridicule. Keep this tone throughout.

After your essay, add a paragraph stating your attitude toward your subject, your purpose in writing about it, and your tone.

## Writing Assignment One
## Sample 1. Grade: High

*August*

As the hot Arizona sun beats down on the diving board, the chrome standards shine and reflect everything in the swimming pool. The board is about three feet off the deck, secured by two rear anchor pipes and two U-shaped pipes at its middle, along which a bar slides to give the board more or less spring. Except for the chrome supports, the board is a dull silver color, and very hot to the touch. The entire structure is quivering slightly from the force of a dive that has just been made into the pool. On closer examination, the chromium standards are entirely rust-free, as are the large wing nuts which tighten the sliding bar. The rubber on the bar is cracking, due to the summer heat and the fact that it hasn't been moved for years. A small patch of fog on the chrome where the diver stepped is receeding rapidly. The surface of the board is rough, made of aluminum molded with innumerable small imperfections in the smooth surface, making the board a good base for diving but terribly uncomfortable for sunbathing. The rough aluminum is a little cooler than the chrome, and the footprints of the diver are still outlined as small puddles of water. In spite of the fact that the aluminum is divided at two inch intervals, the entire surface is somewhat damp, both from splashings from the pool below and drippings from the bathing suits of people as they dived into the pool. Every three or four feet in the length of the board, the grain of the roughness changes for an inch or so, indicating suitable places to start the runup for the dive. The only other thing breaking the roughness of the surface of the board are the two round-headed bolts and plate which secure the board to the rear supports. A small, faded, and barely distinguishable label on the side of the board reads "Whitaker Pools".

*December*

Like a hand of ice with a protruding finger, the diving board juts out above the snow which threatens to reduce it to a lump as it has all the other structures about the swimming pool. No sun breaks through the overcast, and the only visible parts of the board are the six sections of supporting pipe between the snow below and the icicles above. These show no color, reflecting only the dingy gray of the water and the dull white of the snow. Because the snow has been drifting, little bases have formed for each of these pipes. Everything is extremely cold, sticking to the wet glove that scrapes the snow from the board. As the chrome parts become visible, they appear with small spots of rust accumulated in the fall and deadening even further the reflections. Icicles break off the edge of the board, taking with them particles of paint from the aluminum. Viewed from below, the rubber bar is unravelling in tatters, at last giving in to the extreme temperature changes. The entire structure sags slightly as it is meant to under weight, but offers no spring to the wet and ponderous snow. Beneath the board, the separations in the aluminum try to let water through, but succeed only in forming rows of icicles. From each side, a wing nut protrudes from the blanket, but it too has been disfigured by a coat of ice. The rest of the board is entirely hidden, and as the snow begins to fall becomes only a fleeting outline in the murky storm.

My two descriptions are of a diving board at two different times of year: one during the summer on a hot day and the other during the winter in a snowstorm. In the first, I have tried to illustrate the board as I see it when there is lots of action around it, and it is an integral part of the action. This paper is mostly objective, but I think I can feel what I'm talking about: the warmth of the aluminum, the coolness of the water, the lightness of the atmosphere at the time. In other words, my emotions at this time are of happiness, relaxation, and simple appreciation of summer. I described the board very closely because all of the details are part of my mind's eye's picture of the board.

The second description, as the first, is of an actual scene I remember. It is the description of the board, a symbol of summer, in the winter during a snowstorm. My purpose here was to show the fact that I possess an intense hatred for snow in all forms. This is why I used unusual adjectives to describe snow (murky, dull, ponderous as opposed to more conventional "snow adjectives" such as sparkly, light, brilliant, etc) I also bring up the point about rust because the board does rust every winter and the rust further defeats its purpose of providing joy to swimmers, as does the snow. The "cracking rubber in the first essay was a thing to be expected: it didn't hurt the board and was just another illustration of the intense heat I was trying to show. However, the rubber in the second scene is shredding and unraveling, completely useless because of the effects of the snow.

My emotions in these two essays can be explained by

the fact that I am fond of warmth and feel rather opposed to cold. The first essay uses adjectives of warmth and happiness together, for to me they are one and the same. The second essay takes the opposing view and illustrates a very cold and hence depressing scene.

## Writing Assignment One
## Comment on Sample 1. Grade: High

A diving board would seem an object difficult to describe interestingly even once, still more difficult to describe twice—with genuine differences in the description. This student, however, overcomes the difficulties, largely because of the fullness and accuracy of his details and their appropriateness to the two seasons. His analysis is thorough; if the whole production has a weakness, it is that the first descriptive paragraph is too objective to convey the sense of happiness the writer says he feels in summer. Many papers depend too heavily on a lush use of adjectives to portray the differences; this student's prose, while not brilliant, is relatively spare and sinewy. There is one misspelling.

## Writing Assignment One
## Sample 2. Grade: Average

CAR *morning*

Encased in the crystal frost of the pre-dawn darkness, my car sits in the drive awaiting the day. Its black tires are damp and musty, while the pink sides glisten dully in the chill twilight. The windshield is shrouded in a crackling crust of silver ice and stares into a vacuum of mist. The steal body is icy to the touch without the beat of the motor for warmth, and must wait for the sunrise for its life.

CAR *sunset*

Scarlet bursts exploding from its polished surfaces, my car sits in the brilliance of the blood-red sun setting behind the dark mountain. Its pink sides are now a burnished copper, contrasting with the jet-black tires and shiny tar of the driveway. Mirrored in its chrome are all the glories of the sunset, and the windows flash its dying rays to all sides. The uneven surfaces catch the light at different angles, and the car comes alive with the warmth and the color and the beauty of the day's end.

The two descriptions are very different in the the picture of the car they give. The purpose was to show the car in two different aspects, as a cold machine, and as something beautiful, almost alive. The tone of the first paragraph is dark and still, while the second paragraph is alive with warmth and color. Because of its quality of life and beauty I felt more involved with the car in the second paragraph.

## Writing Assignment One
## Comment on Sample 2. Grade: Average

A score of *high* is probably right for the first section of this paper in which the writer paints a morning and an evening picture of the car. The details and the wording have the same compact richness that makes the first sample superior. Every phrase helps to define the chilly unaliveness of the early morning picture just as every word and every detail in the second sketch is alive with the warmth and the brilliance of the sunset; yet the student never overwrites for the sake of vividness. The last sentence of the early morning scene is a notable example of this writer's unpretentious skill. What differentiates this paper from the first, however, is the slightness and the obviousness of its second section, where the student examines what he has done and how he has done it. His almost perfunctory disposal of this vital part of the assignment is the readers' main reason for rating the paper *average* instead of *high*.

## Writing Assignment One
## Sample 3. Grade: Low

*Our Pear Tree in Spring*

In our back yard the predominant sight in the Spring time is our large pear tree.

Just after all things turn green, Our pear tree blosoms with beautiful white flowers, creating a terrific contrast with the, newly turned green, large hill in the back ground.

After the limbs have been laiden with snow all winter, the limbs are in a hanging and bent state. It almost looks as if it is mourning for someone or something.

Our pear tree is a beautiful sight in the spring.

*Our Pear Tree During Summer Months*

After the flowers of Spring have wilted and start to grow into fruit, You can almost watch the tree take on a new like. Each day the bends in it's limbs straighten out more and more. The tree gets stronger. Once the limbs are straight the weight of the fruit starts to bend the limbs once more.

This time the tree looks proud to be a bearer of one of God's miracles.

*Explaination*

I had no purpose when I wrote the two descriptions. The only difference in the two descriptions is that of the seasons themselves.

I have no difference in attitude because I am indifferent to pear trees in any season.

As for the effect of my attitudes on my purpose, I can explain this easily. I had no attitude towards the subject and my only purpose was to fulfill this assignment. So there couldn't have been any effect.

I have no emotional point of view because I can't see how anyone could get emotional over a pear tree.

Had I know what this assignment was for I would have chosen some object I could have envolved myself with.

## Writing Assignment One
## Comment on Sample 3. Grade: Low

Perhaps the best comment on this paper is that two readers independently call it "my favorite *low*." A very honest student, who "can't see how anyone could get emotional over a pear tree," and who has considerable difficulty in expression, has been faced with an assignment beyond his capacity. His descriptive paragraphs show how he strained to reach a higher level of aesthetic appreciation than he really feels; his "Explaination" is sincere enough to atone for the insincerity of his descriptions; but it is couched in the same rudimentary paragraphs as the others, with many of the same technical errors.

## Alternate Writing Assignment
## Sample 1. Grade: High

The representation of the Canterbury cathedral, as seen in the color photograph, does not reveal the time or age in which it was taken as its composition is of basic elements of foreground (a mass of trees), background (hills), the sky, and the cathedral as the definite center of interest. All these elements exist there today, just as they did 1000 and more years ago, whereas the numerous uninteresting details of the black & white photo, betray it as a recently-taken picture of a stuffy old church in the midst of a bunch of buildings and trees. The flexibility of the color photo, in that it could depict any era of the development of the town equally well, wins out and makes it by far the better candidate for use in a Canterbury history volume.

## Alternate Writing Assignment
## Comment on Sample 1. Grade: High

There is no accounting for tastes. Many people would disagree with this student's description of the black and white photograph as having "uninteresting details" of "a stuffy old church." But his purpose is to persuade his audience that the colored photograph is the better one for a history of Canterbury—and this he does with ingenuity and logic, his premises being granted. His writing seems better than average for an eleventh grader—as far as it can be judged by a single paragraph.

## Alternate Writing Assignment
## Sample 2. Grade: Average

*As an illustration for a history of Canterbury*

I think that I would use the black and white picture. It has many advantages over the color picture for this topic. The black and white picture is sharply defined and has sharp details and the color picture is blurred and darker. When you think of history you think of details which are defined very well. There is also less emphasis on the cathedral and the title says history of Canterbury and not the cathedral.

## Alternate Writing Assignment
## Comment on Sample 2. Grade: Average

Though the student claims "many advantages" for the black and white picture as an illustration for a history of Canterbury, he is hard put to it to list three, one of which is not very convincing. His literal-mindedness is shown by his last sentence. In the broad group of *average* ratings, this sample would be in the lower half.

## Alternate Writing Assignment
## Sample 3. Grade: Low

In an illustration for the town of Canterbury, the colored picture would probabily make the most interesting picture of the two. An individual would use a picture which presents a feeling of age which this picture does do. The color illustration also is blurred causing a viewer to believe that their is, not a clear history of the town of Canterbury itself. The color picture presents a mood which is much more suitable for the reading and the studying of history.

## Alternate Writing Assignment
## Comment on Sample 3. Grade: Low

Faulty grammar and punctuation plus thin material and shaky logic make the grade of this paragraph *low*.

## Writing Assignment Four
## Sample 1. Grade: High

*The Mayor of Casterbridge*

1 Michael Henchard definitely is a tragic hero in the Aristotelian sense. He fits the requirements perfectly. His character is good, consistent, appropriate, and true to life. His is prosperous and highly renoun, and his change of fortune occurs because of a frailty in his character. A reversal of situation starts his decline. Finally recognition, and Aristotelian necessity, takes place in which Henchard gains self-knowledge. All these elements combine to make Henchard a very tragic hero.

2 Henchard's character is good. He has a purpose in life—to punish himself for selling his wife—and by trying to carry it through he is elected Mayor of Casterbridge. The people like his intense energy, which he shows in his hay business and his completion of his vow. It is fitting that he should punish himself for breaking the moral order by vowing not to drink for twenty-one years.

3 Henchard is highly renoun and prosperous, but he has faults just like anyone else. These weaknesses make him tragic because he is so true to life. He is jealous. For example, he objects to Farfrae's interest in Elizabeth-Jane because he fears that she will love her admirer more than she does Henchard. And Henchard does anything to win her love. Another of Michael's frailities is his impulsiveness. He irrationally tells Newson that Elizabeth-Jane has been dead for over one year. However if he told Newson the truth there would have been nothing left for Henchard to live for in his depressed condition, had Newson taken Elizabeth-Jane. Henchard's pride is also a fault in his character. He is too proud to apologize to Farfrae for his fight in the loft. These are all good qualities, but Henchard consistently carries them to extremes. Consequently they lower his public image. This brings about his change of fortune from prosperity to poverty. Aristotle says this must happen to the tragic hero.

4 The reversal of situation acts as a stimulus in Henchard's decline. He set out to find the papers which would prove to Elizabeth-Jane that he is her real father. Oppositely he discovers a note from his late wife that says Henchard's Elizabeth-Jane died. This is Newson's. Henchard is extremely disappointed and this is an unjust act of the gods. He takes it out on Elizabeth-Jane. He finds many difficulties when she moves to Lucetta's to escape his uncalled for treatment.

5 Aristotle says that reversal of situation and recognition should occur at the same time. In Hardy's novel, Henchard's recognition occurs at the end of the book when he is writing his will. He gains the knowledge that people can "turn the other cheek", as Able Little did. He realizes how unfair he has been to his employee. Henchard also perceives that he is so full of wrongs, that he is not worthy of a funeral or even remembrance after death. He does not want Elizabeth-Jane to know. This is an advance. He is not thinking of himself but of someone else's feelings. He has done wrong to lie to Newson, and now he does not want to bother them any more. Henchard suffers for his recognition, but pathos is a necessity in tragedy.

6 Thomas Hardy has formed a tragic hero, Michael Henchard, who fits Aristotle's requirements. Through his experience we learn and pity him because he is so much like ourselves.

The purpose of my paper is to convince the reader that it is valid to describe Michael Henchard as a tragic hero in the Aristotelian sense. I give Aristotle's requirements for a tragic hero, and then try to give examples to support these statements. I find that I do not arrange my ideas in a logical development. I use short, abrupt sentences that comment rather than analyze. These elements only weaken my speaker whose purpose is to inform.

I try to choose the best details that demonstrate Henchard fits Aristotle's requirements for a tragic hero. For example, Aristotle says the hero must have a weakness in character. I back this up by giving pride in paragraph three as one of Henchard's faults. He is so proud that he cannot apologize to Farfrae for the near fatal fight in the loft. I describe Henchard's recognition which is another requirement. He realizes that people can "turn the other cheek" as Able Little does. Another detail I use in the fact that his character is appropriate. It is fitting that he should punish himself for breaking the moral order. These are a few of the details that give support to the statement that Michael Henchard is a tragic hero in the Aristotelian sense.

I try to select words that relate to my purpose. For instance I describe Henchard's character as appropriate and true to life. I list jealousy, impulsiveness, and pride among his weaknesses. I state he is renoun and prosperous until his fortune changes. He has recognition. Finally I say he is true-to-life. All these words inform the reader what Aristotle's requirements are for a tragic hero, and how Michael Henchard fits them.

However I do have poor choices of words, too. I describe him as good, but I should explain Aristotle's definition of good. He means the hero must have an intensity of character or in other words a purpose in life. I also say Henchard acts irrationally, but I do not clearly explain how it is irrational. These mistakes in diction do not fulfill my purpose to inform.

My sentence structure is not very effective in this paper. In paragraph four, for instance, I use too many sentences. They could have been combined into two or three well-structured sentences, instead of five that give useless plot summary. My best sentence structure is in the introduction. The structure is simple, and I focus on the main idea.

I use too many short sentences in this paper. This is especially apparent in in the third and fifth paragraphs. They do not analyze which is their main purpose. The do not keep the writing smooth or the reader interested.

My sentences do not follow any logical order. This is obvious in paragraph three which is my weakest paragraph. These sentences confuse the reader and distract from the purpose.

The short sentences, ineffective sentence structure, poor use of "good" and "irrational", change of tense, and rough style form an unconvincing speaker. He is supposed to describe why Michael Henchard is a tragic hero in the Aristotelian sense. This paper is a good example of how correct, but poorly organized ideas weaken the purpose and the speaker.

## Writing Assignment Four
## Comment on Sample 1. Grade: High

This total production deserves a *high* rating mainly because of the ruthless honesty of the student's criticisms of his own paper, and because some of the criticisms are deserved. He gives Henchard too many different faults to satisfy the Aristotelian "tragic flaw"; he seems to have been convinced that short sentences are a weakness in his style; and he attributes to mistakes in diction some faults (such as his failure to define Aristotle's idea of "good") that go deeper than a mere wrong choice of words. Taken alone, perhaps neither the original theme nor the analysis of it would be graded *high;* but together they show clearly what the student meant to do and where he fell (in his own opinion) short of his aim. This power of self-criticism is what the exercise is designed to show, and there can be little doubt that this student has it in a high degree. And though the writing is never brilliant, it is, also, seldom at fault technically. One wishes that he would write "renowned" instead of "renoun"—see paragraph 3 of the theme—or that he had, sometimes, a lighter touch, but weighed against his virtues, these flaws are not enough to bring his grade down.

## Writing Assignment Four
## Sample 2. Grade: Average

*The Clock*

It was seven in the morning and the girl awoke to the ring of her alarm. Sitting up, she decided she wouldn't let herself lie back down in bed. Her amount of will power shocked her as she literally jumped out. Oddly (for she had started school before) she was nervous with anticipation. She tried to analyze this fear as she dressed but she came to no conclusion.

She continued thinking as she walked to her first day at the new summer school. Again the fear she couldn't understand came upon her. Breathlessly she walked into her first two hour class and found herself among forty excited faces and eager tongues. She stood looking at the faces and imagining hers as one of them. She glanced at the clock and saw that were almost two hours left in that first class. She passed the rest of the period gazing at the teacher as she expressed the opening day words of, "I want to welcome all of you to school today. I know that all of you who know your way around will help all those who feel lost." The girl felt that she was the only one in the room listening.

The bell rang and she sat quietly waiting for some sign of recognition from her fellow classmates: she got none. She wondered why no one thought to talk to her. As she sat waiting, one group in particular interested her. They joked with the teachers and wanted notice.as they treated the school as an old friend. She watched them more closely and realized she had been one of them. She had ignored those new like herself for she had been shielded by the security of belonging. She turned from the now blank faces and looked at again at the clock: $1\frac{1}{2}$ hours to go.

The rest of the day went relatively quickly for she now felt at ease with the blank faces around her. She felt pleasure when one even smiled at her. She couldn't feel bitter for she had been one of them too, a part of the group ignorning all those who felt out of place. This, oddly enough, seemed to be a great discovery to her. It filled the blank place in her with a feeling, unrecognizable at first, but there. She looked again at her watch and saw nothing but its two hands, strangely close and almost touching.

A bell rang and she walked home.

The purpose of my writing was, for the most part, to create a believable experience and character. I wanted to convey this to the reader so that he could gain something from my realization.

In selecting details I looked most for those which would add realism and relate to other's past experiences. In describing the girl's feelings as she entered the classroom, I hoped to do this. I also wanted an image to run through the story to reinforce the total meaning. This was the word "blank". I used the clock as a symbol, referred to in the beginning, middle and end of the story. I tried to use words that appeal to the senses as well as move the story and characterization: Breathlessly, excited faces and eager tongues, blank faces, are a few examples. I also used metonomy in a few places as shown above. I paid little attention to the length or structure of my sentences and I don't believe my paragraphs had any particular organization except in time.

I hope that by my use of words to convey a theme of recognition my speaker was effective. My speaker, in being an omniscent observer, was able to watch the girl, know her thoughts and relate this to the reader. By using this observer I believe I was able to characterize the girl more fully than had I merely created a narrator.

The relationship between the purpose and speaker is almost too close to be defined. The voice of the speaker is the most important technique the writer has in achieving his ultimate purpose. In creating a perceptive speaker and through this using important details, I hoped to achieve my goal of a sucessful story.

## Writing Assignment Four
## Comment on Sample 2. Grade: Average

This student first wrote a short, short story and then an analysis in which she makes clear that she knows what she meant to do in her story and how she tried to do it. But the story itself is not a success: intended to present "a believable experience and character," it has so little action—and what there is, is vague—that neither character nor experience is believable. The specific assignment is to write an analysis of the "speaker." This job the student performs about as well as anyone could perform it, given the shapelessness of the "speaker" in the story. The quality of the analysis is better than that of the material analyzed, but its upper limit is still restrained by the weakness of the story. Grade: *average.*

## Writing Assignment Five, Question 1
## Sample 1. Grade: High

*Back to Summer Camp*

Sancton and I both spent some time in a Boy Scout Summer Camp. Sancton was far more gung-ho than I, spending a multitude of summers whereas I spent only one (and one too many) summer.

Allowing for differences in climate, the camps were very similar—neat, clean, with both open space, and wooded areas. What my camp lacked in Sancton's cypress it more than made up for with poisen ivy. Our camp had no bayou, however we did have a polluted lake which we used for canoeing and rowing and in addition we had a large, heated (just above the melting point) swimming pool.

Sancton and I both had experiences with Negroes. Sancton had his Joe, the caretaker, a true friend and all that. I had Henry Williams, who hailed from Detroit, and helped me through camp.

My experience with Henry was a bit different from the one Sancton had with Joe. The main difference was Joseph Johnson, lately moved north from Alabama, a devoted apostle of Robert Shelton but otherwise a fine person. Joe and I constantly argued about civil rights, I defending the Negro, and Joe saying: "Look at the Lion! Nobody elected *him* King of the beasts! Why then is he the King of the beasts? He is the King of the beasts because for thousands of years God has named him King of the beasts. He is genetically superior by vast numbers of mutations from his subjects. He does not treat his subjects as equals, he treats them as subjects. Man's the same way. For thousands of years, God in his infinite justice has ordained the white man to be king of all men. Genetically speaking . . ." and so on for 15 minutes of illogic. Once this was happening and I inadvertantly glanced behind me. Henry Williams was standing there, listening avidly to every word. He was stone white.

It is a tribute to Henry that he never let my friendship with Joe Johnson interfere with my friendship with him.

Sancton learned a lot at camp. He learned about thinking, living, females—the touchiest of all subjects, hard labor, philosophy, and in general matured greatly. I mainly learned how to shoot a rifle straight. For the two weeks I was in camp, every morning I would spend over in the rifle range. During that period, I progressed from an absolute novitiate to a reasonable proficiency. The quarter-mile hike between my camp and the range proved highly beneficial to my waistline, which was already displaying the ravages of inflation, and due to a hereditary skin condition (epidermolysis bullora simplex) I learned much about the care of blisters. Indeed, it was at that time I first imitated Christ in that I walked on water. Nevertheless, I can't really say I got very much out of camp.

It is strange to me that Sancton should omit any mention of food. As my friends will testify, food is one of my major vices. This is not to say that camp food is at all worth writing about. To be as complimentary as possible, the food they gave us at camp fell just short of being inedible. We wolfed it down by the ton, proving the adage that "men eagerly take shoe leather when there is no meat." At best, that is.

Finally, Sancton had many more interesting characters in his camp. He had Joe, the hike leader, the girls were nearby, the trumpet player, et. al. . All I had were a red-neck southerner and a Negro. Sancton's characters are all idealized. Mine are human. And that, I suspect, was the main difference.

*Explanation*

The purpose of this paper was rather simple, namely, to compare my camp experiences with those of Sancton the writer for the benefit of the Council on English. Nothing else: I desired to show nothing, etc.

The attitude I take in this piece is a nostalgic tongue-in-cheek tone. I didn't really hate camp, I'm quite vituperative when I have to be and this paper is anything but vituperative. It boils down to an old philosophy I read in some dusty old book: "Life you have only once. Live it and have fun!" In that light I have viewed my camp experiences.

I have the horrible feeling there is something else about my theme that I must write. Since there is so little contained in the theme, what I have not already pointed out is so minuscule so as to deserve attention only by slightly batty professors. For, as the philosopher said, er, well, skip it.

## Writing Assignment Five, Question 1 Comment on Sample 1. Grade: High

This student follows the themes of Sancton's essay as closely as he—with quite different experiences—can. He describes his attitude as "a nostalgic tongue-in-cheek tone," which is an accurate description. By the end of the second sentence the reader knows that there will be ridicule; by the end of the essay, the reader knows that the writer's sense of humor is acute, sometimes brash, but also that he has it under pretty good control. And by the end of the "Explanation," most of these discoveries have been reinforced. The dangers for a young writer with a keen sense of humor who indulges in ridicule are (a) going too far and (b) becoming monotonous. Some will think that in his comments on his blisters this student goes too far. In general, however, his control is good, and he can move from ridicule to seriousness effectively—as he shows by turning from his exposure of the Alabaman's illogic to a genuine tribute to his Negro friend, Henry Williams. His attitude toward his model, Sancton, seems just right: he is respectful of the wider camp experiences Sancton genuinely enjoyed, incidentally turning the ridicule on himself. His final paragraph shows his tongue still in cheek, but is also a tersely accurate criticism of Sancton's essay. This young man must be fun to teach.

## Writing Assignment Five, Question 1 Sample 2. Grade: Average

*Life at Camp*

Camp is a wonderful place, if you happen to be a Boy Scout or a bird watcher. For most, though, it is an ordeal to be dreaded. The day you arrive, everything looks like its going to be fun, because it is new to you. Now is the time to prepare for the weeks ahead. You will probably first become aware that there is something you weren't told about camp when you eat your first meal. Camp food is difficult to describe, not so much for a lack of words, but because descriptions vary, depending on how sick you are. After a while you learn to swallow it with as little chewing as necessary. After eating, it is time for a "nature walk", a deceptive name given to their obstacle course. The goal of these walks is to see if we can find some rare bird that everyone but the counselors knows is either nonexistant or extinct. After everyone is sufficiently worn out, we return to where we left the counsilors consuming candy bars and reading, and, as a group, return to camp as the sun sets. Everyone is bushed, so we turn in for the night. The bunks, though, are more like torture racks, so by morning everyone is bent like pretzils. When the bugle sounds, shattering our nightmares, we all fall from our bunks, landing in a pile on the floor. Today is handicrafts day, so we all head for the crafts center. This is a do-it-yourself torture house, where the unsuspecting and less nimble of us are always wounding themselves with knives, needles, hammers and other devices to numerous to mention. The casualties in this area are heavy.

After a summer at camp, when it is time for open house, everyone is joyous, even the counsilors, who look on with relief. Now is the time to be most wary. If you are asked how you liked camp, don't say you did, to speed your departure, just moan a little.

## Writing Assignment Five, Question 1 Comment on Sample 2. Grade: Average

This paper takes a satirical attitude toward camp life, approaching that of the McKenney essay, but is far more limited in scope. There is no specific reference to the model, but this paper's nature walk is reminiscent of the bird walk in the model. It should be pointed out, however, that this student not only treats familiar targets from a fresh point of view but also—in the handicraft passage, for example—brings in new targets. What prevents the paper from receiving a better grade is partly its failure to add an analytical paragraph, as the assignment requires, and partly its technical troubles. There were several places where the main long paragraph might have been broken, to advantage. There is a shift from "you" to "we"—and back again in the final sentence; there are some misspellings and errors in punctuation. But revision and the addition of a paragraph of analysis might have pulled the paper up to a grade of *high.*

## Writing Assignment Five, Question 1 Sample 3. Grade: Low

I went to a church camp in Maine. The name of this camp was Geneva Point and it was on the beautiful Lake Winnipesaukee. We had to get up at 7:30 a.m. every morning. During the morning we had discussion groups. Some of these groups delt with religion and others were on family life. There was a minister, priest, and rabbi up there. In this way we got to know more about our religion as well as others.

Everyone made alot of friends up there. In the evening dances, and movies were held. One night we went on a sunset cruise around the lake. This cruise was beautiful, and everyone was sad when it was over.

I look back on this week at camp with enjoyment. It showed me how to make friends easier, and developed me spiritually.

## Writing Assignment Five, Question 1 Comment on Sample 3. Grade: Low

Off to a bad start, the paper grows steadily weaker; and it comes rapidly to a poor ending. If the preceding sample answer is a good *average,* this one is surely a low *low.* Among its defects is its lack of an analytical paragraph such as the assignment requires, but there really is not much to analyze.

*A Composition Unit*
*Based on Cartoons*
*Grades 11 and 12*

use them in their printed sequence; they are designed to be so used.)

1. List as many items as you can in Cartoon 3 that characterize the men. If you were drawing the cartoon, what details would you consider adding?

2. What is the difference between what the speaker is saying and what the cartoonist is saying? What is the artist satirizing in 3?

3. Assume that you agree with the speaker in Cartoon 3. What happens to the humor in the cartoon? What does this consideration teach you about the nature of satire?

4. The humor of the two cartoons depends somewhat on use of euphemism. Substitute other terms for *"have-not"* in the caption of 3, some euphemistic and some blunt, and talk about how these terms work in the statement. (If the students do not suggest *"disadvantaged,"* suggest it to them.)

5. What is the effect of the exaggerated metaphor in Cartoon 4? Contrast the speaker's words with what the cartoonist might have had him say: "Let's just say that we're floating on rough and changing waters." Work out statements that compete with "we're adrift on the stormy sea of economic vicissitude" in euphemistic quality and in ornateness. (As students develop and talk about these statements, they are likely to discover the ambiguity in "we": we the two bums and we the nation.) Talk about the specific choices of words that the cartoon writer had to make and about how successfully he made them.

6. You may have decided that the cliché "adrift on the stormy sea" works well in the context of comedy; perhaps it works even better than equally ornate but more original language would. What do these conclusions imply about the usefulness of ornate clichés in language that is intended to be taken seriously?

7. Contrast the appearance of the characters in Cartoon 4 with the language of the speaker. Write a one-sentence statement about how the principle of contrast works in the cartoon.

8. Assume that the speaker in 4 intends his comment to be humorous and that his listener accepts his little joke as just that, a little joke. Now assume that the speaker is sincere and that his listener accepts his comment seriously. How does the humor in these two interpretations differ?

9. Try to explain why you respond more sympathetically to the speaker in one of the cartoons than to the speaker in the other.

10. Some readers will smile only momentarily at Cartoon 3 but will continue to smile at Cartoon 4 each time they read it. Try to explain these different reactions to the two cartoons.

11. What specific advantages and disadvantages do the two cartoonists have that a writer trying to make the same points would not have? (A dialogue on this subject between the teacher of English and a teacher of art could be fascinating and informative. Such a dialogue should give way to student participation during the latter part of the discussion.)

## Writing Assignment Two

Choose one of the following writing assignments; use *either* Cartoon 5 *or* Cartoon 6 (from the envelope in the back of this book) as the basis for your essay, which is to be written outside class. Your classmates are your audience.

1. The humor of a successful cartoon can have as its source a situation that is quite serious. The reader of the cartoon smiles at the clever interpretation the artist has given the situation, but then the reader realizes that the situation underlying the cartoon is not humorous. Write an essay that (1) shows that the cartoon is based on such a situation and (2) comments on the situation.

2. Write an essay in which you (1) analyze the nature of the humor of the cartoon and (2) comment on the success of the cartoon in achieving its humor.

## Class Discussion of Papers

Arrange follow-up discussions similar to those that follow writing assignment one. If you can afford only one day for discussion this time, choose two or three papers, ditto them, and hand them to students the day before the discussion. Again, see that the discussion concentrates on clarity, rhetorical techniques, and content.

# *A Composition Unit Based on Cartoons Grades 11 and 12*

## Writing Assignment One

(This assignment, to be done outside class, is based on Cartoons 1 and 2 in the envelope in the back of this book.)

Write a 300-word essay about an idea that *either* Cartoon 1 *or* Cartoon 2 suggests to you. You may refer to the cartoon early in your paper if you wish, but move quickly into a discussion of the idea that the cartoon suggests. Be certain that your paper is developed around a thesis (a general truth or proposition). Your classmates are your audience.

## Class Discussion of Papers

This discussion of the papers from writing assignment one will take two class periods. Arrange the students into groups of four or five people for reading and discussing papers the first day. The papers a group considers should be their own. Students should go about their work the first day with a minimum of directing from you. Once you have read the set of papers, choose two or three for class discussion that you will direct on the second day of the unit. See that the discussion concentrates on clarity, rhetorical techniques, and content. If you have the material and equipment that will enable you to ask the students to write their papers on master copies, the students can have a copy of each paper they read on the first day. Even if you cannot use this technique, ditto the papers to be used on the second day of the discussion.

## Class Discussion of Two Cartoons

(This discussion is based on Cartoons 3 and 4 in the envelope in the back of the book. Use as many of the following problems as seem to be appropriate for your class. The large number of problems may wear down the patience of some of your class. Some of the problems may be too subtle and others too obvious. But if you find the problems generally right for your class,

## Suggestions for Teachers Who Wish More Cartoon-based Assignments

1. In devising additional assignments based on cartoons, avoid telling the student that he must write on one particular problem about one particular cartoon. Give him some alternatives in either problems or cartoons, or both. These alternatives should help the student avoid writing statements that he doesn't believe.

2. If you permit students to choose their own cartoons, require them to have you approve the cartoons before they begin writing. (Suppose that you assign a problem similar to problem 1 in writing assignment two and that the student chooses a cartoon that is just funny and nothing else. His paper is certain to be less than successful.) This arrangement seems to be a good one: give the students one or two cartoons that you think will work well for an assignment but tell them that they may choose others, subject to your approval.

3. After the discussion of Cartoons 3 and 4, you may want to have students write about cartoons (chosen by you) with captions that invite discussion of how language works.

## Writing Assignment One, Cartoon 1
## Sample 1. Grade: High

*Commentary on Cartoon 1*

Face it; if you are college age and still content with the world as it is, you are just not with it. Basically it is not a new thing. The young Left Bank anarchists believed themselves of a superior ilk as compared to bourgeois France. Even in old Greece, we find a bunch of complainers led by Socrates. However, the numbers of discontented souls in these cases were relatively and daringly small while the number of college picketeers increases with each September.

Now if you are within the age limit and want to be with it but cannot think of anything traumatically important to be against, do not fret. What you are against, what has made you discontent, is unimportant as long as you are discontent. After all, once you reach thirty or thirty-five you can be as content as you like, for you will find yourself transformed like Cinderella at midnight into a dull, solid, middle class citizen of the type you have been against.

What happens when you are discontent? How do you go about letting it be known that you are discontent? What benefits does discontent offer you? When discontent you are rebellious. You demonstrate for or against, usually against, to let it be known that you are rebelling. Probably the favorite unpopular causes today are Viet Nam and the draft. The racial issue is no longer one of the big three because it has become too popular with everyone else.

Demonstrating is the nicest way of being rebellious because it is safe and does not involve too much work, so you are not too exhausted when you go to the frat party afterwards. And it actually serves a double purpose when you think about it. First of all, you are showing the world that you are discontent with its beuracracy, and second,, you are getting the chance to meet new people. The friendships you form may last a lifetime, and the boys you meet! They are all absolutely gorgeous.

You have seen the facts. You see my point now, don't you? If you are in college and want to have a marvelous time and do something for humanity at the same time, be a rebel and picket.

## Writing Assignment One, Cartoon 1
## Comment on Sample 1. Grade: High

Cartoons are meant to be at least wryly amusing. The student who wrote this paper (obviously a girl—see the next to last paragraph) has the sense and the skill to write about a cartoon amusingly, with a lighthearted irony that pricks some of the bubbles of the rebels. She strikes the tone in her opening sentence and maintains it throughout, keeping her tongue in cheek in spite of her dead-pan, factual style. This is no mean feat, and it is so deftly accomplished that the readers willingly forgave a bad misspelling and a wrong use of "ilk." Brief though it is, the paper has a beginning, a middle, and an end; moreover, each paragraph makes its own point, all leading to the conclusion.

## Writing Assignment One, Cartoon 1
## Sample 2. Grade: Average

The caption to cartoon 1, "Oh Gerald, I'm so marvelously discontent," is amusing because two opposite ideas are in conflict. One can not usually compare similarities in the concept of happiness, or contentness, and discontent. The resulting statement would be seemingly impossible; on the surface a falsehood. To be content with discontent, however, is a paradox. It appears false at first, but after further thought, the ironic possibilities appear. The paradox is a beautiful thing in that it takes some mental gymnastics to decern and decipher them. The paradox of "Discontent is content," is of the same general type as Orwell's jewel in his book *1984,* "War is Peace". This particular paradox revolved around the fact that in the year 1984, the economies of the world were so war orientated, that peace, in conventional usage, would mean total calapse. The peope of *1984*'s society were so used to the idea of unending war, to remove this familiar state of being, would have severe psycological effects. The people were so completely surrounded with war, for such a long period of time that War became peace, and peace would become war.

In the cartoon, the two main characters are obviously young, and have been currently ivolved in a protest march. The older generation of today might tag them "alienated youth." Their parents might say they are just going through a stage. But today, there have been too many young people invoved in some sort of protest movement. It is dangerous to take this identify and ignore attitude. The protest movement is becoming almost a way of life with some young people, and when it does, the effects will be perilous and lasting. The paradox "Discontent is Content" could very well become the epitaph of the twentieth century.

## Writing Assignment One, Cartoon 1 Comment on Sample 2. Grade: Average

This paper, with its intelligent remarks on paradox, its apt reference to Orwell's *1984*, and its explanation of how different groups might characterize the couple in the cartoon, comes close to a grade of *high*. The readers, however, decided on a rating of *average*, recognizing at the same time that the essay is at the top of that classification. Their reasons are twofold: they feel that not enough evidence has been given to justify the prophecy of doom in the final paragraph, effective though its last sentence is. They are also disturbed by a series of technical flaws—at least one example of faulty reference, several misspellings, errors in punctuation, and at least two cases of dubious diction: "contentness" and "orientated." In a theme of less than 300 words there are too many flaws, of various kinds, to justify a grade of *high*.

## Writing Assignment One, Cartoon 1 Sample 3. Grade: Low

*Time of Confusion*

It seems in today's world that people are in a state of discontent and confusion, as though peace was a thing that wasn't meant to exist or be fostered in our time. The peace of set rules and regulations are constantly being criticized and fought against. People now want freedom from those things which meant more than life itself in earlier times. These topics which were once mentioned in whispers and behind closed doors such as sex and birth control are now becoming subjects for open discussion. Freedom in situations of morality have become the sought after goal. Set rules and set standards have become too rigid and old-fashioned in our advanced times. Peace and tranquility rests in confusion and lack of order. People are no longer concerned with the basic necessities of life but are more concerned with provoking thought and searching for hidden meanings which sometimes are not there to be found. Before man can possibly look outside himself as to the emotional needs of others, man has to search into his inner soul to understand himself.

Man wants to free himself from his position and escape to a sort of "haven for thinkers." Instead of being concerned with what he thinks and knows is right according to his place in society and in relation to God, he is more concerned with what his fellowman thinks of and about him. Man was meant to be a social being. When he goes against this basic need, he causes inner confusion and disorder.

Man no longer revolts against the set way of doing things because it is necessary, but because it is the thing to do. People are constantly striving for new and better material things, which is good. But when this striving is never satisfied with a goal and is constantly fostered for the sake of being "better than the Jones'," it can only lead to further discontent and utter confusion.

## Writing Assignment One, Cartoon 1 Comment on Sample 3. Grade: Low

The assignment calls for an essay about an idea that the cartoon suggests to the writer. One trouble with this paper is its total lack of direct reference to the cartoon, or explanation of how the idea "Time of Confusion" was suggested. Freedom is mentioned in two sentences; the couple under the tree, in the cartoon, have signs about freedom; and the essay uses the word "discontent," but in a sense quite other than that of the cartoon.

A second difficulty is with grammar. "The peace of set rules and regulations are constantly being criticized" is soon followed by "Peace and tranquility rests in confusion"; in both cases the meaning is as vague as the verbs are wrong.

The third trouble with this paper is its failure in logical organization. The connection between sentences three and four, or between sentences two and three of the second paragraph—to cite only two instances—is difficult to discover. The student tries to give the essay unity by repetition of the words "discontent and confusion"—see first and last sentences—but throughout there is a lamentable lack of coherence.

## Writing Assignment One, Cartoon 2 Sample 1. Grade: High

Villians are aliens. Criminals have foreign names which associate them with ethnic, language or racial groups unlike the majority of the society in which they live. American criminals are black-haired Italians, bearded Socialists, teamster-union Communists or trench-coated members of the Mafia. Their accents are foreign and their English is broken. They wear white socks, black pointed shoes, baggy pants and white ties. They have beady, guilty eyes, bad breath and poor complexions. Gangsters eat in cheap restaurants, drink in dirty bars, keep poor company and late hours, wear leather shoulder holsters and live in the underground. However, the professional apprehenders of these criminals are clean shaven (except when they're on the job), mingle with luscious female companions, lead a more dignified office life and are essentially all-American. They represent what every anemic American wants to be—a champion of national causes in the face of foreign infiltration.

Every man wants to be a champion of his own country. He does not understand other countries and probably will never be able to see the Universe as a whole rather than a sectionalized map-full of misunderstanding enemies. His country is green and the one next door is yellow. Black lines fit comfortably and impregnably between the two clumps of color. His neighbors are either the same as him or different. If they are different, they are categorized as aliens; if they are the same, they are of course Americans. Man cannot muster the foresight or power to jump over his picket fences and black borders. His aliens remain villains. The have sinister ideas, criminal appearances and dangerous plans, and they are constantly peering over window sills and the tops of wrinkled newspapers. Just as we have established a typical villian for the purposes of our own society, other countries have conceived of similar trademarks. Foreign villians are American supermen, and will remain so until we have demolished all of the fences or found a way to communicate with one another through the pickets.

## Writing Assignment One, Cartoon 2 Comment on Sample 1. Grade: High

This paper starts out dubiously, with the misspelling "Villians" the very first word. (The second time round "villains" is correctly spelled, but alas! the word appears twice more misspelled.) There is also a "him" that ought to be "he." But the readers feel strongly that against the positive values of ingenious diction, competent sentence handling, and appropriate thought, these flaws are insignificant. This student, like the one who wrote the *high* paper on Cartoon 1, has a sense of humor well under control, and the idea suggested to him by the cartoon is sound and well developed.

## Writing Assignment One, Cartoon 2 Sample 2. Grade: Average

The purpose of cartoon 2 is, obviously, to tell the reader in a picture that his way of looking at things is not always right. The cartoon is aimed at the person who is capable of realizing this. The two Chinese children, seated on a step, are obviously stereotypes as a Western person would see them. The exaggeratedly slanted eyes and the prominent cheekbones of the children, coupled with their traditional and therefore stereotyped dress, are parallels of the typical image of the Western child. The words of the cartoon directly imply this ("the round blue eyes and pink face"). The whole scene is a parody of the concept of stereotyping and chauvinism. The cartoon here is probably the most direct way of getting the parody across. It would have taken hundreds of attempts to put this across to the average American, the recipient of the point of the cartoon. All of those attempts would, as well, have to be worded delicately so that any latent shreds of prejudice would not be offended. This drawing is a way to get the idea across gently, and to make the reader laugh at himself. The caption here is so typical of the average American's concept of other nations—he sees them as enemies to the flag of his country and, therefore, suspicious, the heavies in the black and white game of life. It then follows that other nations must, by the same token, also be guarding their nationalism suspiciously. This cartoon merely points it out and lets the reader draw his own conclusions.

## Writing Assignment One, Cartoon 2 Comment on Sample 2. Grade: Average

This paper is practically free from technical errors, and its writer sees the point of the cartoon as clearly as does the writer of the preceding paper. He fails to develop the idea suggested by the cartoon into sound generalizations, as his predecessor does not fail, and clings very closely to the cartoon itself. In even greater contrast is the rather solid, pedestrian style of this paper and the colorful wit of the one graded *high*. When he does attempt a figure of speech, his touch is unsure: how can "latent shreds of prejudice" be "offended"? The real topic of his essay is the value of the cartoon as a means of communicating criticism, but the writer does not state this as an idea suggested to him by the cartoon.

## Writing Assignment One, Cartoon 2
## Sample 3. Grade: Low

People of different nationalities "see" each other in about the same "light". This means that the things people look for in other persons are the same as looked for in them. One reason this is true might be because people are usually impressed by the stronger characteristics of others. One such strong characteristic seems to be looks.

Many Americans have a set pattern that covers the total looks of the people of a country. For example, the Japaneze look might consist of black, straight, hair and slanted, squinty eyes and sallow skin. People have trouble distinguishing one Japaneze from another because the all seem to look alike. It makes one wonder whether or not foreigners have this same problem. Since Americans consider themselves to have a variety in looks, it seems very improbable, but then again, Americans might notice characteristics of their own kind that otherwise go unnoticed.

What seems a good envirbnment for the people of one country is criticized by others. For example, Americans might be skeptical about the customs of uncivilized African tribes, but those Africans are just as skeptical about the American way of life. If one person prefers his government, it is always possible to find a foreigner that is just as content with his own. Usually the things a person criticizes in another person's environment are the same things criticized about his environment.

People like to characterize foreigners as the villain in stories. An example of such is the Nancy Drew series. One of the culprits in these books is always a Chineze man. This is probably because people tend to believe they look evil.

One of the major problems of human existence is, and has always been, the lack of understanding of other people. With better understanding, peace and prosperity might be achieved.

## Writing Assignment One, Cartoon 2
## Comment on Sample 3. Grade: Low

This paper is far from illiterate, and its writer sees the point of the cartoon. But his style is clumsy, ponderous, and repetitive. His topic is really the lack of understanding among nations, but he does not get around to stating it until his final paragraph. Paragraphs two and three are illustrations of that topic, but until a reader finishes the theme it is not easy for him to perceive any connection between them. It is characteristic that he writes "Many Americans have a set pattern that covers the total looks of the people of a country," when what he means is that Americans tend to think people of a foreign country look alike. And if he had written it in this simpler form, he might have realized that Americans do not believe that all the English look alike, or all the French, and so forth. Distinctions of this kind seem beyond him. The readers feel that this paper belongs somewhere in the middle of the numerous class *low*.

## Writing Assignment Two, Cartoon 5
## Sample 1. Grade: High

*Laughing at Sorrow*

Humor and laughter are everyday · human responses which we usually take for granted. But if we pause to try to analyse why a particular cartoon, for instance, is "funny" what we often find makes it difficult to understand why humor is enjoyable. For when we remove the elements of surprise and cleverness of presentation, the underlying situation is quite often based on a serious, or even tragic incident. At first we laugh at such a cartoon, but then we realize that the cartoonist also had the intent of presenting a serious situation and commenting on it.

The cartoon "I'm Lonesome!" is an example of this "tragic" type of humor. After we remove the humorous presentation of the cartoonist, who has his none too glamorous subject shouting her problem from her tenement window, we are faced with a common tragedy of urban life. In the urban centers today the often heard complaint that individuals are treated as no more than statistics is true. For example, this woman may be told tomorrow, as many city dwellers have, that the urban renewal computers have calculated that for the greatest good to the greatest number of people, her home is to be torn down. Nor is it likely that her cries will be answered by her neighbors. Recent incidents in New York, where people had not even the interest in their fellow city dwellers to call the police to their aid when they saw them in trouble, show the barriers that people surrounded by other people can put up around themselves. Certainly the futility of declaration of the woman in the cartoon makes her situation pitiful.

It is obvious that the cartoonist does not think that the situation he is presenting is right. He makes us pity the woman because she is so homely, and her situation must be desperate if she is driven to the extreme of yelling her problem out the window. The artist also comments on the coldness of the city through his stark and barren depiction of the buildings, and the absence of people, except the subject. There is no sign of life in any other window, and the woman appears to be alone with the concrete.

The cartoonist, then, had two motives in drawing this cartoon, and each complements the other. First, it makes the reader laugh, but the source of this humor is a serious situation, which the artist states is wrong.

## Writing Assignment Two, Cartoon 5 Comment on Sample 1. Grade: High

This paper is clearly and competently written, and follows directions to the letter. Its writer sees the humor in the cartoon, but sees with equal clarity the seriousness of the situation humorously portrayed. He illustrates his generalization about the "tragic" type of humor, and concludes with a justified speculation about the cartoonist's purposes. It is probable that Mr. Steig would agree with this writer.

Students in general saw the seriousness underlying the humor of this cartoon, but few stated it as succinctly and as well as does this writer. The paper is not brilliant, but intelligent and effective.

## Writing Assignment Two, Cartoon 5 Sample 2. Grade: Average

The humor in cartoon 5 is the thought that anyone living in a huge city could possibly be lonesome. A city offers a variety of meeting places. Surely there is someone else who shares this woman's interests and could be a friend. People dream of going to the city to meet people. Many small town girls head toward that center of opportunity, the city, to find a career and seek a husband. It is paradoxical to think that a resident of this desirous site is lonely.

However this cartoon is as serious as it is humorous. The lose of individuality in the anonymous city is a frightening thought. The apathy of a city dweller to his fellow man is a common story. The murder of a woman while 38 "neighbors" watched is something which is becoming less and less an unusual occurence. These so called humans had no other thought than concern for their own involvement. The city goes on; the buildings —and the people who dwell within—don't care.

## Writing Assignment Two, Cartoon 5 Comment on Sample 2. Grade: Average

The trouble with writing a comment on a truly *average* paper is that there is frequently little to say. Part of being in the *average* category is having sufficient intelligence to grasp the main ideas: this student so qualifies. Another part is having learned enough about writing to avoid a mass of egregious errors: here, too, the criterion is met, though in so short a theme a couple of misspellings and "desirous" for "desirable" are unfortunate. But this student fails to develop an idea or a topic convincingly. This paper is obviously intended as an analysis of the humor in Cartoon 5, but the analysis is very limited; what there is is accurate enough, but, like the rest of the paper, it is thin.

## Writing Assignment Two, Cartoon 5 Sample 3. Grade: Low

*Are You Lonely?*

In the world around us there are many challenges to be met. One of the greatest challenges to overcome stems from the fact that people are lonely. Loneliness is an undesirable feeling that one seldom wants. One person that we know for sure is lonely is the hermit, but the other person that is lonely could be you or it could be me. It is the person that acts and seems happy, but in actuality is not satisfied with himself.

The hermit to most people is the loneliest of all for he is outwardly noticable. Some people usually become hermits through some action that turns them away from the world. One of the loneliest introverts was Heidi's grandfather in the storybook about Heidi. Some incident caused this poor old man to withdraw from society, and to live on the mountain, lonely and secluded. Psychologically, hermits can not tolerate the imperfections of human beings, and so they withdraw from reality. However, they still need companionship whether it be human or animal. The Shade Gap affair proved that a hermit needed something, and he happened to find it in an unfortunate girl. The man owned some dogs, and, as everyone knows, dogs are basically loyal to their master, and tolerant of his actions. The person who cannot stand the imperfections of others, and through his actions becomes a hermit is the most common type of lonely persons.

There are many people that seem very content and happy, but are really lonely and complex. For example, the actor who sees many people like directors and stage people, and who has many fans may in reality be a lonely person, because he cannot cope with his own problems. Marilyn Monroe had many fans all over the world, showing that she was a very wonderful actress, but, on the inside, she had many conflicts giving her a lonely, artificial life. Here is a strange situation because she, as an actress, could put herself into the parts of the persons she was playing, but could not play the part which she found herself in. Some people have very high standards of perfection, striving all their lives to meet these standards, and when they do not reach their goal become rejected people. One prime example of this was Napoleon, who died in exile. He was a man of great perfection, wishing to conquor Russia. When he failed he became a broken man living in sheer misery. It is usually hard to identify this type of loneliness in a person because he will do anything to mask or conceal his true feelings.

So it is hard to tell who the lonely person is. It might be the person sitting next to you, or it might be the hermit on the hill, or even someone famous. One cannot tell. To correct and improve the situation, one should go out of his way to say something friendly to someone today.

## Writing Assignment Two, Cartoon 5 Comment on Sample 3. Grade: Low

The assignment gives a choice of topics: either a discussion of the serious situation underlying the cartoon or an analysis of its humor. This student avoids both; having omitted any reference whatever to the cartoon, he obviously cannot analyze its humor.

Instead, he plunges into a disquisition on loneliness and lonely people, managing to bring together a strange fellowship of lonely hearts: Heidi's grandfather, hermits ("the most common type of lonely persons"), Marilyn Monroe, and Napoleon after his failure in Russia. And "the other person that is lonely could be you or it could be me," for many are able to conceal their pangs under an outward appearance of happiness.

The writing in this paper, as such, is passable, but a certain incoherence would keep it in the *low* group even if it focused on one of the required topics.

## Writing Assignment Two, Cartoon 6 Sample 1. Grade: High

The situation depicted in cartoon 6 is quite a familiar one. The cartoonist is commenting on dogmatism and pomposity in the realm of intellectual (or cultural) pursuits, in particular the artistic sphere. One often assumes a role of superiority if his knowledge exceeds that of others; the humor lies in the word "like", because of its subjective, non-factual connotations. How can one be told what to like? Many people assume that they have this prerogative to guide and inform in the matter of taste. The cartoonist uses the art gallery to imply "the arts", and children to comment wryly on the state of naïve adults.

This cartoon may be enlarged in its interpretation to include almost all spheres of activity. To an emerging Asian nation, the U.S. says: "Democracy works for us, so you'll like it." To an unsuspecting audience, Salvador Dali quips: "I'm Dali, and so you will enjoy my 'happening.' " Of course, this line of reasoning, to use the term loosely, is hardly valid, constituting a dangerous fallacy in many peoples' thinking.

## Writing Assignment Two, Cartoon 6 Comment on Sample 1. Grade: High

The combination of Cartoon 6 and the topics assigned for papers in writing assignment two produced a number of *averages* and *lows,* but almost no *highs.* The readers agree that this paper belongs in the *high* category, though they tend to qualify it as *high minus* because of its brevity. The student is obviously able; it seems clear that he chose the first topic, for he shows that the cartoon is based on a serious idea, but he could have spent, to advantage, more time and space in showing how the cartoon comments on the situation.

At the same time, this student is able to say a great deal in a few, well-chosen words. He expects his reader to be able to expand his compressed points. "The humor lies in the word 'like', because of its subjective, non-factual connotations." To be understood clearly, this clause needs the context of the first half of its sentence and the caption of the cartoon; at first reading, the connections are not quite clear. The readers have a common belief that what appears in the essay is of *high* quality; they only wish for more.

## Writing Assignment Two, Cartoon 6 Sample 2. Grade: Average

The nature of the humor presented in the cartoon is that of recreating an uncomfortable situation that is funny in retrospect. It additionally offers a humorous situation with an underlying, disturbing significance.

The cartoon itself is highly successful in each case. Everyone has been intimidated by intelligent or pseudo-intelligent people presuming to impose their superior knowledge on others. Modern art is a loaded topic and the confusion surrounding its meaning immediately catches a knowing response from most people.

An additional vehicle for humor lies in the age of the three people. One child speaking to her peers in such a knowing manner, coat off, with slightly bohemian clothes brings a laugh from most adults. Parents in particular remember situations when children "think they know."

In regard to the more serious implications is the fear of someone's ideas pushed on one. Cultural and political propaganda immediately come to mind. Most people take this sort of "Big Brother" intimidation as a direct affrontery to their democratic ideals. The cartoon grows in seriousness in that children are involved; such words coming from so young a mouth!

Young people, however, would laugh at the cartoon as it reminds them of adult's assumed superiority because they are adults. The child-speaker is the oldest, and the biggest of the three. An adolescent, while gathering the political and cultural implications, also will recall the equally serious indoctrination of themselves by their parents.

The cartoon is a successful example of the funny-serious type of humour in its use of loaded topics and vehicles. It lacks audience limitations and has skillfully combined caregully chosen elements to create this universal situation.

## Writing Assignment Two, Cartoon 6 Comment on Sample 2. Grade: Average

This student attempted the more difficult of the two topics suggested: an analysis of the nature of the humor in Cartoon 6 and comment on the success of the cartoon in achieving its humor. But the second sentence of the first paragraph pulls in the other topic, also, and the writer recurs to this theme in the fourth paragraph, with some damage to the unity of his essay.

One might question the first sentence. Does the cartoon recreate "an uncomfortable situation that is funny in retrospect"? The pictured children, certainly, seem not to be uncomfortable; indeed, their attitudes indicate gleeful anticipation.

This writer is a serious-minded soul, however; when he generalizes from the cartoon, he moves immediately to propaganda and 1984. But he has shown no "intimidation" of her young companions by the senior member of the cartoon's trio, so that his "serious implications" seem a bit far-fetched.

Aside from these questions of content, there are some flaws in technique—particularly bad is the faulty reference in the last sentence of the fifth paragraph. Yet, in general, the writing is adequate.

For an eleventh grader to tackle the topic it takes either courage or blissful ignorance; that the resulting analysis is thin and pushed to extremes should perhaps be expected.

## Writing Assignment Two, Cartoon 6 Sample 3. Grade: Low

Art, to many people, is a mysterious subject to be understood only by those in the know. If often takes many years to fully understand all the elements and components of good art. After these years of training, a person may still not be a good art critic. A small child may recognize the unity that exists in a painting and label it good. Chronological age should therefore have no relation to the amount of art awareness one possesses. Most people realize this and humor results from the little girls mistaken assumption.

What may appeal to one person in art, may irritate someone else. What is right and wrong is dictated by the present standards of society. A painting called ridiculous twenty years ago, may be recognized as a masterpiece tomorrow. It is sort of humorous to consider that the little girl should be able to dictate the likes and dislikes of another person.

## Writing Assignment Two, Cartoon 6 Comment on Sample 3. Grade: Low

Here is another attempt to deal with the difficult topic involving an analysis of the humor in Cartoon 6 and its success. This effort is less successful than the previous one, partly because some of its premises are dubious. To say that "Chronological age should therefore have no relation to the amount of art awareness one possesses" is a rash statement as long as it is unqualified. And while it is true that "After . . . years of training, a person may still not be a good art critic," it is more than likely that he is better equipped than a babe in arms.

Comment on the success of the cartoon in achieving humor is limited to the final sentence in this short paper, and amounts only to "It is sort of humorous. . ."

The technique is generally good; the paper is in the *low* category because of its thinness and illogic.

*An Essay and a Poem*
*on the Same Subject*
*Grade 11*

will and testament, and it thereby revokes all other wills and codicils at any time heretofore made by me. I hold Basic A Mileage Ration 108950, O. P. A. Form R-525-C. The number of my car is 18-388. Tickets A-14 are valid through March 21st.

3 I was born in District Number 5903, New York State. My birth is registered in Volume 3/58 of the Department of Health. My father was a man of medium height. His telephone number was 484. My mother was a housewife. Her eyes were blue. Neither parent had a social security number and neither was secure socially. They drove to the depot behind an unnumbered horse.

4 I hold Individual Certificate Number 4320-209 with the Equitable Life Assurance Society, in which a corporation hereinafter called the employer has contracted to insure my life for the sum of two thousand dollars. My left front tire is Number 48KE8846, my right front tire is Number 63T6895. My rear tires are, from left to right, Number 6N4M5384 and Number A26E5806D. I brush my hair with Whiting-Adams Brush Number 010 and comb my hair with Pro-Phy-Lac-Tic Comb Number 1201. My shaving brush is sterilized. I take Pill Number 43934 after each meal and I can get more of them by calling ELdorado 5-6770. I spray my nose with De Vilbiss Atomizer Number 14. Sometimes I stop the pain with Squibb Pill, Control Number 3K49979 (aspirin). My wife (Number 067-01-9807) takes Pill Number 49345.

5 I hold War Ration Book 40289EW, from which have been torn Airplane Stamps Numbers 1, 2, and 3. I also hold Book 159378CD, from which have been torn Spare Number 2, Spare Number 37, and certain other coupons. My wife holds Book 40288EW and Book 159374CD. In accepting them, she recognized that they remained the property of the United States Government.

6 I have a black dog with cheeks of tan. Her number is 11032. It is an old number. I shall renew it when I get time. The analysis of her prepared food is guaranteed and is Case Number 1312. The ingredients are: Cereal Flaked feeds (from Corn, Rice, Bran, and Wheat), Meat Meal, Fish Liver and Glandular Meal, Soybean Oil Meal, Wheat Bran, Corn Germ Meal, 5% Kel-Centrate [containing Dried Skim Milk, Dehydrated Cheese, Vitamin $B_1$ (Thiamin), Flavin Concentrate, Carotene, Yeast, Vitamin A and D Feeding Oil (containing 3,000 U.S. P. units Vitamin A and 400 U.S.P. units Vitamin D per gram), Diastase (Enzyme), Wheat Germ Meal, Rice Polish Extract], 1½% Calcium Carbonate, .00037% Potassium Iodide, and ¼% Salt. She prefers offal.

When I finish what I am now writing it will be late in the day. It will be about half past five. I will then take up Purchase Order Number 245-9077-B-Final, which I received this morning from the Office of War Information and which covers the use of certain material they want to translate into a foreign language. Attached to the order are Standard Form Number 1034 (white) and three copies of Standard Form Number 1034a (yellow), also "Instructions for Preparation of Voucher by Vendor and Example of Prepared Voucher." The Appropriation Symbol of the Purchase Order is 1153700.001-501. The requisition number is B-827. The allotment is X5-207.1-R2-11. Voucher shall be prepared in ink, indelible pencil, or typewriter. For a while I will be vendor preparing voucher. Later on, when my head gets bad and the pain radiates, I will be voucher preparing vendor. I see that there is a list of twenty-one instructions which I will be following. Number One on the list is: "Name of payor agency as shown in the block 'appropriation symbol and title' in the upper left-hand corner of the Purchase Order." Number Five on the list is: "Vendor's personal account or invoice number," but whether that means Order Number 245-9077-B-Final, or Requisition B-827, or Allotment X5-207.1-R2-11, or Appropriation Symbol 1153700.001-501, I do not know, nor will I know later on in the evening after several hours of meditation, nor will I be able to find out by consulting Woman 067-01-9807, who is no better at filling out forms than I am, nor after taking Pill Number 43934, which tends merely to make me drowsy.

I owe a letter to Corporal 32413654, Hq and Hq Sq., VII AAF S.C., APO 953, c/o PM San Francisco, Calif., thanking him for the necktie he sent me at Christmas. In 1918 I was a private in the Army. My number was 4,345,016. I was a boy of medium height. I had light hair. I had no absences from duty under G.O. 31, 1912, or G.O. 45, 1914. The number

# *An Essay and a Poem on the Same Subject Grade 11*

*Works:* E. B. White, "About Myself," from *Second Tree from the Corner,* and W. H. Auden, "The Unknown Citizen"
*Approximate Time:* 4 days

## First Assignment

Read "About Myself," an essay by E. B. White.

### *About Myself*

E. B. White

I am a man of medium height. I keep my records in 1
a Weis Folder Re-order Number 8003. The unpaid balance of my estimated tax for the year 1945 is item 3 less the sum of items 4 and 5. My eyes are gray. My Selective Service order number is 10789. The serial number is T1654. I am in Class IV-A, and have been variously in Class 3-A, Class I-A(H), and Class 4-H. My social security number is 067-01-9841. I am married to U. S. Woman Number 067-01-9807. Her eyes are gray. This is not a joint declaration, nor is it made by an agent; therefore it need be signed only by me—and, as I said, I am a man of medium height.

I am the holder of a quit-claim deed recorded in 2
Book 682, Page 501, in the county where I live. I hold Fire Insurance Policy Number 424747, continuing until the 23 day of October in the year nineteen hundred forty-five, at noon, and it is important that the written portions of all policies covering the same property read exactly alike. My cervical spine shows relatively good alignment with evidence of proliferative changes about the bodies consistent with early arthritis. (Essential clinical data: pain in neck radiating to mastoids and occipito-temporal region, not constant, moderately severe; patient in good general health and working.) My operator's licence is Number 16200. It expired December 31, 1943, more than a year ago, but I am still carrying it and it appears to be serving the purpose. I shall renew it when I get time. I have made, published, and declared my last

of that war was Number One.

## To the Teacher

Comedy—including irony and satire—is notoriously difficult to teach. A quip or joke that has to be explained loses most of its humor in the process. White's essay, and the Auden poem, will be delights to the able students without explication. The less able will need some help, but it is suggested that in all classes students be encouraged to make discoveries about the humor, the satire, the underlying meanings, as far as possible by themselves. Nothing is so likely to kill their enjoyment of these two pieces as a rigidly followed plan of thorough analysis. The teacher must be able to follow, for part of the time at least, wherever the class discussions lead him, but so to guide the students that the most important points are brought out and understood. The questions for discussion that follow should probably not be asked in the order they are printed in; some may not need to be asked at all.

## Questions for Discussion

*I. "About Myself" as an autobiographical essay, as it purports to be.*

1. What evidence in the essay would allow you to write a description of the author's appearance? Would an artist be able to draw or paint a likeness? Why or why not?

2. From the information about himself presented by the author, would you be able to write a reasonably accurate character sketch? What traits does he—consciously or involuntarily—reveal? What important information about an individual does he conceal (his education, occupation, interests and hobbies, religious affiliation if any)?

3. After considering these matters, to what extent do you think the title appropriate? What is White writing about? The question may be posed here, but answers should be deferred.

*II. Fun and games.*

1. It has been reported that Mr. White admitted that he had fun writing this piece. Can you detect any evidence to support this rumor?

2. Much of his enjoyment may have come from his ability, in the essay, to poke fun at a wide variety of targets. What are some of these?

*Note to the teacher.* It will probably be useful to list on the board the targets as the class suggests them—always requiring evidence from the essay. The list can be used to identify cases where the satire cuts more ways than one. Following are targets that should find places somewhere in the list:

a. the increasing modern habit of identifying people, animals, and things by numbers. How do you know he is making fun of this habit? (One evidence is the equal importance, so far as the essay indicates, of the numbers of his four automobile tires and the number of his life insurance policy.);

b. regulations—governmental—that affect private lives;

c. the language of official documents—quoted, parodied, becoming (cf. paragraph 7) more obscure as it attempts to be more precise;

d. the author's parents;

e. the author's wife;

f. the author's dog;

g. the author himself (some of these points may have been covered in I.2 above).

Items d, e, f, and g are those in which the satire is double-edged. For example, consider the paragraph about the dog (6): what effects are produced by (a) the phrase "cheeks of tan"; (b) the elaborate chemical analysis of her "prepared food"—after all, it's dog food; (c) the food the dog prefers? Is the paragraph making fun of the makers of dog food, of the modern passion for scientific or pseudoscientific analysis, or of the dog? Or all three? Explain. A similar technique can be used with the author's parents and wife and the author himself.

*III. Points that may have come out in the previous discussion* (if they have, don't belabor them, but they should not be missed).

1. About the author.

a. He refers twice to licenses he has not renewed. Does he sound guilty? Is he making fun of himself or of regulations that are not enforced, perhaps are not enforceable?

b. Several times the author refers to himself, and once to his father, as "of medium height." Can you suggest a reason for this repetition?

2. About some of White's satirical devices.

a. A play on words: consider "social security" in

paragraph 3; "vendor" and "voucher" in paragraph 7.

b. The non sequitur: consider the last sentence of paragraph 1. What other examples can you find? (The last sentence of paragraph 5—in context; sentences 2, 3, and so forth of the final paragraph.)

c. Contrast—unexpected, sometimes concealed. (Something important—his "last will and testament"—immediately followed by his "Basic A Mileage Ration," paragraph 2.) Many other examples are available. (Insurance—tires; father—phone number.)

*IV. Towards the end.*

1. The essay contains references to wars. Which wars? How do you know? To what extent does White seem affected by the current war?

2. In the final paragraph White identifies a corporal only by his serial number. What does he gain by going on to specify the corporal's Christmas gift?

3. What functions do you think a final paragraph should perform? To what extent do you think White's final paragraph performs these functions? In arriving at your answer, pay special attention to the sound, and the implications of the war's name, in the final sentence.

4. Go back to I.3 to get a class consensus on what White is writing about. (There should be a place for his interest in a less-regulated life—when his parents could drive "behind an unnumbered horse," paragraph 3.)

## Second Assignment

Read "The Unknown Citizen," by W. H. Auden.

### *The Unknown Citizen*

(To JS/07/M/378 This Marble Monument
Is Erected by the State)

W. H. Auden

He was found by the Bureau of Statistics to be
One against whom there was no official complaint,
And all the reports on his conduct agree
That, in the modern sense of an old-fashioned word, he was a saint,
For in everything he did he served the Greater Community.
Except for the War till the day he retired
He worked in a factory and never got fired,
But satisfied his employers, Fudge Motors Inc.
Yet he wasn't a scab or odd in his views,
For his Union reports that he paid his dues,
(Our report on his Union shows it was sound)
And our Social Psychology workers found
That he was popular with his mates and liked a drink.
The Press are convinced that he bought a paper every day
And that his reactions to advertisements were normal in every way.
Policies taken out in his name prove that he was fully insured,
And his Health-card shows he was once in hospital but left it cured.
Both Producers Research and High-Grade Living declare
He was fully sensible to the advantages of the Installment Plan
And had everything necessary to the Modern Man,
A phonograph, a radio, a car and a frigidaire.
Our researchers into Public Opinion are content
That he held the proper opinions for the time of year;
When there was peace, he was for peace; when there was war, he went.
He was married and added five children to the population,
Which our Eugenist says was the right number for a parent of his generation,
And our teachers report that he never interfered with their education.
Was he free? Was he happy? The question is absurd:
Had anything been wrong, we should certainly have heard.

### Questions for Discussion

1. If the citizen's file number is known, and if he has been investigated by so many organizations and groups, how can he be called "Unknown"?

2. Why should the State erect a monument to JS/07/M/378? In what ways is this similar to the monument to The Unknown Soldier? Suggest reasons for capitalizing "Greater Community" (line 5).

3. Consider the organizations and individuals that allegedly knew about the citizen's conduct (there are

about a dozen). Do they all exist? Does the poem imply that they are governmental agencies? How would you relate Auden's use of these groups to White's use of numbers?

4. Auden calls "saint" an old-fashioned word, applicable to the citizen in a "modern sense." Contrast this meaning with the "old-fashioned" one. What is the poet implying about religion today?

5. What is suggested about the citizen by lines 23 and 27? Is there an analogous idea in the White essay?

6. "We" and "our" occur often in the poem. To whom do these words refer? Do they include the speaker of the poem? Or the author? Explain your answers.

7. What knowledge about the citizen is not revealed by statistics and official investigations? Does Auden think this knowledge important? How do you know? Explain the effect of his use of "absurd" (line 28).

8. What seems to be Auden's belief about modern man's relationship to the State? Judging by "About Myself," do you think White would agree?

9. Both the essay and the poem purport to be about an individual. To what extent do you think this apparent subject is the real subject of the essay and the poem? Explain your answer.

10. On similar subjects, one author writes in prose, the other in verse. Which medium seems to you more effective? Why?

11. How important a role does *ridicule* play in the poem and in the essay? What are the targets for ridicule in each? To what extent does each rely on such techniques as exaggeration, understatement, irony, reduction to absurdity? Ridicule can be gentle, tender, understanding or bitter, contemptuous, intolerant. Do any of these words define the ridicule in either the essay or the poem? If not, what terms would you use to define that ridicule?

## Writing Assignment

Write an account of a day in the life of "the Modern Man" (a phrase used in line 20 of "The Unknown Citizen") as you see him after reading this poem and essay. Develop from your experience the problems he encounters and his solutions. Write your account for *one* of these audiences:

a. A group of modern men whom you are trying to persuade that their way of life is undesirable. You are a lecturer with a mission.

b. A group of older citizens who do not accept the modern man's way of life but who you think should accept it.

c. A group of modern men whose votes you want and whom you are reminding of the virtues of the modern way of life, which you promise to work to maintain. In this case, create a speaker who admires the modern way of life while you, the author, like Auden, deplore it.

d. Your fellow Martians, to whom you are reporting on the daily life of the modern Earth Man after your recent journey to Earth in a flying saucer.

e. Secondary school students in the year 4023 for whom you are writing a history textbook. You have only these two documents by White and Auden as first-hand source material for constructing a description of the daily life of twentieth century man (known to historians as Modern Man).

*A Composition Unit in Persuasion*
*Grades 11 and 12*

mates, asks you to attend a dance at your high school. The two dances are on the same Saturday night. You have dated Joe two or three times, and you would like him to ask you to go out with him on future occasions. Tell two people of your plans to attend the university dance: (1) your best girl friend and (2) Joe. Write the explanations in language that will sound as if you were making the explanations orally. Tell the truth in both accounts.

3. (For boys.) Your older brother has asked you to go on a weekend hunting (or fishing) trip with him. You accept, and you do not tell him that you have a three-page paper that is due Monday in English class. You assure yourself that you will take writing materials with you and stay in camp all one morning and write the paper while the others are gone. What better setting, you ask yourself, could one possibly find in which to write? After all, look at Thoreau. You are convinced that you owe it to yourself, and especially to your writing talent, to go. But the hunting (or fishing) is good, and on Monday you do not have the paper finished. Tell (1) your friends at school and (2) your English teacher about your weekend. Write in the language you would use if you were making the explanations orally. Tell the truth in both accounts.

### Second Day

Divide the students into groups of four or five. Each student should read both of his explanations to his group. Then his listeners will tell him whether they hear two separate voices in the two accounts.

### Third Day

(The third day of the unit should be held as soon as the teacher can read, but not mark, all the papers and ditto the three or four sets most suitable for the third day's work.) Do not distribute all the sets at the beginning of the period: discuss each set before new papers are distributed. Have both pages of a set read aloud. Then ask the class to discuss these problems:

1. Cite specific words in each paper of the set that are used because of the speaker's audience. These words would not be used in his explanation to the other of his two audiences. (Before this part of the discussion is completed, the teacher should use the word *diction* in a context that will make the word clear to any students who do not already know it.)

2. Are there differences in grammatical constructions, spelling, or punctuation that can be accounted for by considering the audiences for whom the explanations are intended? (Verb tense, verb voice, contractions, variant spellings, and dashes are likely to be cited here, but the material should determine the content of the discussion.)

3. If there are significant differences in the order in which the material is presented in the two explanations, try to decide why the narrator chooses to organize his material differently for the two audiences.

4. Now talk about the differences in tone caused by the differences in problems 1, 2, and 3 above.

## Study of a Student's Paper

### Fourth Day

The author of "My Opinions on Compulsory Physical Education in High School," a college freshman, is asked to assume an audience of secondary school physical education instructors who are attending a conference on physical education programs. During the conference the teachers hear a number of speakers with varying qualifications in and attitudes toward physical education programs. This freshman is asked to try to persuade his audience to accept his points about physical education in secondary schools. He is to read his paper to his audience.

### *My Opinions on Compulsory Physical Education in High School*

For many years we Americans, as if with one mind, 1
have jumped with both feet into the battle for physical fitness. In health bars we consume gallons of carrot juice. We go on health diets, and ruin our health. We take up, and give up, hiking and skiing. We read health magazines from cover to cover, without getting out of our chair; and we can hardly pick up any magazine without seeing advertisements of body-building equipment featuring skinny-before and muscle-bound-after pictures of young men who have already spent their money in the worthy cause of physical fitness. The fact is that physical fitness has become a fad.

# *A Composition Unit in Persuasion Grades 11 and 12*

## To the Teacher

The primary purposes of this unit are (1) to teach the student that the relationship between the speaker and his audience in a particular situation should influence the stylistic elements of his composition and (2) to give him experience in applying this knowledge in his own writing.

Teachers of English know that questions about persuasion do not stand alone. To what extent does subject matter determine style? How important are principles of argument in persuasive discourse? These are fundamental questions that certainly should not be neglected in a student's training in composition, and they should not be entirely disassociated from persuasion. But they are secondary in this unit to the question of how one persuades his audience to react favorably to his argument.

## Writing Assignment One (and Study of Papers)

### First Day

Ask each student to select *one* of the following writing assignments and to begin work on it in class. He should bring his completed papers to class the second day. Each assignment requires two short papers; neither paper should be longer than one page.

1. You drove the family car off a slippery road; it became so mired that you had to call a service truck to pull your car out of the mud. Write two explanations in the language that you would use if you were giving the explanations orally: the first to your father when you arrive home later than you should, the second to your friends next day. Tell the truth in both accounts.

2. (For girls.) You have an older brother who is a freshman at the state university. He has invited his girl friend to attend a dance at the university, and he wants you to come with her—to date his new roommate. Your brother says his roommate is one of the most likable fellows he knows. Shortly after you learn of your brother's plans, Joe, one of your class-

One of the most important branches of the physi- 2
cal fitness movement is the teaching of physical education in public schools. Teachers of basketball and football have equal status with teachers of English and mathematics. Colleges have separate schools where earnest young men and women are taught to play volleyball correctly so that they may in turn teach earnest boys and girls to play volleyball correctly.

What is it all for? Some people say, "To keep us 3
fit." Those same people explain how shocking it was to discover during the Korean War how many of our young men and women were actually in poor physical condition. They go on to explain that the physical education program is set up to prevent such deplorable conditions. Ergo, we need compulsory physical education in high school.

I admit that it sounds like a good idea. But, for 4
the years before the Korean War, there were physical education courses in almost every public school. Therefore, if physical education courses were actually worthwhile, more of the draftees would have been in good condition. If playing volleyball and basketball for forty minutes twice a week will not keep Johnny fit, why make him keep on doing it? To boys who are already spending much of their time engaged in extracurricular activities involving physical exercise, this eighty minutes a week means even less. Either way, it is a waste of time.

There is no place in public schools for fads or other 5
ways of wasting time. The time that Johnny and Susie now waste by hopping around on one foot in some gymnasium might better be spent on important things. Johnny and Susie might benefit by some classes in how to meet and get along with people, or classes in dancing—not twisting, but real dancing—or classes in the fast dying out art of conversation. If none of these appealed, perhaps they might be more interested in a couple of courses in ancient history, world literature, or art and music appreciation. Johnny and his classmates would surely find knowledge of these subjects more useful in later life than they would knowledge of the correct way to do a handstand on the rings in the gym. Unless, of course, Johnny plans to quit school and join a circus.

One might get the impression from what I have 6
said that I am against physical exercise, which is certainly not the case. I like it. I believe, however, that it should be kept in its place, which is as a pastime indulged in in one's leisure hours. I dislike being the victim of some fad, I know that eighty minutes a week will not make me a prize physical specimen, and I didn't have to go to high school to keep fit.

### Questions for Discussion

Copies of "My Opinions on Compulsory Physical Education in High School" should be given to your students at the end of the third day. They should be asked to read the paper before class the fourth day and to prepare to respond to the problems listed below, which should accompany the paper.

1. Cite specific words and larger elements in the paper that are likely to so offend the audience that the young man's argument may not get a fair hearing. [Be certain your students do not overlook the second sentence in paragraph 2, the last sentence in paragraph 4, "fad" (1), "earnest young men and women" (2), "fads or other ways of wasting time" (5), "hopping around on one foot" (5), "indulged in" (6), "victim of some fad" (6).]

2. What advantages and disadvantages does the speaker have in his role as a recent participant in a high school physical education program? He should have been aware of these as he prepared his comments.

3. What sort of beginning might have caused the young man's audience to consider his criticism of physical education?

4. Assume that you are asked to talk to the writer about how to do a better job of persuading. How will you begin? What can you say that is true and that will cause him, your audience, to accept your comments?

## Writing Assignment Two

### Fifth Day

Talk with the students for a few minutes about the following writing assignment. Caution them against assigning themselves responsibilities they cannot fulfill. For example, a student should not assume the role of a constitutional lawyer trying to convince the Supreme Court justices to overrule a lower court's decision, nor should the student try to convince Old Testament scholars of the authenticity of the early miracles. Encourage the students to discuss the kinds of problems they can work with satisfactorily. Ask the students to begin to plan their work during the class period, but to write the paper out of class. Give the students a certain date on which you will check to see that the rough draft has been written. This date should be about three days before the final draft is due.

### Directions

Assume an audience that cannot be expected to agree entirely with the thesis of the paper you will write. Then write a paper in which you attempt to convince the audience that a particular idea is true or that a particular action should be taken.

On the title page indicate your audience and your relationship to the audience; tell, too, whether your audience will read your paper or will hear you present it. For example:

1. I am a student addressing the curriculum director of my high school. He will read my paper.

2. I am addressing my classmates in Junior English. They will hear me present my paper.

3. I am assuming the role of a P.T.A. president addressing the city councilmen. They will hear me present my paper.

## Study of Leacock's Essay "Americans Are Queer" (Optional, Grade 12)

### To the Teacher

This part of the unit is optional for able twelfth grade students. The essay by Stephen Leacock faces the student with the deliberate use of illogic as a sophisticated technique of persuasion. Every well-trained ninth grader learns the dangers of the sweeping generalization whose validity a single exception can demolish. Here the students meet an obviously astute writer who is doing the very thing they have been told they mustn't do. Their problem is to figure out why he is doing it, how he is doing it, and with what calculated effects on his audience he is doing it. (Teachers will note—and should point out to their students—where and how some details of Leacock's essay are "dated," with or without the loss of effect.)

### *Americans Are Queer*

Stephen Leacock[1]

Americans are queer people: they can't rest. They have more time, more leisure, shorter hours, more holidays, and more vacations than any other people in the world. But they can't rest. They rush up and down across their continent as tourists; they move about in great herds to conventions; they invade the wilderness, they flood the mountains, they keep the hotels full. But they can't rest. The scenery rushes past them. They learn it, but they don't see it. Battles and monuments are announced to them in a rubberneck bus. They hear them, but they don't get them. They never stop moving; they rush up and down as Shriners, Masons, Old Graduates, Bankers—they are a new thing each day, always rushing to a reunion or something.

So they go on rushing about till eventually the undertaker gathers them in to a last convention.

Americans are queer people: they can't read. They have more schools, and better schools, and spend more money on schools and colleges than all Europe. But they can't read. They print more books in one year than the French print in ten. But they can't read. They cover their country with 100,000 tons of Sunday newspapers every week. But they don't read them. They're too busy. They use them for fires and to make more paper with. They buy eagerly thousands of new novels at two dollars each. But they read only page one. Their streets are full of huge signs. They won't look at them. Their street cars are filled with advertisements; they turn their eyes away. Transparent colors, cart wheels, and mechanical flares whirl and flicker in the crowded streets at night. No one sees them. Tons of circulars pour through the mails, through the houses, and down the garbage chute. The last American who sat down to read died in the days of Henry Clay.

• • • • •

Americans are queer people: they can't play. Amer

1. Stephen Leacock was himself Canadian, but his books are printed in this country and his "audience" for this essay is largely American.

icans rush to work as soon as they grow up. They want their work as soon as they wake. It is a stimulant—the only one they're not afraid of. They used to open their offices at ten o'clock; then at nine; then at eight; then at seven. Now they never shut them. Every business in America is turning into an open-all-day-and-night business. They eat all night, dance all night, build buildings at night, make a noise all night. They can't play. They try to, but they can't. They turn football into a fight, baseball into a lawsuit, and yachting into machinery. They can't play. The little children can't play; they use mechanical toys instead—toy cranes hoisting toy loads, toy machinery spreading a toy industrial depression of infantile dullness. The grown-up people can't play: they use a mechanical gymnasium and a clockwork horse. They can't swim: they use a float. They can't run: they use a car. They can't laugh: they hire a comedian and watch him laugh.

Americans are queer people: they don't give a 5
damn. All the world criticizes them and they don't give a damn. All the world writes squibs like this about them and they don't give a damn. Foreign visitors come and write them up; they don't give a damn. Lecturers lecture at them; they don't care. They are told they have no art, no literature, and no soul. They never budge. Moralists cry over them, criminologists dissect them, writers shoot epigrams at them, prophets foretell the end of them; and they never move. Seventeen brilliant books analyze them every month; they don't read them. The Europeans threaten to unite them; they don't mind. Equatorial Africa is dead sour on them; they don't even know it. The Chinese look on them as full of Oriental cunning; the English accuse them of British stupidity; the Scotch call them close-fisted; the Italians say they are liars; the French think their morals loose; the Bolsheviks accuse them of Communism.

But that's all right. The Americans don't give a 6
damn; don't need to—never did need to. That is their salvation.

## Questions for Discussion

*Reaction.*

1. While you are reading this essay, does it irritate you as an American?

2. If so, do you conclude that the author deliberately sets out to irritate and insult Americans?

3. If not, what do you think keeps Leacock's statements from being offensive to Americans?

*Examination of the essay.*

1. What accusations does Leacock make against Americans? How does he give them specific support in his essay?

2. To what extent do you find his evidence persuasive?

3. To what extent do you see his arguments as vulnerable? Is it likely that the author is unaware of this vulnerableness? If he is aware of it, why doesn't he do something about it?

4. In what order does Leacock present the ideas in his essay? Where is the climax?

5. What effect does he achieve by the unusual number of short sentences? What is the effect of the frequent repetition?

6. Examine the following phrases:

"or something," paragraph 1

"to make more paper with" (instead of "for making more paper"), paragraph 3

"a toy industrial depression of infantile dullness," paragraph 4

How would you describe the level of formality of each of these expressions? What do your findings tell you about the speaker?

7. Comment on the effectiveness of the underlined wording in each of the following expressions:

"a *rubberneck* bus," paragraph 1

"*a last convention,*" paragraph 2

"an *open-all-day-and-night* business," paragraph 4

"writers *shoot* epigrams at them," paragraph 5

8. Cite examples of Leacock's use of parallelism and comment on the effectiveness of this parallelism for his purposes.

9. How would you describe the tone of the essay and why?

10. Look again at the section in paragraph 5 describing the attitudes of other peoples, other nations toward America. What effect do these statements have on the meaning—and the tone—of the essay? Does Leacock supply more or less logical proof for these statements than he does for the earlier ones about Americans?

11. What effect does the last paragraph have on the meaning—and the tone—of the essay?

*Considered judgment.*

1. Now that you have carefully examined the essay, what do you think the author's purpose is?

2. How are the reasoning and the tone of the essay related to this purpose?

## Writing Assignment Three (Optional)

Using the Leacock essay as a point of departure, write an essay in which you try to persuade your audience by a deliberate technique of exaggeration and by the use of generalizations too sweeping to be either logical or offensive. Adopt a tone and voice deliberately fashioned to win your intended audience. When you have written your paper, add a statement in which you describe your purpose, your tone and voice, and your audience. Here are three topics modeled on Leacock's, but you are free to devise your own topic if you prefer:

(1) Teachers Are Queer

(2) Adolescents Are Queer

(3) Parents Are Queer

This paper should be prepared at home with plenty of time for revision and proofreading.

## Writing Assignment One, Topic 1
## Sample 1. Grade: High

"Gee Dad, I have never felt more like a fool than tonight. I had to wait by the car stuck in the mud with cars going by looking at me.

"I was going down Deepdene, and just as I was coming around the bend, a car came around the other way with his lights on bright. It all happened so quickly that I just misjudged the side of the road. The other driver was nice enough to go down to the gas station, and send up the service truck. I think that the whole thing was my fault so I will take all the blame for what happened. I will be glad to pay all the towing costs with my own money if you want me to."

"The next guy that asks me about the mud on my car I will punch in the nose.

"I was going down 'Dead Man's Hill' at a safe 35 when this jerk comes around the bend with his lights on bright and hogging the road. He must have been going 60 miles an hour. All I could do was to swerve out of his way, and ended up in the ditch stuck in the mud.

"I was amazed that the studge stopped to help me. What really floored me was that he offered to get the tow truck for me. That guy down at the gas station must be as slow as a tortoise, because it wasn't until after a good half hour before he got there.

"When I got home, my old man really laid into me. I thought that he was going to have a Heart attack right there. I ended up paying for the towing costs; I'm lucky I didn't bash-up the old machine.

## Writing Assignment One, Topic 1
## Comment on Sample 1. Grade: High

This paper is skillful in its manipulation of tone and language. Its first part strikes a discreet balance between frigid formality and slangy unconcern. The tone is courteous but not obsequious. The language is careful with that carefulness that adolescents save for their elders, but it never stiffens to pompousness. The opening admission of folly is calculatedly disarming—to prepare the way for an explanation designed to allay parental wrath and win respect for the speaker's willingness to assume responsibility for his actions. The opening of the second part strikes an entirely different note—this time a tone of pugnacious bravado used to shield the speaker from chagrin. Terms like "guy," "jerk," and "studge" are as appropriate here as they would have been inappropriate in the explanation to a possibly disgruntled father. The other obvious strength here is the skill with which the student keeps the facts the same in both accounts, letting the differences in the two accounts derive only from tone, diction, and arrangement of material.

## Writing Assignment One, Topic 1
## Sample 2. Grade: Average

Situation: Evening time and I approach my dad in the living room.

"Good evening, Dad! I got into a slight accident this evening but there's no cause for an alarm. As you noticed today the road was quite slippery and pretty dangerous for the cars. Well, what happened was that when I was driving along the highway, my car was starting to slide a little. To avoid an accident with an oncoming car, I drove the car off to the side of the road. When I drove the car off the road, it got stuck in the mud and it got all muddy and mired. I had to the service truck to pull the car out. I payed the service men since I had money with me and I got the car cleaned and washed before I drove it into the garage. I also checked it for damages and there weren't any.

Situation: I approach my friends who are sitting on the grass.

"Hi, fellas! What are you guys doing? Oh yeah! You should have seen what happened to me yesterday. I had to drive my dad's car off the road yesterday because the road was very slippery and my pop's car was sliding all over the place. The funny thing was that when I drove the car off the road it got stuck in the mud. The car was all dirty and muddy when I decided to call the service truck because the car couldn't come out of the paste-like mud. I had to pay the service men for their service since I had money and I didn't want my Pop to pay for it. When I told my Pop he was very surprised but after a while he felt okay because the car didn't have any damages and I had taken responsibility for my actions.

## Writing Assignment One, Topic 1
## Comment on Sample 2. Grade: Average

This is an acceptable but less subtle handling of the car incident than that of Sample 1. Here, too, in his first section, the speaker indicates his awareness of his responsibility for what has happened but nowhere admits that he is in any way to blame, thus missing an invaluable device for forestalling or dissolving parental disapproval. The language in the exchange between son and father is just about formal enough to suggest the speaker's discomfort in the situation. Diction and sentence structure are carefully correct but not unduly formal. The statement that the car " 'got stuck in the mud and it got all muddy and mired' " provides an excess dosage of mud, but the redundancy may be deliberately intended to indicate the speaker's lack of verbal ease with his father. Even so, the term "mired" is a bit fancy for this occasion. What differentiates the paper from Samples 1 and 3, however, is the writer's failure to achieve a sharply different tone and to employ an entirely different level of language in the second installment where the speaker is talking to his peers. Except for the initial " 'Hi, fellas!' " and the " 'Oh yeah!' " the tone is too polite, the English too good, too careful, too like what should have been reserved for adult ears. There is no note of bravado here such as might have contrasted with the deprecatory tone needed in the first part. In talking with other boys, a normal, red-blooded high school student is not going to use such adult platitudes as " 'I had taken responsibility' " nor such descriptive theme phrasing as " 'paste-like mud.' " In fact the almost assertive note of conscious rectitude that permeates both versions is irritating rather than persuasive to ears that are sensitive to tone.

## Writing Assignment One, Topic 3
## Sample 3. Grade: High

I walked into English class Monday morning without my paper. I was hoping that someone else would be unprepared. I started to ask Steve about his paper.

"How long is yours?"

"About seven hundred words; I decided to do a real good job on this one. It took me three hours! How long's yours?"

"Didn't do it."

"What?!"

"I went hunting all weekend. Didn't have time. My brother came around Saturday morning and asked me to go duck shooting. So I went. I took some paper and a pen, so I could do the paper one morning while everyone else was out hunting. But the ducks were everywhere, so I just decided I'd rather shoot than write. We got our limit both days. Anyway, who cares? Most he can do is take off five points."

"What are you going to tell him?"

"Same thing I told you."

"You better get started; here he comes."

"Sir, I have a problem."

"Yes?"

"Sir, I don't have my theme."

"Why not?"

"Well, on Saturday morning my brother asked me to go hunting with him. I thought that I could stay in-camp one morning while he and his friends were hunting, and I could do my paper then. So I took a pen and some paper with me. I really intended to do the paper; but circumstances kept occurring which prevented me from writing the paper in the morning. On Sunday night, we didn't get home until twelve-thirty, so I decided to wait till this morning and ask you what to do. Is there a possibility I could do the paper tonight? Maybe I could write it about the hunting trip. That way, the trip will not have been a complete waste of time."

## Writing Assignment One, Topic 3
## Comment on Sample 3. Grade: High

This paper meets the demands of the assignment with apparently effortless competence. Its first section is relaxed enough in language and sentence structure to create the illusion of student talking to student. The occasional omission of the sentence subject (" 'Didn't have time.' ") furthers the illusion of actual talk. The tone strikes just the right compromise between brazenness and concern. And a glint of welcome humor comes through in the final exchange:

"What are you going to tell him?"

"Same thing I told you."

Then comes the second installment—stiffened at once into deference with that initial " 'Sir,' " after which the speaker does present the same facts. But this time he wraps them in a mollifying package of deprecation and disarming frankness. The opening " 'I have a problem' " is astute. The student knows that the word "problem" will command a sympathetic hearing from anyone in the teaching business. The student also knows the practical value of the question form: " 'Is there a possibility I could do the paper tonight?' " And note the deft tentativeness with which he phrases the question, the tone of almost humble entreaty. A final even more astute touch is the suggestion that the hunting trip might be turned to account as fodder for the overdue paper.

## Writing Assignment One, Topic 3
## Sample 4. Grade: Low

A you guys, you should have been on the fishing trip with me. Had plenty of fish. We went to this guy's ranch that stay by the fishing area and nobody goes there because it's private land. My Uncle got a pass for us that's why we could go in. Every time you throw the line in, one fish bite. We was fishing all day. I suppose to do a paper for English but I neva do it. Was more intresting fishing and when I went back at night I couldn't say-up. I think I get one "F" in English.

Mr. Tiernan, I didn't do my paper. I was going to do it but I went on a fishing trip. We were fishing all day and at night I couldn't stay up to do it. So I don't have a paper to hand in.

## Writing Assignment One, Topic 3
## Comment on Sample 4. Grade: Low

This student does vary the language and the sentence structure of his two versions, using a curious mixture of pidgin English and American schoolboy talk in his first version—a possibly justifiable choice for this particular student. The serious weakness here comes in the second part, the interchange between student and teacher, where in a situation calling for subtle strategy and calculated diplomacy, we get nothing but a blunt, factual announcement with no indicated desire to set matters right, no hint of self-censure, and no suggestion of apology.

## Writing Assignment Two
## Sample 1. Grade: High

*Mercy Killing*

Spoken to an audience of contemporaries.

Modern medical research has advanced to achieve great successes previously not dreamed of. Every year man gets closer to his goal of wiping out the killer diseases and discovers new preventative measures. However, for every cure that is found, it seems that a new illness is discovered, just as serious or perhaps more so than the one just cured. A vicious circle is present, but man is thankful for every ailment he has illiminated, and can only hope for relief when struck with an incurable sickness.

One form of relief which is very contraversial is mercy-killing. Many people, without really thinking about it, give 'No' as a flat, final answer. But perhaps if they would put themselves into a situation where the question of Mercy-killing would arise, their ideas would change. The methods are many—a painless injection is administered—death is immediate. Of course the procedure would have to be agreed to by either the patient—if of sound, sane, mind or, if unconscious, by a relative. Consider the birth of an infant piteously disfigured, and mentally damaged. Life for this creature, a horrible word, but not a human being, would surely be no blessing, no joy. He could never know beauty, love. His short existence would be spent in an institution—never knowing a family, truely knowing nothing—a vegetable.

Or, consider an intelligent person struck down with an incurable, progressing disease; malignant cancer—leukemia. He knows his condition, his days are numbered—one would think surely if they were few he would want to live them out—but who would want to live days in excruciating pain, for death? If the patient asks for a mercy killing to spare him this torture, who could refuse him?

Or, think of someone struck with a severe Cerebral Hemmorage. Here I am referring directly to a specific incident. The patient's mind is useless—he is totally unconscious—no thoughts, reflexes, nothing. If the victim is not to recover, there is a certain stage at which he can be either dead or alive, according to varying definitions of the terms. If life is synonomous with an aware being, bright and energetic, then, in truth, he is dead. The body has technically stopped functioning but life, in it's basic definition can be maintained—through intravenous feeding and automatic heart pulsators—this can go on indefinitely. Shouldn't the relatives put a stop to it? Can they honestly believe that this is life, being kept alive by machines? This can go on and on—this person can remain in a suspended state—neither dead nor alive.

The only real objections are on moral grounds. Many say—"Who are we to play God?" "Only God can give and take away life." But then how can these people advocate wars? Is war more acceptable, the slaughter of millions of men, than bringing the end to one's suffering? How could anyone even conceive of a Bomb? Mercy killing is a natural function—animals will naturally kill any member of their group if it is dying—out of pity. Why is it beneath man? Why do we have to try to hang on to life as long as possible even though there isn't any life left to cling to?

## Writing Assignment Two
## Comment on Sample 1. Grade: High

This paper has at least five misspellings. All but one of these are of not very common words; none poses a problem of comprehension to the reader. Against these flaws, however, are many virtues. One is a tone of utter sincerity: the writer is totally convinced of the rightness of his cause. Another is structure: the case for mercy killing is buttressed by four examples, each more telling than the last: there is a real climax. Furthermore, the writer is aware of the arguments of the opposition; he states conditions under which mercy killing might be agreed to (second paragraph) and then, after the series of case studies, returns to the opposing forces in a final paragraph. The writer can handle effectively a variety of sentence structures and a vocabulary of unusual range. It is likely that the "audience of contemporaries" is deeply impressed. So are the readers.

## Writing Assignment Two
## Sample 2. Grade: Average

My Audience: A Group of Parents
My Topic: The Necessity of College

If I were to ask you what your main concern as a parent is, you would probably answer, "My child's future," and justifiably so, since it is natural for a parent to want his child to be successful, to be someone. But what is success and what does it mean to become someone? In a technical-minded world such as ours most people have come to use college as a synonym for success. When I mention college, what comes into your mind? A degree? A good job? A substantial salary—enough money to live comfortably on with some to spare. Probably, since you are experienced adults who over the years have found evidence which in some way proves that statement. But, to the dedicated college student, college basically means hard work—the type of hard work that can be handled effectively only by those who are capable mentally, psychologically, and physically.

A child wants his parents to be proud of him; but it is also necessary to understand that all children are not capable of performing college work or really want to. And if you truly don't want to do something, if you find no fulfillment in doing something, of what use will it be? It will be of no use. A College degree might get your child a job, but it will not keep the job for him—that he must do himself—and this cannot be done if there is no interest.

So, when it is time to decide, if your child confronts you with a preference for a career other than college, will you give him a chance? Or will you force him into what you think is best for him? I realize that you have had experience and know, to some extent, what might be best for your child; but I don't believe anyone has so much insight into a person as to know his deepest thoughts and desires. Remember that you don't have to find your child, he has to find himself; and he can only do so when he is following a way of life in which he knows and feels he will be able to express himself as a person, an individual, a someone.

## Writing Assignment Two
## Comment on Sample 2. Grade: Average

The assignment calls for a paper that would attempt to persuade an audience not in entire agreement with the thesis of the paper. The student is also supposed to indicate the kind of audience and his relationship to it. This student tells us that he is addressing a group of parents, but nothing about his relationship to the group. Is he representing some youth group? Are his own parents in the audience? How does he happen to be addressing them on this topic? These questions obviously have some relevance to any judgment of his paper, but the student gives no answers. This failure is one reason for a grade of *average*. Another is in the structure of the piece: the introduction takes up too much space and time, and the concluding ideas seem to need further development. Still another is the writer's apparent confusion over a child's lack of interest in a job that a college degree will not help him keep—see the second paragraph.

But this paper has some positive merits: the writing is generally competent; the plea for broadmindedness is forthright; and the writer's attitude is respectful.

## Writing Assignment Two
## Sample 3. Grade: Low

Title: The Validity of High School Activities
Audience: High School Seniors and Juniors
Aim: To stimulate the audience into evaluating their own participation in High School activities

High school activities offer many challenges and rewards for those who use them wisely. Many a year has been made by that extra night spent putting up decorations for a prom. But what is the purpose behind all this pomp? To answer this—Come, let us reason together.

High school activities have value when they have meaning. Since the future belongs to those who will pursue it, elementary steps on a social scale must be taken in high school. Co-curricular clubs are such steps. Organized for the promotion and benefit of a common objective we can infer the presence of a working bond of unity among the members. This is good, in that the stability of our society will be dependant on how well the members can accept and work together with their peers.

Paradoxically, the student can also develope a greater awareness of his own insignificance, through a broader outlook he sees that no man is indispensible and life will sustain without him as well as with him.

However, social activities must be a mutual contract between the organization and the individual. The constant demands put a person can develope in him, unconscious character traits. Through difficult trials he can learn perserverance, through sacrifice he can learn self denial and through perserverance and self denial he can conquor himself.

Ideally the cycle is completed. A person seeks, finds and facilitates his true nature through his own contributions—but this is not always so. People are not forced to help themself.

Think back to your own last club meeting. Did everyone participate in the planning of activities and carry them out? Or did your meeting follow the routine procedure of yawning and clock watching? If this is so, isn't it time something was done?

Let's stop pointing the finger. Why do many students go to a lot of trouble for nothing, more specifically why do students join a club if they don't want to be members? One of the most popular reasons is status. How impressive is the 'big brass" with 5 club pins on her jacket when compared to the girl who has none. And there will always be comparisons. Or how about last year's activity sheet? How many blanks did you fill? Perhaps you deserved the awards, only you know.

Another reason for club darting is the 'pressure." In analogy and context students are forced to be carbon copies of other

Where have you come up from? This is for each to decide, but now is the time to turn around and see where you're headed

## Writing Assignment Two
## Comment on Sample 3. Grade: Low

This paper starts off well—title, audience, aim are clearly stated, and the first paragraph runs smoothly. Misspellings begin to creep in before the end of the second paragraph; a comma fault hurts the single-sentence third paragraph, and from there on, technical errors become more and more abundant, even including lack of any punctuation at the end of sentences. In addition to these flaws, the paper's organization is confused. The writer has ideas, some of them good, but they tend to be poured out helter-skelter, with the result that the reader is unsure about the writer's real attitude toward the activities. Here is a paper that, pruned, proofread, and reorganized, could well move into the *average* rating.

## Writing Assignment Three (Optional)
## Sample 1. Grade: High

Parents are queer. Funny queer. Some are strange queer. But most are funny queer. . . . Funny . . . .

Parents are a mass of contradictions. They take you to the beach and say you can't go in the water. They tell you not to smoke, and then ask you to get them another pack. They tell you not to make a rolling stop at stop signs while they make rolling stops at stop signs.

Parents worry alot. They worry when you don't date, and they worry more when you do date. They tell you not to cheat on an exam, but they wont let you do your own homework. You might get it wrong. They tell you to put a sweater on because they're cold.

Parents are silly. They ask you what you want for your birthday. When you tell them they say it is stupid, ridiculous, and out of the question. Then you get it on your birthday. They ask you one question a hunddred times. When you answer it the hundredth time, they ask you what you said.

Parents certainly are queer.

1. audience—children over 16 or parents (seperate groups—not together)

2. tone—not serious, light

3. purpose of paper—show lighter side of parents as viewed from child.

## Writing Assignment Three (Optional)
## Comment on Sample 1. Grade: High

This assignment calls for a satirical essay after the model of Leacock's "Americans Are Queer," along with a brief analysis describing purpose, tone, and audience. This student's "Parents are queer" manages, in the opinion of the readers, to catch the tone of light-hearted exaggeration that Leacock uses, and maintains it through an admittedly brief essay. Only those who read many essays on this topic are likely to realize how hard it is for high school seniors or juniors either to capture this satirical tone without using sheer invective or to maintain it through several paragraphs. No doubt this student was wise to keep the essay short. The appended statement on audience, and so forth, shows ability to say a good deal in a few words. The paper is graded on its quality, not its quantity.

This writer catches both the spirit and the form of Leacock's essay and applies them creatively to parents. For example, he uses the Leacock trick of repetition with variation at the beginning of each new paragraph. And practically every sentence within the paragraphs juxtaposes contradictions in the Leacock manner. The examples are close enough to the truth to have bite but exaggerated enough to inflict no damaging pain. The writer deliberately uses short, choppy sentences and even the fragment "funny queer" in his first paragraph; but these informal abrupt sentences are expressly designed to jolt parents into taking a new look at themselves through the eyes of an amused and amusing teen-ager. The suddenness and the tepidness of the closing are the main weakness in this otherwise competent response to the assignment. An exceptional student would somehow have managed an ending designed to reveal the tongue-in-cheek tone of all that goes before it.

## Writing Assignment Three (Optional)
## Sample 2. Grade: Average

*Rock-and-Roll Singers are Queer*

Rock-and-roll singers are queer. They all have long shaggy mops for hair. You can't tell if you are looking at them from the front or the rear. Sometimes you wonder if they are human beings or English sheep dogs.

Rock and roll singers are queer. They can't speak English. The words of the songs they sing sound like a mixture of an early Chinese dialect and Hebrew and the music sounds as if it had been written on the spot, and none of the musicians could agree on the tune.

Rock and roll singers are queer. They make unkind remarks about different subjects. They degrade their God and their beliefs. They have no sense of pride in who or what they have made of themselves.

Rock and roll singers are queer. They are all the same. They all sing the same songs with the same tunes. There is no difference in the way they dress, eat, sleep, breath, smoke, drink, or respond to their screaming fans. They have lost their identity if they ever had one.

The audience is anyone who is a fan of the Beatles, the Rolling Stones, the Dave Clark Five, or others. I am trying to point out how ridiculous these groups are.

## Writing Assignment Three (Optional)
## Comment on Sample 2. Grade: Average

This is a decently written paper that captures the outer trappings but not the inner spirit of the Leacock essay. Like Leacock, this writer starts each paragraph the same way, thus achieving Leacock's deliberate repetition but not his variation. Dutifully the student fulfills the more obvious demands of the assignment, but there is no real drollery here, no genuine humor, no such skill in paradox as livens the first sample.

## Writing Assignment Three (Optional)
## Sample 3. Grade: Low

*Teachers are Queer*

In our modern world today our teachers at school directly influence and shape our minds, morals, and lives. They are far too often either too busy concerning themselves with some obsolete idea or they themselves are too antiquited to aid the stagnated student. In a progressive era, progressive ideas should be brought forth, for example sex. Sex should be brought forth and discussed openly with no cause for embarressment, as I am sure every senior has encountered it in some way.

A teacher is supposed to be a friend or rather a buddy, someone to talk to, yet he or she is always critical of our appearance, our ideas, or our beliefs as students. Granted we are younger, but time passes, while they remain passive. Never does the teacher act as a friend, only as a guard to quell any riots or grumblings which may arise from the discontented student.

In general teachers really are queer. Aware of their superiority, the condesension is almost unbearable. One must propitiate disgustingly in order to raise one's average, and disgustingly enough the teacher laps it up like milk drenched with honey. How we bear their moods, tear and shares, unfair tests on material we have never covered, and their cigarettes in their shirt pockets is truly amazing!

So why not revolt? Because we as students are forced to realize that their time has come and gone and unhappily we remain as the scapegoat. We are also forced to realize their superiority, not because they are any smarter than we, only that they are older. We humor them, laugh at their dry jokes, and try desperatly not to fall asleep during their classes. Above all we are sent to school to learn, and learn we will, even if it is only devious ways in which to torture those teachers which fail us in their absurd courses.

This paper is obviously exaggerated to a great degree. I used alliteration and short sentences to add tone. Sarcasm is the theme throughout the paper. The audience, our class, is able to visualize each teacher, while listening to this, and this was my purpose.

## Writing Assignment Three (Optional) Comment on Sample 3. Grade: Low

Both of the previous papers succeed to some extent in catching the Leacock tone; this paper never does. What should be a rapier is a bludgeon, and not too well-shaped even for a club. Diction, spelling, sometimes grammar, are shaky: "they themselves are too antiquited to aid the stagnated student." The final sentence of the paper illustrates this student's difficulties both with tone and with grammar. A comparison of this paper with the *high* sample brings out the gap between them. And the final sentence of the explanation is revealing: the student is quite unaware of having given his audience no real aid in visualizing each teacher.

*This book was designed by Freeman Craw. It was composed in Garamond types by Connecticut Printers, Inc., Hartford, Connecticut, and printed by offset at Offset Reproductions, Inc., New York. The section dividers, printed by offset and silk screen, were produced by Offset Reproductions, Inc., and by Masta Displays, Inc., New York. The illustrations were printed by Tri-Arts Press, Inc., New York. The cover was printed by offset at Leeart Press, Inc., New York. The book was bound by Fisher Bookbinding Co., Inc., New York.*